The Surveillance Studies Reader

The Surveillance Studies Reader

Sean P. Hier and Joshua Greenberg

Open University Press

Open University Press
McGraw-Hill Education
McGraw-Hill House
Shoppenhangers Road
Maidenhead
Berkshire
England
SL6 2QL

email: enquiries@openup.co.uk
world wide web: www.openup.co.uk

and Two Penn Plaza,
New York, NY 10121-2289, USA

First published 2007

A catalogue record of this book is available from the British Library

ISBN10: 0 335 22026 6 (pb)   0 335 22027 4 (hb)
ISBN13: 978 0 335 22026 7 (pb)   978 0 335 22027 4 (hb)

Library of Congress Cataloging-in-Publication Data
CIP data has been applied for

Typeset by RefineCatch Limited, Bungay, Suffolk
Printed in Poland EU by OZGraf S.A.
www.polskabook.pl

The *McGraw·Hill* Companies

We dedicate this book to our teacher, Graham Knight, in partial acknowledgment of his guidance and support.

Contents

Editors' introduction: contemporary surveillance studies

Surveillance and uncertainty

One of the Canadian editors of this book was recently invited to the USA to speak about surveillance practices and social problems in the twenty-first century. The people who were hosting our editor agreed to reimburse him for expenses when he arrived at their university. The first part of the journey involved booking an airline ticket. Our editor chose to do this online. He turned on his computer, entered a password that protected confidential research files, and double-clicked his Internet Explorer icon. When he logged onto his web browser, his identification was automatically checked against his Internet Service Provider's client database to ensure that payments were up-to-date and that his subscription was active. While this was happening, his anti-virus software notified him that his account was in good standing and that only 632 days of his service privileges remained. In the span of less than two minutes, our editor noticed that his identity (as a computer owner and as a consumer) was verified at least three times. This reminded him of how deeply automated surveillance systems structure the routine aspects of daily life even before we leave home.

Once granted access to the WWW, our editor 'Googled' his intended airline. He was reminded of an article he had read about search engines in the *Los Angeles Times*. The article revealed that federal investigators in the USA obtained, under court order, a week's worth of search requests by users of major websites run by Yahoo, Microsoft, and America Online (Menn and Gaither 2006). Familiar with the literature on web-based surveillance, he wondered about David Lyon's (2002: 345) argument that '[u]sing the latest technology, someone else can track each click of your mouse, survey each website you have visited, even read your e-mail messages and rifle through your financial records and legal correspondence'. Was this argument more hype than reality, more possible than probable? Our editor thought back to what he had 'Googled' over the past week and contemplated how much web-based user information governments can and should have access to under the provisions stipulated in the American PATRIOT Act, Canada's Anti-Terrorism Act and counter-terrorism laws in the UK. He was also reminded of George W. Bush's chilling disregard for the provisions of The Foreign Intelligence Surveillance Act and Bush's declared intention to authorize government eavesdropping without court orders. Our editor wondered if a government 'sniffer', that is, an automated program that monitors data traveling over networks, had tracked his online communications or flagged one of his emails recently. He also contemplated what kinds of online and offline surveillance data the Canadian Security Intelligence Service was collecting without his knowledge.

Having received a number of 'hits' on his search engine, our editor accessed his intended airline's website and discovered that they had already created a 'profile' for him based on his previous travel history. He took note of the fact that his name and phone number, travel history and address appeared in the profile. As he examined the data, he wondered if his 'mouse tracks', that is, web surfing activities, were being monitored using a 'cookie' stored on his hard drive (placed there without his direct consent). He also wondered if the disclaimer to protect personal privacy that appeared on the screen before him was reliable. Could the airline use his travel history to build general or aggregated travel profiles for the purposes of flight planning, our editor wondered? Had his profile data been accessed by a data mining program to construct consumer profiles and marketing strategies? Would that be a violation of his 'personal' privacy? Should he be concerned?

Our editor proceeded to book the flight. When he selected the flight, the automated service required a credit card number. Our editor was also presented with options to enter an AirMiles number and to join a frequent flyer club. He decided that he had enough personal information stored in databases beyond his control and only entered his credit card number. During the process, a credit card verification system appeared on the screen; it required him to enter the password that he had entered the last time he had undergone this process. Did anyone else have his password, he wondered? Could someone else get the password? Did any of these concerns really matter? The card number was checked against another, external, database to ensure his credit card bills were being paid. He was also required to enter a valid email address. Would the email address end up on a distribution list for products related to travel, he wondered? Would promotional advertisements for rental cars, hotels or restaurants soon appear in his inbox? Would pornography arrive? In the ten minutes that had passed since he first turned his computer on, our editor reflected on how many automated databases enabled him to make this seemingly innocuous transaction – and how many databases were storing his personal data for reasons unbeknown to him!

A few weeks later our editor was off to the airport. He decided to drive. His automobile, of course, was registered with the state, his insurance company and the car dealer he had bought it from. His licence plates were also registered with the state, and his licence plate number (and his driver's licence number) linked him to the insurance industry and to the police. All these data were stored in interconnected searchable databases. As our editor made his way to the airport, he stopped to purchase fuel. Pulling up to the pumps, he noticed a surveillance camera overhead. He wondered who was monitoring the camera. Would 'they' store his digital biometric facial image for a day, a week or a year? Why is it necessary to submit a biometric measurement to the fuel station simply to purchase fuel? Did the sign informing customers that the area is under surveillance justify the intrusion? Was it, in fact, an intrusion? And what did it intrude on? Was the camera even functional? As our editor swiped his credit card to pay for the fuel, he was again reminded of the databases that make his life as a consumer possible and the visibility demanded of consumers who wish to participate in the consumer market.

With his car full of fuel, our editor was on his way. Driving to the airport, he passed through a number of intersections where cameras were mounted to control traffic flows and monitor intersections for vehicles running red lights. He passed a police officer, apparently too fast, and was pulled over for exceeding the designated limit (a personal failure to engage in self-surveillance and regulate his speed, he thought). Although our editor was aware that the officer had access to a computer that would bring up his relevant personal information (including criminal record), he was still asked to produce photo ID and insurance documents. The reliance on a laminated card to authenticate his identity seemed somehow antiquated. What if there was a discrepancy between his card and the computer information? What if the computer falsely indicated that he had a number of outstanding fines? What if it wrongly indicated that he was wanted for kidnapping? Would the police officer accept his word? Could such a misunderstanding happen? He also wondered how long it would be before thumbprints or retinal scans would replace photographs on licenses. How long before a hologram would be used, he wondered? And he speculated if new, technologically enhanced, tokens of trust would reduce the uncertainties of identifying human beings. As he waited for his expensive ticket to be issued, he received a call on his cell phone. He pressed the receive button and wondered who could intercept the call or trace his location. Was a global positioning satellite looming overhead? Of course it was.

When our editor got moving again and neared the airport, he passed under a sign reading 'speed kills', presumably designed to stimulate the kind of disciplinary self-surveillance that he had minutes earlier failed to realize. When he arrived at the airport, he paid for parking with a credit card and contributed more personal transaction data to a remote database. Our editor proceeded to the terminal building at the airport where he noticed several surveillance cameras; many security officials monitoring travellers attentively; a woman with blue gloves scrupulously inspecting a bag; a very long line of frustrated people clutching all sorts of documentation that presumably attested to their true identity; and a number of machines designed to detect metal, suspicious shapes, bombs, guns, knives and other objects deemed to be of high risk. He joined the line of anxious travellers and began to search for his own identification. Our editor's curiosity was piqued after one man in the line ordered his child to 'look normal' and 'shut up'. Suspicious, our editor thought: what are they trying to hide?

When our editor made it to the counter, he was asked to produce photo identification. The woman at the counter also asked if he had packed his own bag and whether the bag had been out of his sight between the time of packing and the present. Although our editor took some comfort in this rare person-to-person, embodied exchange, he nevertheless wondered who else would have packed his bag? He recalled that the bag had been out of his sight while he pumped fuel, dealt with the police officer and paid for parking at the airport. Did this count? The bag had also been out of his sight at home. Could he trust his family members? Should he? Did the woman at the counter even care?

A few minutes later, our editor walked directly from the check-in counter to the boarding line where he was asked to produce ID again, along with his boarding pass, as he passed under several surveillance cameras. Who was behind the cameras, he wondered? Was there someone watching him specifically? What would attract this kind of special attention? What about the young blonde woman a few people ahead in the line? The tattoo on her lower back might attract attention, he thought. Or were they watching the Indo-Canadian man in the corner? Was there a 'they' at all? This uncertainty reminded him of Margaret Atwood's novel, *The Handmaid's Tale*: who were the Eyes? Within 60 seconds he was asked to start his laptop before the airport official tested it for explosive residue with a cotton swab. As he removed all contents from his pockets and his belt (shoe removal was required later that day in American airports), our editor was reminded of a website about laptop scams in inspection lines and stepped up his own powers of surveillance among his fellow travellers. After passing through a metal detector, he was then asked to stand like a scarecrow while a young man ran a security wand across his body. What was this procedure doing to his internal organs, he wondered? Should he trust medical experts' advice? Once authenticated as a low-risk flyer, our editor entered a waiting area, which was again monitored by surveillance cameras and airport security officials. On his way to the boarding area, he bought a coffee at a conveniently situated coffee shop. Finding himself short on cash, he swiped his debit card and punched in a personal identification number. The magnetic strip on the card activated a remote digital bank account, the account was verified and debited, and he proceeded on his way. As he searched for a seat, he wondered if it was possible that one of the camera operators could read his PIN number and steal his identity. Presumably, the cameras were equipped with pan, zoom and tilt functions enabling extremely clear and exact imaging. Could the camera operator be in cahoots with the coffee stand worker? As he contemplated these uncertainties, a voice on an overhead speaker reminded him never to leave carry-on luggage unattended. In case he forgot, the voice continued to remind him every few minutes.

All of the aforementioned social monitoring, information gathering and procedural verification took place in the first two hours of our editor's trip (and nothing has yet been said about the kinds of person-to-person surveillance that takes place daily; about television viewing as a form of 'synoptic' or bottom up form of surveillance where the many watch the few – think of all those TV screens in airports; or about the forms of self-surveillance that we engage in daily – diet, exercise, hair styling, clothing, etc.). Over the course of that day, our editor passed through three additional airports in the USA (after producing ID to get on the first plane), where he encountered a number of customs agents demanding answers to seemingly irrelevant questions; several computer automated pre-screening flight programs; X-ray machines requiring the removal of his belt and shoes; more closed circuit TV cameras than he could count, some equipped with facial recognition software and algorithmic movement detection functions (just in case he made the wrong turn); officers of various ranks and degrees, all demanding positive identification and assessing his trustworthiness; more remote searchable computer databases containing his personal data than he was aware existed; and above all, an unrelenting supply of suspicion. Ironically, after proceeding through all these security checks, he felt less secure than he did when he had awakened that morning.

These examples, drawn from only a small sample of everyday life, speak to the uncertainties that pertain to contemporary surveillance. While such uncertainties raise a number of important ethical and practical questions about the character of contemporary surveillance practices, we can be certain that more questions pertaining to a wider range of surveillance practices also require attention. Surveillance structures are embedded into the routines of everyday life to such an extent that we rarely consider how significant surveillance data are – and rarely do we consider personal data such as consumer transactions and cell phone calls surveillance data. Surveillance functions ambiguously in everyday life to enable efficiency, convenience and security while simultaneously constraining the opportunities and life chances of individuals and social groups with shared characteristics – be they economic, sexual, racial, geographic or cultural. The ambiguous nature of surveillance also facilitates the penetration of information and data gathering/storage systems into the deeper recesses of everyday life, and the pervasiveness of surveillance systems, although put in place to increase safety and provide security, tends to generate greater levels of insecurity, anxiety and fear. As will become clear in the chapters that follow, surveillance begets surveillance.

Contemporary surveillance studies

While there has long been interest in surveillance, the development of contemporary surveillance studies traces to Max Weber's writings on bureaucracy and to George Orwell's (1949) *Nineteen Eighty-Four*. James Rule's (1973) *Private Lives, Public Surveillance* represents an important contribution to the study of computerization and bureaucratization and Gary Marx's *Undercover: Police Surveillance in America* stimulated interest in surveillance and power relations in the 1980s. Theoretically, Michel Foucault's (1979) *Discipline and Punish* attracted a huge amount of attention. Anthony Giddens' (1985) *Nation State and Violence* and Zygmunt Bauman's (1989) *Modernity and the Holocaust* consolidated interest in structures of surveillance. A number of high profile contributions appeared in the 1990s, including but not limited to, Christopher Dandeker's (1990) *Surveillance, Power, and Modernity*, Oscar Gandy's (1993) *The Panoptic Sort* and Kevin Haggerty and Richard Ericson's (1997) *Policing the Risk Society*. David Lyon has also contributed a series of studies that have significantly advanced the ways we conceptualize and think about surveillance, including *Surveillance Society* (2001), *Surveillance as Social Sorting* (2003) and *Surveillance After September 11* (2003). Scholarly articles that accompanied these important contributions have also brought coherence to the field.

Surveillance studies continue to develop and expand. While surveillance is an intrinsic feature of human social relationships, it is only in the past few years that information and data-gathering techniques have emerged as a sustained multi-disciplinary topic of investigation and theorization. As international scholars continue to examine the importance of information and data storage systems in the administration of social life, we gain deeper insights into the significance of surveillance.

The expanding field of surveillance studies has begun documenting the changing character and consequences of surveillance techniques around the globe. The readings presented in this book represent one more step towards developing a coherent statement on surveillance studies.

The cultural significance and the pervasiveness of surveillance came into focus following the 11 September 2001 (9/11) terrorist attacks on Washington and New York. After the 9/11 attacks, the term surveillance was increasingly used in everyday dialogue, and concepts like biometrics, CCTV and information sharing made their way into news reporting and the popular lexicon. The events of 9/11 also facilitated the intensification, automation, integration and globalization of surveillance systems (Lyon 2003). In an effort to better assess the kinds of information about surveillance that the public received after 9/11, Haggerty and Gazso (2005) enumerated political and institutional responses to the terrorist attacks in *The New York Times* and *The Globe and Mail*. They found that the long list of surveillance responses appearing in the coverage ranged from gamma ray screening, ionscan spectrometers, and thermal imaging technologies to communication interception and intensified record access. Still, although certain media agencies relentlessly promoted the need for enhanced security, often identifying the porous character of border security as a central problem, it was not just newspaper and television reporting, governmental claims making, and Hollywood films[1] that brought increased attention to the realities of contemporary surveillance.

Soon after 9/11, numerous academic and popular books were published as well. David Lyon, perhaps the most prolific writer on surveillance, contributed to popular and academic interest with the publication of *Surveillance After September 11* (2003). Lyon argues that 9/11 catalyzed a 'global panic regime'. This term does not suggest that governmental response to the attacks on Washington and New York was unjustified or that all increased security measures have been out of proportion to the actual threat posed by international terrorism. The problem for Lyon, rather, is that the speed with which security provisions were put into place after 9/11 came at the expense of analysis, critique, reflection and debate concerning who would be affected, how deeply, in what social locations and what would be the long-term consequences of expedient actions. He argues that many of the security provisions were quick solutions to long-term problems, knee-jerk reactions that will take a long time to undo. And he argues that post-9/11 publics, repeatedly exposed to the planes hitting the Twin Towers, were willing to accept more intrusion, scrutiny, interrogation and, ultimately, delay in daily affairs in order to feel safer and more secure.

While these arguments are important ones, Lyon also argues that the continuities in surveillance practices which link the pre- and post-9/11 period are at least as important as the legislative and technological changes that followed 9/11. For example, before 9/11, surveillance was accomplished at a distance. Remote searchable databases were integrated in a variety of social, commercial, governmental, and military locations to verify identities and to authenticate transactions and security clearances. In fact, the images of the planes hitting the Twin Towers, which were broadcast around the world, exemplify what Anthony Giddens (1991) conceptualizes as time–space distanciation. Thousands of people living outside the USA were moved to tears when they saw the planes hit the towers, and thousands more called for immediate action. Yet the vast majority of people who were moved by the images were not in New York at the time of the attacks, and it is probable that a large number had never been to New York. Nevertheless, the images transcended the natural barriers of time and space to the extent that they became personal and intimate. Those images were enormously powerful, but their meaning and significance remained to be interpreted and understood. After 9/11, news reporting and governmental claims making continued to invoke the images. This had the effect of accelerating the development and implementation of more surveillance technologies, and resulted in greater levels of already-existing surveillance integration.

A second continuity linking the pre- and post-9/11 periods is declining levels of trust. Prior to 9/11, trust was constituted, not through human respect and dignity – not through one's good word – but rather through a reliance on 'tokens of trust' like PIN numbers, passwords, credit history, property holdings, personal wealth and, in certain arena such as professional athletics, blood and urine samples and DNA. After 9/11, there was a frenzy to introduce biometric surveillance technologies including iris, finger and retinal scans; software that assesses hand geometry and vein patterns; voice and facial recognition software to sort high-risk from low-risk persons. Caught up in heavy media reporting and governmental claims making, the primary marketing strategy of the high tech industry continues to draw on emotions like fear and suspicion to introduce a variety of technological devices and gadgets to authenticate and verify people's identities.

A third continuity linking pre- and post-9/11 periods is trends towards the integration of information processing and data storage systems. For example, throughout the 1990s many countries had made efforts to implement national identification cards containing small chips in order to link information embedded in the card (e.g., facial images, fingerprints and retinal patterns) with a remote database. Before 9/11, the development and refinement of facial recognition software that links biometric readings with images in remote databases were well underway, and software that could make decisions as to certain human movements was continually being advanced. By 9/11, the Royal Canadian Mounted Police and the Federal Bureau of Investigations had established a strong interest in facial recognition software, and other social locations like casinos, banks and certain workplaces were also targeted. Far from the totalitarian dystopia prophesied by Orwell, the surveillance measures introduced after 11 September do not represent centralization so much as integration (Lyon 2003). These mechanisms were not new, but they were intensified and further elaborated, particularly in select social locations.

These developments in surveillance practices represent some of the foundations of contemporary surveillance studies. The 9/11 attacks have certainly sharpened the analytical edge of surveillance studies, but surveillance studies are concerned with so much more than post-9/11 systems of surveillance. As Lyon argues, 9/11 is a prism through which the intensification of existing surveillance practices can be understood. What this means is that a qualitative shift in surveillance took place after 9/11, and there are important studies still to be conducted on post-9/11 media reporting, information and communication technologies, anti-terrorism legislation and global systems integration. But there are also important studies that remain absent from the literature on the pre-9/11 forms of surveillance that made post-9/11 surveillance possible. Despite the fact that surveillance has become a fashionable topic of theorization and debate, we should not forget that people have always watched over one another. Throughout the modern period, records of various sorts have been kept for such purposes as taxation, military service, immigration and land distribution. Innovations in the form of writing and the dissemination of text, census taking, statistics gathering and the telegraph revolutionized practices of surveillance. As these examples suggest, surveillance always takes place in the context of social and political forces.

The Surveillance Studies Reader

The Surveillance Studies Reader is organized into six parts. The first part, 'Surveillance, the nation-state and social control', presents five classical or foundational readings that address surveillance at the level of the state. The readings demonstrate how surveillance operates as a modern mechanism of social control, and they address the role of surveillance in the formation of the nation-state; how surveillance at the level of the state structures people's daily behaviour; and how state surveillance practices structure everyday life.

The second part of the *Reader*, 'Computers, simulations and surveillance', presents four readings that address the changing character of surveillance and social control in the context of computerization. These readings consider the continuing significance of state forms of power through surveillance, as well as surveillance beyond the state. The readings in Part II address questions such as: What is the new surveillance? Can we understand surveillance exclusively as a top-down, state-driven process? In what ways can surveillance be understood to operate on the basis of simulation or a 'data double' or 'digital footprint'? And in what ways can newer forms of surveillance be understood as democratizing?

The readings presented in the third part of the *Reader*, 'Surveillance and everyday life', illustrate the increasingly banal character of surveillance. This is an important section because it bridges older, more explicit forms of surveillance and social control with the ethical and privacy dimensions addressed in Part VI. Emphasizing the multifaceted nature of surveillance as a social process, the section also addresses forms of dataveillance and the significance of biometric measurements.

The fourth part of the *Reader*, 'Surveillance, social inequality and social problems', demonstrates how surveillance matters in the contexts of digitalization, CCTV, welfare, parental drug testing and racism. These chapters focus on the nuances of surveillance practices and social inequality, drawing attention to some of the most pressing social issues in contemporary western societies. The readings pose important and challenging questions, including: How does surveillance differentially affect human beings? What are some of the ways that surveillance programs are promoted? How does surveillance touch groups of people differently in everyday life? How can various forms of social inequality be understood to influence surveillance practices?

Part 5, 'Surveillance and public opinion', presents three reading excerpts that examine different dimensions of public opinion about surveillance. Several of the chapters appearing in the other sections address how public opinion about surveillance practices is influenced, but the chapters in this section take a more explicit approach to public opinion and public opinion formation.

The final part of the *Reader*, 'Mobility, privacy, ethics and resistance,' presents four readings. Issues of privacy, ethics, and the future of surveillance studies are combined to stimulate thought on how surveillance can and should be studied and how surveillance in its more insidious applications can and should be resisted.

Each part of the *Reader* opens with a section introduction to frame the general, unifying themes. The introductions situate the readings in the context of contemporary surveillance studies, and they also briefly summarize each excerpt.

Note

1   As we write this Introduction, *United 93* is set to hit theatres. Michael Moore's documentary *Fahrenheit 9/11* was another influential film. Readers are also strongly encouraged to view Adam Curtis's *The Power of Nightmares: The Rise of the Politics of Fear* (BBC documentary film series).

References

Giddens, A. (1991) *Modernity and Self Identity: Self and Society in Late Modern Age*. Stanford, CA: Stanford University Press.

Haggerty, K. and Gazso, A. (2005) Seeing beyond the ruins: surveillance as a response to terrorist threats, *Canadian Journal of Sociology*, 30(2): 169–87.

Lyon, D. (2002) Surveillance in cyberspace: the Internet, personal data, and social control, *Queen's Quarterly*, 109(3): 333–44.

Lyon, D. (2003) *Surveillance After September 11*. Cambridge: Polity Press.

Menn, J. and Gaither, C. (2006) US obtains Internet users' search records, *Los Angeles Times*, 20 January.

PART 1

Surveillance, the nation-state and social control

In his seminal statement on social monitoring in everyday life, David Lyon (2001) reminds us that the rise of modern surveillance societies has everything to do with disappearing bodies. What he means is that advances in information and communication technologies have enabled us to do things at a distance. Doing things at a distance – for example, making telephone calls, sending emails and shopping on the Internet – reconfigures the way in which social relationships and human interactions are conducted. At one point in time, people negotiated their daily affairs in the presence of others, and they relied on face-to-face interactions to make decisions and authenticate identities. While face-to-face interaction is still an important part of everyday human interaction, it has become increasingly common practice to also rely on tokens of trust (e.g., PIN numbers and passwords) and electronically mediated networks to accomplish daily tasks that do not involve other human beings at the point of contact (e.g., withdrawing money from an ATM machine).

The rapid expansion of computerization and communication technologies over the past 40 years has had a major impact on how information is gathered, stored, accessed and used to make decisions in the realms of consumerism, leisure activity, personal life management, military, policing and state governance. We should not forget, however, that developments in communication technologies, and concomitant changes in practices of surveillance, profoundly influenced the disappearance of bodies long before the advent of computerization. Harold Innis (1950), for example, argues that the Roman conquest of Egypt, tracing to the fourth century BC, was important to the expanding Empire because of the large quantities of papyrus growing in freshwater marshes along the Nile River. Paper is made from papyrus plants, and control of papyrus supplies not only facilitated the wider distribution of administrative documents and decrees (compared to communication media that were fixed and difficult to move, such as stones or parchment), but it also facilitated developments in state governance over greater distances (i.e., the disappearance of bodies). With the advent of the European printing press in the fifteenth century AD, the administrative capabilities of the state were again widened (Giddens 1985; Anderson 1991). Developments in the distribution and storage of information enabled shifts in the scale and form of surveillance that both enabled and constrained people's lives (see the first reading passage below) – for example, in record keeping, file sharing, taxation, welfare, military and law enforcement – and computerization since the 1960s has further advanced the surveillance capacities of the state for better and for worse.

In addition to understanding the actual features of specific surveillance systems, then, it is important to also consider the general form of surveillance as a social relationship. Georg Simmel (1950), the famous German intellectual, encouraged social researchers to resist the temptation to merely describe the contents or manifest features of human social life. What mattered for Simmel was an understanding of general forms of human association. It is important, argued Simmel, not only to differentiate the content of social life from its general forms, but also to appreciate how changes in the composition of a group from only two to three members realigns the entire form of human group interaction. In a manner similar to Karl Marx and Emile Durkheim, who studied religion, not on the basis of the contents or features of, say, Christianity or Buddhism, but rather as a projection of societal organization, Simmel deemed it important to explain how general forms of human association give rise to patterns of conflict and cooperation, subordination and superordination, in different times, places and social settings.

Section readings

In the first reading passage, Chapter 1, James Rule helps us to think about the form of surveillance and social control processes in the context of 'the scale' of social life. Rule's passage tellingly begins, not with a discussion of surveillance and social monitoring per se, but rather with the nature of collective human living and modern forms of social control. He explains that processes or systems of social control, found in diverse social institutions and societies, involve formal and informal controls. In small-scale societies, where social life is likely to be a public matter, informal face-to-face social controls are viable. This is not to suggest that small-scale societies inhabited by a comparatively small number of people lack the capability to develop elaborate institutionalized apparatuses of formal control. It is to suggest that based on the interactional form of human associations in the small-scale society, where the public and private domains converge, all that is required to ensure conformity to social norms are informal mechanisms. In large-scale, cosmopolitan societies, however, public censure is much easier to escape. In the latter social settings, the staging of mechanisms of social control is different from those found in small-scale societies.

Refining and extending systems of surveillance is crucial to managing a mobile and mostly anonymous public. Surveillance systems, Rule explains, involve knowing the population through the collection and management of information, and being able to identify, locate and apprehend rule-breakers. But systems of surveillance allow agents of social control to manage behavior and the routine daily goings-on of social life as well. The 'clientele' of systems of surveillance and social control includes prisoners and criminals (parolees, for example), but also ordinary citizens (e.g., monitoring potential shoplifters in a department store). In the shift from small- to large-scale social settings, relatively informal face-to-face sanctions are replaced by formal mechanisms of social control that 'link people to their pasts' (Rule 1973: 28) – mechanisms such as passports, credit cards and other 'tokens of trust'. No matter how sophisticated social monitoring systems become (e.g., see-through walls technologies, global positioning satellites and thermo-imaging technologies), what matters for Rule is the scales of social life, forms of group interaction and the concomitant social ordering mechanisms that facilitate collective social living.

One question that consumes Rule is the extent to which changes in the form of human associations and social scale give rise to forms of extreme social control that approximate authoritarianism and totalitarian state repression. Writing in the late 1960s, these were questions that did not have clear answers. One analytical strategy that Rule uses to assess the extent of surveillance and social control is to compare a paradigmatic case or ideal type of totalitarianism (e.g., Orwell's Big Brother) with existing systems of mass surveillance. In limited social settings (e.g., prison), the staging of surveillance allows for total surveillance. But the realization of a present-day total surveillance society is unlikely, not least because of the prohibitive costs associated with such a system. Nevertheless, Rule offers four accounts or forms of limitations on surveillance systems to enable theoretical and practical comparisons. The accounts are important because too often we assume that contemporary surveillance systems are all powered by high-tech, high-speed computers that store large amounts of information in centralized databases. There remain, however, many limitations on surveillance systems today – as there did when Rule wrote over three decades ago.

Anthony Giddens explores the theme of modern tendencies toward totalitarian political power in the next reading passage (Chapter 2). Perhaps more than any other contemporary sociologist, Giddens has sought to explicate the connections between surveillance, industrialism, war, totalitarianism and the administrative power of the modern nation-state. In the reading passage, Giddens begins by arguing that the term 'totalitarianism' is of relatively recent political origin, traced to criticisms of Italian Fascism in the 1920s. The most common understandings of totalitarianism, says Giddens, not only involve the extreme ideological concentration of ideas backed by a narrow, identifiable leadership. They also entail a fully developed secret police force and a state monopoly on communications, weapons and organizations. This circumscribed understanding of totalitarianism, he suggests, may actually hide more than it reveals about the tendential properties of totalitarianism that exists at the core of all modern nation-states.

The maximization of surveillance is of undeniable importance to authoritarian state-control on the social scale of the modern nation-state. As Giddens explains, totalitarian rule depends on a social infrastructure sufficiently developed to enable the state to penetrate the daily lives of the majority of its citizens (see the fourth reading passage for a critique of the state's 'penetration' of society). Ubiquitous state penetration of the everyday lives of citizens was hampered in traditional (small-scale) states, not only because of relatively low levels of literacy and a concomitant restricted public sphere, but also because of the limited scope and influence of state policing. In modern nation-states, by contrast, state-coordinated surveillance functions are such that information garnered from the citizenry is derived from multiple forms of documentation that can be used to exercise force and achieve compliance with state goals and desires.

Provocatively, Giddens argues that surveillance as a source (or means) of administrative power and social control is not simply available for purposes of repression and subordination. Rather, Giddens also argues that in societies of the scale of modern nation-states, the centralization of administrative power allows for the actualization of citizenship rights. The latter include provisions under the welfare state. In this regard, totalitarianism, says Giddens, is not, paradoxically, a total system of control through mass surveillance. The expansion of surveillance does, however, radically transform the relationship between the state and civil society. For Giddens, then, what is important to remember is that totalitarianism is not about a specific type of society – Italian Fascism or German Nazism, for example – but rather it is about a type or form of rule containing certain key institutional components.

In the third reading passage, Chapter 3, Christopher Dandeker begins by elab-orating an idealized typology of bureaucratic surveillance systems. He observes that the rational-legal type of surveillance structure that has been most approximated by western nation-states, with their attendant capabilities of administration over large distances, is made possible through processes of bureaucratization. He argues that bureaucratization, as a type of social organization, is bound up with systems of power and surveillance. To better understand modern western bureaucratic forms of surveil-lance, he identifies four dichotomized systems of rule: personal versus bureaucratic administration and autocratic versus liberal interests. In personalized administrative systems, whether underscored by autocratic or democratic interests, the powers of surveillance and, necessarily, political rule are limited. The means of surveillance are personal and informal, and specialized functions or intermediaries are absent. By con-trast, bureaucratic forms of surveillance, in their dictatorial or rational-legal form, involve durable structures capable of reaching across large distances and compiling large amounts of information on the population.

The key difference between bureaucratic dictatorships and rational legal structures, says Dandeker, is that rulers in the latter are more accountable to the subject popula-tion. Examining four attributes of the development of public authorities, he explains in greater detail that modern nation-states possess bureaucratic systems for the internal policing of their populations, as well as for the management of external relations. The expansion of citizenship rights is at the centre of these developments, made possible by military and economic struggles within and between nation-states, as well as by expanding bureaucratic structures as modes of public administration and surveillance. The bureaucratization of war and military organization were of central importance to the internal and external means of power projection – from external resource exploitation to internal systems of taxation. As Dandeker argues, there were distinct phases in the bureaucratization of military power, from the seventeenth-century military revolution to the nineteenth-century industrialization of war, and it was the bureaucratization of mili-tary power that exacerbated developments between and among the fields of external and internal relations of power. While the development of the public authority of the state entails the institutional separation of the state and society, the rational modern bureau-cracy intensifies this process through its sheer surveillance capabilities. Facilitated by the interrelated forces of economic taxation systems, demographic population scale, technology and transport, the administrative penetration of society not only enhances the capacities for administering the population over distance. It also enables states to plan for the future.

One of the central arguments running through the first three reading passages is that as populations disperse and become more fluid, as in a society of strangers, the state introduces a greater number of mechanisms to monitor, administer and control the population. John Torpey puts a different spin on these developments in the fourth reading passage (Chapter 4). For Torpey, it is not so much that modern states monitor where people go, but rather that they restrict or monopolize the means of movement. As societies became more heterogeneous following the Medieval Period, and as populations grew larger, citizens became more reliant on state authorization for the legitimization of the means of movement across space. Torpey argues that these processes emerged in tandem with states' monopoly of the means of violence, and that they not only demonstrate the centrality of surveillance practices in state regulation and social control. They also demonstrate how the 'state-ness' of states is constituted in part through the right to authorize and regulate movement – an argument alluding to the importance of analytical focus on the form of social life.

The final reading passage, Chapter 5, is extracted from Michel Foucault's *Discipline and Punish: The Birth of the Prison*. In a manner somewhat different than Torpey, Foucault examines changes to human subjectivity in the eighteenth century – what happened rather than how – yet he achieves the former through an examination of the social architecture of the latter. Foucault introduces his passage with a discussion of how a seventeenth-century town addressed the threat of plague. First, an encompassing system of surveillance was enacted, to the extent that each community member's age, sex and name were centralized in the context of lockdown. Occupants of each household were called to show themselves at regular intervals in a steady regime of discontinuous surveillance. In the interests of the public good, the town was made known through a system of registration, reinforced by 'the great review of the living and the dead' (Foucault 1979: 196). Plague management called for multiple separations and an organization of in-depth surveillance and control, to the extent that even those who carried out quarantine procedures were not beyond the gaze of inspectors. The exercising of power, however, involved much more than asymmetrical inspection; it involved the individualization of pathology through classification, categorization and, in the case of house inspectors, search of person. For Foucault, plague management was the ideal political dream, and it did not even matter if there was a 'real' threat of plague. As he contends, the plague as a form, once real and imaginary, required only the haunting memory of contagions.

The significance of plague management, as a mechanism of surveillance and disciplinary control, is made clearer in the context of control mechanism applied to lepers. Whereas plague victims were surveilled by differentiation, segmentation and training, says Foucault, lepers were managed through segregation, exclusion and exile. Foucault argues that the exclusion of the leper and the arrest of the plague victim, although not bringing with them the same political dream, were nevertheless compatible projects, having slowly merged in the nineteenth century. What this reveals is that panoptical forms of surveillance through codification and data gathering techniques are dialectical, involving both inclusionary and exclusionary impulses. They are exclusionary in that they segregate the deviant from the community, individualizing categorical exclusions. They are inclusionary in that segregation does not simply involve punishment of the deviant; it entails, rather, the training of the community through disciplinary governmental techniques – a productive formation of the self (see Hier 2004). In Foucault's assessment, plague management facilitates understanding of the context in which

Bentham's writings on panopticon can be generalized as panopticism throughout the whole of society as a form of power and control.

Questions

Chapter 1 (Rule)

1   What does Rule mean by social scale? How does social scale influence systems of surveillance?
2   Differentiate systems of surveillance from the staging of social control. Think of a few contemporary examples to illustrate the differences.
3   What are the different ways that small- and large-scale societies provide the surveillance infrastructures necessary to stage systems of social control? What relationship, if any, does surveillance in small- and large-scale societies share?

Chapter 2 (Giddens)

1   Explain how Giddens understands totalitarianism. Why does he resist equating totalitarianism with a specific type of state?
2   In Giddens's assessment, is totalitarianism a component of traditional societies? Explain your answer with reference to totalitarian tendencies in modern nation-states.
3   What are the institutional features of totalitarianism? How does surveillance figure in this political type of rule?

Chapter 3 (Dandeker)

1   What are the four modes of surveillance identified by Dandeker? Discuss their corresponding systems of rule.
2   Identify two broad bureaucratic administrative structures that characterize modern societies. What are the key differences between the two structures?
3   What is the general role that surveillance occupies in the emergence of modern nation-states?

Chapter 4 (Torpey)

1   What does Torpey mean by the monopolization of the legitimate means of movement as a form of state surveillance?
2   What is the relationship between the development of modern bureaucratic states, as explored in the first three reading passages, and states' monopolization of the means of movement, as explored in the fourth reading passage?

Chapter 5 (Foucault)

1   In what ways can Foucault's example of plague management be used to illustrate the importance of studying forms of social surveillance?
2   What is disciplinary surveillance? How does it differ from more overt or explicit forms of social control?
3   How does Foucault explain panopticism as a socio-historical pattern of social control?

Suggested reading

1   Orwell, G. ([1949] 2004) *Nineteen Eighty-Four*. London: Gardner's Books.
    Nineteen Eighty-Four is the first of three dystopian novels discussed in the suggested readings. In *Nineteen Eighty-Four*, Orwell explores the life of Winston Smith and his efforts to think for himself. Winston Smith tries to evade Big Brother by challenging the propaganda of the Party. Although Orwell wrote *Nineteen Eighty-Four* in 1949, its basic lessons continue to appeal to a wide readership.

2   Kafka, F. ([1937] 1992) *The Trial*. New York: Alfred A. Knopf.
    The Trial focuses on Joseph K., a man who finds himself accused of a crime he did not commit. Joseph K., moreover, is not aware of the charges. He is released from custody, but required to constantly answer questions about his daily life. The novel explores the uncertainties of bureaucratic surveillance.

3   Atwood, M. (1985) *The Handmaid's Tale*. Toronto: McClelland-Bantam Inc.
    The Handmaid's Tale is the third dystopian novel discussed here. The novel portrays a police state that regulates all aspects of human life in a gendered and, more damaging, status-stratified society. Not only does Atwood remind us of the human social dimensions of surveillance, but she also captures the contingency of democracy and democratic parity.

4   Haggerty, K. and Ericson, R. (1999) The militarization of policing in the information age, *Journal of Political and Military Sociology*, 27(2): 233–55.
    Haggerty and Ericson argue that existing accounts of military dynamics overlook the broader social implications of the military's commitment to developing and using high technology. They contend that the spread of high technology into wider society has led to the American government's efforts to institutionalize a closer military/policing technological establishment.

5   Higgs, E. (2001) The rise of the information state: the development of central state surveillance of the citizen in England, 1500–2000, *Journal of the History of Sociology*, 14(2): 175–97.
    This article develops an argument that centralized forms of state surveillance predate industrialization. Contrary to popular argumentation, Higgs contends that the development of information gathering by state elites had more to do with the desire to maintain the status hierarchy of the English polity. He explores some the nuances of local versus state surveillance prior to the Industrial Revolution.

References

Anderson, B. (1991) *Imagined Communities*. London: Verso.

Foucault, M. (1979) *Discipline and Punish: The Birth of the Prison*. London: Peregrine.

Giddens, A. (1985) *The Nation State and Violence*. Berkeley, CA: University of California Press.

Hier, S. P. (2004) Risky spaces and dangerous faces: surveillance, social disorder, and CCTV, *Social and Legal Studies*, 13(4): 541–54.

Innis, H. (1950) *Empire and Communications*. Toronto: University of Toronto Press.

Lyon, D. (2001) *Surveillance Society: Monitoring Everyday Life*. Buckingham: Open University Press.

Rule, J. (1973) *Private Lives, Public Surveillance*. London: Allen Lane.

Simmel, G. (1950) *The Sociology of Georg Simmel*. New York: Free Press.

1

Social control and modern social structure[1]
by James B. Rule

Why do we find the world of *1984* so harrowing? Certainly one reason is its vision of life totally robbed of personal privacy, but there is more to it than that. For the ugliest and most frightening thing about that world was its vision of total *control* of men's lives by a monolithic, authoritarian state. Indeed, the destruction of privacy was a means to this end, a tool for enforcing instant obedience to the dictates of the authorities.

And yet, such thoroughgoing, relentless social control represents nothing other than an extreme manifestation of one of the ubiquitous processes of social life. Ubiquitous, and actually vital. True, sociologists have generally accepted the argument that social life would be impossible unless men felt a measure of willing commitment to abide by its rules. The social order would collapse, according to this argument, if everyone felt free to lie, steal, rape or cheat whenever he or she could avoid punishment for doing so.[2] But social life would be equally impossible without special means for making disobedience difficult or unattractive. For men's willingness to obey the strictures of established social forms is never wholly automatic, never merely a result of their inner commitment to the established rules. No, such conformity depends as much on a host of specific mechanisms of social control, ranging from gentle reproof to mass execution, from locks on doors to driving licences. Without them, we would find our world both unrecognizable and unviable.

Social control

By social control I mean all those mechanisms which discourage or forestall disobedience, which either punish such behaviour once it has occurred, or prevent those with inclinations to disobedience from acting on those inclinations. These mechanisms reinforce and sustain the most diverse social units. From the family to the state, from the most fanatical sect to the most hidebound bureaucracy, social bodies have their means of excluding those apt to break the rules, and their means of ensuring specific unpleasant consequences to those who disobey. Even lovers come both to recognize what each expects of the other and to be influenced by the unpleasant consequences of violating such expectations. Of course, the conspicuousness of the sanctions varies immensely. Some sanctions are informal and subtle, while others are flaunted as intimidating deterrents. But one may be confident that, wherever there are rules to guide men's behaviour and to constrain their selfish desires, there will also be mechanisms of social control to ensure that these rules are obeyed.

The workings of social control, and particularly efforts to impose or resist it, give rise to some of the bloodiest, most conflict-ridden chapters of social life. The growth of centralized states from groups of smaller, autonomous principalities, or the creation of an empire from a group of smaller states, represent cases in point. The efforts of the constituent elements to avoid subordination under a single system of control are bound to lead to serious tests of strength among them, and often violent ones at that. Once the issue is settled and the predominance of the new authorities is evident, social control may proceed more routinely, without repetition of the violent contests necessary to instate it in the first place. Nevertheless, the fact that the state or any other social unit may sustain itself by inconspicuous, routine manifestations of control should not obscure the considerable forces of social control implicit in the existence of such units.

It would be wrong to imply that contests over the imposition of social control occur only in the context of politics. The same dynamics are evident in the development of a new, inclusive religious faith which incorporates or supersedes an earlier array of smaller, parochial sects. Or, in the attempt of powerful business interests to overcome or take control of their localized competitors in order to found a national or international monopoly. The underlying process in all such cases is the same. Where there have been a plurality of centres of direction and coordination – of control, in short – a single centre attempts to assert its domination over these elements or, by destroying the old structures themselves, over the people who had comprised them. It is through such struggles that new social units of all kinds are born.

If new social units come into being with the extension of social control, failure of control can lead to their death. The challenge of a provincial revolt against a centralized state, after all, is nothing if not an attempt to deny the centre its ability to maintain control. Should such a revolt succeed, the state dies, even though its constituent parts, the provinces, may remain. The growth and breakup of states, again, is only one example. The same process is evident in the splintering of a broadly based political movement into a congeries of sects, or the dismantling of a corporate empire into its constituent firms. The point is, maintenance of some measure of control over any social unit is one way of identifying the unit as such. When social control fails, when the centre can no longer enforce its customary directives, the state, political movement, corporate entity or whatever loses its coherence and hence its identity.

Most social systems, in fact, have points of special vulnerability to failure in social control. These are points where disobedience is especially likely to occur, and where failure of control leads especially quickly to the unviability of the body as a coherent social unit. For an empire threatened by revolt, the salient problem might be the enforcement upon the provinces of customary obligations of taxation and military service. For an established church facing a rash of heresy, the preoccupation might be the enforcement of doctrinal or liturgical orthodoxy. In cases like these, the regime will also have other tasks of social control, other norms which it desires to see enforced. But first concerns are apt to go to these more pressing problems. An empire about to lose its grip on its territories, or a church about to lose its religious authority and hence its following, must concern itself with the preservation of these things before it can afford to be concerned about anything else. One can identify similar 'fault lines' in most social units, points at which disobedience is especially likely and the failure of control especially dangerous to the system. The leadership of such bodies, if it is shrewd, will not begrudge the attention necessary to assure compliance at these points, even at the cost of neglecting other forms of control.

Those who seek to maintain social control must accomplish two sorts of things. First, they must maintain what one might call *powers of control*. This means, for one thing, that they need to be able to apply sanctions, or inducements sufficient to discourage the sanctioned person from repeating his disobedient acts. The sanctions, of course, can be positive or negative, physical or symbolic, formal or informal, so long as they really do influence behaviour. Second, if the system is not to rely only on reward or punishment after the fact, it must possess means of excluding would-be rule-breakers from the opportunity to disobey, for example, by refusing in some way to deal with them. Many systems, . . . can afford to be weak in the first respect, so long as they remain strong in the second. And many forms of punishment, such as execution and imprisonment, work both to make misbehaviour undesirable from the standpoint of the would-be deviant, and to insulate others from his behaviour.

Neither of these two powers does any good, however, without . . . a system of *surveillance*. In the first place, surveillance entails a means of knowing when rules are being obeyed, when they are broken, and, most importantly, who is responsible for which. In some instances these things may be easy to accomplish, e.g., a flagrant armed robbery by notorious criminals. In the case of other forms of disobedience, such as income tax evasion, it may be extremely difficult. A second element of surveillance, also indispensable, is the ability to locate and identify those responsible for misdeeds of some kind. Again, this may be simple in many cases . . . however, it may be the most difficult condition of all to fulfil.

In practice, it is often very difficult to draw boundaries between processes of surveillance and the application of what had been termed the powers of control . . . [F]or example, the same people and the same bodies are often engaged in the collection of information and in the application of sanctions. Nevertheless, when I want to emphasize those activities having to do with collecting and maintaining information, I speak of *systems of surveillance*. Where the concern lies more with the actual management of behaviour, through sanctioning or exclusion, I refer to *systems of control*. To designate the organizations, persons or interests seeking to maintain control, I use the terms *agency, regime*, or more broadly, just 'the system'. Finally, those from whom compliance is sought are called the 'clientele' of any particular system of control . . .

The staging of social control

Because of both cost considerations and other factors, rules enforceable in one setting may be quite incapable of enforcement elsewhere. It may be easy to enforce, say, a tax on the use of a particular road simply by erecting a toll gate and exacting payment from all who pass. Here the task of control is relatively simple and inexpensive; anyone who fails to pay is easily noted, apprehended and sanctioned. Much more problematic, however, is the enforcement of a tax on the distillation of whisky. For there the authorities have difficulty in knowing that the violation is occurring in the first place, and perhaps even more difficulty in determining who is responsible for the violation. Because of such tactical considerations, agencies of control often try to manipulate the social setting of the behaviour in question so as to gain the maximum advantage over their clienteles. In Britain, for example, international travellers may legally land and depart only from a limited number of recognized seaports and air-fields, staffed by the 'Special Branch' or political police and immigration authorities for this purpose. Were this not the case, control over movement in and out of the country would be more expensive at best, and perhaps impossible in any case.

. . . [S]uch tactical considerations in enforcement are called the *staging* of social control. More specifically, one might define staging as the relative advantage and disadvantage to system and clientele posed by the social structural context of surveil-lance and control. Thus the staging of any forms of control may be favourable to the system, in that it makes enforcement easy, or to the clientele, in that it facilitates evasion . . .

More than anything else, [we are] . . . concerned with the effects upon the staging of social control of changes in the *scale* of social life. Social scale is a concept some-times used by sociologists and economists to describe the extent of interdependence among people in different social units.[3] The scale of any social unit is seen as pro-portional to the numbers of people comprising it, and to the intensity of relations among them. The unit itself may either be the whole of a society, or some smaller element of social organization, like a family or a bureaucracy. In the instance of whole societies, the smallest-scale cases would be the isolated, autonomous group of primi-tives, self-sufficient as a band of even a few hundred people. Few social groupings like this actually remain, but so far as one knows all men once lived in very small-scale units like these. Of middling social scale, by these criteria, would be loosely integrated, ancient states, where a single capital theoretically rules a considerable area, but actually impinges rather little on the lives of those in the province. England during feudal times is a tolerable example. Even when the nation was united under a single monarch, there was little in the way of central administration, and both local govern-ment and the balance of local social and economic life went on in considerable parochial autonomy.

By contrast, the large-scale organization of the modern nation-state both embraces very large numbers of people and orders their lives in very close dependence upon one another. The highly centralized, powerful polities of modern states, with their powers to tax the entire population, to raise massive military forces, and to maintain uniform legal systems throughout their boundaries are only one manifesation of this interdependence. Their closely integrated economic systems, where the failure of one firm can immediately endanger the jobs of workers in a different industry thousands of miles away, is another. No less significant are the comprehensive, interdependent structures which dominate education, communications, religion or any number of other social activities. Indeed, the growth of the modern nation-state is very much the story of the destruction of old forms of local and regional autonomy, and of their replacement by social forms which bring the affairs of all the populace into closer coordination . . .

. . . [T]he scale of different social settings has everything to do with the viability of different forms of social control, and specifically with the staging of control. Forms of behaviour easily controlled in small-scale social settings may be almost impossible to control elsewhere, and vice versa. Hence changes in the scale of social life have drastic effects on the relations between agencies of control and their clienteles.

Small-scale social units, whether they are primitive tribes, small towns, or something else, generally rely on highly informal but nonetheless effective means of social control. In such settings, after all, social behaviour is much more likely than elsewhere to be a public matter. Instances of thievery, an illicit love affair, or any other breach of commonly accepted rules are not apt to escape general attention. Moreover, given that people in such settings are apt to know their fellows through face-to-face acquaintance, the perpetrator is unlikely to escape the resulting sanctions of community disapproval. Gossip spreads the news of misbehaviour throughout one's entire social world, and one's past is thus virtually an open book. In more cosmopolitan settings, however, escape from one's past may be much easier. The simple fact that these societies comprise so many participants makes it impossible for everyone to know about everyone else. Nor are the standards of 'correct' behaviour so uniform. Given these differences in the staging of social control, one wonders whether the conformity often noted in small-scale settings necessarily stems, as many anthropologists have felt, from some special moral solidarity.[4] A more likely explanation, one suspects, is the effectiveness of specific mechanisms of social control.

By contrast, consider the position of the state or any other agency seeking to obtain compliance from a mass clientele in a large-scale social setting. Attempting to make the members of such a body pay their taxes, or obey the motoring laws, or refrain from subversive political activities, any regime automatically faces enormous problems of surveillance. No one person could possibly be acquainted with all members of such a public, still less keep track of them all at the same time. Nor is it easy to maintain surveillance over all points where disobedience might occur, so as to note violations of the rules. Faced with the problem of securing compliance from a mobile, anonymous public, any regime must do its best to develop techniques to replicate the functions of gossip and face-to-face acquaintance in small-scale social settings.

Still, means do exist to this end. The commonest solutions to the problem of mass surveillance in large-scale societies lie in the use of documentation. Whether in discursive prose, standardized data-sheets or computer records, the formal rendering of information about people comes to take the place of informal mechanisms of surveillance found in small-scale settings. The crucial function of such documentation is to link people to their pasts, and thereby to provide the surveillance necessary for the exercise of social control. Given the anonymity of large-scale societies, the mobility of persons within such societies, and the time lapses involved in encounters between agency and client, it is only through documentation that the former can keep track of who is who, and who has done what. Without passports, credit records, licences and the host of other documents which link flesh-and-blood men and women to their past statuses, misdeeds, accomplishments or whatever, all sorts of critical relations would be impossible – including the relations of control which subsist between the members of mass societies and their major institutions . . .

The growth of mass surveillance and control, then, seems somehow bound up with the changing structures of modern societies. But just what is the nature of this association? And what new forms of social organization and control do further developments along these lines promise? Does the continued extension of mass surveillance promise the advent of more and more oppressive forms of social control? Is the association between rigid mass surveillance and authoritarian rule accidental or inevitable? Again, one recalls uneasily the very large-scale, very tightly controlled world of *1984*. Does the continued growth of mass surveillance draw us relentlessly into a world like Orwell's? Or will a closer, more analytical look at these developments yield a more complex and subtle set of predictions?

The growth of mass surveillance

Since the mid-1960s, these developments have received increasing public attention, both in Britain and in America. Journalists, legislators, jurists and others have identified in the growing collection and use of personal information both the seeds of destruction of personal privacy and the beginnings of *1984*-style authoritarianism. The cause of the alarm has not only been the growth of mass surveillance in the sense used here, but also in the development of sophisticated eavesdropping techniques, data banks, census inquiries and other forms of intrusion into men's private lives. Such concerns have led to a good deal of writing on these topics, by both academics and other interested observers. These authors have generally decried the growth of such activities, offered grave predictions concerning their imminent effects, and proposed various solutions to avert such calamities.

Anyone concerned about the growth of mass surveillance, and about the moral and social issues which it poses, will be grateful for this response, . . . Nevertheless, I feel that the inferences drawn by these authors, even the most conscientious of them, have sometimes been excessively glib. This tendency is most serious at that delicate point where discussion moves from observed fact to inference and prediction.

A case in point might be drawn from the recent study by Malcolm Warner and Michael Stone. At one point the authors provide an interesting and useful discussion of data files, and the issues inherent in their centralization and confidentiality, only to have their imaginations run wild in conclusion. Commenting on the possibility of adopting a single number for the files of every individual, they write:

> Probably a unique number would mean that there would have to be an issue of identity cards – to be carried at all times so that the number could be quoted at all times. That seems harmless, but once you make any piece of paper obligatory it is a very easy step into tyranny – witness South Africa. If you haven't got it, it's a crime; if it is taken from you, you're stuck – you become a 'non-person'.[5]

Here one feels that the authors have stopped thinking critically, and instead are contenting themselves with playing to the grandstand of alarmed public opinion.

Even Alan Westin, whose book *Privacy and Freedom* is widely and justly regarded as the best review of recent developments on these topics, is not invulnerable to the temptation to make unhelpfully rash speculations. One passage in that book discusses the possibility of a universal credit system where no financial transaction would take place in cash:

> ... the life of [the?] individual would be almost wholly recorded and observable through analysis of the daily 'transactions' of 'Credit Card No. 172,381,400 . . .' Whoever ran the computers could know when the individual entered the highway and where he got off; how many bottles of Scotch or Vermouth he purchased from the liquor store; who paid the rent for the girl in Apartment 4B; who went to the movies between two and four p.m. on a working day at the office; who was at lunch at Luigi's or the Four Seasons on Tuesday, September 15; and the hotel at which Mrs Smith spent the rainy afternoon last Sunday . . . There would be few areas in which anyone could move about in the anonymity of personal privacy and few transactions that would not be fully documented for government examination.[6]

These two statements are representative of an extremely widespread trend among recent writings on these topics. Such statements are not factually incorrect; their speculative nature makes it impossible to submit them to proof or disproof. But they are unhelpful in that they carry speculation to such an extreme as to blur the distinction between concrete, verifiable trends and fancy. More seriously, they seem to take for granted precisely the questions which are most problematic and most challenging. *How* does the use of identity cards lead to tyranny? *How* does computerized credit accounting conduce to state control over persons' private lives? Is it *necessarily* true that the development of unique numbering for personal identification brings any society within 'a very easy step' to tyranny? Would universal reliance on credit *inevitably* and *inherently* lead to a situation where 'there would be few areas in which anyone could move about in the anonymity of personal privacy and few transactions that would not be fully documented for government examination'?

The most pressing need of all in these cases is to judge the real possibilities of such developments, to assess the concrete forces which conduce to or contravene the feared results. The installation of a central water supply for a large city may in itself open the possibility of poisoning the entire populace with a single lethal dose. But one's concern about such an event clearly turns on the concrete conditions which would make such an event likely or unlikely. So it should be with the development of mass surveillance . . .

. . . [L]et me sketch a model of the most extreme possible development of mass surveillance, an ideal type of a social order resembling the one portrayed by Orwell, though perhaps even more extreme. This I call a *total surveillance society.*

In such a world, first of all, there would be but a single system of surveillance and control, and its clientele would consist of everyone. This system would work to enforce compliance with a uniform set of norms governing every aspect of everyone's behaviour. Every action of every client would be scrutinized, recorded and evaluated, both at the moment of occurrence and for ever afterwards. The system would collate all information at a single point, making it impossible for anyone to evade responsibility for his past by fleeing from the scene of earlier behaviour. Nor would the single master agency compartmentalize information which it collected, keeping certain data for use only in certain kinds of decisions. Instead, it would bring the whole fund of its information to bear on every decision it made about everyone. Any sign of disobedience – present or anticipated – would result in corrective action. The fact that the system kept everyone under constant monitoring would mean that, in the event of misbehaviour, apprehension and sanctioning would occur immediately. By making detection and retaliation inevitable, such a system would make disobedience almost unthinkable.

One should never expect to encounter a real system like the one just described. That is just the point. The only usefulness of this paradigm is as a foil for comparison to real systems, as a case guaranteed to be more extreme than the real world could ever produce. True, some agencies may develop something like systems of total surveillance over very limited numbers of people, for short periods of time. Police may keep constant watch over a small group of conspirators, or the staff of a hospital may exercise something like total surveillance over those in the intensive care ward. But difficulties of staging, and especially prohibitive costs, rule out such techniques for larger clienteles over longer periods of time. No, the usefulness of the paradigm lies in its making it possible to compare systems of surveillance and control now in existence to this theoretical extreme, and to one another in terms of their proximity to this extreme . . .

For example, any real surveillance system is limited in *size*. This means, for one thing, limitation to the numbers of persons whom it can depict in its files. Second, there is always a limitation in the amount of information with which a system can cope, the amount which it can meaningfully use in its decision-making on each person. Indeed . . . the amount of *usable* information is often less than that which is theoretically available on file. And such limitations on the amount of usable data kept per person correspond in turn to limitations in the amount of the subject's life depicted in the files. Third, surveillance systems also face limitations in what one might term the *subtlety* of their decision-making based on filed data. In the world of *1984* the authorities seemed to use information cunningly enough to know what their people were going to do even before they themselves did . . .

Second, real surveillance systems are limited in the *centralization* of their files . . . Centralization of data is extremely important in the staging of social control, in that it prevents clients from escaping the effects of their past by moving from one place to another. If the single central record can be applied wherever the fugitive goes, such movement does no good. Thus, to be fully effective, any system of surveillance should be able to collect information on a person's behaviour from any point in a society, and use it to enact measures of control on the same person at any other point. . . .

Third, real systems fall short of the total surveillance extreme, and vary considerably among themselves, in terms of the *speed* of *information-flow* and *decision-making* which they exhibit. In Orwell's world, all misbehaviour presumably was registered with the authorities immediately, and resulted in immediate retribution when necessary. [Today's systems] by contrast, are not nearly so sophisticated. They are slow, for one thing, in their intake of information: relevant facts may be available for some time before the system can bestir itself to incorporate them in usable form. Moreover, these systems vary in the speed of movement of data once it is incorporated in their files, and in the application of such data to decision-making about people. Limitations like these make it easier for the individual to escape the effects of his past, for example, in cases where the agency of surveillance and control cannot bring its data to bear on a client quickly enough to act against him.

Fourth, and finally, real systems of mass surveillance and control are limited to varying degrees in what I term their *points of contact* with their clienteles. This again involves several things. First, existing systems are limited in the numbers of points at which they can incorporate information on the people with whom they must deal. Whereas in *1984* the authorities could 'tune in' on virtually every moment of every person's life, real surveillance systems restrict themselves to limited points of intake – for example, through the courts and a few other junctures in the case of police surveillance, and through credit-granting institutions, in the instance of consumer credit reporting. Similarly, existing systems are limited in terms of their ability to 'get back at' – to locate, accost and apprehend – those who have broken the rules. Unlike Orwell's world, modern societies provide many opportunities for those who wish to avoid the attention of the authorities simply to drop out of sight. To be sure, systems of mass control have their own ways of countervailing against these opportunities. But the point is clear; systems vary in their ability to penetrate the anonymity of mass society so as to make the disobedient available for sanctions. A final and equally important element of contact between system and clientele is the ability of the former to identify individual clients . . . [T]he position of the agency of control suffers unless it can quickly and unerringly link any single client to his record. Since clients themselves often wish to avoid such linkage, the strength of identification systems represents one of the important elements of the hold of the system on those with whom it deals.

These four forms of limitations of present-day surveillance systems, in relation to the total surveillance extreme, are at the same time criteria of their *capacity* or effectiveness. As any system develops along any of these dimensions, it improves in its ability to carry out the tasks of mass surveillance and control. Nor are the four criteria only theoretical toys, for . . . these same four issues are of immense practical concern to those who run systems of mass surveillance . . .

Notes

1   This chapter is an extract from J. Rule (1973) Social control and modern social structure, *Private Lives and Public Surveillance*. London: Allen Lane, pp. 19–43.
2   This assumption is the stepping-off point for all the immensely influential work of Talcott Parsons. The key reference, of course, is *The Social System*, London, Tavistock Publications, 1952.
3   To the best of my knowledge, this concept was originally developed in Godfrey and Monica Wilson, *The Analysis of Social Change*, Cambridge University Press, 1945, see especially Chapter II. Another application is in Eshref Shevky and Wendell Bell, *Social Area Analysis*, Stanford, California, Stanford University Press, 1955.
4   More persuasive, in this context, are the arguments of Malinowski. See Bronislaw Malinowski, *Crime and Custom in Savage Society*, London, Kegan Paul, Trench, Trubner and Co., 1926; especially Chapter XI.
5   Malcolm Warner and Michael Stone, *The Data-Bank Society*, London, George Allen and Unwin, 1970, p. 77.
6   Alan F. Westin, *Privacy and Freedom*, New York, Atheneum, 1967, p. 165.

2

Modernity, totalitarianism and critical theory[1]
by Anthony Giddens

In his speech of acceptance for the Nobel Literary prize in the late 1950s, Camus observed that those

> born at the outset of World War I became twenty at the time both of Hitler's ascent to power and of the first revolutionary trial. Then, to complete their education, they were confronted in turn by the Spanish Civil War and World War Two – the universal concentration camp, a Europe of torture and prisons. Today they must raise their children and produce their work in a world threatened by nuclear destruction. Nobody, surely, can expect them to be optimists.[2]

. . . Camus's remarks were motivated in some part both by a certain repugnance towards modernity in general and by an awareness of the dangers of totalitarian political power in particular. Totalitarianism, I shall claim, is a tendential property of the modern state. An understanding of the origins of totalitarianism, as a specifically twentieth-century phenomenon, presumes analysing the consolidated political power generated by a merging of developed techniques of surveillance and the technology of industrialized war. Looming behind this is the question of the relation between states and the deployment of military power in current times – not just as an analytical issue but as a problem for normative political theory. How might the monopoly of the means of violence on the part of states be reconciled with established political ideas of the 'good society'? . . .

Totalitarianism: surveillance and violence

The history of the term 'totalitarian' is well-known, even if the concept itself is one of the most fiercely debated in political theory. When Gentile spoke of '*uno stato totali-tario*' on behalf of Mussolini, he can have had little idea of the uses to which the term would later be put, or the controversies in which it would figure. The word was first coined as one carrying a favourable connotation in respect of the political order to which it referred, at a period when Mussolini was still advocating freedom of the press, accepting the existence of other parties and favouring a competitive market economy. 'Totalitarian' began to be used in critical attacks upon Italian fascism in the late 1920s, when opposition parties were brutally suppressed, all trade unions except state-sponsored ones abolished, the Chamber of Deputies dissolved and concentration camps set up, with the death penalty being instituted for political offences.

Since then the concept has undergone numerous vicissitudes. It has been applied to movements, parties, leaders and ideas, as well as more commonly to political systems.[3] States or governments that have been labelled totalitarian include above all fascist Italy, Nazi Germany and Stalin's Soviet Union, but also Russia under the Czars, a range of traditional states, especially Egypt and Rome, absolutist states, and fictional societies like Plato's republic. Small wonder that the notion has been called 'a conceptual harlot of uncertain parentage, belonging to no-one but at the service of all'.[4] Amid the welter of usages there are some general lines of agreement accepted by many writers. Most argue that totalitarianism is, in fully developed form at any rate, recent in origin, dating from about the time at which the term itself was invented. The concept is usually taken to be above all a political one, referring to a mode of organizing political power, involving its extreme concentration in pursuit of objectives defined by a narrowly circumscribed leadership. Friedrich's definition is the one perhaps most often quoted in the literature. Totalitarianism, he says, is distinct 'from other and older autocracies' and from 'Western-type democracies'. It has six characteristics:

> (1) a totalist ideology; (2) a single party committed to this ideology and usually led by one man, the dictator; (3) a fully developed secret police; and three kinds of monopoly or, more precisely, monopolistic control: namely that of (a) mass communications; (b) operational weapons; (c) all organisations, including economic ones.[5]

The contrast between totalitarianism and 'Western-type democracies' is of key importance in explaining the popularity of the concept in the period since the Second World War. Totalitarian states were regarded by liberal political observers as including those forms of social order that have an advanced industrial base, but do not display the institutional characteristics of liberal democracy. Whereas when referring to Italy or Germany totalitarianism designated a relatively transitory phase in social development – terminated by war – in the case of the Soviet Union and the East European countries it was used to refer to a definite type of socio-political order separate from the capitalist states, continuing as long as that order remained in existence. Applied as a characteristic of the East European states, 'totalitarian' refers to a political system supposedly displaying the characteristics mentioned by Friedrich. The USSR and the state socialist societies are portrayed as monolithic systems of political power, founded upon cultural and social conformity deriving from the suppression of interest divisions. This standpoint is often linked to an equation of Marxist socialism with authoritarianism, producing an all-pervasive state, subordinating the needs or wishes of the populace to the arbitrary policies of the state authorities. Collectivism, as Belloc observed, may stem from noble motives, but leads in practice to omnipotent state power. 'The capitalist state breeds a collectivist theory which *in action* produces something utterly different from collectivism: to wit, the servile state.'[6]

If this type of view is correct, totalitarianism cannot be regarded as a phenomenon that could potentially come about in all modern states. It is a type of rule associated with fascist and Soviet-type societies, that could only come into being in liberal democratic states if they succumbed to collectivism. Two questions therefore arise. How far does it make any sense to describes the Soviet Union and the Eastern European states in the terms listed by Friedrich? Do these characteristics, once identified, bear close comparison with episodes of fascism in Europe and elsewhere? For we should accept, I think, that totalitarianism is a different phenomenon to the forms of autocracy found in traditional states . . .

If we compare, not Soviet-type society to liberal-democratic capitalism as a whole, but Stalinism, Nazism and Italian fascism, both in their theory and in their practice, we find some marked similarities. These for the most part do indeed tend to involve the points mentioned by Friedrich. In each case a dictatorial ruler shaped pre-existing symbolic systems into a consolidated ideological basis of rule, accompanied by the pervasive use of coercion to suppress dissidence. Italian fascism was by far the least murderous of the three. The secret police force OVRA was specifically established in the late 1920s to dissolve internal political opposition, with heavy political censorship imposed upon antagonistic groups. Nonetheless, in the 1930s some 20,000 people in Italy were arraigned before special courts and 10,000 imprisoned without trial. As in the other states, in Italy the law was personalized, giving the individual ruler a range of sanctions at his disposal for the control of recalcitrants. Thus, in 1926, Mussolini was accorded the right to issue legally binding decrees, many thousands of which were promulgated during the course of his rule. As the Supreme Leader of the Soviets, Stalin was able personally to dominate many aspects of overall state policy. The Enabling Act of 1933 in Germany gave Hitler, as Chancellor, the right to make laws for a certain period without the need for ratification.[7] In each country the 'total ideology' of which Friedrich speaks was based upon a strong stimulation of nationalism, stressing radical distinctions between the national community and 'out-groups', and associated with the figure of the leader. Party organization was also constructed around affiliation to the leader, this affiliation again being couched in the language of a self-sufficient nationalism.

The use of terror marked all three regimes, although loss of life was much lower in Italy than in the case of the other two states. Terror was justified by appeals to national unity and to the involvement of the mass of the people in the governmental system. 'The German people', according to Hitler, 'has elected a single deputy as its representative with 38 million votes . . . I feel myself just as responsible to the German people as would any parliament.'[8] In Italy it needed more than four years to effectively suppress other political parties, but in Germany this was accomplished in an immediate and radical fashion, with mass imprisonment and the building of large concentration camps. By the outbreak of the War, there were in Germany over a quarter of a million people imprisoned for political reasons and three times this number by the end of the hostilities. During this period possibly as many as twelve million people were systematically exterminated. If these figures are staggering, they were probably surpassed in the Soviet Union during Stalin's rule. In the purges some one

million people lost their lives and some twelve million more died in the labour camps;
perhaps some twenty million people died as a direct result of the use of violence as a
means of political repression during the whole period of Stalin's ascendancy.[9] In the
Soviet Union, like Germany, the labour camps made a major contribution to the
country's performance in the war. Twenty per cent of the country's railways were
constructed by workers from the camps and 75 per cent of the gold mined was
extracted by such workers. But in neither case was the rationale for the existence of
the camps more than marginally economic.[10]

In all three societies, the systematic use of violence was combined with the use of
networks of secret police, having extensive and frequently employed powers of arrest
for political transgressions, these phenomena being closely connected with rigid state
direction of cultural activity.[11] The widespread use of terror, according to Arendt,
tends to be integrated with strict control over cultural production, because the point
of the threat of violence is not so much to instil fear as to create a climate in which
acceptance of propaganda will be facilitated.

> [When] Stalin decided to rewrite the history of the Russian Revolution, the
> propaganda of his new version consisted in destroying, together with the older
> books and documents, their authors and readers: the publication in 1938 of a new
> official history of the Communist Party was the signal that the superpurge which
> had decimated a whole generation of Soviet intellectuals had come to an end.
> Similarly, the Nazis in the Eastern occupied territories at first used chiefly
> antisemitic propaganda to win former control of the population. They neither
> needed nor used terror to support this propaganda. When they liquidated the
> greater part of the Polish intelligentsia, they did it not because of its opposition,
> but because according to their doctrine Poles had no intellect, and when they
> planned to kidnap blue-eyed and blond-haired children, they did not intend to
> frighten the population, but to save 'Germanic blood'.[12]

This does not imply, she adds, that in totalitarianism terror is secondary to the
regimented control of cultural production. On the contrary, terror continues to be
used by totalitarian regimes even when a population, or the relevant section of the
population, is completely quiescent. Terror is, as it were, the very medium of government. This seems valid from one respect, but questionable from another. Having been
used to subdue certain social groupings, or to secure particular policies, the orchestrated use of violence tends to continue just as before. On the other hand, in each of
the three examples, the acquiescence of the majority was not purchased through the
use of force against them, or even by the dissemination of propaganda. All three
regimes, particularly their leaders, secured a considerable level of active and enthusi-
astic support from diverse sectors of the population. The student of totalitarianism
must explain this as well as the role of terror in mobilizing subject populations for the
doctrines advocated by the state authorities. Of course, mass support was in some
part fostered by programmes carefully orchestrated to achieve that end. For example,
the National Socialists gave a great deal of attention to planning the leisure activities of
the population in order to develop the spirit of national unity they deemed desirable
and proper. All manner of types of communal recreation were organized through

local party cadres, under central direction.[13] But the enthusiasm with which much of the population embraced the Nazi cause and expressed active support for their leader can hardly be accounted for entirely by such programmes.

Let me sum up at this point where the preceding comments lead. I consider Friedrich's concept of totalitarianism to be accurate and useful. Totalitarianism is not characteristic of traditional states, but only of nation-states and nation-states in relatively recent times at that; its main features can be represented according to Friedrich's criteria. But 'totalitarian' is not an adjective that can be fruitfully applied to a type of state, let alone to Soviet-style states generically. It refers rather to a *type of rule*, unstable in major aspects, yet capable of bringing about the most horrendous consequences for the populations that suffer the brunt of its concentrated power. Totalitarianism is, thus far at least, a phenomenon associated mainly with Italian fascism, Nazism and Stalinism, but there are other examples which fall into the same category – for example, the brief rule of Pol Pot in Kampuchea. While, of course, there are major differences between all these examples, they share very important threads in common. These common characteristics relate to features of the modern state in general; there is no type of nation-state in the contemporary world which is completely immune from the potentiality of being subject to totalitarian rule.[14]

. . . Nation-states differ in a fundamental way from traditional ones in respect of the maximizing of survellance which, in combination with internal pacification, generates an administrative unity corresponding to definite borders. Totalitarianism cannot exist in traditional states because their segmental character is incompatible with the necessary mobilization of concentrated resources. Several of the features of totalitarian control are present in some traditional states, but not in the same overall combination with one another. Thus what Friedrich calls a 'totalist ideology' is almost the norm rather than the exception in class-divided societies. The confinement of literacy to small groupings of the population, the typical fusion of theocracy and military power, allied to the absence of a 'public sphere' in the modern sense, usually make for the dominance of a confined symbolic culture. But this cannot become effective 'propaganda' so far as the majority of the subject population are concerned, since it is not possible for the state authorities to ensure that it is systematically channelled to the mass. Secret police are common in traditional states, but normally the scope of their influence is limited to the locales of the elite and of government officialdom. Terror, in the sense of the large-scale use of violence to subdue or intimidate subject groups, particularly conquered populations, is exceedingly common in the pages of history. But in the scale of historical massacres and brutalities there is nothing that can more than remotely match the degradations of totalitarianism.

The possibilities of totalitarian rule depend upon the existence of societies in which the state can successfully penetrate the day-to-day activities of most of its subject population. This, in turn, presumes a high level of surveillance . . . the coding of information about and the supervision of the conduct of significant segments of the population. Totalitarianism is, first of all, an extreme focusing of surveillance, devoted to the securing of political ends deemed by the state authorities to demand urgent political mobilization. Surveillance tends to become concentrated (a) in respect of a multiplication of modes of the documenting of the subject population by the state – identity cards, permits of all sorts, and other kinds of official papers, have to be held by all members of the population and used to follow even the most ordinary of activities; and (b) this is the basis of an expanded supervision of those activities, carried out by the police or their agents.

The ends to which totalitarian rule is mobilized tend to be strongly involved with nationalism, since nationalist sentiments offer the prime ideological means of binding together otherwise diverse populations. Nationalism is important in supplying the 'total' aspect of totalitarian doctrines because it carries its own 'symbolic historicity', providing a myth of origins of a people, but also supplying the people with a common destiny to be striven for in the future. Fascist thought tends to draw upon those elements of nationalist ideals that make up the aggressive, exclusivist side of the nationalist Janus. Marxism, as its critics have long pointed out, can readily be adapted to messianic goals and is the *locus classicus* of historicity conceived of as linking the past to an immanent future. But Stalinism, nonetheless, involves a considerable admixture of nationalist thought, to which the notion of 'socialism in one country' was admirably suited. Whether linked with Marxist-Leninism or not, nationalism lends itself readily to mass propaganda, since the fate of the whole community is considered to be a shared one.

Elements of totalitarian rule

1   *Focusing of surveillance* as:
    (a) information coding, documentation of activities of the population,
    (b) supervision of activities, intensified policing.
2   '*Moral totalism*': fate of the political community as embedded in the historicity of the people.
3   *Terror*: maximizing of police power, allied to disposal of the means of waging industrialized war and sequestration.
4   *Prominence of leader figure*: appropriation of power by leader depending not upon a professionalized military role, but the generation of mass support.

Surveillance involving the use of intensified policing rapidly tends to dissolve into terror, for fairly self-evident reasons. The most obvious one – although arguably the least consequential – is that policing tends to become allied to the application of methods of torture to obtain confessions, in contexts in which crimes involve the holding of deviant political views, rather than involving specified infractions of the law. Much more important are the capabilities of police or paramilitary forces to deploy the technology of industrialized war against an unarmed or poorly armed population. Tanks, mortars, machine-guns deployed with reference to a civilian population, even if presented as a threat rather than actually put to use, can for policing purposes allow a temporary physical control of populations well in excess of anything that could be accomplished in traditional states. This is especially true if the means of violence are focused upon particular groupings in those populations, rather than being used as an instrument of government of the overall political community. When combined with methods of sequestration already well pioneered in other contexts of deviance, the concentrated application of the use of force against minority groupings can become extremely intense. The term 'concentration camp' already carries this meaning and is the most 'total' of 'total institutions', thus being the prototype of totalitarian terror. Terror here, as Arendt says, is not concerned with the causing of fear for its own sake, but rather expresses the extremity of the 'deviance' attributed to those interned, from which the majority outside needs to be protected.

A key aspect of totalitarianism, without which the rest would not be possible, or at least would not be unified into a cohesive system of rule, is the presence of the leader figure. The leader abrogates powers previously belonging to the law courts, political assemblies, or separate state officials. This can be achieved partly on the basis of the use of terror, purging those who disagree with particular policies or who might in some way be a source of resistance to them. But a high level of personal affiliation to the leader on the part of the police and the military is also demanded, as well as the active support of large segments of the general population . . .

In spite of its name, totalitarianism is not an all-or-nothing phenomenon and has direct links to a range of less cataclysmic potentialities of modern states. Let me briefly indicate these, moving from 4 to 1 in the preceding characterization of totalitarian rule. So far as point 4 goes, the issue concerns that of the possibility of personalized rule in modern states. Such a form of domination was prototypical of traditional states, there only having been two known exceptions to it – Classical Greece and the Roman Republic. The existence of 'dictatorships' today has to be understood against a background of universal acknowledgement of polyarchy. A fairly high degree of personalizing of leadership can appear in all polyarchic systems, as Weber pointed out and indeed actively advocated as desirable. What he called 'charisma' probably rests upon the very psychological dynamics of leadership just discussed, in so far as personalized leadership is able to generate mass support. Personalized leadership may, of course, be associated with military government. An individual achieves political power not through available electoral mechanisms, but through its seizure by the armed forces, of which that individual is either the overall commander or rises to prominence within the ruling military cabinet. Such rulers may become 'dictators' in the sense that, controlling the means of violence, they are able to impose a range of policies upon a largely recalcitrant population, at least for a certain period of time. But given the difficulties inherent in sustaining military government, 'dictatorship' of this sort is not likely to persist unless the individual in question is able to generate widespread commitment among a considerable section of the civilian population.

By far the most common circumstance in which strongly personalized rule emerges is where a government is established as a result of the influence of a social movement – again indicating the importance of 'charisma'. Such was the case in each of the three major circumstances of totalitarian rule, the conditions giving rise to the movements involved no doubt also influencing the strength of the personal affiliations the leaders were able to achieve. Stalin was the 'inheritor' of the mantle of Lenin, but was able to sustain a style of personalized leadership because the impetus of the changes initiated by the October Revolution were still strong, Lenin having died too soon after his assumption of government for there to have begun a full-scale process of the routinization of charisma. Since the influence of social movements in the political life of modern nations is bound to remain marked, in the light of the 'fields of historicity' afforded by modern culture, personalized leadership is certain to remain a prominent feature of the political life of many states.

It is partly the association of the charismatic leader with a social movement achieving governmental power that explains why the fostering of terror becomes a possibility. Social movements are dynamic modes of association, concerned to mobilize change in accordance with convictions that do not necessarily allow much space for alternative opinions. The 'moral leverage' which a popular leader is able to achieve over a followership, combined with control of modern instruments of violence, generates repressive capabilities of a very formidable kind indeed. Since the French Revolution, terror has been associated particularly with the activities of post-revolutionary regimes and continues to be so in the twentieth-century world. But on a more minor scale it has to be regarded as an ever-present possibility within modern political systems wherever there are acute problems of governability. Here the issues involved merge with some of those raised by considering the internal role of armed force confronting the pacified populations of nation-states. Policing based upon the pervasive use of violence, supported by paramilitary forces or the army, is in principle a possibility within states of all types. Its importance in the modern state raises questions of political theory concerned with control of the means of violence generally, and these I shall consider in a following section.

'Moral totalism' I connect particularly with the pervasive influence of historicism in the culture of modernity. In the sphere of politics it is most particularly associated with nationalist doctrines in the modern world but, in a more general way, relates back to the influence of social movements. To talk of 'totalism' here does not imply acceptance of the sort of thesis advanced by Talmon and others, which traces tendencies towards totalitarianism to the generalized influence of doctrines regarding the 'popular will' as the arbiter of political organization. The overall significance of polyarchy in modern states is not unrelated to totalitarianism – in my formulation of the concept rather than that employed by Talmon – because polyarchic involvement in political systems provides for possibilities of mass mobilization otherwise precluded.[15] But the 'totalizing' effect of symbol systems depends mainly upon how far they can be appropriated in such a way as to couple historicity with a hostile attitude towards 'out-groups'. Marxism can be utilized in this fashion, as can various other streams of modern thought which nominally are quite opposed to any vision of totalitarian rule. But, like nationalism, Marxism is Janus-faced and can fuel the most radical critiques of totalizing doctrines.

These problems have been much discussed in the literature of political science, however, and it is upon the influence of surveillance that I want to concentrate most attention. The essential importance of surveillance as a medium of power has not been grasped within either liberal or socialist traditions of political theory. In both cases this is bound up with the same emphases that tend to obstruct a satisfactory account of the control of the means of violence in influencing social organization and social change. Economic exchange is taken to be the elementary binding force in modern societies. In socialism in general, and Marxism in particular, oppressive forms of rule are examined in relation to class dynamics and in some sense or another – directly or indirectly – traced to the impact of class domination. Marx's celebrated analysis of Bonapartism is a case in point. The 'autocratic power' that the state developed under Louis Bonaparte is explained as originating in the 'balance' between contending classes which allowed the state apparatus to step in.[16] Subsequent Marxist authors have gone through all sorts of conceptual contortions to acknowledge the administrative power of the state while still finding its origins in class domination.[17] For liberal writers on the other hand, state power is associated particularly with bureaucracy, bureaucratic regulation being necessary to coordinate the economic framework of a complex division of labour.

Neither of these traditions of thought places surveillance, or the mechanisms of control of 'deviance' associated with the administrative consolidation of the modern state, as central. Surveillance may interact in various ways with class domination but, as has been previously stressed, is certainly not derivative of it. Bureaucracy involves forms of surveillance activity, in both senses of surveillance. But the themes upon which most writers (including Weber) have concentrated when analysing bureaucratic administration tend to marginalize those with which I am principally concerned here. Bureaucratic power, as conceived of by Weber at any rate, is the power of the expert and the specialized official. The problem of surveillance, in the overall context of the nation-state, is rather different.

The expansion of surveillance in the modern political order, in combination with the policing of 'deviance', radically transforms the relation between state authority and the governed population, compared with traditional states. Administrative power now increasingly enters into the minutiae of daily life and the most intimate of personal actions and relationships. In an age more and more invaded by electronic modes of the storage, collation and dissemination of information, the possibilities of accumulating information relevant to the practice of government are almost endless. Control of information, within modern, pacified states with very rapid systems of communication, transportation and sophisticated techniques of sequestration, can be directly integrated with the supervision of conduct in such a way as to produce a high concentration of state power. Surveillance is the necessary condition of the administrative power of states, whatever ends this power be turned to. It is not only intimately connected with polyarchy, but more specifically with the actualization of citizenship rights.[18] Consider, for example, economic rights. The provision of welfare cannot be organized or funded unless there is a close and detailed monitoring of many characteristics of the lives of the population, regardless of whether they are actually welfare recipients or not. All such information thus collected is a source of potential freedom for those whose material wants are provided for through welfare schemes. But it can also be a means of regulating their activities in a coordinated fashion according to political doctrines promulgated by the state authorities,[19] which is not unconnected with the fact that authoritarian governments may promote generous welfare schemes in combination with the severe curtailment of political and civil rights.

The connection of surveillance with policing makes for other possibilities of political oppression, going back again to totalitarianism, but separable from it in their less immoderate forms. The creation of 'deviance', within the modern state is contemporaneous with the fact of its suppression.[20] 'Deviance' is not a set of activities or attitudes separate from the surveillance operations of the state, but is formed in and through them. Now as opposed to most – although not all – traditional modes of punishment, the correction of 'deviance' is specifically a moral matter, however much it may be overlain by pragmatic considerations. The policing of modern states can never be something which is merely a 'technical' question of administration. Within this are buried a whole range of complex issues of normative political theory. One need not go so far as to say that every criminal act is an indictment of the existing social order, or that the speech of the 'mentally ill' discloses alternate universes of reality to that accepted by the majority, to see that the Soviet practice of placing dissidents in mental hospitals connects closely with modern 'correctional' treatment as a whole. Totalitarian rule produces sweeping and comprehensive categories of 'deviance', but these cannot be regarded as wholly separate phenomena from those integral to modern states.

The implications of this discussion are two-fold. First, surveillance (in its various forms and aspects) must be regarded as an independent source of power, maximized in the modern state, which has to be as much of a concern in social critique as questions of material inequality or the nature of polyarchy. The writings of its most subtle analyst, Foucault, demonstrate both that the oppressive possibilities of surveillance cannot be countered merely by appeal to class dynamics or to the extension of democracy, and that there is no obvious and simple political programme to develop in coping with them. But we must also conclude that aspects of totalitarian rule are a threat in all modern states, even if not all are threatened equally or in exactly the same ways. Whether we like it or not, tendencies toward totalitarian power are as distinctive a feature of our epoch as is industrialized war . . .

Notes

1 This chapter is an extract from A. Giddens (1985) Modernity, totalitarianism and critical theory, in *The Nation-State and Violence*. Cambridge: Polity Press, pp. 294–310.

2 Quoted in A. J. May (1966) *Europe Since 1939*. New York: Holt, Rinehart and Winston.

3 Carl J. Friedrich et al. (1969) *Totalitarianism in Perspective: Three Views*. London: Pall Mall, p. 6ff.

4 Benjamin R. Barber (1969) Conceptual Foundations of Totalitarianism, in C. J. Friedrich (ed.) *Totalitarianism in Perspective*, London: Pall Mall, p. 19.

5 Carl Friedrich (1954) *Totalitarianism*. Cambridge, MA: Harvard University Press; cf. also C.J. Friedrich and Z. K. Brzezinski (1967) *Totalitarian Dictatorship and Autocracy*. New York: Praeger Press.

6 Hilaire Belloc (1932) *The Servile State*. Indianapolis: Liberty, p. 125.

7 Aryeh L. Unger (1974) *The Totalitarian Party*. Cambridge: Cambridge University Press, p. 13ff.

8 Quoted in Michael Curtis (1969) Retreat from Totalitarianism, in C.J. Friedrich et al. (eds) *Totalitarianism in Perspective*. London: Pall Mall, p. 76.

9 Robert Conquest (1968) *The Great Terror*. New York: Macmillan.

10 cf. James Millar and Alec Nove (1976) Was Stalin really necessary? *Problems of Communism*, 25.

11   cf. Claude Lefort (1981) *L'invention démocratique*. Paris: Fayard, p. 85ff.
12   Hannah Arendt (1967) *The Origins of Totalitarianism*. London: Allen & Unwin, pp. 341–2.
13   cf. A. L. Unger (1974) *The Totalitarian Party*. Cambridge: Cambridge University Press, p. 170ff.
14   *CPST*, pp. 143–4.
15   J. L Talmon (1961) *The Origins of Totalitarian Democracy*. New York: Praeger Press. As Menze emphasizes, totalitarianism has a 'thoroughly ambivalent relationship to modern democracy . . . Totalitarianism is inconceivable and unrealisable without the democratic notion of popular sovereignty and its concrete realisation in the modern state.' See Ernest A. Menze (1981) *Totalitarianism Reconsidered*. London: Kennikat, p. 15.
16   Marx, 'The Eighteenth Brumaire of Louis Bonaparte'.
17   See Nicos Poulantzas (1973) *Political Power and Social Classes*. London: New Left Books.
18   *CCHM*, vol. I, chapter 10.
19   cf. F. F. Piven and R. A. Cloward (1972) *Regulating the Poor*. London: Tavistock Publications.
20   Foucault, *Discipline and Punish*.

3

Surveillance: basic concepts and dimensions[1]
by Christopher Dandeker

Bureaucracy, power and surveillance: towards a typology of surveillance systems

Personal and bureaucratic surveillance

The main concern [of this chapter] is to analyse the development of bureaucratic systems of surveillance in the key organizations of modern society and, as a result, to show how these organizations expanded their surveillance capacities . . .

This long-term process involved what Weber referred to as a shift from personal and patrimonial forms of administration to the rational and bureaucratic organizations of modernity. In the former, rulers have few means of controlling their subject populations beyond their personal powers of supervision and information gathering. They have no reliable, disciplined administrative staffs who can act on their behalf at a distance. Circuits of administrative control and information-flow are therefore extremely limited in terms of spatial and temporal extent. In respect of political structures, these limits have been breached by rulers through the adoption of a number of strategies: the delegation of administrative powers to members of a number ruler's household, as in the creation of patrimonial regimes, or the delegation of administrative rights to autonomous power-holders in exchange for military service and loyalty, as in feudal patterns of rule. A third strategy involved the creation of rationally disciplined bureaucracies (M. Weber 1978: 255–65).

Modern bureaucracies are extremely durable structures. The economic and technological resources of modern industrial society provide the means of establishing permanent and rationally disciplined bureaucracies to an extent which would have been the object of envy to all pre-modern rulers for whom bankruptcy and administrative weakness or disintegration were routine features of the political landscape. Their resilience through time is matched by their surveillance capacities or the effect with which they can integrate and administer mass populations across vast spaces: for instance, compare the areas occupied by the contemporary USA and Soviet Union with the effective jurisdictions of the great agrarian empires of China and India (J. Hall 1986: 173–92). In this context, one should refer to 'time-space' as each dimension implies the other. For example, the barrier which spatial distance can pose to rulers who wish to ensure that their instructions are complied with by subject populations, can only be determined by considering the time required to ensure that sufficient resources are mobilized and delivered to any points of disobedience. Depending upon the social structure, 100 or 1,000 miles can have similar consequences in terms of the ease with which rulers can supervise their subjects. Modern systems of transport and communication have overcome natural barriers in ways quite beyond the capacities of non-industrial civilizations. Such conditions enable modern rulers to have a high 'presence availability' at the most distant points of their administrative networks (A. Giddens 1985: 172–91). Indeed, in many respects, industrial states, once defeated, are easier to administer than non-industrial ones simply because it is easier to identify strategic points which, when captured, are decisive for the effective control of a state.

Modern bureaucratic systems of surveillance not only provide effective means of administering subject populations; they also constitute a basis for 'willing the future'. This involves the collection of information from diverse time-space locations, including scientific forecasts of projected trends in order to plan the future of an organization. Thus the process of bureaucratization can be viewed in terms of an extension of the strategic horizons of the rulers of those organizations which undergo it at the same time as subject populations are increasingly made the objects of rulers' policies.

Surveillance in autocratic and liberal systems of rule

While the process of bureaucratization is central to a discussion of the growth of the surveillance capacities of the organizations in modern society, a second issue cuts rights across it. This concerns the connections between power and surveillance.

. . . [I]n considering the ways in which surveillance activities reproduce systems of rule, a distinction needs to be drawn between rule over and rule on behalf of subject populations. This dichotomy derives in part from Mosca's social theory. In autocratic systems, the authority of rulers is generated at the top of the society as in doctrines of the divine right of monarchs. In what Mosca referred to as 'liberal' regimes, authority derives from the lower reaches of society and is couched explicitly in terms of the voluntary consent of the subordinate population (R. Bellamy 1987: 50–1). At this point it is necessary to clarify some terminological issues. The distinction between autocratic and liberal principles encompasses two related issues:

(1) the degree to which the ruled can exercise supervision over rulers and their administrative staffs; (2) the extent to which the prerogatives of rulers are concentrated so as to facilitate arbitrary rule.

Mosca was careful to point out that, as he viewed it, 'democracy' cut right across the contrast between liberal and autocratic systems. That is to say, it is possible for rulers in both types to be recruited from a relatively narrow (aristocratic) or broad (democratic) social base. For example, he pointed to Imperial China and the Venetian Republic as examples respectively of autocratic democracy and liberal aristocracy.

However . . . there is a sense in which 'democracy' is constitutive of modernity if, following Tocqueville, this term is used to refer to the condition of social and political equality. In this context, the rise of the masses as participants in the modern state has been associated with both liberal and autocratic systems (what Tocqueville viewed as republican and despotic regimes). For Tocqueville, as for Weber, modern democracy in this sense is 'Janus-faced' and can be expressed in bureaucratic dictatorship or the rational-legal bureaucracies of liberal capitalism (J. Stone and S. Mennell 1980: 348–80).

As Hall and Mann have argued recently, although it is possible to identify a long-term trend in the growth of the surveillance capacities, or 'penetrative' and supervisory powers of the modern state, the spectre of totalitarianism in the twentieth century indicates that the same cannot be said of a shift from autocracy to liberal structures (J. Hall 1985; M, Mann 1988). This argument echoes Tocqueville's view: it is one thing to establish a bureaucratic state but it is quite another to establish durable arrangements under which rulers act on behalf of a subject population yet are also prevented from using the 'tyranny of the majority' (as in the one party state) to rule arbitrarily and to exclude the interests of large sectors of society.

Hall uses some of these ideas as the basis for a discussion of capstone and organic government and links this with a broader argument concerning the 'uniqueness of the west' and the rise of modernity (J. Hall 1986; C. Ashworth and C. Dandeker 1986). An organic system is strong in terms of its surveillance capacities; however this administrative power is made to serve interests that express a fairly broad social consensus. In contrast, capstone government is arbitrary in terms of the narrow range of social interests it serves yet severely limited in its capacities to gather information about and supervise the subject population. Hall uses the contrast between capstone and organic government to explain how modern capitalism, based on the primacy of the market and private business enterprise, developed so vigorously in north-western Europe. Crucial in this development was the impact of organic government. Modern capitalism flourished in the context of the administrative and legal framework of the early modern state. The surveillance capacities of the state evolved especially in the fields of taxation, law and military administration.

Two conditions prevented the development of bureaucratic despotism or autocracy and the dysfunctional consequences of such arrangements for market capitalism. First, the marked rivalries between nascent western nation-states prevented the formation of a despotic hegemonic empire in Europe along the lines of Imperial China. Second, for reasons explored by Max Weber, the west was characterized by more liberal political structures, particularly from the standpoint of the capitalist classes. States either accommodated the interests of these classes, or, if political conditions for capitalist enterprise worsened in one society, the rivalry between nation-states enabled entrepreneurs to move to those states prepared to offer more favourable conditions for capitalist economic activities.

In the early modern west, a rare institutional complex thrived: this comprised 'strong' government in terms of its administrative power to 'penetrate' society – not so strong as to inhibit enterprise and initiative, yet not so weak as to discourage market transactions altogether. At the same time, this administrative power was linked with more liberal political structures than those prevailing in, say, Imperial China.

The conclusion to be drawn from the preceding discussion is that surveillance systems can be analysed in terms of two cross-cutting dimensions: first whether their capacities are rooted in personalized or bureaucratic administrative structures; and second whether those systems reproduce autocratic or liberal systems of rule . . .

In figure [3.1], four modes of surveillance are distinguished in ideal typical form. These can be described as petty tyranny, bureaucratic dictatorship, direct democracy and rational-legal bureaucracy. Petty tyranny and direct democracy will be referred to briefly before turning to the issue of patronage and what are viewed as the two main types of modern bureaucracy.

Under a petty tyranny, autocratic power is exercised over a subject population by a single person whose means of supervision and information gathering do not extend much beyond his or her own personal capacities. Their limited reach confines the realistic ambitions of such a person to a local area and population. As Weber argued, charismatic warrior bands, religious groups and criminal gangs through the ages have, on occasion, approximated to these arrangements (M. Weber 1978: 241–54).

In direct democracies, surveillance activities are carried out by all members of the collectivity in pursuit of popular interests, although this may result in the tyranny of the majority over the liberties of particular individuals or minorities. As is the case with petty tyranny, the means of surveillance are personal and informal; for example, in the ways in which some communities rely on gossip networks to ensure general compliance with normative standards (N. Elias 1965). In this context one can also refer to some anthropological discussions of the processes through which simple, stateless societies maintain social order without recourse to bureaucratic administrative structures (see S. Roberts 1979). In both petty tyrannies and direct democracies, surveillance activities are performed with little or no recourse to intermediate specialist officials.

Patronage and surveillance

What has been referred to in figure [3.1] as the zone of patronage concerns transitional modes of surveillance that fall mid-way between personal and bureaucratic systems on the one hand and autocratic and liberal principles on the other. Under arrangements based on patronage, surveillance activities and the reproduction of systems of rule are tenuous social processes characterized by personalism as well as the anonymous or impersonal features more prevalent in modern societies. At the

	Personal Administration		Bureaucratic Administration
Autocratic Interests	Petty tyranny		Bureaucratic dictatorship
		Patronage	
Liberal Interests	Direct democracy		Rational–legal

Figure [3.1] Systems of rule

same time, surveillance activities are performed by specialist intermediaries who are autonomous from both the controls of the subject population and of the discipline normally imposed by modern bureaucratic systems.

The term patronage is used here in two senses: to refer to a social relation and to a social system (T. Johnson and C. Dandeker 1989). In all societies, one can identify patronage relations defined as durable, reciprocal relations of vertical or lop-sided friendship. As Bourne has argued, the essence of patronage comprises inequality of power resources, the reciprocity of services and the intimacy of friendship (J. Bourne 1986: 5). To this should be added the principle of voluntarism as the social basis for participation in patronage relations. These features distinguish relations between patron and client from those between lord and serf, master and slave and the contractual relations between employer and employee characteristic of modernity.

However, the social significance of patronage in societies fluctuates. In some societies, patronage relations play a strategic role. Here one can identify a patronage system defined not as a relationship but as complex, hierarchically organized chains of such relationships that provide the socio-economic and administrative basis of a system of rule: here patronage constitutes a means of surveillance.

There are two important structural features of patronage systems: (1) the dominance of vertical over horizontal relations of social solidarity; and (2) the effects of voluntarism in inhibiting the formation of inherited forms of power holding.

The existence of vertical relations connecting patrons with clients in a deferential social hierarchy inhibits the social significance of class or status forms of horizontal solidarity as well as undermining the potential legitimacy of egalitarian forms of ideology. Communal, status or class actions are not unknown but patronage ties and loyalties reduce the salience of these forms of group mobilization and integration.

Similarly, the institutionalization of personalized ties which are in principle the outcome of individual choices has the generalized effect of undermining the emergence of stable, hereditary structures of power holding. The incorporation of voluntarism into a system of resource allocation introduces a destabilizing factor as patronage operates as a competitive and pluralistic system: patrons are dependent on maintaining a high level of client support in a situation where clients are neither owned nor totally controlled and where client choice is a significant resource and dynamic in the system. In a deferential social order, the subordinate population can shift their client loyalties or have multiple patrons. At the same time, patrons as 'entrepreneurs' can compete for clients and are neither members of a hereditary status group nor disciplined bureaucratic subordinates of a ruler.

Societies based on patronage are associated essentially with transitional phases in state development and the wider process of modernization. Patronage provides the administrative basis of systems of rule where, 'political integration and social mediation are limited by the weakness of market forces and the ineffectiveness of central government' (J. Bourne 1986: 8). It emerges to facilitate economic and political relationships where the personal ties of kinship are no longer effective and the integrative and distributional effects of the market and rational-legal state cannot operate . . .

Bureaucracy and surveillance

Attention can now be turned to the other two modes of surveillance indicated in figure [3.1]. In modern societies, surveillance of subject populations is performed largely by bureaucratic officials in the context of formal organizations. However, two broad variants of modern bureaucracy need to be distinguished, each reflecting the broader institutional differences between capitalist (with the exception of fascist or similar authoritarian regimes) and the great majority of state socialist societies These two administrative structures are defined respectively as rational-legal public bureaucracy and bureaucratic dictatorship.

Clapham has discussed the differences between these systems in terms of two conditions: first, the effective enforcement from above of a public ethic of correct behaviour; that is to say, a legal code commanding general acceptance which requires officials to administer the population impersonally through the application of abstract, formal rules to particular cases. Second, the enforcement from below of the accountability of the bureaucracy to the subject population. As Clapham argues,

> either the ruler or the public have an interest in bureaucracy run on correct Weberian lines: the ruler because it promotes effective hierarchical control and efficiency in carrying out the agency's defined task; the public because the rules reduce the opportunities for bureaucrats to exploit the clientele. Meanwhile, the bureaucratic officials, in the middle so to speak, possess considerable scope for discretion in respect of the gap between their actual powers, deriving from occupancy of their official positions, and the formal rules which define their use.
>
> (C. Clapham 1982: 26)

In circumstances where neither the ruler nor the bureaucracy itself are accountable to the subject population through some robust system of interest representation, the possibility of impersonal control of the bureaucracy and of the way it supervises the subject population will decline. The ruler is likely to become in practice accountable only to the bureaucracy itself on which he or she depends for the maintenance of a system of rule, rather than to the subject population. In other words, if all the bureaucracy has to fear is the wrath of the ruler, its power will be greater than in a system where the subject population also has the means of ensuring the accountability of bureaucratic behaviour. And then the bureaucracy itself will be able to maximize its powers of manoeuvre and, as in the context of the administrative history of the Soviet Union, become 'the sole corporation, whose interests . . . [the ruler] cannot afford to offend while as the agency for implementing the ruler's policies, it will be well placed to block any initiatives which threaten it' (ibid.: 26–8). Furthermore, in order to carry out any policies at all, the ruler may have to reconcile him or herself to a strategy of patronage as a means of overcoming sources of bureaucratic resistance.

Of course, in the relational sense defined earlier, patronage is a universal feature of bureaucratic organizations; the key issue is whether patronage is the key or strategic principle of organizational behaviour. In bureaucratic dictatorships, it is likely that the autocratic ruler(s) may be forced into patronage as the principal way of managing the bureaucracy. Meanwhile, the subject population, armed with few means of guaranteeing the accountability of the bureaucracy to themselves, have only the choice of accepting its arbitrary behaviour or joining in the patronage game of bribery and corruption in order to divert scarce organizational resources their own way.

In bureaucratic dictatorships then, personalism and competition pervade the system; factionalism operates in such a way that the ruler cannot relate to the bureaucracy as if it were a dependable administrative machine.

This line of argument has important implications for a view of modern totalitarian systems of rule (A. Giddens 1985: 294–341). If a given system has little or grudging consent from the subject population, then while the latter might experience bureaucratic administration as arbitrary and something over which they have little control, the rulers themselves would have little effective means of supervising or knowing about what was carried out in their name. If consent is a significant factor in the maintenance of a system of rule, the possibilities for control over and knowledge about a subject population, somewhat paradoxically, would be rather limited from a ruler's point of view. Indeed it might be suggested that the scope for effective action by autocratic rulers would be relatively less than those situated in a rational-legal system and who, in principle, could command the more willing consent of broader sections of the population. In the former, bureaucratic surveillance would be ineffective but arbitrary; in the latter the reverse would be the case.

Thus in systems of rule reproduced by rational-legal bureaucracies, both ruler and bureaucracy are accountable effectively to the subject population and distribute resources according to a widely held ethic of acceptable bureaucratic behaviour. The ethic is enshrined in the legal and wider value system and secured through liberal structures of interest representation.

It should be borne in mind that the contrast between bureaucratic dictatorship and rational legal bureaucracy is an ideal typical one. It is a means of contrasting the different ways in which bureaucratic surveillance can reproduce systems of rule in different types of society – liberal capitalist, state socialist, authoritarian capitalist. Moreover, its purpose is to define the framework in terms of which more substantive themes can be considered below. The view to be defended here is that the organizations of modernity in the west have managed to come closer to approximating the ideal type of rational-legal bureaucracy than their equivalents in state socialist societies have managed to do so far.

Surveillance and modernity

. . . As Giddens has suggested, sociology and its object of study – society – are in large part the products of modernity (A. Giddens 1985: 172). If by society one means a clearly demarcated and internally well-articulated social entity, it is only relatively recently that large human populations have lived under such arrangements; and these have been the administrative achievements of modern nation-states. From a political point of view, the modern world comprises a network of competing nation-states and collectivities aspiring to that status.

Modern nation-states have well-developed bureaucratic systems for the internal policing of their populations as well as for the management of their external relations.

Their systems of rule are legitimated in terms of the politics of citizenship and the bonds of national solidarity as expressed in language and customs, although of course, many nation-states are multi-ethnic or multi-national units. These distinctive features of modern nation-states can be outlined in more detail before focusing more specifically on the impact of war and military organization on the development of their surveillance capacities.

The nation-state: bureaucracy, citizenship and military power

Bendix has argued that, 'the central fact of modern nation building is the orderly exercise of a nation wide public authority' (R. Bendix 1969: 22). In the west, there were four aspects of this political transformation. First, there was a long-term concentration of political authority. The political structure of absolutism anticipated one of the constituitive features of modern nation-states: 'where all people have rights, where all are subjects of one king; where the king in turn exercises supreme authority over everyone, we get a first intimation of national citizenship and one supreme authority over all public affairs' (ibid.: 57). With the French revolution, the 'democratic' will of the people replaced monarchy as the agency that wielded nation-wide political authority.

Second, the concentration of political authority was accompanied by a shift from functional to more individualistic systems of political representation with the extension of citizenship rights. In this context, Bendix, Marshall and, more recently, Giddens have discussed three types of citizenship rights: civil rights are those concerned with freedom of association, movement (including the right to sell labour and own property), freedom of speech and the rule of law. Political rights are concerned with the participation of subject populations in the exercise of political power and thus in the supervision of rulers. In contrast, economic rights 'concern the right of everyone within a state to enjoy a certain minimum standard of life, economic welfare and security' (A. Giddens 1985: 201).

Bendix argues that in the modern nation-state, 'each citizen stands in a direct relation to the sovereign of the country, in contrast with medieval polity' (R. Bendix 1969: 89–90). Although Bendix recognizes the importance of Marshall's discussion of three types of citizenship rights, in his own analysis he focuses mainly on the extension of civil and political rights to the lower classes. This process meant that wider sections of subject populations could speak for their own interests rather than depending on the patronage of their social superiors in whose houses or estates they served.

For Marshall, the emergence of citizenship involved a sequential development of civil, political and social (or what Giddens prefers to call economic) rights. Thus, in the British context, the civil rights realized in the seventeenth and eighteenth centuries provided the basis for an extension of political and economic rights in the nineteenth and twentieth centuries respectively.

Giddens's analysis of citizenship draws on Marshall's discussion but also departs from it in three important respects. Empirically, Giddens suggests that the extension of citizenship rights has been a more complex process than Marshall acknowledges. For instance, in Britain some civil rights were not extended until the twentieth century while yet others have been diminished. In Germany, Bismark's social reforms – the extension of welfare or economic rights – were instituted in order to forestall concessions on the political front (A. Giddens 1985: 205).

Secondly, Giddens prefers to view citizenship rights not simply in terms of phases of social development but rather as recurrent 'arenas of contestation" between rulers and ruled. Each cluster of rights is focused on a particular organizational and thus surveillance context: the police and society (civil rights); the electorate and the political organs of the state (political rights); and the relations between capital and labour within the business enterprise (economic rights). Thus in modern capitalist societies, a crucial area of citizenship rights are 'beyond' the state and anchored in an organization based on private property.

Thirdly, in explaining the rise of modern citizenship, Giddens departs from both Bendix's and Marshall's views. In sharp contrast with Marxist analysis, Bendix relegates class conflict to the periphery of his discussion of political modernization. On the other hand, Marshall views modern citizenship rights as providing a basis of (social democratic) compromise between the main classes of modern capitalism. Although Giddens accepts Marshall's view of some of the consequences of modern citizenship, he prefers to interpret class conflict as a medium for the extension of citizenship rights. This is in contrast to both Marshall's own suggestion that such rights have 'blunted' class divisions, and Bendix's marginalization of class in the social analysis of these issues. In the present argument, one qualification of Giddens's analysis will be to suggest that a significant motive for the extension of citizenship has been competition for military and economic power amongst states as well as struggles between classes within states.

The extension of citizenships rights in the modern nation-state has been dependent on the concentration of political authority: the allocation of equal rights to more and more citizens presupposes the development of an agency 'above' those individuals. However, the extension of citizenship rights is connected not only with this process of concentration but also with other features of the modern nation-state. These concern two aspects of modern bureaucracy: as a mode of public administration and as a means of surveillance.

In the modern nation-state, the administrative instruments of power become the property of the public rather than being privately owned by the monarch. The impersonal, public authority of the state is extended in modern polities and this process entails an institutional separation between state and society. The administrative functions of government generally become 'removed from the political struggle in the sense that they cannot be appropriated on a hereditary basis by privileged estates and on this basis parcelled out among competing jurisdictions' (R. Bendix 1969: 128–9). This entails the 'development of a body of officials whose recruitment and policy execution were separated gradually from the previously existing involvement of officials with kinship loyalties, hereditary principles and property interests' (ibid.). As was observed earlier, this change means that patronage declines as the strategic mechanism in the recruitment to and operation of the administrative structures of the modern nation-state (pp. 46–9).

The fourth attribute of the modern nation-state concerns its surveillance capacities: these are produced by the use of rational bureaucracy for the administrative penetration of society. As Giddens and Poggi have argued, this development suggests a quite different meaning of separation from the one referred to above as a way of analysing the relationships between the modern state and society (A. Giddens 1981: 169–81; G. Poggi 1978: 92–116).

The modern state is separated from society in respect of the emergence of a public power from pre-existing patrimonial regimes. However, from an administrative point of view, pre-modern states and their rulers were far more separated from their societies than are their modern counterparts. They could not subject their populations to the fine mesh of bureaucratic surveillance evident in modern states.

In the context of the European *ancien régime*, the rulers of even the most absolutist states found it difficult to supervise and gather information about their populations. The presence availability of rulers was limited by a number of conditions.

A series of technical problems shortened considerably the radii of effective administration from a central point. Poor transport and communications, with roads impassable to wheeled traffic for much of winter made it difficult to administer subject populations in any detailed way. This remained the case until the end of the eighteenth century.

Demographic considerations were also significant: the population was small compared with those characteristic of modern societies, and widely dispersed in relatively self-sufficient communities. Only a small proportion lived in towns and cities. The limited social division of labour favoured a disperal of effective administrative control to the localities.

Economic factors reinforced transport and demographic limitations. The economy produced only a limited surplus for the tax system to channel into state coffers. Here was a vicious circle from the standpoint of rulers: limited economic resources made it difficult for rulers to build (expensive) reliable tax and military bureaucracies. In turn, limited bureaucratic development meant that it was difficult to channel those resources that the economy could produce into the hands of the state. Major state functions such as taxation and military force were, in varying degrees, decentralized to private contractors. This process of 'sub-contracting', and, in the absence of strategic financial control by the state bureaucracy, the corruption that went with it, constituted important obstacles to the will of the central authorities. However, this line of argument is not to deny the genuine advances made in central government administration during the late seventeenth and eighteenth centuries (pp. 62–3) . . .

The emergence of the modern nation-state can then, be identified in terms of a combination of four attributes: the concentration of political authority; citizenship as the political basis for the relationships between rulers and ruled; administration by public bureaucracy rather than by patronage; and administration of society through bureaucratic surveillance.

In this overall process, war and military organization were of central importance. First of all, the armed forces constituted the most significant branch of the early modern state in terms of relative size, organizational complexity, consumption of state expenditure, and means of power projection – both internally and externally. Second, war was the most important motive for the establishment of the modern state as a durable and well-articulated social entity. As Paul Kennedy has argued, 'the post 1450 waging of war was intimately connected with the "birth of the Nation state"'

(P. M. Kennedy 1988: 70). The bureaucratization of military power in the west was connected symbiotically with the development of the capitalist economic system: an expansion of military power depended on the technical, financial and organizational resources of commercial and industrial enterprises; at the same time military power, and especially naval weaponry, aided the global economic expansion of the west overseas in respect of new markets for raw materials and exports. It also provided an important stimulus to capitalist industry and commerce by way of demands for textiles, timber, iron and later steel, chemicals and other goods. All these resources of the capitalist system were channelled into military activities through loans raised by states on the developing financial markets and revenue secured through the tax system (W. McNeill 1983: 79–101; T. M. Cipolla 1965; M. Howard 1976: 38–74).

Bearing in mind this symbiotic relationship between economic and military resources, war was an important motive for the conduct of the state and military organization, the most important feature of its administrative structure. Thus, military organization provides a clear example of the association between bureaucratic surveillance and the modern nation-state.

There were distinct phases in the bureaucratization of military power. In the argument defended here, particular attention is paid to the effects of what Roberts has called the 'military revolution' of the late sixteenth and early seventeenth centuries (M. Roberts 1958). During this period, the foundations of the modern armed forces as a fusion of professional and bureaucratic principles were laid. This process can be discussed by focusing on changes in the relationships between three groups: the central authorities, the officers' corps, including the important NCO or supervisory class, and the ordinary soldiers and sailors themselves. The state transformed military organization from a system comprising autonomous, largely self-equipped mercenary formations, employed by contracting captains, to one based on professional servants of the state, disciplined in a bureaucratic hierarchy and owing allegiance to the state alone. This process constituted a shift from a system based on petty and competing patrimonialisms to a unified rational-legal order for the administration of military violence. By 1700 the outline of all that is modern about the modern armed forces was visible (M. Howard 1976: 54).

By the eighteenth century,

> the enhanced authority and resources of the state . . . gave to their armed forces a degree of permanence which had often not existed earlier . . . Power was now national power, whether expressed through the enlightened despotisms of eastern Europe, the parliamentary controls of Britain or the later demagogic forces of revolutionary France.
>
> (P. M. Kennedy 1988: 75–6)

In the nineteenth century, further developments in the bureaucratization of military discipline can be linked with the impact of the industrial and democratic revolutions. In that context, attention can be focused on the ways in which modern technology and the national citizenship state altered the relationships between military organization and society and increased substantially the capacity of the state to deploy bureaucratized military power.

In the twentieth century, two particular aspects of the bureaucratization of military power stand out: first, the relationships between modern technology and surveillance in military organizations; and second, the impact of the demands of war on the growth of state surveillance beyond the military sphere into the wider society.

During the two world wars and beyond, the seemingly ever-increasing pace of technological change continued to enhance the capacities of the state to mobilize, deploy and control military power. The technical demands of war not only led to an enhancement of the ability of the state to exercise surveillance over its armed forces but also to a tightening of the networks of surveillance over the rest of society. Although this process was rooted in the industrialization of war in the nineteenth century – particularly in the equation linking citizenship and military service – the main connections between war and what is referred to here as the rise of the 'security state' were forged during the two world wars and the subsequent nuclear age. Whilst some of the advanced societies have lessened their dependence on mass conscripted armies, it remains the case that defence and security issues have provided important grounds for supervising the civilian population in time of war or threat of war.

The bureaucratization of military power has, then, been an important aspect of the rise of the modern nation-state. War has been perhaps the most significant motive for the formation of the modern nation-state in the west, and military organization its most crucial arm, particularly of course, in the field of external relations (M. Mann 1988). Yet as was pointed out earlier, the institutional differentiation of internal and external relations was itself an achievement of the nation-state. As Giddens has suggested, the process of modernization is accompanied by a decline in the routine use of military power within the territorial boundaries of states and an increased focus on police surveillance as a means of supervising subject populations (A. Giddens 1985: 103–21, 172–92) . . .

To sum up . . . [t]he growth of surveillance in modern societies is understood in terms of a growth in the surveillance capacities of organizations. This process is understood in terms of a shift from personal to bureaucratic control via intermediate forms of patronage. In modern capitalist societies, bureaucratic surveillance comprises a combination of control over and on behalf of subject populations. This is certainly not to underplay the hierarchical nature of surveillance in these societies, but it is to draw a distinction between the systems of administrative power in liberal capitalist, authoritarian capitalist and state socialist societies. This was the point of the dichotomy between liberal and autocratic principles . . .

Capitalism – that is to say, generalized commodity production as the economic core of class societies – has been a central force in these administrative developments. Its importance can be seen in the establishment of the feedback loop between military and economic power and thus the formation of modern nation-states; in the undermining of patronage and personalized forms of surveillance as the principal media of societal integration and thus in providing the material basis of police surveillance; and in creating the mass markets for labour and other commodities as a context in which the modern bureaucratic business enterprise could flourish.

While capitalism was a major force behind the growth of bureaucratic surveillance, bureaucracy was also linked with other features of modernity: the constraints of industrial technologies, the power interests of professional occupations linked with emergent bureaucratic organizations; the power needs of states; and, of course, as Weber stressed, the inherent technical advantages and momentum of bureaucracy itself . . .

Note

1   This chapter is an extract from C. Dandeker (1990) Surveillance: basic concepts and dimensions, in *Surveillance, Power and Modernity: Bureaucracy and Discipline from 1700 to the Present Day*. Cambridge: Polity Press, pp. 37–65.

References

Ashworth, C. E. and Dandeker, C. (1986) 'Capstones and organisms: political forms and the triumph of capitalism': a critical comment, *Sociology*, Feb., 20(1); 82–7.

Bellamy, R. (1987) *Modern Italian Social Theory*. Cambridge: Polity Press.

Bendix, R. (1969) *Nation-Building and Citizenship*. Garden City, NY: Doubleday Anchor.

Bourne, J. (1986) *Patronage in Nineteenth Century England*. London: Edward Arnold.

Cipolla, C. M. (1965) *Guns and Sails in the Early Phase of European Expansion, 1400–1700*. London: Collins.

Clapham, C. (1982) *Private Patronage and Public Power: Political Clientelism in the Modern State*. London: F. Pinter.

Elias, N. (1965) *The Established and the Outsider*. London: Cass.

Giddens, A. (1981) *A Contemporary Critique of Historical Materialism*, vol. 1. London: Macmillan.

Giddens, A. (1985) *The Nation-State and Violence*. Cambridge: Polity Press.

Hall, J. A. (1985) 'Capstones and organisms: political forms and the triumph of capitalism', *Sociology*, May, 19(2).

Hall, J. A. (1986) *Powers and Liberties: The Causes and Consequences of the Rise of the West*. Gretna, LI: Pelican.

Howard, M. (1976) *War in European History*. Oxford: Oxford University Press.

Johnson, T. J. and Dandeker, C. (1989) 'Patronage: Relation and System,' in A. Wallace-Hadrill (ed.) *Patronage in the Ancient World*. London: Croom Helm.

Kennedy, P. M. (1988) *The Rise and Fall of the Great Powers*. London: Unwin Hyman.

Mann, M. (1988) *War, States and Capitalism*. Oxford: Blackwell.

McNeill, W. (1983) *The Pursuit of Power, Technology, Armed Force and Society Since 1000 AD*. Oxford: Blackwell.

Poggi, G. (1978) *The Development of the Modern State*. London: Hutchinson.

Roberts, M. (1958) *Gustavus Adolphus*, 2 vols, London.

Roberts, S. (1979) *Order and Dispute: Introduction to Legal Anthropology*. London: Penguin.

Stone, J. and Mennel, S. (1980) *Alexis De Tocqueville: On Democracy, Revolution and Society*. Chicago: University of Chicago Press.

Weber, M. (1978) *Economy and Society*, 2 vols. Berkeley, CA: University of California Press.

4

Coming and going: on the state monopolization of the legitimate 'means of movement'[1]
by John Torpey

In his writings, Karl Marx sought to show that the process of capitalist development involved the expropriation of the 'means of production' from workers by capitalists. The result of this process was that workers were deprived of the capacity to produce on their own and became dependent upon wages from the owners of the means of production for their survival. Borrowing this rhetoric, Marx's greatest heir and critic, Max Weber, argued that a central feature of the modern experience was the successful expropriation by the state of the 'means of violence' from individuals. In the modern world, in contrast to the medieval period in Europe and much historical experience elsewhere, only states could 'legitimately' use violence; all other would-be wielders of violence must be licensed by states to do so. Those not so licensed were thus deprived of the freedom to employ violence against others. Following the rhetoric used by Marx and Weber, [this chapter] seeks to demonstrate the proposition that modern states, and the international state system of which they are a part, have expropriated from individuals and private entities the legitimate 'means of movement,' particularly though by no means exclusively across international boundaries.

The result of this process has been to deprive people of the freedom to move across certain spaces and to render them dependent on states and the state system for the authorization to do so – an authority widely held in private hands therefore. A critical aspect of this process has been that people have also become dependent on states for the possession of an 'identity' from which they can escape only with difficulty and which may significantly shape their access to various spaces. There are, of course, virtues to this system – principally of a diplomatic nature – just as the expropriation of workers by capitalists allows propertyless workers to survive as wage laborers and the expropriation of the means of violence by states tends to pacify everyday life. Yet in the course of each of these transformations, workers, aggressors, and travelers, respectively, have each been subjected to a form of dependency they had not previously known.

Let me emphasize that I am not claiming that states and the state system *effectively* control all movements of persons, but only that they have monopolized the *authority* to restrict movement vis-à-vis other potential claimants, such as private economic or religious entities. Such entities may play a role in the control of movement, but they do so today at the behest of states. Nor am I arguing that states' monopolization of the legitimate means of movement is a generalization valid for all times and places; the monopolization of this authority by states emerged only gradually after the medieval period and paralleled states' monopolization of the legitimate means of violence. My argument bears strong similarities to that of John Meyer when he addresses the delegitimation of organizational forms other than the nation-state in the emerging 'world polity.' Various non-state associations, Meyer writes

> are kept from maintaining private armies, their territory and property are subject to state expropriation, and their attempts to control their populations are stigmatized as slavery ... although states routinely exercise such controls with little question. A worker may properly be kept from crossing state boundaries, and may even be kept from crossing firm boundaries by the state, but not by the firm.[2]

To be more precise, firms may keep a worker from crossing the boundaries of the firm, but they do so under authority granted them by the state.

An understanding of the processes whereby states monopolized the legitimate means of movement is crucial to an adequate comprehension of how modern states actually work. Most analyses of state formation heretofore have focused on the capacity of states to penetrate societies, without explicitly telling us *how* they effect this penetration. Such analyses have posited that successful states developed the ability to reach into societies to extract various kinds of resources, yet they typically fail to offer any specific discussion of the means they adopted to achieve these ends ...

Meanwhile, analyses of migration and migration policies have tended to take the existence of states largely for granted, typically attributing migration to a variety of socioeconomic processes ('push-pull' processes, 'chain migration,' 'transnational communities,' etc.) without paying adequate attention to territorial states' need to distinguish 'on the ground' among different populations or to the ways in which the activities of states – especially war-making and state-building – result in population movements. The chief exception to this generalization has been to be found in the writings of Aristide Zolberg, who has been urging for two decades that the state-building (and state-destroying) activities of states should occupy a central role in studies of human movement or its absence, alongside the more routine examination of states' immigration policies.[3] Rather than ignoring the role of states, studies of immigration policies take them as given and thus fail to see the ways in which regulation of movement contributes to constituting the very 'state-ness' of states.

These approaches are inadequate for understanding either the development of modern states or migration patterns. In what follows, I seek to supersede these partial perspectives and to show that states' monopolization of the right to authorize and regulate movement has been intrinsic to the very construction of states since the rise of absolutism in early modern Europe. I also attempt to demonstrate that procedures and mechanisms for identifying persons are essential to this process, and that, in order to be implemented in practice, the notion of national communities must be codified in documents rather than merely 'imagined'[4] ...

Monopolizing the legitimate means of movement

States have sought to monopolize the capacity to authorize the movements of persons
– and unambiguously to establish their identities in order to enforce this authority –
for a great variety of reasons which reflect the ambiguous nature of modern states,
which are at once sheltering and dominating. These reasons include such objectives as
the extraction of military service, taxes and labor; the facilitation of law enforcement;
the control of 'brain drain' (i.e., limitation of departure in order to forestall the loss
of workers with particularly valued skills); the restriction of access to areas deemed
'off-limits' by the state, whether for 'security' reasons or to protect people from
unexpected or unacknowledged harms; the exclusion, surveillance and containment
of 'undesirable elements' whether these are of an ethnic, national, racial, economic,
religious, ideological or medical character; and the supervision of the growth, spatial
distribution and social composition of populations within their territories.

States' efforts to monopolize the legitimate means of movement have involved a
number of mutually reinforcing aspects: the (gradual) definition of states everywhere
– at least from the point of view of the international system – as 'national' (i.e., as
'nation-states' comprising members understood as nationals); the codification of laws
establishing which types of persons may move within or cross their borders, and
determining how, when and where they may do so; the stimulation of the worldwide
development of techniques for uniquely and unambiguously identifying each and
every person on the face of the globe, from birth to death; the construction of bureaucracies designed to implement this regime of identification and to scrutinize persons
and documents in order to verify identities; and the creation of a body of legal
norms designed to adjudicate claims by individuals to entry into particular spaces and
territories. Only recently have states actually developed the capacities necessary to
monopolize the authority to regulate movement.

To be sure, despotisms everywhere frequently asserted controls on movement
before the modern period, but these states generally lacked the extensive administrative infrastructure necessary to carry out such regulation in a pervasive and systematic fashion. The *successful* monopolization of the legitimate means of movement by
states and the state system required the creation of elaborate bureaucracies and technologies that only gradually came into existence, a trend that intensified dramatically
toward the end of the nineteenth century. The process decisively depended on what
Gérard Noiriel has called the '*révolution identificatoire*,' the development of 'cards'
and 'codes' that identified people (more or less) unambiguously and distinguished
among them for administrative purposes.[5] Such documents had existed previously, of
course, but their uniform dissemination throughout whole societies, not to mention
their worldwide spread as the international passport with which we are familiar today,
would be some time in coming. Once they became available to (almost) anyone,
however, they also became a requirement for legitimate movement across territorial
spaces.

Things have not always been this way. The great migrations that populated many
of the world's inhabited regions would otherwise have been greatly hampered, if
not rendered impossible. Where the right to authorize movement was controlled by
particular social groups before the coalescence of the modern state system (and

indeed until well after it had come into being), these groups were as often private entities as constituted political authorities. Indentured servants' right to move, for example, was under the control of their masters. Under serfdom, the serfs' legal capacity to move lay in the hands of their landlords, who had jurisdiction over them. Slavery, even when it did not involve actual shackles, entailed that slaveholders held the power to grant their slaves the right to move.[6]

As modern states advanced and systems of forced labor such as slavery and serfdom declined, however, states and the international state system stripped private entities of the power to authorize and forbid movement and gathered that power unto themselves. In doing so, they were responding to a considerable extent to the imperatives of territorial rule characteristic of modern states, as well as to the problem of 'masterless men'[7] as personal freedom advanced. The phenomenon is captured nicely in Karl Polanyi's discussion of the emergence of 'the poor' as a distinctive group in early modern England:

> [T]hey became conspicuous as *individuals unattached to the manor,* 'or to any feudal superior[,]' and their gradual transformation into a class of free laborers was the combined result of the fierce persecution of vagrancy and the fostering of domestic industry . . .[8]

The transition from private to state control over movement was an essential aspect of the transition from feudalism to capitalism.

The process through which states monopolized the legitimate means of movement thus took hundreds of years to come to fruition. It followed the shift of orientations from the local to the 'national' level that accompanied the development of 'national' states out of the panoply of empires and smaller city-states and principalities that dotted the map of early modern Europe. The process also paralleled the rationalization and nationalization of poor relief, for communal obligations to provide such relief were an important source of the desire for controls on movement. Previously in the domain of private and religious organizations, the administration of poor relief gradually came to be removed from their purview and lodged in that of states. As European states declined in number, grew in size, and fostered large-scale markets for wage labor outside the reach of landowners and against the traditional constraints imposed by localities, the provision of poor relief also moved from the local to the national arena.[9] These processes, in turn, helped to expand 'outward' to the 'national' borders the areas in which persons could expect to move freely and without authorization. Eventually, the principal boundaries that counted were those not of municipalities, but of nation-states.

The process took place unevenly in different places, following the line where modern states replaced non-territorial forms of political organization[10] and 'free' wage labor replaced various forms of servitude. Then, as people from all levels of society came to find themselves in a more nearly equal position relative to the state, state controls on movement among local spaces within their domains subsided and were replaced by restrictions that concerned the outer 'national' boundaries of states. Ultimately, the authority to regulate movement came to be primarily a property of the international system as a whole – that is, of nation-states acting in concert to enforce their interests in controlling who comes and goes. Where pronounced state controls on movement operate *within* a state today, especially when these are to the detriment of particular 'negatively privileged' status groups, we can reliably expect to find an authoritarian state (or worse). The cases of the Soviet Union, Nazi Germany, apartheid-era South Africa and Communist China (at least before the 1980s) bear witness to this generalization.[11]

The creation of the modern passport system and the use of similar systems in the interior of a variety of countries – the product of centuries-long labors of slow, painstaking bureaucratic construction – thus signaled the dawn of a new era in human affairs, in which individual states and the international state system as a whole successfully monopolized the legitimate authority to permit movement within and across their jurisdictions. The point here is obviously not that there is no unauthorized (international) migration, but rather that such movement is specifically 'illegal'; that is, we speak of 'illegal' (often, indeed, of 'undocumented') migration as a result of states' monopolization of the legitimate means of movement. What we now think of as 'internal' movement – a meaningless and anachronistic notion before the development of modern states and the state system – has come to mean movement within national or 'nation-states.' Historical evidence indicates clearly that, well into the nineteenth century, people routinely regarded as 'foreign' those from the next province every bit as much as those who came from other 'countries.'

None of this is to say that private actors now play no role in the regulation of movement – far from it. Yet private entities have been reduced to the capacity of 'sheriff's deputies' who participate in the regulation of movement at the behest of states. During the nineteenth and into the twentieth century, for example, governments in Europe pressed steamship companies into overseeing for them whether particular people should be permitted to travel to the destinations they had chosen. Since the development of air travel, airline companies have been subjected to similar obligations. Both shipping enterprises and air carriers have frequently resisted carrying out the sheriff's deputy function, mainly because they fear that their participation in such quasi-governmental activities will hurt their profitability. Not wanting to appear guilty of mere cupidity, however, they are likely to say that they regard the regulation of movement as the proper province of the state – and so it is.[12]

If, along with their efforts to monopolize the legitimate use of violence, modern states also seek to monopolize the legitimate means of movement, they must have means to *implement* the constraints they enunciate in this domain. In order to do so, they must be able to construct an enduring relationship between the sundry agencies that constitute states and both the individuals they govern and possible interlopers. This fact compels us to reconsider the principal line of sociological argumentation concerning the way modern states have developed.

Modern states: 'penetrating' or 'embracing'?

Previous sociological discussion of the development of modern states has focused attention primarily on their growing capacity to 'penetrate' or 'reach into' societies and extract from them what they need in order to survive. Discussions of states as 'penetrating' societies more effectively during the modern period can be found in almost any major recent sociological discussion of the nature of modern states.[13] Going the state theorists one better, Jürgen Habermas expanded the metaphor of 'penetration' to characterize the activity of both the modern bureaucratic state and the capitalist economy. Habermas thus speaks of the 'colonization of the life-world' by the 'steering media' of money and power.[14] Yet Habermas's analysis shares the weaknesses of the 'penetrationist' paradigm of state theory, for 'money' is rather more concrete than 'power' as a mechanism for enabling and constraining social choices. But we may correct for the abstractness of 'power' relative to that of money by seeing that identification papers of various kinds constitute the bureaucratic equivalent of money: they are the currency of modern state administration.

The traditional (and unmistakably sexual) imagery of societies being 'penetrated' by the state, however, unnecessarily and misleadingly narrows our analytical vision about the nature of modern states. In particular, the 'penetrationist' approach has had little to say about the mechanisms adopted and employed by states to construct and sustain enduring relationships between themselves and their subjects, the 'social base' of their reproduction. The metaphor of the 'penetration' of societies by states thus distorts the nature of the process whereby states have amassed the capacity to reconfigure social life by focusing our attention almost exclusively on the notion that states 'rise up' above and surmount the isolated societies that seem, in this metaphor, to lie prostrate beneath them. Willingly or unwillingly, the now-standard imagery of penetration suggests, more or less weak societies simply receive the advances of more or less powerful states. Having been penetrated, societies give up – to a greater or lesser extent – what states demand of them. But how does this actually happen? How are the people who make up 'societies' compelled to 'render unto Caesar what is Caesar's'?

In order to extract resources and implement policies, states must be in a position to locate and lay claim to people and goods. This fact suggests an alternative imagery to that of 'penetration' for understanding the accumulation of infrastructural capacity by modern states. Foucault has of course stressed the importance of 'surveillance' in modern societies, but it often remains unclear in his writings to what particular purposes surveillance is being put. I believe we would do well to regard states as seeking not simply to penetrate but also to *embrace* societies, 'surrounding' and 'taking hold' of their members – individually and collectively – as those states grow larger and more administratively adept. More than this, states *must* embrace societies *in order to* penetrate them effectively. Individuals who remain beyond the embrace of the state necessarily represent a limit on its penetration. The *reach* of the state, in other words, cannot exceed its *grasp*. Michael Mann is correct that the 'unusual strength of modern states is infrastructural'[15] and their capacity to embrace their own subjects and to exclude unwanted others is the essence of that infrastructural power.

My use of the term 'embrace' derives from the German word *erfassen*, which means to 'grasp' or 'lay hold of' in the sense of 'register.' Thus, for example, foreigners registered at the *Ausländerbehörde* (Agency for Foreigners) are said to be '*ausländerbehördlich erfasst*' – i.e., registered for purposes of surveillance, administration and regulation by that agency. People are also '*erfassen*' by the census. It says something important about the divergent processes of state-building on the European continent and in the Anglo-American world that we lack ordinary English equivalents for the German '*erfassen*' (as well as for the French verb *surveiller*). Whether or not our language adequately reflects this reality, however, the activities by which states 'embrace' populations have become essential to the production and reproduction of states in the modern period.

In contrast to the masculinized image of 'penetrating' states surmounting societies, the metaphor of states' 'embrace' of societies directs our awareness to the ways in which states bound – and in certain senses even 'nurture' – the societies they hold in their clutches. In this regard, the imagery of 'embracing' states shares similarities with Michael Mann's notion of the way states 'cage' social activity within them, particularly the way in which the rise of national states tended to reorient political activity from the local or regional to the national level.[16] Yet Mann's 'caging' metaphor fails to get at the way in which states metaphorically 'grasp' both entire societies and individual people in order to carry out their aims. My metaphor of states 'embracing' their populations is much more akin to James Scott's idea that states seek to render societies 'legible' and thus more readily available for governance.[17]

The notion that states 'embrace' individuals goes further, however, by calling to mind the fact that states hold *particular* persons within their grasp, while excluding others. This consideration is especially important in a world of states defined as nation-states – that is, as states comprising members conceived as nationals – and concerned successfully to monopolize the legitimate means of movement. In contrast, the imagery of 'penetration' is blind to the peculiarities of the society that the state invades. Surely the metaphor of 'embrace' helps make better sense of a world of states that are understood to consist of mutually exclusive bodies of citizens whose movements may be restricted as such.

Systems of registration, censuses, and the like – along with documents such as passports and identity cards that amount to mobile versions of the 'files' states use to store knowledge about their subjects – have been crucial in states' efforts to achieve these aims. Though not without flaws and loopholes, of course, such registration systems have gone a long way toward allowing states successfully to 'embrace' their populations and thus to acquire from them the resources they need to survive, as well as to exclude from among the beneficiaries of state largesse those groups deemed ineligible for benefits.

Modern 'nation-states' and the international system in which they are embedded have grown increasingly committed to and reliant upon their ability to make strict demarcations between mutually distinct bodies of citizens, as well as among different groups of their own subjects, when one or more of these groups are singled out for 'special treatment.' The need to sort out 'who is who' and, perhaps more significantly, 'what is what' becomes especially acute when states wish to regulate movement across external borders. This is because, as Mary Douglas wrote some years ago, 'all margins are dangerous . . . [A]ny structure of ideas is vulnerable at its margins.'[18] The idea of belonging that is at the root of the concept of citizenship is threatened when people cross borders, leaving spaces where they 'belong' and entering those where they do not.

Yet the nation-state is far more than a 'structure of ideas.' It is also – and more importantly for our purposes – a more or less coherent network of *institutions*. In this respect, recent developments in sociology turn our thinking in a fruitful direction when we try to make sense of how states actually embrace the societies they seek to rule, and to distinguish their members from non-members. Rather than merely suggesting the way institutions shape our everyday world, the 'new institutionalism' directs our attention to the 'institutional constitution of both interests and actors.'[19]

This point has a special relevance with regard to identities. Too frequently in recent academic writing, identities have been discussed in purely subjective terms, without reference to the ways in which identities are anchored in law and policy. This subjectivistic approach, given powerful impetus by the wide and much-deserved attention given to Benedict Anderson's notion of 'imagined communities,' tends to ignore the extent to which identities must become codified and institutionalized in order to become socially significant. Noiriel has made this point in the strongest possible terms with respect to immigrants: 'It is often overlooked that legal registration, identification documents, and laws are what, in the final analysis, determine the "identity" of immigrants.'[20]

But the point is more general. The cases of 'Hispanics' (as opposed to Caribbeans or South or Central Americans, for example) or 'Asian Americans' (as opposed to Japanese-Americans, Korean-Americans, etc.) in the United States, categories designed for the use of census-takers and policy-makers with little in the way of subjective correlates at the time of their creation, are here very much to the point. Whether substantial numbers of people think about themselves subjectively in these terms is an open, empirical question; that they would not be likely to do so without the institutional foundation provided by the prior legal codification of the terms seems beyond doubt.

As nation-states – states of and for particular 'peoples' defined as mutually exclusive groups of citizens[21] – modern states have typically been eager to embrace their populations, and to regulate the movements of persons within and across their borders when they wish to do so. Their efforts to implement such regulation have driven them toward the creation of the means uniquely and unambiguously to identify individual persons, whether 'their own' or others. In order to monopolize the legitimate means of movement, states and the state system have been compelled to define who belongs and who does not, who may come and go and who not, and to make these distinctions intelligible and enforceable. Documents such as passports and identity cards have been critical to achieving these objectives. Beyond simply enunciating definitions and categories concerning identity, states must *implement* these distinctions, and they require documents in order to do so in individual cases.

Getting a grip: institutionalizing the nation-state

In order to make sense of the notion that states exist 'of and for particular peoples' generally understood today as 'nations,' we must first consider what a 'nation' is. The concept of the nation, according to Weber, entails that we may 'expect from certain groups a specific sentiment of solidarity in the face of other groups,' without there being any determinate 'empirical qualities common to those who count as members of the nation.'[22] Following in Weber's footsteps, Rogers Brubaker has stressed the 'contingent, conjuncturally fluctuating, and precarious' quality of 'nation-ness,' pointing out that: 'We should not ask "what is a nation" but rather: how is nationhood as a political and cultural form institutionalized within and among states?'[23] Brubaker's institutionalist constructionism provides an important correct-ive to those views (typically held above all by nationalists themselves) that suggest that 'the nation' is a real, enduring historical entity. Failing their institutionalization, 'nations' must remain ephemeral and fuzzy.

How, indeed, is nationhood institutionalized? More specifically, precisely how is the nexus between states, subjects and potential interlopers generated and sustained? In order to extract the resources they need to survive, and to compel participation in repressive forces where necessary, states must embrace – that is, identify and gain enduring access to – those from whom they hope to derive those resources. Alternatively, states must be in a position to establish whether or not a would-be entrant matches the criteria laid down for authorized entry into their domains. Charles Tilly has noted that the French Revolution's inauguration of what he aptly calls 'direct rule' gave rulers 'access to citizens and the resources they controlled through household taxation, mass conscription, censuses, police systems, and many other invasions of small-scale social life.'[24] Yet this listing leaves the matter too vague for adequate comprehension of the way in which states have, in fact, 'invaded' small-scale social life and sought to render populations available to their embrace.

In particular, Tilly's enumeration of invasions leaves unclear how taxation and conscription grew to depend decisively on mechanisms of surveillance such as cen-suses, household registration systems, passports (internal and external) and other identity documents. The activities classically associated with the rise of modern states only became possible on a systematic basis if states were in a position successfully to embrace their populations for purposes of carrying out those activities. Such devices as identity papers, censuses and travel certificates thus were not merely on a par with conscription and taxation as elements of state-building, but were in fact essential to their successful realization and grew, over time, superordinate to them as tools of administration that made these other activities possible or at least enforceable.

Sociologists of the state have begun in recent years to address more adequately the problem of how states construct a durable relation between themselves and their subjects/citizens in furtherance of their own aims. This concern has been especially prominent in the work of Anthony Giddens. In his important study *The Nation-State and Violence*, Giddens pays considerable attention to the growing role of surveillance in the development of 'direct rule.' In contrast to 'traditional states,' Giddens noted that modern states presuppose a regularized administration and that much of the necessary administrative capacity of modern states is rooted in *writing*. It is through written documents – such as identification papers – that much of the surveillance entailed by modern state administration is carried out: '[A]dministrative power can only become established if the coding of information is actually applied in a direct way to the supervision of human activities . . .'[25] Max Weber had earlier noted the importance of 'the files' as an important element of bureaucratization, of course, but he failed to indicate their enormous role in the construction of states' enduring embrace of their citizens. Yet despite the heightened attention to the relationship between states and their subjects/citizens in recent writing on the development of state capacities, we still have little idea of how this relationship is actually constructed and sustained . . .

Against this background, let us briefly examine the imposition of passport controls in early modern European states, as rulers increasingly sought to establish untrammeled claims over territories and people.

> Such rulers began to move away, however unintentionally, from a political map [that] was an inextricably superimposed and tangled one, in which different juridical instances were geographically interwoven and stratified, and plural allegiances, asymmetrical suzerainties and anomalous enclaves abounded.[26]

In doing so, they cleared away some of the medieval underbrush that stood between them and the nation-state.

The prevalence of passport controls in absolutist Europe

Passport controls in Europe are hardly a recent invention. The exigencies of rule in early modern Europe led states to take a considerable interest in strengthening their power to regulate the comings and goings of their subjects. The mercantilist policies pursued by these states entailed the general presupposition that population was tantamount to, or at least convertible into, wealth and military strength. Accordingly, these rulers had a powerful interest in identifying and controlling the movements of their subjects. This they sought to do with a variety of strictures on movement that frequently involved documents as the means for their enforcement.

For example, with Prussia's Imperial Police Ordinances of 1548, beggars and vagrants 'were banned as a threat to domestic peace, law, and order.' Shortly thereafter, an edict of the Imperial Diet prohibited the issuance of 'passes' to 'gypsies and vagabonds [*Landstreicher*],' suggesting both that these two groups were in bad odor and that passes were required as part of the normal procedure for removing from one place to another, at least for those of the lower orders.[27] By the seventeenth century, German rulers made laws intended to tie servants more firmly to their masters, and thus also to squelch those bogeys of the officialdom, vagrancy and itinerancy.[28]

Meanwhile, across the Channel, similar developments had been afoot for some time. Despite the guarantee of the English subject's freedom to depart in the Magna Carta, a statute of 1381 forbade all but peers, notable merchants, and soldiers to leave the kingdom without a license.[29] Early modern English rulers were especially concerned that uncontrolled departures would facilitate religious deviance.[30] Then, not long after the English Civil War, an alleged upsurge in itinerancy generated by the desire of the destitute to turn up more generous rates of poor relief than were available in their native villages led the English monarch Charles II to adopt a law severely restricting movement from one parish to another. The 'Act for the better Reliefe of the Poore of this Kingdom' of 1662[31] empowered the local authorities to remove to their place of legal settlement anyone 'likely to be chargeable to the parish' – or, to put it in terms that would later become familiar in American immigration legislation, anyone 'likely to become a public charge.' At the same time, the law allowed migration for purposes of performing seasonal or other temporary labor, provided that the person or persons involved 'carry with him or them a certificate from the minister of the parish and one of the churchwardens and one of the overseers for the poore' attesting to their legal domicile, to which they were required to return upon completion of such work. These laws governing movement helped to codify in law – and to implement in practice – a distinction between 'local' and 'foreign' poor, and notably referred to the place to which illegal settlers should be removed as their 'native' residence. The act of removing oneself from one's place of birth thus appears to have been regarded as an anomaly, and may indeed have constituted a violation of the law without proper papers.

To the east, trends toward enhanced documentary controls on movement received a powerful boost from Russian Czar, Peter the Great. Eager to advance Russia's standing among the Continental powers, Peter's modernizing reforms arose primarily from a desire to improve the country's military capabilities. In this enterprise Peter was smashingly successful, for by 1725 he had created the largest standing army in Europe.[32] Such armies required extensive recruitment and, consequently, systematic access to the young men of the country. One means for the state to gain such access was to restrict mobility by requiring documentation of movement and residence. Consistent with this aim, the Czar in the early eighteenth century promulgated a series of decrees regulating the domicile and travel of Russian subjects. An edict of 1719 required anyone moving from one town or village to another to have in his (or less likely her) possession a pass from his superiors.[33] This ukase only broadened the provisions of the legal code of 1649 that had originally consolidated the Russian pattern of serfdom, the very essence of which lay in its controls on peasant movements.[34] The use of documents as mechanisms of control made serfdom's legal restrictions on peasant movements easier to enforce.

These examples demonstrate clearly that restrictions on personal freedom of movement related directly to two central questions facing burgeoning modern states: (1) how the economic advantages available in a particular area were to be divided up, whether these involved access to work or to poor relief; and (2) who would be required to perform military service, and how they would be constrained to do so. In other words, documentary controls on movement were decisively bound up with the rights and duties that would eventually come to be associated with membership – citizenship – in the nation-state.

Until the ultimate triumph of capitalism and the nation-state in nineteenth-century Europe, however, controls on movement remained predominantly an 'internal' matter. This fact reflected the powerfully local orientation of life and the law, as well as the persistence of mercantilist ideas about population-as-wealth and the relatively inchoate character of states and the international state system. Gradually, competition among states set in motion processes of centralization that resulted in a winnowing of the number of competitors, such that only those states capable of mobilizing sufficient military and economic resources survived.[35]

In the course of these developments, rulers seeking to expand their domains and their grip on populations increasingly asserted their authority to determine who could come and go in their territories. For example, during the late medieval period in France, the legal concept of the 'foreigner' shifted from the local to the 'national' level (at this point the term can still only be applied anachronistically), and from the private realm to that of the state, as a consequence of the royal usurpation from the *seigneurie* of the so-called *droit d'aubaine,* according to which foreigners had been defined as those born outside the *seigneurie.*

> This [shift] created for the first time a kingdomwide status of foreigner and, correlatively, an embryonic legal status of French citizen or national. The legal distinction between French citizen and foreigner thus originated in the late medieval consolidation of royal authority at the expense of seigneurial rights.[36]

The monopolization of the legitimate means of movement by states entailed their successful assertion of the authority to determine who 'belonged' and who did not. The state's complete expropriation of the power to authorize movement would take some time to achieve, of course, but they were well on their way to making this monopoly a reality.

To these more strictly political considerations must be added Karl Polanyi's compelling portrayal of the decisive role of the early modern state in weaving together local into national markets, a process that frequently involved the triumph of the central state against fierce local resistance. This gradual transformation facilitated a sea-change in conceptions of 'internal' and 'external' territory and thus in the nature of the restrictions on who could come and go, and with whose authorization.[37] As markets for labor power, in particular, became 'nationalized,' states asserted dominion over the right to determine who could move about and under what conditions. The general result of the process was that local borders were replaced by national ones, and that the chief difficulty associated with human movement was entry into, not departure from, territorial spaces. The spread of identification documents such as passports was crucial to states' monopolization of the legitimate means of movement. But this would take some time to achieve in practice, and began by facing a sharp challenge from the libertarian elements in the French Revolution.

Notes

1 This chapter is drawn from J. Torpey (2000) Coming and going: on the state monopolization of the legitimate 'means of movement', in *The Invention of the Passport: Surveillance, Citizenship and the State.* Cambridge: Cambridge University Press, pp. 4–20.
2 Meyer (1987: 53).
3 See, e.g., Zolberg (1978, 1983). It seems to me that Zolberg's pleas have only recently begun to be heeded; see, e.g., Skran (1995).
4 See Anderson (1991). Michael Mann (1993: 218) has noted that 'Anderson's "print capitalism" could as easily generate a transnational West as a community of nations' in the absence of the institutionalization of the latter.
5 On the 'identification revolution,' see Noiriel (1991); he develops the notion of 'The Card and the Code' (1996, chap. 2). In her work on laws relating to naming, Jane Caplan (2000) speaks of the emergence of a 'culture of identification' during the nineteenth century.
6 For a comparative analysis of slavery and serfdom as systems of control over movement, see Kolchin (1987, especially chap. 1, Labor Management).

7 For an in-depth study of such persons in one country, see Beier (1985).

8 Polanyi (1944: 104, my emphasis); see also Chambliss (1964).

9 For an analysis of the origins of modern poor relief systems, see Gorski (1996, 1997). On the 'nationalization' of poor relief in Germany, see Steinmetz (1993). One may well wonder whether recent changes in US welfare law that shift responsibility from the federal down to the state level have begun to reverse this trend.

10 On such organizations, see Spruyt (1994).

11 On passport controls in the Soviet Union and China, see Torpey (1997).

12 On this issue, see Gilboy (1997).

13 See, for instance, Mann (1993); Skocpol (1978); Tilly (1990). Randall Collins used the term 'penetration' as a sort of taken-for-granted shorthand for understanding the essential activities of modern states in his comments on a presentation by Michael Mann at the Center for Social Theory and Comparative History, UCLA, 27 January 1997.

14 See Habermas (1987).

15 Mann (1993: 60).

16 Mann (1993: 61).

17 See Scott (1998). If I may borrow the metaphor with which Scott describes how he and Stephen Marglin arrived at roughly similar views about the functioning of states, he and I seem to have taken different trains to much the same destination; his train, however, was a 'local,' whereas mine was an 'express.' That is, Scott explores a variety of ways in which modern states have sought to make societies 'legible,' while I have tried to focus on one particular aspect of that effort – namely, identification documents deployed for the regulation of movement.

18 Douglas (1966: 121).

19 Brubaker (1996: 24); see also Powell and Dimaggio (1991).

20 Noiriel (1996: 45).

21 See Brubaker (1992).

22 Weber (1978: 922).

23 Brubaker (1996: 16, 19).

24 Tilly (1990: 25).

25 Giddens (1987: 47). Leonard Dudley (1991) has noted that writing originated (in ancient Sumeria) not as a means of recording speech, but in order to facilitate taxation.

26 Anderson (1974: 37–8).

27 Bertelsmann (1914: 17–18).

28 Raeff (1983: 74, 89–90).

29 5 R. II, stat. 1, c. 2 (1381) section 7, cited in Plender (1988: 85, n. 12).

30 See Warneke (1996).

31 14 Charles II *c.* 12. This law appears to be what Karl Polanyi refers to as the 'Act of Settlement (and Removal).'

32 Bendix (1978: 501ff).

33 Matthews (1993: 1–2).

34 See Kolchin (1987).

35   On this process, see Burke (1997); Elias ([1939] 1978; [1939] 1982); Tilly (1990).

36   See Brubaker (1992: 37). It is suggestive that, at least according to one historian, the term 'passport' was first attested to in France during this period. See Nordman (1987: 148).

37   Polanyi (1944: 63–7). I am grateful to Peggy Somers for reminding me of the usefulness of Polanyi's classic for the analysis I am trying to develop here.

References

Anderson, B. ([1983] 1991) *Imagined Communities: Reflections on the Origin and Spread of Nationalism*, revised edn. New York: Verso.

Anderson, P. (1974) *Lineages of the Absolutist State*. New York: Verso.

Beier, A. L. (1985) *Masterless Men: The Vagrancy Problem in England, 1560–1700*, London: Methuen.

Bendix, R. (1978) *Kings or People? Power and the Mandate to Rule*. Berkeley: University of California Press.

Bertelsmann, W. (1914) *Das Passwesen: eine völkerrechtliche Studie*. Strassburg: J. H. Ed. Heitz.

Brubaker, R. (1992) *Citizenship and Nationhood in France and Germany*. Cambridge, MA: Harvard University Press.

Brubaker, R. (1996) *Nationalism Reframed: Nationhood and the National Question in the New Europe*. New York: Cambridge University Press.

Brunialti, A. (1915) Passaporti, in P. S. Mancini (ed.) *Enciclopedia Giuridica Italiana*, vol. 13, Part I. Milan: Società Editrice Libraria, pp. 674–85.

Burke, V. L. 1997. *The Clash of Civilizations: War-Making and State Formation in Europe*. Cambridge, MA: Polity Press.

Caplan, J. (2000) 'This or that particular person': protocols of identification in nineteenth-century Europe, In J. Caplan and J. Torpey (eds) *Documenting Individual Identity: The Development of State Practices in the Modern World*. Princeton: Princeton University Press.

Chambliss, W. (1964) A sociological analysis of the law of vagrancy, *Social Problems*, 11(1): 67–77.

Douglas, M. (1966) *Purity and Danger: An Analysis of Concepts of Pollution and Taboo*. London: Routledge & Kegan Paul.

Dudley, L. M. (1991) *The Word and the Sword: How Techniques of Information and Violence Have Shaped Our World*. Cambridge, MA: Basil Blackwell.

Elias, N. ([1939] 1978) *The Civilizing Process*, vol. 1: *The History of Manners*, Trans. E. Jephcott. New York: Pantheon.

Elias, N. ([1939] 1982) *The Civilizing Process*, vol. 2: *Power & Civility*, trans. E. Jephcott. New York: Pantheon.

Giddens, A. (1987) *The Nation-State and Violence*. Berkeley: University of California Press.

Gilboy, J. (1997) Regulatory relaxation: International Airlines, the Immigration Service, and Illegal Travelers. Paper presented to the Annual Meeting of the Law and Society Assocation, St. Louis, MO, May.

Gorski, P. S. (1996) *The disciplinary revolution: Calvinism and state formation in early modern Europe, 1550–1750*. PhD, dissertation, Department of Sociology, University of California, Berkeley.

Gorski, P. S. (1997) Sixteenth-century social reform: why Protestantism mattered. Typescript, Department of Sociology, University of Wisconsin, Madison.

Habermas, J. (1987) *The Theory of Communicative Action*, vol. 2: *Lifeworld and System: A Critique of Functionalist Reason*, trans. T. McCarthy. Boston: Beacon Press.

Kolchin, P. (1987) *Unfree Labor: American Slavery and Russian Serfdom*. Cambridge, MA: Harvard University Press.

Mann, M. (1993) *The Sources of Social Power*, vol. 2: *The Rise of Classes and Nation-States, 1760–1914*. New York: Cambridge University Press.

Matthews, M. (1993) *The Passport Society: Controlling Movement in Russia and the USSR*. Boulder, CO: Westview Press.

Meyer, J. ([1980] 1987) The world polity and the authority of the nation-state, in G. M. Thomas et al. (eds) *Institutional Structure: Constituting State, Society, and the Individual*. Newbury Park, CA: Sage.

Noiriel, G. (1991) *La tyrannie du national: Le droit d'asile en Europe, 1793–1993*. Paris: Calmann-Levy.

Noiriel, G. ([1988] 1996) *The French Melting Pot: Immigration, Citizenship, and National Identity*, trans. G. de Laforcade. Minneapolis: University of Minnesota Press.

Nordman, D. (1987) Sauf-Conduits et passeports, en France, à la Renaissance, in J. Céard and J.-C. Margolin (eds) *Voyager à la Renaissance: Actes du colloque de Tours 30 juin–13 juillet 1983*. Paris: Maisonneuve et Larose, pp. 145–58.

Plender, R. ([1972] 1988) *International Migration Law*, 2nd revised edn. Dordrecht: Martinus Nijhoff.

Polanyi, K. (1944) *The Great Transformation: The Political and Economic Origins of Our Time*. Boston: Beacon Press.

Raeff, M. (1983) *The Well-Ordered Police State: Social and Institutional Change Through Law in the Germanies and Russia, 1600–1800*. New Haven, CT: Yale University Press.

Scott, J. C. (1998) *Seeing Like a State: How Certain Schemes to Improve the Human Condition Have Failed*. New Haven: Yale University Press.

Skocpol, T. (1978) *States and Social Revolutions: A Comparative Analysis of France, Russia, and China*. New York: Cambridge University Press.

Skran, C. (1995) *Refugees in Inter-War Europe: The Emergence of a Regime*. Oxford: Clarendon Press.

Spruyt, H. (1994) *The Sovereign State and its Competitors*. Princeton: Princeton University Press.

Steinmetz, G. (1993) *Regulating the Social: The Welfare State and Local Politics in Imperial Germany*. Princeton: Princeton University Press.

Tilly, C. (1990) *Coercion, Capital, and European States, A. D. 990–1992*. Oxford: Basil Blackwell.

Torpey, J. (1997) Revolutions and freedom of movement: an analysis of passport controls in the French, Russian, and Chinese Revolutions, *Theory and Society*, 26: 837–68.

Warneke, S. (1996) *A Coastal 'Hedge of Laws': Passport Control in Early Modern England*. Studies in Western Traditions Occasional Papers No. 4, School of Arts, La Trobe University, Bendigo, Australia.

Zolberg, A. (1978) International migration policies in a changing world system, in McNeill and Adams (eds) *Human Migration: Patterns and Policies*. Bloomington, IN: Indiana University Press, pp. 241–86.

Zolberg, A. (1983) The formation of new states as a refugee-generating process, *Annals of the American Academy of Social and Political Science*, May, 467: 24–38.

5

Panopticism[1]
by Michel Foucault

The following, according to an order published at the end of the seventeenth century, were the measures to be taken when the plague appeared in a town.[2]

First, a strict spatial partitioning: the closing of the town and its outlying districts, a prohibition to leave the town on pain of death, the killing of all stray animals; the division of the town into distinct quarters, each governed by an intendant. Each street is placed under the authority of a syndic, who keeps it under surveillance; if he leaves the street, he will be condemned to death. On the appointed day, everyone is ordered to stay indoors: it is forbidden to leave on pain of death. The syndic himself comes to lock the door of each house from the outside; he takes the key with him and hands it over to the intendant of the quarter; the intendant keeps it until the end of the quarantine. Each family will have made its own provisions; but, for bread and wine, small wooden canals are set up between the street and the interior of the houses, thus allowing each person to receive his ration without communicating with the suppliers and other residents; meat, fish and herbs will be hoisted up into the houses with pulleys and baskets. If it is absolutely necessary to leave the house, it will be done in turn, avoiding any meeting. Only the intendants, syndics and guards will move about the streets and also, between the infected houses, from one corpse to another, the 'crows', who can be left to die: these are 'people of little substance who carry the sick, bury the dead, clean and do many vile and abject offices'. It is a segmented, immobile, frozen space. Each individual is fixed in his place. And, if he moves, he does so at the risk of his life, contagion or punishment.

Inspection functions ceaselessly. The gaze is alert everywhere: 'A considerable body of militia, commanded by good officers and men of substance', guards at the gates, at the town hall and in every quarter to ensure the prompt obedience of the people and the most absolute authority of the magistrates, 'as also to observe all disorder, theft and extortion'. At each of the town gates there will be an observation post; at the end of each street sentinels. Every day, the intendant visits the quarter in his charge, inquires whether the syndics have carried out their tasks, whether the inhabitants have anything to complain of; they 'observe their actions'. Every day, too, the syndic goes into the street for which he is responsible; stops before each house: gets all the inhabitants to appear at the windows (those who live overlooking the courtyard will be allocated a window looking onto the street at which no one but they may show themselves); he calls each of them by name; informs himself as to the state of each and every one of them – 'in which respect the inhabitants will be compelled to speak the truth under pain of death'; if someone does not appear at the window, the syndic must ask why: 'In this way he will find out easily enough whether dead or sick are being concealed.' Everyone locked up in his cage, everyone at his window, answering to his name and showing himself when asked – it is the great review of the living and the dead.

This surveillance is based on a system of permanent registration: reports from the syndics to the intendants, from the intendants to the magistrates or mayor. At the beginning of the 'lock up', the role of each of the inhabitants present in the town is laid down, one by one; this document bears 'the name, age, sex of everyone, notwithstanding his condition': a copy is sent to the intendant of the quarter, another to the office of the town hall, another to enable the syndic to make his daily roll call. Everything that may be observed during the course of the visits – deaths, illnesses, complaints, irregularities – is noted down and transmitted to the intendants and magistrates. The magistrates have complete control over medical treatment; they have appointed a physician in charge; no other practitioner may treat, no apothecary pre-pare medicine, no confessor visit a sick person without having received from him a written note 'to prevent anyone from concealing and dealing with those sick of the contagion, unknown to the magistrates'. The registration of the pathological must be constantly centralized. The relation of each individual to his disease and to his death passes through the representatives of power, the registration they make of it, the decisions they take on it.

Five or six days after the beginning of the quarantine, the process of purifying the houses one by one is begun. All the inhabitants are made to leave; in each room 'the furniture and goods' are raised from the ground or suspended from the air; perfume is poured around the room; after carefully sealing the windows, doors and even the keyholes with wax, the perfume is set alight. Finally, the entire house is closed while the perfume is consumed; those who have carried out the work are searched, as they were on entry, 'in the presence of the residents of the house, to see that they did not have something on their persons as they left that they did not have on entering'. Four hours later, the residents are allowed to re-enter their homes.

This enclosed, segmented space, observed at every point, in which the individuals are inserted in a fixed place, in which the slightest movements are supervised, in which all events are recorded, in which an uninterrupted work of writing links the centre and periphery, in which power is exercised without division, according to a continuous hierarchical figure, in which each individual is constantly located, exam-ined and distributed among the living beings, the sick and the dead – all this consti-tutes a compact model of the disciplinary mechanism. The plague is met by order; its function is to sort out every possible confusion: that of the disease, which is transmit-ted when bodies are mixed together; that of the evil, which is increased when fear and death overcome prohibitions. It lays down for each individual his place, his body, his disease and his death, his well-being, by means of an omnipresent and omniscient power that subdivides itself in a regular, uninterrupted way even to the ultimate determination of the individual, of what characterizes him, of what belongs to him, of what happens to him. Against the plague, which is a mixture, discipline brings into play its power, which is one of analysis. A whole literary fiction of the festival grew up around the plague: suspended laws, lifted prohibitions, the frenzy of passing time, bodies mingling together without respect, individuals unmasked, abandoning their statutory identity and the figure under which they had been recognized, allowing a quite different truth to appear. But there was also a political dream of the plague, which was exactly its reverse: not the collective festival, but strict divisions; not laws transgressed, but the penetration of regulation into even the smallest details of every-day life through the mediation of the complete hierarchy that assured the capillary functioning of power; not masks that were put on and taken off, but the assignment to each individual of his 'true' name, his 'true' place, his 'true' body, his 'true' disease. The plague as a form, at once real and imaginary, of disorder had as its medical and political correlative discipline. Behind the disciplinary mechanisms can be read the haunting memory of 'contagions', of the plague, of rebellions, crimes, vagabondage, desertions, people who appear and disappear, live and die in disorder.

If it is true that the leper gave rise to rituals of exclusion, which to a certain extent provided the model for and general form of the great Confinement, then the plague gave rise to disciplinary projects. Rather than the massive, binary division between one set of people and another, it called for multiple separations, individualizing distributions, an organization in depth of surveillance and control, an intensification and a ramification of power. The leper was caught up in a practice of rejection, of exile-enclosure; he was left to his doom in a mass among which it was useless to differentiate; those sick of the plague were caught up in a meticulous tactical partitioning in which individual differentiations were the constricting effects of a power that multiplied, articulated and subdivided itself; the great confinement on the one hand; the correct training on the other. The leper and his separation; the plague and its segmentations. The first is marked; the second analysed and distributed. The exile of the leper and the arrest of the plague do not bring with them the same political dream. The first is that of a pure community, the second that of a disciplined society. Two ways of exercising power over men, of controlling their relations, of separating out their dangerous mixtures. The plague-stricken town, traversed throughout with hierarchy, surveillance, observation, writing; the town immobilized by the functioning of an extensive power that bears in a distinct way over all individual bodies – this is the utopia of the perfectly governed city. The plague (envisaged as a possibility at least) is the trial in the course of which one may define ideally the exercise of disciplinary power. In order to make rights and laws function according to pure theory, the jurists place themselves in imagination in the state of nature; in order to see perfect disciplines functioning, rulers dreamt of the state of plague. Underlying disciplinary projects the image of the plague stands for all forms of confusion and disorder; just as the image of the leper, cut off from all human contact, underlies projects of exclusion.

They are different projects, then, but not incompatible ones. We see them coming slowly together, and it is the peculiarity of the nineteenth century that it applied to the space of exclusion of which the leper was the symbolic inhabitant (beggars, vaga-bonds, madmen and the disorderly formed the real population) the technique of power proper to disciplinary partitioning. Treat 'lepers' as 'plague victims', project the subtle segmentations of discipline onto the confused space of internment, combine it with the methods of analytical distribution proper to power, individualize the excluded, but use procedures of individualization to mark exclusion – this is what was operated regularly by disciplinary power from the beginning of the nineteenth century in the psychiatric asylum, the penitentiary, the reformatory, the approved school and, to some extent, the hospital. Generally speaking, all the authorities exercising individual control function according to a double mode; that of binary division and branding (mad/sane; dangerous/harmless; normal/abnormal); and that of coercive assignment, of differential distribution (who he is; where he must be; how he is to be characterized; how he is to be recognized; how a constant surveillance is to be exercised over him in an individual way, etc.). On the one hand, the lepers are treated as plague victims; the tactics of individualizing disciplines are imposed on the excluded; and, on the other hand, the universality of disciplinary controls makes it possible to brand the 'leper' and to bring into play against him the dualistic mechanisms of exclusion. The constant division between the normal and the abnormal, to which every individual is subjected, brings us back to our own time, by applying the binary branding and exile of the leper to quite different objects; the existence of a whole set of techniques and institutions for measuring, supervising and correcting the abnormal brings into play the disciplinary mechanisms to which the fear of the plague gave rise. All the mechanisms of power which, even today, are disposed around the abnormal individual, to brand him and to alter him, are composed of those two forms from which they distantly derive.

Bentham's *Panopticon* is the architectural figure of this composition. We know the principle on which it was based: at the periphery, an annular building; at the centre, a tower; this tower is pierced with wide windows that open onto the inner side of the ring; the peripheric building is divided into cells, each of which extends the whole width of the building; they have two windows, one on the inside, corresponding to the windows of the tower; the other, on the outside, allows the light to cross the cell from one end to the other. All that is needed, then, is to place a supervisor in a central tower and to shut up in each cell a madman, a patient, a condemned man, a worker or a schoolboy. By the effect of backlighting, one can observe from the tower, standing out precisely against the light, the small captive shadows in the cells of the periphery. They are like so many cages, so many small theatres, in which each actor is alone, perfectly individualized and constantly visible. The panoptic mechanism arranges spatial unities that make it possible to see constantly and to recognize immediately. In short, it reverses the principle of the dungeon; or rather of its three functions – to enclose, to deprive of light and to hide – it preserves only the first and eliminates the other two. Full lighting and the eye of a supervisor capture better than darkness, which ultimately protected. Visibility is a trap . . .

Hence the major effect of the Panopticon: to induce in the inmate a state of conscious and permanent visibility that assures the automatic functioning of power. So to arrange things that the surveillance is permanent in its effects, even if it is discontinuous in its action; that the perfection of power should tend to render its actual exercise unnecessary; that this architectural apparatus should be a machine for creating and sustaining a power relation independent of the person who exercises it; in short, that the inmates should be caught up in a power situation of which they are themselves the bearers. To achieve this, it is at once too much and too little that the prisoner should be constantly observed by an inspector: too little, for what matters is that he knows himself to be observed; too much, because he has no need in fact of being so. In view of this, Bentham laid down the principle that power should be visible and unverifiable. Visible: the inmate will constantly have before his eyes the tall outline of the central tower from which he is spied upon. Unverifiable: the inmate must never know whether he is being looked at at any one moment; but he must be sure that he may always be so. In order to make the presence or absence of the inspector unverifiable, so that the prisoners, in their cells, cannot even see a shadow, Bentham envisaged not only venetian blinds on the windows of the central observation hall, but, on the inside, partitions that intersected the hall at right angles and, in order to pass from one quarter to the other, not doors but zig-zag openings; for the slightest noise, a gleam of light, a brightness in a half-opened door would betray the presence of the guardian.[3] The Panopticon is a machine for dissociating the see/being seen dyad: in the peripheric ring, one is totally seen, without ever seeing; in the central tower, one sees everything without ever being seen.[4]

It is an important mechanism, for it automatizes and disindividualizes power. Power has its principle not so much in a person as in a certain concerted distribution of bodies, surfaces, lights, gazes; in an arrangement whose internal mechanisms produce the relation in which individuals are caught up. The ceremonies, the rituals, the marks by which the sovereign's surplus power was manifested are useless. There is a machinery that assures dissymmetry, disequilibrium, difference. Consequently, it does not matter who exercises power. Any individual, taken almost at random, can operate the machine: in the absence of the director, his family, his friends, his visitors, even his servants (Bentham, 45). Similarly, it does not matter what motive animates him: the curiosity of the indiscreet, the malice of a child, the thirst for knowledge of a philosopher who wishes to visit this museum of human nature, or the perversity of those who take pleasure in spying and punishing. The more numerous those anonymous and temporary observers are, the greater the risk for the inmate of being surprised and the greater his anxious awareness of being observed. The Panopticon is a marvellous machine which, whatever use one may wish to put it to, produces homogeneous effects of power.

A real subjection is born mechanically from a fictitious relation. So it is not necessary to use force to constrain the convict to good behaviour, the madman to calm, the worker to work, the schoolboy to application, the patient to the observation of the regulations. Bentham was surprised that panoptic institutions could be so light: there were no more bars, no more chains, no more heavy locks; all that was needed was that the separations should be clear and the openings well arranged. The heaviness of the old 'houses of security', with their fortress-like architecture, could be replaced by the simple, economic geometry of a 'house of certainty'. The efficiency of power, its constraining force have, in a sense, passed over to the other side – to the side of its surface of application. He who is subjected to a field of visibility, and who knows it, assumes responsibility for the constraints of power; he makes them play spontaneously upon himself; he inscribes in himself the power relation in which he simultaneously plays both roles; he becomes the principle of his own subjection. By this very fact, the external power may throw off its physical weight; it tends to the non-corporal; and, the more it approaches this limit, the more constant, profound and permanent are its effects: it is a perpetual victory that avoids any physical confrontation and which is always decided in advance . . .

The plague-stricken town, the panoptic establishment – the differences are important. They mark, at a distance of a century and a half, the transformations of the disciplinary programme. In the first case, there is an exceptional situation: against an extraordinary evil, power is mobilized; it makes itself everywhere present and visible; it invents new mechanisms; it separates, it immobilizes, it partitions; it constructs for a time what is both a counter-city and the perfect society; it imposes an ideal functioning, but one that is reduced, in the final analysis, like the evil that it combats, to a simple dualism of life and death: that which moves brings death, and one kills that which moves. The Panopticon, on the other hand, must be understood as a generalizable model of functioning; a way of defining power relations in terms of the everyday life of men. No doubt Bentham presents it as a particular institution, closed in upon itself. Utopias, perfectly closed in upon themselves, are common enough. As opposed to the ruined prisons, littered with mechanisms of torture, to be seen in Piranese's engravings, the Panopticon presents a cruel, ingenious cage. The fact that it should have given rise, even in our own time, to so many variations, projected or realized, is evidence of the imaginary intensity that it has possessed for almost two hundred years. But the Panopticon must not be understood as a dream building: it is the diagram of a mechanism of power reduced to its ideal form; its functioning, abstracted from any obstacle, resistance or friction, must be represented as a pure architectural and optical system: it is in fact a figure of political technology that may and must be detached from any specific use.

It is polyvalent in its applications; it serves to reform prisoners, but also to treat patients, to instruct schoolchildren, to confine the insane, to supervise workers, to put beggars and idlers to work. It is a type of location of bodies in space, of distribution of individuals in relation to one another, of hierarchical organization, of disposition of centres and channels of power, of definition of the instruments and modes of intervention of power, which can be implemented in hospitals, workshops, schools, prisons. Whenever one is dealing with a multiplicity of individuals on whom a task or a particular form of behaviour must be imposed, the panoptic schema may be used. It is – necessary modifications apart – applicable 'to all establishments whatsoever, in which, within a space not too large to be covered or commanded by buildings, a number of persons are meant to be kept under inspection' (Bentham 40; although Bentham takes the penitentiary house as his prime example, it is because it has many different functions to fulfil – safe custody, confinement, solitude, forced labour and instruction).

In each of its applications, it makes it possible to perfect the exercise of power. It does this in several ways: because it can reduce the number of those who exercise it, while increasing the number of those on whom it is exercised. Because it is possible to intervene at any moment and because the constant pressure acts even before the offences, mistakes or crimes have been committed. Because, in these conditions, its strength is that it never intervenes, it is exercised spontaneously and without noise, it constitutes a mechanism whose effects follow from one another. Because, without any physical instrument other than architecture and geometry, it acts directly on individuals; it gives 'power of mind over mind'. The panoptic schema makes any apparatus of power more intense: it assures its economy (in material, in personnel, in time); it assures its efficacity by its preventative character, its continuous functioning and its automatic mechanisms. It is a way of obtaining from power 'in hitherto unexampled quantity', 'a great and new instrument of government ... its great excellence consists in the great strength it is capable of giving to *any* institution it may be thought proper to apply it to' (Bentham, 66).

It's a case of 'it's easy once you've thought of it' in the political sphere. It can in fact be integrated into any function (education, medical treatment, production, punishment); it can increase the effect of this function, by being linked closely with it; it can constitute a mixed mechanism in which relations of power (and of knowledge) may be precisely adjusted, in the smallest detail, to the processes that are to be supervised; it can establish a direct proportion between 'surplus power' and 'surplus production'. In short, it arranges things in such a way that the exercise of power is not added on from the outside, like a rigid, heavy constraint, to the functions it invests, but is so subtly present in them as to increase their efficiency by itself increasing its own points of contact. The panoptic mechanism is not simply a hinge, a point of exchange between a mechanism of power and a function; it is a way of making power relations function in a function, and of making a function function through these power relations. Bentham's Preface to *Panopticon* opens with a list of the benefits to be obtained from his 'inspection-house': '*Morals reformed – health preserved – industry invigorated – instruction diffused – public burthens lightened –* Economy seated, as it were, upon a rock – the gordian knot of the Poor-Laws not cut, but untied – all by a simple idea in architecture!' (Bentham, 39).

Furthermore, the arrangement of this machine is such that its enclosed nature does not preclude a permanent presence from the outside: we have seen that anyone may come and exercise in the central tower the functions of surveillance, and that, this being the case, he can gain a clear idea of the way in which the surveillance is practised. In fact, any panoptic institution, even if it is as rigorously closed as a penitentiary, may without difficulty be subjected to such irregular and constant inspections: and not only by the appointed inspectors, but also by the public; any member of society will have the right to come and see with his own eyes how the schools, hospitals, factories, prisons function. There is no risk, therefore, that the increase of power created by the panoptic machine may degenerate into tyranny; the disciplinary mechanism will be democratically controlled, since it will be constantly accessible 'to the great tribunal committee of the world'.[5] This Panopticon, subtly arranged so that an observer may observe, at a glance, so many different individuals, also enables everyone to come and observe any of the observers. The seeing machine was once a sort of dark room into which individuals spied; it has become a transparent building in which the exercise of power may be supervised by society as a whole.

The panoptic schema, without disappearing as such or losing any of its properties, was destined to spread throughout the social body; its vocation was to become a generalized function. The plague-stricken town provided an exceptional disciplinary model: perfect, but absolutely violent; to the disease that brought death, power opposed its perpetual threat of death; life inside it was reduced to its simplest expression; it was, against the power of death, the meticulous exercise of the right of the sword. The Panopticon, on the other hand, has a role of amplification; although it arranges power, although it is intended to make it more economic and more effective, it does so not for power itself, nor for the immediate salvation of a threatened society: its aim is to strengthen the social forces – to increase production, to develop the economy, spread education, raise the level of public morality; to increase and multiply.

How is power to be strengthened in such a way that, far from impeding progress, far from weighing upon it with its rules and regulations, it actually facilitates such progress? What intensificator of power will be able at the same time to be a multiplica-tor of production? How will power, by increasing its forces, be able to increase those of society instead of confiscating them or impeding them? The Panopticon's solution to this problem is that the productive increase of power can be assured only if, on the one hand, it can be exercised continuously in the very foundations of society, in the subtlest possible way, and if, on the other hand, it functions outside these sudden, violent, discontinuous forms that are bound up with the exercise of sovereignty. The body of the king, with its strange material and physical presence, with the force that he himself deploys or transmits to some few others, is at the opposite extreme of this new physics of power represented by panopticism; the domain of panopticism is, on the contrary, that whole lower region, that region of irregular bodies, with their details, their multiple movements, their heterogeneous forces, their spatial relations; what are required are mechanisms that analyse distributions, gaps, series, combinations, and which use instruments that render visible, record, differentiate and compare: a physics of a relational and multiple power, which has its maximum intensity not in the person of the king, but in the bodies that can be individualized by these relations. At the theoretical level, Bentham defines another way of analysing the social body and the power relations that traverse it; in terms of practice, he defines a procedure of sub-ordination of bodies and forces that must increase the utility of power while practising the economy of the prince. Panopticism is the general principle of a new 'political anatomy' whose object and end are not the relations of sovereignty but the relations of discipline.

The celebrated, transparent, circular cage, with its high tower, powerful and knowing, may have been for Bentham a project of a perfect disciplinary institution; but he also set out to show how one may 'unlock' the disciplines and get them to function in a diffused, multiple, polyvalent way throughout the whole social body. These disciplines, which the classical age had elaborated in specific, relatively enclosed places – barracks, schools, workshops – and whose total implementation had been imagined only at the limited and temporary scale of a plague-stricken town, Bentham dreamt of transforming into a network of mechanisms that would be every-where and always alert, running through society without interruption in space or in time. The panoptic arrangement provides the formula for this generalization. It programmes, at the level of an elementary and easily transferable mechanism, the basic functioning of a society penetrated through and through with disciplinary mechanisms . . .

Notes

1   This chapter is an extract from M. Foucault ([1977] 1995) Panopticism, in *Discipline and Punish: The Birth of the Modern Prison*. New York: Vintage, pp. 195–209.

2   *Archives militaires de Vincennes*, A 1,516 91 sc. Pièce. This regulation is broadly similar to a whole series of others that date from the same period and earlier.

3   In the *Postscript to the Panopticon*, 1791, Bentham adds dark inspection galleries painted in black around the inspector's lodge, each making it possible to observe two storeys of cells.

4   In his first version of the *Panopticon*, Bentham had also imagined an acoustic surveillance, operated by means of pipes leading from the cells to the central tower. In the *Postscript* he abandoned the idea, perhaps because he could not introduce into it the principle of dissymmetry and prevent the prisoners from hearing the inspector as well as the inspector hearing them. Julius tried to develop a system of dissymmetrical listening (Julius, 18).

5   Imagining this continuous flow of visitors entering the central tower by an underground passage and then observing the circular landscape of the Panopticon, was Bentham aware of the Panoramas that Barker was constructing at exactly the same period (the first seems to have dated from 1787) and in which the visitors, occupying the central place, saw unfolding around them a landscape, a city or a battle? The visitors occupied exactly the place of the sovereign gaze.

References

Archives militaires de Vincennes, A 1,516 91 sc.
Bentham, J. (1843) *Works*, ed. Bowring IV.
Julius, N. H. (1831) *Leçons sur les prisons*, I, Fr. trans.

PART 2

Computers, simulations and surveillance

The reading passages presented in Part I demonstrate the importance of centralized forms of state surveillance in the administration of everyday life. The state certainly continues to occupy a key role in maintaining surveillance infrastructures globally. We need only to consider the expanded legislative powers of policing, detention, profiling and judicial intervention that were ushered in after 11 September 2001 in the USA, Canada, Austria, Denmark, Germany, India, Singapore, Sweden, France and the UK to appreciate the continuing surveillance capacities of the state. But information gathered by non-state agencies and organizations also occupies an increasingly significant component of surveillance systems today. Surveillance is designed into the flows of everyday existence (Rose 1999), and surveillance data enable consumers to perform a wide range of functions. Among these functions are accessing bank accounts and health records, constructing customer profiles to facilitate efficient service, making cell phone calls, and sending and receiving electronic mail. It is important to realize, however, that the same data that enable citizens to easily negotiate everyday life in consumer markets can also be used by government agencies to construct profiles, risk assessments and activity histories. Following the attacks on 11 September 2001 (USA) and 7 July 2005 (London), it was surveillance data from 'everyday activities' such as credit cards, cell phone use and movement through public space (i.e., biometric facial images garnered from CCTV surveillance cameras) that were used by law enforcement officials to track the activities of the attackers (despite the praise afforded to CCTV surveillance). While these examples are unique, far more mundane examples of the convergence of public and private information and data storage systems are readily available.

Moreover, the processes by which data stored in state and non-state databases are garnered from ordinary citizens are far from homogenous. It is true that people routinely surrender all kinds of personal data to benefit from discounts, services and sales. It is also becoming increasingly common that consumers and citizens must provide personal data to benefit from privileges and gain access to (or renew) services, even when they are wary of doing so. To offer one example of this growing tension, a survey of 5000 online shoppers in the US found that 75 per cent of respondents reported heightened security concerns with buying goods online, but only 33 per cent of respondents reported that they actually reduced their online consumerism because of security concerns.[1]

From public health information to aggregated data on residential shopping patterns, it is difficult to avoid leaving a 'data footprint' when dealing with government and non-government databases. In fact, front line (desk or counter) workers in the public and private sector are rarely able to perform the routine tasks of their jobs (e.g., taking an order) without first gathering, entering and storing customers' or users' personal information. What happens to data that are collected and stored is anyone's guess – both when agencies store data and when computer equipment is sold (or, in rare but not unheard of cases, stolen or hacked into). It is increasingly common to learn that personal, financial, health, consumer and credit data have been compromised by inadequate security provisions and careless handling practices. As surveillance systems continue to proliferate beyond the state, those interested in understanding and explaining surveillance struggle to define precisely what surveillance is, how privacy protection can be maintained, and to what extent consumer convenience trumps data protection in the minds of consumers in the context of rapid advances in computerization, information gathering, and data analysis.

Section readings

In the first reading passage, Chapter 6, Gary Marx addresses 'the new surveillance'. In the 1980s, Marx warned of the growth of 'soft' forms of secret surveillance, and he pointed to the decentralized and expanding nature of surveillance in society (Marx 1985, 1988). In the reading passage, Marx continues to examine these developments. He argues that the last half of the twentieth century witnessed a dramatic increase in the use of surveillance technologies. Compared to previous times, surveillance technologies are today more numerous, routine and intrusive. Contemporary explanations for, and understandings of, surveillance, says Marx, have hitherto failed to grasp the characteristics of present-day monitoring. Popular explanations continue to emphasize suspects, asymmetrical monitoring, embodied persons, close observation and the salience of human vision. Today's surveillance practices, by contrast, involve routine rather than atypical targeted monitoring. They involve categorical as well as individual monitoring practices, and they take place across a greater number of social contexts. A growing number of surveillance systems also exist outside the immediate realm of policing and law enforcement.

Marx conceptualizes the differences between 'traditional' and 'new' surveillance in terms of ideal-typical forms of social monitoring. As ideal types, the traditional and new forms of surveillance can be classified on the basis of a number of general dimensions. As an ideal-typical form, the new surveillance tends to be involuntary, routine and remote. It tends to be less visible, categorical, relatively cheap and automated. And it tends to involve multiple and intense measures that operate at a distance, often beyond the capacity of the human senses. It is important to note, too, that Marx emphasizes the supplemental nature of the new surveillance. It is not that new forms of surveillance have entirely replaced traditional modes of social monitoring. Rather, new forms of surveillance supplement older, more traditional ways of gathering information. As Marx observes, it is difficult to definitively decide whether these developments in surveillance techniques empower or dis-empower citizens. With developments in surveillance technologies come developments in data protection – technologically and legally. It is, nevertheless, certain that surveillance technologies will continue to proliferate in the future, and with them technologies of counter-surveillance will proliferate.

The multi-dimensional character of power, surveillance and developments in digital and electronic infrastructures is a theme continued in the second reading passage, Chapter 7, where William Bogard addresses the simulation of surveillance: the disguising of an absence with a presence. The simulation of surveillance, says Bogard, is a control strategy. He explains that surveillance technologies are, paradoxically, not simply about surveillance; they operate as machines of vision and in terms of a kind of surveillance in advance of surveillance. Police forces create risk profiles, for example, to categorically monitor groups of people for potential acts of terrorism, thievery, or criminality. But as Bogard strikingly observes, in the world of virtual profiling sooner or later cases of intervention – be they police-, medical-, consumer- or education-based – come to resemble simulated profiles rather than vice versa. This is a case of profile-verification prior to intervention: it is a self-fulfilling prophecy in that the profile produces the guarantee of suspects irrespective of any one individual's identity. Indeed, international travelers of Middle Eastern background learned this fact all too well after the 2001 attacks on Washington and New York.

Considering Bogard's argument, readers might be reminded of the Hollywood movie, *The Matrix*. *The Matrix* tells the story of Thomas A. Anderson (a.k.a. Neo), an ordinary man confronted by Morpheus. Morpheus is a resident of the last human city of Zion, and he is leading the search to find 'The One' (i.e., Neo). Morpheus informs Neo that the world he has been living in is a dream world, a virtual computer simulation called The Matrix. Morpheus removes the 'context' of The Matrix for Neo to reveal 'the desert of the real': the once human-inhabited city of Chicago that is desolated after global war. Readers who have seen *The Matrix* will recall Morpheus's prophetic words following a simulated Jujitsu fight: 'Do you think the air you are breathing is real?' The point, as it relates to Bogard's argument, is that virtual imaging systems of surveillance simulate facticity, exploit uncertainty and function to intervene in social life before the fact (readers might also be reminded of the Hollywood movie, *Minority Report*). In the world of virtual simulation, subject relations are reconfigured in a context where we increasingly monitor our own activity and behaviour. So much is this the case that Bogard speculates about a 'supernormalization' taking place in most institutional settings to the extent that they actually reconfigure the boundaries between what is real and what is simulated. Still, he is careful to avoid arguing that we exist in a purely simulated world.

The first two reading passages address the interrelations of new surveillance, changing subject relations and virtual simulation. The third reading passage, Chapter 8, is helpful, in that it brings greater conceptual clarity to these interrelated developments in practices of surveillance. In the reading passage, Haggerty and Ericson formulate the concept of the 'surveillant assemblage'. For too long, they observe, surveillance has been caught up in explanations that rely on Orwell and Foucault. The problem with relying on Orwell and Foucault is that, as Marx, Poster and Bogard demonstrate, contemporary information and data gathering systems exist beyond the state, they cannot be based on the metaphorical workings of the nineteenth-century prison (or other social architecture), and they increasingly eschew asymmetrical forms of monitoring and social control. As the population itself is transformed into a signifier for proliferating surveillance systems, say Haggerty and Ericson, it is time to explore other, more appropriate metaphors to capture the essence of surveillance today.

To think otherwise about surveillance, Haggerty and Ericson use Gilles Deleuze and Félix Guattari's notion of 'assemblages' to denote the increasing convergence of once discrete systems of surveillance. They argue that we are witnessing the rhizomatic expansion of information and data gathering systems. A rhizome is a plant that grows horizontally and that throws up shoots in different locations. Rhizomes, however, are tenacious; they grow and expand to such an extent that their expansion cannot be halted by breaking them in a single location. In a manner very different from a central-ized arborescent trunk, the rhizome is everywhere and its growth is continual. The metaphor of the rhizome better captures the character of surveillance, Haggerty and Ericson assert, because surveillance in multiple forms is appearing in so many social locations throughout our societies. These systems, however, do not simply mark important changes in the form and intention of surveillance. Through the rhizomatic expansion of surveillance, Haggerty and Ericson also argue that a partial democraticiza-tion of surveillance hierarchies is taking place. This involves more and more sectors of the population becoming susceptible to surveillance. Far from top–down forms of social control, bottom–up or synoptic forms of surveillance are now at work, drawing more people into the surveillant assemblage.

The extent to which surveillance hierarchies are becoming democratized is taken up in the final reading passage, Chapter 9, where Hier reminds us of the human dimensions of the surveillant assemblage. In a sympathetic but critical assessment of Haggerty and Ericson's arguments, Hier contends that the surveillant assemblage model places too much emphasis on the technological aspects of contemporary surveillance practices and their concomitant social effects. For Hier, we are not witnessing the levelling of surveillance hierarchies. What we are witnessing, he contends, is a polarization effect, whereby surveillance hierarchies are simultaneously flattened and intensified in differ-ent social locations. To illustrate the polarization of surveillance practices as processes of social control, Hier uses the example of claims making pertaining to welfare recipients, and he links these activities conceptually to the 'synopticon'. For Hier, the explanatory importance of the human intentions and desires behind surveillance systems – even the most technologically advanced ones – cannot be underestimated.

Questions

Chapter 6 (Marx)

1   What is the new surveillance? Think of the ways that new forms of surveillance touch your daily life.
2   Does the new surveillance make obsolete questions of privacy and data protection? Explain.
3   What is the place of traditional forms of surveillance in the new surveillance society?

Chapter 7 (Bogard)

1   What is the simulation of surveillance?

2   In what ways do simulated forms of surveillance influence your daily activities?
3   What does Bogard mean by supernormalization? What influence does supernormaliza-
     tion have on the distinction between and public/private and real/virtual?

Chapter 8 (Haggerty and Ericson)

1   What is the surveillant assemblage? How does it differ from traditional forms of
     surveillance?
2   How does the surveillant assemblage transform surveillance hierarchies, according to
     Haggerty and Ericson?
3   What are the different characteristics of the surveillant assemblage? Identify and
     describe at least four.

Chapter 9 (Hier)

1   What does Hier mean by the argument that surveillance practices are dialectical?
2   What is the relationship between panoptic and synoptic forms of surveillance? How does
     this help us to rethink the sources of power and social control in society?
3   Do you agree with Hier's critique of Haggerty and Ericson's argument? Is he correct to
     argue that Haggerty and Ericson place too much emphasis on the social and cultural
     effects of contemporary surveillance technologies?

Suggested reading

1   Staple, W. (1997) *The Culture of Surveillance: Discipline and Social Control in the United
     States*. New York: St. Martin's Press.
     William Staples examines how citizens in the United States are subjected to more intru-
     sive form of social control in their daily lives. He develops a continuum of surveillance,
     spanning relatively innocent forms of surveillance to explicitly intrusive forms, and
     considers the social consequences of control cultures.
2   Fiske, J. (1999) Surveilling the city: whiteness, the black man, and democratic totali-
     tarianism, *Theory, Culture, & Society*, 15(2): 67–88.
     Fiske's article examines the rapid expansion of video surveillance in American cities
     in terms of control mechanisms that differentially target black men. He argues that
     Orwellian and Foucauldian conceptions of social control are racialized, and that surveil-
     lance is a technology of whiteness.
3   Haggerty, K. and Ericson, R. (1999) *Policing the Risk Society*. Toronto: University of
     Toronto Press.
     Policing the Risk Society has quickly become a benchmark contribution to surveillance
     studies. The book details how changing police surveillance practices are interlinked with
     other organizations and agencies such as insurance companies. These technologies of
     surveillance operate on the logic of risk reduction, and the bureaucratization of police
     work establishes parameters in which decisions are made. The authors daringly try to
     link risk society theory to a governmentality framework.
4   Lyon, D. (2003) *Surveillance as Social Sorting: Privacy, Risk, and Digital Discrimination*.
     New York: Routledge.
     Surveillance as Social Sorting conceptualizes surveillance as a threat to social inequality
     rather than simply to individual freedoms. The book presents a number of original essays
     on topics ranging from CCTV surveillance to health risks.

5   Baudrillard, J. (1994) *Simulation and Simulacra*. Ann Arbor: University of Michigan Press. Although not a direct contribution to surveillance studies, *Simulation and Simulacra* develops an argument that the world we live in is a simulation comprised of signs and symbols. It is a hyperreality reliant on models and maps, to the extent that reality imitates the simulations.

Note

1   http://news.zdnet.co.uk/internet/security/0,39020375,39205460,00.htm

References

Althusser, L. (1971) Ideology and ideological state apparatuses, in L. Althusser (ed.) *Lenin and Philosophy and Other Essays*. New York: Monthly Review Press.

Hall, S. (1988) The toad in the garden: Thatcher among the theorists, in C. Nelson and L. Grossberg (eds) *Marxism and the Interpretation of Culture*. Urbana: University of Illinois Press.

Marx, G. (1985) I'll be watching you: reflections on the new surveillance, *Dissent*, Winter, 32: 26–34.

Marx G. (1988) *Undercover: Police Surveillance in America*. Berkeley: University of California Press.

Rose, N. (1999) *Powers of Freedom*. Cambridge: Cambridge University Press.

6

What's new about the 'new surveillance'? Classifying for change and continuity[1]
by Gary T. Marx

Introduction

In an interview with the individual responsible for an all-purpose student id access card used for building entrance, the library, meals and purchases at a large Southern university I encountered the following case:

> The registrar came into his office and discovered an arson effort that failed. A long burn mark on the carpet led to a Gatorade bottle full of flammable liquid in a closet. In an adjacent building police found the area where the bomb was assembled. They requested card access records for that building. A review of the logs found some early morning card swipes which looked suspicious. They also checked the lot number on the Gatorade bottle that was holding the liquid and determined it had been delivered to a campus convenience store. Upon matching the records of purchasers of Gatorade with those entering the building where the bomb making materials were found, the police got a hit. They confronted the suspect and he confessed to arson. His motive was to burn up his academic records, as he was failing several classes and didn't want to disappoint his parents.

This high tech discovery of human spoors needs only to be bolstered by a video camera, DNA matching and thermal lie detection to serve as a paradigmatic case of the 'new surveillance' (Marx 1988). New technologies for collecting personal information which transcend the physical, liberty-enhancing limitations of the old means are constantly appearing. These probe more deeply, widely and softly than traditional methods, transcending natural (distance, darkness, skin, time and microscopic size) and constructed (walls, sealed envelopes) barriers that historically protected personal information . . .

The last half of the 20th century has seen a significant increase in the use of technology for the discovery of personal information. Examples include video and audio surveillance, heat, light, motion, sound and olfactory sensors, night vision goggles, electronic tagging, biometric access devices, drug testing, DNA analysis, computer monitoring including email and web usage and the use of computer techniques such as expert systems, matching and profiling, data mining, mapping, network analysis and simulation. Control technologies have become available that previously existed only in the dystopic imaginations of science fiction writers. We are a surveillance society. As Yiannis Gabriel (forthcoming) suggests, Weber's iron cage is being displaced by a flexible glass cage.

Three common responses to changes in contemporary surveillance technology can be noted. One general historical and functional view holds that there is nothing really new here. All societies have certain functional prerequisites which must be met if they are to exist. These include means for protecting and discovering personal information and protecting social borders. Any changes are merely of degree, not of kind.

An opposing, less general view is that we live in a time of revolutionary change with respect to the crossing of personal and social borders. There are two variants of this. One is that the sky is indeed falling and, 'you never had it so bad'. Some journalists and popular writers claim 'privacy is dead'.

A related view holds that while the technologies are revolutionary, the way they are used reflects social and cultural factors. In that regard the forces of modernity operate to extend individual control. The trend on balance, whether through counter-technologies or changing customs, policy or law, is for protection of personal information to become stronger as new threats appear, although given the piecemeal approach to privacy legislation in the United States (in contrast to that in much of Europe in which protections are based on a broad principle such as 'respect for human dignity'), there is usually a lag.

Yet simple sweeping assertions about such a complex, dynamic and varied topic are not very helpful. Broad concepts may in Neil Smelser's (1959: 2) words 'shroud a galaxy of connotations'. However useful as an intellectual shorthand, ideal types such as 'developed vs. undeveloped nations' or 'traditional vs. the new surveillance' must be considered in light of the multiple dimensions which usually run through them.

The academic literature on particular surveillance technologies is gradually expanding. In contrast this [chapter] offers a minimalist rendering of the most basic dimensions which cut across and can be used to characterize any surveillance activity. It is at the middle range, situated (and offering a bridge) between more abstract theoretical explanations and empirical description. As a prelude to specifying dimensions let us note some shortcomings of popular definitions.

A deficient definition

One indicator of rapid change is the failure of dictionary definitions to capture current understandings of surveillance. For example in the *Concise Oxford Dictionary* surveillance is defined as 'close observation, especially of a suspected person'. Yet today many of the new surveillance technologies are not 'especially' applied to 'a suspected person'. They are commonly applied categorically. In broadening the range of suspects the term 'a suspected person' takes on a different meaning. In a striking innovation, surveillance is also applied to contexts (geographical places and spaces, particular time periods, networks, systems and categories of person), not just to a particular person whose identity is known beforehand.

The dictionary definition also implies a clear distinction between the object of surveillance and the person carrying it out. In an age of servants listening behind closed doors, binoculars and telegraphic interceptions, that separation made sense. It was easy to separate the watcher from the person watched. Yet self-monitoring has emerged as an important theme, independent of the surveilling of another. In the hope of creating self-restraint, threats of social control (i.e. the possibility of getting caught) are well-publicized with mass media techniques.

A general ethos of self-surveillance is also encouraged by the availability of home products such as those that test for alcohol level, pregnancy, menopause and AIDS. Self-surveillance merges the line between the surveilled and the surveillant. In some cases we see parallel or co-monitoring, involving the subject and an external agent.[2] The differentiation of surveillance into ever more specialized roles is sometimes matched by a rarely studied de-differentiation or generalization of surveillance to non-specialized roles. For example regardless of their job, retail store employees are trained to identify shoplifters and outdoor utility workers are trained to look for signs of drug manufacturing.

The term 'close observation' also fails to capture contemporary practices. Surveillance may be carried out from afar, as with satellite images or the remote monitoring of communications and work. Nor need it be close as in detailed – much initial surveillance involves superficial scans looking for patterns of interest to be pursued later in greater detail.

The dated nature of the definition is further illustrated in its seeming restriction to visual means as implied in 'observation'. The eyes do contain the vast majority of the body's sense receptors and the visual is a master metaphor for the other senses (e.g., saying 'I see' for understanding or being able to 'see through people'). Indeed 'seeing through' is a convenient short hand for the new surveillance.

To be sure the visual is usually an element of surveillance, even when it is not the primary means of data collection (e.g. written accounts of observations, events and conversations, or the conversion to text or images of measurements from heat, sound or movement). Yet to 'observe' a text or a printout is in many ways different from a detective or supervisor directly observing behavior. The eye as the major means of direct surveillance is increasingly joined or replaced by hearing, touching and smelling. The use of multiple senses and sources of data is an important characteristic of much of the new surveillance.

A better definition of the new surveillance is the use of technical means to extract or create personal data. This may be taken from individuals or contexts. In this definition the use of 'technical means' to extract and create the information implies the ability to go beyond what is offered to the unaided senses or voluntarily reported. Many of the examples extend the senses by using material artifacts or software of some kind, but the technical means for rooting out can also be deception, as with informers and undercover police. The use of 'contexts' along with 'individuals' recognizes that much modern surveillance also looks at settings and patterns of relationships. Meaning may reside in cross-classifying discrete sources of data (as with computer matching and profiling) that in and of themselves are not of revealing. Systems as well as persons are of interest.

This definition of the new surveillance excludes the routine, non-technological surveillance that is a part of everyday life such as looking before crossing the street or seeking the source of a sudden noise or of smoke. An observer on a nude beach or police interrogating a cooperative suspect would also be excluded, because in these cases the information is volunteered and the unaided senses are sufficient.

I do not include a verb such as 'observe' in the definition because the nature of the means (or the senses involved) suggests subtypes and issues for analysis and ought not to be foreclosed by a definition, (e.g. how do visual, auditory, text and other forms of surveillance compare with respect to factors such as intrusiveness or validity?). If such a verb is needed I prefer 'attend to' or 'to regard' rather than observe with its tilt toward the visual.

While the above definition captures some common elements among new surveillance means, contemporary tactics are enormously varied and would include:

- a parent monitoring a baby on closed circuit television during commercials or through a day care center webcast;
- a data base for employers containing the names of persons who have filed workman compensation claims;
- a video monitor in a department store scanning customers and matching their images to those of suspected shoplifters;
- a supervisor monitoring employee's e-mail and phone communication;
- a badge signaling where an employee is at all times;
- a hidden camera in an ATM machine;
- a computer program that monitors the number of keystrokes or looks for key words or patterns;
- a thermal imaging device aimed at the exterior of a house from across the street
- analyzing hair to determine drug use;
- a self-test for level of alcohol in one's system;
- a scanner that picks up cellular and cordless phone communication;
- mandatory provision of a DNA sample;
- the polygraph or monitoring brain waves to determine truthfulness;
- Caller ID.

Dimensions of surveillance

The differences between traditional and new surveillance can be approached in terms of the categories in Table [6.1]. Traditional surveillance tends to be characterized by the left side of the table. The traditional means have certainly not disappeared. They have, however, been supplemented by the new forms which tend to fall on the right side of the table.

I don't claim that the values on the right side of the table cleanly and fully characterize every instance of contemporary surveillance that has appeared since the development of the microchip and advances in microbiology, artificial intelligence, electronics, communications and geographic information systems. Nor do the values on the left side perfectly apply to every instance of the old surveillance prior to this. Social life is much too messy for that. There is some crossing over of values (e.g. informers, a traditional form, have low visibility, drug testing, a new form,

Table [6.1] Surveillance dimensions

Dimension	A Traditional surveillance	B The new surveillance
Senses	Unaided senses	Extends senses
Visibility (of the actual collection, who does it, where, on whose behalf)	Visible	Less visible or invisible
Consent	Lower proportion involuntary	Higher proportion involuntary
Cost (per unit of data)	Expensive	Inexpensive
Location of data collectors / analyzers	On scene	Remote
Ethos	Harder (more coercive)	Softer (less coercive)
Integration	Data collection as separate activity	Data collection folded into routine activity
Data collector	Human, animal	Machine (wholly or partly automated)
Data resides	With the collector, stays local	With 3rd parties, often migrates
Timing	Single point or intermittent	Continuous (omnipresent)
Time period	Present	Past, present, future
Data availability	Frequent time lags	Real time availability
Availability of technology	Disproportionately available to elites	More democratized, some forms widely available
Object of data collection	Individual	Individual, categories of interest
Comprehensiveness	Single measure	Multiple measures
Context	Contextual	Acontextual
Depth	Less intensive	More intensive
Breadth	Less extensive	More extensive
Ratio of self to surveillant knowledge	Higher (what the surveillant knows, the subject probably knows as well)	Lower (surveillant knows things the subject doesn't)
Identifiability of object of surveillance	Emphasis on known individuals	Emphasis also on anonymous individuals, masses
Emphasis on	Individuals	Individual, networks systems
Realism	Direct representation	Direct and simulation

(Continued overleaf)

Table 6.1 (continued)

Dimension	A Traditional surveillance	B The new surveillance
Form	Single media (likely or narrative or numerical)	Multiple media (including video and/or audio)
Who collects data	Specialists	Specialists, role dispersal, self-monitoring
Data analysis	More difficult to organize store, retrieve, analyse	Easier to organize, store, retrieve, analyse
Data merging	Discrete non-combinable data (whether because of different format or location)	Easy to combine visual, auditory, text, numerical data
Data communication	More difficult to send, receive	Easier to send, receive

is discontinuous). These are after all ideal types whose virtue of breadth often comes with the vice of combining elements that show significant variation at a less abstract level. But if the categories are useful in analyzing big variation (or more useful than the descriptive ad hoc naming we presently have), they will have done their job.

For limitations of space, here I offer only a summary of the new and traditional surveillance in the abstract terms of Table [6.1]. The dimensions emphasize elements that I think have changed. I thus exclude other very important dimensions useful for comparing types of surveillance apart from the issue of changes. These include the extent of deception and ease or difficulty of neutralizing a technique, factors which appear not to have changed significantly over the last century. I also exclude others such as degree of invasiveness and validity about which the evidence of change is mixed.

The new surveillance relative to traditional surveillance extends the senses and has low visibility or is invisible. It is more likely to be involuntary. Data collection is often integrated into routine activity. It is more likely to involve manipulation than direct coercion. Data collection is more likely to be automated involving machines rather than (or in addition to) involving humans. It is relatively inexpensive per unit of data collected. Data collection is often mediated through remote means rather than on scene and the data often resides with third parties. Data is available in real time and data collection can be continuous and offer information on the past, present and future (ala statistical predictions). The subject of data collection goes beyond the individual suspect to categories of interest. The individual as a subject of data collection may also become the object of an intervention. There may be only a short interval between the discovery of the information and the taking of action.

The new surveillance is more comprehensive often involving multiple meas-ures. But since it is often mediated by physical and social distance (being more likely to be acontextual) it is not necessarily more valid. It is more intensive and extensive. The ratio of what the individual knows about him or herself relative to what the surveilling person knows is lower than in the past, even if objectively much more is known. Relative to the past the objects of surveillance are more likely to be an anonymous individual, a mass or an aggregate. The emphasis is expanded beyond the individual to systems and networks. The data often goes beyond direct representation to simulation and from narrative or numerical form to also include video and audio records. The monitoring of specialists is often accompanied (or even replaced) by self-monitoring. It is easy to combine visual, auditory, text and numerical data and to send and receive it. It is relatively easier to organize, store, retrieve and analyze data. Traditional surveillance is the reverse of the above.

The Talmud states, 'for instance is not proof'. In contrasting traditional and new forms of surveillance in light of these categories I am convinced that significant change has occurred. Yet given the breadth of the net cast and limited resources, this has been argued by illustration. A next step is to operationalize concepts and collect quantitative measurements.

Given the nature of perception, lists imply an egalitarianism among terms that is often unwarranted. The dimensions in Table [6.1] are hardly of equal significance. They can be clustered or ranked in various ways. Among those on the new surveillance side with the clearest social implications are extending the senses, low visibility, involuntary nature, remoteness and lesser cost. These create a potential for a very different kind of society and call for stringent vigilance. In extending the senses (the ability to see in the dark, into bodies, through walls and over vast distances etc.) they challenge fundamental assumptions about personal and social borders (these after all have been maintained not only by values and norms and social organization, but by the limits of technology to cross them). Low visibility and the involuntary and remote nature of much contemporary surveillance may mean more secrecy and lessened accountability, less need for consent and less possibility of reciprocity. Lesser costs create a temptation to both widen the net and thin the mesh of surveillance. For example what if brain scan technology lives up to the claims of its advocates to identify what people feel, know or are thinking? (*New York Times*, 9 Dec., 2001) In the interest of preventing terrible things from happening (which after all it would be irresponsible not to do, not to mention legal liability), the sacred value traditionally placed on interior life would be eroded . . .

Empowerment, disempowerment or 'both'?

It is not easy to reach a conclusion about what the changes in surveillance technology imply for western democratic conceptions of individualism, as expressed in the issue of control over personal information . . .

Looked at broadly across time periods, has the ability to protect forms of electronic communication been increasing or decreasing? It is difficult to say. Almost as soon as the telegraph appeared so did wiretapping and the same holds for efforts to intercept every new form of communication. The absolute amount of intercepted telecommunications has increased as the telephone has become nearly universal and as population and the various forms for communication have increased.

However, we do not have adequate information to reach strong conclusions about whether the interception of telecommunications has increased in a relative, as well as an absolute sense, declined or remained roughly constant. An assessment of this would require determining the number of involuntary interceptions as a percentage of all telecommunications. It would be ideal to have this broken down by type – interceptions by domestic law enforcement, by NSA and other domestic and foreign intelligence agencies, by telephone company employees, by employers and by private citizens and by factors such as number of, and length of interceptions and number of persons intercepted. Beyond the use of technical means, it would as well be ideal to have interception data for other forms such as the extent of uninvited listening in on a party-line (when they were in existence) or on an extension or speaker phone.

With recent developments estimates should also include overhearing cordless and cellular conversations and intercepting fax, email and webcam communications. Those making loud use of their cell phones in public also have their conversations partially intercepted (although this is not quite the same since it is more voluntary). The appearance and gradual disappearance of phone booths would also be of interest.

We would also want measures for other aspects of interception beyond direct listening and recording such as for call and trap devices which can be used by law enforcement without a warrant to identify when and what number was dialed. The extent of the use of newer techniques that permit identifying networks of communication beyond the traditional one line to another is also of interest. When a communication has been intercepted whether the content stays secret (as is often the case with intelligence agencies) or becomes public (as is often the case with journalistic snooping on film stars and politicians) would ideally also be considered.

Interception issues apart, these means also have implications for protecting some aspects of personal information. Telecommunications has traditionally offered freedom from visual observation. In permitting interactions on a vastly expanded scale without the need to travel and physical co-presence, they greatly enhanced the ability to communicate, while increasing control over information such as appearance, body language, facial expressions, exact location, who one is with and even who the communicator was.[3] Contrast this with a conversation visible to a third party overheard in a public place such as a restaurant.

Over time, elements of the telephone's intrusive potential were curtailed even as other intrusive potentials appeared. Claims must be time, as well as component specific. For example the eavesdropping potential present when all calls had to be made through an operator (the classic telephone operator of Lily Tomlin) disappeared as automatic switching spread, starting in the 1930s. Greater affluence and technical changes have led to the almost complete disappearance of the party line in which several households shared a phone line and conversations could easily be overheard by just picking up the phone. Initially the service monitoring of phone lines required an operator to listen to conversations but can now generally be served by merely checking electronic signals.

While it took almost a century, non-court approved wiretapping eventually was prohibited with the Katz decision (*Katz vs. United States*, 389 U.S. 347, 1967) which found that there is a right to privacy even in a 'public' phone booth. The Court held that the Fourth Amendment applied to persons not to places and to electronic, as well as physical searches. Title III of the 1968 Omnibus Crime Control and Safe Streets Act made unauthorized wiretapping a felony. To judge from impressionistic accounts, the amount of wiretapping without a warrant appeared to have declined after that.

Cordless and cell phone communication, appearing in the 1980s, which rely on radio transmissions were technically easy to legally intercept with scanners and even some UHF television channels. But 1986 legislation made their interception without a warrant illegal. Greater technical protection also came to be built into the phones.

Starting in the 1980s as analogue voice communications carried over copper wires began to be replaced by digital based technologies and services carried on fiber optic wires, interception in principle became easier. Messages whether by phone, fax or e-mail routinely arrived with identifying details that were much more difficult to locate with the analog system. Phone numbers could be automatically linked to reverse directories for additional information. In addition, communication content could be tapped directly through remote computer entries, rather than having to go through the risky procedure of directly tapping into the line at the location of interest. However, without appropriate design of the system, locating the actual transmission carrying a message was apparently more difficult. The controversial Digital Telephony Act of 1994 is intended to change that by requiring communications manufacturers to engineer systems that make remote wiretapping easy via computer.

However, no matter how much more communication there is to intercept, or how much easier it becomes to do, this can be thwarted, or at least inhibited by use of encryption. While it took almost a century, public encryption of telecommunications is now widely available, offering an unprecedented level of communications privacy. On the other hand there are technical efforts via remotely (or directly) planted sniffers to get to a message before it can be encrypted.

The silent recording capability now built into many answering machines makes it easier to secretly record conversations and the marketing to the public of telecommunications surveillance equipment once available only to police may also have increased the interception of communication. However, this is matched by the marketing of equipment for protecting communications.

E-mail could be legally intercepted until the passage of the Privacy Protection Act of 1986. The sending of junk fax and automated phone dialing was prohibited not long after. Until the appearance of Caller-ID in 1988, the caller was not required to reveal his or her phone number. Then by technological fiat all callers, even those who were unlisted had their number delivered. This reversed the previous advantage for callers of anonymity and the ability to intrude at will. Caller-ID as initially offered increased the control of the caller, while decreasing control of the person called, since his or her phone number and other information could be involuntarily delivered (and by implication all the other information this can be automatically related to through data bases). Yet several years later a public outcry over Caller-ID led to a blocking option, restoring some of the status quo.

Other forms are more difficult to label as involving an increase or decrease in control. What should we make of the ability to record conversations? On the one hand if this is done secretly and/or against the will of one of the parties, their control is weakened. But if done with their consent, it may increase control by offering a means of validating claims as to what was communicated. This cuts against the natural tilt toward favoring the claims of the more privileged and those of higher status.

Developments such as video phones, internet web transmissions, use of phone technology to transmit biometric data and the merging of the cell phone and still camera further illustrate the dynamic nature of the situation and the mixture of empowering and controlling elements. A central question of course is just who is being empowered or controlled, and for what ends? In the case of Caller-ID is this the caller or recipient of a call, or both relative to third parties? Since all of us play a variety of roles the technology both empowers and lessens power, although hardly to the same degree across roles, institutions and broad contexts.

Within any measure of the amount of personal information collected is the tricky question of the ratio of involuntarily to voluntarily provided information. The new surveillance is of social concern partly because of its ability to gather information secretly and involuntarily. For many observers, if the ratio stays constant or even moves toward an increase in voluntarily provided information, that is progress. As a formal matter, there has never been more informed consent in our society and the amount seems to be increasing. Consider the ratio of voluntarily recorded phone conversations vs. those from wiretaps. Most recorded phone conversations are for- mally consensual, as with the millions of service calls each day in which persons are told their conversation is being recorded. In most work settings it is also now standard practice to inform employees of the kind of communications monitoring (phone, e-mail, etc.) they face.

Yet we must also ask just how 'voluntary' such recording is. In principle the individual can always hang up or choose not to work for a super-surveilling employer. Sometimes there is a choice and a request not to record a phone call will be honored. But usually such consent is specious since one needs the service, information or job and just saying 'no' denies these. The role of manipulation and deception in obtain- ing consent also need to be considered, as does the relative ease of consenting (note the contrast between 'opt in' and 'opt out' systems). Still in general a principle of consent is to be preferred to secrecy and non-consent . . .

In summary even with just one technology such as telecommunications, no simple empirical conclusion can be drawn about whether the control of personal information has increased or decreased. Holding apart crisis periods such as wartime, the pattern is neither consistent over time, nor equivalent across different kinds of personal information or border crossings. How much more difficult then to draw conclusions about improvement across all means of surveillance, particularly in the absence of broad empirical research. Even with an empirical pattern that lends itself to conclusions, the issues of moral evaluation are far from simple.

It is also necessary to consider technologies in relation to each other and in toto. Functional alternatives in which if one way of meeting a goal or need is blocked another will be found, must also be considered. Thus restrictions on wiretapping may result in an increase in the use of informers or undercover operations which are alternative, less restricted means of obtaining information. Or these may increase

together as informers' tips are used to justify obtaining wiretaps.[4] Efforts to successfully limit the application of the polygraph through legislation (Regan, 1995) resulted
in a decline in its use, but were accompanied by a significant increase in other, even
less validated, forms such as paper and pencil honesty tests.

In democratic free market societies along with more powerful technologies, may
come counter-technologies and the strengthening of individual rights to protect personal data. Nor are individuals (or groups) simply passive reeds in a technological
hurricane. They have resources to fight back. (Marx forthcoming) A dialectical process can often be seen in which changes in behaviour patterns and the development of
extractive technologies lead to new rules and technologies for limiting their application. Technologies are both determined and determining. They do not enter a neutral
culture, but one with informal and formal protections for personal information, as
well as one with value and organizational supports for collecting such information.
Yet, having appeared, their distinctive attributes may have independent and
unanticipated impacts . . .

Notes

1   This chapter is an extract from G. Marx (2002) What's new about the 'new
    surveillance'? Classifying for change and continuity, *Surveillance and Society*,
    1(1): 9–29.
2   The self-restraint and voluntary compliance favored in liberal democratic theory
    receive a new dimension here. The line between the public and the private order
    maintenance becomes hazier. The border may be blurred in the sense that there
    can be a continuous transmission link between sender and receiver as with brain
    waves or scents. Other broken and reconstructed borders are discussed in Marx
    1997. Consider also a federally funded 'Watch Your Car' program found in
    11 states in 2001. In this program vehicle owners attach a decal to their car
    inviting police to pull them over late at night to be sure the car is not stolen. To the
    extent that this 'co-production' of social order becomes established it is easy to
    imagine individuals wearing miniature video, audio, location and biological moni-
    tors sending data outward to protective sources. New borders and forms of neu-
    tralization will of course appear, but it will be a new senses-transcending ball
    game and we will become more aware of the extent to which the limits of the
    physical world shape cognition and norms.
3   However, this may change to the extent that video phones become widespread
    and manners (or technology) mandate their use. In principle one would be
    free to choose whether or not to have this and then whether or not to turn it
    on. Yet subtle and not so subtle social pressures may tilt toward continual use.
    Lack of reciprocity on an individual's part (failure to use it) may lead the
    other party to a communication to wonder what the individual is hiding. There
    is some parallel to expectations about not wearing a mask in face-to-face
    interactions.
4   This raises an issue of when one technology displaces another, rather than serv-
    ing to simply pile on what is already there. Gilliom (2001) for example notes that
    the appearance of an elaborate computerized monitoring system for those on

welfare has supplemented rather than displaced the traditional system of 'rat calls' as a means of information on violations.

References

Gabriel Y. (forthcoming) The glass cage: flexible work, fragmented consumption, fragile selves, in J. Alexander, G. Marx and C. Williams (eds.) *Self, Social Structure and Beliefs: Essays in Honor of Neil Smelser*. Berkeley: University California Press.

Gillion, J. (2001) *Overseers of the Poor*. Chicago: University of Chicago Press.

Marx, G.T. (1988) *Undercover: Police Surveillance in America*. Berkeley: University of California Press.

Marx, G.T. (1997) The declining significance of traditional borders (and the appearance of new borders) in an age of high technology, in P. Droege (ed.) *Intelligent Environments*. Amsterdam: Elsevier.

Marx, G.T. (1998) An ethics for the new surveillance, *The Information Society*, 14(3): 171–85.

Marx, G.T. (forthcoming) A tack in the shoe: neutralizing and resisting the new surveillance, *Journal of Social Issues*, Special Issues on technology and privacy.

Regan, P. (1995) *Legislating Privacy: Technology, Social Values and Public Policy*. Chapel Hill: University of North Carolina.

Smelser, N. (1959) *Social Change in the Industrial Revolution*. Chicago: University of Chicago Press.

7

Surveillance, its simulation, and hypercontrol in virtual systems[1]
by William Bogard

Panic for nothing

A true story. Driving out of the Medicine Bow range of the Rocky Mountains toward Laramie, Wyoming, you pass through the little town of Centennial. It's not much more than a truckstop – a gas station/cafe, a small motel, some outbuildings. You wind around a blind curve before dropping onto the valley floor. It's been downhill for twenty miles, almost no traffic, and you're oblivious to how fast you're driving. Just at the edge of town, you spot a patrol car parked on the side of the road by the cafe. Speed trap. You panic and hit the brakes, thinking you might have time to slow down, but it doesn't matter. You've certainly been spotted, probably scanned with a radar gun. You start to pull over. But as you get closer, you notice that no one is sitting inside the car, that in fact it's not really a patrol car at all, just an old junker painted black and white, topped with some fake flashers, and set by the road to make people like you slow down in a hurry. It's probably been sitting there for years. Maybe the owners of the cafe just wanted you to stop and have lunch, spend some money; maybe the highway patrol put it there for local pedestrians, because it doesn't have the money to spend on a real car and driver. Someone, in any case, is playing a bad joke on you. It works. And if you pass through town again, just knowing the patrol car isn't real, that there's no cop inside, doesn't totally overcome the uncertainty of that last curve. You think: there's no trap, don't worry, it's a fake. Or is it? Maybe this time it *is* real. You slow down just to be safe. After a couple of times of this, of course, the apprehension wears off. After all, even the best ruse becomes transparent if it's repeated too often. When that happens, the patrol car becomes just another curiosity along the road (. . . but still, you slow down).

This is an everyday example, although not a perfect one, of what I mean by the simulation of surveillance. As a strategy of control, it's a simple and also ancient idea, but one that from the beginning develops enormous complexity: feign an observer or a field of observation, and divert, enhance, or arrest a flow – in this case, the motion of your car, but in practice, it could be any process, activity, or rhythm. Virilio (1986: 15) shows how contemporary power – the 'observation machine' of postindustrial societies – is *dromological*; it operates on speed, on the *time* of movement. Dromology, literally, is the 'logic of the race' – in the present context, the race to *see first*. Who sees first, ultimately, who *foresees* or sees in advance, wins. Virilio begins his analysis of dromo-logic with a consideration of how political power is organized to control the movement of crowds in the street and immediately links this to the problem of police observation, not, as is conventionally the case, to the dynamics of class struggle:

> The State's political power, therefore, is only secondarily 'power organized by one class to oppress another'. More materially, *it is the polis, the police, in other words highway surveillance*, insofar as, since the dawn of the bourgeois revolution, the old communal poliorcetics . . . has confused social order with the control of traffic.
>
> (ibid.)

In the abstract, then, power is the policing of speed, of material flows, by the machinery of observation.

If we link the dromological concept of surveillance to simulation, we arrive at a strategy of war as old as war itself (bourgeois society did not discover it).[2] Make the enemy waste time sorting out appearances. Generate uncertainty and unplanned changes in movement, temporary paralyses, breaks in flows. Deflect the enemy's attention, make him hesitate or misread the conditions of his observation, by using decoys and surrogates, disguising *an absence with a presence*, then surprise him from another direction. In its highest forms, this kind of deception can lead the enemy to hide in the very places that are the most exposed. Power here is not simply the 'polis'; ideally, it has no specific locus at all but is always 'somewhere else.' It is never *the* center but rather *what* centers (see Shorris 1985), not the focus but *what* focuses, a force working along the periphery of its object's vision, at the limits of its perceptual field, behind its back. Or again, it's the force that makes *every place a center* – i.e., a target – *every time a midpoint* between observation and capture. Power here operates as the simulation of surveillance, a projection or a screen. In our own example of 'highway surveillance,' we might even say that power does not exist at all (at least, not in *this* space or *this* time). That's *not*, however, what whoever stationed the fake patrol car by the side of the road wants speeders to know, namely, that their panic is for nothing, that the trap isn't real.

The simulation of surveillance is a control strategy that informs most of the latest diagnostic and actuarial technologies we associate with the information age – computer profiling and matching, expert decision-systems and cybernetic intelligence, electronic polling, genetic mapping and recombinant procedures, coding practices of all sorts, virtual reality. These technologies *simulate* surveillance in the sense that they *precede and redouble a means of observation*. Computer profiling, for instance, is understood best not just as a technology of surveillance, but as a kind of *surveillance in advance of surveillance*, a technology of 'observation before the fact.' A profile, as the name suggests, is a kind of prior ordering, in this case a model or figure that organizes multiple sources of information to scan for matching or exceptional cases. Resembling an informed form of stereotyping, profiling technology has become increasingly popular in targeting individuals for specialized messages, instructions, inspection or treatment. Advertisers use it to determine the timing and placement of ads to reach the widest segment of selected audiences. Educators use it to adjust course content to specific populations of students, police to target potential offenders. Profiling, in turn, is only one of a host of increasingly available computer-assisted actuarial and diagnostic procedures that are being used, among other things, to identify individuals for various tasks or entitlements, to define potential risks or hazards, and to forestall or enhance certain behaviors or traits. Unlike stereotypes, however, profiles are not merely 'false images' that are used to justify differences in power. Diagnostic profiles exist rather at the intersection of actual and virtual worlds, and come to have more 'reality,' more 'truth and significance,' than the cases to which they are compared. Rather than the profiles resembling the cases, increasingly the cases start to resemble the profiles. In Florida, for example, the highway patrol uses criminal profiles to spot potential drug carriers traveling along a stretch of Interstate 95, long known as a route for drugs moving up the coast from Miami to New York. Based on prior search and arrest records, and criminological simulations, profiles function as preliminaries to surveillance, means of training and selection, allowing the police to scan the passing traffic more efficiently and quickly. If your skin color, sex, age, type of car, state license plate, number of passengers, direction of movement, etc., matches the computer profile each officer carries while on duty, you're a target, whether you've actually done anything wrong or not. Here, the image of the typical offender initiates a series of actions designed to eliminate a risk – in effect, a statistical artifact – rather than respond to an actual offense. The image is not false; it is more like a self-fulfilling prophecy – it creates the offense. If a driver is pulled over and found to be carrying drugs, it doesn't 'confirm' the profile, which is always true before the event. The driver – his identity, history, biography – isn't really important. What's important is how the profile is drawn and that it operates in accordance with the parameters around which it was designed. The profile neither fails nor succeeds (here, in capturing an offender); rather, however it's drawn, it *guarantees or serves up* an offender for surveillance. Such higher-order surveillance technologies speed the sorting and analysis of information in an effort to develop full front-end control. They are, in essence, a form of verification prior to identification (if you don't fit the profile, no one really cares who you are; for all practical purposes, you don't exist).[3]

Because they function so efficiently as apparatuses of selection and training, these kinds of technologies undoubtedly extend the already vast surveillance capabilities of the modern bureaucratic state. They are like, if you will, the new 'gatekeepers' of the bio-electronic order of the future: if you have the right password (or profile, genetic configuration, image), you can continue on – with your work, with your relations with others, with your life. If not, you're a target. But they are also simply quite unlike earlier forms of surveillance. For one thing, they do not just passively record facts (on the model, for instance, of photography), they *simulate facticity* (on the model of virtual imaging systems); rather than document the truth of events, they exploit and reinforce the uncertainty, the wavering line, between truth and fiction. Finally, they favor deterrence over the punishment aspect of disciplinary strategies, proactive or preventative over reactive measures (Bogard 1991).[4] Our patrol car example conforms to a basic pattern in the development of surveillance technologies: get rid of the 'external' surveillor once and for all. Who needs the police? Get the traveler to police himself, and save the time and effort of policing him. In the high-tech imaginary of today's surveillance societies, *you're* in the patrol car, you see yourself coming, so to speak, compare yourself to the profile. You participate in and are responsible for your own observation.[5]

But it's even more complicated than that. In this fantasy, you *are* the patrol car, which is to say, the *apparent* means of observation. 'You,' the 'agent' in all this, as it turns out, exist only as a function of the total simulation – eliminate the car, wipe out the scene, and you eliminate the speeder. 'You' aren't the center here, because there is no center. 'You' don't control yourself but are only a mobile node in a highly dispersed control environment. In this scenario, the whole polarity of Subject and Object, observer and observed, collapses[6] – 'you' aren't even driving down the mountain at all; written into the program, you've already driven down this mountain and been busted, over and over again. And no one is watching because you've already been seen. Violation, arrest, sentencing, everything is over, mapped out, before it's begun – at least that's the fantasy. Power has no 'place' whatsoever in these systems, not even along the periphery. Rather, it is always diffuse, atmospheric, and delusional.

When the simulation of surveillance forms the basis of social control strategy, everything suddenly becomes reversible, including the sense and location of control itself – who the authorities are, who breaks the law, who gets caught, all this becomes a tangle, as we shall see. There's no sense to getting 'caught' here (unless we mean caught before the act), and no law and no police either, in the sense we normally have come to associate with traditional surveillance practices. Instead, the entire field of observation and all its elements are projected into a scene where everything is capable of circling back in on itself, where the offender is 'netted' or captured in advance, the violation is already committed, the sentence already handed down, the time already served. Simulated surveillance is like a Möbius strip, with neither an inside nor an outside surface, or a Mandelbröt function that opens onto endless, nested levels of control, recording, speed traps.

Certainly, it is an unwieldy and strange sounding concept – the simulation of surveillance – but it is what telematic societies are really all about; when they are simulated, the strategic forms and applications of surveillance are almost unlimited. As more human functions – decision-making, calculation, communication, sociation, thinking, seeing, feeling, imagining (especially imagining!) – go 'online' today, as more essentially 'human' powers are sacrificed or given over to virtual systems – allowing screens to substitute for experience, profiles to make our judgments – the greater the refinement, and the invisibility, of the surveillance apparatus.

As I use it here, the simulation of surveillance refers to a 'map' or 'diagram' of forces, in Michel Foucault's sense, a display of relations of power and knowledge which are general in, if not exclusive to, a given age, and to an extent serve to define its coherence (when Foucault speaks of 'disciplinary societies,' this is what he has in mind) (Foucault 1979: 205). Or again, it is like Deleuze's (1988: 37ff.) notion of an 'abstract machine,' a 'singularity' that sets forces in motion and generates concrete functions across a multiplicity of practices. It refers, again, to a social order or generalizable way of ordering, although one that paradoxically calls into question both the idea of the social and the possibility of order. In this order, the 'social' tends to disappear (i.e., go online, onscreen); and in this society, order and chaos are often difficult to distinguish (what appears online to be highly ordered in fact masks the radical absence of order) (Baudrillard 1983a; Bogard 1990) . . . telematic societies, simulated orders, virtual societies, the postindustrial or postmodern age, the information age, cyborg world. All of these descriptions are interchangeable, and none of them works perfectly. At some point, they all tend to fall back into language that is fundamentally inadequate to their object, specifically, into dualist and categorical frames like human:machine, true:false, fictional:real, male:female, domination:subordination, power:ideology – all distinctions that . . . virtual systems themselves function so efficiently to deconstruct.

The diagram of simulated surveillance appears to us in concrete form as a fantastic bionic-machinic *assemblage* – networks or webs of computer technology, screens, data entry and exit points, sensors, jammers, prosthetic, genomic, and ergonomic devices, software, hardware, wetware, linking bodies to flows of information. It is an assemblage that not only functions to normalize relations among individuals, and of individuals to themselves, but, if you will, to *supernormalize* those relations in simulation. While normalization, in the sense developed by Foucault, refers to the multiplicity of individualizing and totalizing practices in surveillance or disciplinary societies, supernormalization is the reduction of all differences and similarities to modulations of basic codes. The biomachinic assemblage works to erase permanently the already tenuous distinction between the individual and the totality in modern 'mass societies,' and substitute instead a kind of pure, cybernetic operationality or connectivity that scales evenly across all levels of experience. The apparent complexity of this assemblage masks a rather simple aim to develop a closed system, where all processes can be translated and managed as flows from and back into information – no longer conformity to a historically variable and continuously contested system of norms, but rather, if you will, production from and return to a singular, universal 'norm of norms.'

The fact that surveillance as a means of social control can be simulated is nothing new. Cybernetic assemblages are only one example of many technologies dating back to antiquity that web simulation to practices of observation or inspection. Simulation and surveillance have gone hand in hand . . . in war and espionage since their origins. Today, they are routine control functions in most institutional settings, to such an extent that they now almost define the operations and the limits of those institutions . . . the simulation of surveillance infuses work, private life, war, and sexuality, but as privileged fields of the exercise of power which cut across traditional institutional boundaries. Increasingly, these technologies force us to adopt a science fiction vocabulary to account for them. In the 'brave new world' of surveillance and its simulation, work, privacy, war, and gender become hyperreal, and workers, soldiers, women, and men become cyborgs, plugged in, electrified, coded bodies. On the information highway, the domestic sphere becomes a global marketplace, a public forum, an electric theater of sex, pleasure, and power, even as the globe, markets, public spaces, sexuality, and power shrink and finally disappear onscreen. The new technologies of this world are those that virtualize perception and experience, and their means of control is cybernetic. Or rather, all their control is hypercontrol, in which the code governs the interactivity of the organism and the machine . . . I want to emphasize how difficult it is, in relation to these technologies, to continue to think in conventional terms like social control, institution, discipline, the normalized

individual, indeed, surveillance itself; and how hard it is today to define the boundaries of work that is 'informated,' or when and where electronic wars begin and end,
or how sex intersects with, and is to a large degree neutralized by, computerization
and biotechnologies.

What does it mean for surveillance to be simulated? It does *not* mean, above all,
that surveillance no longer exists, or that it does not produce material effects. Nor
does it mean, as in the example with which we began, simply that surveillance practices are deceptive or masked (although this is often the case in its earlier forms,
especially when we consider police or military surveillance). In this context, we need
to guard against the common idea of simulation as a kind of 'illusion.' The simulation of surveillance does not exactly mean the 'illusion' of surveillance. Modern
surveillance is not so much 'illusory' as it is elevated to a kind of higher reality or,
more exactly, pushed to its spatial and temporal limits by simulation. Simulation
always aims for the 'more real than real'; as a technical operation . . . it works to
eliminate, not foster, illusion. The better a simulation, the less awareness there is of the
artifice that identifies it *as* a simulation. If we could imagine a perfect simulation of
surveillance, of observational control, something that we'll do many times in this
book, the question of its 'staging' wouldn't even arise, because everything would
appear 'too real' to leave any room for doubt, for even the slightest suspicion that
what was observed was 'in reality' a simulation. The simulation of surveillance, then,
is not about creating an illusion of surveillance, but about rendering indiscernible, if
you will, the fact of its illusion, viz., that control by observational technologies always
involves, to some degree or other; the diminution of the *appearance* of deception.

Even more, to call these technologies of illusion is to give them far too much
credit. Human beings can perhaps create illusions, can deal in artifice and deception.
But any *vital* power of illusion, any of the deeper, creative subtleties of artifice, ultimately are beyond these devices – they are, in the end, just machines, designed and
programmed to do what they do and nothing more (see Baudrillard 1993b: 54–55).
At best, they can make the line between human and machinic forms of artifice vacil-
late. Where the imaginary of simulation is the focus, it is always a question of the
implosion of poles, the play between illusion and reality, human and machine, the
shifting meaning and location of power, Subject and Object, the undecidability of
who is watching and who is watched. To analyze simulation is to involve oneself
immediately in paradoxes, bleeding concepts, and floating senses. We shouldn't view
this as a problem, however, but as an essential and productive uncertainty that defines
the operation of simulation itself. We can deal with that uncertainty to some extent by
following Baudrillard's convention in thinking about these technologies in terms of
the creation of hyperreal spaces (and times) rather than simple illusions, which always
prompts us to search for something real in distinction to them.

Simulation technologies are not strictly or exclusively observational or 'inspec-
tional' in nature. Computers are one example, perhaps the main example today, of a
technology whose control functions are fully integrated into its mode of operation
rather than imposed externally as a form of inspection. Computers do not 'watch'
individuals, although they are used routinely to record their performance (behavior,
thoughts, traits, transactions). Unlike panoptic systems, their 'architectures' of
control, their orders of spatial and temporal relations, are virtual (i.e., orders of

information). In the case of computers, control is more adequately conceived in terms of the network itself, specifically, the set of human–machine interfaces considered as a whole, rather than an effect of an external, contingent relation between a 'recording' machine and its operator, between an observer and what it observes.

Simulated surveillance, in its imaginary form, aims for a state of perfect deterrence, in fact a state where deterrence is no longer necessary. Its strategy is always control *in advance*, hyperized, front-end, programmed control – regulation as a matter of feedback, models, circuitry design, interface, and integration. It is an operation that passes *through* bodies and connects them to the storage and retrieval functions of digital systems, and to the instructions coded in genetic sequences. Control as perfect deterrence is, in one sense, not really control at all, but rather a permanent condition of deferral and elusion, a final solution to all the 'problems' arising out of the desire to eliminate surprise and risk – all contingencies are planned for in advance, all problems are dodged, all effects are modulations or permutations of their code. Probably the readiest and most intelligible examples of hypercontrol in telematic societies are video games and virtual reality technologies, where control is a function of the *circuit* established between the operator and the machine, and not the property of either pole considered separately (all surprises in a video game are programmed surprises). With the development and proliferation of computers, imaging technologies, coding and decoding equipment, and the like, this form of control becomes radically trans-institutional, i.e., a universal schematics working indifferently across institutions (economic, cultural, political), translating them as so many flows and breaks of information. All this represents a further refinement – and in some ways the refinement *ne plus ultra* – of the process Max Weber (1958: 155) at the beginning of the century referred to as disenchantment, or what Benjamin (1969: 217ff.) described as the loss of aura in a mechanical age. Computerization, of course, has been the major force in this process recently, but we should remember that it is only the current technological manifestation of a rationalization and standardization of disciplinary methods that 'took off' in the modern age but whose real roots are lost in the distant past . . .

Notes

1   This chapter is an extract from William Bogard 1996 Surveillance, its simulation, and hypercontrol in virtual systems, in The Simulation of Surveillance. Cambridge: Cambridge University Press, pp. 25–34.

2   The principles that war (military power) is based on deception and demands foreknowledge of the enemy for its successful conduct are, of course, Sun Tzu's, and date back to the Warring States period in China in the fifth century BC. See *The Art of War* (1963: 66). Virilio discusses the 'observationmachine' as a logistics of perception linked to deception in *War and Cinema* (1989) . . .

3   Literally, you don't *matter*, you're not even real, or more exactly, 'less real' than the profile. For an interesting and provocative discussion of how cultural and historical productions create 'bodies that matter' versus bodies that are assigned to the margins of indifference, see Judith Butler, *Bodies That Matter* (1993).

4   On deterrence as dominant strategy of postindustrial, telematic culture, see also Baudrillard, *Simulations* (1983b: 59–60), and 'The Beaubourg Effect: Implosion and Deterrence' (1982).

5   In *Discipline and Punish*, Foucault shows how panoptic surveillance is designed to foster self-control (1979: 201ff.). Mark Poster also emphasizes the self-participatory and self-regulatory nature of contemporary informational systems of control in *The Mode of Information: Poststructuralism and Social Context* (1990).

6   On how informed control systems produce 'mobile' or floating subjects, see Scott Lash and John Urry, *Economies of Signs and Space* (1994). We shall return to this idea many times . . . one of the fundamental ironies of virtual systems [is] in being able to 'travel' anywhere onscreen (e.g., channel cruising), the subject who views the screen remains fixed and immobile in front of it, collapsing the dialectic of mobility and immobility. The collapse of the poles of mobility and immobility, Subject and Object, human and machine, observer and observed, is a general theme in much of the postmodern literature on technology and control. Again, one of the main theorists here is Baudrillard, especially his book *Fatal Strategies* (1990b). See also the collection of articles in Michael Benedikt (ed.), *Cyberspace* (1992). For a critique of Baudrillard's position on this subject, see Douglas Kellner, *Jean Baudrillard: From Marxism to Postmodernism and Beyond* (1989): 154–167.

References

Baudrillard, J. (1982) The Beaubourg effect: implosion and deterrence, *October* (Spring) 20: 3–13.

Baudrillard, J. (1983a) *In the Shadow of the Silent Majorities or . . . The End of the Social*. New York: Semiotext(e).

Baudrillard, J. (1983b) *Simulations*. New York: Semiotext(e).

Baudrillard, J. (1990b) *Fatal Strategies*. New York: Semiotext(e).

Baudrillard, J. (1993b) *The Transparency of Evil: Essays on Extreme Phenomena*. New York: Verso.

Benedikt, M. (ed.) (1992) *Cyberspace*. Cambridge, MA: MIT Press.

Benjamin, W. (1969) The work of art in the age of mechanical reproduction, in H. Arendt (ed.) *Illuminations*. New York: Schocken Books, pp. 217–51.

Bogard, W. (1990) Closing down the social: Baudrillard's challenge to contemporary sociology, *Sociological Theory*, 8(1): 1–16.

Bogard, W. (1991) Discipline and deterrence: rethinking Foucault on the question of power in contemporary societies, *Social Science Journal*, 28(3): 325–46.

Butler, J. (1993) *Bodies That Matter*. New York: Routledge.

Deleuze, G. (1988) *Foucault*. Minneapolis: University of Minnesota Press.

Foucault, M. (1979) *Discipline and Punish: The Birth of the Prison*. New York: Vintage.

Kellner, D. (1989) *Jean Baudrillard: From Marxism to Postmodernism and Beyond*. Stanford, CA: Stanford University Press.

Kellner, D. (1992) *The Persian Gulf TV War*. Boulder, CO: Westview Press.

Lash, S. and Urry, J. (1994) *Economies of Signs and Space*. Thousand Oaks, CA: Sage Publications.

Poster, M. (1990) *The Mode of Information: Poststructuralism and Social Context*. Chicago: University of Chicago Press.

Shorris, E. (1985) Reflections on power: a dissenting view, *Harper's*, (July), pp. 51–4.

Tzu, S. (1963) *The Art of War*. Oxford: Oxford University Press.

Virilio, P. (1986) *Speed and Politics*. New York: Semiotext(e).

Virilio, P. (1989) *War and Cinema: The Logistics of Perception*. London and New York: Verso.

Weber, M. (1958) Bureaucracy, and science as a vocation, in H. H. Gerth and C. Wright Mills (eds.) *From Max Weber*. New York: Oxford University Press, pp. 129–56, 196–244.

8

The surveillant assemblage[1]
by Kevin Haggerty and Richard Ericson

Introduction

One of the most recognizable figures in cultural theory is the flâneur as analysed by
Walter Benjamin (1983). A creature of nineteenth-century Paris, the flâneur absorbs
himself in strolling through the metropolis where he is engaged in a form of urban
detective work. Concealed in the invisibility of the crowd, he follows his fancies to
investigate the streets and arcades, carving out meaning from the urban landscape.
Possessing a 'sovereignty based in anonymity and observation' (Tester 1994: 5), the
flâneur characterizes the urban environment and the experience of modernity.

There has been an exponential multiplication of visibility on our city streets.
Where the flâneur was involved in an individualistic scrutiny of the city's significa-
tions, the population itself is now increasingly transformed into signifiers for a multitude of organized surveillance systems. Benjamin recognized the importance of even
the earliest prototypes of such technologies, observing how the development of photography helped undermine the anonymity which was central to the flâneur by giving
each face a single name and hence a single meaning (Benjamin 1983: 48) . . .

Our aim is to reconsider some of the more familiar theoretical preoccupations
about this topic. We do so by drawing from the works of Gilles Deleuze and Félix
Guattari to suggest that we are witnessing a convergence of what were once discrete
surveillance systems to the point that we can now speak of an emerging 'surveillant
assemblage'. This assemblage operates by abstracting human bodies from their territorial settings and separating them into a series of discrete flows. These flows are
then reassembled into distinct 'data doubles' which can be scrutinized and targeted
for intervention. In the process, we are witnessing a rhizomatic leveling of the hierarchy of surveillance, such that groups which were previously exempt from routine
surveillance are now increasingly being monitored.

Theorizing surveillance: Orwell and Foucault

Writing well in advance of the contemporary intensification of surveillance technologies, Orwell (1949) presented a prescient vision. In his futuristic nation of Oceana,

citizens are monitored in their homes by a telescreen, a device which both projects images and records behaviour in its field of vision. The 'thought police' co-ordinate this extensive monitoring effort, operating as agents of a centralized totalitarian state which uses surveillance primarily as a means to maintain social order and conformity. Not all citizens, however, are singled out for such scrutiny. The upper and middle classes are intensely monitored, while the vast majority of the population, the underclass 'proles', are simply left to their own devices.

The fact that we continue to hear frequent cautions about '1984' or 'Big Brother' speaks to the continued salience of Orwell's cautionary tale. In the intervening decades, however, the abilities of surveillance technologies have surpassed even his dystopic vision. Writing at the cusp of the development of computing machines, he could not have envisioned the remarkable marriage of computers and optics which we see today. Furthermore, his emphasis on the state as the agent of surveillance now appears too restricted in a society where both state and non-state institutions are involved in massive efforts to monitor different populations. Finally, Orwell's prediction that the 'proles' would largely be exempt from surveillance seems simply wrong in light of the extension and intensification of surveillance across all sectors of society.

Michel Foucault's (1977) analysis of the panopticon provides the other dominant metaphor for understanding contemporary surveillance. In part, Foucault extends Orwell's fears, but his analysis also marks a significant departure, as it situates surveillance in the context of a distinctive theory of power . . .

Foucault's analysis improves on Orwell's by reminding us of the degree to which the proles have long been the subject of intense scrutiny. In fact, Foucault accentuates how it was precisely this population – which was seen to lack the self-discipline required by the emerging factory system – that was singled out for a disproportionate level of disciplinary surveillance. Foucault also encourages us to acknowledge the role surveillance can play beyond mere repression; how it can contribute to the productive development of modern selves. Unfortunately, Foucault fails to directly engage contemporary developments in surveillance technology, focusing instead on transformations to eighteenth and nineteenth century total institutions. This is a curious silence, as it is these technologies which give his analysis particular currency among contemporary commentators on surveillance. Even authors predisposed to embrace many of Foucault's insights believe that rapid technological developments, particularly the rise of computerized databases, require us to rethink the panoptic metaphor. For example, Mark Poster (1990: 93) believes that we must now speak of a 'superpanopticon' while Diana Gordon (1987) suggests the term 'electronic panopticon' better captures the nature of the contemporary situation. But even these authors are in line with a general tendency in the literature to offer more and more examples of total or creeping surveillance, while providing little that is theoretically novel. For our purposes, rather than try and stretch Foucault's or Orwell's concepts beyond recognition so that they might better fit current developments, we draw from a different set of analytical tools to explore aspects of contemporary surveillance.

The surveillant assemblage

The philosopher Gilles Deleuze only occasionally wrote directly on the topic of surveillance, usually in the context of his commentaries on Foucault's work (Deleuze 1986, 1992). In conjunction with his colleague Félix Guattari, however, he has provided us with a set of conceptual tools that allow us to re-think the operation of the emergent surveillance system, a system we call the 'surveillant assemblage' . . .

Deleuze and Guattari introduce a radical notion of multiplicity into phenomena which we traditionally approach as being discretely bounded, structured and stable. 'Assemblages' consist of a 'multiplicity of heterogeneous objects, whose unity comes solely from the fact that these items function together, that they "work" together as a functional entity' (Patton 1994: 158). They comprise discrete flows of an essentially limitless range of other phenomena such as people, signs, chemicals, knowledge and institutions. To dig beneath the surface stability of any entity is to encounter a host of different phenomena and processes working in concert. The radical nature of this vision becomes more apparent when one realizes how any particular assemblage is itself composed of different discrete assemblages which are themselves multiple.

Assemblages, for Deleuze and Guattari, are part of the state form. However, this notion of the state form should not be confused with those traditional apparatuses of governmental rule studied by political scientists. Instead, the state form is distinguished by virtue of its own characteristic set of operations; the tendency to create bounded physical and cognitive spaces, and introduce processes designed to capture flows. The state seeks to 'striate the space over which it reigns' (Deleuze and Guattari 1987: 385), a process which involves introducing breaks and divisions into otherwise free-flowing phenomena. To do so requires the creation of both spaces of comparison where flows can be rendered alike and centres of appropriation where these flows can be captured.

Flows exist prior to any particular assemblage, and are fixed temporarily and spatially by the assemblage. In this distinction between flows and assemblages, Deleuze and Guattari also articulate a distinction between forces and power. Forces consist of more primary and fluid phenomena, and it is from such phenomena that power derives as it captures and striates such flows. These processes coalesce into systems of domination when otherwise fluid and mobile states become fixed into more or less stable and asymmetrical arrangements which allow for some to direct or govern the actions of others (Patton 1994: 161).

It is desire which secures these flows and gives them their permanence as an assemblage. For psychoanalysts, desire is typically approached as a form of lack, as a yearning that we strive to satisfy. In contrast, Deleuze and Guattari approach desire as an active, positive force that exists only in determinate systems. Desire is a field of immanence, and is a force 'without which no social system could ever come into being' (May 1993: 4). As such, desire is the inner will of all processes and events; what Nietzsche refers to as the 'will to power'. As we demonstrate below, a range of desires now energize and serve to coalesce the surveillant assemblage, including the desires for control, governance, security, profit and entertainment . . .

Component parts

The analysis of surveillance tends to focus on the capabilities of a number of discrete technologies or social practices. Analysts typically highlight the proliferation of such phenomena and emphasize how they cumulatively pose a threat to civil liberties. We are only now beginning to appreciate that surveillance is driven by the desire to bring systems together, to combine practices and technologies and integrate them into a larger whole. It is this tendency which allows us to speak of surveillance as an assemblage, with such combinations providing for exponential increases in the degree of surveillance capacity. Rather than exemplifying Orwell's totalitarian state-centred Oceania, this assemblage operates across both state and extra-state institutions.

Something as apparently discrete as the electronic monitoring of offenders increasingly integrates a host of different surveillance capabilities to the point that

> no one is quite sure any longer what [Electronic Monitoring] is. Voice, radio, programmed contact, remote alcohol testing, and automated reporting station ('kiosk') technologies proliferate and are used both singly and in a dizzying array of combinations.
>
> (Renzeman 1998: 5)

The police are continually looking for ways to integrate their different computer systems and databases, as exemplified by ongoing efforts by the FBI forensics section to link together databases for fingerprints, ballistics and DNA (Philipkoski 1998). Still another example of such combinations is the regional police computer system in Central Scotland

> Phone conversations, reports, tip-offs, hunches, consumer and social security databases, crime data, phone bugging, audio, video and pictures, and data communications are inputted into a seamless GIS [geographic information system], allowing a relational simulation of the time-space choreography of the area to be used in investigation and monitoring by the whole force. The Chief Constable states: 'What do we class as intelligence in my new system in the force? Everything! The whole vast range of information that comes into the possession of a police force during a twenty-four-hour period will go on to my corporate database. Everything that every person and vehicle is associated with.'
>
> (Norris and Armstrong (1997) quoted in Graham 1998: 492)

In situations where it is not yet practicable to technologically link surveillance systems, human contact can serve to align and coalesce discrete systems. For example, various 'multi-agency' approaches to policing are institutionalized. Originally, such efforts were wedded to a welfarist ideology of service delivery, but in recent years social service agencies have been drawn into the harder edge of social control (O'Malley and Palmer 1996; Ericson and Haggerty 1999). The coming together (face-to-face, or through electronic mediation) of social workers, health professionals, police and educators to contemplate the status of an 'at risk' individual combines the cumulative knowledge derived from the risk profiling surveillance systems particular to each of these institutions.

The body

A great deal of surveillance is directed toward the human body. The observed body is of a distinctively hybrid composition. First it is broken down by being abstracted from its territorial setting. It is then reassembled in different settings through a series of data flows. The result is a decorporealized body, a 'data double' of pure virtuality.

The monitored body is increasingly a cyborg; a flesh-technology-information amalgam (Haraway 1991). Surveillance now involves an interface of technology and corporeality and is comprised of those 'surfaces of contact or interfaces between organic and non-organic orders, between life forms and webs of information, or between organs/body parts and entry/projection systems (e.g., keyboards, screens)' (Bogard 1996: 33). These hybrids can involve something as direct as tagging the human body so that its movements through space can be recorded, to the more refined reconstruction of a person's habits, preferences, and lifestyle from the trails of information which have become the detritus of contemporary life. The surveillant assemblage is a visualizing device that brings into the visual register a host of heretofore opaque flows of auditory, scent, chemical, visual, ultraviolet and informational stimuli. Much of the visualization pertains to the human body, and exists beyond our normal range of perception.

Rousseau opens *The Social Contract* with his famous proclamation that 'Man was born free, and he is everywhere in chains'. To be more in keeping with the human/machine realities of the twenty-first century, his sentiment would better read: 'Humans are born free, and are immediately electronically monitored'. If such a slogan seems unduly despairing, one might consider the new electronic ankle bracelet for infants, trademarked HUGS, which is being marketed to hospitals as

> a fully supervised and tamper-resistant protection system that automatically activates once secured around an infant's ankle or wrist. Staff [are] immediately alerted at a computer console of the newly activated tag, and can enter pertinent information such as names and medical conditions. Password authorization is needed to move infants out of the designated protection area and – if an infant is not readmitted within a predetermined time limit – an alarm will sound. An alarm also sounds if an infant with a Hugs tag is brought near an open door at the perimeter of the protected area without a password being entered. The display console will then show the identification of the infant and the exit door on a facility map. Alternatively, doors may also be fitted with magnetic locks that are automatically activated. As well, Hugs can be configured to monitor the progress and direction of the abduction within the hospital. Weighing just 1/3 of an ounce, each ergonomically designed infant tag offers a number of other innovative features, including low-battery warning, the ability to easily interface with other devices such as CCTV cameras and paging systems and time and date stamping.
>
> (Canadian Security 1998)

Professor Kevin Warwick of Reading University is the self-proclaimed 'first cyborg,' having implanted a silicon chip transponder in his forearm (Bevan 1999). The surveillance potential of this technology has been rapidly embraced to monitor pets. A microchip in a pet's skin can be read with an electronic device which connects a unique identifying number on the microchip to details of the pet's history, ownership and medical record. Warwick has proposed that implanted microchips could be used to scrutinize the movement of employees, and to monitor money transfers, medical records and passport details. He also suggests that

> anyone who wanted access to a gun could do so only if they had one of these implants . . . Then if they actually try and enter a school or building that doesn't want them in there, the school computer would sound alarms and warn people inside or even prevent them having access.
>
> (Associated Press 1998)

These examples indicate that the surveillant assemblage relies on machines to make and record discrete observations. As such, it can be contrasted with the early forms of disciplinary panopticism analysed by Foucault, which were largely accomplished by practitioners of the emergent social sciences in the eighteenth and nineteenth centuries. On a machine/human continuum, surveillance at that time leaned more toward human observation. Today, surveillance is more in keeping with the technological future hinted at by Orwell, but augumented by technologies he could not have even had nightmares about.

The surveillant assemblage does not approach the body in the first instance as a single entity to be molded, punished, or controlled. First it must be known, and to do so it is broken down into a series of discrete signifying flows. Surveillance commences with the creation of a space of comparison and the introduction of breaks in the flows that emanate from, or circulate within, the human body. For example, drug testing striates flows of chemicals, photography captures flows of reflected lightwaves, and lie detectors align and compare assorted flows of respiration, pulse and electricity. The body is itself, then, an assemblage comprised of myriad component parts and processes which are broken-down for purposes of observation. Patton (1994: 158) suggests that the concept of assemblage 'may be regarded as no more than an abstract conception of bodies of all kinds, one which does not discriminate between animate and inanimate bodies, individual or collective bodies, biological or social bodies' . . .

In the figure of a body assembled from the parts of different corpses, Mary Shelly's *Frankenstein* spoke to early-modern anxieties about the potential consequences of unrestrained science and technology. Contemporary fears about the implications of mass public surveillance continue to emphasize the dark side of science. Today, however, we are witnessing the formation and coalescence of a new type of body, a form of becoming which transcends human corporeality and reduces flesh to pure information. Culled from the tentacles of the surveillant assemblage, this new body is our 'data double', a double which involves 'the multiplication of the individual, the constitution of an additional self' (Poster 1990: 97). Data doubles circulate in a host of different centres of calculation and serve as markers for access to resources, services and power in ways which are often unknown to its referent.

They are also increasingly the objects toward which governmental and marketing practices are directed (Turow 1997). And while such doubles ostensibly refer back to particular individuals, they transcend a purely representational idiom. Rather than being accurate or inaccurate portrayals of real individuals, they are a form of pragmatics: differentiated according to how useful they are in allowing institutions to make discriminations among populations. Hence, while the surveillant assemblage is directed toward a particular cyborg flesh/technology amalgamation, it is productive of a new type of individual, one comprised of pure information.

Rhizomatic surveillance

Deleuze and Guattari (1987) outline how 'rhizomes' are plants which grow in surface extensions through interconnected vertical root systems. The rhizome is contrasted with arborescent systems which are those plants with a deep root structure and which grow along branchings from the trunk. The rhizome metaphor accentuates two attributes of the surveillant assemblage: its phenomenal growth through expanding uses, and its leveling effect on hierarchies.

Rhizomatic expansion

Rhizomes grow across a series of interconnected roots which throw up shoots in different locations. They 'grow like weeds' precisely because this is often what they are. A rhizome 'may be broken, shattered at a given spot, but it will start up again on one of its old lines, or on new lines' (Deleuze and Guattari 1987: 9). Surveillance has comparable expansive and regenerative qualities. It is now estimated that there are 500,000 surveillance cameras operating in Britain (Freeman 1999), where a city dweller can now expect to be caught on film every five minutes (Duffy 1999). Paul Virilio argues that this growth in observation has transformed the experience of entering the city: 'Where once one necessarily entered the city by means of a physical gateway, now one passes through an audiovisual protocol in which the methods of audience and surveillance have transformed even the forms of public greeting and daily reception' (Virilio 1997: 383). Resounding echoes of his point can be heard in the effusive boastings of an operation's director for a British surveillance firm who recounts how 'The minute you arrive in England, from the ferry port to the train station to the city centres, you're being CCTV'd' (Freeman 1999). The study by Norris and Armstrong (1999) of British CCTV also demonstrates how this ostensibly unitary technology is in fact an assemblage that aligns computers, cameras, people and telecommunications in order to survey the public streets.

Deleuze and Guattari emphasize how 'the rhizome operates by variation, expansion, conquest, capture, offshoots' (1987: 21). No single technological development has ushered in the contemporary era of surveillance. Rather, its expansion has been aided by subtle variations and intensifications in technological capabilities, and connections with other monitoring and computing devices. Some of the rhizomatic offshoots of the surveillant assemblage derive from efforts to seek out new target populations that ostensibly require a greater degree of monitoring. The list of such populations is limited only by imagination, and currently includes, for example, the young, caregivers, commuters, employees, the elderly, international travelers, parolees, the privileged and the infirm. Much of this expansion is driven by the financial imperative to find new markets for surveillance technologies which were originally designed for military purposes (Haggerty and Ericson 1999).

For Orwell, surveillance was a means to maintain a form of hierarchical social control. Foucault proposed that panoptic surveillance targeted the soul, disciplining the masses into a form of self-monitoring that was in harmony with the requirements of the developing factory system. However, Bauman (1992: 51) argues that panopticism in contemporary society has been reduced in importance as a mechanism of social integration. Instead of being subject to disciplinary surveillance or simple repression, the population is increasingly constituted as consumers and seduced into the market economy. While surveillance is used to construct and monitor consumption patterns, such efforts usually lack the normalized soul training which is so characteristic of panopticism. Instead, monitoring for market consumption is more concerned with attempts to limit access to places and information, or to allow for the production of consumer profiles through the *ex post facto* reconstructions of a person's behaviour, habits and actions. In those situations where individuals monitor their behaviour in light of the thresholds established by such surveillance systems, they are often involved in efforts to maintain or augment various social perks such as preferential credit ratings, computer services, or rapid movement through customs . . .

The public is slowly awakening to the profits that are being made from the sale of their data doubles. One consequence of this recognition has been the further commodification of the self. Parallel to how the emergence of the wage economy necessitated the fixing of monetary prices to labour power, citizens and economists are now contemplating what, if any, compensation individuals should receive for the sale of their personal information. Dennis (1999) reports on a recent study which found that 70 per cent of Britons were happy to have companies use their personal data, on the condition that they receive something in return, such as more personal service or rewards. Privacy is now less a line in the sand beyond which transgression is not permitted, than a shifting space of negotiation where privacy is traded for products, better services or special deals.

In addition to a desire for order, control, discipline and profit, surveillance has voyeuristic entertainment value. Clips from CCTV's are now a staple of daytime talk shows while programmes such as *America's Dumbest Criminals* have helped soften the authoritarian overtones of mass public surveillance (Doyle 1998). The proliferation of hand-held video cameras has also given rise to *America's Funniest Home Videos*, as well as the more morbid *Faces of Death* videos which portray a procession of accidental fatalities which have been captured on film.

As the surveillant assemblage transcends institutional boundaries, systems intended to serve one purpose find other uses. In his early analysis of paper-based records, Stanton Wheeler (1969) pointed out that it is a characteristic of such records that they can be combined to serve new purposes. The computerization of record-keeping has greatly expanded this ability. For example, police organizations have secured routine, and often informal, access to a host of non-police databases, such as those from insurance companies and financial institutions. Research by Northrop,

Kramer and King (1995) indicates that the police have become the primary users of many systems originally established for other governmental purposes, and Gordon (1990) reports on proposals to link the US federal NCIC police database to computers from Social Security, Internal Revenue, Passport, Securities and Exchange and the State Department. Davis (1998: 381) recounts how in some Southern California communities the police now have direct computerized access to school records.

In surveying the informational horizon for ever more potentially useful sources, police organizations have recently recognized the surveillance and investigative potential of corporate databases. Files from telephone and utilities companies can be used to document an individual's lifestyle and physical location (Ericson and Haggerty 1997), and marketing firms have developed consumer profiling techniques that contain precise information on a person's age, gender, political inclinations, religious preferences, reading habits, ethnicity, family size, income, and so on (Gandy 1993; Turow 1997). When these sources are combined through computerized data matching, they allow for exponential increases in the amount of information the police have at their disposal. Burnham (1997: 164–7) relates that the FBI has employed commercial databases for undisclosed investigative purposes, and that the US Drug Enforcement Agency has developed its own in-house registry with information culled from mailing and telephone listings, direct marketers, voters records, and assorted commercial sources. Although cloaked in secrecy, this registry was expected to contain 135,000,000 records as of its inception in 1991 and would subsequently receive regular updates of corporate and residential data.

Ostensibly non-criminal justice institutions are being called upon to augment the surveillance capacities of the criminal justice surveillance system. In Canada, for example, in an effort to deter money laundering, financial institutions are compelled to monitor and report 'suspicious' transactions. More recently, regulations have been introduced to require American banks to compare the financial holdings of their clients against an electronic list of parents who owe child support. Educators and medical practitioners are already legally compelled to report suspected instances of child abuse, and the police have started to request or confiscate media tapes of public disturbances in efforts to identify lawbreakers.

Rhizome and hierarchy

For both Orwell and Foucault, surveillance is part of a regime where comparatively few powerful individuals or groups watch the many, in a form of top-down scrutiny. Contemporary studies of surveillance continue to emphasize this hierarchical aspect of observation. For example, Fiske concludes his insightful analysis of the surveillance of American Blacks (particularly Black men), by proclaiming that 'although surveillance is penetrating deeply throughout our society, its penetration is differential. The lives of the white mainstream are still comparatively untouched by it' (Fiske 1998: 85). And while the targeting of surveillance is indeed differential, we take exception to the idea that the mainstream is 'untouched' by surveillance. Surveillance has become rhizomatic, it has transformed hierarchies of observation, and allows for the scrutiny of the powerful by both institutions and the general population.

All contemporary institutions subject their members to forms of bureaucratic surveillance. Individuals with different financial practices, education and lifestyle will come into contact with different institutions and hence be subject to unique combinations of surveillance. The classifications and profiles that are entered into these disparate systems correspond with, and reinforce, differential levels of access, treatment and mobility. Hence, while poor individuals may be in regular contact with the surveillance systems associated with social assistance or criminal justice, the middle and upper classes are increasingly subject to their own forms of routine observation, documentation and analysis. The more institutions they are in contact with, the greater the level of scrutiny to which they are subjected. In the case of the powerful, this can include the regular monitoring of consumption habits, health profile, occupational performance, financial transactions, communication patterns, Internet use, credit history, transportation patterns, and physical access controls.

It is not exclusively powerful social groups and institutions which observe the powerful. Mathiesen (1997) accentuates the tendency toward 'bottom-up' forms of observation in his claim that a process of *synopticism* is now at work which parallels Foucault's panopticism. Synopticism essentially means that a large number of individuals are able to focus on something in common. New media, particularly television, allow the general public to scrutinize their leaders as never before (Meyrowitz 1985). We need only consider the media circus which surrounds Britain's royal family to acknowledge this point. Furthermore, the monitoring of the powerful has been eased by the proliferation of relatively inexpensive video cameras. These allow the general public to tape instances of police brutality, and have given rise to inner-city citizen response teams which monitor police radios and arrive at the scene camera-in-hand to record police behaviour. Such monitoring culminates in those surreal situations of labour unrest where picketing workers film the police while the police film the strikers. While not a complete democratic leveling of the hierarchy of surveillance, these developments cumulatively highlight a fractured rhizomatic criss-crossing of the gaze such that no major population groups stand irrefutably above or outside of the surveillant assemblage.

A further distinction is needed, however, if we are to fully appreciate the distinctive form that the observation of the powerful now assumes. Such surveillance is often a mile wide but only an inch deep. The depth, or intensity, of the surveillance directed at the powerful generally exists as a potentiality of connections of different technologies and institutions. It is activated, or intensified, when there is some perceived *ex post facto* or prospective need to profile their movements, consumption patterns, reading preferences, tastes in erotica, personal contacts, such that they coalesce into a remarkably detailed data double. The O.J. Simpson case provides a telling example of the intensity that this potentiality can assume when put into motion. Included among the reams of information that the L.A.P.D. were able to collect about O.J. Simpson were details about which pornographic movie he watched in his hotel a few days prior to the murders. The police also approached a private company which sells satellite surveillance photographs to try and discern whether Simpson's now (in)famous white Bronco was in the driveway of Nicole Brown Simpson's home on the night of the murders (Fiske 1998).

Conclusion: the disappearance of disappearance

Premodern living arrangements typically consisted of individuals residing in rural villages where they knew and were known by their neighbours. The mass movements of individuals into cities ruptured these long-standing neighbourly and familial bonds. Individuals in cities became surrounded by streams of unknown strangers. Sociologists have drawn a wide range of implications from this social transformation. Anonymity allowed for new possibilities in self-creation: the freedom to partake in experiments with identities and life projects. Simmel believed that the metropolis 'grants to the individual a kind and an amount of personal freedom which has no analogy whatsoever under other conditions' (1950: 416). Others have accentuated the darker side of these possibilities for self-creation, cautioning how this new found 'freedom' could also be experienced as a daunting obligation, as modern individuals are now compelled to be free, to establish identities and life projects in the face of radical uncertainty about correct courses of action. Bauman (1997: 20–1) observes that modernity transformed 'identity from the matter of ascription into the achievement [sic] – thus making it an individual task and the individual's responsibility,' and these 'individual life-projects find no stable ground in which to lodge an anchor'.

From the beginning, however, this general narrative of anonymity and invisibility contained a subplot, one which involved countervailing efforts by institutions. The rise in credentials and surveillance systems was a way to create institutional reputations and provide for ways to differentiate among unknown strangers (Nock 1993). These new forms of reputation lack the deep subjective nuances which characterized familial and neighbourly relations in the idealized premodern rural village. Instead, knowledge of the population is now manifest in discrete bits of information which break the individual down into flows for purposes of management, profit and entertainment. While such efforts were originally a footnote to the historical rise of urban anonymity, they now constitute an important force in their own right.

The coalescence of such practices into the surveillant assemblage marks the progressive 'disappearance of disappearance' – a process whereby it is increasingly difficult for individuals to maintain their anonymity, or to escape the monitoring of social institutions. Efforts to evade the gaze of different systems involves an attendant trade-off in social rights and benefits. Privacy advocates bring this point home in their facetious advice that individuals who are intent on staying anonymous should not use credit, work, vote, or use the Internet. Two quite different historical examples accentuate the extent to which the possibilities for disappearance have narrowed.

A recent biography of a female activist recounted how she was followed in the 1950s by secret service agents. Unbeknownst to her, at one point she managed to evade her pursuers by simply taking an ocean cruise which rendered her beyond the reach of their abilities to track her movements. Clearly, this would not be the case today. Even on the ocean a person's whereabouts could still be discerned through the monitoring of credit card transactions, computer connections, travel arrangements and telephone calls.

Our second example also concerns ship travel, but this time it involves the greatest naval armada ever assembled – the allied invasion of Normandy in 1944. At that time the Germans were reasonably certain that an invasion of France was imminent, but it was not until the fog lifted on the morning of June 6th to reveal a fleet of over 5,000 ships off the coast that they knew the invasion had truly begun. Again, the contrast between yesterday and today is telling. With advanced military sensing devices that now include globe-scanning satellites and submarines equipped with sensors that can detect the propeller of a ship traveling on the opposite side of the ocean, the surprise appearance of such a massive military grouping is simply inconceivable.

The invisible armada and elusive activist have faded into historical memories. From now on, such matters will be readily captured by a surveillant assemblage devoted to the disappearance of disappearance.

Note

1   This chapter is an extract from K. Haggerty and R. Ericson (2000) The surveillant assemblage, *British Journal Sociology*, 51(4): 605–22.

References

Associated Press (1998) Professor gets first chip implant, *Associated Press*, 27 August.

Bauman, Z. (1992) *Intimations of Postmodernity*. London: Routledge.

Bauman, Z. (1997) *Postmodernity and Its Discontents*. New York: New York University Press.

Benjamin, W. (1983) *Charles Baudelaire: A Lyric Poet in the Era of High Capitalism*. London: Verso.

Bevan, S. (1999) Chips may dip into work-place sanity, *The Windsor Star*, 10 May.

Bogard, W. (1996) *The Simulation of Surveillance: Hypercontrol in Telematic Societies*. Cambridge: Cambridge University Press.

Burnham, D. (1997) *Above the Law: Secret Deals, Political Fixes, and Other Misadventures of the U. S. Department of Justice*. New York: Scribner.

Canadian Security (1998) The importance of Hugs, November/December.

Davis, M. (1998) *Ecology of Fear: Los Angeles and the Imagination of Disaster*. New York: Henry Holt.

Deleuze, G. (1986) *Foucault*. Minneapolis: University of Minnesota Press.

Deleuze, G. (1992) Postscript on the societies of control, *October*, Winter, 59: 3–7.

Deleuze, G. and Guattari, F. (1987) *A Thousand Plateaus*. Minneapolis: University of Minnesota Press.

Dennis, S. (1999) 75% of Brits happy to give firms their personal data, *YAHOO News Asia*, 18 May.

Doyle, A. (1998) 'Cops': television policing as policing reality, in M. Fishman and G. Cavendar (eds) *Entertaining Crime: Television Reality Programs*. New York: Aldine de Gruyter.

Duffy, J. (1999) Something to watch over us, *BBC News Online*, 4 May.

Ericson, R. and Haggerty, K. (1997) *Policing the Risk Society*. Toronto: University of Toronto Press and Oxford: Oxford University Press.

Ericson, R. and Haggerty K. (1999) Governing the young, in R. Smandych (ed.) *Governable Spaces: Readings on Governmentality and Crime Control*. Dartmouth: Ashgate.

Fiske, J. (1998) Surveilling the city: whiteness, the black man and democratic totalitarianism, *Theory, Culture & Society*, 15(2): 67–88.

Foucault, M. (1977) *Discipline and Punish: The Birth of the Prison*. New York: Vintage.

Freeman, A. (1999) Big brother turning into a Big Bother, *The Globe and Mail*, 25 May.

Gandy, O. (1993) *The Panoptic Sort: A Political Economy of Personal Information*. Boulder, CO: Westview.

Gordon, D. (1987) The electronic panopticon: a case study of the development of the national crime records system, *Politics and Society*, 15(4): 483–511.

Gordon, D. (1990) *The Justice Juggernaut: Fighting Street Crime, Controlling Citizens*. New Brunswick: Rutgers University Press.

Graham, S. (1998) Spaces of surveillant simulation: new technologies, digital representations, and material geographies, *Environment and Planning D: Society and Space*, 16(4): 483–504.

Haggerty, K. and Ericson, R. (1999) The militarization of policing in the information age, *The Journal of Political and Military Sociology*, 27(2): 233–45.

Haraway, D. (1991) *Simians, Cyborgs and Women: The Reinvention of Nature*. New York: Routledge.

Kanaley, R. (1999) 'States' sale of data: at what price? *Philadelphia Inquirer*, 13 June.

Mathiesen, T. (1997) The viewer society: Michel Foucault's 'Panopticon' revisited, *Theoretical Criminology*, 1(2): 215–33.

May, T. (1993) The system and its fractures: Gilles Deleuze on Otherness, *Journal of the British Society for Phenomenology*, 24(1): 3–14.

Meyrowitz, J. (1985) *No Sense of Place*. New York: Oxford University Press.

Nock, S. (1993) *The Costs of Privacy: Surveillance and Reputation in America*. New York: Aldine de Gruyter.

Norris, C. and Armstrong, G. (1997) Categories of control: the social construction of suspicion and intervention in CCTV Systems, Report to ESRC; Department of Social Policy, University of Hull.

Norris, C. and Armstrong, G. (1999) *The Maximum Surveillance Society*. Oxford: Berg.

Northrop, A., Kramer, K. and King, J. L. (1995) Police use of computers, *Journal of Criminal Justice*, 23(3): 259–75.

O'Malley, P. and Palmer, D. (1996) Post-Keynesian policing, *Economy and Society*, 25(2): 137–55.

Orwell, G. (1949) *Nineteen Eighty-Four*. New York: Penguin.

Patton, P. (1994) MetamorphoLogic: bodies and powers in *A Thousand Plateaus*, *Journal of the British Society for Phenomenology*, 25(2): 157–69.

Philipkoski, K. (1998) A crime-sniffing network, *Wired News*, 11 August.

Poster, M. (1990) *The Mode of Information*. Chicago: University of Chicago Press.

Renzeman, M. (1998) GPS: is now the time to adopt? *Journal of Offender Monitoring*, 11(2): 5.

Simmel, G. (1950) The metropolis and mental life, in G. Simmel (ed.) *The Sociology of Georg Simmel*. New York: The Free Press.

Tester, K. (1994) Introduction, in K. Tester (ed.) *The Flâneur*. London: Routledge.

Turow, J. (1997) *Breaking Up America: Advertisers and the New Media World*. Chicago: University of Chicago Press.

Virilio, P. (1997) The overexposed city, in N. Leach (ed.) *Rethinking Architecture*. London: Routledge.

Wheeler, S. (1969) Problems and issues in record keeping, in S. Wheeler (ed.) *On Record*. New York: Russell Sage Foundation.

9

Probing the surveillant assemblage: on the dialectics of surveillance practices as processes of social control[1]
by Sean P. Hier

Problematics

In the early pages of her essay *When Old Technologies Were New*, Carolyn Marvin (1988) argues that the history of electronic media reveals less about the evolution of technical efficiencies in communication than a series of arenas for negotiating issues crucial to the conduct of social life. Among those issues, who is 'inside' and who is 'outside', who may speak and who may not and who possesses authority to be believed. Here, she maintains, the focus of communication is shifted from 'the instrument' to 'the drama' in which diverse social groups perpetually negotiate power, authority, representation and knowledge with whatever resources they have at their disposal. It follows that, although the development of advanced forms of electronic media may serve to alter the perceived effectiveness of one group's surveillance over others, the enduring drama of human agents and technological innovations has more to do with the social conflicts and practices which serve to illuminate new communication devices than it does with the particular instrument of mediation, surveillance or social control.

In the last two decades, significant alterations in the technological character of surveillance practices have transpired to the extent that researchers have started to rethink dominant theoretical and conceptual assumptions, particularly where the role of the state is concerned. Offering what has become a conceptual benchmark in the surveillance literature, Kevin Haggerty and Richard Ericson (2000) incorporate the notion of assemblages to denote the increasing convergence of once discrete systems of surveillance. They argue that the late modern period has ushered in the proliferation of information and data gathering techniques which operate to break the human body into a number of discrete signifying data flows. Reassembled as 'functional hybrids' whose unity is found solely in temporal moments of interdependence, resulting surveillance simulations bring together a seemingly limitless range of information to formulate categorical images or risk data profiles which render otherwise opaque flows of information comprehensible. Conceptualizing the surveillant assemblage as a sequence of processes which approach the human body as a cyborg/flesh amalgamation which is secondarily directed back towards embodied individuals for a plethora of reasons, not only do they deduce that there has transpired important changes in the form and intention of surveillance, but this line of reasoning is extended to affirm that a partial democratization of surveillance hierarchies has ensued.

Whilst it can be conceded that the manifest character of surveillance has been significantly enhanced through technological and communicative innovation, enabling certain transformations in the purposes of surveillance, this [chapter] probes certain key assumptions of the emergent 'surveillant assemblage'. It is argued that the assemblage model places an exaggerated degree of importance, however implicitly, on the social and cultural *effects* of the technological capabilities of contemporary surveillance practices which serves to obscure rather than clarify the enduring drama of human agents and surveillance technologies. The problem derives from the fact that the fundamental object of contestation, or the primary point of conceptual departure, is the supposition that the impetus to surveillance comes ostensibly from above (variations on which take the form of the panoptic power of the state), so when surveillance technologies began to facilitate the monitoring of a wider population base this has been interpreted as a shift in the cultural character of surveillance (op. cit:610) with its concomitant leveling of hierarchies. In an effort to account for the more fundamental forces and desires which give rise to, and sustain, surveillant assemblages, the functioning of a dialectic embedded in many surveillance practices is revealed in the present analysis to contribute to a polarization effect involving the simultaneous leveling and solidification of hierarchies. The impetus, however, is not located in powerful social actors or elite bodies. Rather, it is purported that considerable foundational support derives from popular social grievances, various antagonisms directed at a variety of socially constituted risk groups *from below*, which come to secondarily culminate in the intensification of top-down regimes of surveillance . . .

The surveillant assemblage

The contemporary literature concerned with surveillance has demonstrated a tendency to gravitate towards the metaphoric imagery expatiated in George Orwell's prescient vision of Oceania and, more commonly, Michel Foucault's abstraction of the panoptic. For Orwell, the future promised state totalitarianism, exemplified by the 'telescreen', the 'thought police' and categorically selective social monitoring practices. So went the argument, the constant visibility of Big Brother served as a mechanism of repression oriented towards inducing and maintaining compliance and social order. Foucault, by contrast, understood the visible manifestations of modern surveillance as having been increasingly rendered unnecessary through the normalizing gaze of the disciplines and the constitution of self-regulating subjects. Well beyond a mechanism of repression, panoptic observation involved a productive reflection on the self to the extent that the dispersion of truth claims across a range of social institutions served to generate disciplinary practices and the exercise of power over oneself.

In Haggerty and Ericson's assessment (2000), what emerges as problematic through this protracted reliance on Foucault and, less commonly, Orwell is that such accounts fail to embrace seriously contemporary developments in surveillance techniques. Among other things, they contend that contemporary surveillance practices stretch far beyond the state, their technological capabilities problematize a reliance on

18th and 19th century total institutions and, far from the negative connotations that tend to be attached to surveillance, many surveillance practices today are not only supported but encouraged by those who serve as the primary targets of data gathering systems. What this intimates for Haggerty and Ericson is that, rather than recasting Orwellian or Foucauldian imagery to fit the technological particularities of contemporary surveillance (i.e. electronic panopticon, super panopticon), it is more beneficent to chart alternative theoretical and conceptual terrain.

In doing so, they invoke Deleuze and Guattari's concept of assemblages to denote the increasing convergence of once discrete information and data gathering systems. Pronouncing surveillance as one of the main institutional components of late modernity, the 'surveillant assemblage' is put forth to distance their conceptual endeavor from the episteme of discretely structured objects of stability and constancy. Incorporated to explicate the functional multiplicity of a heterogeneity of objects whose unity is located in moments of interdependence, the notion of the assemblage is adopted to capture the configurational character of the present – in the words of Deleuze and Guattari (1987: 406), 'veritable inventions'.

For Haggerty and Ericson, what is notable about the emergent surveillant assemblage is that, driven by desires to bring component parts together into functional systems – variations on which take the form of control, governance, security and profit – an exponential increase in, and convergence of, surveillance technologies has ensued. They explain that surveillance capabilities are increasingly directed towards the human body as a distinctive composition of life forms and webs of information. These processes involve abstractions from, or data doubles on, organic hybrids, such that a protracted reliance develops on machines not only to register but record otherwise discrete observations. Maintaining that we are only beginning to appreciate how surveillance is driven by the desire to integrate component parts into wider systems, they insist that data simulations are not simply 'representational' by nature, but involve a more advanced form of pragmatics having to do with their instrumental efficacy in making discriminations among divergent populations.

What this indicates about contemporary systems of surveillance is that they do not approach the embodied individual for purposes of punishment or control. Instead, with the assistance of various information technologies the body is broken into a series of data flows, such that the introduction of 'breaks' or divisions into otherwise free-flowing phenomena contributes to the creation of physical and cognitive spaces that capture, striate and appropriate flows. In this sense, it is not the personal identity of the embodied individual but rather the actuarial or categorical profile of the collective which is of foremost concern to the surveillant assemblage. The temporal culmination of the striation or appropriation of flows, in turn, serves as a mechanism to make visible that which is opaque, to bring tangibility and coherence to informational stimuli which reside beyond the normal range of human perception. The surveillant assemblage, in other words, can be understood as a mechanism of 'visualization', giving rise to a cyborg flesh/technology amalgamation comprised of pure information which is only then redirected back towards the body for a multitude of reasons.

To complete their conceptualization, Haggerty and Ericson highlight the 'rhizomatic' character of the surveillant assemblage. Borrowing from Deleuze and Guattari, they explain that rhizomes are plants which grow in surface extensions through interconnected roots oriented in a vertical fashion. That the rhizome grows across interconnected roots which throw up 'shoots' in different locations, fracture or discontinuity in the root structure is inconsequential for the overall growth potential of the infrastructure. The rhizome serves as a fitting metaphor to capture the essence of contemporary surveillance, they contend, for it is not that there exists a centralized structure (or arborescent 'trunk') which coordinates contemporary 'branches' of surveillance, but that surveillant technologies operate by variation and disjunction, intensification and horizontally fragmented expansion.

There is no doubt that developments in contemporary surveillance techniques have opened spaces not previously accessible (or not on such a wide scale) to divergent agencies and organizations. The problem which emerges, however, is that Haggerty and Ericson deduce from their conceptualization that the rhizomatic character of contemporary surveillance has worked to transform previously existing hierarchies of surveillance. In contrast to panoptical conceptions of surveillance, where the few are able to visualize the many, they maintain that the rhizomatic expansion of surveillance throughout all sectors of society '. . .cumulatively highlight a fractured rhizomatic criss-crossing of the gaze such that no major population groups stand irrefutably above or outside the surveillant assemblage' (op. cit.:618). They attribute this partial democratization of surveillance hierarchies to the fact that surveillance *has become* rhizomatic (op. cit.:617), recognizing that although surveillance monitoring remains differential in its various application(s), there has transpired a 'synoptic shift' of sorts, whereby bottom-up forms of observation are *now at work* (op. cit.:618) which parallel Foucault's conception of panopticism. The point they wish to make is that the 'creeping' character of surveillance infrastructures, made possible by advances in information and communication technologies across state and extra-state agencies, has enabled the many to scrutinize the few like never before, rendering a more extended range of the population susceptible to surveillance in its many forms.

Probing the surveillant assemblage

Whilst it can surely be conceded that advances in information and data gathering capabilities have facilitated the formation of new data gathering techniques through a rhizomatic expansion well beyond the state, it is crucial to remain cognizant of the fact that these new patterns or 'shoots' are neither random nor is their fundamental character unique to the present. They involve, in the words of David Lyon (2001), 'leaky containers', once discrete public and private sector informational infrastructures increasingly coming into contact. Although this characterizes an increasing pattern in surveillance, particularly where electronic or automated surveillance is concerned, it is important not to lose sight of the fact that these infrastructures remain connected to, or develop out of, 'early modern' systems of surveillance, underscored by the desire to coordinate and control populations, to make 'visible' that which evades immediate perception – the panoptic impulse. By arguing that there has transpired a 'late modern' rhizomatic expansion in the cultural constituent which is surveillance, Haggerty and Ericson place an exaggerated degree of importance on the social and cultural effects of the capabilities of contemporary surveillance technologies. For it is not that surveillance has become rhizomatic in that elusive temporality identified as the late modern period, but rather surveillance, as intimately tied to the expansion of information and communication technologies, and hence to the rise of modernity, has always been rhizomatic. Considering that the metaphor of the rhizome is used not only to capture the expansion and resilience of surveillant assemblages but to simultaneously signify its leveling effect on surveillance (and, by corollary, social) hierarchies, to achieve a more complete appreciation of the significance of manifesting surveillance technologies ('shoots') it is necessary to probe deeper into the divergent social and cultural forces and desires which give rise to, and are component parts of, surveillant assemblages.

One intriguing line of reasoning is found in Mathiesen's (1997) discussion of the 'viewer society', where he calls into question Foucault's (1977:216) invocation of Julius' proclamation that the problem of the modern age is '. . . [t]o procure for a small number, or even for a single individual, the instantaneous view of a great multitude'. For Mathiesen, what is missing – or more accurately, ignored – in Foucault's account of the panoptical-surveillance society is an incorporation of the role of the mass media. He explains that accompanying the shift observed by Foucault from the theatrical expression of the sovereign to the disciplinary-surveillance society has been the parallel rise of the modern mass media. What this implies for Mathiesen is that, whereas the few are vested with the ability to see the many under panoptical surveillance, the many have increasingly become accustomed to seeing, and thereby contemplating, the actions of the few with the rise and expansion of mass mediated communication systems, particularly television.

Captured by the appellation of the synoptic, Mathiesen postulates that synopticism may be used to represent situations whereby large numbers of people are able to focus on something in common. Conceptualized as an opposing situation to panoptical supervision, he contends that synoptical observation represents a concurrent force which accelerated through the modern period in intimate interaction – even fusion – with the panoptic. For as Mathiesen outlines, it was at precisely the same time that Foucault identified the rise of the modern prison and panopticism that the media of mass communications in the form of the press emerged. Presupposed by important social conditions including the changing role of the citizen and the development of a sizable middle class, the mass distribution of the newspaper enabled those of similar social status to visualize on a much wider scale not only others with whom they presumably identified but the actions and intentions of those with whom they did not. The subsequent communicative expansion of other media – film, radio, television – significantly contributed to the advancement of this capability, but it was also facilitated by the distributive capacities of technological flows in the form of the train, steamship, telegraph and the harnessing of electricity. It is important to note, too, that developments in the expansion of mass communications were presupposed by a social structure which increasingly desired mobility, speed and information, facilitating the distanciation of time and space and the disembedding of social relations.

That synoptical processes developed in tandem with panoptical ones, from the Inquisition to the Internet, leads Mathiesen to the argument that the synoptic and the panoptic are mutually implicating processes which serve reciprocal functions. What is unique to the contemporary context, he adds, is that it is technologically feasible for panoptical and synoptical impulses to merge through the same technology. When abduction footage from video surveillance tapes showing two-year-old James Bulger being escorted out of the Bootle Strand Shopping Centre near Liverpool were synoptically revealed to a worldwide audience in the early 1990s, for example, the panoptic impulse was strikingly apparent: more surveillance, tighter security. The video coverage neither served to deliver James Bulger from the wrath of his murderers any more than footage from a Soham recreational centre camera contributed to the deliverance of Holly Wells and Jessica Chapman. To paraphrase Colin Hay (1996), what the footage of James Bulger's abduction did do is explicate how the society of the spectacle reaps its revenge upon the society of surveillance: the private, depersonalizing CCTV coverage of the failed disciplinary routines of the mall became public spectacle, as footage showing James Bulger escorted from the centre was thrust into newspapers, magazines and television news broadcasts for the visual consumption, and condemnation, of an international audience.

Hence, in contrast to Foucault's understanding of the modern subject as the culmination of dispersed, non-visible panoptical processes oriented towards the transformation of the soul, Mathiesen finds it more feasible to explain these processes as fulfilled by the visibility of modern synopticon. Far from Foucault's panoptical gaze, where surveillance and punishment are removed from open view, the synoptic embraces the visual in the most emphatic manner because the synopticon is thoroughly visual and visualizing. Not only do synoptical processes enable the many to focus on something of common stock but Mathiesen argues that they constitute a more or less total pattern of visualization, intimately tied to the impulse to panoptic visualization. In recent memory, no event exemplifies the dialectical interaction of synoptical forces and panoptical desires more cogently than the mediation of the terrorist attacks on the World Trade Center of 11 September 2001. Through sustained graphic visual representation of the collapsing Twin Towers, the fusion of the synoptic and the panoptic was revealed: repeated exposure to the fantastic spectacle served to invite a global audience to consume the hybrid image of fascination and repulsion whilst those same images served as, and remain, the central discursive resource oriented towards consolidating panoptical aspirations through the intensification of information gathering, data sharing and risk management techniques. In its many forms, surveillance stands as a cause as well as an effect of intensified practices of social monitoring and information gathering.

Surveillance practices as processes of social control

With an exaggerated degree of importance assigned to the social and cultural effects of the technological capabilities of contemporary surveillance practices, the surveillant assemblage rests on the assumption that the impetus to surveillance comes fundamentally from above, from elite, police or government. As surveillance technologies increasingly made possible the monitoring of a wider portion of the population, this has been interpreted as a shift in the cultural character of surveillance hierarchies. Yet, the fallout of an acceleration in the expansion of surveillance infrastructures has not been the tearing away of surveillance hierarchies *sui generis*, but rather a polarization of hierarchies has ensued in the form of a simultaneous leveling and solidification of already existing fractures.

One form in which the solidification of surveillance hierarchies assumes is a dynamic set of practices conceptualized in terms of social control processes. Admittedly, the epistemology of social control, which has enjoyed a long history in sociological writings, has tended to produce a kind of determinism implying that there exists an acting 'society', 'social structure' or remote governmental body that acts upon an otherwise homogenous population in a singular and uniform manner. It is for this reason that recent sociological discourse on social control has sought to understand the workings of governmental projects by drawing attention to the importance of the intersection of state practices with processes and techniques of self formation. Maintaining a conceptual emphasis on the role of human agency, as well as the configurational character of state policy, the popular dimensions that presuppose social control processes in their manifest form have been prioritized (cf. Hunt 1999 . . .). What has hitherto been ignored is the role that surveillance practices in terms of the mutual conditioning of synoptical forces and panoptical desires have to play in the formation of processes of social control.

Perhaps no example demonstrates how the dialectical constitution of surveillance finds stability in social control processes better than contemporary approaches to single mothers and welfare. Welfare recipients have long been subjected to moralized regimes of surveillance. Little (1994, 1997), for instance, presents compelling analyses of the extent to which the actions and agency of single mothers collecting welfare in the Canadian province of Ontario have been surveilled by agents of the state as well as those acting in collusion with the state – neighbours, teachers, landlords and charity workers. Whilst these forms of morally regulating the activities of poor single mothers, relying to a large extent on 'informers' or 'rats', remain prominent, Gilliom (1997, 2001) has reported on how 'old forms' of morally regulating poor single mothers in Ohio have combined with the potentialities of 'CRIS-E', the Client Registration System-Enhanced.

A high-tech surveillance system capable of monitoring all 'legitimate' forms of welfare recipients' income for risks of infraction or abuse, CRIS-E brings together state-wide databases to manage and evaluate, surveil and administer welfare allowances. What is so alarming about the system is not the state's stronghold over poor single mothers, but the disciplinary effects of CRIS-E. As Gilliom relates through interview data, although single mothers accessing welfare fully realize that the state does not provide enough in allowances to meet basic necessities, many refrain from taking 'side jobs' for fear of termination from welfare or, equally as feared, the 'inspection'. What the latter involves is state agents interrogating recipients to ascertain their 'deservingness' or 'worthiness' under conditions of secrecy as to the purpose of the inspection. Indeed, Gilliom is correct to observe that it is hard to image a more compelling example of the politics of vision and how surveillance operates as a form of domination over the body, contributing to the exasperation rather than leveling of hierarchies of surveillance.

The implementation of CRIS-E draws attention to important 'panoptic' developments in the regulation of poor single mothers, but Gilliom's discussion fails to fully account for the synoptical desires motivating the development of such a system.

Going some distance to accommodate for this shortcoming, Margaret Little (2001) has sought to understand the consequences of New Right politics on the surveillance of poor single mothers accessing welfare in Ontario since 1995. As she argues, by play- ing on myths surrounding single mothers who access government allowance as lazy criminals who present a significant risk to the welfare system, the state and ultimately the moral underpinnings of 'society', the government has been afforded *popular legitimacy* to significantly reduce allowances for poor single mothers whilst at the same time enhancing a variety of surveillance mechanisms which govern their lives.

When the conservative government under the leadership of former Premier Mike Harris ascended to power in Ontario in 1995, it was on a New Right policy platform combining a neo-liberal emphasis on reducing the size and role of government with a neo-conservative focus oriented towards 'getting tough' with moral deviants. One of the central discursive objects of contention in the Harris Tories' campaign strategy was 'the welfare recipient'. Riding on a populist platform reflected in the nation's mainstream press, the conservatives' agenda included a strong codified discourse focusing on welfare dependency, responsibilization and levels of benefits that 'we can't afford' (Knight 1998:109). At the start of their campaign, the conservatives were significantly behind the liberals in the polls, as the liberals enjoyed over 50% support with the conservatives at 25%. Voicing a consistent and clear commitment to cutting government spending, introducing mandatory workfare and cutting welfare costs, as well as taking a hard line with juvenile offenders and rescinding 'useless' employment equity/race relations policies, the conservatives' media strategies mem- orably involved Mike Harris standing in front of a mock road sign reading 'Welfare, Ontario', to the point that by the fourth week of the campaign the liberal's lead was vanishing (ibid).

Particularly noteworthy about the conservatives' election platform was not simply that they assigned a conflated sense of blame for high levels of government spending to moral deviants, welfare recipients and criminals, but an additional level of failure was attributed to the structure of government itself. This strategy effectively served to set up two discursive antagonisms: first it situated 'honest citizens' against those on the social and moral margins, individualizing blame and social responsibility; and second, it problematized the role of the state in social welfare, identifying responsible government as a problem in and of itself. As Mathiesen maintains, the visual domain of synopticon vis-à-vis the press represents a totalizing message system tailored to the 'requirements' of modernity, functioning to constrain popular consciousness in the interests of power and control. 'Inside synopticon', he laments, '. . . the material is purged of everything but the criminal – what was originally a small segment of a human being becomes the whole human being – whereupon the material is hurled back into the open society as stereotypes and panic-like, terrifying stories about indi- vidual cases' (op. cit:231). By articulating a generalized sense of crisis along the dual axes of the political and the transgressive, the Harris campaign served to tap into populist anxieties pertaining to middle-class discontentment with state spending, public safety and welfare abuse.

Understood in the context of the wider political landscape of the early 1990s, the conservatives' ascendancy to power was set against the backdrop of rising provincial debt, severe recession, growing unemployment and an NDP government perceived as a failure in the eyes of business and labour. Attributing responsibility to careless government spending, able-bodied workers who refuse to participate in the labour force and single mothers living in subsidized housing projects with male partners akin to brothels (cf. Little 1999), the Harris Tories managed to muster enough momentum to win 45% of the popular vote. Their first term in power brought a reduction in welfare benefits by nearly 22%, the implementation of a 'workfare' programme and reduced allowances to those who seek retraining and educational advancement. But nothing was so devastating as the mechanisms of surveillance implemented under the Harris government's anti-fraud provisions.

Designed to 'stamp out fraud', several 'verification measures' were enacted which involved welfare workers demanding literally hundreds of pieces of information from poor single mothers (Little 2001). With a wider concern to rationalize the administration of welfare, old paper documents were increasingly transferred to computer files. Over the duration of these processes, it was discovered that several pieces of verifying documentation were missing from welfare recipients' files. Subsequently, everything from assets, documented employment histories and relationships with ex-spouses/lovers to the sale of personal belongings – some of which transpired over a decade prior to the request for documentation – were demanded. The stresses placed on women who were faced with fewer financial resources to track down such information (to offset childcare, travel fees and service charges), combined with barriers such as those faced by aboriginal women who were forced to deal with The Department of Indian and Northern Development, women who had to contact abusive ex-spouses or immigrant women forced to seek documentation in other countries.

Added to which, these 'personal' verification measures were augmented by the coming together of data gathering systems which function to compare information on income tax returns, student loans and welfare benefits through enhanced automated computer networks. The Harris Tories even introduced a provincial fraud telephone hotline, granting anonymity to anyone who reports on welfare fraud. As Little reveals, callers are exonerated from responsibility and accountability for their accusations, opening a window for any number of personal grievances to be energized into vindictive attributions of welfare fraud. Since the invigoration of these surveillance mechanism, Little reported that over 10 000 recipients have been cut off assistance, 89% of whom were women. The number is much higher if welfare reductions are considered, to the extent in 2000–01 17 734 people were either reduced or terminated from social assistance.[2] And what is so disappointing is that through the intersection of these categorical/computer assisted and individual-moralized monitoring techniques, there are no hearings, explanations or second chances under the Tories' 'Zero Tolerance' policy.

There is no doubt that the potential for the policing of welfare has been drastically enhanced with the sharing of information across government sites, but what these examples of welfare policing serve to highlight is the intersection of 'new' and 'old' forms of surveillance. The most devastating consequence of amendments to Ontario welfare surveillance came in August of 2001, when college student Kimberly Rogers died eight months' pregnant while under 'house arrest' in her apartment. Purported by anti-poverty activists to have succumbed to extreme temperatures of the late summer, Rogers was legally confined to her apartment for six months when it was discovered through verification measures she had accessed the provincial student loan fund at the same time as she was accessing welfare. The dangers of 'leaky containers' and risk management techniques had never been so devastatingly revealed in Ontario under the auspices of the Harris government's 'common sense revolution'. Amazingly as the inquest into the death of Kimberly Rogers commenced, calls for biometric finger scanning to prevent 'double-dipping' could be heard as the Tories' second term in office continued. Essentially, what the new measures function to do is *create* rather than detect conditions of fraud, revealing surveillance as a cause as well as an effect of intensified forms of social monitoring and information gathering. In the end, when the morally-laden language of fraud and verification is removed, what remains are prejudicial evaluations, populist underpinnings and poor women confronted with ever increasing intrusions into their personal lives in the pursuit to feed and clothe their families . . .

Notes

1   This chapter is an extract from S. P. Hier (2003) Probing the surveillant assemblage: on the dialectics of surveillance practices as processes of social control, *Surveillance & Society*, 1(3): 399–411.
2   Ontario Welfare Fraud Control Report, 2000–1. Government of Ontario.

References

Deleuze, G. and Guattari, F. (1987) *A Thousand Plateaus*. Minneapolis: University of Minnesota Press.
Ericson, R. and Haggerty, K. (1997) *Policing the Risk Society*. Toronto: University of Toronto Press.
Foucault, M. (1977) *Discipline and Punish*. New York: Pantheon.
Gilliom, J. (1997) Everyday surveillance, everyday resistance. *Studies in Law, Politics and Society*, 16: 275–97.
Gilliom, J. (2001) *Overseers of the Poor: Surveillance, Resistance and the Limits of Privacy*. Chicago: University of Chicago Press.
Haggerty, K. and Ericson, R. (2000) The surveillant assemblage, *British Journal of Sociology*, 51(4): 605–22.
Hay, C. (1996) Mobilization through interpellation: James Bulger, juvenile crime and the construction of a moral panic, *Social and Legal Studies*, 4: 197–223.
Hunt, A. (1999) *Governing Morals*. Cambridge: Cambridge University Press.
Knight, G. (1998) Hegemony, the media and new right politics: Ontario in the late 1990s, *Critical Sociology*, 24(1–2): 105–29.
Little, M. (1994) 'Manhunts' and 'Bingo Blabs': the moral regulation of Ontario single mothers, *Canadian Journal of Sociology*, 19(2): 233–47.
Little, M. (1997) *No Car, No Radio, No Liquor Permit: The Moral Regulation of Single Mothers in Ontario*. Toronto: Oxford University Press.
Little, M. (1999) 'The pecker detectors are back': regulation of the family form in Ontario welfare policy, *Journal of Canadian Studies*, 34(2): 110–36.
Little, M. (2001) A litmus test for democracy: the impact of Ontario welfare changes on single mothers, *Studies in Political Economy*, 66: 9–36.

Lyon, D. (2001) *Surveillance Society: Monitoring Everyday Life*. Buckingham: Open University Press.

Marvin, C. (1988) *When Old Technologies Were New*. New York: Oxford.

Mathiesen, T. (1997) The viewer society: Michel Foucault's 'Panopticon' revisited, *Theoretical Criminology*, 1(2): 215–34.

PART 3

Surveillance and everyday life

In January 2006, American President George W. Bush's administration came under intense criticism for authorizing the National Security Agency (NSA) to conduct electronic surveillance on citizens' telephone and Internet correspondence without court approval. Defending his administration's policy, President Bush argued that the NSA would only monitor people with links to al-Qaeda, and that they would only intercept messages where one end of the correspondence was based overseas. This is a small price to pay, President Bush proclaimed, for the ongoing 'war on terror'.

The NSA's ability to monitor daily communications is made possible by the willingness of some large telecommunications companies in the US (e.g., Verizon, BellSouth, MCI, Sprint, AT&T) to use data mining techniques to comb through telephone and Internet records to detect 'suspicious behaviour'. Data mining entails the extraction of implicit, previously unknown information from vast amounts of data (Frawley et al. 1992). Once these patterns are established, the telecommunication firms provide the names of potential suspects to the authorities, setting off intensified cycles of surveillance.[1] Despite the still unsettled legal and ethical questions about the Bush administration's surveillance practices, recent survey results showed that 53 percent of Americans support unrestricted government eavesdropping on citizens if it helps to reduce the threat of terrorism (Stolberg 2006).

The NSA program illustrates the relationship between exceptional forms of state surveillance and monitoring practices involving the otherwise mundane aspects of everyday life. From text-messaging lovers and friends to shopping online for new books or chinos, seemingly trivial daily consumer activities leave visible traces of our identities, desires and interests. These digital footprints enable states, corporations and other powerful groups to monitor people's activities and produce detailed demographic and behavioural profiles of each citizen. Although many data mining activities involve attempts by commercial retailers to improve marketing strategies, the NSA example reveals the ambiguous character of surveillance and the extent to which these seemingly innocuous activities may have more dangerous applications. It also reveals how we are unwittingly enlisted as participants in a new configuration of governmental strategies aimed at monitoring and controlling our everyday actions.

Given that social monitoring increasingly takes place at the level of everyday life, it is important to rethink how we understand surveillance practices. There is no doubt that political elites continue to observe, calculate, categorize and manage the behaviours of citizens through a myriad of surveillance techniques. Indeed, the example of the NSA illustrates how use of surveillance techniques to achieve social control remains a fundamental component of modern statecraft. Nevertheless, other practices and activities are also woven into the fabric of surveillance societies, and many of these techniques are not governed by the same logic, rationale or ordering principles as state-sponsored espionage.

Section readings

The first reading passage, Chapter 10 by David Lyon, theorizes the many ways new technologies allow people to enjoy the conveniences of everyday life while simultaneously creating a greater capacity for authorities to monitor, regulate and order citizens' lives and life chances. Lyon suggests that surveillance has a Janus face: increasingly sophisticated communication and information technologies enable us to purchase clothes, obtain a health card, board an airplane and withdraw and transfer money, all at the click of a mouse. In doing so, however, we are required to surrender a great deal of information about our interests and identities. This has resulted, Lyon argues, in the transformation of human subjects into 'data subjects'. Communication no longer demands physical co-presence; the 'disappearing body' requires only informational footprints to represent people's needs, interests and desires.

According to Lyon, the increased centrality of surveillance in everyday life is an inherently contradictory process. As the ever-changing world of new technologies extends the abilities of powerful groups (e.g., government, corporations) to monitor and track citizens and consumers, we are constantly demanding assurances that our privacy rights will be protected and respected. Yet surveillance is contradictory because, just as the financial and political self-interests of corporations and governments fuel the will to observe, categorize and codify, privacy is itself a key generator of surveillance. Increasing surveillance begets demands for better privacy protection, which in turn beget more sophisticated computer programs to organize our personal information, which again prompt calls for more privacy protection, *ad infinitum*.

For Lyon, however, privacy is not the most important consideration in everyday surveillance. Focusing on privacy, which is usually understood as an individual issue, detracts analytical and political attention away from the social consequences of surveillance. Using Foucault's concept of 'biopower', Lyon maintains that surveillance systems serve as an effective means of governing the population through the regulation of subjectivity. Surveillance organizes social relationships and constitutes individuals into larger categories using 'governmental technologies' like statistics and probabilities. When telecommunications companies employ data mining to detect patterns of suspicious telephone or Internet use, they are essentially classifying and categorizing people on the basis of the information they collect about customers (e.g., cell phone calls, Internet traffic, online purchases). Lyon concludes with a number of recommendations for data protection.

The second reading passage, Chapter 11 by Oscar Gandy, focuses on the rise of data mining practices immediately following the terrorist attacks of 11 September

2001. Gandy takes an explicitly normative position in relation to data mining, arguing that the extraction of meaningful knowledge or intelligence from databases amplifies risks to society and poses long-term consequences that will be hard to remedy.

Gandy provides several examples to illustrate the range of post-9/11 data mining applications and to highlight some of the implications of this mode of everyday surveillance. In the video rentals business, for example, data mining can help retailers determine patterns in audience tastes and preferences. If the majority of movie viewers who rent *Syriana* also rent *Good Night and Good Luck*, both starring George Clooney, administrators at the video store would learn that this group of renters either enjoys George Clooney movies or that they enjoy critical movies about American politics. Furthermore, if viewers rent one film but not the other, the check-out clerk will likely have this information on hand to suggest the other rental on a subsequent visit.

Similar practices occur when we shop for books online. When shopping on Amazon.com, for example, it is common to receive a recommendation for at least one other book that bears a thematic resemblance to a book we looked at or purchased. In the aviation industry, data mining can provide analyses of accident descriptions from on-board data recorders (i.e., black boxes), and, with enough aggregate data, it is possible to predict which attributes or combinations of variables correlate strongly with aviation accidents. Motor vehicle targeting by police forces has always been a source of contention, particularly when drivers' skin colour is used to assist police in identifying stolen vehicles or in robbery or drug-related investigations. Data mining becomes useful in these cases, Gandy argues, but for cynical and strategic reasons.

In addition to outlining the range of post-9/11 data mining applications, Gandy demonstrates how the commercial data mining industry experienced a major boom in business following the terrorist attacks on the Pentagon and World Trade Center. Citing a *USA Today* report, he shows how the information and communications technology sector scrambled to compete for Pentagon and State Department business in developing ideas and technologies that could aid in the behavioural profiling of citizens. The social implications of this massive expansion of data mining technologies are numerous, including discrimination against communities as defined along racial-, gender-, age- or class-based lines. Gandy contends that prioritizing efficiency and economics over democratic principles will destroy the social fabric, and he concludes that the best strategy available to citizens and researchers concerned about the social implications of data mining and other forms of everyday surveillance is to mobilize public opinion by drawing media attention to the implications for civil rights violations.

Whereas Lyon and Gandy focus on the application of data mining and related monitoring schemes, the third reading passage, Chapter 12 by Susan Hansen, presents a historical analysis of employee assistance programs (EAPs) in the United States. Through EAPs, employers provide their employees with a range of benefits, normally in conjunction with a broader health care plan, which are designed to help employees deal with everyday problems affecting their workplace performance. EAPs include a repertoire of programs, from assisting employees with substance abuse problems or emotional distress to providing personal financial management tips, child-rearing advice, and health and fitness programming. EAPs do more than just intervene to help correct current problems that may be hampering employee productivity, however.

They also enable employers and employees to identify behavioural risk and its impact on prospective efficiency.

EAPs are worthy of attention from surveillance scholars, Hansen argues, because they problematize previous workplace surveillance studies which have tended to focus on the use of surveillance practices as technologies of social control (e.g., Kiss and Mosco 2005). She draws on Lyon's (1993) argument that surveillance involves a relationship between control and care, which helps her to address broader theoretical question about why workers have embraced the very 'technologies' designed to control their behaviour. Situating contemporary EAPs in relation to historical practices of employee surveillance, Hansen examines the Ford Motor Company's scientific and moral management practices and how workplace-based assistance programmes changed over the twentieth century.

The important aspect of EAPs is that they do not entail 'direct interference' on the part of management, but rather a 'projective assessment' of individualized risk factors in order to warrant heightened monitoring of employees' personal and emotional problems. This has involved the mobilization and application of psychological concepts, principles, and investigative methods (e.g., psychometrics, non-directive interviews, etc.) as a way of rendering visible the 'troubled employee' – both to the managers of the workplace and to the workers themselves. For Hansen, surveillance is thus not only an *effect* of discourse but also a *cause*. The 'troubled employee' emerges from the conceptual tools and theoretical principles of psychology (as an institutional field), but additionally sets in motion a range of responses designed to prioritize the psychologically balanced 'enterprising self' (Rose 1992) as the central unit of the workplace and society.

The final reading passage, Chapter 13 by Kevin Walby, introduces institutional ethnography (IE) as a methodologically innovative approach to surveillance studies. Deriving from the work of Dorothy Smith, IE 'problematizes social relations at the local site of lived experience, whilst examining how *sequences of texts* coordinate consciousness, actions, and ruling' (Walby 2005: 158, emphasis added). The focus of IE on texts enables researchers to examine how manifest and observable social actions (e.g., the video monitoring routines of private security guards) at the local level are informed and circumscribed by extra-local relations. In other words, IE seeks to understand how, in the complexity of everyday lived realities, individuals draw upon experiential knowledge that is formed at a more abstract level of social organization than they are aware.

Walby provokes surveillance researchers to look beyond their speculative theorizing, and he demands that more rigorous empirical attention be granted to the everyday lived reality of public video surveillance. Specifically, he focuses on the socio-technical dynamics of closed-circuit television (CCTV) surveillance in a suburban shopping mall in Victoria, BC, Canada. In this context, Walby demonstrates the extent to which everyday surveillance reproduces racialized discourses of inequality, and his analysis troubles the assumption that surveillance necessarily entails processes of 'disciplining' and 'normalizing' human agents that are subject to the gaze of authorities (Foucault 1977). Specifically, Walby focuses on how social relations are shaped by and reproduced through the video monitoring work of two key informants. Video is the textual device of surveillance, and it is both active and activated because it requires the operator to read the body language, dress, skin colour, age, etc. of shoppers to determine if they are normal or suspicious and to then enter into new sequences of action.

Walby's analysis reveals that, when situated within the framework of ruling capitalist relations, video monitoring in suburban British Columbia creates and reproduces the image of the 'flawed consumer'. True to the IE tradition, Walby shows that already existing discourses of domination shape monitoring routines such that the shopping experience of *all* individuals at Suburban Mall is subject to exclusionary practices that cut across racial and class lines. Whether it is 'Natives' or people with 'bad shoes', Walby shows how CCTV monitoring in this particular locale distinguishes 'desirables' from 'dirtbags', the latter requiring more intensified surveillance. Importantly, Walby demonstrates that through their embeddedness in a ruling discourse and set of organizational practices, it is the CCTV operators whose behaviours and activities are normalized along institutional lines.

Questions

Chapter 10 (Lyon)

1   In what ways does Lyon suggest that the 'fading face' and 'disappearing body' are both a cause and effect of surveillance?
2   What does Lyon mean when he writes that surveillance produces 'categorical suspicion' at one end and 'categorical seduction' at the other? How does this relationship between suspicion and seduction illustrate the paradoxical nature of surveillance?
3   What are the two main types of responses to surveillance to emerge over the past 30 years? Which do you think is more effective and why?

Chapter 11 (Gandy)

1   What are three social implications Gandy associates with the expansion of data mining technology? Do you think that these are reasonable 'trade offs' if data mining and related forms of surveillance can help track and identify suspected terrorists? Why or why not?
2   What has been the regulatory response from the Federal Trade Commission (FTC) to the discriminatory social segmentation that results from data mining practices? Why does Gandy find this response to be unsatisfactory?
3   How does the Cherry case illustrate the dangerous social segmentation effects of data mining?

Chapter 12 (Hansen)

1   In what ways does Hansen's analysis of Employee Assistance Programs advance our knowledge of workplace surveillance?
2   How do contemporary Employee Assistance Programs differ in nature and scope from the Ford Motor Company's pioneering model of scientific and moral management?
3   How has the development of new communication technologies augmented the range of services provided by EAPs? Do you think these developments in new technology have made it more difficult to see the problematic nature of workplace surveillance?

Chapter 13 (Walby)

1   In what way(s) does Walby conceptualize video as an 'active text'? What are the implications of this definition of video for understanding how local lived realities are constituted extra-locally?

2   Describe the relationship between 'rolling text' and 'initiating text'. In what ways does Walby's discussion of CCTV surveillance illustrate this relationship?

3   How does Walby's analysis of the CCTV system at Suburban Mall challenge the conventional view of video surveillance as involving panoptic practices?

Suggested reading

1   Mykhalovskiy, E. and Weir, L. (2006) The Global Public Health Intelligence Network and early warning outbreak detection: a Canadian contribution to global public health, *Canadian Journal of Public Health*, 97(1): 42–5.

This commentary discusses emerging approaches to global infectious disease surveillance in the context of the recent SARS epidemic. Its focus is a Canadian initiative called the Global Public Health Intelligence Network (GPHIN). The authors argue that the development of new communication platforms, such as Internet-based medicine (e.g., ProMED-mail) and real-time news service providers (e.g., Factiva), has enabled public health practitioners and policymakers to more closely monitor global media coverage of health events and create new early warning outbreak detection practices and policies. The article illustrates the notion that surveillance is inherently ambiguous and has both negative and productive qualities.

2   Kiss, S. and Mosco, V. (2005). Negotiating electronic surveillance in the workplace: a study of collective agreements in Canada, *Canadian Journal of Communication*, 30(4): 549–64.

This article focuses on the surveillance technologies that enable corporate owners and managers to measure and monitor worker activity, and the responses of the labour movement in Canada to ensure protection of privacy rights in new collective agreements. Content analysis of existing agreements reveals that limited attention to surveillance by unions is suggestive of the hierarchy of trade union and worker bargaining priorities. At the same time, the information sectors (which make up the fastest growing sector of the union movement) are more likely to make electronic surveillance a significant priority in negotiating new collective agreements.

3   Rose, N. (1999) *Governing the Soul: The Shaping of the Private Self*, 2nd edn. London: Free Association Books.

Drawing on Foucault's studies of psychology and ethics, and Bruno Latour's notion of governing 'at a distance', Rose argues that the 'soul' is a product of the discourses and techniques in psychology that emerged throughout the mid- to late twentieth century. Focusing on the construction of the self in warfare, industrial productivity and childhood, he contends that the soul is brought into existence through institutional processes and personal interventions. A second edition, published in 1999, offers the reader a more clearly articulated methodological framework and updated reviews of research on governing subjectivity.

4   Gamson, J. (1998) Look at me! Leave me alone! *The American Prospect*, Nov/Dec, p. 78.

The cult of celebrity is based on our obsession to know more and more about the personal details of other people's lives. Tabloids and television talk shows, and increasingly Internet chat rooms, provide a forum for us to channel our curiosities and feed our obsession with the private lives of celebrities, but it has also made us more willing to open up our own lives to the gaze of others. We live in an 'extraordinarily ocular culture', writes Gamson, 'that rewards the looked-at, so it ought not be surprising that lots of people are ready to be watched . . . Being looked at, being visible, being known about, is a currency.' Gamson's essay provokes a new way of thinking about how publics so readily embrace technologies that erode, limit or annihilate their personal privacy.

5   Jones, A. (2004) Social anxiety, sex, surveillance, and the 'safe' teacher, *British Journal of Sociology of Education*, 25(1): 53–66.

Jones situates changes in teacher union policies and practices around teacher–student interaction in relation to Foucault's notion that bodies inscribe the relations of power and control or discipline human interaction. The paper focuses upon social anxieties among New Zealand primary school teachers regarding touching of children. One effect of 'safe distance' relationships between teachers and young students has been an intensification of discipline and self-control by teachers. To be seen as innocent, teachers must be constantly visible – this continually constitutes teachers as categorically suspicious, already guilty and potentially sexually abusive. Teachers' responses have entailed modifying their everyday actions and developing and formalizing new policies to protect them from being accused of inappropriate behaviour.

Note

1   Not all telecommunications firms agreed to participate in the NSA's surveillance project. For example, Qwest refused, making it the darling of the civil liberties movement. For representative media coverage, see National Public Radio (2006) Homeland security in the digital age, (*Talk of the Nation*), 3 January. Available online at: http://www.npr.org/templates/story/story.php?storyId=5080992; and *USA Today* (2006) Telecoms let NSA spy on calls, 6 February, A1.

References

Foucault, M. (1977) *Discipline and Punish: The Birth of the Prison*, Alan Sheridan (trans.). New York: Random House.

Frawley, W., Piatetsky-Shapiro, G. and Matheus, C. (1992) Knowledge discovery in databases: an overview, *AI Magazine*, 13(3): 213–28.

Kiss, S. and Mosco, V. (2005) Negotiating electronic surveillance in the workplace: a study of collective agreements in Canada, *Canadian Journal of Communication*, 30(4); 549–64.

Lyon, D. (1993) An electronic panopticon? A sociological critique of surveillance theory, *Sociological Review*, 41: 653–78.

Rose, N. (1992) Governing the enterprising self, in P. Heelas and P. Morris (eds.) *The Values of Enterprise Culture*. London: Routledge, pp. 141–64.

Stolberg, S.G. (2006) Balancing act by Democrats at hearing, *The New York Times*, 7 February, p. 17.

Walby, K. (2005) Institutional ethnography and surveillance studies: an outline for inquiry, *Surveillance & Society*, 3(2/3): 158–72.

10

Everyday surveillance: personal data and social classifications[1]
by David Lyon

Introduction

Surveillance by electronic means is an increasingly significant mode of governance in so-called knowledge-based or information societies. As Rose nicely puts it, 'surveillance is "designed in" to the flows of everyday life' (1999: 234). Daily routines are now subject to myriad forms of checking, watching, recording and analysing, so much so that we often take for granted the fact that we leave trails and traces wherever we are and whatever we do (Staples 2000). But those trails and traces, however justified, are not innocent. Taken together, they are located within a network of relationships that service us, situate us and help to organize and order our social lives. Surveillance contributes increasingly to the reproduction and reinforcing of social divisions.

Surveillance in this context means a focused attention to personal details aimed at exerting an influence over or managing the objects of the data, or 'data subjects' as they are sometimes called. Although the word surveillance often has connotations of threat, it involves inherently ambiguous processes that should not be considered in a merely negative light. Much everyday convenience, efficiency and security depends upon surveillance. Moreover, it occurs in a world where other kinds of 'mediated visibility' (Thompson 1995: chapter 4) – particularly through television, but also using webcams and so on – are available, and have a variety of effects. Surveillance is just one aspect of this mediated world. It also exhibits both hard and soft faces, which need to be distinguished. Nonetheless, surveillance does also raise questions about power, citizenship and technological development, and about information policy, regulation and resistance.

In what follows, I offer a straightforward and simple argument about everyday surveillance but one that is at odds in some significant respects with other treatments of the same themes. I argue, for example, that the rise of routinized, systematic surveillance has rather mundane origins that should not in the first place be construed as socially sinister. Surveillance is seen here as a response to the 'disappearing body' from integrative social relationships, enabled by modern means of communication and information-handling. The outcomes of this process, however, are not inconsequential as far as social order and social control are concerned. The rise of invisible information infrastructures that facilitate the classification and processing of personal data and the increasing porousness of their storage containers generate distinctive questions about everyday surveillance. These questions invite critical responses, ones that go well beyond the conventional discourses of privacy that are so often trotted out as counterpoints to surveillance.

How did surveillance become so central?

For most of human history, most social interaction has been face-to-face. I say 'has been' rather than 'was' to emphasize the point that face-to-face interaction continues to be significant. But communication that takes place with the other person or persons present . . . has been supplemented by many forms of communication that do not involve co-presence and that are stretched over space. It is a key feature of modernity that using new media of communication people can interact and even remain in relationships that are integrated with others despite being divided by distance.

Fresh forms of interaction have developed as a result of this stretching of relations over space and, in some ways, over time. The new technologies are implicated in those new relationships, just because they are the means that enable them. The forms of relationship are not caused by the new technologies (which often have different uses and effects than those intended by their producers and their proponents) but the new technologies mediate them. It is striking, for example, that neither the telephone nor the Internet were conceived as means of helping ordinary people to chat with each other but that is just how they have come to be used (Marvin 1988; Slevin 2000). Some forms of mediated interaction have emerged over the past two centuries that are much less obviously reciprocal than phone calls or e-mail conversations. One thinks of the so-called mass media, where messages may be largely one-way, but where people are nonetheless linked in communication and symbolic exchange. Today, of course, phone-in shows on the radio and e-mail responses to television shows or newspaper articles increase the dialogical possibilities of these media.

I mention this variety of new kinds of mediated relationships to indicate that surveillance is just one among many forms of communication that have emerged as face-to-face relations of co-presence have been supplemented by so many others (Lyon 1997). So, what is special about surveillance? I suggest that as new technologies enabled more and more to be done at a distance, some compensations are sought for the fading face, the disappearing body. In earlier times, suitable compensations included a signature or a seal on a letter to authenticate its personal origin. But in the increasingly complex social settings of modernity, other tokens of trust were sought, to make up for the lack of visual, body clues and cues, such as handshakes, eye contact, and so on. Of course, the tokens of trust were sought by powerful institutions as well as in more informal contexts, which is why a critical analysis is called for.

By the twentieth century, not only the passport (Torpey 2000) or national identification papers, but also other forms of documentary evidence were required for administrative and commercial purposes: for identification at school, the workplace or to police, for admission to certain sites, to obtain cash from a bank or to pay for purchases, tokens of trust, of worthiness, of authentication. Today our wallets and

purses are stuffed with credit cards, membership numbers, phonecards, social insurance cards, driver's licences, library cards, health cards and loyalty club cards that can
either be used when no other body is present for the transaction – say, at a bank
machine – or when the other party is a complete stranger who needs some kind of
validation for the exchange to take place.

The body has steadily disappeared from these relations but communication
continues, at a distance, mediated overwhelmingly today by electronic means. From
the point of view of the organization or agency that issues the magnetic strip, the
barcode or the PIN, of course, the process of checking for inclusion or of verifying
identity is a means of classifying and categorizing data subjects. What of the view the
other way? Personal data may be released – wittingly or unwittingly – by those to
whom they refer and communicated to others (the bank, the welfare department, the
airline) who have some interest in them. These data are likely to be the basis of
communication with the data-subjects as well but beyond this, the data are frequently
combined in new ways and communicated between machines much more than with
data subjects. What happens to those data as they are processed is largely unknown
by data subjects, although some of it may be guessed when the road-toll invoice,
personalized advertising or spam (electronic junk mail) appears in the mailbox or on
the screen.

Paradoxes abound. Privacy, which so often is felt to be endangered by these
developments, can equally be considered as a key generator of surveillance. As the
more anonymous arrangements of the modern 'society of strangers' emerged, and
privacy was more valued, so the reciprocal need for tokens of trust grew as a means of
maintaining the integrity of relations between those strangers (Nock 1993). As the
locally-known, embodied person slid from view in the web of social relations, so
the importance of credentials, identification and other documentary evidence was
amplified. The other paradox, as I have hinted, is that the same process displays quite
different faces. The means of keeping trust between strangers are at the same time the
means of keeping track of the details of daily life. Privacy produces surveillance that,
it is said, threatens privacy. But not only privacy. As surveillance became a central,
constitutive component of modernity, so it became increasingly a social ordering
device on a steadily greater scale. This happened as more and more bureaucratic
organizations undertook surveillance activities in order to maximize their efficiency
and their efficacy. Keeping track is a crucial means of ensuring organizational efficiency, as Max Weber classically demonstrated (Dandeker 1990). But keeping track
requires more and more sophisticated means of classification and categorization, that
both feeds on surveillance data and stimulates the organizational appetite for them . . .

Surveillance depends, then, on information infrastructures, invisible frameworks
that order the data according to certain criteria, purposes and interests. In the later
twentieth century, information infrastructures were decisively computerized, which
simultaneously made them even less visible and even more powerful, and also produced some specific kinds of coding (Lessig 1999). The kinds of interests behind
social classifications expanded to include not only government departments and
policing or security services, but also a multitude of commercial organizations as
well (Gandy 1993; Lyon 1994). Beyond this, particular kinds of agencies have
become prominent – above all insurance companies – and their interests often

transcend those of either governmental or commercial domains. They have become, albeit as an unintended consequence of their activities, very powerful social actors on the contemporary landscape (Strange 1996).

To take just one example, there is plenty of evidence that insurance companies contribute strongly to police work in Canada. As Richard V. Ericson and Kevin D. Haggerty show, the 'risk logics' and classification schemes of external institutions such as insurance companies profoundly influence the police, who become in effect knowledge workers for them. Insurance demands lead to a shift from territories to classes of populations with varying risk levels. Biographical data are sought on populations in order to profile them in terms of probabilities and possibilities, which makes surveillance more and more systematic. Computerization simply extends the whole process such that in the end, they claim that:

> Coercive control gives way to contingent categorization. Knowledge of risk is more important than moral culpability and punishment. Innocence declines, and everyone is assumed to be 'guilty' until the risk communication system reveals otherwise.
>
> (Ericson and Haggerty 1997: 449)

But it is not merely that information infrastructures have significant connections with the rise of risk management and insurance classifications. Information infrastructures also enable the expansion of surveillance capacities (Rule 1973) in several important respects. The first is that they allow for plug-ins from other sorts of technological devices ... Two of the plug-ins that I have in mind are video and closed circuit television (CCTV) surveillance on the one hand, and biometrics and genetic surveillance on the other. The one has to do with the visibility of body behaviours, including in some cases the recognition of body identities, and the other, with personal identification using unique body parts and the prediction of behaviours and conditions from reading genetic sequences.

It is important to note that these plug-ins depend upon the information infrastructure for their heightened surveillance capacities. For while in their own right each may contribute in specific ways to the augmenting of surveillance ... it is their dependence on computer-based information infrastructures that give them their peculiar power. Without the assistance of complex and sophisticated data processing power, these new technologies would remain relatively weak as means of surveillance. From the point of view of policy, this is a telling development because at present the level of unquestioning acceptance of information and communication technologies is far higher than that of ethical and political critique and assessment.

The second way that information infrastructures tend to bolster surveillance capacities is that they enable networked communication between different databases. Whereas once it was fairly safe to assume that personal records kept for purposes such as health, policing, social insurance, banking and driver licensing would be stored in relatively watertight containers, the computerization of these records means that they are readily amenable to different forms of integration. Given the immense value placed on personal data, both for commercial exploitation and for risk management, huge pressure is placed on these containers to yield their secrets in shareable ways . . .

A related issue of what might be called 'floating data' is that as some dot.com firms have failed, their databases of personal records are among the assets that can be sold off to pay creditors. So, for instance, when in 2000 a defunct company called ToySmart.com tried to sell its personal data they were challenged, and obliged to sell only the entire website, and only to a related company (Stellin 2000). Other cases may not come to light, or may be less clear cut. Again, there are both technical and legal limits to this in most jurisdictions (Flaherty 1989, Bennett, 1992) but this does not mean that the leaky containers will suddenly stop data seeping from one to the other.

One of the key characteristics of what Manuel Castells calls the 'network society' is precisely that it is a 'space of flows' (Castells 1996: 412). Along with the nodes and hubs in the system, dominant groups determine how and in what interests the material infrastructure operates. Among the sequences of exchange and interaction that form the flows are surveillance data, risk communication and personal information, and they, no less than any other flows, circulate according to logics embedded in asymmetries of organizational power. Concrete examples of this are offered by Norris and Armstrong (1999: 8) in discussing closed circuit television (CCTV). Soccer stadia are under the camera's eye to check for (likely signs of) disorder, workplaces are watched to ensure compliance with health and safety regulations, and city centres are monitored to create and maintain ideal conditions for consumption. Differing dominant groups ensure the dispersal of discipline and its undulating, shifting quality as different sectional interests each play their part.

One outcome of this that should not be overlooked is that so-called information societies are thus by their very constitution also surveillance societies. Surveillance societies are not an accidental or malevolent result of perverse developments within information societies. Information societies – or, perhaps better, network societies (Castells 1998) – in which advanced electronics-based information infrastructures are a central means of co-ordination and exchange, operate by means, among other things, of advanced surveillance operations. But they are not necessarily *maximum* surveillance societies . . . While totalitarian potential is always present, particularly in regimes that already exhibit such tendencies, the more subtle development of surveillance power is more likely.

As understood here, surveillance societies are not characterized by a single all-embracing and all-penetrating system . . . As Norris and Armstrong say of camera surveillance, 'CCTV has been implemented not as one pervasive system but as a series of discrete, localised systems run by a myriad of different organizations rather than a single state monolith' (Norris and Armstrong 1999: 7). The fact that there is no single all-embracing system is no call for complacency, however. The system – or, perhaps better, 'assemblage' (Haggerty and Ericson 2000) – expands and mutates constantly. It is augmented not only within hierarchical organizations of the sort that depict Big Brother overseeing all from the apex or the Panopticon inspector gazing out from the tower, but also, more frequently, within networks that spread horizontally, reaching out here, contracting there, but always finding more ways of seeking and processing personal data with a view to management and influence.

Why does surveillance matter?

Earlier I proposed that surveillance has become a significant means of governance, and of the reinforcing of social difference, and that is why the issues are important. I do not wish to downplay the fears of those who may feel that their privacy may be impugned or invaded by new kinds of surveillance technologies. They are real fears and deserve to be addressed, but to consider only personal fears about privacy distracts us from the public issues surrounding surveillance (Regan 1995). By suggesting that surveillance has become a means of governance, I mean that it serves to organize social relationships and contributes to patterns of social ordering. It does so largely through what Michel Foucault called biopower, making people up by classifying them according to categories . . .

Categorizing is an ancient process but became crucial to the rationalized social organization of modernity. Through social convention and custom people accept their place within the hierarchy or learn to see themselves in relation to the status of others. What happens when traditional lines of authority and relationship are dismantled, to be replaced by bureaucratic rules and organizational practices? These too, are eventually accepted, even though they may now be seen as much more mutable . . . As the body disappears from integrative social relationships, and is replaced by abstract tokens, so the categories too become more abstract and actuarial, and thus apparently benign. When information scientists design, delegate and choose classification systems they seldom see them as 'embodying moral and aesthetic choices that in turn craft people's identities, aspirations, and dignity' (Bowker and Star 1999: 4). But as Suchman pithily notes, 'categories have politics' (1994).

The massive systems of computer-assisted classification that have been developed over the past thirty years are the taken-for-granted infrastructure of informational societies. They represent a concatenation of standards, practices and codes that are more or less interconnected, such that – in the case of the surveillance classifications considered here – personal and population data flows constantly through the nodes and hubs of the network. Though obvious asymmetries of power exist, no one person or body is in charge of surveillance systems; no one person or body can change them. Yet, they help to make us up, to naturalize us to the institutions and agencies that invent and elaborate the categories. And they help to create the sense of who and what is rightly included and excluded; who is this, that, or other (Bourdieu 1984: 470–8). Of course, it is an empirical question as to how far and under what conditions people accept as their own the categories in which they are placed by contemporary surveillance systems (Jenkins 2000). This is a reflexive process. But the history of medical, moral, criminal and consumer categorization suggests that plenty of people accept such labels and live likewise.

. . . I am not suggesting that classification and surveillance are socially negative processes. They are necessary aspects of all social situations and serve social purposes, from the vital to the vicious. The point is that as powerful means of governance, of social ordering, they are also increasingly invisible and easily taken-for granted. The risk management (and other) classifications of surveillance societies involve categories that are inherently political, that call for ethical inspection. I am not suggesting either that such classifications are each powerful in the same way. Surveillance as understood here exists on a long continuum along which data is collected and processed for a range of purposes from policing and security to consumption and entertainment. It produces categorical suspicion at one end (such as ethnic profiling at airport security checks) and categorical seduction (such as targeting of potential car rental customers from lists of airline loyalty club members) at the other. Cities are increasingly splintered into socio-economically divided consumption and security enclaves by these practices (Graham and Marvin 2001). But either way, the categories have ethics; the codes have politics.

This, then, is why surveillance matters. It does indeed provoke privacy concerns from time to time. But, as expressed, these personal concerns are frequently temporary and contingent ones, often relating to mistakes and errors in databases or telecommunications systems, or to loss of access to the tokens of trust such as credit cards or driver's licenses. They are not high on any political agenda. And when, for example, surveyed Internet users claim to care about online privacy, it turns out, paradoxically, that the very same persons key-in PINs and credit card numbers online! (*Washington Post* 2000.) They want the benefits of e-commerce even if they also want assurances that their personal details are secure and not being used for purposes beyond the immediate transaction. When it comes to legal restrictions on surveillance, whether construed as data protection or as privacy laws, it is usually the data-subject who has to make an appeal. The law only acts as a guarantee of some right to self-protection. This is why legal limits, though not insignificant, scarcely scratch the surface of the social issues raised by rapidly rising surveillance levels in everyday life . . .

What can be done about surveillance?

It would make sense if some social practices and technological systems that affect everyone were also understood and actively negotiated by everyone. Such is not the case. All too often, convenience and efficiency are all that get noticed in systems that have surveillance aspects, with the result that data subjects are often unaware of the broader discriminatory and classificatory dimensions of such systems. Data protection and privacy policy and legislation have made significant strides in recent decades, even though in some cases they may be minimalist and even cynical. Data protection and privacy remain vital concerns, even if their impact on the negative aspects of social categorization does not yet amount to much. On the other hand, what I refer to as minimalism would be seen in rules that allow only for a right of self-protection, and cynicism may be evident in cases where laws have been enacted in order to facilitate business with a trading partner rather than out of actual concern with the effects on the lives and prospects of data-subjects.

At the same time, surveillance does not simply go on behind people's backs. We participate in and actively – though not always consciously – trigger the data-capture by making telephone calls, using credit cards, passing our hands over entry scanners, claiming benefits, walking down the camera-watched street, surfing the net, and so on. Not enough is known about how people in everyday life comply with, negotiate and resist surveillance. But it is clear that workers are cautious if not negative about some electronic devices such as video, audio and computer-use monitoring, not to mention the use of biometric and genetic checks and screens. People using public spaces such as streets and private ones such as shopping malls are aware of and avoid or play up to closed circuit television systems and video surveillance. Users of Web-based e-mail accounts and online shoppers are often wary of divulging personal data, when requested to do so, especially when those data seem to have little to do with the immediate transaction in question. They are aware that some other data image of them circulates in cyberspace and may well accept this as the price paid for some benefit or reward.

But it is not enough to assume that over time people will somehow 'get wise to' mushrooming surveillance systems. Such systems are a largely uninspected and unregulated means of social classification, of social ordering. They affect people's chances and their choices, and as such demand to be recognized. Beyond this, their growth calls for ethical scrutiny and democratic involvement. Of course, there is an ambiguity to all such systems. Of course, surveillance exhibits more than one face. But the face that is publicized is that of the smoothly running organization, the rapid response to consumer demands or to security calls, the flexibility of the management structure, and not the negative and possibly undesirable aspects of personal data processing. The discriminatory power of contemporary surveillance is wielded by large organizations that have strong interests in valuable personal data. The persons from whom such data are abstracted face a built-in disadvantage in this respect.

Various kinds of responses to surveillance have emerged over the past two or three decades. They may be thought of as regulative and mobilizing responses (Lyon [2001]: chapter 8). The first is seen most obviously in the various data protection and privacy laws that now exist in most countries dependent on information infrastructures. But it is also evident in a number of voluntary, market and technical remedies for what is most usually construed as threats to privacy. Voluntary measures include company-based adherence to fair information principles. Most banks and many website operators proactively offer details of their 'privacy policies' today. Market solutions include the growing idea of making personal data earn the equivalent of royalties, such that the data subject has a tangible return for the use of his or her abstracted data. Technical solutions are various, and often relate to security. The most publicized example is that of the electronic signature.

'Fair Information Principles' (that require those collecting data to use them only for the purposes stated and not for others, to obtain only that which is nedeed for their immediate purposes and to ensure that the data has been obtained with the knowledge and consent of the data subject, and so on) to which most privacy legislation makes reference, do not address directly the issue of the categorization carried out by surveillance systems. They depend, implicitly but importantly, on the idea that data-subjects may have an interest in controlling the flow of personal information about them. This relates to an ethically appropriate desire to disclose oneself to others only in a voluntary and limited way, and within relations of trust. And it must be said that such fair information practices, when installed, may well mitigate some negative effects of discriminatory categorization . . .

Mobilizing responses, on the other hand, have grown in number and volume since the 1980's. Non-government groups and consumer movements have attempted to get to grips with the realities of the rhizomic expansion of surveillance. They may take the form of organized protest or watchdog groups – such as Privacy International or the Electronic Privacy Information Center – or *ad hoc* responses to specific issues. Thus, attempts to create an electronic 'Australia Card' for all citizens in the mid-1980s spawned a social movement that successfully turned down the proposal, as did similar, later attempts in South Korea. Campaigns have also been mounted against specific firms and products such as the Lotus 'Marketplace: Households' software in 1994, or the Intel Pentium III chip with its unique identifier for all computers, in 1999. The use of the Internet to mobilize resistance is an important part of the process.

These mobilizing responses may point the way to new modes of negotiating and resisting negatively construed aspects of surveillance in the twenty-first century. It is the codes, both symbolic and electronically inscribed, that provide the means for surveillance power to flow. As Deleuze (1986) argues, physical barriers and constraint within places matter less today than the codes that enable and disable, admit and exclude, accredit or discredit . . . As Melucci (1996) observes, social movements today are increasingly concerned with perceiving risks and identifying them as public issues, with a process of 'challenging codes'. He argues that as everyday concerns about personal identification and life-chances become more obviously set against global flows of data and of power, new kinds of oppositional politics will emerge, appropriate to the 'information age' . . .

The question, 'what can be done?' may thus be answered practically rather than abstractly. Many responses to surveillance have emerged and are emerging, as I suggested above, this is entirely appropriate given the increasing monitoring of everyday life. While the lead, in some instances, may be taken by legal initiatives, other responses are also called for, at many levels. The law, at best, can only help to create a culture of carefulness about the processing of personal data, it cannot possibly speak to all issues, let alone keep up with each development in data mining, profiling, database targeting and marketing, locational tracking of vehicles or cellphones, and so on.

Conspiratorial and paranoid responses are counter-productive, not least because negative aspects of surveillance often arise as unintended consequences or by-products of other acceptable or unquestionable processes of risk management or marketing. They are also inappropriate to situations of networked, rhizomic surveillance, where no panoptic inspection tower and no omnipotent Big Brother exists. Rather, constant vigilance on the part of government departments, companies, advocacy and consumer groups, and ordinary users and citizens is called for, especially in light of the panic regimes consequent on the terrorist attacks of 11 September 2001. Focused ethical attention, along with serious proposals for democratic accountability, and educational and awareness-raising initiatives, are needed if everyday surveillance is properly to be understood, and when necessary, confronted and challenged.

Note

1   This chapter is an extract from D. Lyon (2002) Everyday surveillance: personal data and social classifications, *Information, Communication & Society*, 51(1): 1–16.

References

Bennett, C. (1992) *Regulating Privacy: Data Protection and Public Policy in Europe and the United States*. Ithaca: Cornell University Press.

Bourdieu, P. (1984) *Distinction: A Social Critique of the Judgement of Taste*. London and New York: Routledge.

Bowker, G. and Star, S. L. (1999) *Sorting Things Out: Classification and its Consequences*. Cambridge, MA: MIT Press.

Castells, M. (1996) *The Rise of the Network Society*. Oxford and Malden, MA: Blackwell.

Castells, M. (1998) Materials for an exploratory theory of the network society, *British Journal of Sociology*, 51(1): 5–24.

Dandeker, C. (1990) *Surveillance, Power, and Modernity*. Cambridge: Polity Press.

Deleuze, G. (1986) Postscript on the societies of control, *October*, 59: 3–7.

Ericson, R. V. and Haggerty, K. (1997) *Policing the Risk Society*. Toronto: University of Toronto Press.

Flaherty, D. (1989) *Protecting Privacy in Surveillance Societies*. Chapel Hill: University of North Carolina Press.

Gandy, O. H. (1993) *The Panoptic Sort: A Political Economy of Personal Information*. Boulder, CO: Westview.

Graham, S. and Marvin, S. (2001) *Splintering Urbanism: Networked Infrastructures, Technological Mobilities, and the Urban Condition*. London and New York: Routledge.

Haggerty, K. and Ericson, R. V. (2000) The surveillant assemblage, *British Journal of Sociology*, 51(4): 605–22.

Jenkins, R. (2000) Categorization: identity, social process, and epistemology, *Current Sociology*, 48(3): 7–25.

Lessig, L. (1999) *Code and Other Laws of Cyberspace*. New York: Basic Books.

Lyon, D. (1994) *The Electronic Eye: The Rise of Surveillance Society*. Cambridge: Polity Press; Malden, MA: Blackwell.

Lyon, D. (1997) Cyberspace sociality: controversies over computer-mediated communication, in B. Loader (ed.) *The Governance of Cyberspace*. London and New York: Routledge, pp. 23–37.

Lyon, D. (2001) *Surveillance Society: Monitoring Everyday Life*. Buckingham: Open University Press.

Marvin, C. (1988) *When Old Technologies Were New*. Oxford and New York: Oxford University Press.

Melucci, A. (1996) *Challenging Codes: Collective Action in the Information Age*. Cambridge, New York and Melbourne: Cambridge University Press.

Nock, S. L. (1993) *The Costs of Privacy: Surveillance and Reputation in America*. New York: Walter de Gruyter.

Norris, C, and Armstrong, G. (1999) *The Maximum Surveillance Society: The Rise of CCTV*. London: Berg.

Regan, P. (1995) *Legislating Privacy: Technology, Surveillance, and Public Policy*. Chapel Hill: University of North Carolina Press.

Rose, N. (1999) *Powers of Freedom: Reframing Political Thought*. Cambridge, New York and Mclbourne: Cambridge University Press.

Rule, J. (1973) *Private Lives, Public Surveillance*. Harmondsworth: Allen Lane.

Slevin, J. (2000) *The Internet and Society*. Cambridge: Polity Press.

Staples, W. G. (2000) *Everyday Surveillance: Vigilance and Visibility in Postmodern Life*. Lanham MD: Rowman and Littlefield.

Stellin, S. (2000) Dot-com liquidations put consumer data in limbo, *The New York Times*, 4 December.

Strange, S. (1996) *The Retreat of the State: The Diffusion of Power in the World Economy.* Cambridge, New York and Melbourne: Cambridge University Press.

Suchman, L. (1994) Do categories have politics? The language/interaction perspective reconsidered, *Computer-Supported Cooperative Work*, 2: 177–90.

Thompson, J. (1995) *The Media and Modernity.* Cambridge: Polity Press.

Torpey, J. (2000) *The Invention of the Passport: Surveillance, Citizenship, and the State.* Cambridge, New York and Melbourne: Cambridge University Press.

Washington Post (2000) Internet users seek assurances over on-line use of personal data, *Washington Post*, 20 August. Available online at: http://washingtonpost.com/wp-dyn/articles/A60984–2000Aug20.html>

11

Data mining and surveillance in the post-9/11 environment[1]
by Oscar H. Gandy

In his wildly successful book on the future of cyberspace Lawrence Lessig (1999) responded to a general challenge to privacy activists: tell us what is different about surveillance in the computer age. Lessig suggested that the difference is to be seen in the ease with which the data generated from the routine monitoring of our behaviour can be stored, and then searched at some point in the future.

Indeed, because more and more of our daily life involves interactions and transactions that generate electronic records, our lives become fixed in media that can be examined and reviewed at will. Lessig and others who are concerned about threats to privacy (Lyon, [2001]) have identified the countless ways in which our behaviour in public places, as well as in the privacy of our homes, generates records that come to reside in the computers of corporations and government agencies.

As Lessig suggests, while a sales clerk in the local store might take note of a shopper's interest in different pieces of jewellery or clothing as she makes her way from counter to counter, their monitoring does not generate a searchable record of each of her visits to the store. Indeed, unless they are security guards, and she is looking particularly suspicious that day, the guards usually don't follow her from floor to floor. It is only when she actually purchases those socks or gloves that a searchable record is made. However, the generation of searchable records of 'transactions' in electronic network environments (cyberspace) is many times more extensive than it is in the world of bricks and mortar. Web servers generate a record each time a visitor clicks on a banner ad, or follows a link in order to learn more about some commodity or service.

In addition, because of the ways in which Web technology facilitates the linkage of records, the click streams, or mouse droppings that surfers leave behind as they browse around much of the Web, make it easy for marketing service providers like DoubleClick to develop a cumulative record (Sovern, 1999). Because DoubleClick manages the serving of ads for several thousand publishers on the Web, individual profiles may contain information about a broad range of goods and services about which an individual may have indicated some interest.

Because the cost of storing data in electronic form continues to drop . . . there is less of an incentive for organizations to discard any transaction-generated information

(Gates, 1999). The problem that businesses and government agencies are then left with is determining how to make sense of these growing mountains of data (Green et al., 1999).

Enter the mathematical wizards who brought us both the bell curve and the ballistic missile, and *voilà!* we have the science of data mining, or as the specialists would prefer, the science of Knowledge Discovery in Databases.

Data mining, as a tool for the discovery of meaningful patterns in data, is the product of some rapidly developing techniques in the field of applied statistical analysis. Of particular importance for those of us who are concerned about the implications of data mining for individual and collective privacy, is the fact that data mining software, products, and services are being introduced into the market place by a large number of competing vendors. The increasing sophistication of these software packages, and the rapidly declining prices for custom, as well as off-the-shelf data mining products mean that these techniques will soon be in widespread use (Danna & Gandy, 2002).

In addition, governments' heightened concern with security following the events of September 11, 2001 (9/11) means that an infusion of tax dollars for research and development is likely to attract a swarm of competitors. We can expect this increase in demand to support an even more rapid development of the capacity of data mining programs to produce strategic 'intelligence' from what would ordinarily be meaningless bits of data stored in remote computers around the globe. The consequences of such a development are quite troubling, and they are the focus of this chapter . . .

Data mining

. . . The goal of any data mining exercise is the extraction of meaningful intelligence, or knowledge, from the patterns that emerge within a database after it has been cleaned, sorted and processed. The routines that are part of a data mining effort are in some ways similar to the methods that are used to extract precious minerals from the soil. However, whereas the extraction of precious metals is often labour intensive, and represents risks to both workers and the environment, the extraction of intelligence from computer databases is increasingly automated in ways that reduce the direct risks to labour at the same time that they amplify the risks to society in general. Indeed, as I will argue, the impact of data mining on the social environment may, in the long run, be more destructive than strip mining for coal.

Imagine if you can, the mountains of transactional data that are generated each time a consumer purchases commodities that have been marked with universal product codes (UPCs). When consumers use credit or cheque verification cards, or any of a number of retail vendors' discount cards, individually identifiable information is captured and linked with the details of those purchases. There is little wonder that large retail chains like Wal-Mart have been forced to invest substantial resources in the development of data warehouses to allow them to extract some of the hidden value in the terabits of data being generated each day throughout their expanding global networks (Gates, 1999, p. 232).

Our interactions with government agencies, as well as with the component parts of the massive health care system, also generate detailed records. However, because these data are not gathered in standard forms with classification schemes akin to the UPC code, there are tremendous pressures within these industries to move toward greater standardization and comparability across transactions (Bowker & Star, 1999).

Although progress is being made somewhat more slowly in translating voice messages into text for automated processing, no such barriers exist for classifying e-mail text or the posts that are made to newsgroups. The textual components of Web pages are also relatively easy to classify and describe, although the graphics on those pages still represent something of a problem for developers.

Even more problematic, in terms of the need to develop common codes and classification standards, is the digitized output of surveillance cameras. However, it seems likely that the rate of success in developing classification techniques in this arena will increase substantially in response to research and development initiatives rushed through the legislature in response to the events of 9/11.

The goals of data mining

In general, data mining efforts are directed toward the generation of rules for the classification of objects. These objects might be people who are assigned to particular classes or categories, such as 'that group of folks who tend to make impulse buys from those displays near the checkout counters at the supermarket'.

The generation of rules may also be focused on discriminating, or distinguishing between two related, but meaningfully distinct classes, such as 'those folks who nearly always use coupons', and 'those who tend to pay full price'.

Among the most common forms of analysis are those that seek to discover the associative rules that further differentiate between clients or customers. For example, video rental stores seem to be interested in discovering what sorts of movies tend to be rented together, and what sorts of movies tend to be associated with the sale of microwave popcorn or candy.

In an attempt to develop reliable sorting tools, data miners seek to discover patterns of association between demographic characteristics and a host of commercial behaviours. Discriminant analyses within the commercial sphere are often applied to the task of differentiating between high-value and low-value customers. For example, in the case of urban retailers negotiating the placement of radio advertisements, this sort of analysis may help them to determine what sorts of ads are more likely to generate 'prospects, rather than suspects' (Ofori, 1999, sec. 2, p. 27). That is, advertisers make use of strategic assessments based on estimates of the racial composition of the audiences they purchase access to when buying broadcast time. These choices are based on the belief that African-American and Hispanic youth are more likely to steal than to purchase certain retail products.

Businesses seek to maximize profits by minimizing risk. They do this by identifying individuals, who, by virtue of their profiles, ratings, or comparative scores, should probably be ignored, avoided or treated with the utmost deference and respect. Some business service providers may also rely upon the pattern recognition features of data mining programs to determine whether a credit card is likely to have been stolen, or if the legitimate owner of the card is at increased risk of default, or is likely to make a fraudulent claim . . .

Risk management takes on a slightly different character when the decision makers are involved in the protection of public safety or 'national security'. Data mining specialists at the MITRE Corporation described one project that involved developing a strategy for identifying or targeting vehicles for inspection by law enforcement officers (Rothleder, Harris & Bloedorn, (n.d.)). The challenges involved in selecting one vehicle from among many are presented as being similar to the problems involved in discovering patterns in aircraft accidents that would allow risk managers to identify the 'precursors' of dangerous situations in the air.

In the aviation example, an analysis of accident descriptions derived from on-board data recorders, or in the transcripts of witnesses, might reveal a meaningful pattern. For example, an analysis of accident reports might produce a suggestion that accidents often occurred following an indication in the records of air traffic controller commentary that the plane 'veered to the left following take-off'. Further analyses of accident records might indicate that such references were also more likely to be made when a particular class of malfunctions occurred under winter weather conditions. Each accident that is accompanied with a voice record provides data that can be transformed into text which can be searched for keywords, or terms that become more meaningful with each recorded accident. Over time, such terms become associated with a specific technical problem, while at the same time they can be distinguished from other terms or phrases that might indicate a mistake, or a pilot error. Ideally, the analysis of subsequent accidents adds to the power of the explanatory models that data mining helps to produce.

In the case of motor vehicle targeting, the focus of the data mining effort is slightly different. Here the effort is directed towards identifying the attributes of both the driver and the vehicle, as both are parts of the profile that is used to identify likely targets. In the case of airplane accidents, each one is examined in great detail. Not all automobiles are stopped, and all those stopped are not subject to detailed examination. However, each time a vehicle is subjected to a more detailed inspection, considerably more information is added to the pool of data about drivers and vehicles. Clearly the sorts of data that can be gathered during a full inspection, to say nothing of the data that might be gathered after an arrest, are substantially different from data that can be gathered on the basis of observation of a moving vehicle, or a cursory inspection of a vehicle when stopped.

Much has been written about the use of a driver's race as an element in the profiles used by state police to identify vehicles they believe are likely to be involved in the transportation of contraband drugs (Allen-Bell, 1997). Because of the adverse public response to the use of race as a predictor, data mining efforts are being turned toward finding other cues that the police may find to be equally useful, but less politically sensitive, indicators of a basis for justifying a non-random stop and search.

Data mining technology

The technology of data mining becomes more sophisticated with each passing day. Neural networks are just one of the more sophisticated analytical resources being used more widely in data mining applications. Neural nets are said to mimic the ways in which the human brain processes information. These systems learn, or become more accurate, over time. An experience-based learning model attaches and adjusts the weights that are applied to different attributes or variables in response to each correct and incorrect prediction or determination.

A common application of neural networks by insurers is in support of fraud detection. In deciding whether a reported accident could have been staged, an analytical model is likely to have been developed on the basis of an assessment of detailed records from thousands of reported accidents. A relatively small proportion of these accident reports will have been determined to be fraudulent. At each iteration in the development cycle, varying weights will be assigned to potentially relevant factors such as the age and gender of the driver. As the model is developed, other, potentially more reliable, indicators may emerge. It will matter, for example, whether the injured party called an attorney. More importantly, perhaps, information about whether the claimant's physician was called before or after the attorney was called, might be added to the model. As usual, the desired outcome is an improved ability to make a prediction, and provide an estimate of its accuracy. The decision support system asks 'How likely is a particular item to be a fraudulent claim?' It is up to the client or user of the software to decide whether or not to just pay the claim, or risk angering the insured by requesting additional information about the accident . . .

Commercially available data mining software

A number of firms have begun to offer data mining services and software products that are supposed to make it easier for Web-based marketers to transform transaction-generated data into intelligence that can be used to facilitate customer segmentation. Well-defined segmentation schemes often become the primary resource of a marketing campaign. Among the leaders of this emerging market are firms with names like digiMine, Accrue, NetGenesis and Personify. These firms provide analytical services to Web-based companies.

The emerging market also includes familiar providers of statistical software such as SPSS (Statistical Package for the Social Sciences), which includes neural networks and rule induction features in its Clementine Service resource. Some comprehensive software packages, or client service products, are designed to facilitate customer relationship management (CRM). Within marketing circles the philosophy of CRM is no longer one of capturing the largest share of the market; rather it is capturing the largest share of the most valuable customer's business (Peppers & Rogers, 1997). This is an orientation to the market that reflects a belief that 20 per cent of a firm's customers will provide 80 per cent of its revenue. Corporate strategists believe that capturing that revenue can be assured only by 'growing the customer' through 'cross-selling' . . .

Increased demand for data mining tools

While the firms that are providing the bulk of these data mining products and services will continue to try and shape consumer demand through aggressive marketing, they are also likely to realize something of a windfall in terms of the increased attention to the development and implementation of data mining applications following the events of 9/11.

Less than a week after the assault on the Pentagon and the World Trade Center towers, an article in the business section of *USA Today* asked, 'What can tech companies do?' Jump-start the development and implementation of data mining techniques, was the unequivocal response. One executive from one of a handful of still-active Internet communications firms suggested that '[we] are experts at data mining and we have vast resources of data to mine. We have used it to target advertising. We can probably use it to identify suspicious activity or potential terrorists' (Maney, 2001, p. 613). This executive was probably referring to applications such as 'Online Preference Marketing' (OPM), through which an Internet user's browsing activities are classified into 'types of inferred interests or behaviors that may be attractive to advertisers' (Agreement, 2002, p. 7). It seems likely that it was one or more 'volunteers' within the communications industry who provided the information that was used to identify some of the so-called 'material witnesses' in the United States detained by the FBI. The primary change, of course, would be the development of indicators and categories that would be of interest to government offices charged with insuring 'homeland security' in the US (*National Strategy*, 2002).

Much more cautious responses were offered by other technology developers who suggested that we were probably still years away from the kinds of data mining technology that might have allowed us to predict and interrupt the plans of the hijackers (Maney, 2001). Nevertheless, in response to what they perceived to be a continuing threat of terrorism, the Pentagon announced a major initiative designed to speed the development of technologies that could actually be deployed in the 'war against terrorism' within 12–18 months (Streitfeld & Piller, 2002).

At the top of the government's wish list was an appeal for 'ideas to identify and track down suspected terrorists, and to predict their future behavior'. This goal was linked with a desire to 'develop an integrated information base and a family of data mining tools and analysis aids'. What the Pentagon was looking for was an analytical resource that would assist in the

> identification of patterns, trends, and models of behavior of terrorist groups and individuals . . . The system would allow 'what if' type modeling of events and behavioral patterns and result in predictive analysis products.

Ideally, the Pentagon sought a system that could efficiently scan data in the nation's computer networks and if they 'discover that a member of an extremist group also bought explosives and visited a Web site about building demolition, they might be able to halt a potential attack' (France et al., 2001) . . .

There are of course a great many reasons for being concerned about the sorts of dramatic changes in the ways in which the American government plans to escalate the surveillance of its citizens, their associates, and any visitors who might be defined as threats to the security of the 'homeland' under the broad powers granted under the USA PATRIOT Act (Bowman, 2002). These concerns are multiplied in the face of evidence that the United States government has been able to win compliance, if not active support, for its plans to increase the level of communications and data surveillance to be carried out on the citizens of other nations. Yet, there are, in my view, still more important concerns that are raised by visions of a tidal wave of commercial applications of data mining that will follow rapidly behind a Schumpeterian swarm of innovations (Preston, 2001) brought into being by this most recent activation of the military industrial complex.

The exchange of data mining applications between the government and commercial sectors is likely to be accelerated as a result of increased pressure and latitude for surveillance and data-sharing activities that have been approved under the extensive powers authorized by the USA PATRIOT Act (2001). There is particular concern about the availability of details about individuals' searching of the Web (Bowman, 2002), in that the capture of URLs from public terminals and private computers provides easy access to the content of files accessed by individual users (FBI asks . . ., 2002; Government, Internet Industry, 2002; Madsen, 2001) . . .

Social implications of data mining

Why should the expansion of data mining systems and applications concern us? As I have suggested, data mining systems are designed to facilitate the identification and classification of individuals into distinct groups or segments. From the perspective of the commercial firm, and perhaps for the industry as a whole, we can understand the use of data mining as a discriminatory technology in the rational pursuit of profits. However, as members of societies organized under more egalitarian principles, we have come to the conclusion that even relatively efficient techniques may be banned or limited to the degree that they are accompanied by negative social consequences, or externalities.

For example, Marsha Stepanek (2000) of *Business Week* referred to the application of data mining techniques in electronic commerce as 'Weblining'. I suspect she chose this term precisely because she believed that it would activate the collective distaste that Americans have expressed toward spatial, or geo-demographic, discrimination against neighbourhoods and communities defined by race. Indeed, these are techniques that the courts and legislatures have banned as 'redlining' when used by banks and mortgage firms.

However, because the Internet is only marginally defined by geography (Graham & Marvin, 2001), the 'neighbourhoods' that will be excluded from access to goods and services are primarily conceptual or analytical, rather than spatial. Because of this, the victims of 'Weblining' are less likely to be aware of their status as victims of categorical discrimination. As a result, they will be even less likely to organize as an aggrieved group in order to challenge their exclusion from opportunities in the market place, or in the public sphere.

Let me be clear. There are some people who argue that even the use of race, gender and age as elements within predictive models should be allowed because they are economically efficient (Hausman & McPherson, 1996) . . .

On the other hand, those of us who argue against this sort of discrimination are concerned that if we allow decision makers to use race, and gender, and other markers of group identity as the basis for exclusion from opportunity, then we will only strengthen the correlation between group membership and social status . . .

Of course, it is not only discrimination on the basis of race, gender or age that should concern us. Our concerns should be based more generally on what we understand to be the social consequences that flow from using a decision system that systematically bars members of groups or segments of the population from acquiring the informational resources that are essential to their individual development and their collective participation in the economy and in the public sphere.

As a communications scholar, I am especially sensitive to the use of discriminatory technologies like data mining to determine which people will have access to the information that they need to make sense of the world. When data mining systems are used by companies in the communication or information fields to segment their audiences in the service of profitability rather than the public good, we should assume that disparities in access to information will worsen. Such applications are already available in the market place.

'Digital Silhouettes' is the name used by Predictive Networks for one of their products. The resource uses demographics, including race, to characterize Internet consumers' orientations toward 90 content subcategories that are determined on the basis of the firm's analysis of click stream data. Their promotional materials claim that their 'artificial intelligence engine derives individual preferences from web-surfing behavior'. Their promotion claims that 'over time, as more and more sites are visited, the appropriate level of confidence in the accuracy of the Digital Silhouette is established allowing Predictive Networks to accurately model user preferences, affinities and demographics while protecting their privacy' (Predictive Networks, 2001).

While segmentation and targeting may be efficient, and it may serve the competitive and strategic interests of media organizations and their clients, it is also likely to be destructive of the social fabric. Consider the services provided to advertisers by DoubleClick, Inc. DoubleClick identifies itself as a 'Third-party ad service' (Agreement, 2002). DoubleClick 'derives revenue from its ability to record, analyze and target Online Ads based upon User Data, to "help marketers deliver the right message, to the right person, at the right time, while allowing Web publishers to maximize their revenue and build their business in the process" ' (Agreement, 2002, p. 5) . . .

Segmentation reinforces difference, while it obscures those things we share in common. This is a point that has been made by Cass Sunstein (2001), in his book, *Republic.com*. Although Sunstein suggests that the increasing polarization we observe is the product of consumer choice, I believe he underestimates the influence of strategic marketing.

It is important to remember that access to information is often determined by the kinds of subsidies that advertisers are willing to provide to publishers in order to gain access to the consumers (and I might add, the voters) whom they value the most. Financial support from advertisers not only provides subsidies to the people who need it least, but by withholding support from media that serve the less desirable audiences, these publishers must either deliver a lower quality product, or seek advertisers with less wholesome commodities for sale. Once again, the differences between us are drawn more sharply, and ironically, they seem to make even more sense because they strengthen the correlations between attributes that actually have no genuinely causal links (Gandy, 2001).

So, what are we to do? The standard responses of governmental agencies like the Federal Trade Commission (FTC) to this sort of discriminatory segmentation are, in my view, unlikely to provide much protection from the dangers that are likely to accompany the widespread use of data mining.

Most recently, the orientation of policy makers in the United States has been toward corporate self-governance, and away from regulation. The FTC has emphasized the value of a much-modified standard of 'fair information practices', which is supposed to ensure that the public enjoys 'notice and choice' regarding the collection and use of personal information.

While consumer-oriented legislation may provide some increased security for individuals in their dealings with the health care establishment, and with regard to their children's exploration of the Web, these regulations are for the most part meaningless as a defence against the social harms that data mining represents.

First of all, the dominant privacy framework is one that emphasizes 'individually identified information'. Although much of the talk in policy circles is about the development and use of consumer profiles, the power of data mining lies not in its ability to target specific individuals, but in its ability to increase the benefits to be derived from controlling the behaviour, on the average, of members of well-defined groups . . .

Second, citizens and consumers cannot expect to be meaningfully informed about the uses to which their transaction-generated information will be applied. This is the case, in part, because even those who manage these data warehouses have only the most general awareness of those future uses. As a result, individuals who encounter tokens of 'notice and choice' really only choose between doing without, and providing an unfettered consent for whatever future uses of information a data manager may discover to be relevant.

In general, consumers somewhat naively believe that their interests are being protected in some way by government regulations that guarantee them access to the information about them being held in some database. The idea is that having this access will enable them to challenge the accuracy of the data that have been recorded in these files. I doubt that there is any meaningful way for an individual consumer to understand, much less challenge, the cumulative score they have been assigned by some data mining operation based on neural net technology.

I recall the classic case of one Claire Cherry, a white woman in Georgia who claimed that she had been a victim of discrimination because Amoco denied her a gasoline credit card. It seems that her application had been denied in part because she lived within a zip code that included a high proportion of African-Americans. The problem that Ms Cherry faced was that the scoring system used by Amoco made use of a multivariate model that included 38 variables. Understandably, she was unable to specify the impact that her zip code, and its underlying racial component, actually had on the determination of her credit status (*Claire Cherry*, 1980). Contemporary scoring models use hundreds of variables and, even more problematic from the perspective of today's consumers, many of these analytical models are adjusted continuously in order to incorporate the latest information that recent transactions provide.

It may be possible for privacy advocates to demand that organizations limit the storage of transaction data for longer than is absolutely necessary (Kang, 1998). They may also attempt to limit the use of this information for purposes unrelated to the initial transaction. This sort of use limitation had been applied to US government agencies in the past, but it seems unlikely, however, that one sector of government would seek the elimination of data in its files at the same time that other sectors are trying to require their secure storage, and increased sharing with any who can claim a legitimate interest. Although the Foreign Intelligence Surveillance Court was extremely critical of the intelligence-sharing proposals of the FBI (United States, 2002), the US Attorney General has enjoyed somewhat more success in gaining acceptance of extended data gathering and sharing between the US and its foreign allies (Scheeres, 2002).

In the final analysis, the best strategies available to those of us who are concerned about the social costs of discrimination may involve the mobilization of public opinion. People tend to be outraged when they discover, or are informed that, they have been discriminated against. There is some value, therefore, in supplying the press with egregious examples of individuals, or communities, or classes of people, who have been victimized by data mining, and by the use of profiles based on irrelevant attributes like race or ethnicity.

On the other hand, it is also likely that the use of data mining in the so-called 'war against terrorists' will soften the public up for its use in a now quiescent war against global competitors, and the threat to shrinking profits. An occasional 'horror story' about some 'so-called victims' of discrimination may do very little to shift the tide of public opinion (Democracy Online Project, 2002; Sullivan, 2001).

Note

1   This chapter is an extract from O. Gandy (2003) Data mining and surveillance in the post-9/11 environment, in K. Ball and F. Webster (eds) *The Intensification of Surveillance: Crime, Terrorism, and Warfare in the Information Age*. London: Pluto Press, pp. 26–41.

References

Agreement between The Attorneys General of the States of Arizona, California, Connecticut, Massachusetts, Michigan, New Jersey, New Mexico, New York, Vermont and Washington and DoubleClick, Inc. (2002), August 26.

Allen-Bell, A. (1997) The birth of the crime 'Driving While Black' (DWB), *Southern University Law Review*, Vol. 25.

Bowker, G. and Star, S. (1999) *Sorting Things Out: Classification and Its Consequences*. Cambridge, MA: MIT Press.

Bowman, L. (2002) FBI wants to track your web trail, *ZDNet News*, 6 June. Available at: zdnet.com.com/2100–1105–933202.html

Claire Cherry v. Amoco Oil Co., 490 F.Supp. 1026 (N.D. Ga. 1980)

Danna, A. and Gandy, O. (2002) All that glitters is not gold: digging beneath the surface of data mining, *Journal of Business Ethics*, 40.

Democracy Online Project (2002) Report. Privacy and Online Politics. Is Online Profiling Doing More Harm Than Good for Citizens in Our Political System? The George Washington University. Available at: dop@gwu.edu

FBI Asks Libraries for Records of People Suspected of Terror Ties (2002) *The Wall Street*

Journal Online, 24 June. Available at: online.wsj.com/article/0,, SB1024963982754360320 .djm,00.html

France, M., Kerstetter, J., Black, J., Salkever, A. and Carney, D. (2001) Privacy in an age of terror, *Business Week*, 5 November. Available at: http://businessweek.com/ magazine/ content/01_45/b375600/.htm

Gandy, O. (2001) Dividing practices: segmentation and targeting in the emerging public sphere, in W. Bennett and R. Entman (eds) *Mediated Politics: Communication in the Future of Democracy*. Cambridge: Cambridge University Press.

Gates, W. with Hemingway, C. (1999) *Business @ the Speed of Thought: Using a Digital Nervous System*. New York: Warner Books.

Government, Internet Industry in Anti-Terror Eavesdropping Partnership (2002) *Silicon Valley.com*, 26 May. Available at: http://www.siliconvalley.com

Graham, S. and Marvin, S. (2001) *Splintering Urbanism: Networked Infrastructure, Technological Mobilities and the Urban Condition*. London: Routledge.

Green, H., Himelstein, L., Hof, R.D. and Kunii, I. (1999) The information gold mine, *Business Week*, 26 July.

Hausman, D. and McPherson, M. (1996) *Economic Analysis and Moral Philosophy*. Cambridge: Cambridge University Press.

Kang, J. (1998) Information privacy in cyberspace transactions, *Stanford Law Review*, 50(4).

Lessig, L. (1999) *Code, and Other Laws of Cyberspace*. New York: Basic Books.

Lyon, D. (2001) *Surveillance Society: Monitoring Everyday Life*. Buckingham: Open University Press.

Madsen, W. (2001) Homeland Security, Homeland Profits. CorpWatch, 21 December. Available at: http://www.corpwatch.org/issues/PID.jsp?articleid=1108

Maney, K. (2001) What can tech companies do? *USA Today*, 19 September.

National Strategy for Homeland Security (2002, July) US Office of Homeland Security. Available at: http://www.whitehouse.gov/homeland/book/nat_strat_hls.pdf

Ofori, K. (1999) *When Being No. 1 is Not Enough: The Impact of Advertising Practices on Minority Owned & Minority Formatted Broadcast Stations*. Report to the Federal Communications Commission. Civil Rights Forum on Communications Policy, Washington DC

Peppers, D. and Rogers, M. (1997) *The 1:1 Future: Building Relationships One Customer at a Time*. Norfolk: Currency.

Predictive Networks (2001) *Digital Silhouettes* Available at: predictivenetworks.com

Preston, P. (2001) *Reshaping Communications*. London: Sage.

Rothleder, N., Harris, E. and Bloedorn, E. (n.d.) *Focusing on the Data in Data Mining: Lessons from Recent Experience. Online report* The MITRE Corporation. Available at: http:// www.mitre.org

Scheeres, J. (2002) Europe passes snoop measure, *WIRED News*, 30 May. Available at: http:// www.wired.com/news/print/0,1294,52882,00.html

Sovern, J. (1999) Opting in, opting out, or no options at all: the fight for control of personal information, *Washington Law Review*, 74(4).

Stepanek, M. (2000) Weblining, *Business Week*, 3 April.

Streitfeld, D. and Piller, C. (2002) Big Brother finds all in once-wary High Tech *LATimes.com*, 19 January. Available at: http://www.latimes.com/news/nation-world /nation/ la-011902techshift.story

Sullivan, B. (2001) Warming to Big Brother, *MSNBC.com*, 14 November. Available at: http:// www.msnbc.com/news/654959.asp?cp1=1

Sunstein, C. (2001) *Republic.com*. New Haven: Princeton University Press.

United States Foreign Intelligence Surveillance Court (2002) *Memorandum Opinion*, 17 May.

USA PATRIOT Act of 2001, Pub. L. No. 107–56, 115 Stat. 272 (2001).

12

From 'common observation' to behavioural risk management: workplace surveillance and employee assistance 1914–2003[1]
by Susan Hansen

Introduction

Currently, in the US, close to 80 percent of workers are subject to some form of electronic surveillance in the workplace (AMA, 2001). Two-thirds of American workers are members of employee assistance programmes (EAPs) (CONCERN, 2003). In other regions of the world, the proportion of workers subject to either form of workplace regulation is far less striking: in the UK, while half of all workers are subject to 'infrequent' electronic monitoring, only 11 percent are likely to be subject to daily monitoring (KPMG, 2001); and barely 10 percent (or 2.26 million) of British workers belong to an EAP (Hansen et al., 2003). The discrepancy in these figures, across cultures, illustrates the historical contingency of what have become commonplace disciplinary practices in the postindustrial American workplace.

Workplace monitoring and EAPs are genealogically interdependent disciplinary practices. This article traces the emergence and transformation of these mutually contingent phenomena, with particular attention to the kinds of problematizations, explanations and technologies that have enabled the proliferation of EAPs. This approach draws on the genealogical strategy of Foucault (e.g. Foucault, 1980), and the extension of his approach by Rose (e.g. Rose, 1999) and others (e.g. Kendall and Wickham, 1999; Copeland, 1997). Here, in presenting excerpts from a more comprehensive genealogical study, attention is drawn to the convergence of disciplinary technologies of power, to encompass the surveillance of the minutiae of the once private realm of the home lives of workers.

Sewell (1999) and Lyon (1993) have called for a '*critical* theory of [surveillance] which attempts to consider ". . . the place of love, care, trust and enabling within surveillance systems"' (Lyon, 1993: 675; emphasis added). Indeed, it could be argued that late modern surveillance systems, such as the EAP, rely upon such positive and *enabling* methods in the micro-exercise of *productive* power. For such systems, therapeutic and pastoral forms of care are inextricable elements of the array of productive forms of disciplinary power that define the daily experience of the postindustrial western worker. However, these 'traditional' forms of disciplinary power (e.g. Foucault, 1980) are, in contemporary versions of the EAP, increasingly augmented by a peculiarly neoliberal attention to the systematic pre-detection of problems *in potentia* (e.g. Castel, 1991) – or 'behavioural risk management' (e.g. Yandrick, 1996) – which is in turn part of a wider 'surveillant assemblage' (Haggerty and Ericson, 2000). Such an assemblage radically extends the number of mundane sites subject to surveillance (e.g. Moore and Haggerty, 2001), and renders it 'increasingly difficult for individuals to … escape the monitoring of social institutions' (Haggerty and Ericson, 2000: 619).

The emergence of employee assistance programmes

Employee assistance programmes, in their current form, are an assemblage of knowledge, practices, tactics and strategies designed to detect, prevent and ameliorate the psychological or personal problems of employees. Their present composite is based on the amalgamation of an array of practices, including governmental practices from the last century, 'reinvented' for the postindustrial workplace, and novel practices that have emerged from the possibilities presented by the new inscription and visualization technologies of the 21st century – electronic communication and monitoring; data collection, linkage and processing capabilities – and from the new logic of risk proffered by the New Public Health movement, together with, in the US, the symbiotic ascendance of managed behavioural healthcare.

EAPs have worked alongside employee monitoring practices for much of the last century. The neophyte discipline of psychology played a major role in the emergence and administration of these disciplinary practices. However, while Taylor's time-and-motion studies informed the burgeoning subdiscipline of industrial psychology, EAPs were more properly an offshoot of the mental hygiene movement that came to problematize key social sites, including the workplace, the home and the school. The mental hygiene movement was, significantly, the first population-based approach to the newly desirable attribute of 'mental health'. Modelled on the social measures adopted to promote health and hygiene, psy-practitioners of the earlier part of this century enjoined workers, mothers and students to 'master the art of living according to simple psychological truths' (Weatherhead, 1934: 6) in the name of ensuring proper mental hygiene, across society. Poor mental hygiene was argued to lead to (newly psychological) problems such as antisocial conduct, unhappiness and inefficiency at work (e.g. Montgomery, 1938).

The strategies for 'scientific management' developed in the first two decades of the 20th century – collectively known as Taylorism – were programmes designed primarily to increase efficiency. By such programmes, workers were governed as 'productive subjects', and observed and individualized through such methods as time-and-motion studies, the division of work into standardized tasks, and other technical interventions designed to increase the efficiency of workers (Rose, 1992). Taylorism is often cited as an early example of the kinds of industrial workplace monitoring practices that have expanded to overwhelm the postindustrial workplace (e.g. Marx, 1999). Less often cited as relevant to the history of workplace regulation and monitoring are those *psychological* programmes for ensuring the productivity of workers that were developed in the early years of the 20th century. The neophyte psychology of 'adjustment' developed by psychologists to assist with, and account for the resettlement of soldiers after the First World War was key to the development of organizational interest in the psychological affairs and moral conduct of workers (Rose, 1985).

Thus, in parallel with the scientific management of workers as 'productive subjects' in the workplace, organizational attention also shifted to encompass the moral management of the home life and habits of the 'productive subject'. The first systematic organizational effort to monitor and improve the private lives of employees occurred in 1914, in the shape of a profit-sharing plan designed by the Ford Motor Company to motivate workers to adopt more efficient and virtuous habits in the home and the factory (Gunther, 1947). The Ford Company created a Sociological Department to administer the plan, and sent field agents on home visits to assess the quality of employees' personal habits and home lives, according to set criteria. In order to qualify for the 'profit-sharing plan' – which included a shorter working day, and higher wages – each worker was required to 'show himself to be sober, saving, steady, industrious and must satisfy . . . staff that his money will not be wasted in riotous living' (Meyer, 1981: 37) . . .

In the US, the history of employee assistance has a peculiar trajectory. Though 21st-century EAPs have become all-encompassing, ever-available work–life management systems (e.g. APSHelpLink™, 2003) they existed, for the greater part of the 20th century, in the form of workplace programmes designed to identify and intervene in alcohol, and subsequently alcohol and drug, abuse. Prior to the turn of the 19th century, alcohol use was not of particular concern to employers as a threat to productivity. Indeed, Compton and Buon (1990: 2) note that, in the 18th and 19th centuries, 'it was common practice for employers to supply employees with alcohol as an inducement to work harder, and, in some cases, even to go to work'. It was also unremarkable for a portion of wages to be available in liquid form – or for a workplace alcohol allowance to be deducted from a worker's salary – whether consumed or not (George, 1925). While the American Temperance movement of the 1890s saw the first concerted attempt to guard against the 'dangers' of alcohol use in the workplace, systematic efforts to discourage alcohol use by workers were more properly part of the new era of 'scientific management', which formulated the problem as belonging to that class of undesirable practices that may pose a threat to efficiency and productivity.

However, in the US, the first formal workplace alcohol programmes were not a product of Taylorism. Rather, the appearance of workplace-based programmes in the 1940s is usually attributed to the efforts of the now (in)famous self-help-based organization, 'Alcoholics Anonymous' (e.g. Wilkey, 1986), which was a proactive lobby for the curtailment of alcohol use in the workplace; and to the scientific credibility that accompanied the formal listing of alcoholism as a disease by the World Health Organization. During this time, the insistent demands for efficiency and increased productivity that came with the Second World War were instrumentalized in the form of especially close attention to the monitoring and measurement of (threats to) productivity (Rose, 1999). These early programmes sought to make alcohol users newly visible in the workplace. Supervisors were enjoined to be alert to such 'symptoms' as the excessive use of breath mints, overly rosy noses, and 'bleary eyes' (Buon, 1988). This vigilance was extended to returning veterans, at the close of the war. However, supervisors were initially 'resistant' to this extension of their responsibility into the 'personal affairs' of their colleagues. Indeed, the 'resistance' of supervisors to monitoring the personal lives of employees persisted for some time – in the 1960s and into the 1970s, 'problems related to a person's private life [that do] not affect . . . their work performance . . . [were] NOT [considered to be] the business of the employer' (Compton and Buon, 1990: 4).

Alcohol use in the workplace was, at this time, understood primarily as a problem in and of itself – though, as we have seen, the link between the alcohol use and morally problematic personal habits of employees has been the focus of organizational attention since at least 1914. Nevertheless, it was not until the early 1970s that this self-evident 'problem' came to be redefined as a 'symptom' of underlying personal or psychological problems. Indeed, the 'failure' of these early programmes to significantly reduce workplace alcohol use tends often to be attributed, by contemporary EAP providers, as being due to the 'misplaced focus' of these early programmes on workers' behaviour, rather than on primary, and now self-evidently causative, psychological issues (e.g. Van den Burgh, 2000).

In the late 1950s, an AA-endorsed series of articles appeared in more than 250 newspapers and magazines across the US. These articles presented 'the problem' in economic terms, using the catchphrase banner, 'The Billion Dollar Hangover' (Trice and Schonbrunn, 1981). By the rhetoric of these articles, employee alcohol use, far from being a private matter, was now an *economic* problem of epidemic proportions; a threat to the productivity of the nation; and a *public* health issue. By the early 1960s, 'occupational assistance programmes' (OAPs) for the detection and treatment of workers with alcohol problems were offered in many US workplaces. The addition of 'drug problems' to alcohol problems coincided with the close of the Vietnam War, and the public concern over the imminent return of large numbers of addicted servicemen. As it happened, despite the widespread drug usage of US soldiers while overseas, upon their return, the predicted 'local epidemic' never eventuated . . .

Workplace alcohol programmes have in common across these transformations a reliance on augmenting and formalizing the workplace monitoring skills of supervisors. Methods for enabling the visibility of employees with a drug or alcohol problem became a staple of staff development courses. These methods had, in common with earlier techniques, a reliance on the 'observational skills' of supervisors and on the effective monitoring of work performance, with a view to identifying those workers declining in efficiency due to alcohol or drug use. However, until the 1970s, supervisors were advised against raising personal matters, about which they were warned that they '[were] not qualified to counsel'; similarly psy-professionals were issued a similar caution on the dangers of 'trying to make every supervisor a counsellor' (Speroff, 1955: 375).

Though the programmes of the 1960s and the early 1970s were, in policy, designed to focus on work *performance*-related alcohol and drug problems, contemporary employee assistance professionals are sceptical of the extent to which this was carried out in practice. Compton and Buon (1990) note disparagingly that '[this] supposed focus on work performance [was] ignored in preference to a reliance on *common observation*' (Compton and Buon, 1990: 5; emphasis added). However, as we have seen, methods of common observation are themselves a historically recent – and indeed technical and taught – method for identifying employees with alcohol problems. The traditional focus of workplace alcohol programmes, on the identification of unproductive employees, gave way, during the 1970s, to a series of new and old supervisory obligations: to monitor performance levels with a view to identifying declines in performance levels, to offer a referral to an EAP, to motivate the employee to seek *professional* help, to work with counsellors, and to monitor performance levels following employee assistance (Kuzmits and Hammons, 1979).

The passage of the Comprehensive Alcohol Abuse, and Alcoholism Prevention, Treatment and Rehabilitation Act (also known as the Hughes Act) in 1970 provided funding for workplace intervention programmes to detect, confront and refer alcoholic employees to treatment. In 1971, a key US federal government agency – the National Institute of Alcohol Abuse and Alcoholism (NIAAA) – was created. These conditions enabled the proliferation of OAPs in workplaces across the nation – the growing staff of which sought heightened credibility through professionalization in 1974. As a professional body, the Association of Labor and Management Administrators and Consultants on Alcoholism (ALMACA) lobbied for the expansion of the employee problems within their purview. OAPs, which were specifically directed at 'drug and alcohol problems', were felt to 'stigmatize' potential users of OAP services, and to discourage workers from presenting for problem assessment and counselling. Thus, in the 1980s, OAPs were 'repackaged' as employee assistance programmes, and ALMACA became EAPA (or the Employee Assistance Professionals Association) and the scope of relevant employee *problems* was radically broadened to include marital and family difficulties, legal problems and other 'personal' matters. However, the range of *services* offered by EAPs remained within a therapeutic or pastoral logic of care – counselling was offered as the panacea for a plethora of self- and employer-identified 'personal problems'.

This broadening of the 'problem base', and the legislative and financial support of the US government, saw the number of EAPs swell from 300 in 1972 to 2400 in 1977 (Van den Burgh, 2000). Three years later, in 1980, the number had nearly doubled to 4400 programmes (Compton and Buon, 1990). By the 1980s, 'modern EAPs' were defined as:

> . . . a set of company policies and procedures for identifying, or responding to, personal or emotional problems of employees which interfere, directly or indirectly, with job performance.
>
> (Walsh, 1982)

. . . [F]rom this new professional definition . . . 'direct interference' with job performance was no longer a necessary condition for employee intervention. Rather, a projective assessment of *indirect* interference was, for the first time, sufficient warrant for the heightened monitoring of the personal and emotional problems of employees.

Along with this novel definition came a raft of technologies for the identification of 'personal and emotional problems'. It is at this juncture that the 'core technology' of EAPs was more firmly grafted onto psychological assessment methods – technologies that have been appropriated successfully by a range of professionals and para-professionals, from lawyers to telemarketers. The inscription and visualization technologies first developed to track and record the 'intersubjective world of the factory' (Rose, 1996) have made it possible for managers to monitor the 'inner lives' of workers through the application of psychometric measurement and scaling, through non-directive interviews, and through the provision of detailed tables, charts and other forms of technical output which made the psychological realm newly visible – and newly *problematic* . . .

The troubled employee

In the 1980s, the figure of the 'troubled employee' was key to accomplishing this shift from a narrow focus on identifying those workers whose *performance* was observably affected by drug or alcohol use to identifying those workers who may be at direct or indirect *risk* of becoming unproductive due to personal or emotional problems – or 'troubled employees'. The 'core technology' for identifying and dealing with the 'troubled employee' (e.g. Roman and Blum, 1985) is a formalized procedure designed to instruct supervisors on how to identify the 'troubled employee'; how to confront them; and how to arrange for problem assessment and referral, and 'a return to the workplace as productive' (Van den Burgh, 2000: 3).

The troubled employee is constructed, in economic terms, as a figure likely to incur significant ongoing costs to the organization. The categories included in the estimation of this cost are broad and inclusive. One contemporary EAP advises that:

> . . . The average cost of troubled employees has been estimated at $3300.00 per employee per year . . . Using conservative estimates, the cost of a troubled employee who uses EAP services can be expected to be about $1100.00 per employee per year. Employers who establish and maintain an EAP program can save an average of $2200.00 per employee per year.
>
> (www.addictionrecov.org/wrkguide_interv.htm)

As is evident from this estimate, the language of economics, enterprise and efficiency has been seamlessly incorporated into the terminology of employee assistance, in an extension and elaboration of Ford's early rationale in seeking to retain workers whose personal habits and home lives were conducive to productivity. These once self-evidently moral matters are now normatively described in psychological and economic terms. Indeed, in both the popular and the academic press, personal or emotional problems are characterized as, above all else, *costly* – the impact of distress is overwhelmingly rendered in economic terms (see Yandrick, 1996; Petersen et al., 2002, for examples), of career and productivity costs, family and relationship costs, social costs and so on. Similarly, the solutions proffered by EAPs in particular, and by the mental health industry, and popular self-help versions of official psychological wisdom more generally, draw upon the now commonsensical notion of the *enterprising* self (e.g. Rose, 1992) as the ideal model for emotional well-being:

> The vocabulary of enterprise provides versatile tools for thought: the worker is no longer construed as a social creature seeking satisfaction of his or her need for

> security, solidarity and welfare, but as an individual actively seeking to shape and manage his or her own life in order to maximize its returns in terms of success and achievement.
>
> (Miller and Rose, 1993: 100)

This new vocabulary expands on the cultivation of the self-regulating employee, encouraged by psychologists since the 1950s. However, the notion of the enterprising self is unique in conjoining 'the economic health of the nation and the private choices of individuals' (Miller and Rose, 1993: 99).

Thus, although the figure of the 'troubled employee' is still deployed to invoke the projected benefits of EAP services, the 1990s have seen a further expansion of the core clientele – rendering *all* employees – and indeed, their families – as legitimate subjects of employee assistance programmes:

> One premise upon which the EAPs are based is the belief that organizations employ the whole person, not just 40 hours per week of the person . . . in most cases, you are in many ways employing not just one person, but the partner, and a number of children.
>
> (Compton and Buon, 1990: 4)

Again, though seldom mentioned in contemporary reviews of the field (e.g. Van den Burgh, 2000; Compton and Buon, 1990), the expansion of the EAP to encompass aspects of the home and family lives of employees draws upon the early welfarist model of organizational governance deployed by Ford. However, in contrast to the unwelcome visits of the field agents of the Sociological Department, to inspect at first hand the character and habits of employees, contemporary EAPs rely upon the willingness of workers to *want* to manage their work and family responsibilities, with the assistance of these programmes.

Behavioural risk and work–life management

The key selling point of the 21st-century EAP is the claimed ability to prevent many *potentially* troubled employees from reaching behaviourally problematic limits. In the 1990s, both the previously central notions of the 'core technology' and of the 'troubled worker' were problematized by EAP providers, and were progressively replaced by more 'positive' and 'personal' terms: 'Rather than seeing a client system as "troubled", one conceptualises the individual as "challenged" ' (Van den Burgh, 2000: 2) . . .

This emphasis on proactive prevention coincides with the parallel ascendance of the 'New Public Health' movement (e.g. Baum, 1998), which expounded the benefits of 'early intervention' and 'prevention' as the most efficient means to reduce health and mental healthcare costs across society. The closely related subfield of mental health promotion (e.g. Barry, 2001) found, in EAPs, a fertile site for practice. In contrast to the work of mental health practitioners, mental health *promotion* practitioners are concerned with the identification of risks to mental health, and endeavour to work prophylactically to identify strengths and to reduce risks.

The transition of EAPs from a supervisory model of observation and limited reporting, to a focus on the prevention of personal problems through the early identification of psychological problems *in potentia* and the reduction of risk through the identification of personal strengths, marks the transition of EAPs from a form of governance characterized by a pastoral mode of control and care to a neoliberal form of discipline, marked by an increasing reliance on the *motivation* of workers towards self-management, self-monitoring and self-correction.

The identification and management of behavioural risk, and the cultivation and monitoring of self-directed efforts at 'work-life management' are key to the contemporary EAP. The application of EAPs to behavioural risk management (e.g. Orbach, 2001) is a telling instance of the shift from a disciplinary concern to identify particular troubled employees, to the prophylactic management of risk across organizations. Behavioural risk management systems are capable of monitoring the behavioural risk status of employees, across large and variable populations . . .

Castel (1991: 296) argues . . . that, rather than being about 'discipline', the new order is about *efficiency* – the most extreme form of which would constitute 'a system of prevention perfect enough to dispense with both repression and assistance, thanks to its capacity to forward-plan social trajectories from a "scientific" evaluation of individual abilities'. Indeed, as we have seen, the contemporary forms of 'repression' and 'assistance' in the workplace – workplace monitoring practices and EAPs – are both invested in the rhetoric of efficiency and enterprise. Workplace monitoring claims primarily to enhance the *efficiency* of organizations (e.g. Sewell, 1999). Other benefits touted include: enhancing safety in the workplace; increasing productivity; accurate and objective performance appraisal and reward; consumer empowerment; and the protection of corporate assets. However, Marx (1999) notes that, despite rhetoric to the contrary, very few organizations collect data which could support these claimed benefits – and indeed, that there may be compelling reasons to suspect that overzealous workplace monitoring may be 'counter-productive', and may 'negatively impact' on the physical and mental well-being of workers. In support of these 'suspicions' Marx cites the 1993 World Labor Report, which claims that 'stress costs American employers $200 billion a year through increased absenteeism, diminished productivity, higher compensation claims, rising health insurance fees and additional medical expenses' (US Senate, 1993: 19).

Here, the interlinked rationale for contemporary EAPs becomes particularly compelling. The programmes promise to identify and address those very *personal* problems that may directly or indirectly 'negatively impact' the well-being of workers, and, in turn, the 'health' of the organization. One American EAP company claims that:

> EAP service outcome studies for the past twelve months indicate employee productivity up by 16 percent, work relationships improved by 27 percent, and absenteeism/tardiness down by 80 percent for employees using [EAP services].
>
> (www.concern.com)

Indeed, it is now commonplace for EAPs to be promoted as 'an effective and affordable way to encourage healthy lifestyles and detect problems that could impact the workforce if not addressed' (APS HelpLink™, 2003). EAPs are now also 'designed to solve problems early before they become costly to the employer and the employee' (CONCERN, 2003). In this attention to *personal* problems – as the source of potential costs to productivity – workplace monitoring practices and other 'stress-inducing' workplace practices are effectively excluded from serious consideration as a credible *source* of unease, discontent and associated grounds for inefficiency – though, as we have seen, they may provide the *source data* for estimations of their probable manifestation.

The identification and management of behavioural risk mark one aspect of the expansion of employee assistance towards a new mode of surveillance characterized by 'systematic pre-detection' (Castel, 1991). However, employees are also increasingly enjoined to self-directed employee assistance via new, 'user-friendly' work–life management systems that provide convenient and engaging methods for preventative correction, monitoring and referral. The two are, of course, intimately linked: by the 1990s, EAPs were increasingly provided by larger external companies which often also offered managed behavioural healthcare. The parallel genealogy of the specifically American (behavioural) healthcare system is interdependent with that of the EAP (see Hansen et al., 2003). By this system, and particularly during the 1990s, larger companies have become intimately – and financially – directly involved with their employees' behavioural health history and care (Newhouse, 2000). The touted cost-saving benefits of preventative EAPs to the managed behavioural healthcare costs for industry are integral to their steady growth and current prevalence in the US . . . Managed behavioural healthcare is devoted to 'empowering' consumers to solve their mental health problems 'inhouse' – and preferably, while they are still amenable to some form of 'self-help' – that is, before personal problems have been respecified as 'billable disorders'.

Electronic employee assistance

The range of services provided by EAPs has been augmented by electronic technology, by the rapid growth of computers in the workplace, and by the increasing availability of the Internet – with many providers moving towards an online interface for electronic and increasingly automated EAP services (e.g. CONCERN, APS Healthcare). In the US, 65 million of the 115 million employed adults aged 25 and over use a computer. However, in recent years, while the increase in the percentage of employees using computers has been modest (52 percent in 1998 to 57 percent in 2001), the percentage using the Internet at work grew from 18 percent in 1998 to 42 percent in 2001 (US Department of Commerce, 2002). The Internet has been described as an ideal vehicle for delivering 'cost-effective' mental health-care (Bashshur, 1997). To this end, some contemporary EAPs have developed web-based programmes or 'life management systems' designed to be accessible and convenient for 'everyday use' . . .

Contemporary providers argue that the Internet is an ideal medium for accessible and engaging EAP services:

Today, the Internet is integrated into all aspects of our lives. The Internet represents the vehicle, which brings individuals, companies, and providers together. It's the place where people gather information, search for life management resources and referrals, and solutions to everyday life events and challenges ... [The] Internet will help us connect people in convenient and compelling ways, providing them with quality information that will enable them to navigate the emotional challenges of everyday life. With our Internet product, APSHelpLink.com™ we will reach a much wider audience. APS Healthcare has invested significant resources in developing a web-based Life Management product that is designed to help people help themselves with issues that impact their health, quality of life, and well being.

(www.apscare.com/helplink/helplinkcom_index.htm)

The acceptance of contemporary EAPs has been facilitated by their association with the 'objective expertise' of the psy-professional, which offers a 'caring' and morally defensible basis for making disciplinary decisions; and by association with neutral and objective methods of recording and measurement. Electronic technology augments these associations through the apparent neutrality of the machine; by the apparent 'privacy' offered by the 'personal' computer, and by the possibility of disembodied participation in online para-therapeutic activities and discussions ...

APSHelpLink.com™: 'Helping people help themselves to lead healthier lives'[2]

APS Healthcare is a private, for-profit, managed behavioural healthcare organization. It provides 'managed behavioural health, employee assistance programs, and specialty care management services to 9.4 million 'covered lives' in the United States and Puerto Rico'. During 1995–1999, APS grew by 935 percent, and currently provides 'assistance' to more than 14 percent of the 65 million US workers currently covered by an EAP. As such, APS Healthcare is an example of the increasingly dominant external EAP provider, which is also invested in the provision of managed behavioural health. APS Healthcare's marketing material asserts that 'unresolved personal problems' can pose a serious threat to productivity, and that at least one in five workers is afflicted by such a problem. They provide 'ongoing education and prevention, early intervention, and short-term problem resolution', and describe employee assistance as 'an effective and affordable way to encourage healthy lifestyles and detect problems that could impact the workforce if not addressed [which in turn will] reduce the risk of unnecessary health care costs' (APS Healthcare, 2003).

APSHelpLink.com™: 'Helping People Help Themselves to Lead Healthier Lives' provides 'life management tools' to help people with 'behavioral health problems; financial and legal issues; child and elder-care concerns; and work/life issues'. These 'self-help tools' are designed to help people to 'clarify problems and plan ways to resolve them'. APSHelpLink™ is a 'high-value low-cost benefit' that promises to help both employers and everyday consumers. Employers are promised 'reduced absenteeism, employee retention, and increased visibility', while employees are assured of the benefits of the 'ease of access, convenience, consumer information, and interactive self-help tools and resources' offered by APSHelpLink.com™.

The website has been 'designed and written to be accessible to everyday people living in the real world'. Thus it is 'dynamic and brief' and offers a 'high degree of interactivity' to/with the user. Through a 'unique combination of upbeat appeal and hopefulness', with 'down-to-earth usefulness and caring for the individual', APSHelpLink™ aims to be 'compelling', 'convenient' and 'fun' . . .

The APSHelpLink™ site is not only designed to assist employees to identify and alleviate early signs of personal or psychological problems: according to the promotional material on the parent-site, 'the organisation of the site, the choice of content, and its structure are based on the latest research on how the brain works and on the most effective methods and theories of how people change'. Specifically, Prochaska and DeClemente's 'readiness to change' model (e.g. Bunton et al., 2000) has been used to inform the site's design. This is a cognitive-behavioural model often employed in the public health and (mental) health promotion field in efforts to persuade people to recognize and change their undesirable habits. Thus, 'APSHelpLink™ is *motivational* in nature and operates on the assumption that people are curious and *want* to work towards solutions in their lives'. By this logic, APSHelpLink™ offers an unambiguous benefit to all employees – and indeed, 'people in general' – through the offer of structured guidance through self-directed life change.

This comprehensive site (1800 pages) goes beyond either the provision of psycho-educational information, or professional advice. Rather, APSHelpLink™ promises to:

> . . . encourage and empower people to do something useful with the information that is available on our site and elsewhere . . . APSHelpLink™ goes beyond *helping people change the way they feel* about their lives. We want to empower people to make changes that are concrete and measurable in behavioral terms.
>
> (www.apscare.com/helplink/helplinkcom_index.htm)

These concrete and measurable changes are available for perusal both by the empowered employee, and by concerned employers. APS offers employers access to the results of a 'utilization analysis' for their employees: number and percentage of online visits (by topic, content and function); duration of visits; number of visits spent in life problem areas; number and percentage of visits to online features (Search, Phone A Counselor, Chats, Find A Clinician, etc.); user visit frequency by area. With respect to the Bridge to Change evaluation, APSHelpLink™ advises that they can track, by problem type, an individual's success on following through on the goals that they set for themselves. This promise – to render the potentially problematic inner lives of employees into an accessible and calculable form – makes the data compiled by EAPs all the more amenable to incorporation by behavioural risk management information systems.

Conclusion

This investigation has pursued a historically particular problem, i.e. how it is that employee assistance programmes have come to be, on the whole, 'actively welcomed' by workers. In contrast to the largely positive, but somewhat 'mixed reception' of workplace monitoring practices (e.g. Rule, 1996; Mason et al., 2002), EAPs tend to be received as unambiguously benign and even 'empowering', and to be unproblematically welcomed as a 'benefit', rather than as a potential infringement to one's privacy – as the recent appropriation of the EAP format by many US unions as MAPs – or 'member assistance programmes' – attests (Molloy and Kurzman, 1993).

As we have seen, the home lives of workers have long been of interest to organizations, as a potential indicator of a less than efficient character – and this interest has also historically been presented as constituting a tangible *benefit* for workers. However, it is only relatively recently that the private lives of employees have come to be problematized in psychological terms, as posing a series of identifiable behavioural risks to *prospective* efficiency. By this process of problematization, previously unremarkable aspects of the private lives of workers have become simultaneously 'troubling' and 'intelligible' (see Rose, 1999); and indeed, 'normality' has become a delicately balanced achievement, to be maintained through constant self-management – and self-monitoring.

Contemporary EAPs are concerned to detect and avert potentially costly personal problems, via self-directed and motivational programmes such as those contained in structured web-based applications. The 'motivational logic' of electronic EAPs marks the transition of the programmes from an earlier focus on the scientific management of the productive subject, and the moral management of the 'sober, saving, steady, industrious' employee, to the neoliberal governance of the 'life and life conduct of the ethically free subject' (Miller and Rose, 1993), who strives for self-fulfilment, personal growth and autonomous work–life management. Thus the exercise of authority has become a therapeutic matter – as perhaps the most efficient way of acting upon the actions of others is to change the ways in which they will govern – or 'care for' – themselves . . .

According to Lyon (2001), care and control define the 'two faces' of surveillance – the suasive logic by which postindustrial surveillance systems operate. EAPs offer a form of preventative surveillance organized overtly around the logic of 'concern' (or assistance) rather than 'control' (or repression). This mode of preventative surveillance, unlike classic disciplinary forms, does not rely on the coercive co-presence of the 'watcher and the watched' (Castel, 1991) – and indeed, web-based electronic employee assistance has been seamlessly incorporated as a 'convenient and compelling' *benefit* of relevance to all employees and their families, and as an ever-accessible tool for managing the everyday details of one's life and work. For, as Lyon (2001) reminds us, 'our daily experiences of surveillance . . . occur in mundane moments rather than in special searches . . . 'surveillance is "designed in" to the flows of everyday existence' (Rose, 1999: 234)'.

Notes

1   This chapter is an extract from S. Hansen (2004) From 'common observation' to behavioural risk management: workplace surveillance and employee assistance 1914–2003, *International Sociology*, 19(2): 151–71.

2   An earlier version of this section has appeared in Hansen et al. (2003).

References

AMA (American Management Association) (2001) *Workplace Monitoring and Surveillance Survey*. New York: AMA.

APS Healthcare (2003) Available at: www.apshealthcare.com (accessed 4 April 2003).

APSHelpLink™ (2003) Available at: www.apshelplink.com (accessed 4 April 2003).

Barry, M. (2001) Promoting positive mental health: theoretical frameworks for practice, *International Journal of Mental Health Promotion* 3(1): 25–34.

Bashshur, R. (1997) Telemedicine and the health care system, in R. Bashshur, J. Sanders and G. Shannon (eds) *Telemedicine: Theory and Practice*. Springfield, IL: Charles C. Thomas, pp. 265–90.

Baum, F. (1998) *The New Public Health: An Australian Perspective*. Oxford: Oxford University Press.

Bunton, R., Baldwin, S., Flynn, D. and Whitelaw, S. (2000) The 'stages of change' model in health promotion: science and ideology, *Critical Public Health*, 10: 55–70.

Buon, T. (1988) Beyond Drug and Alcohol Treatments in the Workplace. Paper presented at the ICAA Third Pan Pacific Conference, Kuala Lumpur, Malaysia.

Castel, R. (1991) 'From dangerousness to risk', in G. Burchell, C. Gordon and P. Miller (eds) *The Foucault Effect*. Hemel Hempstead: Harvester Wheatsheaf, pp. 281–98.

Compton, R. and Buon, T. (1990) *Employee Assistance Program – The Australian Way*, Centre for Employment Relations Working Paper No 1: 90. Nepean: University of Western Sydney.

CONCERN (2003) Available at: www.concern.com (accessed 4 April 2003).

Copeland, I. (1997) Pseudo-science and dividing practices: a genealogy of the first educational provision for pupils with learning difficulties, *Disability and Society*, 12(5): 709–22.

Foucault, M. (1980) Two lectures, in C. Gordon (ed.) *Michel Foucault: Power/Knowledge: Selected Interviews and Other Writings 1972–1977*. Brighton: Harvester.

George, M. (1925) *London Life in the 18th Century*. New York: Knopf.

Gunther, J. (1947) *Inside USA*. London: Hamish Hamilton.

Haggerty, K. and Ericson, R. (2000) The surveillant assemblage, *British Journal of Sociology*, 51(4): 605–22.

Hansen, S., McHoul, A. and Rapley, M. (2003) *Beyond Help: A Consumer's Guide to Psychology*. Ross-on-Wye: PCCS Books.

Kendall, G. and Wickham, G. (1999) *Using Foucault's Methods*. London: Sage.

KPMG (2001) *The Uneasy World of E – Klegal Management Survey*. London: KPMG.

Kuzmits, F. and Hammons, H. (1979) Rehabilitating the troubled employee, *Personnel Journal*, April, pp. 239–50.

Lyon, D. (1993) An electronic panopticon? A sociological critique of surveillance theory, *Sociological Review*, 41: 653–78.

Lyon, D. (2001) *Surveillance Society: Monitoring Everyday Life*. Buckingham: Open University Press.

Marx, G. T. (1999) Measuring everything that moves: the new surveillance at work, in I. and R. Simpson (eds) *The Workplace and Deviance, JAI Series on Research in the Sociology of Work*. Greewich, CT: JAI Press.

Mason, D., Button, G., Lankshear, G., Coates, S. and Sharrock, W. (2002) 'On the poverty of a priorism: technology, surveillance in the workplace and employee responses, *Information, Communication and Society*, 5(4): 555–72.

Meyer, S. (1981) *The Five Dollar Day: Labor Management and Social Control in the Ford Motor Company, 1908–1921*. Albany: State University of New York Press.

Miller, P. and Rose, N. (1993) Governing economic life, in M. Gane and T. Johnson (eds) *Foucault's New Domains*. London: Routledge, pp. 75–106.

Molloy, D. and Kurzman, P. (1993) Practice with unions: collaborating toward an empowerment model, in P. Kurzman and S. Akabas (eds) *Work and Well-Being: The Occupational Social Work Advantage*. Washington: NASW Press, pp. 46–60.

Montgomery, E. (1938) *Can Psychology Help?* London: Rich and Cowan.

Moore, D. and Haggerty, K. (2001) Bring it on home: home drug testing and the relocation of the war on drugs, *Social and Legal Studies*, 10(3): 377–95.

Newhouse, J. (2000) Managed Care: Lessons in Healthcare Reform. Paper presented at the Academy of Business and Administrative Sciences International Conference, Prague, July.

Orbach, N. (2001) EAPs as a risk management tool, *Behavioral Health Management*, 21(4): 44–7.

Petersen, A., Kokanovic, R. and Hansen, S. (2002) Mental health care in a culturally diverse society, in S. Hendersen and A. Petersen (eds) *Consuming Health: The Consumer Model in Health Care*. London: Routledge, pp. 121–139.

Roman, P. and Blum, T. (1985) The core technology of Employee Assistance Programs, *Almacan*, 8–9 March, pp. 18–19.

Rose, N. (1985) *The Psychological Complex*. London: Routledge.

Rose, N. (1992) Governing the enterprising self, in P. Heelas and P. Morris (eds) *The Values of Enterprise Culture*. London: Routledge, pp. 141–64.

Rose, N. (1996) *Inventing Our Selves: Psychology, Power, and Personhood*. Cambridge: Cambridge University Press.

Rose, N. (1999) *Governing the Soul: The Shaping of the Private Self*, 2nd edn. London: Free Association Books.

Rule, J. (1996) High-tech workplace surveillance: what's really new? in D. Lyon and E. Zureik (eds) *Computers, Surveillance and Privacy*. Minneapolis: University of Minnesota Press.

Sewell, G. (1999) *On the Possibility of a Sociology of Workplace Surveillance*, Department of Management Working Paper in Human Resource Management, Employee Relations and Organisation Studies No 4. Melbourne: University of Melbourne.

Speroff, B. (1955) There's danger in trying to make every supervisor a counsellor, *Personnel Journal* 33(10): 375–7.

Trice, H. and Schonbrunn, M. (1981) A history of job-based alcoholism programs 1900–1955, *Journal of Drug Issues*, Spring, pp. 171–98.

US Department of Commerce (2002) *A Nation Online: How Americans Are Expanding Their Use of the Internet*. Washington, DC: US Department of Commerce.

US Senate (1993) *The Privacy for Consumers and Workers Act*, Senate Bill 984. Washington, DC: US Senate.

Van den Burgh, N. (2000) *Emerging Trends for Employee Assistance Programs in the 21st Century*. New York: Haworth Press.

Walsh, D. (1982) Employee Assistance Programs, *Health and Society*, 60(3): 483–517.

Weatherhead, L. (1934) *Psychology and Life: Sound Psychology Made Vivid and Practical*. London: Hodder and Stoughton.

Wilkey, W. (1986) The influence of Alcoholics Anonymous on alcoholism treatment, *Employee Assistance Quarterly*, 1: 1–17.

Yandrick, R. M. (1996) *Behavioral Risk Management: How to Avoid Preventable Losses from Mental Health Problems in the Workplace*. Tiburon, CA: Jossey-Bass.

13

How closed-circuit television surveillance organizes the social: an institutional ethnography[1]
by Kevin Walby

Introduction

. . . In most western nation-states during the last decade, there has been a rapid diffusion of closed-circuit television (CCTV) surveillance into open-streets, apartment complexes, and places of consumption. Within the new paradigm of neo-liberal governance, CCTV has been implemented to 'reaestheticise' particular . . . locations throughout the city and to promote consumer friendliness (Fyfe and Bannister, 1996; Coleman and Sim, 2000; 1998). Inside the . . . space of the shopping mall, the body language of citizens is relentlessly scrutinized from a distance by CCTV operators, though a high number of people remain unaware of the cameras (Honess and Charman, 1992:6). Ethnographic research has been conducted in CCTV control rooms,[2] but, to the knowledge of this author, no study of CCTV monitoring has been conducted from the perspective of institutional ethnography. What differentiates institutional ethnography from other forms of ethnography is its focus on texts as coordinating social organization both in local and across extra-local settings . . . This study falls roughly into the category of ethnographic 'workplace studies' which are concerned with the practical details of organizational activity and the use of technology (Heath, Luff, & Svensson, 2002; Heath, Hindmarsh & Luff, 1999).

In order to examine CCTV from the perspective of institutional ethnography, it is key to conceptualize CCTV video images as a form of text . . . which is central to the coordination of peoples' activities. This coordination can occur in two ways, both of which depend on an interpretive activation of the text by a CCTV operator: (1) understood as a 'rolling text,' CCTV video can result in the real time concerting of a sequence of events . . . (2) understood as an 'initiating text,' CCTV video is rewritten and reinterpreted as a series of texts which can coordinate social activity between different complexes of social organization. By means of video as a 'rolling text,' the shopper-turned-risk is caught in the act of shoplifting by the CCTV operator. Through the video as an 'initiating text,' the act of the offender is written up and distributed to various institutions in a process involving televisual mall surveillance, risk detection and risk communication.

This [chapter] will show how CCTV video, conceptualized as a televisual text . . . coordinates actions/events and subsequently plays a role in reproducing social relations. Institutional ethnography offers a novel methodological approach to analyzing camera surveillance. Research for this [chapter] was conducted with camera operators in a Suburban Mall's CCTV control room located in Victoria, BC. The data are a combination of unstructured interviews and observations that occurred in the CCTV control rooms while the CCTV operators worked . . .

Reading video through the lens of institutional ethnography: texts as 'active' and 'activated'

Institutional ethnography

Institutional ethnography sees texts as active in shaping and reproducing social relations.[3] For Dorothy E. Smith, participants in social relations are not necessarily known to one another, but are connected through texts and the organizational features which envelope work processes. *Institutions* identify a 'complex of relations forming part of the ruling apparatus, organized around a distinctive function,' and *ethnography* commits us to an exploration of 'the persons whose everyday world of working is organized thereby' (Smith, 1987:160). Institutional ethnography draws on Marx and his conception of political economy and class structure arising from the activities of people (Smith, 1990:94), but also on ethnomethodology, in which the institutional ethnographer finds significant the common-sense knowledges of people and how they think, intend, and feel in the local settings of their work (Smith, 1999:75).

Institutional ethnography goes further to focus on texts as they structure our thinking, intending, and feeling, and seizes critical advantage of texts as they are accessible for research. As a method of inquiry, institutional ethnography exposes both our own engagement with textually-mediated interaction and the ruling practices which texts organize. The text must be seen as active; there is always something in the text which . . . enters into the organization of what is to come (Smith, 2001:174). For this to happen, the text must be activated by a reader. Activation involves a reading of the text, and each reader brings with her/him a set of informal rules about how to approach the text. These rules are manifestations of the institutional ruling practices in which the reader is embedded . . .

. . . Texts are not inert, but through activation have the capability to do untold work upon bodies, consciousness, and social organization.

Video surveillance in modernity

. . . We live in a surveillance society (Lyon, 2002; 2001), which doubles as a televisual culture. Visualization is essential to knowledge reproduction and therefore bound up in the exercising of social power (Jenks, 1995; Jay, 1995; Macphee, 2002). Video has challenged the written word for top status as the characteristic textual medium. Anthony Giddens asserts 'the development of writing greatly extends the scope of distanciated interaction in space as well as in time' (1979:204). To conceptualize video as a text, we must see video, aided by the technologies of satellite and fiber optics, as extending the scope of distanciated interaction beyond the spatial potential of written texts. The possibilities of new visual technologies like CCTV are implicated in a complex new arrangement of social relations, transforming what it means to be visible, who can be visible and when (Crang, 1996:2103). Images increasingly influence political decisions. CCTV is a distanciated form of governance,[4] which dismantles long established time-space boundaries and therefore alters the mode of interaction between authorities and citizens . . .

One of the most distinguishing features of modernity is the power of the visual, evidenced in Foucault's discussion of the Panopticon and panopticism (1979). The Panopticon is the predominant, if not over-indulged in, metaphor used to describe modern surveillance practices. Foucault sees the Panopticon as a technique used to administer or discipline large numbers of people within a particular institution (Poster, 1984:101). The Panopticon forces people into enclosed spaces where they can be watched so as to normalize their behaviour along institutional contours (Bauman, 1998:52). Despite contentions to the contrary (Deleuze, 1990; Lianos, 2003), and serious problems with the Panopticon metaphor,[5] it is important not to jettison Foucault's concept of panopticism because it reminds us of the presumptuous ambition of both state and non-state organizations to *see* and to *know* everything, and of the ways in which data collection and knowledge are intertwined (Webster, 1995; Boyne, 2000). CCTV cameras involve a relationship of power between the watcher and the watched, signifying the continued resonance of panopticism in the 21st century (Norris and Armstrong, 1999a:5).

The postmodern mall is instrumentally designed to promote purchasing, and hyperreal fixtures mask its highly controlled nature (Gottidiener, 2003: 132). Citizens shop in malls for the perceived advantages of heightened security and levels of safety which streetscape shopping spaces do not provide. The sense of safety in the quasi-public space[6] of the mall reflects the intensity of surveillance provided by private security personnel and CCTV (Fyfe and Bannister, 1998:258). The perception of order, its 'agreeable ambiance' (Lianos and Douglas, 2000:115), makes the mall a favorite place of the consumer for purchasing commodities and services. CCTV is the televisual means to govern visions of order and disorder in spaces of consumption . . .

CCTV serves as an authoritative tool which aids in policing those persons unwilling or unable to subscribe to consumerist ideology out of the mall. CCTV control rooms operate as the 'nerve centre' of shopping malls, where risk information is managed and communicated, and where decisions are made immediately (Helten and Fischer, 2003:21). Plugged into the information circuitry and organizational interests of the mall, the CCTV operators use the camera technology, as well as their practical knowledge and familiarity with the store (Heath, Luff, & Svensson, 2002:186), to collect and collate televisual data which they use to manage the flow of shoppers.

Video as text: active and activated

Video is the textual device of CCTV surveillance, and is *active* in that it is used to coordinate lived realities and facilitate organization at the institutional, extra-local level. In one sense, I conceptualize CCTV video as a 'rolling text,' used to mediate sociality and work processes within the local setting directly in the moment. In a second sense,

I conceptualize CCTV as an 'initiating text,' akin to how a written text would be dealt with in institutional ethnography. The 'initiating text' overlaps with a series of texts, facilitating extra-local organization of the social and the production of information. A discussion of video as text is entirely consistent with the theoretical underpinnings of institutional ethnography.[7] Moreover, the 'rolling' and 'initiating' texts are bound up in the two dialectically related characteristics of surveillance: the collation and storage of information concerning a subject population, and the direct supervision of that population's conduct (Giddens, 1981:5, 1991:15; Dandeker 1990:37).

Beyond . . . analyses of content, texts help organize courses of concerted social action (Smith, 1990:121). Video is active in that it can serve as an 'initiating text,' being rewritten and reinterpreted into a series of non-video texts which can coordinate social activity between different complexes of social organization. Like the field notes of a police officer or sociologist, the video data is rewritten within an institutional discourse which frames the text in light of a ruling practice. Wrenched out of social relations and transcribed into written text, the televisual data are a constituent in concerting future events, actions, and work. In the case of CCTV video, video's function as an 'initiating text' is evident in its transcription by a CCTV operator into other documents (e.g. incident reports, logbooks) which are then used to coordinate relations between authorities, social services, Courts, etc.

As a 'rolling text,' CCTV video is active in the immediate sense, being a constant display of people and their behaviours. The CCTV operator ['reads'] the embodied ambiguities of shoppers/citizens as they move on and off the screen; this reading of the video frames the body language, dress, skin colour, age, etc., of the shoppers/citizens as normal or abnormal, suspicious or unsuspicious. The 'rolling text' is active because it informs consciousness and social organization in real time, as the text unfolds itself to the CCTV operator. A particular reading of the text by the CCTV operator can lead to security work on the floor level. The experience of the shopper/citizen can be radically altered. What was before a leisurely period of shopping can become a threatening experience, inundated with authorities. A CCTV operator, informed by the video, may communicate to a floorwalker to track a shopper, issue a security alert, or contact police authorities . . .

In order to coordinate interaction, texts need to be read and *activated*. Activation of a text is bound up in the interpretative and subjective processes of human consciousness, reading, and action:

> That it is activated by the reader means that the activity or operation of the text is dependent upon the reader's interpretative practices. These too are constituents of social relations rather than merely the idiosyncrasies of individuals.
>
> (Smith, 1990:121)

This interpretative aspect is an unfailing characteristic of televisual social monitoring: '[operators] rely on a set of normatively based, contextual rules to draw their attention to any behaviour that disrupts the "normal"' (Norris, 2003:265). The reader both activates and responds to the text. Activation is therefore informed by a subjective reading which has in part been structured by institutional discourses and other informal socialization processes.

In conceptualizing 'video as text,' one must consider how video is interpreted by the camera operators, and how this interpretation is translated into an institutionally-fit language which then orchestrates action. Of particular concern are the body language . . . of citizens which are classified and interpreted by camera operators . . . and which are written into the text during the work of reading, interpretation, transcription, and activation . . . [T]extually-mediated work occurs within specific organizational settings, and is couched in discursive and ruling practices.

Textually-mediated discourse and ruling relations

Any co-ordinated form of human interaction that involves reciprocal, multiple, and overlapping relations, in which the actions of some social actors guide the actions of others, can be a ruling relation. Textually-based ruling relations structure consciousness . . . in such a way that social relations are seen as disconnected. Smith writes,

> The ruling relations 'extract' the coordinative and concerting of people's everyday/everynight activities and subject them to technological and technical specialization, elaboration, differentiation, and objectification. They become independent of particular individuals . . . Coordination and concerting are leached out of localized and particularized relations . . .
>
> (1999:77)

The use of texts in work processes has the effect of objectifying social relations, making them appear as mere moments as opposed to ongoing social courses of action (Campbell and Manicom, 1995:7). This form of social consciousness is a property of organization, which is manifested in the creation of institution-linking texts or series of texts. Discourses . . . within ruling relations affect social actors in such a way that they conceptualize their own position within the field of relations as disconnected from the position of other social actors (Sharma, 2001:420), rendering the organizational features of a particular institution invisible . . . Particular to specific locales, discursive processes are continuously re-oriented by the CCTV operators. The status of discourse is as much an outcome of interactions between operators and video as it is an input which frames practices of camera surveillance.

The expansion of textually-mediated discourses of ruling has largely occurred over the past century, and this expansion has been enabled by the development of technologies that permit the rapid reproduction and circulation of texts in multiple sites (McCoy, 1995:184). I am arguing that video, and more specifically of CCTV video surveillance, should be conceptualized similarly, as a text which is active, activated, and contributing to the organization of sociality and work processes within an identifiable ruling framework.

Several discourses inform the 'activation' of CCTV video. In commercial settings, a discourse of the flawed consumer and underclass informs the consciousness of CCTV operators. Flawed consumers are those citizens 'who are unable to respond to the enticements of the consumer market because they lack the required resources' (McCahill, 2002:11), or those who respond through illicit activity (e.g. shoplifting);

the underclass are those who constitute the growing army of unemployed and homeless increasingly seen not as a social group to be integrated, but as dangerous 'anti-social' groups, as "risks to be policed" (ibid.: 16; Goldberg, 1993: 169; Rose, [2000]: 195) . . . CCTV facilitates the coordination of action and events in settings far removed from the local, coordinating social relations through the orchestration of events which safeguard capitalist accumulation. It is through discursive processes that common knowledge of this coordination is subverted.

An institutional ethnography of CCTV surveillance

Method of inquiry

. . . Embedded in informants' talk about their work is their tacit knowledge of how to concert their own pieces of the work with the work of others. Interviewing in institutional ethnography differs from other styles of interviewing, as the method attempts to locate the multiple points of textually-mediated coordination of action within/ between organizations.[8] When interviews are used in this approach, 'they are used not to reveal subjective states, but to locate and trace points of connection among individuals working in different parts of institutional complexes of activity' (Devault and McCoy, 2002:753) . . .

Research for this [chapter] was conducted with camera operators in a . . . CCTV control room located in Victoria, BC. The control room was situated in a large department store, part of an even larger suburban shopping complex. The interviews went on for lengthy periods of time, and the transcribed versions of the interviews are not fully presented here. This study utilized open-ended interviewing and observation; freedom in research design is important because it allows the informants to tell the story of their work . . .

The aim of the interviews was three-fold: (1) to explicate the interpretive aspects of the CCTV operators' work, which indicates how they read and activate the 'video as text,' but also indicates the textually-mediated discursive processes which envelope their work process; (2) to listen for and ask about texts or series of texts which are the active constituents of work-related activity and sociality (Devault and McCoy, 2002:765); (3) to connect the active text(s) and its activation to an extra-local organizational complex. Police authorities and Courts are the principal extra-local organizational complexes, although the Suburban Mall is connected to many other extra-local organizations. The terms and forms of language derived from the interview are those of the informant, not the institutional ethnographer (Smith, 1987:189). To protect the anonymity of the informants and organizations, pseudonyms are substituted for their names.

Research findings and analysis

Resource Protection Officers W & T at Suburban Mall

Resource Protection Officers W & T are both white males in their late twenties. The retail outlet . . . wholesales over $50 million in merchandise a year. W & T are 'resource protection officers,' and are less concerned with filling arrest quotas than with preventing the loss of capital . . . Officers W & T work as both the CCTV operators and the floor-walkers, communicating between the floor and the control room with mobile phones, plugged into the information network of the municipal police. Officers W & T work eight hour shifts, either between 9 a.m. and 5 p.m. or 1 p.m. and 9 p.m. Several other CCTV operators are employed by the department store, but Officer W is the lead supervisor and therefore responsible for administrative duties. Incentives for pay raises are related to the annual amount of 'resources protected,' and the individual allocation of pay raises is supervised by Officer W.

The department store at Suburban Mall has a 27-camera monitoring system, one of the most sophisticated in Victoria, BC. Three multiplexers condense the 27 cameras into three, recordable screens. Cameras are used primarily to track and record the actions of those citizens deemed suspicious, but cameras are also used to monitor the work of employees and for internal audits . . . The CCTV control room is located near the back of the store, closest to the exit leading into Suburban Mall and furthest away from the exit leading onto a main street in the city. Before the implementation of the camera system, Suburban Mall lost nearly $1 million to theft each year. This figure has been cut back by several hundred thousand in the five years since the camera system was implemented. Both Officer W and Officer T were present in the control room at the time of the interviews.

Officers W & T and the 'rolling text' at Suburban Mall

When CCTV video is conceptualized as a 'rolling text,' of interest is how the text *immediately* transforms social relations at the local setting. Officers W & T read the actions of people on the screen. In interpreting the CCTV text, Officers W & T assume 'everyone is a thief' (Officer W) 'until proven innocent . . . [laughs]' (Officer T). They read the video text from the interpretative-institutional frame which presumes each person who enters the store is a potential risk – a potential shoplifter . . . As explicated later in the data, Officers W & T do not target suspicion equally towards all shoppers; rather, their informal watching rules direct intensified surveillance at racialized minorities, single mothers, persons receiving income assistance, and other socially constructed categories of citizens coded as 'abnormal.' This influences W & T's reading of the video text . . .

K: What do you look for in people's actions?

OFFICER W: On a camera system, you are twelve feet up, so it is a different perspective than on the floor, you can see a lot more . . .

OFFICER T: You can also get in a lot closer, you know, zoom in and see how old their shoes are . . .

OFFICER W: What they are doing with their hands . . .

OFFICER T: First thing you look for is if they are *sketchy*, if they are dirty and sketchy . . . if they are scruffy . . . either they are shopping or they are not shopping.

OFFICER W: Shopping behaviours, you know, you see someone walk in the store and they go straight for a high-end item. Most people they walk in, they browse, they ask for help, but if they go straight for the boom box . . .

OFFICER T: If they are carrying bags, if they come in the store with a big GAP bag, you know, what are they doing with the bag? They probably came on the bus from a different mall . . .

Shopper behaviour seen as inherently abnormal by Officers W & T would not be self-evident to the lay viewer. Normative judgments about what constitutes a regular shopper are implicit in Officers W & T's reading of the text; these normative judgments are manifestations of the organizational features of the institution where they work. Given the volume of people potentially monitored at any given moment, 'operators utilize their already existing understanding of who is most likely to commit crime or be troublesome to provide potential candidates for targeted surveillance' (Norris and Armstrong, 1999b:119) . . .

K: Do you have a list of things you look for . . . things which would make you think someone was suspicious?

OFFICER T: You always look at their shoes. If they got dirty shoes . . .

OFFICER W: 99% of the time a shoplifter will have bad shoes . . .

OFFICER T: Except sometimes a shoplifter might have good shoes, 'cause they stole them . . .

OFFICER W: Baggy coats, everyone has their own method. A big one is their hands, what are they holding, what are they carrying. If they aren't looking at the price tags, they are just grabbing stuff, you know, people don't shop like that . . . we'll look for grab-n-runs, we'll look for people leaving their bikes right by the front door . . .

OFFICER T: Sometimes someone will grab something, like a couple pairs of underwear, then they'll go and get a pair jeans and lay them over top, or they'll leave something in one part of the store and come back to it, so you wait for them to come back and then you nab them . . .

OFFICER W: Or they'll bunch something up in their hands . . .

OFFICER T: Or they will have been in the store a couple days before, they'll have a receipt for something, they'll grab the same item and walk up to counter and try to exchange it, they'll say they have a receipt for it and they'll try to return it.

OFFICER W: A lot of the time people will be touching their faces, they'll be very nervous, even the experienced ones. It is like poker – everyone has a tell!

Both Officers W & T received university educations in psychology. Officer W completed his M.A. in behaviourism. Clearly, the reading of people and their actions is a central part of the CCTV operator's job at Suburban Mall. They not only read the screen for criminal behaviour, but also for behaviour they treat as indicative of potential criminal behaviour (Norris and Armstrong, 1999b: 130; Graham 1998:-490), like the parking of a bicycle near the front door or the wringing of hands. CCTV becomes activated when the officer's reading of the text influences his next action, orchestrating a sequence of social events.

> OFFICER T: Sometimes you can zoom in, catch the number on a credit card, type it in on the computer, and it says the account holder is born in 1921, but the guy with the card is only a twenty-year old. It is reasonable to say that it is not his card . . . sometimes you type it in and it is a stolen card, so you let them buy the stuff and then you get them outside and arrest them.

> OFFICER W: Sometimes we don't even have to move. Like if we recognize a person who has come in, we can just page them, say 'so and so please come to the Resource Protection office.' So they'll know we're watching them, they'll get spooked, and they'll leave. Or we'll flash our radios. That is where the prevention side of it comes in. Or, if a person we recognize comes in, they steal, and they get off with some merchandise, we can just phone the cops and tell them and they can go to their house and arrest them.

In both these instances, the CCTV as 'rolling text' is used to coordinate a sequence of events in real time. In the credit-card fraud scenario, the social event takes place in the local setting. In the case of the grab-n-run shoplifter who escapes the store, the event is coordinated via communication with police in the extra-local setting . . . In the case of the known offender, the public address system allows the operator to make announcements directly to the offender, which also alerts other workers in the store. Suspicious activity is sometimes first identified by workers in other sections of the building (Heath, Luff, & Svensson, 2002:190). Mobile phones aid communication within the store, so that the operator on the floor can contact the operator in the CCTV control room and vice versa:

> K: So one of you is in the control room and one of you is out on the floor, how do you communicate?

> OFFICER T: We got walkie talkies and portable phones, so when three of us are in, maybe we'll have one in the control room, one on the floor and one at the exit. So Officer W will say 'heh he is going out,' and we'd make the arrest . . .

When citizens are detected as shoplifters, they are placed under citizens' arrest by officers W & T. The experience of the shopper-turned-risk is immediately altered. The criminal code, a text in itself and part of a series of texts (which includes the video), directly informs their work:

> K: So you call in the police?

> OFFICER W: Yup, every time we make an arrest.

> OFFICER T: Section 494 of the criminal code states that to arrest a person you

have to report it to the police, if not you will be charged for acting as a cop when you are not a cop . . .

K: So you're making citizens' arrests?

OFFICER W: Yup, we have the right to detain someone for shop theft.

Officers W & T and the 'initiating text' at Suburban Mall

The 'initiating text' can be rewritten and reinterpreted into a series of texts which overlap and facilitate extra-local organization of the social. Writing practices are crucial to collecting and processing information and to classification; they also play a key role in constructing and objectifying consumers (Callon, 2002: 199). At Suburban Mall, CCTV video is put into words, written into a logbook, rewritten into an incident report (sometimes referred to as an RCC by Officers W & T), which is subsequently sent to a host of interrelated organizational complexes. They are interrelated through administrative practices which are co-textually-mediated.

K: Do you write happenings down in a logbook?

OFFICER T: Yeah, we write it down in the logbook, and also we have reports . . .

K: Incident reports?

OFFICER W: But today, a known shoplifter was in the store, she was looking around, and we recognized her. So we went down to talk to her, we spooked her, she left the mall, so I called mall security and said, 'Hey, look, a known shoplifter just exited the store and went into the mall, she is probably looking for vacuum cleaners . . .'

K: So this would get written in the incident report?

OFFICER W: This would get written in the logbook, what she was wearing, the time, what she was looking at . . . If there is an arrest we'll start an RCC, we'll call the police and we'll start an official file . . .

K: So the logbook is used to build an incident report, and the RCC is an official incident report?

OFFICER W: A lot of times it is . . .

OFFICER T: We have our store incident report which gets emailed to Toronto . . .

OFFICER W: And it gets catalogued nationally . . .

OFFICER T: Then there is a report to Crown Counsel. That becomes a Crown document, on file, and the police handle that, it goes to the Courthouse, and it is used if we have to testify if they don't plead guilty.

K: So what will you write?

OFFICER T: We'll note down physical characteristics, they were looking around, here and there, they were paying more attention to their surroundings than normal shoppers do . . .

OFFICER W: And then if you're off for a couple of days you come in and you always review the logbook, see what happened, find out who has been in . . .

K: So the RCC it . . .

OFFICER W: It is the same form that the police use . . .

OFFICER T: It is the same program on the computer that the police have.

The video as text is interpreted as a 'rolling text,' and then transcribed, taking the form of an 'initiating text.' It initiates a series of texts which orchestrates a future sequence of social events. Officers W & T transcribe the CCTV image, which is reinterpreted and re-transcribed into the incident report, which can be sent to a host of interrelated organizational complexes including the police, the Crown Counsel, the Courts, and the head office in Toronto via email. Moreover, the incident report exists at the outset as a computer file which is compatible with the method of police record-keeping. Further probing revealed the organizational depth to which the incident report coordinates action:

K: Who else receives the incident reports?

OFFICER T: John Howard Society, through the Crown.

OFFICER W: Yeah, whoever needs to get a copy of it just talks to the Crown and can get one. Yeah, the John Howard Society gets them, 'cause they deal with a lot of offenders. They rehabilitate offenders. They get a copy of the incident report and make them realize what they did wrong and they have to write an apology to the store.

OFFICER T: Baby strollers are a hot thing too. Yeah, because they are new moms and they don't work, and they have their kid all day long, they need something to do and apparently they shoplift. A lot of them will go, fill up the bottom of the stroller . . . sometimes Social Services gets involved, especially around the children . . .

K: Do they get a copy of the incident report?

OFFICER W: Oh yeah.

OFFICER T: And if you're caught on tape, well, most people plead guilty. And if they don't, and we got them on tape, we just forward it to the defence attorney and they usually change their plea.

K: So how does the video get used by the Courts?

OFFICER W: If I actually had to testify it would be played by the Court as part of the testimony, and basically I'd be describing it as if I am the camera operator. I'd be explaining what I was doing, what he was doing, like, 'here he is folding some clothes over some others,' you know?

K: Where else does the incident report go?

OFFICER T: Every RCC we fill out, the video evidence is available upon request, so that's why we try to get everything on tape, 'cause if all you have is your logbook notes, the defence attorney will cross examine you and try to screw you up.

K: What about the tapes?

OFFICER W: It depends on the level of interest, like sometimes on a big case the video evidence can go to the regional manager in Vancouver, and it might make it up all the way to Toronto to the national manager.

OFFICER T: And we're not really allowed to give away the video footage, but if there is a known offender then we can make a photo from the video and forward it to other store locations.

An incident report for each offender, initiated by the video text, is forwarded to the Crown Counsel, the defence attorney, the Court, and in some cases to the John Howard Society and to Social Services. These are examples of how the video as text becomes a written text and then facilitates further work processes. The video as text itself is sent to the regional manager in Vancouver or the national manager in Toronto, and can also be used as a standardizing piece of evidence within the Court room. Within the Court room, the tape is reinterpreted using the professional language and interpretative-institutional frame of the CCTV operator (Goodwin and Goodwin, 1997), who is located within a specific organizational framework within the shopping complex. 'Professionals,' like the CCTV operator, have the power to legitimately visualize and put into words the events which unfold on video.

Officers W & T, discourse, and ruling practices at Suburban Mall

As people located within the framework of ruling, Officers W & T construct objectified versions of citizens using televisual and non-televisual texts. CCTV video, and the incident report, guide their work in a manner which has both immediate and extra-local effects on the people who are made objects of surveillance. Officers W & T's talk makes clear the particular discursive approach they partake in through CCTV monitoring, and indicates the organizational complex which frames their work:

OFFICER W: A lot of it is facial recognition, we have known offenders . . .

OFFICER T: About fifty percent of them are repeat offenders . . .

OFFICER W: They are probably IV drug users and this is their livelihood, to steal for a living . . .

K: So you build a profile about known offenders?

OFFICER W: Well every month or two there are Resource Protection meetings, we talk and swap photos . . .[9]

OFFICER T: But we don't get a lot of the worst of the worst up here, you know, drug addicts who are homeless, they don't come up from the downtown core . . .

K: So do you make a lot of arrests?

OFFICER W: Not right now 'cause it is after 'welfare Wednesday,' so they have money, but once they run out of money things will pick up again.

Recall from an earlier section the discourses of the flawed consumer and underclass. The flawed consumer, a veritable member of the socially constructed underclass, is unable to respond to the enticements of the consumer market for lack of required resources. In the act of surveillance, the 'shopper deemed suspicious' becomes a risk to be policed. From the perspective of the organizational complex, it is suspicion which is directed towards people who receive social assistance, not compassion or understanding. This discourse informs the work of Officers W & T, directing asymmetrical levels of organizational surveillance at those presupposed to not belong. Norris and Armstrong suggest that the area surveyed by the CCTV operator is an area of 'normative ecology,' and that people regarded as not belonging are treated as 'other' and made objects of intensified surveillance (1999b: 140). This presumptuous reading of the text by Officers W & T constructs future shoppers as suspicious *ipso facto*, as illegitimate, as depersonalized 'things' to be watched. More importantly, and akin to the 'colour-coded' profiling Norris and Armstrong discovered in their CCTV study (ibid.: 124; see also Fiske, [1998]), camera monitoring at Suburban Mall constitutes a racialized exclusionary practice . . . :

OFFICER W: As for what we look for [pause] Natives. Hate to stereotype, but I know in Central Saanich they have houses on their reserves that are basically a shopping store of merchandise stolen from real stores . . .

K: An urban reserve?

OFFICER W: Yeah, where the police can't go, without a warrant.

OFFICER T: I've been told that the Elders give the younger ones a list of what they actually want them to steal, and if they do get caught, the punishment is handed over to the band, so nothing gets done because the band does nothing.

K: They come in contact with the police?

OFFICER T: Yeah, you still get hauled down to the police station and it gets turned over to the band.

K: And the incident report?

OFFICER T: It goes to the band, but nothing happens, they aren't punished, so they come back. What else? Basically, if they look like a dirtbag, then they are. So you watch, and figure out . . .

OFFICER W: Like a construction worker might come, and they are dirty, but we know the ones who aren't . . .

Those 'dirty ones' are not aesthetically dirty like the construction worker. Rather, Officers W & T *know* it is some innate quality of the young, Aboriginal shopper which necessitates intensified surveillance. In this instance, it is not embodied ambiguity but skin colour which acts as the 'signifier of suspicion.' CCTV operators engage in racialized profiling because they feel they are more likely to 'protect resources' if particular categories of shoppers are monitored. Aboriginality is the indicator onto which the CCTV operator projects the shopper-as-risk discourse. The racialized profiling practice noted in this study indicates the prevalence of exclusionary, rather than inclusionary, forms of social control.[10] Racialized profiling through camera surveillance will become a serious social problem in Canadian society if policy initiatives are not enacted to regulate the rules of watching that CCTV operators use to classify, sort, and exclude citizens.

Discussion and conclusion

CCTV video is used to mediate activities within the work setting and facilitate organization at the institutional level. The institutional ethnographer is acutely interested in mapping out textually-mediated work processes. [Figure 13.1] explicates the coordinating role of televisual and non-televisual texts within Suburban Mall. The video as text instigates the process, acting as a 'rolling text' of embodied persons which is read by the CCTV operator from an interpretative-institutional frame. The 'rolling text' is interpreted in real time, and informs Officers W & T's work of resource protection in Suburban Mall. The CCTV operators do the work of activating the video text, making citizens' arrests, and translating the video into a written text. This written text, or 'initiating text,' takes the form of the logbook, and, in cases where it is warranted, an incident report. However, video of offenders can be freeze-framed and distributed to other stores as a picture text, and the video itself can be sent to Crown Counsel, the defence attorney, and the Court. This underlines the *replicable* form of the video text as one linkage in the technique of inscription. The incident report also goes to Crown Counsel, the defence attorney, and the Court. The Court can then distribute the incident report to the John Howard Society, Social Services, or the Band Counsel, depending on the given situation. The same copy of the incident report can be sent to the Regional Manager in Vancouver, the National Manager in Toronto, and Police authorities.

The CCTV video, in original or transcribed form, is active in coordinating sequences of sociality and work in each institution shown in [Figure 13.1]. Through video as 'rolling text,' the shopper-turned-risk is caught in the act of shoplifting by the CCTV operator. Via the video as an 'initiating text,' the act of the offender is written up and distributed to various institutions in a process involving televisual mall surveillance, risk detection and risk communication. Contained within the text is a dialogue, a dialectic of reading and writing which reveals the organizational arrangement of an institution. Video is active when used as a constituent of social and work processes, despite indication that the participants in these interactions are not necessarily known to one another. Televisual texts, in both the 'rolling' and 'initiating' senses, contribute to the construction of an objectified reality, displacing the subject.

What we see in the Suburban Mall is not Foucault's automatic functioning of power (1979:201), where the behaviour of shoppers is normalized by the perpetual gaze of the CCTV camera. Rather, the imperative of capital accumulation induces a

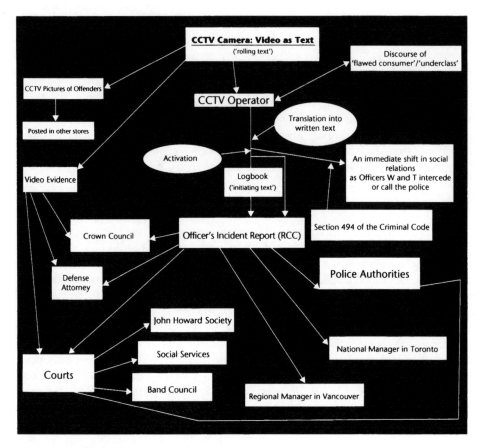

[**Figure 13.1**] Officers W and T at Suburban Mall

desire to exclude flawed consumers from territories of consumption (McCahill, 2002: 196), leading to a form of CCTV-mediated 'moral regulation' (ibid.: 14). As Officer T explains, 'Sometimes you're all gung-ho because you really want to catch them, *it is like they are stealing from you.*' The evidence presented in this [chapter] demonstrates how, through their own reading and rewriting of the video text, Officers W & T actively participate in the discourses which are fundamental to the relational aspects of the organizational complex where they work.

For Foucault, the 'disciplinary individual' is always the inmate – the object of the guards' scrutiny – never the observer in the central tower (Goodlad, 2003:543; Lyon 1991). As an interesting twist to the Panopticon metaphor, it is the CCTV operators' watching behaviour which is normalized along institutional lines by being behind the camera at Suburban Mall, not the shoppers' behaviour by being pored over by the all-seeing eye. Officers W & T occupy a position in the ruling structure, so they come to view the world in distinctive ways by virtue of their participation in the discourse that underpins their work processes; Officers W & T presuppose and internalize the propriety of the organizational complex in which they work.

Through the construction and use of classificatory rules for watching, the cognitive activity of the CCTV operator is trained, producing the objects of knowledge around which the institutional discourses of the profession are organized (Goodwin, 1994:628). CCTV operators employ ways of seeing and acting which are subjective as well as manifestations of the organizational interests of Suburban Mall. The textually-mediated experience of participating in discourse also displaces the officers' own experiences of watching and reading the CCTV video. CCTV operators are best conceptualized as 'control workers' (Rose, [2000]:199–200). It is their job to administer the marginal in the . . . mall, to protect communities of consumption from . . . individuals socially constructed as inherently risky, and to identify, assess, and reduce or eliminate the possibility of profit loss. The targeted surveillance and exclusion of the Aboriginal shopper is bound up in the racialized subjectivities of the CCTV operator, but also the Suburban Mall's prerogative of resource protection. CCTV operators use codes to classify and sort the shopper population. Activity by Aboriginal shoppers is automatically considered as suspicious, as 'anti-social,' and threatening to the flow of capital . . .

Utilizing institutional ethnography, the talk of CCTV operators in their work settings explicates how CCTV video, conceptualized as a text or as a primary source in a series of texts, is used to coordinate lived realities and facilitate organization at the institutional, extra-local level. In their work processes, CCTV operators employ a diverse array of texts, including the logbook, the criminal code, the incident report, pictures, and the video itself. The video as text – in picture, written, and original form – is an active constituent of sociality. In Suburban Mall, and many other institutions, video contributes to both the immediate and extra-local coordination of work processes. The events which video as text are active in shaping take place within the discourses which permeate the organizational complex, discourses that the CCTV operators actively participate in . . .

Notes

1 This chapter is an extract from K. Walby (2005) How closed-circuit television surveillance organizes the social: an institutional ethnography, *Canadian Journal of Sociology*, 30: 189–214.

2 See McCahill (2002), Heath, Luff, & Svensson (2002), and Norris and Armstrong (1999b) for the most in-depth studies.

3 This is not to reduce institutions to texts, but rather to show that texts are the foundational media in co-ordinating people's work activities in institutional complexes (Smith, 2001: 175) . . .

4 It is now common for banks and other commercial entities to outsource their video monitoring to settings situated thousands of kilometers away. The cameras remain local, but 'the watchers' are now extra-local. As a Canadian example, banks in downtown Victoria and Vancouver transmit the live images caught on their CCTV to Toronto via fiber optic connections. The CCTV operators in Toronto then alert authorities in the given city if need be, thereby orchestrating subsequent social events.

5 The prevalence of discreet and mundane surveillance practices does not create

the automatic functioning of power that Foucault had envisioned. For instance, CCTV cameras are sometimes not noticed by the people who fall under the optical gaze. The presence of cameras does not directly alter people's behaviour. Citizens regularly commit litigious acts, despite knowing they are likely to be caught. While we have not seen the closure of agency implied in Foucault's disciplinary society, the desire to know, watch, classify, and exclude – panopticism – remains central to CCTV surveillance.

6   Increasingly there is confusion over what constitutes public versus private space. For Slater, 'the shopping mall indicates the most profound contemporary confusion of public and private: it is a private development which "simulates" a public sphere which has all but disappeared from contemporary society' (1998: 150). Implementation of CCTV constitutes the privatization of public spaces. For Christian Parenti (2003: 110), public space is a resource, a democratic platform, and this holds true for the Greek polis through to the town square and the contemporary city streetscape. Parenti writes, 'destroying or controlling these public spaces has always been a political tool by which rulers battle restive populations' (ibid).

7   Smith writes that textual-mediation co-ordinates work organization in two senses: 'one the actual local setting in which it goes on and the other the hook-ups it creates with other setting and text-reader conversations of other people reading the same text' (2001:175).

8   The focus of the interviews was not the informant herself, but rather the institutional complex in which she worked.

9   The text can also be broken down into pictorial representations which are shared between store locations. Photographs are records or texts which are viewed in socially organized ways within a particular discourse.

10   This statement must be qualified by acknowledging that computerization, digitization, and automation, particularly in forms of consumer dataveillance and database amalgamation, move the inclusion/exclusion dialectic towards inclusive forms of surveillance. The tension between inclusion/exclusion is a key dialectic informing surveillance studies. Linking facial and movement recognition software with CCTV monitoring systems has not yet become routine, so camera monitoring is still contingent on assessing multiple factors of human sociality, and therefore based on subjective decision-making processes pertaining to who should be barred entry from particular locales.

References

Bauman, Z. (1998) *Globalization: The Human Consequences*. New York: Columbia University Press.

Boyne, R. (2000) Post-Panopticism, *Economy and Society*, 29(2): 285–307.

Callon, M. (2002) Writing and (re)writing devices as tools for managing complexity, in J. Law, and A. Mol (eds) *Complexities: Social Studies of Knowledge Practices*. Durham and London: Duke University Press.

Campbell, M. and Manicom, A. (1995) Introduction, in M. Campbell and A. Manicom (eds) *Knowledge, Experience and Ruling Relations: Studies in the Social Organization of Knowledge*. Toronto: University of Toronto Press.

Coleman, R. (1998) From the Dockyards to the Disney Store: surveillance, risk and security in Liverpool city centre, *International Review of Law, Computers & Technology*, 12(1): 27–45.

Coleman, R. and Sim, J. (2000) You'll never walk alone: CCTV surveillance, order and neo-liberal rule in Liverpool city centre, *British Journal of Sociology*, 51(4): 623–39.

Crang, M. (1996) Watching the city: video surveillance and resistance, *Environment and Planning A*, 28(12): 2099–104.

Dandeker, C. (1990) *Surveillance, Power, and Modernity: Bureaucracy and Discipline from 1700 to the Present Day*. New York: St. Martin's Press.

Deleuze, G. (1990) Postscript on the societies of control, *L'Autre journal*, 1: 1–8.

Devault, M. and McCoy, L. (2002) Institutional ethnography: using interviews to investigate ruling relations, in J. F. Gubrium and J. A. Holstein (eds) *Handbook of Interviewing: Context and Method*. Thousand Oaks, CA: Sage Publications.

Fiske, J. (1998) Videotech, in Mirzoeff, Nicholas (ed). In *The Visual Culture Reader* London: Routledge.

Foucault, M. (1979) *Discipline and Punish: The Birth of the Prison*. New York: Vintage Books.

Fyfe, N. (1996) City watching: closed circuit television surveillance in public spaces, *Area*, 28(1): 37–46.

Fyfe, N. R. and Bannister, J. (1998) 'The Eyes Upon the Street': Closed-circuit Television Surveillance and the City, in N. R. Fyfe (ed.) *Images of the Street: Planning, Identity, and Control in Public Space*. London: Routledge.

Giddens, A. (1979) *Central Problems in Social Theory: Action, Structure and Contradiction in Social Analysis*. London: The Macmillan Press, Ltd.

Giddens, A. (1981) *A Contemporary Critique of Historical Materialism: Vol. 1 Power, Property, and the State*. London: The Macmillan Press Ltd.

Giddens, A. (1991) *Modernity and Self-Identity: Self and Society in the Late Modern Age*. Cambridge: Polity Press.

Goldberg, D. (1993) *Racist Culture*. Oxford: Blackwell.

Goodlad, L. M. E. (2003) Beyond the Panopticon: Victorian Britain and the critical imagination, *PMLA: Papers of the Modern Language Association of America*, 118(3): 539–556.

Goodwin, C. (1994) Professional vision, *American Anthropologist*, 96(3): 606–33.

Goodwin, C. and Goodwin, M. H. (1997) Contested vision: the discursive constitution of Rodney King, in B.L. Gunnarsson, P. Linnel and B. Nordberg (eds) *The Construction of Professional Discourse*. London: Longman.

Gottdiener, M. (2003) Recapturing the center: a semiotic analysis of shopping malls, in A.R. Cuthbert (ed.) *Designing Cities: Critical Readings in Urban Design*. Oxford: Blackwell Publishers, Ltd.

Graham, S. (1998) Spaces of surveillant simulation: new technologies, digital representations, and material geographies, *Society and Space*, Vol. 16, Environment and Planning Dept., pp. 483–504.

Heath, C., Hindmarsh, J. and Luff, P. (1999) Interaction in isolation: the dislocated world of the London Underground train driver, *Sociology*, 33(3): 555–75.

Heath, C., Luff, P. and Svensson M.S., (2002) Overseeing organizations: configuring action and its environment, *British Journal of Sociology*, 53(2): 181–201.

Helten, F. and Fischer, B. (2003) Video surveillance on demand for various purposes? Berlin shopping malls as socio-technical testbeds for CCTV. Available at: Urbaneye: http://www.urbaneye.net/results/ue_wp11.pdf

Honess, T. and Charman, E. (1992) Closed-circuit television in public places: its acceptability and perceived effectiveness, Home Office Research Development and Statistics. Available at: http://www.homeoffice.gov.uk/rds/prgpdfs/fcpu35.pdf

Jay, M. (1995) *Downcast Eyes: The Denigration of Vision in Twentieth-Century French Thought.* Berkeley, CA: University of California Press.

Jenks, C. (1995) The centrality of the eye in western culture: an introduction, in C. Jenks (ed.) *Visual Culture.* London: Routledge.

Lianos, M. (2003) Social control after Foucault, *Surveillance & Society,* 1(3): 412–30.

Lianos, M. and Douglas, M. (2000) Dangerization and the end of deviance: the institutional environment, in D. Garland and R. Sparks (eds) *Criminology and Social Theory.* Oxford: Oxford University Press.

Lyon, D. (1991) Bentham's Panopticon: from moral architecture to electronic surveillance, *Queen's Quarterly,* 98(3): 596–617.

Lyon, D. (2001) *Surveillance Society: Monitoring Everyday Life.* Buckingham: Open University Press.

Lyon, D. (2002) Everyday surveillance: personal data and social classifications, *Information, Communication & Society,* 5(2): 242–57.

Macphee, G. (2002) *The Architecture of the Visible. Technology and Urban Visual Culture.* London: Continuum.

McCahill, M. (2002) *The Surveillance Web: The Rise of Visual Surveillance in an English City.* Cullompton, Devon: Wilan Publishing.

McCoy, L. (1995) Activating the photographic text, in M. Campbell and A. Manicom (eds) *Knowledge, Experience and Ruling Relations: Studies in the Social Organization of Knowledge.* Toronto: University of Toronto Press.

Norris, C. (2003) From personal to digital: CCTV, the panopticon, and the technological mediation of suspicion and social control, in D. Lyon (ed.) *Surveillance as Social Sorting: Privacy, Risk, and Digital Discrimination.* London: Routledge.

Norris, C. and Armstrong, G. (1999a) Introduction: power and vision, in C. Norris, G. Armstrong and J. Morton (eds) *Surveillance, Closed Circuit Television, and Social Control.* Aldershot: Ashgate.

Norris, C. and Armstrong, G. (1999b) *The Maximum Surveillance Society: The Rise of CCTV.* Oxford: Berg.

Parenti, C. (2003) *The Soft Cage: Surveillance in America from Slavery to the War on Terror.* New York, NY: Basic Books.

Poster, M. (1984) *Foucault, Marxism and History: Mode of Production versus Mode of Information.* Cambridge: Polity Press.

Rose, N. (2000) Government and control, in D. Garland and R. Sparks (eds) *Criminology and Social Theory.* Oxford: Oxford University Press.

Sharma, N. (2001) On being not Canadian: the social organization of 'migrant workers' in Canada, *Canadian Review of Sociology and Anthropology,* 38(4): 415–38.

Slater, D. (1998) Public/private, in C. Jenks (ed.) *Core Sociological Dichotomies.* London. Sage Publications.

Smith, D. E. (1987) *The Everyday World as Problematic: A Feminist Sociology.* Toronto: University of Toronto Press.

Smith, D. E. (1990) *Texts, Facts, and Femininity: Exploring the Relations of Ruling.* New York, NY: Routledge.

Smith, D. E. (1999) *Writing the Social: Critique, Theory, and Investigations.* Toronto: University of Toronto Press.

Smith, D. E. (2001) Texts and the ontology of organizations and institutions, *Cultures, Organizations, and Societies,* 7(2): 159–98.

Webster, F. (1995) *Theories of the Information Society.* New York, NY: Routledge.

PART 4

Surveillance, social inequality and social problems

The 2001 Super Bowl in Tampa, Florida, is an important moment in the history of surveillance. Using a software program called FaceIt™, which was developed and donated by the Visionics Corporation, New Jersey, local police strategically placed video surveillance cameras in key locations to scan the faces of thousands of ticket holders entering the stadium. Although no arrests were made, the program identified 19 wanted suspects by matching biometric readings of spectators' facial images with previously stored facial images of convicted felons. Following the 'success' of this experiment, the Tampa police proceeded to install a 36-camera system equipped with the FaceIt™ software in the city's nightlife district. The publicity that this private–public partnership generated was significant for the biometrics industry in general, and for Visionics in particular. Government departments and agencies around the world[1] started to invest millions of taxpayers' dollars in the development of biometric surveillance for terrorism and intelligence purposes (O'Harrow 2001), and the FaceIt™ system became the next 'magic bullet' in the fight against crime.

While several stakeholder groups (i.e., police services, merchants, politicians) argue that biometric applications like FaceIt™ are an effective tool for combating everything from terrorism to child predators on the Internet, critics charge that video surveillance systems and related biometric applications do not reduce violent crime. Critics also argue that the problems with video surveillance programs extend beyond their ineffectiveness. They contend that increased surveillance has a harmful effect on the social fabric because it creates a pervasive sense of suspicion and criminalizes innocent people by submitting every individual to a virtual police lineup. Even citizens who have never had contact with the police might find themselves 'categorically vulnerable' to discrimination by virtue of their membership in social groups defined by the authorities as 'risky' or 'dangerous' (e.g., black men, youth). The American Civil Liberties Union (ACLU), the National Association for the Advancement of Colored People (NAACP), the National Asian Pacific Consortium (NAPC), and countless other civil rights organizations argue that video surveillance programs enable the police to engage in 'high-tech racial profiling'[2] with little, if any, accountability.

The problems associated with the escalation in video surveillance use internation-ally speak to the relationship between surveillance practices and social problems generally. Commonly rationalized as a way of addressing what are perceived to be already existing social problems (e.g., fraud, crime and other behaviours deemed to be anti-social and/or criminal), the implementation of surveillance systems often creates or exacerbates a range of social problems (e.g., poverty, over-policing, suspicion and exclusion) under the guise of managing risk and reducing harm. For this reason, surveillance may be conceptualized as both a cause and an effect of social problems. The readings in this section address the multifaceted relationship between surveillance and social problems, examining specific practices such as digital technologies, welfare administration, racial profiling, parental drug testing of their kids, and public camera surveillance.

Section readings

The first reading, Chapter 14 by John Gilliom, examines the history of surveillance practices that have underscored welfare administration in the United States. For Gilliom, before the population can be governed, it must become 'knowable' to state administrators. As such, citizens must be categorized on the basis of characteristics that are observable, assessable and amenable to the management and information in modern bureaucratic systems.

Gilliom traces contemporary population management strategies to the sixteenth century, when British law first empowered local officials to identify, document and later mark destitute persons with badges indicating their status. He shows how similar practices emerged with the Quincy Report of 1821: the poor were separated into categories of 'impotent' poor and 'able-bodied' poor. However, Gilliom maintains that modern forms of welfare surveillance really began with the economic collapse of the Great Depression. The Social Security Act (1935), Gilliom shows, laid out key discursive and administrative differences in how the poor received social assistance. These differences have an important effect on the role of surveillance and its influence on social problems. Unemployment insurance and seniors' pensions (previously referred to as Old Age Insurance) were not seen as forms of 'relief', but rather as 'compensation' for past contributions to the economic well-being of the nation and state. As such, they did not carry with them the same stigma or scrutiny as programmes like Aid to Dependent Children (later renamed Aid to Families with Dependent Children), the so-called mother's pensions, or widows' and orphans' funds. In the aftermath of the economic devastation of the Depression, monies began to flow to local authorities for redistribution to poor families, but they did so with little policy guidance. This resulted in the development of degrading and invasive *tactics* of modern welfare surveillance, and these bore significant implications for women and children.

In the 1960s, welfare administration and surveillance of the poor improved with more progressive national political leadership and sustained social activism on behalf of the poor. Subsequently, high levels of suspicion and investigations declined, and programme administrators placed greater emphasis on accepting the terms and conditions of poor people's needs. Yet these successes, Gilliom contends, were quickly eroded by the decline of the civil rights and welfare rights protest movements, as well as by the 1972 election of the Nixon administration. The latter's punitive welfare policies and practices entailed more intensified scrutiny and surveillance of welfare recipients and state-level bureaucracies. The computer revolution of the 1980s and 1990s changed the nature of welfare administration and enabled authorities to use more powerful tools to centralize control of the welfare rolls. According to Gilliom, the advent of new communications and information technology constructed a world where there is room neither for secrets nor arguments over basic values and knowledge claims. What is significant is how Gilliom shows how surveillance actually produces social problems, and how moralized surveillance practices are influenced by politics and economics.

The second reading passage, Chapter 15 by Stephen Graham and David Wood, begins where Gilliom's analysis ends: considering the social implications of a new array of surveillance practices that have been facilitated by the digital turn in computerization. Graham and Wood explore the nature of digital surveillance in order to explain how it differs in function and scope from other forms of surveillance. Noting how the technology enables information to be more easily stored, transmitted and computed into new categories, they argue that, while the obvious difference between digital and analogue surveillance systems is quantitative, the fundamental difference between them is qualitative.

Whereas surveillance researchers who focus on digitization may be rightfully accused of technological determinism, for Graham and Wood the causal force of the digital turn in surveillance has been the broader political-economic shifts associated with market liberalism (i.e., privatization, deregulation, commodification and consumerism). They offer a critical approach to the study of surveillance, computerization and inequality by explicating the different ways that political and economic processes circumscribe the development of new surveillance technologies, and of how these technologies then bring into existence categories of normal and abnormal, risky and safe, desirable and undesirable. If we are to properly understand the relationship between surveillance and social inequality, they argue, we must become more aware of structural factors that automate social exclusion.

The task of surveillance research, Graham and Wood conclude, is to mobilize the tools of critical analysis to expose the ways computer systems are being used to prioritize the service quality and life chances of citizens who promise corporations premium economic returns, while simultaneously reducing the opportunities and access of less favoured groups. The digitization of surveillance is driven by a dominant political agenda that seeks to dismantle citizens' access to public space, and students of surveillance must stand vigilant in making visible these regime shifts and their effects on democracy. Resistance must also come from within civil society, they argue, and must take a variety of forms and cut across the plethora of policy domains.

In the third reading in this section, Chapter 16, Roy Coleman argues that surveillance re-zones city space to show how, through a number of technologies and legal-moral ordering practices, urban centres in Britain have been re-imagined and structurally transformed into exclusionary spaces. Coleman shows how institutional practices of social control intersect with, and help to organize, 'visualized spectacles'. His theoretical focus is the definitional processes that underscore campaigns to renew city centres through innovative spatial control policies and practices. These definitional processes are imbued with both political-economic and cultural dimensions that enable powerful sources (particularly business groups and local councils) to ascend to positions of social and political decision-making.

Coleman argues that success in the definitional field depends upon the ability of 'primary definers' to mobilize their resources and promote a shared vision of urbanization. In Britain, central government urban design documents have specified the importance of creating within city centres a 'visually pleasing space'. Translated from policy design into strategies of implementation, this has entailed empowering police to monitor and cleanse British towns and cities of the high-spirited youth, homeless people, street traders and other social groups whose activities and modes of existence do not conform to this 'orderly and risk-free' vision. Surveillance practices are integral to the articulation and promotion of 'the visually pleasing city', and their widespread deployment demonstrates how it is not difference per se that is incompatible with urban renewal but inequality (economic, political and socio-cultural) and marginality that demand containment.

The urban regentrification projects identified by Coleman do not operate solely on the basis of a restrictive or controlling logic that depends on the deployment of intrusive surveillance practices, however. The successful regentrification of city centres has also involved a repertoire of corrective strategies aimed at responsibilizing homeless and youth into performing entrepreneurial roles, such as training them to be tourist guides. The discourse of cultural regeneration that is at the centre of urban re-spatialization projects has also entailed the promotion of youth-oriented cultural pursuits that are aesthetically appealing and conducive to tourism. For example, Liverpool hosts a two-day annual event at the city's waterfront park to promote urban skateboarding and spontaneous street art as a way of embracing and celebrating the city's inclusiveness. Nevertheless, Coleman shows how this discourse is an inherently contradictory one in which moral regulative strategies can take place alongside more traditionally coercive surveillance and policing practices. That skateboarders in Liverpool can also be fined up to £1000 for skating outside of designated periods, or may be subject to an Anti-Social Behaviour Order (ASBO), shows how surveillance practices in the UK are having a differentiated effect on groups lacking power and authority.

The theme of surveillance and youth is continued in the final reading passage in this section (Chapter 17). Dawn Moore and Kevin Haggerty focus on the shifting discourses and surveillance policies involved in the so-called 'war on drugs' in the United States. They argue that the emphasis of surveillance research on state practices and strategies should be re-directed in light of the putative failures of official anti-drug initiatives. Specifically, they demonstrate how the rhetoric and policies of the contemporary anti-drugs campaign are beginning to shift, and that this transformation has subsequently shifted responsibility for conducting surveillance away from the state towards the family. In other words, the war on drugs is morphing from a public problem fought in the public sphere into a private problem that is being waged within the home: parents, rather than police, have been deputized to occupy the front lines in this new phase of the war on drugs.

In their analysis, Moore and Haggerty show how rhetorical paradigms, if they are to resonate widely and mobilize action, must be constantly refreshed: new speakers must emerge, the language must be suited to changing audience contexts, and the words must be capable of ringing true. A powerful rhetorical device is metaphor, and the authors show us how the so-called war on drugs offers a good example of a metaphor that has become tired and predictable. They argue that a new metaphor of 'disease' emerged to supplant, or at best augment, the 'war' metaphor. To take the analogy further, Moore and Haggerty claim that if disease is effectively everywhere, then drug use (as a disease) must become everybody's problem. Moreover, because the disease metaphor evokes the possibility of a curative fix, diagnostic technologies become important in ensuring early detection that is necessary to prevent against chronic pain and suffering. In this case study, Moore and Haggerty show us that adolescents are not only vulnerable to intensified efforts to monitor their actions and behaviours; they are also, importantly, capable of utilizing their creativity to strategic effect by resisting the attempts of their parents and formal authority figures to monitor and control them.

Questions

Chapter 14 (Gilliom)

1   According to Gilliom, why did the Great Depression mark a significant historical moment in surveillance of the poor?
2   Does Gilliom's analysis of welfare administration and surveillance of the poor offer any hope or optimism for resistance to state attempts to control the most economically vulnerable in our society?
3   Describe the key differences in welfare administration from the sixteenth century to the contemporary era. What are the most important ways that the relationship between surveillance and inequality has changed over that period?

Chapter 15 (Graham and Wood)

1   What are some of the interconnections Graham and Wood explore between digital techniques and the changing political economies of cities and urban societies? What are the implications of these interconnections for the study of surveillance and inequality?
2   Identify the range of responses that Graham and Wood demand as important for critiquing digitized surveillance. Do you think that some of these responses are more effective than other responses? Why?
3   How does digitized surveillance differ in function and scope from earlier forms of surveillance? Why are these differences important?

Chapter 16 (Coleman)

1   What are the central arguments of the 'primary definer thesis'? Explain in what ways local authorities are able to exercise primary definition to create exclusionary entrepreneurial urban landscapes.
2   What are some of the ways in which local initiatives to create aesthetically pleasing public spaces are both driven by and help give shape to punitive national government policies and programmes?
3   In what ways has entrepreneurial urbanism in the UK adversely affected working-class youth and the less affluent neighbourhoods in which they live?

Chapter 17 (Moore and Haggerty)

1   How do the shifting metaphors in the anti-drugs campaign signify a shift in drug control and surveillance policies and practices over youth?

2   Which two privacy constraints have traditionally hindered anti-drug initiatives? How has the proliferation of home drug testing provided a 'solution' to these constraints?

3   Michel Foucault famously argued that power is paradoxical because it always generates resistance. How does Moore and Haggerty's analysis of the new phase in the so-called war on drugs illustrate this thesis about the paradox of power?

Suggested reading

1   Goldstein, R.A. (2004) Who needs the government to police us when we can do it ourselves? The new panopticon in teaching, *Cultural Studies – Critical Methodologies*, 4(3): 320–8.
     The author takes a critical position in relation to the Bush administration's national education policy 'No Child Left Behind'. She argues that the rhetoric used to promote the government's policy, which has been widely applauded and reproduced in the mainstream media, makes it difficult, if not impossible, for educators to speak up about the policy framework's structural limitations, philosophical problems and negative effects on social justice curricular programming. The discourse around the Bush administration's childcare and education framework acts as a new panopticon, Goldstein argues, silencing and controlling teachers and others who might be critical of the policy model.

2   Mathur, S. (2006) Surviving the dragnet: 'special interest' detainees in the U.S. after 9/11, *Race & Class*, 47(3): 31–46.
     The author challenges the cultural relativism of postmodern theory and its privileging of 'discourse' over material reality. This is done to show that in the post-11 September environment, human rights are regularly violated in countries like the United States, and with significant material and emotional effects. Focusing on the thousands of Muslim, South Asian and Middle Eastern men who were detained indefinitely without warrant in and around New York City, she argues that incarceration was designed primarily for surveillance and intimidation over a social group who would experience only more intensified monitoring and racial profiling.

3   Cooper, H., Moore, L., Gruskin, S. and Krieger, N. (2005) The impact of a police crackdown on drug injectors' ability to practice harm reduction: a qualitative study, *Social Science & Medicine*, 61(3): 673–84.
     Employing ethnographic methods, the authors set out to examine the effects of heavier police surveillance of public space and of drug users' bodies on the ability of addicts to pursue harm reduction strategies. The findings suggest that intensified policing may undermine the efforts to reduce health risks associated with injection drug use because users will be less likely to carry sterile syringes (and thus use syringes they obtain on the street) for fear of search, arrest and detention. Homeless people with drug addiction, the authors note, are particularly vulnerable under the regime of more intensified surveillance for drug use in public space.

4   Gandy, O.H., Jr. (1989) The surveillance society: information technology and bureaucratic social control, *Journal of Communication*, 39(3): 61–76.
     Where most studies of social inequality focus on economic divisions between members of different classes (e.g., proletariat and bourgeoisie), the author argues that in the contemporary era bureaucratic organizations are able to mobilize information technologies to achieve a position of power and dominance over the citizenry. Whereas the legal system has historically provided citizens with access to rights and information, these protections are now compromised by the extension and reach of new 'technologies of control'.

5   Bell, C. (2006) Surveillance strategies and populations at risk: biopolitical governance in Canada's national security policy, *Security Dialogue*, 37(2): 147–65.
    Drawing on Foucault's concept of biopolitics the author examines Canada's first national security policy, *Securing an Open Society* (2004), and argues, first, that it represents a dangerous step toward a deeper integration with the Bush administration and threatens hard-won civic freedoms in Canada. Second, she argues that what distinguishes the new security policy is its emphasis on the health and safety of the population, in contrast to conventional security policy discourses that focus on protecting the state. This purported 'care' for the population depends, she shows, on the deployment of both routine and exceptional surveillance practices designed to manage risk through a culture of suspicion that will undoubtedly affect already marginalized ethnic minority groups.

Notes

1   Among these were included the National Security Agency (NSA), the US Defense and Justice Departments, the Israeli Defense Ministry, the London Borough of Newham, the Mexican Federal Election Institute and the Keflavik International Airport in Iceland.
2   *National Public Radio* (Talk of the Nation) (2001) Police, video surveillance and privacy, 16 July.

Reference

O'Harrow, R. Jr. (2001) 'Matching faces with mug shots,' *The Washington Post*, 1 August, A1.

14

Welfare surveillance[1]
by John Gilliom

In the winter of 1915, the following reports were filed as part of the home examinations required for applicants to the Mother's Pension in Muskingham County, Ohio:

> Mrs. Hooper lives on the top of Owen's Hill in a two story frame house. There are two rooms on each floor. These rooms are scantily furnished but are clean and well taken care of. The house is three stories at the back, but the brick basement has no doors. The kitchen has a door at the back but no steps leading to the yard. The porch was not clean but that is pardonable owing to the very muddy yard and being the only entrance to the home. She has milk from her brother's cow in return for carring for the cow. [*sic*]

> Mrs. Dieter lives with her mother, brother, and two children in three rooms on the second floor of her mother's home . . . The apartment upstairs is crowded with furniture but [she] is one of the clean Germans and no improvements can be made in the keeping of the rooms. The furniture is plain but good and well kept.

In the years of the Great Depression, the family of my Uncle Steve, like most of the steelworker families in Ohio, fell on hard times. Little work was available and many families, including theirs, turned to the government for 'relief.' Among the rules for receiving aid was that families not have a functioning automobile. Uncle Steve's dad, and other men in the neighborhood, met this requirement by putting their cars up on cement blocks and removing the wheels. When a home inspection was made, the investigator could report that no working vehicle was owned by the family. If a rare trip was absolutely necessary, my uncle's family would put the wheels on and make the drive. But for daily travel, like the nine-mile trek to see if there was work at the mills, the men walked while their cars sat on blocks. If the mills were hiring, the fathers would use part of their wages for the return fare on the electric street car. If there was no work, they would turn around and walk home.

More recently, those few applicants for assistance in the state of Ohio who actually read through the many pages of their application and consent form come across the following statement about bureaucratic surveillance and computerized investigations of their financial claims:

> The human services department will use your social security number when contacting people or agencies to obtain information needed to determine your eligibility and verify information you have given. For example, your social security number may be used to check your income and/or employment information with past or present employers, financial resources through IRS, unemployment compensation, disability benefits received from state or federal sources and any other appropriate local, state, or federal agency to verify information you have given . . . Your social security number, as well as other information will also be used in computer matching and program reviews or audits to make sure your household is eligible for food stamps, other federal assistance programs and federally assisted state programs, such as school lunch, ADC and Medicaid.[2]

To complete their application, they were required to sign a broad series of information-access waivers, capped off by the comprehensive and disentitling: 'I give my consent to the agency to make whatever contacts are necessary to determine my eligibility for assistance and to verify information I have given in this application.'

. . . [W]elfare surveillance is nothing new. From today's computerized information systems, to the visit to Mrs. Hooper's home in 1915, and back to the surveying and badging of the poor in sixteenth-century Europe, governments have closely examined those who seek assistance.

. . . [I]mages and understandings of the poor that are created by welfare surveillance are not only strikingly partial, but partial in ways that reflect the political, social, and technological conditions of the era. From the records we learn that Mrs. Hooper's husband has died, that she has a milk supply and a clean two-story frame house, but not if she has significant financial investments or a marketable skill. In the time of Mrs. Hooper and Mrs. Dieter, it was important that the one had a cow and that the other was a 'clean German.' No mention was made of automobiles, because it was beyond imagination that the rural poor could have one at that point, and no mention was made of computer matching, because computers did not exist. By the time of the Great Depression, computers were still absent, but the existence and condition of the family car were the most memorable facet of a family's brush with the scrutiny of welfare officials. By the 1990s, cars are still recorded in computer programs – and there are caps on their allowable value – but there is no mention of family cows, and a caseworker would undoubtedly face some trouble for recording their impression that a woman was one of the 'clean Germans.' For the purposes of welfare administration and surveillance, a simplified depiction of the poor must focus on those characteristics which are both observable and deemed to be important in the execution of state policy. The resulting depictions will always reflect the tenors and dynamics of the time as well as the perspectives and capacities of the state. As we watch the terms, practices, and priorities of welfare surveillance shift with the social and political changes that mark the last century, we can see and begin to understand the extent to which the state's vision of the poor is always a product of particular prejudices, assumptions, values, and technical capacities. Understanding the factors that make up these particular emphases is a critical element in coming to understand the politics of surveillance.

. . . One constant in American welfare surveillance is the emphasis on whether or not a family will be eligible for assistance. At the center of this process is the 'means test' which consists of some mechanism for determining if someone is eligible by assessing their needs, their resources, or their capacity to work. Was there evidence of a man or inordinately expensive furniture in Mrs. Hooper's home? Did a family have a working car? Do utility bills and rent receipts, computer sweeps of income or investment records, and birth certificates and school attendance records all verify the information provided by a contemporary applicant? In the pages that follow, we will see that this one constant in American welfare surveillance, reflecting both our faith in the importance of labor and our suspicion that people will do nearly anything to avoid it, is the central point in the ongoing state examination of the poor.

. . . the state struggles to know as much as it can about the poor – and to use its knowledge with critical consequences for poor people's lives – an inevitable struggle over information and perception comes to define the unfolding politics of surveillance.

Knowing the poor

Despite a common tendency to assume otherwise, poor people are a complex lot – 'a bloomin' buzzin' confusion' as William James put it, or what Jim Scott calls a 'complex and unwieldy reality' (1998, 11). Demographically, 'the poor' includes all races, colors, ethnicities, religions, and ages of people, although it is heavy on women and children. Ideologically, there are conservatives, liberals, radicals, and plenty of enigmas. Physically, there are tall, short, thin, and fat. For most of us, 'the poor' includes family, friends, students, and neighbors. There are urban and rural and some suburban. The adult poor include those who never stood a real chance in the economy because of location, gender, disease, discrimination, or disability, and there are those who stood a chance, but for some combination of bad luck and personal and social failure haven't made it. Among the poor are also men and women with special talents for music, art, mechanical repair, oratory, hunting, cooking, gardening, and a host of other human endeavors. There are people who are immensely kind-hearted, there are scoundrels, and there are many who, like most of us, struggle between the two poles. And 'the poor' shift through time as different people move in and out of the ranks.

In short, those who at some period of time populate the low end of the income distribution scale in the United States are indescribably varied and multifaceted. But for the government to take action with or upon them, they must, as James Scott argues in *Seeing like a State*, be made 'legible' or fit into terms, categories, and characteristics that are observable, assessable, and amenable to the management and information regimes of modern bureaucracy (see also Dandeker 1990; Foucault 1979, 191). He argues that 'Certain forms of knowledge and control require a narrowing of vision. The great advantage of such tunnel vision is that it brings into sharp focus certain limited aspects of an otherwise far more complex and unwieldy reality. This very simplification, in turn, makes the phenomenon at the center of the field of vision more legible and hence more susceptible to careful measurement and calculations. Combined with similar observations, an overall, aggregate, synoptic view of a selective reality is achieved, making possible a high degree of schematic knowledge, control, and manipulation' (1998, 11).

This project of making the poor legible is hardly a new one. As far back as 1531, British law

> decreed that local officials search out and register those of the destitute deemed to be impotent, and give them a document authorizing begging. Almsgiving to others was outlawed . . . [and] for those who sought alms without authorization, the penalty was public whipping till the blood ran.
>
> (Piven and Cloward 1971, 15; see also Torpey 2000, 18)

Soon after, authorized beggars were required to wear badges marking their status (Handler and Rosenheim 1966). In Britain and colonial America, a public office called 'the overseer of the poor' was created in order to monitor the collection and delivery of aid to the poor and keep careful records of their identity and whereabouts. From the sixteenth-century surveys of the poor to the comprehensive computer-based Client Information Systems that most states now use, welfare administration has been inextricably a process of struggling to 'know' the poor; to measure, depict, and examine them in ways which both express and facilitate the power and techniques of modern statecraft.

'To define, locate, and purge'

Like any system of surveillance and administration, welfare programs need to simplify the world by focusing on a limited set of factors. In studying the history of welfare surveillance it is patently clear what the focus is on. At different times, though techniques change, one persistent and fundamental question is the bedrock for all of the state's knowledge about the poor: whether or not they are 'deserving,' 'worthy,' or 'eligible' for assistance. Whether it be the sixteenth-century judgment of economic impotence, a labor test, a woman's status as a widow and worthy mother, a eugenicist's classification of imbecility, an investigator's declaration that a family car is not working, or a modern computer's determination of income eligibility, the center and pivot of the state's efforts to know the poor is the question of whether or not the state will help them.

Michael Katz's *In the Shadow of the Poorhouse* finds early evidence of this pattern in the Quincy Report (1821), a Massachusetts study which divided the poor into two separate categories:

> 1. The impotent poor; in which denomination are included all, who are wholly incapable of work, through old age, infancy, sickness or corporeal debility. 2. The able poor; in which denomination are included all, who are capable of work, of some nature, or other; but differing in the degree of their capacity, and in the kind of work, of which they are capable.
>
> (Quoted in Katz 1986, 18)

Katz continues by noting that the view of the Quincy Report was that 'no one should hesitate to help the first class of poor,' and that the 'real issue' was the problem of the able-bodied poor.

> According to the Quincy Report, all the 'evils' attributable to the current system of poor relief could be traced to the same root: 'the difficulty of discriminating between the able poor and the impotent poor and of apportioning the degree of public provision to the degree of actual impotency.' The able poor, so it was assumed, should fend for themselves. Indeed, it is only a slight exaggeration to say that *the core of most welfare reform since the early nineteenth century has been a war on the able-bodied poor: an attempt to define, locate, and purge them from the roles of relief.*
> (ibid., emphasis added)

Many weapons have been used in the war on the able-bodied poor, but there appear to be just a few primary strategies. One – seen in the preceding excerpt – is the use of categories which divide the poor according to such distinctions as age, gender, parental status, physical condition, and mental acuity. The very young, the very old, the disabled, or mothers of young children have typically been more likely to receive help. Another very important dividing line is drawn between those who are poor enough to receive aid and those that the legislatures deem wealthy enough to go it on their own. These distinctions among the poor establish lines of demarcation which can be drawn during the deployment of tactics falling under a second main strategy, examination. Examination would include things such as the gathering of basic demographics about a family or individual, administering a labor test, visiting the home, or other means of gathering information with which to depict the poor and ensure that they truly meet the criteria set forth for the awarding of assistance. Third, and often accomplished in the design of the examination, is deterrence. Here, the goal is to make the process of applying for and receiving aid – as well as the more general status of 'being on the dole' – so demeaning and onerous that only the most desperate would ever apply. This could range from requiring uniforms, to publishing names, to engaging in exhaustive investigations of poor families.

The strategies of categorization, examination, and deterrence are readily apparent in the almshouse, or poorhouse, era of American relief. As opposed to 'outdoor relief,' which allowed aid recipients to move about in the community, the 'indoor relief' of the poorhouse requires the poor to live within the walls of a total institution, often in uniform, and under strict rules of behavior and mandates of forced labor. By creating a total institution which was the only major source of relief, the poorhouse movement was able to both sort and control the poor and, through the deterrent effect of these institutions, force the poor to sort themselves. As poorhouses began to give way to the more active use of 'outdoor' relief, the overseers of the poor turned to different tactics in the effort to test and judge. One was the 'labor test' in which poor men would split wood or break rock in an enclosed work yard. By requiring hard and long hours of work from aid applicants, officials could combat idleness, keep the subjects under their watchful eye, and deter those who may be able to find other types of work.[3]

Toward the latter decades of the nineteenth century, the 'scientific charity' movement brought new practices to the treatment of the poor and began an evolution that would gradually produce the contemporary profession of social work and the contemporary regimes of welfare surveillance.[4] One of the central principles of scientific charity was the 'friendly visitor,' a prototype of the modern social worker who would go into the homes of the poor to advise, inspect, support, and instruct. These 'visitors were supposed to be both investigators and friends. They were to inspire confidence and radiate warmth as they intruded into the most intimate details of their clients' lives' (Katz 1986, 67) . . .

'A modern-dress version of poor relief'

In the late nineteenth and early twentieth century, countless experiments were tried in the nation's programs for the poor. Under the influence of Social Darwinism and the more broadly conservative turn in American business and politics, public sector assistance – never generous – all but died off. Privately funded scientific charity continued, the Community Chest movement began, and with the rise of the Reform Era came the settlement house movement and numerous experiments regarding public health and welfare in different urban areas (see Trattner 1999; Katz 1986; Ferguson 1984, 34). And it was in this period that we see what Linda Gordon calls 'the first modern public welfare in the United States': the precursors to AFDC known as the Mothers' Pensions. 'State and local governments established programs to aid single mothers, mainly in the decade 1910–20. These authorized assistance to "deserving" poor single mothers with children, to defray the costs of raising children in their own homes and to deter child labor and the institutionalization of fatherless children. The enthusiasm for mothers' aid was so great that forty-six of the forty-eight states had passed such laws within twenty years . . . (Gordon 1994, 37).

The Mother's Funds varied greatly by location, but Winifred Bell's research makes it clear that surveillance and judgment were a critical component in many areas, usually bundled under the requirement that children be raised in a 'suitable home.' Thus

> Massachusetts and Michigan specified that no male boarder, other than the mother's brother or father, could live in the home . . . A number of states defined a tubercular parent as 'physically unfit.' Several states required that the religion of the child be protected and fostered, and, if the mother failed to do so, she was an improper person to have custody of the children.
>
> (Bell 1965, 7–8)

And the list goes on. From the types of visitations and inspection [described above] to the midnight raids in search of male visitors, the watchful eye was a central part of almost any assistance to the poor.

It was with the economic collapse of the Great Depression that the modern era of American welfare really began. The omnibus Social Security Act of 1935 (SSA) created a whole series of programs in the area of social welfare. Some, like the old age fund and unemployment insurance, were not cast as 'relief' and were less encumbered by stigma and scrutiny (Gordon 1994; Fraser 1989).[5] But in another area – focusing on women and their children – the Social Security Act created little more than a 'modern-dress version of poor relief' (Handler and Rosenheim 1966, 379). As noted, under the program called Aid to Dependent Children (ADC, later AFDC for Aid to Families with Dependent Children), the federal government took over much of the financial responsibility for what had been called 'mothers' pensions' or 'windows' and orphans' funds.' These state, county, or township programs had been devastated by the Depression's twin impact of sharply rising need and sharply falling tax revenues. As the SSA brought monetary assistance but little policy guidance, local practices and programs remained largely in place. It was here, in the program for women and children, that the most degrading and invasive tactics of modern welfare would be seen.

Linda Gordon explains that while the original Social Security Act did not mandate that the largely autonomous states undertake intensive surveillance in the administration of the early ADC program, the Social Security Board was encouraging states to do so within just a few years of passage. Describing the board's 'model state bill' for 1936, Gordon notes that it

> called for investigations of the home and periodic reconsiderations of the amount of assistance. Home visits were the norm in casework at this time, and many social workers argued that clients preferred home visits, to protect their privacy against meeting others or being seen by others. The drive to control expenses soon shifted the locus of supervision to offices, which most clients in fact preferred, and surveillance focused more on receipts and budgets and less on housecleaning. But the assumption remained that a public assistance client was in need of counseling and rehabilitation and had fewer privacy rights than others
>
> (1994, 296)

From these beginnings, the politics of welfare surveillance only grew more and more intense. The dynamics of the transformation are summarized in William Trattner's *From Poor Law to Welfare State*:

> Whereas between 1935 and the early 1950s, the elderly received the bulk of federal and state welfare funds, by the middle of the [1950s] recipients of A.D.C. . . . outnumbered all others receiving such assistance. Furthermore, whereas earlier most recipients of A.D.C. were dependent white children with widowed mothers, an increasing number of those who received such funds now were single black women with illegitimate children – a trend that would increase significantly in the following years. Thus, in the late 1950s state after state began instituting punitive administrative policies designed to reduce the number of such welfare recipients and to deter new applicants. State residency requirements were strictly enforced so that migrants (especially blacks moving from the South to the North) would not receive assistance, and all sorts of new eligibility investigations were initiated, including 'suitable home' and 'man-in-the-house' policies.
>
> (1999, 309–310)[6]

It became clear that the enforcement of the means test and the investigative practices surrounding it were one of the key means through which welfare officials could reduce rolls or meet other political goals.[7]

It is, of course, unavoidable that information gathering and record keeping are part of large-scale public administration – indeed modern government cannot begin to function without constructing elaborate structures of rationalized information (Scott 1998; Dandeker 1990). But because the American style of poor relief places so much emphasis on assessing the capacity of people to fend for themselves and on deterring those who can – through means tests, stigmatization, man-in-the-house rules, labor tests, residency requirements, or the scrutiny of the friendly visitors – it must be even more surveillance intensive than it might otherwise be. As Handler and Rosenheim argued, a 'social insurance' system – like Social Security – avoids some of the intrusions seen here because there is 'a detailed statutory definition of eligibility, a statutorily prescribed benefit schedule, and, often, a contributory scheme of finance' (1966, 379). Since Social Security assumes need and works with established terms of eligibility and support, case-by-case scrutiny can be minimized, while AFDC, with its emphasis on the individual determination of need, frequent reporting, and ongoing determinations of 'worthiness,' is driven to engage in some of the most invasive forms of scrutiny imaginable.

The exceedingly invasive aspects of welfare programs such as AFDC and Medicaid are also tied to the fact that they deal with those who would be considered society's least powerful – poor, often minority, women and children. In *Unruly Practices*, Nancy Fraser explores the disparities between the management of entitlement programs such as unemployment and social security, which deal with largely male 'citizens,' and welfare programs such as Food Stamps, AFDC, and Medicaid, which involve dependent and largely female 'clients.' She concludes: 'The relief programs are notorious for the varieties of humiliation they inflict upon clients. They require considerable work in qualifying and maintaining eligibility, and they have a heavy component of surveillance' (1989, 152–153). In sum, the combined impact of the administrative mode of the modern state, the focus on eligibility assessment, the emphasis on deterrence, and the disdain for and powerlessness of welfare clients, means that the welfare poor are subject to forms and degrees of scrutiny matched only by the likes of patients, prisoners, and soldiers.

The declaration era

In the late 1960s, however, things changed somewhat – level of scrutiny declined, application hurdles were lowered, and many welfare clients received fuller benefits. In a nutshell, 1969 regulations for AFDC administration required states to experiment with a 'simplified' method for determining eligibility. The 'declaration method,' as it is known, 'provides for eligibility determination to be based, to the maximum extent feasible, on the information furnished by the applicant without routine applicant interviews or verification procedures' (Congressional Research Service 1977, 30). For some combination of reasons, including urban militancy, relatively progressive national leadership and local administration, litigation and advocacy by progressive attorneys, the effect of War on Poverty policies, and the impact of mass protest and mobilization, the climate of welfare surveillance shifted during that period. The level of suspicion, hassle, and investigations dropped, as program admin-istrators placed greater emphasis on accepting the terms and condition of poor people's needs as they were presented by the poor themselves . . .

. . . Furthermore, through the work of poverty attorneys, welfare rights activists, and social program workers, it was frequently the case that *welfare agencies* were the ones subject to scrutiny and sanction. In New York, in particular, there was a focused effort to monitor local offices for rules-compliance, to widely publicize sources of assistance that the poor might be unaware of, and to provide active counsel to the poor on the ins and outs of living on welfare (Piven and Cloward 1979). The counties of Appalachian Ohio saw their own version of this transformation in the late 1960s and early 1970s when community action workers and other activists began training wel-fare clients on rules and regulations and, frequently, accompanying them to meetings with caseworkers (author's interviews). It was an important transformation.[8]

Quality control

But it was a short-lived transformation. After 'a considerable degree of controversy,' new regulations in 1973 'significantly reversed' the emphasis on declaration and on the capacity of poor families to depict themselves (Congressional Research Service 1977, 30).[9] The end of this experimental period in welfare administration came amid the decline of the broader African American protest movement, the fracturing of the welfare rights movement . . . and the 1972 triumph of a Nixon campaign that had made welfare a key issue in speeches and advertisements (Piven and Cloward 1979, 332). Tellingly, the Nixon administration signaled its more punitive and conservative approach to welfare through intensified scrutiny of the welfare rolls and enhanced surveillance of both clients and state-level human services bureaucracies.

The 'Quality Control' (QC) movement was one of the most important federal policy catalysts for the resurgence of fraud control efforts and related practices of surveillance at the state level. Although the beginnings of the QC program can be traced to the early 1960s, it was really in the early and mid-1970s that the federal government's efforts in this area began having a significant effect on the state and local administration of welfare. The 1973 QC regulations included stiff financial penalties for states that failed to meet federally stipulated rates of accuracy in case administration. These first penalties were ruled unlawful by the courts in 1975. But by the late 1970s Congress had reworked the legislation with a series of financial penal-ties and incentives designed to produce state compliance with target goals for error reduction. As the federal government intensified its scrutiny of state-level AFDC administration by closely reviewing samples of cases, many states began intensifying the scrutiny of their AFDC clients, frequently shifting from income estimates to mandated monthly reporting and beginning the use of computer matching and other means of more closely inspecting their clients.[10] By the early 1990s, the Quality Control movement was so well entrenched that a new verb entered the vocabulary of welfare caseworkers and administrators: to be 'Cue-ceed' (QC'd) was to have a case or caseworker's files pulled for review by the audit division (author's interviews).

Since the 1970s, there has been a consistent and dramatic expansion in the extent and sophistication of welfare surveillance in the United States. Politically, these changes were fueled and capacitated by the increasingly conservative climate in the nation. From Nixon, through Carter, and then particularly through the Reagan and post-Reagan years, the 'right turn' in American politics has been dramatic. And, as might be expected, conservative politicians did not have a lot of love for the poor or the programs that supported them. President Reagan's attacks on mythical 'welfare queens' drinking vodka in their Cadillacs were only the most bizarre and extreme of the attacks on America's neediest. As in the past, the more punitive orientation toward the poor put increased surveillance of the welfare rolls at the top of the agenda for welfare administration. In 1977 President Carter and HEW secretary Joseph Califano undertook the highly publicized Project Match as a demonstration of the capacity of computer matching to ferret out welfare fraud. The same year, Congress mandated the use of 'wage matching' in AFDC administration and sidestepped the largely toothless Privacy Act of 1974 by giving states permission to access Social Security and other data files regarding the income of American citizens (Greenberg and Wolf 1986, 19–20). By the early 1980s, President Reagan had established his Council on Integrity and Efficiency to undertake a 'Long-Term Computer Matching Project' intended to facilitate and improve the use of computer matching and related techniques in federal and state government (ibid., 19).

Other changes and dynamics helped fuel the expansion of information gathering and control. Beginning in the mid-1970s, AFDC administrators began to pursue more seriously the child support payments that many 'deadbeat dads' (and a tiny fraction of deadbeat moms) had failed to pay. Since AFDC clients were required to sign these monies over to the state, these collections emerged as an important budget item and pulled the welfare agencies into great efforts to establish paternity and pursue child support. By the mid-1980s, federal guidelines required that states attempt to establish paternity. County welfare offices were holding monthly 'blood draw days' in which dozens of children were called in to be DNA-typed so that the state could try to identify their fathers (this gave way to saliva-based tests in more recent years).

Today, almost any welfare application triggers a referral to child support enforcement agencies who work, if necessary, to establish paternity and pursue support. Women who refuse to identify sexual partners when paternity is in question can be ruled ineligible for benefits (author's interviews). In important ways, it was as if the notorious man-in-the-house searches of earlier years had returned in a more complex and contemporary form. Until the late 1960s, AFDC administrators in some areas of the country had undertaken midnight or early-morning raids to see if an unreported male was present in an allegedly single-parent home (Handler and Rosenheim 1966, 381–383). These old-fashioned searches were struck down by the courts, but now the search for the man extended beyond the walls of the house – using tools ranging from DNA analysis to the tracing of Social Security numbers in the numerous state and federal data banks, the men were being searched out wherever they might be . . . The transition from the door-crashing search for a 'man in the house' to the high-tech tracing of 'absent parents' is an apt metaphor for the broader transformation in the nature and design of welfare surveillance. A tradition of personalized supervision has given way to forms of technological surveillance and bureaucratic control that may be less face-to-face but are certainly no less pervasive or controlling.

The client information system

... because a machine can do it better than a worker.
John Dempsey, director, Michigan Department of Social Services

I have it *all!* [laugh] But he was very upset that I even knew anything.
AFDC caseworker, Southern Ohio

As with the workplace drug-testing movement of the 1980s (Gilliom 1994), the contemporary changes in welfare surveillance came about through a fusion of political climate and technological innovation. In this case, the computer revolution made possible, for the first time, comprehensive sweeps of huge bodies of data on mainframe computers. Later, the spread of networked desktop computers made it possible for individual caseworkers to be directly connected to the results of those sweeps. The computerization of welfare administration also enabled states to compile their entire caseloads into comprehensive statewide systems, to compare their caseload to that of other states and programs, and to evaluate the performance of individual caseworkers or particular work units. In short, computerization brought an unprecedented level of bureaucratic transparency to welfare administration and facilitated levels and types of surveillance that were simply impossible under previous technologies.

The politics of welfare administration are almost indescribably complex. With some federal funding and guidance, some state funding and guidance, and some local funding and guidance, welfare administration is a chaotic federalism or, perhaps, simply chaos. Although states differ in how they run their AFDC programs, the general scenario is a poorly paid caseworker, in an office or cubicle in a local welfare agency, in the context of a county system, under the guidance of a state-level department, taking leadership from the state legislature, the Congress, the courts, and the federal bureaucracies. Needless to say, guidelines and directives, from whatever the source, are unlikely to flow smoothly through the system (Gardiner and Lyman 1984). Further, before Client Information Systems (CIS) revolutionized welfare administration, immense physical barriers were created by an administrative and record-keeping system based entirely on paperwork and oral exchanges. Because of this, the older systems simply precluded much in the way of cost-effective scrutiny and review of local performance. Gardiner and Lyman describe it as 'organized anarchy' (1984, 55) and Florence Zeller's 1981 study of efforts to reduce AFDC overpayments argued that the welfare system was 'so much like a Chinese wooden puzzle' that the effects of actions or techniques could not even be assessed. Unless, that is, there were 'major changes, *such as a computer system*' (1981, 84–85, quoted in Gardiner and Lyman 1984, emphasis added).

It is for these reasons that the CIS movement was such an important change in welfare administration. Simply put, the CIS brought a revolutionary degree of administrative centralization and transparency to a previously confused and jumbled mass of administrative back streets and dark alleys. In the span of a few years, all state records were moved onto statewide systems capable of managing and manipulating huge amounts of information. A direct link was established between a caseworker's decision – entered on a terminal linked to the CIS – and state-level administrators.

And those state-level administrators could easily examine rates of error or case problems occurring in the county, the office, or even a particular caseworker's desk.

CRIS-E

In the state of Ohio, where this study is based, the new Client Information System was first dubbed CRIS and, later, CRIS-E, for 'Client Registry and Information System – Enhanced.' Bureaucrats and caseworkers pronounce the name as 'Chris (pause) E.'; a respected person with a protected last name. Clients pronounce the name as 'Crissy'; juvenile and disliked. However one chooses to pronounce its name, CRIS-E is an electronic system of surveillance and administration with immense powers for information management. It creates a statewide network that links each caseworker's terminal to a main system containing the complete files of every client. As explained below, the CRIS-E system works with the Income Eligibility Verification System (IEVS) – the program encompassing most of the regular computer number matches – to provide caseworkers and administrators automated access to all federal and state number matches . . . CRIS-E also offers an on-line intake program, in which a program known as 'the driver' leads caseworkers through a screen-by-screen interview of welfare applicants, then calculates eligibility and, if appropriate, authorizes the issuance of emergency assistance . . .

The advances in surveillance, as measured by sheer apprehension and possession of information, were immense. The list of factors loaded into the system covered, among other things, veteran status; living situations; household income and expenditures; age, names and Social Security numbers of children; health information; work history; marital status; race; criminal history; divorce history; medical insurance; savings and checking accounts; burial contracts; cemetery lots; life insurance; Christmas clubs; and retirement plans. The lists go on to include unearned income and queries about alimony, dividends, union pensions, worker's compensation, black-lung benefits, and any 'money from another person.' And always, at the end of every list, 'anything else?'

The data cover costs of telephone, sewer, garbage removal, electricity, and gas. CRIS-E wants to know if you are on strike and, if so, for how long. If you work, the driver wants the job title, the hourly rate, and the monthly hour totals. It will also ask whether there are aliens in the home, if there are people needing long-term care, if there are any pending insurance settlements, and if there are any changes in the household income or composition expected in the near future. One study at the county level concluded that a typical client would be likely to encounter about '770 questions related to her personal and financial circumstances' and that regulations covering these topics cover over '4,300 pages, with another 2,000 pages of clarifications' (Athens County Department of Human Services, in-house study). And all of this information is logged onto a single statewide computer system, bringing the welfare poor of Ohio into one massive digital poorhouse – each and every one of them easily visible to the new overseer of the poor.

The easily accessed statewide filing cabinet created by CRIS-E has obvious relevance to the sort of information panopticon discussed in the literature on surveillance systems (see, among others, Foucault 1979; Dandeker 1990; Gilliom 1994;

Zuboff 1988; Gandy 1993). It places the roughly three-quarters of a million aid recipients in Ohio into one electronically created site in which all relevant data regarding their lives as recipients are stored and easily accessed. The extent to which this transforms the system cannot be overstated . . . Previously the time and space obstacles to case management and client control were insurmountable; paper records were in thousands of filing cabinets spread out across Ohio's eighty-eight counties. The possibilities for centralized surveillance and control were sharply limited by the simple facts of physical distance and the resulting information fragmentation in the system.

But the screens and software of CRIS-E have replaced the file cabinets, the long application form . . . the manual arithmetic of caseworkers, and much of the rule-finding and interpretation involved in case administration until the late 1980s. With pencil, paper, and file cabinets now far from view, caseworkers fill out application data, calculate benefits, and maintain client records in a system that can be accessed by any caseworker or administrator in the state. Further, the computerization of the state's aid administration means that a wide spectrum of state and federal computer matches can be rapidly and automatically processed. Bringing in data from the Internal Revenue Service, the state's tax office, the Social Security Administration, worker's compensation, and a number of other state agencies, the computer matches use clients' Social Security numbers to see if they have told the truth regarding their needs and resources.[11] The IEVS matches (IEVS is actually only one part of a broader array of matches, but the term is used within agencies to refer to all of the matches available) have, according to at least one county Director of Human Services 'revolutionized' the detection system: 'We catch a lot more people. In fact, we'll get any kind of legitimate income' that a client may be receiving. With the major exception of underground income IEVS does appear to have revolutionized control within the agency.[12] The Department of Human Services (DHS) no longer takes the passive pose of waiting for a rat call.[13] The bureaucrats, with their massive computer system, are able to monitor most forms of legitimate income that occur within the United States. As one interviewed caseworker explained:

> Before IEVS we couldn't pin down what our clients were doing without the aid of anonymous phone calls or just client admissions that they had been working. [Now] we get monthly alerts on IEVS matches. Anybody who's been in the system for ninety days, we start getting matches on. So right off the bat we are catching more of our clients lying quicker.

Suddenly whole new capacities for gathering and using information entered the daily practice of welfare administration. An AFDC caseworker (BJ) who was interviewed by the author as a part of this project explains one client's surprise:

> BJ: This gentleman here was very upset with me when I first got his case. He demanded to see me because . . . I had sent him out a form . . . We got this thing [a computer match alert] showing that he had received workman's compensation. I sent him a letter telling him that I had received information that he is receiving workman's compensation [and that he] needed to update

his information so that I could add it to his case. He got *highly* mad at me. He came in here and demanded to see me and demanded to know *how I knew* that he was getting workmen's compensation. And I couldn't show him the screen, I'm not supposed to let him see the screen – I don't know why because it's his information and they can watch us go through the application – so I didn't show him the screen and when he did give me [the document with] the information he crossed *everything* out. He was so upset that he would not let me see anything off of his workmen's compensation paper, he took a black magic marker and [crossed out] everything because he didn't want me to know his claim number or anything else. I have it *all!* [laugh] But he was very upset that I even knew anything.
How did you resolve it?

BJ: I told him, I said we just get alerts, I said we get information through the state with Social Security, unemployment, anything like that. And so he turned the information in to me; he was just upset that I knew it and could find it out without him telling me. And after he realized . . . I wanted to show him the screen so bad. He probably thought it was just words and that I couldn't do it. 'Cause before I couldn't't've, and if they've been on assistance for a very long time, they probably thought I couldn't and [that] they could hide information from me.

Conclusion: an epistemology of the poor

Forms of knowledge and bodies of information are *always* particular ways of seeing the world, with particular premises, agendas, omissions, and genealogies . . . At the center of welfare thinking – and so much else – in the United States are the ideas of patriarchal individualism and the market. The premise of welfare administration is that the normal state of affairs consists of male-headed, two-parent families earning food, shelter, and clothing by obtaining wages through labor in the economy. In a program like the Mother's Pension or AFDC it is upon failure in terms of this model – the male dies or leaves and the woman and children become 'dependent' – that the state provides assistance. With constant hope and suspicion that all could be 'independent' (that is, for the most part, *dependent* upon an employer or male wage earner) and live on their own means, the state constantly searches for traces of resources, earnings, and even signs of 'a man in the house' or, now, a 'man in the nation.'

Adjacent to the specific ideological premises of welfare administration and surveillance is a broader philosophy of knowledge – an epistemology, or way of thinking about what information and knowledge is. The world of welfare surveillance is state-centered, bureaucratic, and rationalist. It is a world of facts, errors, verification, and evidence. Legislatively stipulated figures for eligibility, support levels, and other dimensions of the program are provided, documents, forms, and receipts are gathered, and determinations are made. It is only with a radical leveling or simplifying of the state's understanding of the poor that the necessary uniformity and simplicity of the automated computer information systems can function. We have seen that for a brief time, prior to the era of computerization, the declaration period in AFDC experimented with giving clients a central role in stating their need and situation, but for the most part the poor exist as objects in the system. There is no voice for the poor in the establishment of levels and criteria (and support levels in most regions of the country are widely known to be inadequate). There is usually little voice for the poor in making the case for their need – documents, receipts, and formulae assert it for them . . .

As the historical examples have shown, government agencies have been struggling to know and depict the poor for a long time. Welfare surveillance is certainly nothing new. But the technological transformation brought about by the emergence of the CIS, automated case management, and the capacity for computer matching marks an important shift in the breadth and depth of the state's capacity for knowledge as well as its capacity to apply that knowledge in the execution of policy. Parallel to the society's broader revolution in the capacity and implementation of surveillance technology, welfare surveillance has hit new levels of quality and density. It has constructed a world in which there is little room for secrets and even less room for arguments over basic values and knowledge claims.

These changes, not just in welfare, but in consumer marketing, taxation, drug law enforcement, educational assessment, and the other institutions of our lives, are important social and political transformations. They mark not just an increase in the technical capacity for observation but an increasing reach and force for centrally determined norms, standards, and values. As we experience an unprecedented extension of the institutional power to enforce these norms, we experience a concomitant reduction in the capacity and power for self-definition in our lives. The welfare mother, the health insurance consumer, the taxpayer, the student, and the loan applicant all have different lots in life, different agendas, different needs, and different resources. But they all unite in being increasingly subject to these new systems of power . . .

It has been argued that much of the activity surrounding the production and use of knowledge in welfare administration is part of a broader mission of keeping the welfare rolls down through detecting or deterring those who could possibly do without. Although there are clearly numerous other purposes in the information quest of welfare surveillance – such as matching clients with appropriate programs, identifying particular needs, or intervening in crises – the central and most enduring mission appears to be that of what the modern bureaucracy calls 'eligibility verification,' that is, limiting and controlling access to welfare in the ongoing skirmishes of what Katz called 'the war on the able-bodied poor' (1986, 18).

As the poor struggle to find means of survival, a struggle over the politics of information necessarily ensues. Programs of scrutiny are designed to augment the hassle, intimidation, and humiliation of applicants with an eye toward the policy goal of deterring all but the most desperate from seeking aid. Specific tactics within programs – the poorhouses, the uniforms, the surprise home visits, the invasive questions – align with a broader cultural shaming of the poor in the mass media to create barriers to anyone asking for help. Politicians make frequent attacks on 'welfare fraud,' and as their widely publicized results both stigmatize and frighten the poor, application levels decline. For those who ask for and receive help, of course, the barriers are no longer barriers, but ongoing punishment for their plight. The poor, normally hampered by a partial and unsure knowledge of the complex system, by low education, and by fear, struggle to advance and maintain a version of their 'case' that makes the most of the possibility and level of aid. The state, hampered by a partial knowledge of the poor and cumbersome layers of bureaucracy, struggles to assert its control and detect violations of the order. But the state's arsenal against the poor has gotten a lot more sophisticated in recent years.

Notes

1 This chapter is an extract from J. Gilliom (2001) Welfare surveillance, in *Overseers of the Poor: Surveillance, Resistance, and the Limits of Privacy*. Chicago: University of Chicago Press, pp. 17–40.

2 Application for Income, Medical, and Food Assistance, Ohio Department of Human Services, Form 7100 (Rev. 9/87), p. 31.

3   Most officials and reformers would have agreed that any relief given to the able-bodied should be as unpleasant and degrading as possible . . . Only those men willing to break stone or cut wood for their meager supper and spartan bed should be sheltered from the streets.

(Katz 1986, 92)

4   Scientific charity was not only a set of principles that guided action; it also was a method for gathering data with which to further develop the law of charity and reform. Charity organizations, their leaders felt, should study as well as help the poor. In New York, the Charity Organization Society meticulously classified its cases and mapped their distribution by streets and even houses.

(ibid., 69)

5   When the Social Security Act was passed, only ADC required that clients be 'needy.' To establish need a client had to be not only without income but also without resources, including property or services which many at the time considered essential, such as telephones or automobiles or houses, and which might stave off poverty and help a temporarily reduced client regain position. Cash savings were not allowed. Thus in many instances an ADC applicant would have to get rid of useful resources even at a loss, impoverishing herself in order to qualify . . . By contrast one could have millions and still collect unemployment compensation or OAI (Old Age Insurance).

(Gordon 1994, 297)

6 Enforcement of these rules included inspections of the home and 'midnight raids' by welfare agents trying to uncover evidence of a 'man in the house':

The object of the raid is to discover a 'man in the house' or 'substitute parent,' whose presence, depending on the jurisdiction, either precludes giving assistance altogether or gives rise to an inference of support, which, of course, the public assistance agency is obligated to investigate and to take into account in determining the unmet budgetary need.

(Handler and Rosenheim, 1966, 282–283)

Man-in-the-house rules were deemed unconstitutional by the U.S. Supreme Court in *King v. Smith* 329 U.S. 309 1968; see Trattner 1999, 310.

7   In 'Privacy in Welfare,' Joel Handler and Margaret Rosenheim summarized the state of AFDC surveillance:

[B]y the nature of public assistance, the task of determining eligibility is never-ending. Unlike the duty to pay income taxes, which calls for calculating taxable income accumulated over a prescribed period of time, the obligation of the recipient to report changes in status that alter his needs or his income or resources is continuing. For administrative purposes, enforcement of this obligation is discharged through periodic checks by welfare authorities, but the recipient carries the burden of reporting when his circumstances change, else he is liable to penalties including prosecution for fraud, permanent or temporary termination of his grant, or withholding from future grants the excess deemed to have been paid out in the past. Having satisfied the authority of his initial eligibility the client must regularly submit to a truncated version of the same process. Furthermore, because of the requirement to report changed circumstances he can be requested to furnish explanations of inconsistencies in his own statements or of the allegations of third parties that bear upon his eligibility. 'Failure to comply' suffices to close a case.

(1966, 382)

8   As Blanche Bernstein, then Deputy Commissioner for Income Maintenance from New York, testified in 1977:

from about the early 1960s until about 1971, the administration of welfare in New York City was, indeed, a rather loose affair. It was the days of the self-declaration and the self-recertification, of separation of services, of an era in which . . . no one worker in the system knew anything about any particular family.

(House Committee on Government Operations,
subcommittee hearings, *Administration of the AFDC Program*,
95th Cong., 1st sess., 1977, 161)

9   Critics of the declaration process argued that it allowed impermissibly high levels of fraud and error in AFDC administration, but others disagreed. Complaining about the extensive regulations and verification procedures that had been put in place by the mid-1970s, Leon Ginsberg, commissioner of the West Virginia Department of Welfare, testified before Congress that 'my statisticians tell me that there was no significant difference in error rates under the simplified declaration system and the rather tedious interviews, home visits, and complex eligibility determination we perform now' (ibid., 367).

10   Governors Rockefeller (N.Y.) and Reagan (Cal.) – whose states had over half of
     the nation's welfare clients – began large-scale campaigns against fraud, and other
     states followed suit. In Nevada, the welfare agency responded

> by mobilizing virtually the entire work force of the department to interview
> employers and neighbors of the poor and to study the records of the social
> security and unemployment compensation agencies for any evidence of
> unreported income in the preceding five or more years.

When nearly half of Nevada's welfare recipients saw their benefits terminated or
reduced without notice or consultation, the National Welfare Rights Organization
mobilized 'some forty lawyers and seventy law students' and held mass demon-
strations. 'On March 20 the Federal District Court issued an order reinstating
everyone who had been terminated or who had received reduced grants, and
retroactive payments were ordered' (Piven and Cloward 1979, 333).

11   So, for example, if an applicant has a savings account in Oregon, the caseworker
     in rural Ohio will come into work one morning and find an 'alert' on their
     screen. When the alert is called up, it will show that a computer sweep of the
     Internal Revenue Service 1099 interest and dividend data shows that the client is
     earning enough interest in Oregon to indicate a significant savings account. The
     client is then contacted to account for the situation and the caseworker, as well as
     the county's fraud control officer, work to decide what appropriate actions and
     charges are. (The client will never be told the source of the information, since the
     IRS insists that its role in the process be secret.)

12   One unintended side effect is that with so many small cases of over-payment
     being detected, each of which requires slow repayment by impoverished people,
     one county agency has nearly as many repayment accounts as it does active
     cases.

13   Prior to the computerization of welfare surveillance, caseworkers and fraud con-
     trol officers had few options. They relied almost solely on the 'rat call' – a tip from
     a neighbor or angry relative of a cheater. As Billy G. Davis, head of the National
     Association of State Welfare Fraud Directors put it: 'Nothing was happening
     before computer matching.' Due to limits on the surveillance capacity of the
     state – the gaps or blind spots in its vision – a wide range of income-enhancing
     or survival efforts were possible. Individuals could feasibly receive assistance bene-
     fits while receiving income from a job, worker's compensation, retirement
     benefits, assistance in a neighboring state, or other sources. But the new surveil-
     lance capacity manifest in the computerization of fraud control closes many
     of the gaps and, in turn, many of the opportunities for beating the system.
     Multi-state and federal computer files covering employment, unemployment
     compensation, retirement, Social Security, savings and investments, and other
     recorded holdings are cross-checked on a regular basis, thereby dramatically
     reducing possibilities for resisting the rules and prohibitions of the welfare
     system.

References

Bell, W. (1965) *Aid to Dependent Children*. New York: Columbia University Press.

Congressional Research Service (1977) *Administration of the AFDC Program*. Washington, D.C.: Government Printing Office.

Dandeker, C. (1990) *Surveillance, Power, and Modernity: Bureaucracy and Discipline from 1700 to the Present Day*. New York: St. Martin's.

Ferguson, K. E. (1984) *The Feminist Case against Bureaucracy*. Philadelphia: Temple University Press.

Foucault, M. (1979) *Discipline and Punish*. New York: Vintage.

Fraser, N. (1989) *Unruly Practices: Power, Discourse, and Gender in Contemporary Social Theory*. Minneapolis: University of Minnesota Press.

Gandy, O. H. (1993) *The Panoptic Sort: A Political Economy of Personal Information*. Boulder: Westview Press.

Gardiner, J. A. and Lyman, T. R. (1984) *The Fraud Control Game: State Responses to Fraud and Abuse in AFDC and Medicaid Programs*. Bloomington: Indiana University Press.

Gilliom, J. (1994) *Surveillance, Privacy, and the Law: Employee Drug Testing and the Politics of Social Control*. Ann Arbor: University of Michigan Press.

Gordon, L. (1994) *Pitied But Not Entitled: Single Mothers and the History of Welfare 1890–1935*. New York: Free Press.

Greenberg, D. and Wolf, D. with Pfiester, J. (1986) *Using Computers to Combat Welfare Fraud*. Westport, CT: Greenwood Press.

Handler, J. F. and Rosenheim, M. K. (1966) Privacy in welfare: public assistance and juvenile justice, *Law and Contemporary Problems*, 31: 377–412.

Katz, M. B. (1986) *In the Shadow of the Poorhouse: A Social History of Welfare in America*. New York: Basic Books.

Piven, F. F. and Cloward, R. A. (1971) *Regulating the Poor: The Functions of Public Welfare*. New York: Vintage Books.

Piven, F. F. and Cloward, R. A. (1979) *Poor People's Movements: Why They Succeed, How They Fail*. New York: Vintage Books.

Scott, J. (1998) *Seeing like a State: How Certain Schemes to Improve the Human Condition Have Failed*. New Haven: Yale University Press.

Torpey, J. (2000) *The Invention of the Passport: Surveillance, Citizenship, and the State*. Cambridge: Cambridge University Press.

Trattner, W. I. (1999) *From Poor Law to Welfare State: A History of Social Welfare in America*. New York: Free Press.

Zuboff, S. (1988) *In the Age of the Smart Machine: The Future of Work and Power*. New York: Basic Books.

15

Digitizing surveillance: categorization, space, inequality[1]
by Stephen Graham and David Wood

Introduction

Wherever there has been the creation and enforcement of categories, there has been surveillance. Historically, this was reinforced through religious and cultural norms. With capitalism and the modern state, such practices were systematized through rational organization: bureaucracy, management and policing. Now a further shift is taking place away from those direct supervisory techniques famously analysed by Foucault (1975). Advances in the technologies of sensing and recording have enabled a massive growth in the monitoring of individuals and groups without the need for constant direct observation or containment of those monitored within particular spaces (Deleuze, 1992; Gandy, 1993; Lianos, 2001; Lyon, 1994, 2001; Poster, 1990). For Gary Marx (1988), this 'new surveillance' is characterized by 'the use of technical means to extract or create personal data . . . taken from individuals or contexts' (Marx, 2002: 12).

Our aim in this [chapter] is to critically explore the social implications of the *digital* within the 'new surveillance'. Bureaucratic and electromechanical surveillance systems (a foundation for the modern nation state, public health and welfare) are being supplemented and increasingly replaced by digital technologies and techniques, enabling what Jones (2001) calls 'digital rule'. Digitization is significant for two reasons: first, it enables monitoring, prioritization and judgement to occur across widening geographical distances and with little time delay (Lyon, 1994); second, it allows the active sorting, identification, prioritization and tracking of bodies, behaviours and characteristics of subject populations on a continuous, real-time basis. Thus, digitization encourages a tendency towards automation. Crucially, the work of human operators shifts from direct mediation and discretion to the design, programming, supervision and maintenance of automated or semi-automatic surveillance systems (Lianos and Douglas, 2000).

Digitization facilitates a step change in the power, intensity and scope of surveillance. Surveillance is everywhere. Computers are everywhere. Their combination already has that air of inevitability that can attach itself to the history of technology. Computer technology certainly is, as Henman (1997) argues, a player in social policy processes, but it is crucial not to read social and policy implications and effects of digital surveillance deterministically from the intrinsic capabilities of the technologies involved. As McCahill (2002) and Thrift and French (2002) demonstrate, such techniques are mediated, at all levels, by social practices that interact with all aspects of the making and functioning of the technological system. Even apparently automated systems, far from being inhuman domains, involve continuous complex social practices and decisions that do much to shape digital surveillance in practice.

This is important because a characteristic of digital surveillance technologies is their extreme flexibility and ambivalence. On the one hand, systems can be designed to socially exclude, based on automated judgements of social or economic worth; on the other hand, the same systems can be programmed to help overcome social barriers and processes of marginalization. The broad social effects and policy implications of digital surveillance are thus contingent and, while flexible, are likely to be strongly biased by the political, economic and social conditions that shape the principles embedded in their design and implementation.

Currently, these conditions are marked by the widespread liberalization and privatization of public services and spaces. This reflects a movement from free, universal public services and spaces, based on notions of citizenship, to markets and quasi-markets based on consumerism. These markets continually differentiate between users based on ability to pay, risk or eligibility of access. While there is clearly much variation and detail in particular cases, this broad political-economic bias means that digital surveillance is likely to be geared overwhelmingly towards supporting the processes of individualization, commodification and consumerization that are necessary to support broader political-economic shifts towards markets, quasi-markets and prioritized public services and spaces (see Graham and Marvin, 2001).

This [chapter] seeks, in four parts, to explore the nature, scope and implications of the growth of digital surveillance techniques and technologies. In the first, we outline the nature of digital surveillance and consider how it differs from earlier forms. We argue that, while the changes may be considered merely quantitative (size, coverage, speed, and so on), important new forms of social practice are facilitated by these changes. The second part develops an exploratory analysis of the interconnections between digitization and the changing political economies of cities and urban societies. Here we examine the essential ambivalence of digital surveillance within the context of wider trends towards privatization, liberalization and social polarization. We argue that the techniques may facilitate better services for mobile, affluent citizens, but that this is often paralleled by a relative worsening of the position of more marginalized groups who are physically or electronically excluded or bypassed by automated surveillance. The third part illustrates these points through three examples: algorithmic video surveillance; digital prioritization in transport and communications; and, finally, electronic patient records and genetic research. Finally, in part four, we reflect on the policy challenges raised by the spread of digital surveillance.

Digital surveillance: making a difference?

Digital encoding works by reducing information to the minimum necessary for accurate reconstruction: the binary code of 1s and 0s. In contrast, analogue forms aim at perfect reproduction of the original. Digital surveillance thus makes the information more amenable to storage, transmission and computation. But is it sufficiently different from analogue forms to merit rethinking and retheorization?

Michel Foucault's (1975) concept of 'panopticism' (the tendency towards a disciplinary state based on direct surveillance) is still a dominant metaphor. However, Poster claims that digitization requires a re-evaluation of this concept because Foucault failed to notice that late 20th-century technological and infrastructural developments were qualitatively different from the earlier examples he studied:

> Today's circuits of communication and the databases they generate constitute a Superpanopticon, a system of surveillance without walls, windows, towers or guards. The quantitative advances in the technologies of surveillance result in a qualitative change in the microphysics of power.
>
> (Poster, 1990: 93)

... The obvious differences between digital surveillance and analogue surveillance are quantitative: computer hard drives can store far more information more conveniently and faster than analogue systems. However, the fundamental differences lie in what can be done with the information gathered. There are two basic processes.

Norris and Armstrong (1999), in their study of closed circuit television (CCTV) in Britain, argue that what is of most concern is the linking of cameras to databases and the integration of different databases. Digitization facilitates interconnection within and between surveillance points and systems. To be truly effective, linkage is often *required* so that captured and stored data can be compared. Technological reasons will always be found to integrate. However, political and economic arguments are not always either presented, heard or assigned equivalent importance, and thus a covert process of 'surveillance creep' (Marx, 1988: 2) occurs, whereby integration is presented as necessary or inevitable.

Importantly, digital systems also allow the application of automated processes: algorithmic surveillance. An algorithm is a mathematical term for a set of instructions: algorithms are the foundation of mathematics and computing. However, algorithms need to be translated into a form that computers are programmed to understand, namely software – essentially many coded algorithms linked together. Algorithmic surveillance refers to surveillance systems using software to extend raw data: from classification (sensor + database 1); through comparison (sensor + database 1 + software + database 2); to prediction or even reaction (sensor + database 1 + software + database 2 + alarm/weapon).

Many of the latest surveillance technologies have embedded digital and algorithmic features. A city centre CCTV system providing images that are watched and analysed by human operators may be digitally recorded and stored, but is not algorithmic. If the system includes software that compares the faces of the people observed with those in a database of suspects, it becomes algorithmic. Patient records in a health service computer are digital and are algorithmic to the extent that software determines the format of the information entered. However, the process becomes algorithmic surveillance when, for example, software compares patient records against signs of particular disease risk factors and categorizes patients automatically.

Some have claimed that algorithmic systems improve on conventional systems. Marx argues that algorithmic surveillance provides the possibility of eliminating the potential for corruption and discrimination (1995: 238). For example, a racist police officer cannot decide to arrest any black male when a facial recognition system can decide categorically whether a particular individual is the wanted man. However, algorithmic surveillance can also intensify problems of conventional surveillance and of computerization. Already, in social policy processes, 'the perceived objectivity of computers is used to validate statistics which support partisan views' (Henman, 1997: 335). Algorithmic systems also pose new questions, particularly relating to the removal of human discretion . . .

It is critical to stress here the subtle and stealthy quality of the ongoing social prioritizations and judgements that digital surveillance systems make possible. This means that critical social policy research must work to expose the ways in which these systems are being used to prioritize certain people's mobilities, service quality and life chances, while simultaneously reducing those of less favoured groups. Importantly, both beneficiaries and losers may, in practice, be utterly unaware that digital prioritization has actually occurred. This gives many of these crucial processes a curiously invisible and opaque quality that is a major challenge to researchers and policy makers alike.

Digital surveillance and the changing political economies of the city

As Thrift and French (2002) have shown, there are now so many software-based surveillance and IT systems embedded in the infrastructure of cities that even the UK Audit Commission had enormous difficulties finding them all when trying to ensure that they would all function in the new millennium. They were often unable to discover who was responsible for them and how they could be checked and reprogrammed. Thrift and French (2002) claim that the ubiquity of such systems in the modern city is leading to the automatic production of space.

This opacity and ubiquity mean that it is hard to identify how the shift to automated, digital and algorithmic surveillance practices relates to current radical shifts in the political economies of welfare states, governance, punishment and urban space. Richard Jones (2001), following Deleuze (1992), argues that, as at-a-distance monitoring systems become intelligent and immanent within the city, so notions of traditional disciplinary control are replaced by the continuous electronic disciplining of subjects against redefined norms across time and space (see Graham, 1998).

Social, commercial and state definitions of norms of behaviour within the various contexts of the city are thus increasingly automatically policed by assemblages of digital technology and software. These are less and less mediated by human discretion (Lianos and Douglas, 2000). Normative notions of good behaviour and transgression within the complex space–time fabrics of cities are embedded into software codes. So, increasingly, are stipulations and punishments (for example, electronic tagging).

Increasingly, the encoding of software to automatically stipulate eligibility of access, entitlement of service or punishment is often done far away in time and space from the point of application (see Lessig, 1999). Software is coded across the world:

call centres that monitor the gaze of automated cameras of electronic tags are switched to low-cost labour locations. Digital surveillance therefore promotes a new round of space–time distanciation, which moves us ever further from modern notions of discipline based on the gaze of supervisors within the same space-time as the disciplined subject (McCahill, 2002). Efforts are then made to enforce such norms and boundaries on the ground on a continuing, real-time basis through the withdrawal of electronic or physical access privileges, the detailed stipulation and monitoring of acceptable behaviours and the automated tracking of individuals' space–time paths.

Within contemporary political-economic contexts marked by privatization and consumerization, this proliferation of automatic systems raises clear concerns that social exclusion itself will be automated. Rather than being based exclusively on uneven access to the Internet, the digital divide in contemporary societies is based on the broader disconnections of certain groups from IT hardware *and* the growing use of automated surveillance and information systems to digitally red-line their life chances within automated regimes of service provision (Jupp, 2001). Such systems actively facilitate mobility, access, services and life chances for those judged electronically to have the correct credentials and exclude or relationally push away others (Norris, 2002). They thereby accelerate the trend away from persons towards data subjects. As Norris et al. suggest, the problem with automated systems is that 'they aim to facilitate exclusionary rather than inclusionary goals' (1998: 271) . . .

Digital surveillance techniques therefore make possible the widening commodification of urban space and the erection within cities of myriad exclusionary boundaries and access controls. These range from the electronic tagging of offenders within their defined space–time domains to gated communities with pin number entry systems and shopping malls with intense video surveillance (Davis, 1990; Flusty, 1997). Digital surveillance systems also provide essential supports to the electronically priced commodification of road spaces; to digitally mediated consumption systems; and to smartcard-based public services – all of which allow user behaviours to be closely scrutinized. Crucially, the new digital surveillance assemblage is being shaped in a biased way to neatly dovetail with and support a new political economy of consumer citizenship and individualized mobility and consumption which would otherwise not be possible (Garland, 2001).

This is especially important within a context marked by the increasing privatization of public services, infrastructures and domains (with a growing emphasis on treating users differently based on assessments of their direct profitability). Digital surveillance also provides a new range of management techniques to address the widening fear of crime and the entrenchment of entrepreneurial efforts to make (certain parts of) towns and city spaces more competitive in attracting investors and (selected) consumers.

Digital surveillance and the city: three examples

After this broad examination of the connections between digital surveillance techniques and the changing political economies of cities, we are in a position to examine the links between digital surveillance, exclusion and urban space in more detail. We do this via three examples: first, algorithmic CCTV; second, information, communication and mobility spaces; and, finally, genetic surveillance.

Algorithmic CCTV

Many systems of sorting and analysis can be linked to video surveillance . . .

[A] developing area is movement recognition. Systems in use to detect motion and movement tend to be relatively simple, based on blobs of particular colours that remain constant in sampled frames of a CCTV image, such as the EU funded Cromatica project at King's College, London (see: http://www.research.eee.kcl.ac.uk/vrl/#cromatica). This was designed for crowd flow management but, when piloted on the London Underground, attracted attention for its potential to help reduce the number of suicides, as it had been observed that the suicidal 'tend to wait for at least ten minutes on the platform, missing trains, before taking their last few tragic steps' (Graham-Rowe, 1999: 25, cited in Norris, 2002) . . .

Gait recognition has also attracted significant media attention. Headlines like 'The way you walk pins down who you are' imply a reversion to Victorian notions of a visible criminal character (see: http://www.isis.ecs.soton.ac.uk/image/gait/press/). The reality is more prosaic, if still technically impressive. Researchers at the University of Southampton have been developing algorithms for the individual human gait. These (like faceprints) have the potential to be stored as information to be compared with existing images . . . [A]ccording to group leader Mark Nixon, 'a distant silhouette will provide enough data to make a positive recognition once we get the system working properly' (McKie, 1999) . . .

Certainty about identity is crucial to the argument for algorithmic CCTV: as was argued earlier, one of the main reasons for its increasing popularity is to counter arguments about human fallibility. But there are allegations that the technologies . . . simply do not work . . . Such technical arguments should not, however, detract from fundamental questions about categorization and bypass. As described earlier, there are significant concerns about the way in which such systems rely on and reinforce the categorization of certain sociospatial risk categories: high crime neighbourhoods, known criminals or dangerous socioeconomic groups (Lianos and Douglas, 2000).

Information, communication and mobility services in the city

Our second range of examples involves the use of new information and communication technologies (ICTs) and digital surveillance to subtly differentiate consumers within transport, communications or service provision. Here, algorithms are being used at the interface of databases and telecommunications networks to allocate different levels of service to different users on an increasingly automated basis. This is done to overcome problems of congestion, queuing and service quality and to maximize the quality of service for the most profitable users. Examples include Internet prioritization, electronic road pricing, call centre call queuing and the use of biometrics to bypass international passport and immigration controls (see Graham and Marvin, 2001).

When the Internet first became a mass medium in the late 1990s it was impossible to give one user a priority service over another. All packets of data on the Internet were queued when there was congestion. However, on the commercialized Internet, dominated by transnational media conglomerates, new software protocols are being embedded into the routers that switch Internet traffic. These smart routers automatically and actively discriminate between different users' packets, especially in times of congestion. They can sift priority packets, allowing them passage, while automatically blocking those from non-premium users (Schiller, 1999).

Thus, high quality Internet and e-commerce services can now be guaranteed to premium users irrespective of wider conditions, while non-premium users simultaneously experience 'website not available' signals. This further supports the unbundling of Internet and e-commerce services, as different qualities can be packaged and sold at different rates to different markets (Graham and Marvin, 2001). As Emily Tseng suggests, 'the ability to discriminate and prioritize data traffic is now being built into the [Internet] system. Therefore economics can shape the way packets flow through the networks and therefore whose content is more important' (2000: 12).

The integration of customer databases within call centres provides another example of digital discrimination. Initially, call centres operated through the judgement and discretion of call centre operators. One system installed at South West Water in the UK in the mid-1990s, for example, meant that:

> when a customer rings, just the giving of their name and postcode to the member of staff [a practice often now automated through call-line identification] allows all account details, including records of past telephone calls, billing dates and payments, even scanned images of letters, to be displayed. This amount of information enables staff to deal with different customers in different ways. A customer who repeatedly defaults with payment will be treated completely differently from one who has only defaulted once.
>
> (*Utility Week*, 1995: 12)

Now that call centres are equipped with Call Line Identification (CLI) allowing operators to detect the phone numbers of incoming calls, such practices are being automated. Automated surveillance systems are emerging that can differentially queue calls according to algorithmic judgements of the profits the company makes from them. 'Good' customers are thus answered quickly, while 'bad' ones are put on hold. As with Internet prioritization, neither user is likely to know that such prioritization and distancing are occurring.

New algorithmic techniques are also being used to reduce road congestion, while improving the mobilities of privileged drivers. With road space increasingly congested, electronic road pricing is an increasingly popular political choice. A range of governments have brought in private or public/private regimes to either electronically price entry into existing city centres (for example, Singapore and, from February 2003, London) or build new private premium highways that are only accessible to drivers with in-car electronic transponders (including Toronto, Los Angeles, San Diego, Melbourne and Manila).

In both cases, road space becomes a priced commodity dependent on users having the appropriate onboard technology and resources – and often bank accounts – to pay bills. In some cases, systems allow traffic flow to be guaranteed whatever the level of external traffic congestion. On the San Diego I-15 highway, for example, software monitoring congestion levels on the premium-priced highway can signal real-time price increases when congestion causes the flow to decrease. Communicated to drivers, this reduces demand and reinstates free flowing conditions.

While such systems have environmental benefits, it can also be argued that their implementation is closely related to the changing political economy of cities. This is because, like Internet prioritization and call centre queuing, they facilitate the removal of what might be called cash-poor/time-rich users from the congested mobility network, in the process facilitating premium network conditions for cash-rich/time-poor users (Graham and Marvin, 2001). The Hong Kong government, for example, recently discussed implementing a city centre road pricing system like that in Singapore. This was not to reduce greenhouse gas emissions; rather, it was a direct response to the lobbying of corporate CEOs who were sick of having to walk the last half mile to meetings in hot, humid conditions because of gridlock. These executives had grown used to a seamless door-to-door service, uninhibited by traffic in Singapore's pricey central business district.

Finally, algorithmic surveillance now allows highly mobile, affluent business travellers to directly bypass normal immigration and ticketing at major international airports. This allows them to move seamlessly and speedily through the architectural and technological systems designed to separate airsides and groundsides within major international airports (Virilio, 1991: 10) . . . Selected premium travellers are issued with a smartcard that records their hand geometry: 'Each time the traveller passes through customs, they present the card and place their hand in a reader that verifies their identity and links into international databases', allowing them instant progress (Banisar, 1999: 67) . . . Such systems extend the infrastructure of highly luxurious airport lounges and facilities only accessible to identified elite passengers . . . ICT surveillance assemblages privilege some users, while those deemed to warrant less (or no) mobility (especially illegal immigrants and refugees) face ever increasing efforts to make international boundaries less permeable through new border control systems.

Genetics and medical surveillance

Medicine, particularly public health and epidemiology, has a long history of surveillant practices, largely in the notification and monitoring of outbreaks of infectious disease (Declich and Carter, 1994; Foucault, 1973, 1975; Mooney, 1999). However, digitization is transforming these practices. Two linked cases will be mentioned here: first, electronic patient records (EPRs); and, second, research into genetics. As van der Ploeg (2002: 62) writes:

> Health care systems throughout the Western countries are moving towards on-line accessible EPRs into which all data on medical history, medication, test results from a broad variety of diagnostic (often already computer based)

techniques, and therapies belonging to a particular individual's medical biography are accumulated, and can be accessed by relevant care givers.

EPRs are convenient and contribute to quick and accurate diagnosis of illness and, therefore, patient welfare and public health. However, they also gradually accumulate a mass of personal information, most of which has no direct relevance to any particular medical condition. Such records are protected by law and medical ethics but, as Mooney (1999) has shown in his analysis of debates about public health and privacy in the 18th and 19th centuries, personal rights can lose out to what is considered to be the public good – a slippery and amorphous notion . . . The pressure to integrate, for example, medical and police databases for law enforcement purposes will become more and more intense as forensic science improves and with the increasing popularity of biocriminology and the pressure for pre-emptive law enforcement policies such as DNA screening (Rose, 2000).

But it is not *1984*-style fears of state surveillance that give most cause for concern; it is the increasing influence of the private sector in health care provision. The relationship between public database holders and the private sector is a key issue, one that is again complicated by digitization. Modern medical research, and in particular genetics, depends increasingly on high-powered computing. As Moor remarks, 'it is . . . only through the eyes of computers that we can hope to map and sequence the human genome in a practical period of time' (1999: 257).

Genetic records are also so readily digitizable that Nelkin and Andrews (1999) can give several examples of scientists predicting that smartcards with an encoded personal genome will soon replace current methods of personal identification. Progress towards the convergence of EPRs, personal genome records and private financial interests is already well underway. For example, leaked minutes of a high-level advisory group working towards a new health Green Paper by the UK Labour government show that the group proposes making the results of DNA sampling in NHS hospitals available to pharmaceutical companies (Barnett and Hinsliff, 2001). Iceland has licensed its entire national medical database to the American genetics company deCODE for research and commercial purposes (Rose, 2001) and Estonia is also planning a genetic database of its citizens (Pollack, 2000).

Once state EPRs are commodified; so prospects for democratic control over personal information decrease and the discriminatory potential multiplies. The insurance industry is just one domain that is being transformed by this increasing commodification (Cook, 1999; Pokorski, 1997). Insurance has serious implications for personal wellbeing when individuals are increasingly forced to find private health care and retirement solutions and rely less upon decreasing state provision. Those whose genetic records make them too financially risky for insurance companies could find themselves bypassed by neoliberal health policies. Moreover, mutualized life and health insurance systems, built up over centuries and based on the social pooling of aggregate risks, threaten to be dismantled and individualized in the same ways as are the physical infrastructures of cities. Users defined through their genetic profiles as low-risk/high-profit could secede from generalized rates and gain low-cost cover, whereas those with high risks of long-term costly illness or early death could be excluded from cover (Graham and Marvin, 2001).

Conclusions: research, policy and resistance

As digital surveillance proliferates, the politics of surveillance are increasingly the politics of code. The processes through which algorithms and software are constructed are often now the only parts of the disciplinary chain completely open to human discretion and shaping. Once switched on, many digital systems become supervised agents that continually help to determine ongoing social outcomes in space and time (Lianos and Douglas, 2000).

The research challenges raised here are clear. Software for surveillance is often bought off the shelf from transnational suppliers. Critical researchers into digital algorithmic systems practices face an imperative to 'get inside' the production and implementation of code (Thrift and French, 2002). This might mean switching the focus of research to the social and political assumptions that software producers embed (unconsciously or consciously) into their algorithms years before and thousands of miles away from the site of application. Research is required to systematically track the sourcing, implementation and implications of digital surveillance in practice, across multiple spaces, as the code moves from inception to application. Such research also needs to address time, as another implication of digital surveillance is its use in decreasing the ability of people to escape deemed offences in the distant past (Blanchette and Johnson, 2002).

The policy implications of such research are complex and problematic. Digital surveillance systems tend to be developed, designed and deployed in ways that hide the social judgements that such systems perpetuate. Rates of technological innovation are rapid and policy makers face serious problems in simply understanding the esoteric and technical worlds of the new surveillance. Policy makers also face geographical and jurisdictional problems. Efforts to regulate and control digital surveillance are necessarily bound by the geographical jurisdictions that give them political legitimacy and power. But social assumptions embedded in surveillance software in one context can have major ramifications in distant times and places. The practices of digitally sorting and sifting societies occur through globally stretched sociotechnical relations (Lyon, 2001).

Another major problem concerns the dominant policy approach to surveillance: the concept of privacy. Privacy is fundamentally embedded both in the Lockean notion of property and in the patriarchal dynamics of the household (Lyon, 1994). Its current politics are also dominated by the discourse of individualist, libertarian 'cyberliberties', which renders it inadequate to deal with complex sociogeographical polarization.

We believe that a strong regulatory approach, based on the principle of the mutual transparency of state and individual (see Brin, 1999), could simultaneously work at the many geographical scales at which social and economic regulation occurs. However, two current trajectories make this transparent society less than likely. The first is the post-9/11 climate. Currently, many western policy makers would consider such transparency politically unacceptable, particularly as pressures increase from the Right for *decreasing* civil liberties in the name of security (see Huber and Mills, 2002).

The second is that the new digital surveillance systems are being used to support the dominant neoliberal economic agenda (for example, the generalized privatization envisaged by the proposed General Agreement on Trade in Services) because they can allow the 'unbundling' of previously public infrastructures and spaces and support 'pay per use' and sophisticated consumer monitoring. As public, welfare and social service regimes restructure and are privatized or remodelled through various forms of 'partnership', the automated control and sifting capabilities of digital surveillance techniques are increasingly being utilized to support differentiated service regimes. These practices are closely modelled on those in the private sector; in many cases, private sector firms are colonizing public and welfare service regimes with precisely such practices.

Does this mean that the choice is for a critical response to digital surveillance to be bound by either cyberliberties, resistance to the 'war on terrorism' or anti-globalization struggles? Not necessarily – although placing the spread of digital surveillance within a wider political-economic critique is crucial. People do 'refuse to disappear beneath the imperatives of spatial regulation that favors select target markets' (Flusty, 2000: 156). Resistance exists in many forms, from the playful guerrilla art of the Surveillance Camera Players (see: http://www.notbored.org/the-scp.html), the systematic anti-panopticism of the i-SEE project in New York, calculating 'paths of least surveillance' (Schenke and IAA, 2002; see: http://www.appliedautonomy.com/isee/), to the everyday practices of the targeted . . .

Resistance varies across policy domains; in health, outside professional disquiet, it has been minimal. While Iceland has at least provided mechanisms for public consultation on the role of deCODE (Rose, 2001), the UK government has shown no such inclination. The practices of insurance companies and health providers are similarly opaque, and, unlike the case of CCTV, there seems little space for individual acts of subversion.

Finally, we must stress that digital surveillance systems do have real limits. While the technologies are rapidly increasing their capabilities, they are often still not as reliable as their proponents claim. For example, facial recognition is still prone to misidentification, although the nature of these errors is in itself a matter of concern. In addition, the sheer diversity of identities, social worlds and political pressures in contemporary cities can quickly swamp crude efforts to impose simplistic notions of exclusion and purified urban order. Contemporary cities remain sites of jumbled, superimposed and contested orderings and meanings; they are 'points of interconnection, not hermetically sealed objects' (Thrift, 1997: 143). Multiple 'spillovers' can easily saturate and overwhelm simple attempts at establishing and maintaining 'hard' disciplinary boundaries. Virtually all boundaries remain to some extent porous and perfect control strategies are never possible.

Note

1   This chapter is an extract from S. Graham and D. Wood (2003) Digitizing surveillance: categorization, space, inequality, *Critical Social Policy*, 23(2): 227–48.

References

Banisar, D. (1999) Big Brother goes high tech, *Covert Action Quarterly*, 67: 6.

Barnett, A. and Hinsliff, G. (2001) Fury at plan to sell off DNA secrets, *Observer*, 23 Sept. Available at: http://www.guardian.co.uk/Archive/Article/0,4273, 4262710,00.html (accessed 1 November 2002).

Blanchette, J.-F. and Johnson, D. (2002) Data retention and the panoptic society: the social benefits of forgetfulness, *The Information Society*, 18(1): 33–45.

Brin, D. (1999) *The Transparent Society*. New York: Perseus.

Cook, E. D. (1999) Genetics and the British insurance industry, *Journal of Medical Ethics*, 25(2): 157–62.

Davis, M. (1990) *City of Quartz*. London: Verso.

Declich, S. and Carter, A. O. (1994) Public health surveillance: historical origins, methods and evaluation, *Bulletin of the World Health Organization*, 72(2): 285–304.

Deleuze, G. (1992) Postscript on the societies of control, *October*, 59: 3–7.

Flusty, S. (1997) Building paranoia, in N. Ellin (ed.) *Architecture of Fear*. New York: Princeton Architectural Press, pp. 47–60.

Flusty, S. (2000) Thrashing downtown: play as resistance to the spatial and representational regulation of Los Angeles, *Cities*, 17(2): 149–58.

Foucault, M. (1973) *The Birth of the Clinic*. London: Tavistock.

Foucault, M. (1975) *Discipline and Punish*. New York: Vintage.

Gandy Jr., O. H. (1993) *The Panoptic Sort*. Boulder, CO: Westview Press.

Garland, D. (2001) *The Culture of Control*. Oxford: Oxford University Press.

Graham, S. (1998) Spaces of surveillant-simulation: new technologies, digital representations, and material geographies, *Environment and Planning D: Society and Space*, 16: 483–504.

Graham, S. and Marvin, S. (2001) *Splintering Urbanism*. London: Routledge.

Graham-Rowe, D. (1999) Warning! Strange behaviour, *New Scientist*, 11 Dec., 2216: 25–8.

Henman, P. (1997) Computer technology: a political player in social policy processes, *Journal of Social Policy*, 26(3): 323–40.

Huber, P. and Mills, M. P. (2002) How technology will defeat terrorism, *City Journal*, 12(1). Available at: http://www.city-journal.org/html/12_1_how_tech.html (accessed 1 November 2002).

Jones, R. (2001) Digital rule: punishment, control and technology, *Punishment and Society*, 2(1): 5–22.

Jupp, B. (2001) *Divided by Information?* London: Demos.

Lessig, L. (1999) *Code – and Other Laws of Cyberspace*. New York: Basic Books.

Lianos, M. (2001) *Le Nouveau contrôle social*. Paris: L'Harmattan.

Lianos, M. and Douglas, M. (2000) Dangerization and the end of deviance: the institutional environment, *British Journal of Criminology*, 40(3): 264–78.

Lyon, D. (1994) *The Electronic Eye*. Cambridge: Polity Press/Blackwell.

Lyon, D. (2001) *Surveillance Society*. Buckingham: Open University Press.

McCahill, M. (2002) *The Surveillance Web*. Cullompton, Devon: Willan.

McKie, R. (1999) The way you walk pins down who you are, *Observer*, 12 Dec. Available at: http://www.guardian.co.uk/Archive/Article/o,4273,394102100.html (accessed 1 November 2002).

Marx, G. T. (1988) *Undercover*. Berkeley: University of California Press.

Marx, G. T. (1995) The engineering of social control: the search for the silver bullet, in J. Hagan and R. Peterson (eds) *Crime and Inequality*. Stanford, CA: Stanford University Press, pp. 225–46.

Marx, G. T. (2002) What's new about the 'new surveillance'? Classifying for change and continuity, *Surveillance & Society*, 1(1): 9–29. Available at: http://www.surveillance-and-society.org

Mooney, G. (1999) Public health versus private practice: the contested development of compulsory disease notification in late nineteenth century Britain, *Bulletin of the History of Medicine*, 73(2): 238–67.

Moor, J. H. (1999) Using genetic information while protecting the privacy of the soul, *Ethics and Information Technology*, 1(4): 257–63.

Nelkin, D. and Andrews, L. (1999) DNA identification and surveillance creep, *Sociology of Health and Illness*, 21(5): 689–706.

Norris, C. (2002) From personal to digital: CCTV, the panopticon and the technological mediation of suspicion and social control, in D. Lyon (ed.) *Surveillance as Social Sorting*. London: Routledge, pp. 249–81.

Norris, C. and Armstrong, G. (1999) *The Maximum Surveillance Society*. Oxford: Berg.

Norris, C., Moran, J. and Armstrong, G. (eds) (1998) Algorithmic surveillance: the future of automated visual surveillance, in *Surveillance, Closed Circuit Television and Social Control*. Aldershot: Ashgate, pp. 255–76.

Pokorski, R. J. (1997) Insurance underwriting in the genetic era (workshop on heritable cancer syndromes and genetic testing), *Cancer*, 80(3): 587–99.

Pollack, A. (2000) Gene hunters say patients are a bankable asset, *Guardian*, 2 Aug. Available at: http://www.guardian.co.uk/Archive/Article/0, 4273, 4046698,00.html (accessed 1 November 2002).

Poster, M. (1990) *The Mode of Information*. Cambridge: Polity Press.

Rose, H. (2001) *The Commodification of Bioinformation*. London: Wellcome Trust. Available at: http://www.wellcome.ac.uk/en/images/hilaryrose1_3975.pdf (accessed 1 November 2002).

Rose, N. (2000) The biology of culpability: pathological identity and crime control in a biological culture, *Theoretical Criminology*, 4(1): 5–34.

Schenke, E. and IAA (2002) On the outside looking out: an interview with the Institute for Applied Autonomy (IAA), *Surveillance & Society*, 1(1): 102–19. Available at: http://www.surveillance-and-society.org

Schiller, D. (1999) *Digital Capitalism: Networking the Global Market System*. Cambridge, MA: MIT Press.

Thrift, N. (1997) Cities without modernity, cities with magic, *Scottish Geographical Magazine*, 113(3): 138–49.

Thrift, N. and French, S. (2002) The automatic production of space, *Transactions of the Institute of British Geographers*, 27(4): 309–35.

Tseng, E. (2000) The Geography of Cyberspace, Mimeo.

Utility Week (1995) IT in utilities, *Utility Week*, Special issue, 19 Nov.

van der Ploeg, I. (2002) Biometrics and the body as information: normative issues of the socio-technical coding of the body, in D. Lyon (ed.) *Surveillance as Social Sorting*. London: Routledge, pp. 57–73.

Virilio, P. (1991) *The Lost Dimension*. New York: Semiotext(e).

16

Surveillance in the city: primary definition and urban spatial order[1]
by Roy Coleman

Introduction

. . . In an authoritative essay 25 years ago Stan Cohen (1979) characterized the emergent 'punitive city' as a spatial complex that was beginning to blur boundaries of control and widen nets of regulation in a manner set to 'increase the visibility – if not the theatricality – of social control' (p. 360). In this and other work, Cohen urged criminologists to look beyond 'social control talk' – which veils stigma and punitive practice behind a language of 'community' and 'compassion' – and, instead, cast scrutiny upon the wider changes occurring in urban space and those institutions charged with the construction of quasi-legal 'atlases of vice' that underpin social control practice (p. 358; see also Cohen, 1983; 1985). Taking this cue, we can begin by stating that social control today is strategically entwined with, and organized around, visualized spectacles that promote ways of seeing urban space as benign, 'people centred' and celebratory. Such urban management strategies are not only refashioning the look and feel of city space but are also, at the same time, reconfiguring the development and rationale of social control in the city . . . Various writers have highlighted an intensification in the surveillance of city streets in the UK (McCahill and Norris, 2002), the USA (Davis, 1990; Parenti, 1999; Ferrell, 2001) and in European cities (Belina and Helms, 2003; Koskela, 2004). Understanding the trajectories of particular social control projects requires comparative international studies within which to place debates in relation to changes in urban spatial justice (MacCleod, 2002; Mitchell, 2003; Peck, 2003), the diffusion of a transatlantic orthodoxy on social control (Wacquant, 1999), the local mediation of control strategies (Raco, 2003) and in terms of the impact of surveillance and control practices upon the urban experience of those targeted (Ferrell, 2001; Hayward, 2004a). Alongside these interdisciplinary concerns critical criminology still has work to do in unmasking the organization of social and political power through exploring the changing terrain of contemporary urban statecraft that guides and rationalizes control practice.

Critical criminological work excavating 'spatial control' has done much to 'recall historical patterns of conflict and injustice' (Ferrell, 2001: 17) and remind criminologists that the city cannot be understood from crime-mapping exercises alone (Hayward, 2004b). This article seeks to extend such insights and examine what Mitchell (2003) calls 'the materialization of order' in the urban form (p. 235). A focus on the materialization of social control practices forces a consideration of the shifting terrain of state power and the rationale for state intervention that works and reworks the definitional problematic of 'crime' in a class-based attempt at 'reclaiming the streets' (Coleman, 2004a). Through the use of case material from cities in the UK and by keeping a focus on the shifting terrain of political economy (Hall and Winlow, 2004), the [chapter] examines the materiality of socio-cultural control and its role in reproducing unequal spatial relations. In this context the emergence of 'new' urban forces, or networks of primary definers, whose material and ideological ascendancy in the urban process rule (Coleman and Sim, 2000), has a direct bearing on the shaping of urban narratives of place as well as the production of space and its regulation. It is a contention of this [chapter] that current practices and discourses that are uncritically placed under the banner of 'crime prevention' are actually better understood as socio-spatial ordering practices that, under entrepreneurial conditions, reinforce and reconstruct particular cultural sensibilities around crime, deviance and incivility. Partnerships between powerful local agencies are central to these practices and promote strategic ways of seeing city space that incorporate the targeting of behaviours, and activities that disrupt primary definitions of urban renaissance. These wider visions and definitions of urban change lie outside the remit of formal crime control agendas and, as a consequence, must be examined as crucial aspects of the normative-cultural dimensions inherent in definitional struggles over 'crime' and 'crime prevention' that are part of the governance of urban space.

Others have shown that these urban crime control projects are informed by depoliticized criminological models, propagated and then exported from the United States, including the 'broken windows' thesis (Wacquant, 1999; Ferrell, 2001; Mitchell, 2003) which, through its application in Business Improvement Districts and police-led partnerships on both sides of the Atlantic, has linked crime to its larger cousin 'disorder', in targeting petty street level offences, 'nuisance' and 'unconventional' behaviours. Routine activity theory has similarly come to the fore to stress the need for 'capable guardians' to watch over 'suitable targets' (Felson, 1998: 52), and has served to justify the proliferation of 'capable' eyes now surveying the streets of the UK in the form of cameras and street wardens . . . this understanding of crime and control tells us nothing of the ideological and material power of the agents and agencies authorized to implement these powerful ideas in securing city spaces (Coleman, 2004a). What follows is an exploration of entrepreneurial urbanism that seeks to place these depoliticized models as active components in the production of urban spaces and political forms of domination. In this way, entrepreneurial urbanism is thought of as a complex, and not entirely coherent, set of strategies to 'reclaim' city streets through the fabrication of an idealized class-based performative rationale for citified behaviour. As the latest trope in a reinvigorated pursuit of urban spatial order, camera surveillance in the UK is a normal feature of city development that propagates the idea of 'capable guardians' and symbolizes the state imaginary with respect to urban order in the UK.[2] But cameras are only one dimension in a wider proliferation of surveillance practices (including private security, public warden schemes, legal sanctions, and local councils and businesses who are developing and funding surveillance networks) that this [chapter] explores as a means of scrutinizing the imaginary of the locally powerful. In taking the wider context into account, the [chapter] discusses the discourses that shape the urban spatial form and hail a particular kind of citified individual as a forerunner to examining how these discourses over the definition of urban space intersect with the development and targeting of surveillance practices in the city.

Primary definition and urban space

Following Richard Sparks (2003), criminologists need to explore how 'transitions between state regimes and changes in the practices and politics of punishment are intimately connected' (p. 171). In this sense, an understanding of surveillance in the city necessitates exploring the intersection between urban statecraft and social control rhetoric. This points to a number of issues. First, surveillance should not be grasped as something organized around, or relating to, one discrete phenomenon or entity, such as surveillance cameras. Thus interconnections between legal and non-legal sanctions, the rhetoric of powerful actors inside *and* outside of formal criminal justice arenas and a range of urban public–private partnership campaigns around local quality of life issues need to be brought to analytical attention. Second, attempting to understand the interconnectedness of surveillance practices in the city leads to a consideration of the city-building process itself and of how the political struggles involved in this process give rise to discourses of socio-cultural censure and perceptions of risk. Third, surveillance practices in the city are increasingly understood as being directed to behaviours outside of, or having a loose relation to, traditional criminal sanctioning categories and processes (Ferrell et al., 2004). An expansion of punitive suspicion in the contemporary city can, therefore, be related to the dynamics of contemporary urban rule in its entrepreneurialized form which points us to the changing nature of the organized definition of space . . .

As developed by Hall et al. (1978: 58–9), primary definition indicates a form of cultural power and political authority through which particular ideologies and preferred meanings are circulated throughout the wider social body so as to set limits upon what is, and what is not, linguistically and practically credible in terms of identifying, understanding and responding to social problems. Originally applied to the media, primary definition points to the exercise of definitional power in society. The authors asked, how do the definitions of 'the powerful' become routinized and taken for granted in relation to the framing of particular problems in a wider social sense? For Hall and colleagues, the concern was to locate the 'control culture' (that denoted interconnections between criminal justice agents, media agents and moral entrepreneurs) historically, and to position it within particular state forms and political regimes (p. 195). The work of Hall and his colleagues remains important in recognizing the role of powerful definers in relation to the establishment of law and order agendas, their targets and the connections between agenda-setting procedures and the material and ideological power of social definition. The work has been criticized for presenting 'an atemporal model' of primary definition which fails to take into account 'new forces and their representatives' whose emergence as socially credible and authoritative spokespersons needs to be acknowledged and explained

(Schlesinger and Tumber, 1994: 19). For the purposes of this [chapter] the concept of primary definition is a means to raise questions about *who* is articulating contemporary urban spatiality and with what consequences for socio-spatial control and justice.

Today the forces of primary definition can be understood as central to a contradictory and conflictual process towards the construction of the city as a 'growth machine' (Logan and Molotch, 1987) that interconnects the spheres of business consortia, City Centre Managers, council departments and chief executives, property development, place marketing, the youth industries, education, senior police and private security organizations. The networks of institutional power now governing urban space consist of an officially designated 'partnership' that is understood as reconstituting city spaces within a 'synergy of capital investment and cultural meaning' (Zukin, 1996: 45) alongside 'the self valorisation of capital in and through regulation' (Jessop, 1997: 29) . . . The contours of primary definition and the emergence of specific primary definers in relation to urban spatial rule will vary between localities but, as it is argued here, the discourses of urban primary definition are emerging in a manner that both reflects and reinforces the processes of urban entrepreneurialism that are currently being promoted in international, national and local spheres of influence, including central government policy and European-funded projects.

Current practices of primary definition forge a politics of image that, in permeating local institutions of rule, reinforces a process in which 'entrepreneurial landscapes – both real and imaginary – are ideologically charged' (Hall and Hubbard, 1996: 163) . . . The selective processes of marketing spatial attributes prioritize particular local, national and international audiences (as tourists, investors, consumers) and sideline public debate around 'older' issues to do with social inequality and its visibility so that poverty itself is seen as a normal and/or inevitable part of this landscape (Soja, 2000). The ideological recharging of space as strategically important to the politics of investment is intensifying a notion of space as performative; that is, space as predictable, not least through the imagery of corporate branding along with conventional images of consumerism and advertising. In this context, new circuits of urban spatial definition are articulating an urban vision that collapses distinctions between the look of the urban fabric with other issues to do with the suitability of behaviour in public space . . .

Surveillance targeting and entrepreneurial urbanism

In the UK these definitions relating to urban spatiality are encouraged through central government urban design guidance documents where 'the look' of the urban fabric is tied to successful regeneration (DETR, 2000; Home Office 2003a). Thus representations of the look, feel and ambience of urban space are evident in national and local promotional documents, local press stories, and city branding and flagship developments. These discursive tracts underpin the construction of spaces for consumption alongside the consumption of places as packaged experiences themselves (Urry, 1995).

The notion of visually pleasing space is tied to aesthetic considerations concerning the moral probity and appropriateness of behaviour in public space. As a managerial (or management *in* space) discourse the notion of reclaiming the streets from the 'yobs',[3] over-exuberant youths, petty thieves, drunks, beggars and illicit traders assumes a strategic ideological position within the networks of primary definition and, as already indicated, is buttressed by central government thinking and legislation. For example, the Anti-Social Behaviour Act of 2003 can be connected to the wider rehabilitation of space and is certainly being applied and understood as a desired tool within worked-out strategies for regeneration. The creation of such a space is part of a sustained move towards what Frank Field MP defines as a 'contract based citizenship' that would work through 'a series of contracts which cover the behaviour of all of us as we negotiate the public realm' (Field, in Grier and Thomas, 2003). It is important to explore the spatial-moral regulation of the kind being endorsed here and its complex relationship to aggressive place marketing and the politics of making visually pleasing space. The wider commitment to 'civilize' city space within partnership rule heralds a rejuvenated moral discourse of street civility. Also it is reflected in the emergence of high-salaried anti-social behaviour 'Czars' who, under the 2003 Act, target beggars and other 'harassers' of the public in, for example, Liverpool and Manchester city centres (*Merseymart*, 2004).

In a general sense these discourses and practices have a reclaiming zeal in relation to urban public space and are targeted at activities and people that are deemed incongruous in these entrepreneurialized zones. In this sense contemporary primary definition promotes an ideal of performance-enhancing space geared towards orderly risk-free experiences and modes of interaction (Lash and Urry, 1994). Performance-enhancing space is constituted through, to borrow Butler's (1990) phrase, a 'stylised repetition of acts' (p. 140) underpinned by regulatory and disciplinary discourses that encourage, cajole, support, reward and coerce the actions that make up performative space. Performance-enhancing space works with the visible in mind and encourages not only the performance of consumption and tourism but, increasingly, the performed appreciation of 'culture' and 'art' in the cities that now form part of the consuming experience. Furthermore, urban surveillance partnerships also work with the visible in mind and expand the power and scope of entrepreneurial agendas. The partnerships are partly managed by local business consortia, chambers of commerce and hybrid organizations sponsored by a mixture of local capital and public grants (Coleman, 2004b). The development of entrepreneurial surveillance practices is increasingly geared to the monitoring of performative space and its potential disruption. For example, the development of automated surveillance cameras that detect suspicious bodily movements (see Graham and Wood, 2003), automatically triggers alarms if people stand or sit motionless for too long, walk around too much or stoop around parked vehicles. Depending on the context, the cameras hone-in on unusual and disruptive acts that negate the normalized fabrications of bodies in urban space and provide evidence of a repetitive and performative rationalization being affected in city street space. Powerful definitions of performative space are embroiled with moralizing discourses that constitute what spaces are and for whom they are intended . . .

Non-performing homeless

Backed by national legislation, a 'fear and fury' discourse at the local level gives expression to class-based anxieties about public space within regentrifying cities across the advanced world (Smith, 1996). For those at the centre of partnership power, the path of homeless people into poverty is irrelevant when placed alongside more pressing concerns to do with the 'contamination' of city space that homeless people symbolize. In the UK, attempts have been made to 'responsibilize' the homeless into performing entrepreneurial roles by recruiting *Big Issue* vendors and training them as tourist information guides (Coleman, 2004a). Other training techniques have been geared towards educating *Big Issue* vendors in 'non-aggressive' sales techniques and making them stand in pitch-marked squares while working. 'Educative' strategies such as these have taken place alongside intrusive surveillance and a process of criminalization. Developments at the local level can be understood in the context of stigmatization of the homeless (as 'winos', spongers and pan-handlers) by national governments in the UK and USA (Mitchell, 2003). In Liverpool, for example, an alliance between local council officials, police and private security resulted in 'Operation Manton' in October 2003. The £50,000 undercover operation was justified by a key primary definer as 'a major step forward in creating a cleaner, safer and more attractive city centre'. Moreover, according to the Manager, businesses and consumers 'highlighted the activities of aggressive beggars as the major detraction from the city centre' (*Guardian*, 2003). In carrying out the operation, the 'nuisance' of homeless people (whether they be rough sleepers, beggars or *Big Issue* vendors) on the streets was responded to with the arrest of 54 homeless people . . . In the entrepreneurial city the routines of thought and practice that inform a moral demarcation of space targets the poor people of the city as eyesores or 'broken windows', and as Mitchell (2001) suggests in the US context, the idea has been 'not to repair them but to remove them altogether' (p. 83). The surveillance and removal of the homeless are a desired goal in entrepreneurial cities and are exemplified in Leeds city centre where they are attempting to ban *Big Issue* sellers using the rhetoric of anti-social behaviour and a campaign entitled 'Shape up or Ship Out' (*Yorkshire Evening Post*, 2004). The excessive surveillance of the lifestyle and working practices of the homeless in advanced capitalist cities (see Mitchell, 2003) is bolstered in the UK by central government making begging an arrestable offence and allowing Community Support Officers to detain and arrest beggars (with the police) if they fail to provide specific information, or refuse to move on when ordered to (*Big Issue in the North*, 2004).

Non-performing youth culture

The discourse of cultural regeneration is now a universal phenomenon which has accelerated in the era of 'the city of renewal' (Evans, 2003: 417). The discourse is a contested one and its celebratory and inclusive tone (see Department for Culture, Media and Sport, 2004) veils attacks on cultural pursuits that fall outside officially sanctioned projects and are instead subjected to surveillance and curtailment. A 'war on youth culture' in United States schools (Muzzatti, 2004: 151) and in public spaces (Ferrell, 2001) in advanced capitalist societies has resonance in the UK through the language of 'anti-social behaviour' that places contractual expectations on bodily conduct and demeanour in strategically visible space ... For the new primary definers, the proximity and management of poverty are central to a politics of vision that seeks to avoid an image of a 'bargain basement sector' (Coleman, 2004a: 145).[4]

As a key tool in the politics of vision, surveillance networks in the UK aid the strategic balance between spatial aesthetics and function and any notion of the city as a space of cultural pursuits for younger people continues to be circumscribed. In Liverpool, skateboarders can be fined from between £250 to a £1000 if they break a bylaw banning skating passed by city councillors in July 2002. Liverpool council claimed that skateboarding should be an offence as it is giving the city a bad image in terms of scaring off tourists and shoppers, as well as damaging statues and memorials. The skaters themselves, who can be regularly seen dodging the surveillance net, preferred an alternative 'vision' of the city and their place in it:

> skating in the streets adds to the atmosphere and is part of the fun. It's a real kick in the teeth that the council have decided they want to ban us from the streets in the summer holidays. I don't think the skateboarders are doing any harm. A lot of people enjoy watching us doing our tricks.
>
> (*Liverpool Echo*, 2002)

While spontaneous street art and skating are subject to control, a two-day annual event does cater for these activities (running since summer 2003) on specially erected skating ramps and walls on Liverpool's waterfront. The event – though shunned by some – is directed at tourists and shamelessly used to promote and fabricate the city's idealized cultural scope and status ...

Skaters, Goths ... beggars and buskers as unsightly and 'unwanted' public spectacles are increasingly lumped together and derided as 'the raff element', as indeed one property developer stated before an inquiry into the building of Europe's biggest commercial city centre project now underway in Liverpool. The 42-acre site – including exclusive shopping, residential, hotel and leisure facilities – will operate strict access control and remove undesirables under the remit of a private security force that links in with public police patrols and camera surveillance (Indymedia, 2003). This spatial ordering strategy impinges on the right to decide who walks through a city's streets and promotes 'safety' for the leisured classes in a way that includes removing from public view the right to protest against, for example, shops dealing in sweatshop goods. The corporate branding of space means that those who protest in these spaces are likely to be labelled as transgressors and defilers of the image of apolitical space ...

Working class youth

Entrepreneurial urbanism 'shows no signs of reaching its geographical limits' (Ward, 2003: 116) and the peripheral, less affluent neighbourhoods in and around the entrepreneurial city core increasingly enter the frame in terms of the problem they pose for city/regional image making. It is in these areas that demonization accompanies anti-social behaviour legislation and informs the urban experience of working class youth. One of the striking things about the use of Anti-Social Behaviour Orders in the UK is how they target the cultural milieu of the young – whether through the curtailment of quad biking; the disallowing of certain forms of linguistic expression; drinking behaviour (see *Guardian*, 2004b) and the restrictions placed on youthful free association in particular spaces regardless of whether any 'anti-social behaviour' has actually taken place. In 2004, Liverpool police and business groups narrowed the distance between established youthful fun time and criminal activity by launching a poster campaign in the city urging the public to report young people to the authorities on the night before 'Halloween'. The poster reads: 'Mischief Night October 30: It's Not Just Kids Having Fun, It's Youth Crime and Disorder'. Under Section 30 of the Anti-Social Behaviour Act 2003, all 16-year olds can be photographed and banned from designated spaces, as was the case in Wigton, Cumbria, in February 2004. Here the curfew covered the centre of town and came into effect over several nights after 9pm. Youths who were refused access to the town felt their civil rights had been violated as many went out for a night at the cinema or to eat fish and chips only to be turned away by police (*Guardian*, 2004a). In Liverpool 'no-go zones for yobs' have been set up under Section 30 of the above Act which provides police with powers of dispersal and banishment of groups of two or more youths and to arrest them if they return within 24 hours . . . Primary definers and youth often come into conflict with particularly punitive consequences for the young that, in the UK context, have a long history (Goldson, 2002). As a result of revanchist discourses and punitive policy in the UK, those 'children who are seen to transgress prescribed behavioural codes and behaviours and boundaries (whether civil or criminal)' are suffering a 'violation' of their civil and human rights (Goldson, 2005). The 2003 White Paper 'Respect and Responsibility: Taking a Stand Against Anti-Social Behaviour' states an 'extended police family', that is, public-spirited community wardens should be developed and draw on a range of 'powers to designate areas to disperse groups and use the child curfew' laws (Home Office, 2003b: 54). This 'extended police family' of 'capable guardians' involves not only local residents but business consortia, developers, private police and local authorities in a remoralization of city streets in a manner that is, although not entirely coordinated, indicative of the attempted orchestration of the definitional processes over public space discussed here . . .

Conclusion

The rollout of city surveillance technologies discussed here reflects and reinforces the changing nature of primary definition and its relationship to the production of urban space. In the contemporary setting, the theatricality of social control in the city and its reinforcement in an entertainment-hungry media may in fact represent 'a continuation of the overall pattern [of social control] established in the 19th century' (Cohen, 1979: 359). Moreover, it is not so much that the city is subject to 'governing through crime' (Simon, in Hudson, 2001: 158) but more accurately it is being governed through *very particular* images of crime and incivility that, along with the justificatory discourses aimed at combating them, have their roots in nineteenth-century city building. This suggests that Cohen's original argument is correct in that 'what is new is the scale of the operation and the technologies' deployed and not, in a challenge to the idea of a 'new penology', *what* and *who* is deemed suitable for targeting and punishment by these technologies (Cohen, 1979: 260). Therefore, the propagation of urban sensibilities that focus on the tangible, visible and scenic, has also reinforced some fairly old urban tales of fear and degeneration (Coleman and Sim, 2005). The visible 'differences' that homeless people, the poor, street traders and youth cultures bring to the city, undermine the hegemonic notions of 'public' spatial utility and function. Indeed, for these groups, it is often merely their visibility alone and not their behaviour that is deemed problematic. As such, surveillance practices work alongside ideas of 'the visually pleasing city' and reinforce certain regenerative claims made for city space ... The upshot is the reinforcement of hegemonic definitions of 'risk', 'crime' and 'harm' as categories assumed to emanate exclusively from relatively poor and 'disaffected' people. However, questions remain as to what extent these processes are indicative trends between cities across the globe? Scholars have begun to debate the significance of trends in control as they criss-cross between different national and capitalist social orders. This has been debated in terms of the theories of 'broken windows' and the assumptions around 'crime and safety' they have perpetuated and alongside the promotion of neo-liberal ideology and market growth (Taylor, 1998; Wacquant, 1999). While comparative studies are essential to understanding the unfolding of urban social control, exploring 'the local' must avoid relativism and contribute to a wider empirical and theoretical debate. Local/global dialectics must form the focus of study in that 'every microcosm presupposes a macrocosm that assigns it its place and boundaries and implies a dense web of social relations beyond the local site' (Wacquant, 2002: 1524) ... The ascendance of 'broken windows' spatial control must be understood not merely as a technical set of devices but as constituted alongside, and as a legitimating 'logic' for, moral censures relating to public decorum in a context of increasing urban poverty (Wacquant, 1999; Peck and Ward, 2002). As well as being attuned to these wider factors, researchers of social control need to study the control process in and through its particular *and* general setting, thus highlighting tensions, contradictions and sites of resistance occurring at multiple spatial scales.

Indeed the arguments contained in this [chapter] must be placed alongside other studies of socio-spatial control and the continuities and discontinuities they highlight. In critically interrogating primary defined space, however, it is argued that powerless groups are often 'represented only by their eloquent absence; their silences ... refracted through the glare or gaze of others' (Hall, 1986: 9). Certainly critical criminologists, wherever they find themselves, will have a role – to use Cindy Katz's (2001) words – in 'understanding and "exposing" the ways that things, people, and social relations are made visible or invisible to the public' (p. 96). Part of this project involves unmasking the institutional organization of primary definition and how urban inequality is maintained through the policing of 'urban outsiders' deemed problematic in relation to the current modes of material acquisition (Ferrell, 2001) – not least because, in the visually-obsessed contemporary city, a concern with hiding social problems, or redefining them as criminogenic issues, is being intensified when, paradoxically, spectacles of civic and cultural illumination are being developed. Surveillance in the city – understood in this sense – is tied to a strategy of representation and illumination of urban phenomena as signifying 'normal' city life ...

The value of human activity in public spaces is increasingly assessed using performative criteria that inevitably casts shadows over other spaces and activities not deemed suitable for public consumption through illumination. The rough sleepers, working homeless, street traders, impromptu youth thrill-seekers and those who rely on 'the bargain basement' economy are at risk of being defined negatively (or defined out) of entrepreneurial space. Unhiding their stories provides a role for criminologists, alongside exposing the city building processes that render these stories irrelevant and unintelligible. However, the city is, and always has been, constituted as a contest over space – over its production, representation and regulation; over who is authorized to be in it and who is kept out; over what constitutes an unpolluted space and what constitutes transgression of space. This [chapter] has not addressed the spaces of resistance in the city, although more adventurous criminologists have made the exploration of resistance a central task in order to uncover alternative 'street politics' that kindle 'a revolution against public order, and for public life' (Ferrell, 2001: 197; see also Ferrell et al., 2004). In Liverpool, attempts to criminalize and remove *Big Issue* vendors from the streets faced opposition through public outcry in the letters pages in the local press and the threat of legal action by the *Big Issue in the North* that forestalled the removal of working homeless people from the streets. In Liverpool there have also been 'sleep outs' by community groups to raise awareness of rough sleeping in the city along with challenges to the punitive rhetoric and criminalization of asylum seekers by groups such as 'People Not Profit'. Alternative media also exist in the spaces of entrepreneurial city craft and provide important sources of public information and challenge to entrepreneurial regimes . . .

In the surveilled city it is often bemoaned that 'difference is not so much . . . celebrated as segregated' (Bannister, Fyfe and Kearns, 1998: 27; see also Fyfe, 2004). The eyesores currently targeted for removal from the streets are not merely 'different' . . . but, as some of the campaigns above have highlighted, unequal in terms of economic, political and socio-cultural criteria of marginality. In the 19th century, city policing acted as an 'urban prophylactic' that cleansed from view, by a seemingly 'pointless ritual' (Brogden, 1991: 116), the eyesores of respectable discomfort while maintaining the geographies of inequality (Brogden, 1982). Tracing the dynamics of inequality in the entrepreneurial city today remains an important task (MacLeod, Raco and Ward, 2003) and so too does tracing the role of surveillance practices in reproducing spatial inequality. Inequality is not merely a variation on cultural expression even though the processes of primary definition now constructing cities promote a 'politics that celebrates marginality rather than seeking to redress it' (Mitchell, 2001: 82). Challenging the power behind the gaze remains a significant and difficult task . . .

Notes

1   This chapter is an extract from R. Coleman (2006) Surveillance in the city: primary definition and urban spatial order, *Crime, Media, Culture*, 1(2): 131–48.
2   Under New Labour, the 'roll out' of social surveillance surpassed Conservative enthusiasm for the technology with the allocation of £170 million of Home Office funds to extend closed circuit television (CCTV) by 40,000 extra cameras in

1999 (Home Office, 1999). Between 1992 and 2002 it is estimated that over a quarter of a billion pounds of mostly public money was spent on camera networks with upwards of three billion for the same period when maintenance costs were included (McCahill and Norris, 2002). As it stands today, the UK is the largest market for CCTV in Europe (Graham, 2000: 45) and accounts for one-fifth of all CCTV cameras worldwide (*Independent*, 2004).

3   'Yobs' is a political and media-favoured term used in the UK to deride young people and comes from the 19th-century bourgeois 'respectable' fear of working-class boys (i.e. 'yobs') in and around the spaces of the city.

4   The need of local people for so-called bargain shopping is born out of the fact that three areas in Liverpool are ranked by the government as being among the top five most deprived areas in the UK in terms of unemployment, health, home ownership and educational attainment (*The Times*, 2004). Liverpool was ranked the poorest area in the UK in terms of average incomes with a high proportion of families surviving on around £8,000 a year (*Liverpool Echo*, 1999). This reality of the working class city has been hard to reimage for local marketers.

References

Bannister, J., Fyfe, N.R. and Kearns, A. (1998) Closed circuit television and the city, in C. Norris, J. Moran and G. Armstrong (eds) *Surveillance, Closed Circuit Television and Social Control*. Aldershot: Ashgate, pp. 21–39.

Belina, B. and Helms, G. (2003) Zero tolerance for the industrial past and other threats: policing and urban entrepreneurialism in Britain and Germany, *Urban Studies*, 40(3): 1845–67.

Big Issue in the North (2004) New begging powers, *Big Issue in the North*, 16–22 August.

Brogden, M. (1982) *The Police: Autonomy and Consent*. London: Academic Press.

Brogden, M. (1991) *On the Mersey Beat: Policing Liverpool Between the Wars*. New York: Oxford University Press.

Butler, J. (1990) *Gender Trouble: Feminism and the Subversion of Identity*. London: Routledge.

Cohen, S. (1979) 'The punitive city': notes on the dispersal of social control, *Contemporary Crisis*, 3(4): 339–63.

Cohen, S. (1983) Social-control talk: telling stories about correctional change, in D. Garland and P. Young (eds) *The Power to Punish: Contemporary Penality and Social Analysis*. London: Heinemann Educational, pp. 101–29.

Cohen, S. (1985) *Visions of Social Control*. Cambridge: Polity Press.

Coleman, R. (2004a) *Reclaiming the Streets: Surveillance, Social Control and the City*. Cullompton: Willan.

Coleman, R. (2004b) Watching the degenerate: street camera surveillance and urban regeneration, *Local Economy*, 19(3): 199–211.

Coleman, R. and Sim, J. (2000) You'll never walk alone: CCTV surveillance, order and neo-liberal rule in Liverpool city centre, *British Journal of Sociology*, 51(4): 623–39.

Coleman, R. and Sim, R. (2005) Contemporary statecraft and the punitive obsession: a critique of the new penology thesis, in J. Pratt, D. Brown, S. Hallsworth, M. Brown and W. Morrison (eds) *The New Punitiveness: Current Trends, Theories and Perspectives*: Cullompton: Willan, pp. 101–18.

Davis, M. (1990) *City of Quartz: Excavating the Future in Los Angeles*. London: Verso.

Department for Culture, Media and Sport (2004) *Culture at the Heart of Regeneration*. London: Department of Culture, Media and Sport.

DETR (Department of the Environment, Transport and the Regions) (2000) *By Design – Urban Design in the Planning System: Towards a Better Place*. London: HMSO.

Evans, G. (2003) Hard-branding the cultural city – from Prado to Prada, *International Journal of Urban and Regional Studies*, 27(1): 417–40.

Felson, M. (1998) *Crime and Everyday Life*. London: Pine Forge Press.

Ferrell, J. (2001) *Tearing Down the Streets: Adventures in Urban Anarchy*. New York: Palgrave.

Ferrell, J., Hayward, K., Morrison, W., and Presdee, M., (2004) Fragments of a manifesto: introducing cultural criminology unleashed, in J. Ferrell, K. Hayward, W. Morrison and M. Presdee (eds) *Cultural Criminology Unleashed*. London: Glasshouse Press, pp. 1–9.

Fyfe, N. (2004) Zero tolerance, maximum surveillance? Deviance, difference and crime control in the late modern city, in L. Lees (ed.) *The Emancipatory City: Paradoxes and Possibilities*. London: SAGE Publications, pp. 40–56.

Goldson, B. (2002) New punitiveness: the politics of child incarceration, in J. Muncie, G. Hughes and E. McLaughlin (eds) *Youth Justice: Critical Readings*. London: SAGE Publications, pp. 386–400.

Goldson, B. (2005) Taking liberties: policy and the punitive turn, in H. Hendrick (ed.) *Children and Social Policy: Critical Readings*. Bristol: Policy Press.

Graham, S. (2000) The fifth utility, *Index on Censorship*, 2: 45–9.

Graham, S. and Wood, D. (2003) Digitizing surveillance: categorization, space, inequality, *Critical Social Policy*, 23(2): 227–48.

Grier, A. and Thomas, T. (2003) A war for civilisation as we know it: some observations on tackling anti-social behaviour, *Youth and Policy: A Critical Analysis*, 82: 1–15.

Guardian (2003) Big Issue sellers held in drugs crack down, *Guardian*, 18 October.

Guardian (2004a) Market towns holiday curfew on youngsters, *Guardian*, 2 April.

Guardian (2004b) Last orders, *Guardian*, 20 October.

Hall, S. (1986) Media power and class power, in J. Curran, J. Ecclestone, G. Oakley and A. Richardson (eds.) *Bending Reality: The State of the Media*. London: Pluto, pp. 5–14.

Hall, S., Critcher, C., Jefferson, C., Clarke, J. and Roberts, B. (1978) *Policing the Crisis: Mugging, the State and Law and Order*. London: Macmillan.

Hall, S. and Winlow, S. (2004) Barbarians at the gate: crime and violence in the breakdown of the pseudo-pacification process, in J. Ferrell, K. Hayward, W. Morrison and M. Presdee (eds) *Cultural Criminology Unleashed*. London: Glasshouse Press, pp. 275–86.

Hall, T. and Hubbard, P. (1996) The entrepreneurial city: new urban politics, new urban geographies, *Progress in Human Geography*, 20(2): 153–74.

Hayward, K. (2004a) *City Limits: Crime, Consumer Culture and Urban Experience*. London: Glasshouse Press.

Hayward, K. (2004b) Space – the final frontier: criminology, the city and spatial dynamics of exclusion, in J. Ferrell, K. Hayward, W. Morrison and M. Presdee (eds) *Cultural Criminology Unleashed*. London: Glasshouse Press, pp. 155–66.

Home Office (1999) £170 million package for CCTV and estate regeneration, Home Office press release, 16 March.

Home Office (2003a) *Building Civic Renewal*. London: HMSO.

Home Office (2003b) *Respect and Responsibility: Taking a Stand Against Anti-Social Behaviour* CM5778. London: HMSO.

Hudson, B. (2001) Punishment, rights and difference: defending justice in the risk society, in K. Stenson and R. Sullivan (eds) *Crime, Risk and Justice*. Cullompton: Willan, pp. 144–72.

Independent (2004) Big Brother Britain 2004, *Independent*, 12 January.

Indymedia (2003) The Duke and chums turn the screws on the working class. Available at: www.indymedia.org.uk/en/regions/liverpool/20/03/12/282695.html

Jessop, B. (1997) The entrepreneurial city: reimaging localities, redesigning economic governance, or restructuring capital? in N. Jewson and S. MacGregor (eds) *Transforming Cities: Contested Governance and New Spatial Divisions*. London: Routledge, pp. 28–41.

Katz, C. (2001) Hiding the target: social reproduction in privatised urban environment, in C. Minca (ed.) *Postmodern Geography: Theory and Praxis*. Oxford: Blackwell, pp. 93–110.

Koskela, H. (2004) Urban exclusion and criminological thought: 'spatialising criminology'. Paper presented to the European Group for the Study of Deviance and Social Control, University of Bristol, 16–21 September.

Lash, S. and Urry, J. (1994) *Economies of Signs and Space*. London: SAGE Publications.

Liverpool Echo (1999) We're still the poor relations, *Liverpool Echo*, 25 October.

Liverpool Echo (2002) Skateboard ban in city, *Liverpool Echo*, 24 July.

Logan, J.R. and Molotch, H.L. (1987) *Urban Fortunes: The Political Economy of Place*. Berkeley: University of California Press.

McCahill, M. and Norris, C. (2002) CCTV in Britain, Working Paper No. 3, *Urban Eye*. Available at: www.urbaneye.net/results/eu_wp3.pdf

MacLeod, G. (2002) From urban entrepreneurialism to a 'revanchist city': on the spatial injustices of Glasgow's renaissance, *Antipode*, 34(2): 602–24.

MacLeod, G., Raco, M. and Ward, K. (2003) Negotiating the contemporary city: introduction, *Urban Studies*, 40(9): 1655–71.

Merseymart (2004) 'I will clean the streets of crime': persistent thieves and beggars to be targeted, *Merseymart*, 2 September.

Mitchell, D. (2001) Postmodern geographical praxis? Postmodern impulse and the war against homeless people in the 'postjustice' city, in C. Minca (ed.) *Postmodern Geography: Theory and Praxis*. Oxford: Blackwell, pp. 57–92.

Mitchell, D. (2003) *The Right to the City: Social Justice and the Fight for Public Space*. New York: The Guilford Press.

Muzzatti, S.L. (2004) Criminalising marginality and resistance: Marilyn Manson, Columbine and cultural criminology, in J. Ferrell, K. Hayward, W. Morrison and M. Presdee (eds) *Cultural Criminology Unleashed*. London: Glasshouse Press, pp. 143–52.

Parenti, C. (1999) *Lockdown America: Police and Prisons in the Age of Crisis*. London: Verso.

Peck, J. (2003) Geography and public policy: mapping the penal state, *Progress in Human Geography*, 27(2): 222–32.

Peck, J. and Ward, K. (2002) Placing Manchester, in J. Peck and K. Ward (eds) *City of Revolution: Restructuring Manchester*. Manchester: Manchester University Press, pp. 1–17.

Raco, M. (2003) Remaking place and securitising space. Urban regeneration and the strategies, tactics and practices of policing in the UK, *Urban Studies*, 40(9): 1869–87.

Schlesinger, P. and Tumber, H. (1994) *Reporting Crime*. Oxford: Clarendon Press.

Smith, N. (1996) *The New Urban Frontier: Gentrification and the Revanchist City*. London: Routledge.

Soja, E. (2000) *Postmetropolis: Critical Studies of Cities and Regions*. Oxford: Blackwell.

Sparks, R. (2003) States of insecurity: punishment, populism and contemporary political culture, in S. McConville (ed.) *The Use of Imprisonment*. Cullompton: Willan, pp. 149–74.

Taylor, I. (1998) Crime, market liberalism and the European idea, in V. Ruggiero, N. South and I. Taylor (eds) *The New European Criminology: Crime and Social Order in Europe*. London: Routledge, pp. 19–36.

The Times (2004) Chorleywood is happiest place to live, *The Times*, 6 May.

Urry, J. (1995) *Consuming Places*. London: Routledge.

Wacquant, L. (1999) How penal common sense comes to Europeans: notes on the transatlantic diffusion of the neo-liberal Doxa, *European Societies*, 1(3): 319–52.

Wacquant, L (2002) Scrutinizing the street: poverty, morality and the pitfalls of urban ethnography, *American Journal of Sociology*, 107(6): 1468–532.

Ward, K. (2003) Entrepreneurial urbanism, state restructuring and civilising 'New' East Manchester, *Area*, 35(2): 116–27.

Yorkshire Evening Post (2004) Big Issue faces the boot, *Yorkshire Evening Post*, 10 April.

Zukin, S. (1996) Space and symbols in an age of decline, in A.D. King (ed.) *Re-Presenting the City: Ethnicity, Capital and Culture in the 21st Century Metropolis*. London: Macmillan, pp. 43–59.

17

Bring it on home: home drug testing and the relocation of the war on drugs[1]
by Dawn Moore and Kevin D. Haggerty

Introduction

The award-winning movie *American Beauty* provides a popular depiction of what we suggest is an extension of anti-drug initiatives in which drug testing, coterminous with a change in the anti-drug discourse, is introduced into the homes of white middle-class America. The story unfolds in a stereotypical, middle-class suburb. In one scene an attractive, white, teenage boy sells marijuana to his middle-aged neighbor. The neighbor asks about a container of yellow liquid and the boy responds that it is urine. His parents, he explains, drug test him.

This article explores this most recent extension of America's anti-drug initiatives into a new and relatively untouched space, the realm of middle-class domesticity. Widely proclaimed failures of the 'war on drugs' have prompted a renewed emphasis on attempts to eradicate the demand for drugs. In the process, the metaphor of drug use as a 'disease' has been revived. This trope works in the context of a distinctive constellation of actors, institutions, and interests to advance home drug testing as a potential solution to one manifestation of America's drug problem. Parental drug testing of teenagers advances anti-drug initiatives into the home and into a child's body by effectively deputizing parents, making them unique articulations of private police. We argue that the use of such tests is characteristic of wider trends in neoliberal approaches to governing crime. Home drug testing is part of a turn to technology in governmental strategies which suggests that analysts must pay greater attention to the minutiae of such tools and the social factors that help to position them as potential solutions to crime problems. However, the drug testing example indicates that rather than being embraced exclusively due to their demonstrated abilities to reduce crime risks, governmental technologies can be adopted for a host of less rational reasons. In the process, they can also prompt some highly distinctive forms of resistance.

We draw from various research sources, including approximately 50 websites dealing with drug testing, numerous hard-copy pamphlets and informational pack-ages pertaining to such tests, and advertisements in specialty magazines aimed at drug users. Telephone interviews were conducted with five representatives of companies that market home drug tests. The minutes of hearings into the regulation of home tests by the US Food and Drug Administration provided valuable insights into who originally advocated on behalf of these tests, and the types of problems they thought these technologies might solve (Food and Drug Administration, 1997).

The failed 'war' on drugs and the revitalization of the drug use 'disease'

It has only been over the last century that drug use has been problematized in Europe and North America. During this time, the discourse surrounding opiates, and eventually a cornucopia of psychoactive substances, has oscillated between notions of criminality and notions of disease. The degree of purchase each of these binaries has held at a given point has contributed to how officials have responded to the 'drug problem'. Criminality and disease have acted as useful tropes, repeatedly invoked in the practice of governing populations or behaviours. The criminalization of drug use has revealed itself time and time again as a means of controlling, isolating, and excluding from mainstream society 'problematic' minority populations (Giffen et al., 1991; Tonry, 1995). The notion of disease, in contrast, tends to work with techniques of inclusion, subjecting a population to a scrutiny of its morals, normalizing some behaviours and pathologizing others (Peele, 1995). Each of these tropes is well suited to specific social contexts. Criminalization has served as an effective technique of control over specific populations in social climates where concerns over immigration and xenophobia have run high (Giffen et al., 1991). Disease, on the other hand, is invoked when governance is directed at more privileged populations. Looking at the governance of drug use over the last century, we see that while both tropes have always coexisted, one is typically privileged as the appropriate response to the inevitable failure of the other strategy. Thus, the treatment movement in the 1970s was largely driven by concerns over the failure of heavy-handed drug control strategies in the 1960s to effectively control drug use (White, 1998). Likewise, the war on drugs in the 1980s and 1990s was a response to the inability of the 1970s treatment movement to significantly decrease the number of drug users.

This most recent war on drugs has also failed. Almost 20 years after its official declaration commentators of all political stripes now routinely acknowledge that this campaign has not come close to meeting its proclaimed goal of eliminating the drug supply through the criminalization of certain populations (Chambliss, 1995; Douglas, 1995; Goode, 1993). Although drug warriors remain committed to criminalization, their policies and programs now lack the sense of urgency, moral certainty, and optimism that originally characterized the anti-drug call to arms.

This is not to say that the war on drugs has been inconsequential. The war on drugs has helped to marginalize and criminalize a generation of ethnic minorities (Miller, 1996), reinforced a conservative crime-control agenda, increased law enforcement budgets, and expanded the network of treatment and social work professionals. Such developments have resulted from efforts by disparate individuals and organizations to capitalize on the opportunities offered to them by the drug war. Failure, however, can also provide its own possibilities, and it is partially the recognized failure of the drug war that has opened up a social space for home drug testing. For example, an Internet website that sells such tests claims: 'The sad truth is we're losing the War on Drugs, and our children are the casualties of that war . . . That's why I created the Parent's Alert Home Drug Testing Service' . . .

The failure of the drug war is also acknowledged by individuals at the forefront of the state's anti-drug efforts. In keeping with the tendency to oscillate between criminality and disease, leading public figures have started to adopt a discourse that downplays the war rhetoric in lieu of approaching drug use as a disease. In a recent television appearance, General Barry McCaffery, the self-proclaimed 'Drug Czar' of the United States suggests that in lieu of thinking of anti-drug efforts as a war, we are better advised to conceive of drugs as a 'cancer' that is afflicting the youth of America:

> [W]hen you start talking about that, a cancer affecting American communities, then you start getting the role of prevention, of education . . . Let's understand the biggest investment we can make is not in the prison system . . . but to get on the front end of this problem and recognize that every addicted teenager costs the country probably a couple of million dollars over their lifetime in impact on the health care system, criminal justice, etc.
>
> (PBS Online Newshour, 2 August 1999)

McCaffery's call to focus on the youthful demand for drugs is reflected in the strategies of every major US anti-drug organization. Organizations like ONDCP, DARE, PRIDE, Partnership for a Drug Free America, Empower America, Drug Use is Life Abuse, SAMHSA, and NIDA are all currently running campaigns and programs that aim to curb youth's demand for drugs. The US government also recently launched a $2 billion anti-drug media campaign aimed at youth. Many of these organizations employ some sort of cancer or disease trope in order to propagate their anti-drug messages. The group 'Drug Use is Life Abuse', for example, champions a 'Red-Ribbon' campaign in which individuals are asked to wear red wristbands to demonstrate their support for the 'fight against the drug-abuse disease'. This strategy of symbolically using ribbons is borrowed from highly visible anti-disease campaigns like the now iconic HIV/AIDS red ribbon and the breast cancer pink ribbon.

The disease metaphor helps shape American anti-drug efforts. However, some caution should be taken against the impression that this metaphor alone can 'determine' the types of solutions advanced on the policy front in any straightforward fashion. A metaphor's power is tempered by the unique social, cultural, and technological environment in which it is invoked. The renewal of the disease metaphor, after an approximate 20-year hiatus in which the discourse was dominated by talk of a war on drugs, demonstrates how the *same* metaphor can be aligned with novel policy initiatives and technological solutions. Rather than there being a single cause for the appeal of home drug tests, it is better to consider the unique combination of factors which helps advance home drug testing as an attractive technology of governance directed at a particular segment of American society . . .

Shifting metaphors

There are several reasons why the disease metaphor is supplanting, or at a minimum augmenting, the war metaphor. First, the war metaphor has become tired and predictable. Because metaphors work by innovatively transplanting conceptions associated with one domain of experience to another, repeated use blunts their novelty, resulting in what Rorty (1989) refers to as a 'dead metaphor'. Two decades of 'war on drugs' rhetoric appears to have transformed a metaphor that originally captured the public's imagination into a predictable figure of speech. Second, it is unlikely that the discourse of an anti-drug 'war' could have been sustained in the face of mounting criticism of its obvious failures. In fact, such criticism is an inherent risk in resorting to the 'war' metaphor. As Best (1999) observes, talk of 'war' is particularly unhelpful in dealing with entrenched social problems such as crime. This is because wars are usually temporally limited, allowing officials to fuel short-term enthusiasm that can subside if the campaign drags on. Wars also offer the promise of a decisive victory, which is not a reasonable prospect in efforts to rectify complex social problems. Consequently, anti-crime wars can easily be singled out as failures, as public expectations of quick victory fade and the moral unity that initially characterized the public response wanes.

Efforts to reframe anti-drug efforts in the language of disease offer distinct attractions and possibilities. The disease metaphor promises to renew flagging public support for anti-drug initiatives. The disease frame also suggests new policy targets and tactics. For example, talk of disease breaks down the us/them dualism intrinsic to the trope of criminality that gives rise to such wars. While the racialized other is the target of criminalization through wars, disease – with cancer being the classic example – affects everyone. And while diseases have particular demographic profiles, they are not intrinsic to poor, ethnic, and otherwise marginalized populations. As disease is effectively everywhere, drug use, by analogy, becomes everyone's problem. At the same time, talk of disease does not imply a homogeneity of treatment of afflicted or at-risk individuals. Those with the financial means can receive better private care and more ready access to early detection technologies and other preventative measures. The disease metaphor also encourages the embrace of diagnostic technologies into anti-drug campaigns. Early detection has become the mantra of the medical profession, and such detection is routinely aided by technological tests and screening systems. If drugs equal disease, the 'best defense' against drug use is easily portrayed as involving early detection through drug screening technologies.

This discursive change, however, does not herald an end to the drug war. Cancer, and disease more generally, as Sontag (1977) notes, are also objects of war. Public policy often intermingles disease and war metaphors in complex ways. American state officials have been loathe to discard the law-and-order conservatism characteristic of the drug war and adopt a kinder, gentler drug strategy such as harm reduction. In many G-7 nations, harm reduction efforts have involved efforts to decriminalize illicit drugs and develop needle exchanges and heroin and methadone maintenance programs (Erickson et al., 1997). Instead of helping to fashion an environment where harm reduction might be embraced, the current manifestation of the disease metaphor leaves existing governmental strategies largely unreconstructed, while extending new technologies of governance to populations traditionally outside the main thrust of anti-drug initiatives.

Domestic governance

Parents can now purchase a variety of 'kits' that test for drugs in urine or hair samples, and only very recently, in samples of breath and nail clippings. Home tests can provide results in as little as five minutes, although some require that a sample be sent to a laboratory for analysis. The simplicity of these tests makes them attractive to parents who do not have the clinical skills, facilities, and credentials to test samples of extracted blood (Nickell and Fischer, 1999; Saferstein, 1995; Zonderman, 1999). New tests can also track the presence of a substance in the body through a longer time period than is possible with blood tests. The presence of trace amounts of a drug in the urine, for example, is detectable anywhere from 12 to 96 hours after it exits the bloodstream (Greenblatt, 1993), while traces of marijuana can be detected in hair samples up to two months after drug use.

The extent of home drug testing in America is difficult to gauge. There are no national statistics on such tests, and home tests are frequently a subcomponent of corporations that market drug tests to industry and government. This makes it difficult to disaggregate the specific number of home tests. The testing industry is also highly competitive, a fact which fosters a degree of secrecy. Industry representatives who are otherwise very forthcoming generally have refused to provide precise sales figures for their tests. Nonetheless, one gains the impression that this is a small but growing sector. One company spokesperson suggested that home test kits might come close to representing 10 percent of their $20 million testing business ... Recent decisions by major American retailers, such as Walgreen's, to stock home test kits will likely result in increased sales.

It is tempting to approach the development of these tests as an intensified form of social control. However, the undifferentiated notion of 'social control' often brings with it an image of subjects being forced to yield to an external power. In contrast, we suggest that home drug tests exemplify some of the dominant tendencies in neoliberal approaches to governing deviance. In his later work, Michel Foucault (1991) introduced the notion of 'governmentality', which amounts to an interrogation of how the practical art of government is envisioned and executed. Governance involves rational policies and practices that ... direct behavior towards desired ends. These techniques differ by virtue of how individuals are acted upon and the role played by individuals in their own subjectification. Neo-liberal strategies of governance ideally minimize repression in favor of techniques that work *with* a subject's limited freedom of choice and action. They structure the context of decision making, creating an environment where individuals freely choose to act in the manner desired by governing authorities ...

In the case of home drug tests, this involves efforts to operate on an adolescent's will by making individual behavior more visible. The ultimate aim of these tests is not so much to detect past drug use or current intoxication, as it is to create an environment where youths choose 'freely', in light of this newly intensified surveillance regime, not to use drugs. As such, the tests are a technology that governs the behavior of the tested subject from a distance by structuring his or her choices about drug use. However, because these tests presuppose and target the free will of the tested subjects, they also leave opportunities for subjects to subvert the aims of governance . . .

Echoing the earlier work of Stanley Cohen (1985), Nikolas Rose (2000) has recently suggested that we can divide strategies of crime control into those that seek to govern by situating individuals in circuits of inclusion versus those that operate on pathologies through a series of exclusions. Such a binary helps to situate home testing in relation to other anti-drug strategies. In keeping with the disease trope, home drug testing is a strategy of inclusion, situating the detection and punishment of criminal behaviors in the compassionate embrace of the family. In contrast, the state's anti-drug policies constitute a strategy of exclusion, which follows the trope of criminality, to remove individuals from their usual social settings, subjecting them to more intensive forms of repression.

A characteristic feature of inclusive neoliberal strategies of crime control is the minimal role played by the state. The state increasingly has withdrawn from direct efforts to guarantee security in lieu of seeking to facilitate the development of private networks of security, expertise, and technology. In the context of home drug tests, the state's facilitative role has involved loosening the FDA regulations so that drug tests can be sold legally over the counter. This was done in response to the lobbying efforts of major pharmaceutical, chemical, and drug testing companies (Food and Drug Administration, 1997).

The ultimate target of such tests is the responsibilized individual. No longer able to rely on the state as a source of security, individuals under neoliberal regimes are constituted as their own personal security manager. O'Malley (1996) has character-ized this as a form of prudentialism which can manifest itself in the purchase of private health care, insurance, and various tools that ostensibly reduce the risk of criminal victimization. Governmental experts, both public and increasingly private, offer advice, strategies, and technologies designed to enhance the security of the individual and his or her family. Home drug tests are one in an expanding array of such security-enhancing tools.

Familial circumstances

Home drug tests are being marketed primarily to the middle-class, white, suburban family. As Garland (2000) has pointed out, the specific dynamics of contemporary middle-class professional families provides a fertile bed for the growth of fears about crime and victimization. Able to spend less and less time in the direct supervision of their children, such parents are now turning to technological forms of scrutiny to satiate a desire to know the specific risks a child might face. Some of the tools being employed towards that end include Internet-connected cameras in daycares (and now high schools), devices to monitor adolescent Internet use, and most recently, teen drug tests. Such a longing is apparent also in the remarks of David Evans of the National On-Site Testing Association to the Food and Drug Administration hearings on the regulation of home tests. There he observed,

You know, if my kid was on Sudafed, I'd want to know that. If a drug test would show that to me, I'd like to know that. Prescription drugs can be abused, non-prescription drugs can be abused. Most kids are using marijuana and cocaine . . . I'd like to know everything my kids are doing. Any drug that goes in their body, I'd like to know about it.

Again, drawing on the disease trope, there is a supposition here that 'exposure' to drugs is a grave concern. Following the popular logic, just as exposure to a disease increases one's chances of contracting the illness, exposure to drugs increases the risk that a youth will develop a dependence disorder. This is especially distressing given the attention now focused on the long-standing fact that adolescent drug use and experimentation are relatively common. Early interventions such as drug testing are indicated in the same way that we are encouraged to get flu shots every fall in anticipation of the high rate of exposure to the virus that we all experience through the winter.

While the family has long been a site of surveillance and control, home drug tests intimately connect the home with broader programs of governance. As Foucault (1991: 100) observes, the family has become 'the privileged instrument for the government of the population'. As the material embodiment of social and scientific expertise, drug tests are yet another vehicle that allows the family to be penetrated by a profusion of expert governmental knowledges. The tests contribute to the ongoing historical transformation of parenting as a role where a general competency was assumed, to a series of activities that depend on an array of expert advice, techniques, and technologies. Rather than being something that simply *is* by virtue of kinship and living arrangements, the family is understood as a series of processes to be effectively governed.

The discourse surrounding home testing that can be found in pamphlets, informational packages, talk-shows, and various websites, situates drug tests as one component in a larger effort to rationally govern the white, middle-class family . . . Such sources offer advice on the minutiae of family management so as to increase the probability of raising drug-free children. One website, for example, encourages parents to use drug testing as part of an explicit 'drug policy'. Such a policy could include working in partnership with parental support groups, communicating the risks of drug use to youths, and using a written contract to detail the implications of straying from that policy. Parents are encouraged to 'Explain to your child that you trust them, but recognize the outside pressures and outside conflicts they face' . . . Some drug test websites contain hyperlinks to information about the prevalence and effects of drug use. Such informational sources are usually characterized by a singular emphasis on the harms of drug use and are devoid of any moderating voices that might downplay the risks of recreational drug use or emphasize the dangers of overreacting to such behavior.

The fact that all drug testing companies promise anonymous results speaks to the distinctive fears that these tests seek to allay. In exchange for becoming deputized agents in the anti-drug campaign, white, middle-class parents can divert their child from the state's official system of drug regulation. State-based anti-drug initiatives are actually one of the main risks faced by middle-class families of teens who use recreational drugs. This is apparent in a drug testing website that depicts a white, teenage boy staring plaintively at the viewer from behind prison bars. The caption over the photograph reads, 'Drug Testing would have been a better way for my parents to find out I was doing drugs'. It sends the clear message that while poor, minority parents continue to witness their children repeatedly coming into conflict with the law, white, middle-class parents should not, and need not, rely on the state to monitor and respond to their child's drug use. Furthermore, it implies that the state's strategy in the war on drugs – criminalization – is not the most effective, desirable, or appropriate way to govern this population of offenders. This is in line with more general trends in late-modern forms of governance, where responsible individuals are encouraged to manage their own affairs with a minimal reliance on the state (O'Malley, 1996). Instead, parents can obtain the necessary evidence themselves, and respond in ways that are free from the dangers posed to both the family and child by the official criminal justice system.

Parents use home tests to produce a credential for their child, a marker that speaks to an adolescent's past behavior and future trustworthiness . . . Historically, . . . of personal markers such as degrees, passports, and criminal records were designed to give unknown strangers some indication of a person's reputation (Nock, 1993). In contrast, home drug tests bring the gaze home. They are a standardized means to establish an adolescent's reputation for those individuals who would ostensibly be most intimately aware of the child's character – his or her parents. These tools stand in the place of a host of more traditional paternalistic ways to establish a child's reputation, freeing parents from the need to listen in on their children's phone calls, search their children's rooms, or piece together the various bits of evidence pertaining to their children's drug use, such as withdrawn behavior, constant need for money, general malaise, and weight loss . . .

Home drug tests extend governmental strategies by helping to transcend two privacy constraints that have traditionally hindered anti-drug initiatives. First, the difficulty in definitively determining whether a person uses drugs, outside of those instances where they are obviously inebriated or incapacitated, has long been a problem for anti-drug efforts. Home tests address this problem by penetrating the bodily integrity of tested subjects, forcing their ostensibly private bodily substances to yield to chemical scrutiny. Residing in the legal gray area of adolescence, tested subjects cannot even marshal the limited privacy rights accorded to adults to resist such bodily intrusions. Second, drug tests infiltrate the privacy of the home, which has long been recognized as hindering policing efforts (Reiss, 1987). As an advertisement for the 'Drug Test' company observes, 'The War on Drugs has been fought in the growing fields, the borders, streets and schools. ONLY NOW is there a way to bring it where it matters most – AT HOME' (original emphasis). While middle-class parents would ostensibly oppose the physical intrusion of state agents into their homes, they appear willing to open the door to anti-drug initiatives, on the condition that they maintain exclusive authority over the results of such tests. This incorporation of middle-class parents into anti-drug efforts indicates that privatization, especially in the realm of criminal justice, occurs not just by making private that which was once public . . . but also by encouraging that exemplar of the private realm – the family – to take up crusades that were originally concerns of the state.

Private commodities

Crime control in America has rapidly become a market for private gain, as evidenced by the rise in private policing, prisons, and security commodities (Taylor, 1999). Private interests also lie behind home drug tests, shaping how they are sold, and to whom, while helping to further entrench class divisions in the governance of adolescent drug use.

Drug tests are one in an array of private security products marketed to responsibilized parents. The appeal of such tests rests on a logic similar to that which motivates the use of alarms, handguns, insurance, and gated communities. This 'family resemblance' acquires a more material form in a web page hyperlink that connects a home drug testing site to a site that sells a host of other security products. There one encounters an unambiguous articulation of the late-modern anxieties about crime that help contribute to the appeal of personal anti-crime technologies.

> You hear about it on TV. You read about it in the newspaper. Its [sic] no secret that crime is a major problem in the U.S. today. And criminals are finding it easier to commit crimes all the time. Weapons are readily available. Our cities' police forces have more work than they can handle. Even if these criminals are caught, they know they won't be spending long in our nation's overcrowded jails. And while lawmakers are well aware of the crime problem, they don't seem to have any effective answers.
>
> Well, there is an effective answer. Take responsibility for your own security.

In this situation, 'taking responsibility' translates into buying various anti-crime commodities. In addition to being connected to a home drug test site, this web page links the viewer to other anti-crime tools, including stun guns, pepper sprays, household protection, motion detectors, personal alarms, tasers, and spy cameras.

Earlier we noted the general bifurcation in strategies of criminal justice governance between inclusionary and exclusionary approaches. Ewick's (1993) work on the institutionalization of deviants points out how a class hierarchy can be overlaid on these two extremes. She details how a class-based two-tier system works to exert different modes of control over different social groups. While the lower classes continue to be directed towards prisons, the exemplar of exclusionary institutions, private organizations now use therapeutic approaches to govern the criminal behavior of the middle classes who are able to pay for their services. Private drug testing establishes a similar cleavage in campaigns against drug use. Home drug tests are not concerned with the generalized betterment of all sectors of society, but are specialist tools available to more affluent parents. While some of the kits sell for $5 or $10, most cost $50 to $60. These costs are amplified by the fact that tests are not reusable and many can only trace one substance. A parent who wished to place his or her child on a periodic drug test regime (testing once a month for marijuana, cocaine, and heroin) could easily spend $500 a year or more on such an endeavor.

The spokesperson for a company that sells a hair test kit accentuated the narrow class-based market for these commodities when he noted that the specific demographics for his products were 'upscale, suburban, newspaper-reader, soccer-moms.

Less of the inner-city types'. The racial division embedded in that sociodemographic characterization should be self-evident. This implicit racial targeting is reinforced by the fact that outside of the prominent display of Oprah Winfrey, who has endorsed one particular home drug test, the packaging and advertisements for these products depict almost no people of color.

Middle-class parents who have assumed the responsibility for governing their children's drug use, and who have the resources to purchase the tests, work to keep their children out of the 'hard end' of the system, governing their drug use through an inclusive paternalistic model. The poor and racialized, however, continue to have their illicit drug use regulated through the coercive state-based war on drugs. Indeed, the US 'war on drugs' has become a de facto undeclared war on young African American and Hispanic men. According to the US Sentencing Project, on any given day nearly one-third of all African American men between the ages of 20 and 29 years are under criminal justice supervision, meaning that they are either in prison, on probation, or on parole (Mauer and Huling, 1995). Drug offenders account for the majority of this population (Tonry, 1995). This racialization of the drug war becomes entrenched in policies such as California's 'three strikes' provisions and the federal law which now requires judges, in sentencing drug offenders, to treat 1 g of crack as the equal of 100 g of cocaine. Since more than 90 percent of crack defendants are African American, as opposed to only 20 percent of those accused of possession of powder cocaine, the law further increases the disproportionate number of African Americans in the prison system (Lemann, 1998: 25).

Authors writing about neoliberal forms of governance have accentuated the calculative attitude that responsibilized individuals are encouraged to adopt in making decisions about how to enhance their security. As O'Malley (1996: 201) observes, 'the rational subject or risk takes on the capacity to become skilled and knowledgeable about crime prevention and crime risks'. However, this is a remarkably rationalist image of the prudential subject, perhaps best epitomized by the insurance agent detachedly scrutinizing actuarial tables. In reality, decisions about what technologies, practices, and expertise to embrace in the quest for security can be profoundly irrational, raising questions about how 'skilled and knowledgeable' individuals actually are in making their decisions. For example, many of the tools designed to enhance personal security against crime risks are technological, a fact which suggests that they can be purchased due to the seductions of the commodity itself, rather than their demonstrated use-value in reducing the risk of criminal victimization. Some tools, such as steering wheel locks or home alarms, are now as much about demonstrating middle-class status as they are about reducing crime risks. Furthermore, it can be incredibly difficult for an individual to determine his or her true risk of victimization, or the degree to which a governmental tool might reduce that risk. In the case of home drug tests, these tools are being sold in a profound knowledge vacuum where almost nothing beyond anecdotal evidence is available to determine whether they reduce adolescent drug use . . . Consequently, we must recognize how a host of irrational factors can play a role in individual decisions about which governmental techniques to embrace, chief among such factors being the role of fear.

Parental fear underpins the attraction of home drug tests. At the most general level, the testing industry benefits from the angst generated by the ongoing moral panic surrounding illicit drug use. Individual companies also employ a range of subtle and not-so-subtle efforts to capitalize on, and augment, parental fear. For example, most of the drug testing promotional literature employs the common strategy of invoking 'shocking numbers' (Best, 1989; Orcutt and Turner, 1993) to dramatize the prevalence and dangers of drugs. These figures are typically unreferenced, or consist of sweeping generalizations, such as 'Drug use among our teens is at its highest level in nine years'. Other companies hone in more specifically on the fears of that class of individual who can afford their kits, as is apparent in the 'informational' component of the website for the 'Drug Test' company that claims that 'heroin, PCP and others with high death rates are gaining in popularity; *particularly among more affluent sectors*' (emphasis added). Speaking to the FDA, the representative from Chem Trak made a similar point, suggesting that 'Unfortunately, good children from good homes who live in nice neighborhoods use drugs. The problem is not one limited to the inner city. 60 percent of the problem occurs in suburbs, many of them affluent suburbs.' More disturbingly, Hanson (1993: 128) reports that the National Drug Awareness and Detection Agency of Houston randomly sends postcards to families that state

> we have been informed that your children may be using ILLEGAL DRUGS . . . Please call us IMMEDIATELY . . . Those who call the number on the card are given a lengthy presentation about the dangers of drugs. They are then urged to send $99.95 to purchase a kit that claims to detect drug use by measuring the pupil of a suspect's eye with a pupil-ometer

(original emphasis)

Dialectics of observation and resistance

Governance seeks to shape the behavior of subjects in the directions desired by authorities. The success of a particular governmental technique, however, is not pre-ordained. The targets of governmental strategies can at times resent or resist efforts to modify their behavior. Constituted as relatively autonomous agents, tested subjects can employ their limited scope for agency to subvert governmental ambitions. Privileged adolescents increasingly have at their disposal a range of commodities which purport to beat drug tests. Predictably, such countertechnologies and tactics have sparked further refinements to monitoring regimes and testing procures, resulting in an escalating dialectic of observation and resistance.

The notion of resisting surveillance brings to mind someone standing outside of the gaze, finding cracks and fissures where surveillance does not penetrate. Resisting surveillance, however, can also involve strategies that work creatively within the field of visibility through imaginative engagements with the particularities of an observational regime (De Certeau, 1984). These involve various techniques that use simulations to stand in for or (mis)represent assorted originals (Baudrillard, 1983; Bogard, 1996). Such simulations depend on an intimate familiarity with the minutiae of the tools and procedures of a particular surveillance regime; how it operates; what it scrutinizes, and how.

Various techniques are available to beat drug tests, and these differ in their specifics and efficacy according to what drug is being tested for, the type of sample collected, and the manner through which this is done. Urine tests appear to offer the greatest range for evasion. If one knows when a urine sample is going to be collected, for example, a clean test can be produced by simply abstaining from drug use for a limited period of time prior to the test, often as little as three days. Urine tests can also be defeated through dilution, which can involve adding water to the sample or drinking copious amounts of water prior to the test.

One of the most straightforward simulations employed to defeat a drug test involves replacing a tainted sample with a clean one. Recall the scene in the movie *American Beauty* mentioned above, where the youth relates that his parents test him for drugs. He then proceeds to explain that this does not pose a problem, as he substitutes someone else's clean urine for his own. Drug users can acquire untainted samples from friends who sell or donate their urine. Individuals can also purchase urine in 'natural' or dehydrated form through mail order and Internet-based companies.

Drug users now also have at their disposal a host of purifying commodities sold through specialty drug magazines or over the Internet. With corporate names like 'Urine Luck', 'Clear', and 'Detoxify', these products subvert drug tests by chemically masking the tested-for markers of drug use. Some of these products are added to the sample itself, while others are ingested by the test subject prior to the test. Table [17.1] displays some of these products currently available on the Internet and how they work (Cargain et al., 1998). Adolescents who might want more information on which techniques work and which are spurious can call the 24-hour telephone hotline run by the drug magazine *High Times* that is dedicated exclusively to disseminating information on how to beat drug tests . . .

Not surprisingly, the development of such tools and techniques has introduced an escalating dialectic into drug monitoring regimes, as avoidance techniques are countered by more restrictive and intrusive testing procedures. Testing companies have capitalized on this trend by selling new tests that detect sample alteration. One such product claims to detect various techniques and products that can be used to beat drug tests including excessive fluid consumption, Klear, Urinaid, Instant Clean, bleach, vinegar, eyewash products, sodium bicarbonate, drain cleaners, soft drinks (and other urine look-alikes), and hydrogen peroxide.

Although one might presume that the companies that market these technologies would be aligned with a specific political agenda, with pro-drug organizations selling drug evasion tools and anti-drug advocates selling drug testing tools, this is not necessarily the case. Instead, the greater allegiance at times appears to be to the quest for profit. For example, the web page for TriCorp labs markets a series of drug tests, and also includes a hyperlink labeled 'Need Help Passing a Drug Test?' This connects viewers with a site that markets various technologies designed to *beat* drug tests! A website for the company 'Urine Luck', whose company spokesperson is drug comedian Tommy Chong, sells a variety of flushing capsules, detoxifying drinks, and urine additives that purport to beat drug tests. It also sells its own home tests for detecting THC, cocaine, opiates, amphetamines, and barbiturates. Both the testing of potential drug users and attempts to beat these tests ultimately benefit the same industry, and at times may benefit the same companies.

Table [17.1] Sample of products currently available via the Internet

Product	Price/Quantity	Description
Clear Choices Carbo Cleaning Shake Health Tech Macon, GA	25.00	• effective up to 5 hours • vitamin B-complex and creatinine • just add water
The Liquid Stuff J&J Enterprises Denver, CO	20.00	• orange, grape, fruit punch • works in 1 hour
Ready Clean Detoxify Brand	30.00/bottle	• 1 hour cleansing drink, effective up to 5 hours • grape, orange, tropical flavors
THC Terminator Drink Fontanella's Herbal Solutions Sagamore Hills, OH	47.95	• clean in 3–4 hours • vitamins, minerals, herbs
Fast Flush Detoxify Brand	25.00	• herbal tea • works in 2 hours
2-Hour Quick Tea Fontanella's Herbal Solutions Sagamore Hills, OH	17.95	• works in 2–3 hours • vitamin B-complex and natural creatinine • cinnamon spice, tropical fruit punch
Clear Choices Quick Flush Capsules Health Tech Macon, GA	20.00/18 caps	• flushes all unwanted toxins in under 3 hours • effective up to 5 hours • vitamin B-complex and creatinine
Precleanse Detoxify Brand	14.95/50 caps 24.95/100 caps	• blend of 10 herbs
Whizzies Smoke Screen Laboratories	30.00	• crystal substance • urine additive
Urine Luck Spectrum Labs Cincinnati, OH	30.00	• urine additive • order through the Internet, receive free shipping and handling
Clear Choice Instant Clean Add-it-ive Health Tech Macon, GA	30.00	• destroys all toxins on contact • 6 ml microvial • 2-year shelf life
Klear Testclean Oklahoma City, OK	30.00	• white, crystal substance • urine additive
THC-Free International Health Aurora, IN	29.95	• works instantly • 100% guarantee

Conclusion: towards an ambiguous result

The American campaign against illicit drug use is expanding its vocabulary beyond the 'war' metaphor to reinvoke the image of drug use as a disease. Such terminological oscillations warrant critical attention because new public policy discourses can bring in their wake new problematizations and an attendant set of self-evident solutions. However, we should be cautious not to overstate the role that new metaphors can play in bringing about such transformations. It is not exclusively the discourse that prompts change, but how metaphors resonate with a broader social situation that makes particular governmental strategies thinkable and actionable.

Previous manifestations of the disease metaphor in campaigns against illicit drugs did not lead, indeed could not have led, to the embrace of home drug tests. At the most obvious level, this is because these technologies did not then exist. The advent of such tests produces new possibilities for governing children and families. However, this is not a technologically determinist result, as the mere availability of such tests cannot explain their use. As we have demonstrated, the embrace of home testing can be partially attributed to how private interests have expounded their benefits to a particular class and race of parents. Encouraged to be obsessed about adolescent drug use, responsibilized parents are also persuaded through efforts that capitalize on such fears to employ a host of private commodities to ensure the security of their families.

Part of the parental appeal of drug tests derives from their promise of scientific certainty in determining whether their child is using drugs . . . The tests themselves, however, offer little guidance for what a parent should do in the event that their child tests positive. Given that such tests hold out the promise of keeping white, middle-class children out of the official criminal justice system, parents would be loathe to turn their drug-using child over to the authorities. As yet, however, there are few formal arrangements for a seamless transition from positive test to institutional response. If home-based drug tests become more popular we can anticipate the increasing establishment of a host of drug 'treatment' policies and techniques designed for youths who have tested positive. Such a development would continue the bifurcation between the white, middle-class inclusionary treatment and lower-class racialized exclusionary repression of illegal drug use. However, the efficacy or ethics of such efforts would remain an open question. This is because contrary to the emerging discourse, the drug habits of recreational users – the population most likely to be caught by such tests – are *not* a disease. Notwithstanding recurring moral panics about drug use, there is little evidence that casual use of drugs leads inextricably to addiction and even less evidence to indicate that addiction is itself a disease in the original biological sense of the term. Lacking any precise scientific and biological meaning, the disease trope invokes powerful imagery of teens requiring treatment, irrespective of the lack of a clinical diagnosis of a medically accepted syndrome.

The advent of home drug testing indicates that anti-drug campaigns are far from over. The United States continues to refuse to adopt harm reduction and decriminalization initiatives. If the focus on eradicating drug demand through the private mobilization of families effectively replaced the supply-side, criminal justice responses to the 'drug problem', then techniques like home drug testing might be considered tools of decriminalization. If this was the case, at least it could be said that criminal sanctions were no longer the derivative harms of anti-drug initiatives. This, however, is not the case. The war on drugs continues, having become very much like a disease itself, a cancer that increases in size and works its way further and further into the American social body.

Note

1 This chapter is an extract from D. Moore and K. Haggerty (2001) Bring it on home: home drug testing and the relocation of the war on drugs, *Social & Legal Studies*, 10(3): 377–95.

References

Baudrillard, J. (1983) *Simulations*. New York: Semiotext(e).

Best, J. (1989) Dark figures and child victims: statistical claims about missing children. *Images of Issues: Typifying Contemporary Social Problems*. New York: Aldine de Gruyter, pp. 21–37.

Best, J. (1999) *Random Violence: How We Talk About New Crimes and New Victims*. Berkeley: University of California Press.

Bogard, W. (1996) *The Simulation of Surveillance: Hypercontrol in Telematic Societies*. Cambridge: Cambridge University Press.

Cargain, M. J., Robinson, J. J. and Pinkston, K. P. (1998) Specimen adulteration: who's winning the battle?, *Journal of Offender Monitoring*, 11: 18–20.

Chambliss, W. (1995) Another lost war: the costs and consequences of drug prohibition, *Social Justice*, 22: 101–24.

Cohen, S. (1985) *Visions of Social Control: Crime, Punishment and Classification*. Cambridge: Polity Press.

De Certeau, M. (1984) *The Practice of Everyday Life*. Berkeley: University of California Press.

Douglas, Jr. J. D. (1995) Why is the war on drugs going nowhere? *Conservative Review*, 6: 15–21.

Erickson, P., Riley, D., Cheung, Y. and O'Hare, P. (eds) (1997) *Harm Reduction: A New Direction in Drug Policies and Programs*. Toronto: University of Toronto Press.

Ewick, P. (1993) Corporate cures: the commodification of social control, *Studies in Law, Politics and Society*, 13: 137–57.

Food and Drug Administration (1997) Clinical Chemistry and Clinical Toxicology Devices Panel of the Medical Devices Advisory Committee, Bethesda, MD: US Food and Drug Administration.

Foucault, M. (1991) Governmentality, in G. Burchell, C. Gordon and P. Miller (eds) *The Foucault Effect: Studies in Governmentality*. Chicago: University of Chicago Press, pp. 87–104.

Garland, D. (2000) The culture of high crime societies: some preconditions of recent: 'law and order' policies, *British Journal of Criminology*, 40: 347–75.

Giffen, P. J., Endicott, S. and Lambert, S. (1991) *Panic and Indifference: The Politics of Canada's Drug Laws: A Study in the Sociology of Law*. Ottawa: Canadian Centre on Substance Abuse.

Goode, E. (1993) *Drugs in American Society*. New York: Knopf.

Greenblatt, D. J. (1993) Basic pharmacokenetic principles and their application to psychotropic drugs, *Journal of Clinical Psychiatry*, 54: 8–13.

Hanson, F. A. (1993) *Testing Testing: Social Consequences of the Examined Life*. Berkeley: University of California Press.

Lemann, N. (1998) Justice for blacks? *New York Review of Books*, pp. 25–8.

Mauer, M. and Huling, T. (1995) Young black Americans and the criminal justice system: five years later, Sentencing Project Report.

Miller, J. G. (1996) *Search and Destroy: African-American Males in the Criminal Justice System.* New York: Cambridge University Press.

Nickell, J. and Fischer, J. F. (1999) *Crime Science: Methods for Forensic Detection.* Lexington: University of Kentucky Press.

Nock, S. L. (1993) *The Costs of Privacy: Surveillance and Reputation in America.* New York: Aldine de Gruyter.

O'Malley, P. (1996) Risk and responsibility, in A. Barry, T. Osborne and N. Rose (eds) *Foucault and Political Reason: Liberalism, Neo-Liberalism and Rationalities of Government.* Chicago: University of Chicago Press, pp. 189–207.

Orcutt, J. D. and Turner, J. B. (1993) Shocking numbers and graphic accounts: quantified images of drug problems in the print media, *Social Problems*, 40: 190–206.

Peele, S. (1995) *Diseasing America: How We Allowed Recovery Zealots and the Treatment Industry to Convince Us We are Out of Control.* San Francisco: Jossey-Bass.

Reiss, A. (1987) The legitimacy of intrusion into private space, in C. Shearing and P. Stenning (eds) *Private Policing.* Thousand Oaks, CA: Sage, pp. 19–44.

Rorty, R. (1989) The contingency of language, in *Contingency, Irony and Solidarity.* Cambridge: Cambridge University Press, pp. 3–22.

Rose, N. (2000) Government and control, *British Journal of Criminology*, 40: 321–39.

Saferstein, R. (1995) *Criminalistics: An Introduction to Forensic Science.* Englewood Cliffs: Prentice Hall.

Sontag, S. (1977) *Illness as Metaphor.* New York: Farrar, Straus & Giroux.

Taylor, I. (1999) *Crime in Context: A Critical Criminology of Market Societies.* Boulder: Westview.

Tonry, M. (1995) *Malign Neglect: Race, Crime and Punishment in America.* Oxford: Oxford University Press.

White, W. (1998) *Slaying the Dragon: The History of Addiction Treatment and Recovery in America.* Bloomington: Lighthouse Institute.

Zonderman, J. (1999) *Beyond the Crime Lab: The New Science of Investigation.* New York: Wiley.

PART 5

Surveillance and public opinion

The American sociologist, Herbert Blumer (1948), argued that public opinion must be understood contextually because it is shaped, formed and brought into existence through relationships involving human beings who interact in an assemblage of social, political, cultural and historical arrangements. Politicians, interest groups, journalists and researchers who study public opinion are likely to agree that the techniques used to identify or measure collective attitudes and beliefs influence the outcomes of the political consensus building process. For example, consider a scenario in which a police or merchant survey asks citizens the following question: 'Would the presence of downtown security cameras make you feel safer shopping in the core?' Contrast this with a citizens' organization that uses a survey to ask the same group of respondents: 'Should Big Brother use intrusive surveillance technologies to monitor your every move in public space?' Although the example is contrived,[1] we can reasonably speculate that the police or merchant survey would find positive support for video surveillance programs, while the survey distributed by the citizens' organization would prompt less enthusiasm for public surveillance. The point is that, although both questions address surveillance in public space, the language and form of the questions conjure up different images of what surveillance means and what its potential consequences might be. The scenarios also reveal the potential variability of public opinion and its role in surveillance policy-making.

Scholars who study public opinion are interested in the images of reality that surveys construct about the social and political world, and they are interested in how polls may potentially bring public opinion in line with the interests and goals of ruling elites, media, or, indeed, pollsters themselves (e.g., Ginsberg 1986). When it comes to the relationship between surveillance and public opinion, as Haggerty and Gazso explain, powerful actors increasingly use opinion polling to orchestrate popular support for controversial policies:

> Opinion surveys can now operate as a form of *de facto* plebiscite on important social issues . . . [and are] considerably important to surveillance studies because of their broader political implications . . . Entire policies are drafted, revised, abandoned and legitimated through appeals to public opinion . . . In the aftermath of the

9/11 terrorist attacks politicians have routinely appealed to 'public sentiment' as manifest in various polls to justify hastily developed surveillance policies.

(2005: 173–4)

Haggerty and Gazso accurately identify the importance of 'public opinion' as an under-examined analytical construct in surveillance studies, and their contention that polls can become a problematic (even dangerous) measurement of public opinion merits greater empirical attention by surveillance researchers. In considering the relationship between surveillance and public opinion, it is important to realize that public opinion can change depending on when individuals are surveyed, how questions are asked, who conducts the survey, and, most importantly, whether respondents are adequately informed about the issue(s) being addressed.

Therefore, it is important to consider a number of questions about the nature of the relationship between surveillance and public opinion:

- What role does public opinion play in the formation of surveillance policies and practices?
- How can we characterize citizen responses to surveillance initiatives? Are citizens ambivalent and acquiescent about or critically engaged in surveillance policy debates?
- Where do citizens receive the bulk of their information about surveillance policies and practices? Is public opinion formed through an engagement with other citizens in open discussion and debate, or are opinions based on passive consumption of the images and rhetoric purveyed via the mass media?
- Do media representations of surveillance facilitate or impede the formation of informed public opinion?
- Do advocates and opponents of surveillance policies seek to inform discussion and generate debate among the citizenry? Do they seek to strategically mobilize public opinion in support of their interests and goals?
- Do citizens willingly surrender their privacy rights or yield to the ethical dilemmas associated with increased monitoring by the political elite and other authorities, such as the police and business organizations?
- What kinds of technology facilitate surveillance practices and the formation of public opinion? Do these technologies enable or constrain the abilities of ruling authorities to monitor and control populations?

These and related questions will be explored in numerous ways in the reading passages in this section.

Section readings

In the first reading passage, Chapter 18, British researcher Mike Nellis reflects on his participation in a BBC radio programme about electronic monitoring (EM). In the programme, the host and her callers expressed very little understanding of the broader issues underlying this mode of punishment and surveillance.[2] Interested to know why this was the case, Nellis investigates public knowledge about EM by exploring the everyday cultural resources citizens have available to them. He focuses on contemporary representations of EM in the cinema, press, television and crime novels to determine how popular culture generates typifications of surveillance and punishment that not only shape our current interpretive frameworks, but also structure new ways of 'imagining' surveillance and punishment.

The 'role of popular culture in *generating* the mentalities from which new forms of punishment can emerge' (p. 3) is aptly highlighted in Nellis's account of the influence of a Spiderman comic in 1981 on American judge Jack Love. So 'comical' was the American EM experience to Britons that the *Independent* reprinted two frames from the original cartoon to highlight both the genealogy of EM and to draw reference to its 'alien American' origins. Nellis shows that the media was so profoundly concerned about the importation of 'American-style tagging experiments' (*Guardian*, 1 August 1996, as cited by Nellis, p. 5) that ongoing EM trials in Britain (many of them successful) were often overlooked or ignored altogether. When it comes to British news coverage of EM, Nellis argues, misrepresentation is the order of the day.

Previous research has examined news coverage of surveillance practices to better understand how media contribute to the formation of public opinion (e.g., Hier et al. 2007). Nellis's main contribution to the study of surveillance, media, and public opinion is the attention he pays to representations of electronic monitoring in the *non-news* mass media of popular cinema, television and crime and science fiction novels. To date, there has been minimal empirical attention granted to entertainment media influence on public attitudes and behaviours. This is surprising considering the ubiquitous nature of surveillance practices and technologies in popular dramatic crime television programs (e.g., *CSI, 24* and *Law & Order*). In terms of cinematic portrayals of EM, Nellis focuses on three American films from the 1990s. Although he accepts that his sample is not representative of all cases, Nellis demonstrates how representations of electronic monitoring in these films, primarily monitoring of black youth, operate as a proxy for racial subjugation and inequality. Nellis also focuses on representations of EM in an impressive breadth of television programming, including dramas, daytime serials, news documentaries, and made-for-TV movies. Nellis's sample illustrates that popular cultural representations of EM are far from uniform, and the ways in which popular culture operates as a 'resource' for interpreting and forging meaning about.

In the second reading passage, Chapter 19, Oscar Gandy elaborates on the latter point. Gandy argues that commercial firms operating in the surveillance and information industries have effectively influenced the US Congress to advance a number of legislative initiatives with far-reaching implications for personal privacy. The reading presents a robust analysis of the communicative politics that underlie broader shifts in surveillance practices, and it deftly addresses the philosophical and analytical concerns of privacy advocates, policy analysts and critical political economists alike.

Key to corporate management of privacy-sensitive issues, Gandy argues, has been the presentation of evidence from opinion surveys that show widespread American support for, among other things, restrictions on their privacy rights in exchange for promises of improvements in national security. By focusing on how policy advocates introduce strategic representations of public opinion into legislative debates about privacy policy, Gandy advances our understanding of the relationship between surveillance and public opinion. Although corporate economic interests have been central

to the development of privacy policy in the US, Gandy shows how difficult it is to empirically demonstrate corporate influence on polling results. He does discuss one such
relationship, however, which involved the appointment of privacy scholar Alan Westin as
a consultant for Equifax, a major player in the credit reporting industry. Westin's media
prominence as a privacy expert enabled Equifax to become the most highly visible
source of privacy-related opinion data in the 1990s, Gandy contends. Crucially, Gandy
notes, news media did not report on the dubiousness of Westin's ability to speak
objectively about Equifax's privacy regulations; the financial relationship between
Westin and his corporate client was rarely mentioned in reports featuring Westin's
glowing speech about the improvements in the corporation's privacy policies. His analysis shows that strategic representations of public opinion about the implications of new
surveillance practices for personal privacy tended to cohere around three key themes:
'the public is concerned', 'there is more than one public', and 'the majority of the
public is reasonable'.

The final reading, Chapter 20, by Alasdair Roberts, might appear to be an unusual
contribution to the study of surveillance and public opinion. Roberts is neither a surveillance researcher nor a scholar of public opinion per se. The reading reflects, rather, his
expertise in comparative systems of public administration (in this case between the UK
and Canada). It focuses on how states manage the tension between citizen demands
for greater access to information and the strategic needs of governments to ensure
control over the flow of information from the political arena to the public sphere. Roberts
argues that, although new Freedom of Information (FOI) legislation in Canada (introduced in 2003) appears to have improved governmental transparency, state officials
have, over the years, developed internal routines for restricting sensitive information
from reaching journalists and representatives of political parties. This capacity to
ensure centralized control over communications was enabled by capitalizing on new
communication and information technologies. In other words, FOI policies, procedures
and technologies provide a state mechanism for monitoring and managing the counter-
surveillance practices of political critics and other overseers (e.g., journalists, activists).
When utilized strategically by either authorities or their opponents, FOI legislation can
enable or constrain the formation of public opinion. Roberts argues that policymakers in
the UK should seriously consider the Canadian experiences with FOI reforms as that
country revisits its own FOI policies.

Roberts situates debates about Canadian Freedom of Information policy in historical context, showing how the rhetoric of 'engaging citizens' to participate in public life
and enabling them to better 'monitor government' to 'maintain the probity' of the
administration spoke to the broader political climate of the times. Criticisms of central-
izing power structures, combined with a number of dangerous political circumstances
(declining economic performance, constitutional instability, inter-regional conflicts, and
apparent abuses of power by the national police force), contributed to disillusionment
with the federal government in Canada during the 1970s. This was also the era of 'fear
and loathing' in American politics, as a disgraced presidency and backlashes from
within and outside government against executive authority forced the US Congress to
strengthen FOI laws in that country. This context is important, Roberts argues, not
because it ushered in a new era of transparency on the part of the state, but because
successive federal governments throughout the 1980s and 1990s responded by

developing a more sophisticated central capacity to poll public opinion and 'craft communications'.

The potential of access to sensitive information to disrupt government control over policy development and strategic management was magnified as 'journalists, opposition politicians and non-governmental organizations honed their ability to exploit the opportunities' created by the new legislation and its spirit of openness and transparency. In response to efforts from outside government to monitor the activities of the state, three key strategies were designed to limit the disruptive potential of FOI legislation, as Roberts outlines: litigation, acts of omission, and (of particular importance for our purposes here) the refinement of internal administrative routines for handling politically sensitive information requests. These internal routines and practices were intensified following the development and implementation of new information technologies, as state officials became better able to streamline the process of flagging and tracking sensitive requests on a real-time basis. These surveillance routines and practices, Roberts illustrates, are not easily observed and have the capacity to operate as 'hidden laws' that prevent citizens from accessing or being informed (e.g., by journalists or opposition politicians) about important public information, and thereby restrict their statutory rights.

Questions

Chapter 18 (Nellis)

1   Nellis suggests that electronic monitoring (EM) can operate as a form of surveillance, and as a mechanism for punishment and rehabilitation of criminals. How do media representations of EM speak to these different mechanisms of control?
2   Why does Nellis suggest that the initial response of the British press to EM was negative and misrepresentative of the issue?
3   What are the key strengths and weaknesses of Nellis's study in understanding the relationship between surveillance and public opinion?

Chapter 19 (Gandy)

1   How does Gandy's research illustrate the argument that opinion polls influence policy formation as much by what they measure and report as by what they ignore? What examples beyond those provided by Gandy help to illustrate this argument?
2   What are 'information subsidies', and how are they used to advance the legislative and/ or economic interests of corporations and/or consumer groups in the privacy-sensitive industry?
3   In what ways did Equifax use effective 'issues management' to advance their policy interests in congressional testimonies? Make specific references to partnership arrangements, media coverage, and the strategic use of public opinion to support your answer.

Chapter 20 (Roberts)

1   How does Roberts' analysis of the contradictions between demands for government transparency and elite anxieties about governability inform the study of surveillance and public opinion?

2   What is ATIPflow and how does its use by government officials in Canada enable the state to exercise greater surveillance over the formation of public opinion?
3   How does the government's handling of the Bell request illustrate the ways in which state departments in Canada have designed internal surveillance practices to minimize the disruptive potential of the Access to Information Act?

Suggested reading

1   Bender, J. (1987) *Imagining the Penitentiary: Fiction and the Architecture of Mind in Eighteenth Century England*. Chicago: University of Chicago Press.
Focusing on popular literature and art from the eighteenth century, Bender challenges the conventional thesis that culture reflects broader institutions and structures, and instead argues that novels (e.g., *Moll Flanders, Robinson Crusoe*) and visual art are 'ideological documents', in other words, engines of social change. Here the focus is on how attitudes toward prisons that appear in art and literature precipitate and motivate broader transformations in penology and the conception and construction of the modern penitentiary.
2   Herbst, S. (1998) *Reading Public Opinion: How Political Actors View the Democratic Process*. Chicago: University of Chicago Press.
Drawing on research from across the social sciences, Herbst examines how key political operatives (e.g., legislative staffers, political activists and journalists) envision and attach value to public opinion. Noting that most of these actors possess elitist views about the ability of citizens to participate as informed actors in the democratic process, she concludes that they instead turn to news media and organized interest groups for representations of public opinion. Herbst's book focuses on the mobilization of public opinion and its impact on the democratic process, and should be essential reading for anyone interested in the communicative politics of public policy.
3   Chermak, S. and Weiss, A. (2006) Community policing in the news media, *Policing Quarterly*, 9(2): 135–60.
Chermak and Weiss draw on past research into media coverage of community policing in the United States and build on theoretical developments in the area of source media strategies to discuss how news media report on community policing initiatives. Methodologically, they draw on surveys of police information officers and content analysis of media discourse. The study finds that not only is community policing rarely reported, but communications officers who work within the police services expend little effort in seeking to manage media coverage of this issue despite the available opportunities and existing positive relationships with local journalists.
4   Keen, M.F. (2004) *Stalking Sociologists: J. Edgar Hoover's FBI Surveillance of American Sociology*. New Brunswick, NJ: Transaction Publishers.
This book illustrates the power of the state to develop internal surveillance routines to monitor and control dissenting voices within civil society, and within academe in particular. Keen uses the Freedom of Information Act (FOIA) in the United States to reveal how the FBI, under the post-World War II leadership of J. Edgar Hoover, created a massive internal security apparatus to keep watch over the intellectual currents within American universities, and in sociology especially. Hoover targeted intellectuals like W.E.B. Du Bois and C. Wright Mills, Keen shows, because of the radical nature of their research agendas. The FBI succeeded for the most part in marginalizing the development of a Marxist tradition in American sociology by promoting and supporting empiricist approaches to social analysis.

Notes

1   For published survey research about public video surveillance, see *inter alia* Ditton (2000), Helton and Fischer (2004) and Sætnan et al. (2004).
2   Electronic monitoring is an overt form of surveillance that entails the attachment of an electronic device to a person (commonly an anklet) that allows their location to be monitored from a central location using GPS technology.

References

Blumer, H. (1948) Public opinion and public opinion polling, *American Sociological Review*, 13(5): 542–54.

Ditton, J. (2000) Crime and the city: public attitudes towards open-street CCTV in Glasgow, *British Journal of Criminology*, 40: 792–9.

Gill, M. and Spriggs, A. (2005) *Assessing the Impact of CCTV – Home Office Research Study 292*, London: Home Office Research, Development and Statistics Directorate. Available at: http://www.homeoffice.gov.uk/rds/pdfs05/hors292.pdf

Ginsberg, B. (1986) *The Captive Public: How Mass Opinion Promotes State Power.* New York: Basic Books.

Haggerty, K.D. and Gazso, A. (2005) The public politics of opinion research on surveillance and privacy, *Surveillance & Society*, 3(2/3): 173–80.

Helton, F. and Fischer, B. (2004) *What Do People Think about CCTV? Findings from a Berlin Survey.* Available at: www.urbaneye.net

Hier, S., Greenberg, J., Walby, K., and Lett, D. (forthcoming) The establishment of public camera surveillance programs in Canada, *Media, Culture and Society*.

Sætnan, A., Dahl, J.Y. and Lomell, H.M. (2004) *Views from Under Surveillance: Public Opinion in a Closely Watched Area in Oslo.* Available at: www.urbaneye.net

18

News media, popular culture and the electronic monitoring of offenders in England and Wales[1]
by Mike Nellis

England and Wales first experimented with the electronic monitoring of offenders (EM) in 1989/90, renewed interest in it the mid-1990s, developed it country-wide in the late-1990s and now uses it on a larger proportion of its offenders than any other country ... Thus far, it has been used to enforce home confinement. The present technology consists of a small transmitter fitted to the offender's ankle which, so long as the offender remains close to a signalling device installed in his home, can be monitored by a computer which may be hundreds of miles away. Voice recognition technology has also been experimented with in England, and in the USA experiments have been conducted to track the movements of convicted offenders using orbiting satellites; this latter technology is not yet commercially viable, although it is anticipated that it will become so (Renzema 1998). The capacity to track, rather than the possibly 'interim' measure of home confinement, has long been the ideal of Tom Stacey's Offender Tag Association (OTA), the body which first promoted the technology in Britain, and which has survived to see its once derided ideas become significant realities in criminal justice (Nellis 2001).

EM in England is used in four ways. Firstly, as a community penalty ... Thirdly, EM was made integral to the Intensive Supervision and Surveillance Programmes, a new initiative for young offenders launched in February 2001. Fourthly, young offenders who would otherwise be remanded in custody were tagged from April 2002. Other uses have been foreshadowed in the Criminal Justice and Court Services Act 2000, and may develop in future. A growing body of technical data and criminological analysis is available to those who are professionally, politically and commercially interested in these developments (see Whitfield 2001 for a valuable summary).

But how well informed is the English public – or, more accurately, publics – about this new development in crime control and on what cultural resources are they drawing to make sense of it? One should not assume that, if they know about EM at all, they acquire knowledge only from official sources, as mediated by the press, and radio and TV news programmes – and certainly not from academic criminology. Some professional commentators have expressed fears that EM is an unwelcome Orwellian development in criminal justice (Ball and Lilly 1988; McCulloch 1997), others that it is a gimmicky and trivial technology of limited utility (Fletcher 1997), but does it register with the various publics in either of these ways – or as something different? What moods might be stimulated by popular representations of EM – enthusiasm, reassurance, scepticism, indifference, paranoia? – and for what reasons? . . .

In an important article on surveillance, Gary Marx (1995) mapped the ways in which CCTV, bugging and tagging devices, and databanks generally have been represented in a variety of cultural forms, popular songs, cartoons, comic books, jokes, advertisements and visual art. He is not particularly concerned with EM, although he reminds us in passing that modern developments in this field were inspired by a Spiderman comic in 1981. He concludes that there are images and tropes of both a protective and a threatening nature, guardian angels as well as Big Brothers, and a range of associated emotional tones: of enthusiasm, complacency, despondency and alarm. Overall, he offers 'thick description' of the cultural resources which citizens might use, intermittently and haphazardly (unless they had studied the subject as exhaustively as he has) to learn about, and to develop and bestow meaning on actual developments in surveillance. His view that representations of surveillance in the journalistic, literary and artistic fields serve both to legitimate and delegitimate it simultaneously, is wholly persuasive, and is of relevance to the policy makers and commercial organisations who are seeking support to install EM in the criminal justice systems of contemporary societies.

This [chapter] has more limited ambitions than Marx, although it is written in a similar spirit. It is more narrowly focused, on EM rather than surveillance generally, and whilst recognising the range of popular cultural forms which could be drawn on, it concentrates only on representation in newspapers, on television (in various formats), in cinema and in popular literature . . . Coverage is restricted to England and Wales, whilst drawing inevitably on the American films and novels which are available here. It tentatively goes beyond Marx by drawing on Bender's (1987) analysis of the literary and artistic roots of 'the penitentiary idea', to raise preliminary questions about the role of popular culture in *generating* the mentalities from which new forms of punishment (such as tagging) can emerge, rather than simply *interpreting* them.

Public knowledge of electronic monitoring

A survey of public awareness of and attitudes towards electronically monitored curfew orders (not HDC), based on interviews with a nationally representative sample of 1,850 people in England and Wales, was commissioned by On Guard Plus and undertaken in November 1999 (Taylor et al. 1999). This showed that spontaneous awareness of tagging stood at 19%, although when the phenomenon was explained to them, this increased to 89%. It was still one of the least known community penalties, community service orders being by far the best known. There were age differences in awareness but no gender differences; people in the 25 to 34 years age bracket were the most likely to know of it (24%), those aged over 65 years least likely (13%). Owner occupiers were marginally more likely to have heard of it than tenants. People living in two of the areas where the trials took place – East Anglia and the North West, but also in the South East, were all more likely to be aware of it (above 93%) than people in Greater London, (73%) where no trials had taken place since 1989/90.

Once the nature of curfew tagging had been explained, the respondents were asked to score (on a 1 to 10 scale ranging from strongly disagree, through agree, to strongly agree) the suitability of electronic tagging for certain types of offender and certain types of offence. In essence, the majority of respondents were 'reasonably well disposed' (scores of 6 and 7) towards tagging for unemployed or fulltime education offenders, offenders aged under 16 years, persistent offenders and female offenders with children. There was more scepticism about using it with mentally ill offenders, although there was a strong belief that it could (and presumably should?) be used in conjunction with other measures. Scores of between 5 and 7 were given for its use with the following crimes: burglary, harassment, shoplifting, sex offences, drug dealing, violence and assault, public order, drunk driving and deception and theft. Small percentages from a minority of respondents (n = 284) also volunteered the view that it could also be used in certain cases of homicide (7%) and rape (6%), and on child abusers (16%), car thieves (13%) and perpetrators of criminal damage (7%). While there is room for doubt about the adequacy of the methodology used in the survey – were respondents really able to imagine how tagging might punish or control particular types of offender when its duration could not exceed six months? – it seems clear that respondents did accept that the tag had the potential to exert effective control; it was expressly not dismissed out of hand.

The sample appear not to have been asked to identify reservations or problems with tagging, nor to have volunteered any. Nor were they asked to indicate what the source of their information was, other than the pollster themselves. Spontaneous awareness of only 19%, at the end of a year in which there had been considerable development of tagging, suggests that it had not registered all that strongly in public consciousness. It might reasonably be assumed, given the higher levels of awareness in two of the areas where tagging took place, that local media coverage – or national media coverage of local issues – was an important, if not unique, source of information. Specific studies might validate this, but in their absence the next section offers a preliminary mapping of the themes and issues surrounding EM that appeared in the English press between 1995 and early 2002.

Press coverage of electronic monitoring

News analysis can be a methodologically complex matter (Wykes 2001). What follows does not claim any sophistication, or to be the final word. It distinguishes between broadsheet and tabloid papers (broadly middle class and working class oriented respectively), and identifies recurrent themes and issues in the reporting of electronic monitoring. Both types of paper seem to have relied on Home Office press releases; the same stories tend to be covered in several papers simultaneously, citing the same facts and statistics (or slight variations), quoting the same sources, but sometimes in a tone that reflects the distinctive ethos of each paper. Attentive readers of the broadsheets could, over time have compiled a fairly accurate if superficial account of how tagging policy has evolved, the basic operating procedure, and the costs of the various schemes and the numbers involved. Richard Ford in *The Times*, Alan Travis in *The Guardian* and Jason Bennetto in *The Independent* have shown a consistent and mostly fair-minded interest in it, and their views have sometimes been augmented by feature articles commissioned (or placed) to advance a particular position.

The English press have contributed to the public awareness of EM from the outset; Aldridge (1994, p. 127) notes a 'bifurcation in [its] press treatment' in 1989, within the context of very limited interest at that time. Nonetheless, via the press, the very terms 'the tag' and 'tagging' became the commonest colloquial descriptions of both the overall sentence and the technology, before any schemes were implemented. This reflects the preferred terminology of the Offender Tag Association (OTA), established in 1982 and responsible for the earliest publicity about EM in England, and whose founder, Tom Stacey, was himself a former *Sunday Times* journalist (and novelist) . . .

The American origin of EM has been a significant theme in the English press, indeed more reference has been made to Judge Jack Love's inspiration by a Spider-man comic, (for example, in *The Guardian*, 13 November 1997) (Fox 1987) than to the lobbying role of the OTA. *The Independent* (15 May 1994) had earlier published two frames from the particular comic in an article critical of tagging both because of its comic book origins and because it was perceived as an alien American development. Hostility to it as an American practice was also evident in an article headlined 'Tagging delay as US equipment fails' (*The Independent*, 1 June 1995). *The Guardian* (7 December 1995) commented disparagingly that 'only 17 US-style tagging orders have been made during the first five months of the nine month trials, three of which have broken down'. Later, when the Home Office first announced the use of curfew orders for fine defaulters it referred to 'the further extension of American-style tagging experiments' (*The Guardian*, 1 August 1996).

In 1995, from whence the present expansion of EM in England has occurred, the press were acutely conscious that it had been tried once before, and found wanting. Their stance was sceptical. *The Times* (7 March 1995) referred to Michael Howard 'reviving' tagging and reminded readers that in the original experiment in 1989/90 'the equipment broke down regularly and 29 (out of 50) offenders violated their curfew, or were charged with a new offence'. *The Daily Telegraph* (7 March 1995) noted that it had been 'dropped by Mr. Kenneth Clarke when he was Home Secretary, only to be resurrected by Mr. Howard'. *The Independent* (1 June 1995) referred to tagging as 'a technique that ended in disaster when it was last used in Britain'. *The Daily Mail* (7 March 1995) headlined an article 'Whitehall rethink on technology branded a failure'. Only *The Daily Express*, a very strong supporter of the Conservative government, was upbeat about the prospect of its reintroduction:

> The electronic tagging of young thugs was first tried five years ago, and failed. But the failure was in the technology not in the idea. Now with improved technology, the idea is back, bringing with it a real prospect of effectively combating crime.
>
> (*The Daily Express*, 30 December 1994)

Looked at overall, there has been a tendency in the press to make premature estimates of the likely scale of its development, and some of what has appeared has been mistaken or misleading. Journalists must bear some responsibility for this, but certainly not all, for they have been reliant on official press releases and leaked internal Home Office documents which may themselves have been inconsistent over time. One such document, circulating in the period immediately before reintroduction in 1995, was summarised thus by Alan Travis in *The Guardian*:

> For the first time in the history of British criminal justice, private security companies are to be given powers to prosecute offenders as well as to organise and supervise their sentences. The departure is part of the Government's plans for the electronic tagging of offenders, which the Home Office believes will eventually become the principal community sentence with up to 20,000 orders imposed a year.
>
> (22 September 1994)

These powers never were invested in the private security companies, and the Home Office has never *explicitly and publicly* said that it envisaged electronic monitoring as the 'principal community sentence' . . . Other forms of misrepresentation include a *Daily Express* editorial (30 December 1994) which stated that the monitoring centres for tagging would be located 'at local police stations'. This creates a subtle symbolic link between tagging and policing (as opposed to probation), and quite possibly trades on the public knowledge that CCTV is sometimes monitored from police stations, but it is factually inaccurate; monitoring stations are invariably located in the service providers or monitoring companies' offices. Even *The Guardian* (18 August 1996) is not immune. A definitively headlined article – 'sex offenders face tagging' – made clear in the small print that the government's proposal was *a possibility* not an actuality. Ambiguous references to 'tracking' in this same article meant placement on the sex offenders' register, rather than tracking in the electronic sense – monitoring the movement, rather than simply the fixed location, of the offender.

Some reporting of EM has been openly hostile. Nick Cohen, an investigative journalist with a regular *Observer* column, has been the most hostile. He exposed the failings of the first trial in great detail, and also (a rarity in England) some of the sharp practices associated with its development in America (*The Independent*, 15 September 1994). Soon after the second English trial began he dismissed tagging as an 'expensive fiasco', noting that in the first two weeks of its availability magistrates made not a single curfew order (*The Independent*, 16 July 1995). Later, he used the case of a group of three Manchester women, with children, who were tagged rather than imprisoned for violent offences, but with curfew restrictions (8am to 1pm) which deliberately prevented them from maintaining their employment as nightclub dancers (*The Independent*, 7 April 1996). This was one of the few tagging stories about women offenders, of whom far fewer have been tagged compared to men, and it showed how EM could be destructive of employment, rather than supportive of it. The women appeared to have good grounds for an appeal against sentence, but that story was not followed up: the negative impression of tagging therefore lingers.

Many press reports draw, in brief, on expert opinion. Harry Fletcher, of the National Association of Probation Officers (NAPO), remains by far the most commonly quoted opponent of EM *in all press reports* (and some of Nick Cohen's stories appear to have originated with him). His pithy faultfinding with tagging – he acknowledges no advantages – have undoubtedly irritated the Home Office and the monitoring companies.[2] His tone has rarely altered over the years, whereas that of other expert voices, notably Paul Cavadino of the Penal Affairs Consortium (see letters, *The Guardian*, 7 March 1995) and Mary Honeyball of the Association of Chief Officers of Probation (ACOP), who were once as hostile, has become more muted . . .

Most of the hostile press comment on EM has come from left-leaning individuals and newspapers. Ironically, however, the single worst-case publicity that it received came, in a short-lived burst, from the right. Under devastating headlines 'Tagging puts public at risk', ' "Public endangered" by tagging scheme' and 'Lag tag shock', *The Yorkshire Post, The Daily Telegraph* and *The Daily Star* respectively (all on 4 March 2000), reported the then Shadow Home Secretary, Anne Widdecombe's, discovery that of the 17,871 prisoners released so far on HDC, 185 had 'been charged with offences committed while wearing tags, including two rapes' (*The Daily Telegraph*).[3] Rather than emphasise the 95% success rate of the HDC scheme, Widdecombe high-lighted its failings, and whilst giving enough information to let readers make independent judgments, *The Daily Telegraph* gave her a platform. Widdecombe's real target was the principle of early release, which she deployed to portray New Labour, in time honoured Conservative fashion, as soft on crime, but a clear impression was nonetheless given that tagged offenders were offending with impunity . . .

There has been a mix of human interest and issue-based stories about tagging in both the tabloids and the broadsheets, and to the average, casual reader the more personalised stories probably convey the most vivid and memorable understanding of tagging's strengths and weaknesses. The first person to be given a curfew order, Clive Barratt, age 29, from Kings Lynn, Norfolk was arrested on suspicion of theft after only a fortnight. Under the ambiguous headline 'Alarm bells ring as first "tagged" offender is arrested again' *The Guardian* (19 August 1995) described how the Home Office undertook damage limitation in this case: 'officials admitted disappointment at Mr. Barratt's behaviour, [but] said the fact his breach was spotted was a sign that the scheme worked'. Not all human interest stories are negative. *The Kettering Evening Standard* (30 March 2000) ran a story . . . under the headline 'Man had perfect alibi: electronic tag proved he was innocent' describing how a suspected car vandal was incriminated by a mendacious witness, but exonerated when his presence at home at the alleged time of the offence was verified by the monitoring company. Positive accounts also appeared in *Time Out* (24 October 1999) and *The Big Issue* (8–14 March 1999), based on interviews with offenders who were clearly appreciative of early release, and happy to see the irksome restrictions of the tag as a lesser evil than prison . . . The most humorous of tagging stories – and embarrassing for the monitor-ing company involved, although it attracted no coverage in major newspapers – concerned a released prisoner whose easily unscrewed artificial leg was unknowingly tagged, allowing him to leave home at will (*Birmingham Metro*, 4 July 2000) . . .

It is perhaps ironic that the most concerted attempt to date, (in February/March 2002) by the Home Office to portray tagging as a tough and controlling 'penalty' occurred in relation to its proposed introduction as an adjunct to a remand on bail for young offenders, which was intended to reduce repeat offending by bailees. This coincided with an expected announcement on the expansion of the HDC scheme, in respect of which the Home Secretary, David Blunkett, was determined to face down critics who claimed that it had jeopardised public safety. Both initiatives were connected to steep rises in custodial populations, and were clearly seen by the press, sometimes cynically, sometimes neutrally, as attempts to ameliorate this. Rather unfortunately, they also coincided with a short and intense media campaign in the more right-wing newspapers, (partly orchestrated by the police to pressure the Home Office for more resources and to resist unwelcome reorganisation) to heighten awareness of rising violent crime throughout Britain. Against this background, tagging for juveniles was easily made to look gimmicky and ineffectual, and its credibility was further damaged by police doubts about its likely effectiveness with recalcitrant bailees. Typical headlines were 'Teenage thugs will ignore tag plan, say police' (*The Yorkshire Post)*; 'Police attack Blunkett scheme to tag muggers' (*The Independent*), both on 27 February 2002. The extension of HDC fared little better, with both a *Sunday Times* columnist (Marrin 2002) and *The Sunday Telegraph* (10 March 2002) portraying it as an unacceptable risk to the public. Lumping together both issues, a columnist (and former Conservative MP) (Mellor 2002) in one of the more notorious tabloids, argued along with other papers, including *The Daily Express* (27 April 2002), that tagging would only be viable if backed up by the threat of prison for the slightest infraction. This negative coverage did appear to have an effect in respect of the youth bail tagging; within a month, seemingly to appease critics in the police, the Home Secretary announced increased use of custodial remands, with tagging barely mentioned. The extension of the HDC scheme proved more robust, and survived the press onslaught.

Electronic tagging and American movies

Electronic monitoring has been shown in at least three American movies, which have also been released in Britain (as films and home videos). All three portray the tagging of ethnic minority men – two African-Americans, one Hispanic – and are centrally concerned with questions of crime and race. Two of the films 'One Eight Seven' (1994, d. Kevin Reynolds) and 'He Got Game' (1998, d. Spike Lee) fall midway between mainstream and independent cinema, but both had major Black stars (Samuel Jackson and Denzel Washington respectively, without whose presence they may never have achieved widespread distribution, or even been made). Because of Spike Lee's standing as a significant Black intellectual, 'He Got Game' must be regarded as a film of some cultural importance, which among other things, directs its youthful Black audience towards the view that EM is to be understood as yet another facet of racial oppression. The third film 'First Time Felon' (1998, d. Charles S. Dutton) was made for American television and only released on video in Britain; it is part of a long tradition of 'contemporary-issue' TV movies, inspired in varying degrees by true stories, with which its production company, HBO, is particularly associated. Its view of race in America – and of electronic monitoring – is rather different from Spike Lee's.

EM is neither a central feature nor a major theme in any of these movies; either it is part of the backdrop, or it is simply an episode in the story. Nonetheless, for many people, particularly the young people who comprise contemporary cinema audiences and who rent videos, these images will have been their first sight of EM (unless they have actually been tagged). These cinema images are more realistically contextualised, and probably more vivid, than anything else they might have seen or read about EM, and it would be difficult to believe that they play no part in shaping the perception and understanding of the technology. I will deal with each of the films in turn.

'One Eight Seven' is a sombre account of the failings of the American public education system, dedicated, in a concluding on-screen text, to the one-in-nine teachers who have been assaulted by their pupils. It focuses on a creative and dedicated African-American science teacher, Trevor Garfield (Samuel Jackson), already the victim of an attempted murder by an aggrieved pupil in a New York school, who resumes his chosen career in a poor neighbourhood school in Los Angeles. Most of the teachers are cynical timeservers who struggle, in dilapidated buildings, with an unsupportive Principal, to maintain reasonable order among the mostly insolent and indifferent Hispanic teenagers. Garfield soon encounters 16-year-old Benny Chacon, who, after refusing a simple request, slams his foot on a desktop and proudly displays the electronic signalling device fastened to his ankle. 'I'm already on house arrest', he sneers, 'there's nothing more you can do to me'. Some of Benny's associates – members of the Tagging Crew (graffiti sprayers) – cheer approvingly. Garfield learns that in addition to being subject to EM, Benny is also on probation for violence, and that despite threatening a woman teacher (whom he is probably stalking), attending school had been made a condition of the probation. Neither measure is an adequate curb on his behaviour. This pessimism is affirmed in a later scene when, one evening, Benny and two friends kill a lone youngster who has despoiled some of their graffiti. Even as Benny's anklet bleeps – warning him that his curfew begins in 15 minutes, he explains to his friends – he shoots the fleeing youngster in the back, then stands over him to finish him off. A more telling image of EM's ineffectualness would be hard to imagine . . .

'He Got Game' is also hostile to EM, but in a quite different way. Jake Shuttlesworth (Denzel Washington), a poor black from Coney Island, New York, is serving the sixth year of a one-to-fifteen sentence in the Attica Correctional Facility for the manslaughter of his wife during a row over the pressure he was putting on their 12-year-old son, Jesus, to practice his basketball – the route, in Jake's view, out of the ghetto. Jesus, now 18, has become a star junior basketball player. Self-interestedly, the state governor wants Jesus to sign up for his old university – and bring in lucrative sponsorship deals. The Attica governor is pressured to release Jake for one week to persuade Jesus to choose the 'right' university, the deal being sweetened by the promise of reduced prison time. Jake is released into the company of two watchful parole officers who, the moment he arrives in his hotel room, remove his handcuffs and fit an electronic device to his ankle, simultaneously plugging a slim black box into his telephone. Nothing is said about how the device functions, except that it is to discourage him from absconding – 'in case you get any smart ideas', his parole officer says, 'we will track you down and when we find you we will shoot you'. Ostensibly, the equipment is that used in home confinement, but the impression is vaguely given that it can track his movements rather than just monitor his presence in the hotel. Jake is also expected to keep in pager contact with his parole officers, although beyond the initial mention this is never alluded to again.

Jake is embarrassed when the anklet is seen by a black shop assistant from whom he buys trainers; he passes it off as a treatment for arthritis, but the black youngster smiles knowingly, explaining that his brother also wears one. At one point, Jesus disparages the device on his father's ankle as a 'Lo-Jack' (the brand name of a car tracking device), and it is this which provides the key to the symbolic role which tagging has in the film. In essence, 'He Got Game' is about the control and commodification of black men by schools, universities, media organisations, corporate sponsors, sports agents and, not least, prisons – 'you are not a free man', the parole officer reminds him, 'your ass is ours . . . you understand that? . . . do you?'. Although the tag has little direct bearing on the plot it here signifies the full extent of the power which white society, in this instance via the penal system, has over Jake, a hi-tech synthesis of the shackles, brands and bells once used on slaves.[4] Allowing the vague impression that Jake's tag actually tracks his movements (although technically inaccurate) was a form of artistic licence on Lee's part, adding to its potency as a symbol of racial domination . . .

'First Time Felon', also focused on an African-American offender, is more sympathetic to electronic tagging. Set in Chicago, based loosely on the true story of Greg Yance (Omar Epps), a 20-ish street dealer in heroin (albeit one from a respectable if fatherless family), the film largely showcases the Illinois Impact Incarceration Programme. Yance chooses four months in this intensive military-style 'boot camp' (a measure that has replaced probation for first time offenders) over five years without parole in the penitentiary, where he doubts his capacity to survive the lethal gang rivalries. The rigours of boot camp – which are as much rehabilitative as punitive – force Yance to re-consider his future. He resolves to go straight, and returns home, subject to electronic monitoring for four months. To the chagrin of his mother, his drug dealing friends soon call round to recruit him back to the streets. He shows them the anklet:

> 'Can't go nowhere, can't go 100 feet with that' he explains.
> 'Bust that shit', says his friend, 'by the time they come to fix it it'll be next month'.
> 'No, dog, I'm going to play it straight'.

Despite its evident effectiveness as a constraint on Yance, the tag is not portrayed as an unmitigated good. His mother argues with the parole officer that four months permanent house arrest is unfair and counterproductive, preventing Yance from attending job interviews and visiting the library. She secures some two hour breaks for him, but it is within those breaks, when he is repeatedly refused work because of his record, as well as being tempted to resume lucrative drug dealing, that his problems intensify. The tag is shown being removed – 'feels lighter', Yance says, shaking his leg – but his continual rejection by prospective employers, the derision of his former girlfriend (who mocks his lack of money), and the assassination of an old associate by a rival gang push him to consider suicide. He resists, and a concluding onscreen note informs us that after five months the real Yance did find work and eventually became a youth worker. The film as a whole, however, avoids cheap triumphalism, tempering its initial view of boot camps and electronic monitoring as effective punishments, by questioning whether their impact on young black people can reasonably be sustained after release unless entrenched racism is also addressed, and unless ex-inmates are helped to find satisfying work.

Electronic tagging on English television

The various types of television programme – drama, light entertainment, news bulletins, documentaries and films – are also potential sources of information about EM, the meaning of which may vary according to the type of programme it appears in, and the type of story being told. Although claims must be tentative, because a comprehensive knowledge of everything on TV, and of who watches what and when, even in one country, is increasingly impossible, EM appears to have figured very little, thus far. Key developments, such as the start of the trials in 1995, have been covered briefly in prime time news bulletins, and references have been made to it in documentaries concerned with broader penal issues. No single TV documentary has been devoted to it. Drama seems barely to have touched on tagging – and comedy, perhaps surprisingly, given the ubiquity of living-room based sit-coms – has, as yet, seen no potential in it. It is difficult to ascertain film scheduling on the multiplicity of cable and satellite channels, but 'One Eight Seven' is the only one of the American movies mentioned above to have been shown prime time on a major terrestrial channel in Britain. In this section, the contribution of five programmes to public awareness and understanding of EM will be appraised.

Appropriately enough for something deemed futuristic, a device called 'the Sobrietor', which is used to enforce a prohibition on alcohol consumption by home-confined offenders in Denver, Colorado, was featured on 'Tomorrow's World' (BBC 1, 25 April 2001), an authoritative, early evening 'magazine' series highlighting developments in science and technology. The eight-minute item was introduced as follows by the two presenters:

> Crime and punishment. Thanks to electronic monitoring it may not be the slam of a cell door that marks the start of a sentence, it could be your own front door closing. It might sound a lot more comfortable that way, but electronic jailers are getting tougher every day . . . The next generation of devices will be able to monitor not only where you are but what you do.

The existing form of EM, using a close-up of an anklet being fitted, was briefly outlined, followed by an explanation of the way in which the Sobrietor augmented this, using breathalyser and voice recognition technology – the latter guaranteeing that someone else does not substitute for the offender before the test. An American probation officer extolled the virtues of EM in general – 'it creates a jail setting in their home' – and the Sobrietor in particular for drink-driving offenders, for whom imprisonment would mean loss of employment. An anonymous offender, monitored by the Sobrietor, likened the experience of being phoned three to five times daily by a computer demanding a breath test to the intrusiveness of 'Big Brother . . . When the system was first set up in my home it never felt like I was alone'. Nonetheless, he preferred it to six months in prison, and welcomed retaining his job, despite also having to pay for the device's installation in his home. The presenters concluded cheerily:

> This could be the future of doing time . . . There are obviously huge financial benefits to an electronic monitoring system like this. The one in Denver has already paid for itself.

Among British TV drama series, only 'Bad Girls', first televised in May 1999, has made use of EM. Set in a women's prison, the rather comically-named HMP Larkhall, the series does occasionally address serious and realistic issues (Reynolds and McCallum 2001). By the time it had reached its third series in 2001, it had acquired a weekly audience of 8.6 million, and EM figured in the third episode of that series, (3 April 2001). One of the regular characters, Julie, was released on the tag to a halfway house, in order to spend some time with her teenage son. She had been advised to apply for it by a helpful older inmate, but nothing was shown of the application and assessment process; at the start of episode three the governor simply tells Julie that her application has been successful . . . The impression given was that monitoring was being used to facilitate home leave, rather than early release, and the tag, in fact, was only incidental to the story – an excuse for setting some action outside the prison. The monitoring officer was shown leaving the halfway house after fitting the tag, and Julie, after a close up of her ankle, then briefly explained to the warden how the device worked (as much for the benefit of the TV audience). After this, the tag is never mentioned. There is no sense of Julie's freedom being constrained. The episode ends when she starts to miss her best friend, and kicks up a fuss outside the prison until she is let back in . . .

Unlike the other TV programmes mentioned here, party political broadcasts are specifically intended to influence viewer attitudes in a certain way. The Conservative Party's first such broadcast in the June 2001 election campaign (backed up on radio and by linked billboard posters) sought to damage the Labour government's credibility on law and order. Although not focused on a real individual it palely imitated the infamous advertisement about Willie Horton – a Massachusetts prisoner who committed rape while on home leave – used very effectively by Republicans to discredit a Democratic presidential candidate in 1988 . . . Using actors, it showed a series of uncouth, mean-looking young men leaving prison, patently unreformed, some of whom then rob and assault unsuspecting members of the public, often women (Butler and Kavanagh 2002, p. 151). There was no explicit mention or showing of tagging – it was the *principle and reality* of early release that was targeted – but insofar as there was an intimate connection between the two in this particular policy, this was clearly an indirect criticism of tagging's potential to reduce the use of custody.

'Soaps' – long-running drama serials, showing several nights a week, at peak viewing times – are routinely used as vehicles for exploring topical social issues in Britain – sometimes realistically, sometimes not – and ITV's rural-set 'Emmerdale' was the first to feature tagging, shortly after the expansion of HDC had been announced in early 2002. Several months before, a series regular, decent teenager Marc Reynolds, had been given twelve months' custody for his reluctant participation in a car theft that resulted in a fatality. Prison scenes were periodically included in the series, his eligibility for HDC raised appropriately, and in April 2002, he returned home. The fitting of the tag to his ankle was briefly shown, and the nature of the technology and the rules of his curfew explained to him and his mother (10 April 2002). The white, middle-aged, monitoring officer was portrayed as firm-but-fair, redolent of the better prison officers in the custodial scenes. Securicor had in fact asked for the aggressiveness of the officer to be toned down in this scene when they were originally asked to advise on the script (personal communication, Clare Sims, Securicor, 18 March 2002). Mark is accepting of the tag, happy to be out of prison, and determined to go straight, and, because he is basically a good kid 'Emmerdale's' ten million audience were encouraged to see electronic monitoring as a beneficial measure *in his case*, removing him from undoubted bad influences in prison. The question of whether it would be an effective measure with bad kids did not arise.

Electronic monitoring in a crime novel

. . . This section is concerned with the literary representation of tagging as an actual development in criminal justice, not with the imaginary forms of tagging envisaged in science fiction, which I will deal with later. To the best of my knowledge, the only crime novel in which electronic monitoring is mentioned is Elmore Leonard's (1992) *Maximum Bob*, the nickname of a tough Florida judge. Leonard is one of the world's best-selling, most prestigious and most respected crime novelists and one critic (Taylor 1997) has discerned 'a great deal of surveillance' in his novels generally (for example, stake-outs and undercover operations), *which tends, however, to be easily disrupted and evaded.* In *Maximum Bob*, Tommy Vasco, a wealthy, drunken doctor on probation for writing fake prescriptions for drug addicts, is already under house arrest when the story opens. He is only a minor character, and the fact of his being tagged is of no great relevance to the plot, except that the rather affluent home to which he is confined is the venue in which the story's lead villain, Elvin Crowe, newly released from prison, plans revenge on 'Maximum Bob'. The following dialogue between Crowe and Vasco is probably the first reference to electronic monitoring in contemporary crime writing:

> Elvin said: 'What's that thing on your ankle, looks like a little radio?'
> 'It's how they keep track of me'. Dr Tommy was at the counter now, putting more rum in his drink. 'You never saw an anklet? You wear it, and you can't go no more than a hundred and fifty feet from your telephone. There's a receiver in this thing and a box hooked up to the telephone line, like you have with your cable TV'.
> Elvin didn't have cable TV or know what he was talking about, but said 'Yeah?'
> 'A computer calls my number every now and then and if I am not in the house or close by the computer doesn't get a signal back and it lets them know'.
> Elvin had heard of that. 'You're on probation? Shit, so am I. . . . Why don't you take the goddam thing off and set it by the phone?'

'You'd have to break it'. Dr Tommy struck his leg straight out. 'You can, all it has is the strap holding it on. But there's some kind of sensor in there, tells them if it is not on your leg'.

'You mean you can't ever leave the house?'

'Only to go to Alcoholics Anonymous, twice a week'.

(Leonard 1992, pp. 165–6; see also pp. 250–1)

Tommy Vasco is a minor middle class offender who abides by the conditions of his house arrest, and in that very limited sense (the conspiracy hatched in his house notwithstanding) EM is portrayed in *Maximum Bob* in a positive light. But, didactic as this exchange is, it conveys little or nothing about the implications and significance of EM, nor what it feels like to be subjected to it. The monitoring personnel themselves – and their relationship to other players in criminal justice – never figure. *Maximum Bob* works perfectly well as a story without this – and it is culturally useful that the innovation of EM has at least been acknowledged by a major crime writer – but the fact remains that its depiction here is superficial, and that in the genre as a whole, its presence in the world has been overlooked . . .

Crime *genre* writing, of course, segues into modern mainstream literature (P.D. James, John le Carre, J. G. Ballard), and crime and punishment themes have always figured in the Western canon (Dostoevsky, Dickens, Hugo). Writers as diverse as John Cheever (1977) and Irvine Welsh (1999) have, respectively, conveyed impressions of imprisonment and policing without ever being categorised specifically as 'crime writers', and all such work becomes a cultural resource for understanding, interpreting, and perhaps even *constituting* the emergent realities of criminal justice. Without losing sight of my main theme – the interpretive role of popular culture – I will here draw on John Bender's (1987) work to consider this latter issue.[5] Bender demonstrates the subtle, shaping influence of 18th century novels and paintings on the structures of feeling that gave rise to 'the penitentiary idea'. If we accept his view that 'fabrications *in narrative* of the power of confinement to shape personality contributed to the process of cultural representation whereby prisons were themselves reconceived and ultimately reinvented' (Bender 1987, p. 1, italics added) we can also reasonably ask what narratives, what processes of cultural representation have been shaping more recent developments in criminal justice (such as tagging), and what may have a bearing on the future. Bender was not specifically concerned with art and literature that self-consciously addressed the future but, as future-consciousness became, throughout the 20th century, ever more deeply embedded in Western time horizons, it seems reasonable in this context to examine the genre – science fiction – that has been most directly concerned with such consciousness.

Imaginary forms of electronic monitoring

. . . Science fiction (sf) has often sought to anticipate the future, or to stimulate insight into the present through future-set stories, and, in the midst of countless works which have explored 'the deliberate use of technology to promote an unworthy quiescence' (Amis 1960, p. 196) criminal justice themes have been commonplace. Quite specifically, 'numerous sf stories have anticipated the use of "electronic tagging", although usually the tags were capable of administering on-the-spot punishment' (Clute and Nichols 1992, p. 276) – and, it should be added, have been of the tracking rather than the home confinement variety. *The Reefs of Space* (Pohl and Williamson 1964), and *The Ring* (Anthony and Margroff 1968) both explore the idea of controlling offenders by attaching devices to them. Pohl and Williamson envisaged a potentially explosive, tamper-proof neck collar fitted to dissidents – presciently called 'Risks' – in a future totalitarian society. Anthony and Margroff, whose book was re-issued in 1986, after EM had emerged in the USA, envisaged a surgically implanted ring on a finger or (particularly for women) toe, fitted in court at the point of sentence for between five and ten years, which monitors mental, spoken and enacted infringements of an artificially heightened (computer-imprinted) conscience – 'law by machine', as one character puts it. To avoid agonising pain, ringed offenders condition themselves into becoming good citizens, establishing habits which outlast the eventual removal of the ring; in that sense it is both cure and punishment.[6]

In science fiction films, pain-inflicting tracking tags are almost always intended to be lethal, not merely uncomfortable, and have not been linked to the idea of an imprinted conscience. In director John Carpenter's (1981) 'Escape from New York', for example, the American government order the release of a war veteran/prisoner to undertake a particularly risky rescue mission for them, over a set 24-hour period. To ensure he returns to base as planned a miniature transmitter is implanted in his neck, attached to a small explosive device which can only be deactivated if he returns on time ... 'The Running Man' (1990, d. Paul Michael Glaser), 'Wedlock' (1990, d. Lewis Teague) and 'Fortress' (1998, d, Stuart Gordon), prisons-of-the-near-future movies, all borrowed Pohl and Williamson's basic idea: prisoners are fitted with explosive tags (a collar in the first two, an intestinator in the latter) to prevent escape and to ensure that they keep to prescribed areas within the prison ... In a neglected American film, 'Virtuosity' (1995, d. Brett Leonard) an imprisoned policeman (inside for killing the terrorists who murdered his family) is released to help find a serial killer; to ensure his co-operation with the authorities he is fitted with a 'micro-locater implant', tracked by satellites, 'which can trigger the release of toxins if he needs to be stopped' ...

In contemporary 'technothrillers' – a prevalent and popular genre which combines actual or imaginary science (or both) with the conventions of crime, spy and political fiction – the use of technology to track particular individuals has often been linked to the broader issues of surveillance, the secret state and the (mal)distribution of power (rather than to the more mundane issue of controlling low- and medium-risk criminals). In the ironically entitled 'The End of Violence' (1996, d. Wim Wenders) the possibility is raised that mass surveillance systems, ostensibly designed to deter and prevent crime, are themselves forms of structural violence. In 'Enemy of the State' (1999, d. Tony Scott), a wholly innocent man, unaware that a tiny signalling device has been mistakenly clipped to him is tracked remorselessly throughout Washington DC by rogue agents from the National Security Agency, via satellite and high resolution CCTV. The story unfolds against a backcloth of media debate about the legitimacy of such technology – it is the murder of one of its high-profile opponents that precipitates the chase. Thoughtful viewers of this film, which is set in the present day not the future, might reasonably ask whether the technology shown here is actual or imaginary, and, if actual, whether it could it be used in this way? Although developed for military purposes it clearly has implications for the policing of cities.

As popular cinema, 'Enemy of the State' plays on liberal Western anxieties about the growth of 'surveillance societies' (Lyon 2000) and concomitant fears about loss of privacy (Rosen 2000). George Orwell's (1948) *Nineteen Eighty-Four* remains a touchstone of debate about such issues, although as Lyon (2000, p. 35) points out there now exists a technological capacity for surveillance 'undreamed of in the worst Orwellian nightmare'. The capacity includes the deployment of CCTV in public and private places, monitoring of telephone and internet communications, satellite photography and, above all, dataveillance, the computerised aggregating of the trails and traces left by consumers in the course of electronic commercial transactions. Much surveillance, though significantly not all, has been legitimated in terms of its assumed contribution to crime prevention and public safety, although its roots lie in much deeper shifts in the structures and cultures of contemporary societies. Numerous writers see these developments as fundamental, defining characteristics of the postmodern Western world, which have by no means reached their limit. Lyon (2000), in particular, discerns in those who champion and support them 'an idolatrous dream of omniperception' (p. 147), a desire for God-like knowledge – and power.

Such is the cultural and political milieu in which actual forms of EM have been growing, although insufficient attention has been paid to this, even by criminologists. Lilly (1990) rightly argued, more than a decade ago, that EM should be analysed more broadly as an aspect of surveillance, rather than simply as an innovation in community penalties – but much debate on EM is still framed in terms of the latter. Later, Lilly and Ball (1993) – not entirely consistently – also questioned whether EM was just a passing fashion in criminal justice, and, of course, the *present forms* of technology may well be just that. But if Lyon is right about the hunger for omniperception, and maybe omniscience, on the part of powerful political and commercial interests, a desire to pinpoint and track individual people in the interests of control, consumerism and convenience, which is already deeply embedded in contemporary society, then the pursuit of progressively more viable technologies of omniperception is unlikely to be abandoned. Biometric surveillance, of which fingerprinting was the precursor, and of which voice and iris recognition are simply the latest practical applications, is likely to become more prevalent.

McCormick (1994) and Mair (2001) have both reflected on the burgeoning application of pre-given forms of 'new' technology to crime control, but neither address the processes by which technology is itself shaped. In what cultural milieu does new thinking about technology emerge, and where might signposts to the future be found? There is a complex inter-relationship, a matrix of mutual stimulation, between technology, imagination and desire to which 21st century criminologists may need to pay more attention, starting perhaps with the field of science fiction. Hitherto, with rare exception (see Pease 1978), criminologists have shared in the prevailing highbrow disdain for sf, and the utopian and dystopian literature which has largely been its seedbed, despite the academic attention it now receives (for example, Fekete 2001) and despite its own many forays into criminal justice. Yet Thomas Disch (1998), one of the strongest intellectual commentators on science fiction, whilst acknowledging the crassness, inaccuracy and irrelevance of much the genre has convincingly argued that a great deal of it has impacted on social reality, has supplied 'the dreams our stuff is made of'. Throughout the 20th century there has undeniably been a symbiosis between scientists and technologists and the best of sf writers, each inspiring and intriguing the other. There have been, and are, scientists and engineers who have written sf themselves, extrapolating possible futures from present trends, and sometimes devising devices and scenarios – and narratives of legitimation – that may not even have been imaginable without the stimulus of science fiction. Traditions of speculation, fabulation and prediction can function both as the milieu in which new technologies are conceived and generated, as well as the interpretive lens through which new technologies are initially received and filtered.[7]

All fictitious worlds, even those in mainstream literature, are *alternative* worlds to some degree, counterfactual accounts which create a sense of verisimilitude. By *amplifying* the element of 'cognitive estrangement' which exists in all literature, science fiction simply expands the parameters of the imaginable, some aspects of which are, or become, feasible. The fact that in England EM was first envisaged by a novelist, (albeit not of science fiction),[8] and that in the USA a Spiderman comic helped trigger its initial development are events whose significance for penal reform has not been properly appreciated – the locus of innovation in penal reform, broadly conceived, may be shifting. The cultural resources on which Tom Stacey and Jack Love drew were outside the frame of conventional penal analysis. It seems increasingly likely – even the Department of Trade and Industry (2000) Foresight panel implies it – that new responses to crime might henceforth emerge as much from interaction between government and innovators in the telecommunication, biotechnology, nanotechnology and security industries, as from established penal policy networks. Criminology's past neglect of the socio-technical sphere, and of the mentalities found in science fiction and 'technothrillers', despite many of modernity's deepest fears having been addressed in these declassé genres, may need to change. Even if, with Disch (1998), after Freud, we accept that dystopian entertainments help primarily to make our nightmares manageable, rather than actually to predict the future, we should still be attentive to those stories about pain-inflicting tags, and keep track of those latter-day Judge Loves who might well want them to come true . . .

Conclusion

What has, and has not, been accomplished here? The main accomplishment has been a partial sketch of how news media, various TV formats, novels and films have addressed the issue of EM in the latter part of the decade during which England and Wales became the world leader in the application of this technology. A rough and by no means exhaustive guide has been drawn of the cultural milieu in which policy makers, penal reformers and commercial organisations are vying to position EM as a new criminal justice tool. It must be emphasised that no easy inference can be drawn as to what people actually think about EM – it is better simply to ask them, as Taylor *et al.* (1999) did – but some indication has been given here of the kind of cultural resources on which they *might* conceivably be drawing to form a judgment, which Taylor *et al.* did not do.

The first thing that can be said about representations of EM in the press and popular culture is that they have confounded both the hopes of its supporters and the fears of its detractors – they have neither consistently proclaimed its potential nor consistently warned of its dangers in any clear and compelling way. The tilt has been towards the negative, and includes instances of dramatic hostility, but the overall picture is mixed, and strikingly muted – EM is not seen to raise 'big issues'. Thus, by no stretch of the imagination can tagging be said to have been seriously debated or explored in the journalistic, literary or cinematic fields in England and Wales. Whilst one could not reasonably expect media coverage (in the broadest sense) to be as comprehensive as the specialised EM literature used by professionals and policy makers, it is still worth remarking that this country has become a world leader in the use of tagging without any significant public deliberation . . .

Different segments of the public draw information from different media, and it is a mistake – especially for those professionally and politically involved in positioning EM – to regard mainstream news reports alone (in the press and TV) as definitive and direct influences on public attitudes. Diverse influences are in play, and while audiences rarely react passively to media representations, the fact remains that, all told, few portrayals of tagging in popular culture have sought to inspire confidence in it as a penal measure, and those which have, have been the more transient . . . If one adds in a range of media not covered in this article – advertising, comic books and computer games – the latter two drawing heavily on science fiction, and likely at some point to deploy imaginary forms of tagging – it seems highly unlikely that positive messages and meanings will have been received by the younger generation who mostly use these media.

Let us now turn to two key issues, the efficacy of EM as a form of crime control, and its alleged threat to civil liberties. Firstly, this analysis yields little evidence to suggest that EM is taken seriously as a means of dealing with crime, despite the claims of its supporters that it is a tough punishment capable of restraining offenders who would otherwise be sent to prison, and that it could therefore contribute to a revived strategy of penal reductionism. This argument has quite simply not been won in the press or in popular culture, despite some convincing research evidence that a combination of tagging and rehabilitative measures are effective means of community control (see Whitfield 2001). In this sense the reporting and representation of EM have been the opposite of the reporting and representation of CCTV, which the press (if not popular culture) tends to assume is highly effective, despite continuing doubts in the research community. Quite why the press has been so sceptical about EM is harder to explain. It may reflect a general press scepticism about all community penalties, about any punishment which is 'less than' prison; community service and probation, overall, have not had particularly positive coverage (Aldridge 1994). It may simply be a deflationary reaction to the ostensibly exaggerated claims that have sometimes been made by the boosters of EM. Notwithstanding the fact that EM has expanded considerably in England and Wales *despite media scepticism (and possible indifference)* if it is to stand a chance of contributing to a revitalised penal reduction strategy, as Lilly and Nellis (2001) argue it could, its supporters are in dire need, at the very least, of better public relations. It may even be the case that unless positive media coverage, and public support, can be secured for EM – a controlling measure by definition – it cannot be got for any community penalty at a time of 'popular punitiveness'.

Secondly, in respect of offenders' civil liberties, there is no prevailing sense in the press or popular culture that EM constitutes a threat to them (or, by implication, to us); it is simply not rigorous or invasive enough. EM's supporters can hardly take heart from this ethical judgment, as it is merely the corollary of EM not being perceived as efficacious. There are, of course, particular exceptions. In the context of racial politics in the United States, Spike Lee does see EM as at least a *symbol* of oppression (he does not explore how controlling it actually is) but other films about ethnic minority youth have either simply disparaged it, or even welcomed it as helpful to rehabilitation. Human interest stories in the Anglo-Welsh press have either welcome EM when it has worked, or derided it when it has not – an ethico-political dimension, a larger strategic possibility such as reducing prison numbers has never entered the frame. This may reflect a journalistic assumption that the civil-rights-of-offenders issue is so obviously settled that it needs no airing – that is, EM is patently less of an infringement of civil liberties than prison, and the inroad into the hitherto private zone of the home is therefore a small price to pay . . .

How might these findings be interpreted? Is there a deeper reason, beyond the internal dynamics of the journalistic, literary, and cinematic fields why EM has signally failed to register as a significant penal innovation in the press and in popular culture? A possible and plausible explanation emerges if the distinguishing features of EM (whether in its actual confining forms or its envisaged tracking forms) are conceptualised as *pinpointing* and *locatability*,[9] and if these are set in the context of contemporary developments in punishment and workplace surveillance. Consider: over the same period in which EM has been deployed, and been hailed and represented by its supporters as a thoroughly *distinctive* innovation in community penalties, the technical capacity for, and cultural desirability of locating individuals (and goods) in general has grown enormously (Bloomfield 2001; Sussex Technology Group 2001). To a very great extent, personal locatability has come to be seen, at least in part, as a useful convenience rather than a wholly unwarranted invasion of privacy. The electronic trails left by consumers, and the traces left by pager and cellphone users, have all made it easier to pinpoint and track people, and increasing numbers of employers expect their workers, outsourced or otherwise, to be accessible and 'on call' in this way. Seen in this light, the mechanism of EM is hardly distinctive, it is only a variant (for convicted offenders) of an experience that, in more muted and diffuse forms, is increasingly widespread in contemporary society . . . Contrary to those who, with Stacey (1996), believe that tracking tagging constitutes an even more intrusive and regulatory measure than home confinement, it may all too easily be *perceived* as being only a little further along a continuum shared with ordinary, mobile, law abiding, *locatable* citizens – and therefore hardly much of a punishment.

Clearly, there are still significant differences between being an offender subject to EM and an ordinary person accessible via a mobile phone to employers, customers, friends and relatives – although the technology which makes both events possible has common roots, and innovations in one sphere have the potential to affect the other. Ordinary citizens nonetheless still have choices about how locatable they make themselves, and to whom. But the choice is by no means absolute or unconstrained, for there is a growing expectation of real-time locatability by employer, employees and among families and friendship networks. Communications technology is expanding the possibilities of *remote intimacy* and as with so many aspects of contemporary surveillance we seem to be experiencing it more as convenience than – as Orwell hoped – as threat. In the absence of deep deliberation on the matter there is no reason to think that this sensibility will do other than intensify . . .

Notes

1 This chapter is an extract from M. Nellis (2003) News media, popular culture and the electronic monitoring of offenders in England and Wales, *Howard Journal of Criminal Justice*, 42: 1–31.

2 In conversation with me, in the mid-1990s, an exasperated senior person in the monitoring industry once credited 'the luddite' Harry Fletcher with single-handedly holding back the development of tagging in England. NAPO had launched its Anti-Electronic Monitoring Campaign in June 1989. The campaign has consisted of data-gathering about the operation of tagging, exhortations to its membership, and the placing of critical accounts in the press.

3 All prisoners eligible for HDC are subject to risk assessment and prison governors responsible for this are known to have been cautious in their judgments. Neither of the two taggees charged with rape had previous convictions for this, or for other sex offences. Further monitoring of HDC by HM Inspectorates of Prisons and Probation (2001) convinced the Home Office of its efficacy, and its further use was encouraged (see also Lilly and Nellis 2001).

4 At least in terms of operational principle, 'belled slave collars' have a real claim to being one precursor of electronic tags. These were collars, with small bells hooped above them, locked around the necks of slaves who persistently sought to escape from their master's plantations (Everett 1978, p. 121). The jangling of the bells made it easy for them to be tracked if they attempted escape again. In the late-1980s, at the time of the first trials of EM, I heard a representative of the Association of Black Probation Officers solemnly oppose it on the grounds that 'Black people have been tagged before'.

5 I may be bowdlerising Bender here, for I recognise that his claim relates as much to the form of the 18th century novel *per se* – the novel as a new artistic institution, with its characteristically refined representation of the interior lives of individuals – rather than to the content of particular texts and stories. But, as his analysis of paintings shows, content as well as form is relevant to the shaping of thoughts and feelings, and to the stimulation of imagination. I recognise too the historical specificity of his claim that 'the institutions of eighteenth century culture were arranged to allow for literary discourse to have causative force' (Bender 1987, p. 6). In the 20th and 21st centuries it needs to be acknowledged that cultural institutions, not least because of their own immense diversity, have 'causative force' in much more complex ways, but Bender's general insight remains and informs certain aspects of this article:

> I consider literature and the visual arts as advanced forms of knowledge, as cognitive instruments that anticipate and contribute to institutional formation. Novels as I describe them are primarily historical and ideological documents; the vehicles not the reflections of social change.
>
> (Bender 1987, p.1)

6   Science fiction, like much genre writing, is inveterately self-referential, and Anthony and Margroff may have been doing no more than developing a permutation of a pre-existing idea. *The Ring*, badly written, badly characterised, set in a poorly imagined mid-21st century (at most), with a ridiculous ending, is not a great sf novel – far from Piers Anthony's best. It was nonetheless prescient in respect of tagging, and several aspects of the 1960s milieu in which it was conceived may have contributed to its depiction of the device. Firstly, prominent debates were taking place on the social and political implications of psychologist B.F. Skinner's behaviourism, some with reference to crime control. Skinner had famously anticipated utopian consequences for his theories in a novel of his own (Skinner 1948), and the more didactic elements of *The Ring* may well have been Anthony's critical rejoinder to that debate. Secondly, the Schwitzgebel (1963) experiments using radio telephony to track delinquents – 'pioneers of what has become known as the "house arrest concept"' (Victorian 1999, p. 150; see also Fox 1987) – took place in this period (and were themselves influenced by behaviourism). Thirdly, there are recognisable similarities between *The Ring* and Anthony Burgess's (1962) far richer and more philosophical near-future novel, *A Clockwork Orange*. In the latter a violent young thug is conditioned into harmlessness by a one-off programme of aversion therapy rather than the wearing of a pain-inflicting tag. (See *The Analogues* (Knight 1952) for a pioneering story in this vein.) Because of the conditioning the central characters in both *A Clockwork Orange* and *The Ring* are both rendered incapable of defending themselves against attack, or using force to rescue someone else from attack. But whereas Burgess decides that it is better to allow evil in order to permit courage, Anthony's protagonist finally accepts that if the computer-imprinted conscience were moderated, the ring is a viable means of shaping good citizens. Quite why such a forgettable novel was republished in 1986 is unclear, unless it was to capitalise on the advent of real EM (as the cover of the paperback implies). Piers Anthony lives in Florida, the state which used tagging the most in the early 1980s, and presumably knew of the development.

7   The interplay of literary and techinical elements in the construction of scientific narratives is beginning to be addressed in social constructivist accounts of science, and there is an interesting history of EM yet to be written from this perspective. Writing about the discovery of the fission of uranium atoms in 1938, Robert Pool (1997) writes that 'scientists [then] didn't have to stop and think what this might mean. *Decades of speculation and prediction had already created an image of a world with nuclear power"* (p. 67, italics added). He quotes a famous physicist, Leo Szilard, as saying of this discovery: ' "all the things which H G Wells had predicted appeared suddenly real to me" ' (Pool 1997, p. 67). In a 1914 novel, H. G. Wells had depicted a utopian society which had harnessed atomic

power, which was in turn partly inspired by the innovative work of British radiochemist, Frederick Soddy, which had appeared several years earlier. More recently, sf novelist William Gibson famously invented 'cyberspace' in *Neuromancer* in 1984 and contributed to the narrative by which the internet has come to be publicly understood. Something like the internet itself had been envisaged in a science fiction novella, *True Names*, in 1981, by a reputable computer scientist at San Diego State University, Vernor Vinge (see Frenkel 2001). Vinge, age 56, typifies those scientists of his generation who claim that reading and, in his case, writing science fiction in his youth influenced his world view and choice of career, and 'he is [now] one of several science fiction writers who have worked with Global Business Network in anticipating future situations and plotting strategies for several major companies' (*New York Times*, 2 August 2001). Criminologists need to understand this milieu – it impinges on 'the commercial corrections complex' (Lilly and Knepper 1992).

8 Tom Stacey (b.1930) is a creative thinker, a polymath, politically Conservative, well outside the network of those conventionally regarded as innovators in criminal justice. An ex-journalist, who dropped out of Oxford without completing his degree, he is now a successful publisher. A brief period of imprisonment whilst working abroad, plus many years as a prison visitor in London convinced him that prison was a destructive experience for many offenders. He had little faith in welfare professions like probation, and believed that stronger forms of control were needed if offenders were to be dealt with in the community. The tag was a product of his imagination, and of a general knowledge about what might have been becoming technically possible, which he decided to check with more scientifically-inclined acquaintances. He has written seven well-received novels – of which *Decline* (Stacey 1991) deals well with the experience of imprisonment – one collection of short stories and three works of non-fiction (see Kendall 1991; Nellis 2001).

9 The implications of new technology for the locatability of individuals are debated in other contexts apart from criminal justice. Mountaineers are apparently divided by the use of mobile phones and satellite navigation systems which may well make the sport safer, reducing risk and saving lives, but which also, by definition, reduce the need for courage and self-reliance in the wilderness. In a paper on 'Modern technology and mountaineering', the Mountaineering Council of Scotland argued that mobile phones conflicted with the core values of mountaineering. Mountain rescue services, needless to say, prefer and encourage their use (*The Daily Telegraph*, 28 October 1995).

References

Aldridge, M. (1994) *Making Social Work News*. London: Routledge.

Amis, K. (1960) *New Maps of Hell*. London: Victor Gollancz. (New English Library Edition 1969).

Anthony, P. and Margroff, R. E. (1968/1986) *The Ring*. New York: Tom Doherty Associates.

Ball, R. A. and Lilly, J. R. (1988) Home incarceration with electronic monitoring, in J.E. Scott and T. Hirschi (eds) *Controversial Issues in Crime and Justice*. London: Sage.

Bender, J. (1987) *Imagining the Penitentiary: Fiction and the Architecture of Mind in Eighteenth Century England*. Chicago: University of Chicago Press.

Bloomfield, B. (2001) In the right place at the right time: electronic tagging and problems of social order/disorder, *The Sociological Review*, 49(2): 174–201.

Burgess, A. (1962) *A Clockwork Orange*. Harmondsworth: Penguin.

Butler, D. and Kavanagh, D. (2002) *The British General Election of 2001*. London: Palgrave.

Cheever, J. (1977) *Falconer*. London: Jonathan Cape.

Clute, J. and Nichols, P. (1992) *The Encyclopaedia of Science Fiction*. London. Orbit.

Department of Trade and Industry Foresight Crime Prevention Panel (2000) *Just Around the Corner: A Consultation Document*. London: DTI.

Disch, T. M. (1998) *The Dreams our Stuff is Made of: How Science Fiction Conquered the World*. New York: Simon and Schuster.

Everett, S. (1978) *The Slaves: An Illustrated History of a Monstrous Evil*. New York: G. P. Putnam's Sons.

Fekete, J. (2001) Doing the time warp again: science fiction as adversarial culture, *Science Fiction Studies*, 28(1): 77–96.

Fletcher, H. (1997) Electronic tagging: purpose, reliability and implications for penal policy, *NAPO News*, May, 89.

Fox, R. G. (1987) Dr Schwitzgebel's machine revisited: electronic monitoring of offenders, *Australian and New Zealand Journal of Criminology*, 20: 131–47.

Frenkel, J. (Ed.) (2001) *True Names and The Opening of the Cyberspace Frontier*. South Yarra: Tor Books.

Gibson, W. (1984) *Neuromancer*. London: Vintage.

Kendall, E. (1991) Interview with Tom Stacey, *The Observer Magazine*, 12 March, 64.

Knight, D. (1952/1976) *The Analogues*, in *The Best of Damon Knight*. New York: Nelson Doubleday.

Leonard, E. (1992) *Maximum Bob*. Harmondsworth: Penguin.

Lilly, J. R. (1990) Tagging reviewed, *Howard Journal*, 29: 229–45.

Lilly, J. R. and Ball, R. A. (1993) Selling justice: will electronic monitoring last? *Northern Kentucky Law Review*, 20(2): 505–30.

Lilly, J. R. and Knepper, P. (1992) An international perspective on the privatisation of corrections, *Howard Journal*, 31: 174–91.

Lilly, J. R. and Nellis, M. (2001) Home detention curfew and the future of electronic monitoring, *Prison Service Journal*: 135: 59–69.

Lyon, D. (2000) *Surveillance Society: Monitoring Everyday Life*. London: Sage.

Mair, G. (2001) Technology and the future of community penalties, in A. E. Bottoms, L. Gelsthorpe and S. Rex (eds) *Community Penalties: Change and Challenges*. Cullompton, Devon: Willan.

Marrin, M. (2002) Releasing prisoners early is a crime waiting to happen, *The Sunday Times*, 24 March.

Marx, G. (1995) Electric eye in the sky: some reflections on the new surveillance and popular culture, in J. Ferrel and C. R. Saunders (eds) *Cultural Criminology*. Boston: Northern University Press (reprinted in: D. Lyon and E. Zureik (eds) *Computers, Surveillance and Privacy*. London: University of Minnesota Press).

McCormick, K. R. E. (1994) Prisoners of their own device: computer applications in the Canadian correctional system, in K. R. E. McCormick (ed.) *Carceral Contexts: Readings in Control*. Toronto: Canadian Scholars' Press Inc.

McCulloch, C. (1997) Electronic monitoring: a task for probation officers? *Vista*, May, pp. 12–19.

Mellor, D. (2002) Stop conning us with crime crackdowns, *The People*, 27 February.

Nellis, M. (2001) Interview with Tom Stacey, *Prison Service Journal*, 135: 76–9.

Orwell, G. (1948) *Nineteen Eighty-Four*. London: Secker and Warburg.

Pease, K. (1978) Prediction, British Psychological Society Division of Criminological and Legal Psychology *Newsletter*, August, pp. 11–14.

Pohl, F. and Williamson, J. (1964) *The Reefs of Space*. Harmondsworth: Penguin.

Pool, R. (1997) *Beyond Engineering: How Society Shapes Technology*. Oxford: Oxford University Press.

Renzema, M. (1998) GPS: is now the time to adopt? *Journal of Offender Monitoring*, Spring, 5.

Reynolds, J. and McCallum, J. (2001) *Bad Girls: The Inside Story*. London: HarperCollins.

Rosen, J. (2000) *The Unwanted Gaze: The Destruction of Privacy in America*. New York: Vintage Books.

Schwitzgebel, R. R. (1963) Delinquents with tape recorders, *New Society*, 31 January, 18: 11–13.

Skinner, B. G. (1948) *Walden Two*. New York: Macmillan.

Stacey, T. (1996) Innovations in technology, in K. Schultz (ed.) *Electronic Monitoring and Corrections: The Policy, the Operation, the Research*. Vancouver: Simon Fraser University.

Sussex Technology Group (2001) In the company of strangers: mobile phones and the conception of space, in S. R. Munt (ed.) *Technospaces: Inside the New Media*. London: Continuum.

Taylor, B. (1997) Criminal suits: style and surveillance, strategy and tactics in Elmore Leonard, in P. Messent (ed.) *Criminal Proceedings: The Contemporary American Crime Novel*. London: Pluto Press.

Taylor, Nelson, Sofres and Harris (1999) *Electronic Tagging of Offenders – A Survey of Public Awareness and Attitudes: Executive Summary*. Manchester: Harris Research.

Victorian, A. (1999) *Mind Controllers*. London: Satin Publications.

Welsh, I. (1999) *Filth*. London: Vintage.

Whitfield, D. (2001) *The Magic Bracelet: Technology and Offender Supervision*. Winchester: Waterside Press.

Wykes, M. (2001) *News, Crime and Culture*. London: Pluto Press.

19

Public opinion surveys and the formation of privacy policy[1]
by Oscar H. Gandy, Jr.

. . . Although the events of September 11, 2001, have brought about a dramatic shift in public sentiment regarding the relative importance of personal privacy as it relates to concerns about security (Harris Poll, 2002), there is little doubt that privacy remains an issue of primary importance to the American public (Wessel, 2002). The extent to which the public will be able to enjoy the privacy rights that they have come to expect will be determined in part by the new rules that will be put in place at the national and state levels of government. The reasonableness of a citizen's expectation of privacy will be assessed against the restrictions established by the USA PATRIOT Act (2001) as well as by a wide assortment of bills that are introduced during coming sessions of Congress (Electronic Privacy Information Center, 2002). Although many aspects of personal privacy have been, or will be, affected by legislative action, this [chapter] is concerned primarily with expectations regarding the privacy of personal information.

Informational privacy policy is concerned with rules governing the access, collection, use and, most importantly, the exchange of information about persons. Although there is an active movement to compress a broad range of privacy concerns under a narrow property regime, the future of this legislative approach is uncertain (Cohen, 2000). It is uncertain, in part, because of the ways in which individuals have historically resisted the exercise of power over information that has not been freely granted (Bartlett, 1989; Davies, 1999).

It is also uncertain because it is impossible to predict the outcomes of debates about rules and regulations that are taking place within a variety of organizations and institutions of business and government (Etzioni, 1999). Information about the attitudes and opinions of 'ordinary Americans' is a critical component of these debates, and assessments of the nature and intensity of public opinion have been especially relevant in the formation of policies that govern the commercial use of personal information (Regan, 1995).

Estimates of the character of public opinion are increasingly derived from professionally administered surveys or polls (Herbst, 1993). Opinion polls influence policy formation by what they measure and report, as well as by what they ignore (Ginsberg, 1986). The fact that a particular question is asked may add legitimacy to a policy option that might otherwise not be considered. Questions asked in opinion surveys may, for example, help to establish the legitimacy of a policy framework or orientation, such as one that emphasizes the importance of 'balancing' individual privacy against collective or institutional interests in using personal information (Etzioni, 1999) . . .

Scholars of public opinion often remind us that the assessment of opinion is a formidable task. Opinions may appear to differ, or to have changed, because of subtle differences in the ways in which problems and options are framed (Page & Shapiro, 1992; Zaller, 1992). Concerns related to framing are especially problematic in the realm of privacy policy because of the variety of ways in which privacy interests have been defined (Davies, 1997; Nissenbaum, 1998). In addition to these and other problems of measurement, policy scholars recognize also that there are strategic interests to be served by representing public opinion in particular ways at critical moments in the policy process. Gandy (1982) characterizes the supply of policy-related information by interested parties as an information subsidy.

Like other economic subsidies, an information subsidy reduces the cost of acquiring or consuming policy-relevant information (Gandy, 1982). By reducing the cost of acquisition, the subsidy giver expects to increase the probability that the target of the subsidy will consume more of the preferred information. Thus, it is likely that in the context of a legislative debate about privacy policy, a sponsor or supporter of a bill that would establish a minimal requirement of 'notice and choice' would provide evidence of the public's willingness to accept such protections. That evidence might be in the form of responses to questions asked in a recent national survey. The survey data would be considered to be an 'indirect information subsidy' because its 'source' is assumed to be uninterested and authoritative (Gandy, 1982, pp. 80–86). As with the other sorts of strategic information that policy actors seek to introduce into a policy debate, it is especially important for estimates of public opinion to be perceived by targets of information subsidies as being accurate and unbiased, or objective (Kollman, 1998).

Although policy actors can deliver these information subsidies through a variety of direct and indirect means, including conferences, newspaper editorials, and special events (Gandy, 1982), the presentation of evidence from opinion surveys within congressional hearings actually provides an opportunity for policy-makers to challenge, or raise questions 'on the record' about, the data and their interpretation. Testimony within congressional hearings also provides an opportunity for policy advocates to make reference to, and offer challenges or support for, arguments made by others who have given testimony. Because of the importance of public testimony to the development of privacy policy at the federal level (Kollman, 1998), this [chapter] will focus primarily on the use of public opinion data in congressional hearings on privacy-related legislation.

Background: public opinion and public policy

It is a basic tenet of democratic theory that government is responsive to the public will, and that measured public opinion is increasingly used as an index of the public's interest in and support for particular policy options (Burstein, 1998; Herbst, 1993;

Monroe, 1998). A realistic, rather than cynical, perspective on the amount of attention that politicians pay to public opinion assumes that legislators take due note of the
ways in which the policies they support may affect the willingness of constituents to
vote for them in the next election (Jacobs, Lawrence, Shapiro, & Smith, 1998). The
relationship between constituent opinion and the policies supported by legislators is
likely to be closer at the state than at the federal level, but the underlying concern
about being, or appearing to be, responsive to public sentiment is still felt at the
national level (Sharp, 1999).

In some cases, legislators appear to be responding to their best sense of the public
mood, or the 'broad climate of opinion' rather than detailed estimates of opposition
or support for particular policy options (Sharp, 1999, p. 237; Page, 1999). Indeed,
there are examples within the literature that suggest that members of Congress will
respond to indirect assessments of the public will as reported in the press, even
though the mood suggested by the media was at odds with formally measured opinion
(Cook, 1998).

Public opinion surveys, or polls as they are often called, are used within the policy
process in other ways. Frequently, legislators and their staffs make use of polls for
guidance in their own efforts to bring opinion into line with the policies they intend to
support. Critical observers suggest that policymakers have 'primarily used public
opinion information to craft their arguments, to justify their positions, and otherwise
to shape public thinking' (Jacobs et al., 1998, pp. 27–28) . . .

Policy entrepreneurs, issue advocates, and the press

Much of what policy makers know and understand about public orientations toward
privacy will have been shaped to a large extent by what the media report about that
opinion. This outcome reflects the increasing role that the media have come to play in
making the results of these polls public. It also reflects a more active role being played
by media organizations as the source, or sponsor, of those polls (Cook, 1998; Ladd &
Benson, 1992).

What journalists report about a policy debate is often shaped by their own policy
preferences, as well as by the preferences of the sources of the information upon
which they depend (Gandy, 1982, 1992; Leff, Protess, & Brooks, 1986). Policy entrepreneurs and others who advocate a particular policy response to a social problem or
opportunity regularly attempt to use the press to mobilize and shape public opinion.
Businesses that depend upon unfettered access to personal and transaction-generated
information will be especially concerned to represent the public as unconcerned
about, or supportive of, businesses having that access (Gandy, 1993). They will use
estimates of public opinion to help convince policy makers of the wisdom of supporting the policy options that they prefer (Herbst, 1993). As a result, skillful public
relations often explains the disparity between what the public actually believes and the
character of their beliefs as they are represented in the press (King & Schudson,
1995).

Important policy change frequently occurs during periods in which the attention
of the public has been drawn to an issue in response to a critical event that generates
expanded media coverage that activates and amplifies public concern (Kasperson &

Kasperson, 1996; Sharp, 1999). The Video Privacy Protection Act of 1988 was introduced and passed in record time in part because of the publicity generated by the publication of the videotape rentals of Supreme Court nominee Robert Bork (Regan, 1995). The even quicker passage of the USA PATRIOT Act of 2001, which threatened rather than protected personal privacy, was undoubtedly facilitated by media attention to the threat of terrorism (King, 2001).

In each of these cases, there is evidence to suggest that policy advocates helped to shape the ways in which the interests of the public were characterized in the press, and in the legislative debates. In the case of the Video Privacy Protection Act, the Direct Marketing Association (DMA) was actively involved in an attempt to legitimize the controlled use of consumer information for marketing purposes. They were ultimately successful in transforming key features of the legislation (Gandy, 1993).

In the case of the USA PATRIOT Act, high technology firms rushed to promote the use of their privacy-invasive systems that they framed as a solution to the public's concerns about safety (Streitfeld & Piller, 2002). On September 24, 2001, The Visionics Corporation, one of the emerging leaders in the development of facial recognition technology, issued a widely distributed special report with an extremely lofty title: 'Protecting Civilization From the Faces of Terror' (Visionics, 2001). After describing the way their system might be implemented in order to prevent terrorists from engaging in international travel, the Visionics report claimed that 'there is no doubt that an identification based security infrastructure using biometrics raises privacy concerns.' Those concerns were discounted later in the report's conclusion: 'we should nevertheless emphasize that the threat to privacy is theoretical while that of terrorism is unfortunately very real' (Visionics, 2001, pp. 6–8).

On the same day, the legislative counsel of the American Civil Liberties Union (ACLU) offered testimony before the House Judiciary Committee on what was at that time The Anti-Terrorism Act of 2001 (King, 2001). Much of the ACLU testimony was concerned with sections of the proposed bill that would weaken a citizen's right to privacy. While urging 'calm deliberation,' the ACLU noted, 'Congress is under great pressure to adopt this legislation lest it be perceived as not doing all that it can to help the war against terrorism' (King, 2001, p. 5). Perhaps because the mood of the majority was actually hostile and seeking retribution if not revenge, the ACLU's counsel sought to represent the voice of reason within the public by means of a sample of one: 'I was talking to someone on the phone the other day about the fear in our country in the aftermath of the attack. He said, "I do not fear what will happen to us as much as I fear what we will become"' (King, 2001, p. 5). Following on from that reflection, the ACLU appealed to Congress to rely upon the democratic public sphere and approach this problem in a serious and deliberative way that would involve 'a public hearing process and full public discussion and debate' (King, 2001, p. 5).

Policy scholars have noted that media attention sometimes leads, and sometimes follows, an increase in attention being paid to particular issues within the Congress (Baumgartner & Jones, 1993). Clearly, the relationship is far too complex to suggest that the causal direction is always from Congress to the press, or from the press to Congress, or from advocates or the public at large. The literature does suggest, however, that policy advocates are likely to be involved in shaping each of these causal paths.

The corporate interest in public opinion regarding privacy

Other than elected officials and bureaucrats, representatives of private corporations are among the most important sources of influence within the policy environment (Baumgartner & Jones, 1993). Etzioni (1988) suggests that corporations and other policy actors develop and use 'interventionist power' in an effort to influence government decisions. Indeed, he suggests that for the private firm, the returns on investments in influencing government are often higher than returns on investments in product development. Information is a critical resource in the production of influence over government decisions.

There are a number of industries whose survival depends upon the capture, storage, transmission, and high-speed processing of information about individuals. These industries are at the core of what we define as an information economy (Preston, 2001). In the past 25 years, leaders in these industries (employment, credit, insurance, direct marketing, and telecommunications) have been especially concerned about the sorts of economic and competitive costs that federal privacy regulations seemed likely to impose on their enterprises (Smith, 1994). Historically, members of information intensive industries have tended to be reactive, rather than pro-active, with regard to privacy policy. As Smith (1994) suggests, unless there is some competitive advantage to be gained from stepping out ahead of the pack, businesses tend to just drift along until some crisis demands a response. Nevertheless, like their counterparts in other sectors of the economy, organizations in the information intensive industries have invested in the management of privacy policy.

In this area, as in others, specialists within the corporation have been assigned the responsibility for 'issues management' (Gaunt & Ollenburger, 1995; Renfro, 1993). For many corporations, issues management usually means 'being able to anticipate issues early enough in the development process and respond quickly and effectively to forestall their movement up the public agenda and graduation into major public issues' (Renfro, 1993, p. 37). Demonstrating the power of corporate influence is quite difficult, however, because in many cases, corporations will contract with independent agencies and consultants to deliver strategic information subsidies (Gandy, 1982). Sometimes these relationships are kept private and confidential, and in other cases the relationship is publicized because of the public relations benefits it provides. It seems likely that the credibility of Alan Westin as a noted privacy scholar justified the prominent linkage of his name with a series of corporate sponsored privacy surveys. Through their partnership with Westin, Equifax, one of the major players in the credit reporting industry, became the most highly visible source of privacy-related opinion data in the 1990s.

In the early 1980s, about the same time that public attention was being focused on 'Big Brother' and the threat to civil liberties represented by government databases, Equifax had begun to expand the scope of its privacy-intensive information business. Equifax's product managers actively sought additional markets for its information about consumers (Gandy, 1993). In 1988, there was a dramatic expansion in the scope of Equifax's involvement in the privacy-intensive sector of the information services market. Equifax created a new division, the Marketing Services Sector, and acquired 14 companies that would further develop its capacity to provide sophisticated profiling services (Equifax, 1989). Also, 1988 was the year in which Equifax hired Westin as a consultant on privacy matters (Smith, 2000).

Although the corporation modified some of its information practices and products in response to Westin's advice, the company also enjoyed the less tangible benefits of 'having a noted "privacy expert" vouch for its good faith' (Smith, 2000, p. 322). Smith notes that Westin was frequently quoted in the newspapers as indicating that the credit-reporting industry was making improvements in its handling of personal information, but that these articles rarely identified Westin as being 'on the payroll of one of the bureaus' (p. 322) . . .

The use of public opinion surveys in hearings on privacy legislation

There are remarkably few studies of the ways in which public opinion surveys have been used strategically by interest groups in an attempt to shape the outcome of a legislative debate (Cook, Barabas, & Page, 2002; Kollman, 1998). None have focused specifically on privacy policy. Traugott (2000) examined the references to public opinion surveys in federal government deliberations during four months in 1997. He was concerned primarily with the quality of the data that were being introduced into legislative debates, and he sought to characterize the actors most likely to make such references. Although Traugott's analysis included statements about public opinion made by officials on the floor of the House or Senate, he observed that more than half of the references to public opinion polls came from congressional testimony. Traugott's observation reinforces the importance of such testimony as an entry point into the policy process. It will be important at some stage to trace the path that survey data make from sponsors, through congressional testimony, to references made on the floor of the House and Senate as the merits of a bill are explored in open debate. This project begins such an analysis at the level of congressional testimony.

I examined hearings for each of the key privacy bills identified in Regan's (1995) analytical history of privacy legislation for references to public opinion surveys. In addition, I examined published reports from 70 hearings that were included in the legislative history of all privacy-related bills that were passed between 1974 and 1999. Only testimony, or letters submitted for the record, which made explicit reference to a survey or poll were selected in order to limit the analysis to formal and broadly available assessments of public opinion. Of course, as Cook, Barabas, and Page (2002) have observed, very few of the references by policy makers to public opinion actually cite specific surveys or facts. Formal statements and the oral testimony of a single witness in a hearing were treated as a single contribution. As a result of this quite restrictive screen, only 64 contributions were retained for analysis.

Explicit references to public opinion surveys or polls in privacy-related hearings were not evenly distributed across the period examined for this study. Many years had no references at all; several had four or fewer. The years in which references to public opinion polls were most frequent were 1990 ($n = 6$), 1991 ($n = 18$), and 1999 ($n = 6$). The distribution of references reflects the substantial reliance of those giving testimony on public opinion polls financed by corporate sponsors.

Over the years, the surveys produced by Louis Harris & Associates for sponsors within the privacy sensitive industries were cited most frequently (44% of the contributions mentioned Harris polls). The surveys administered by Harris for Equifax were identified by name most often (23% of contributions examined). There were 12 references to Westin's role either as an advisor to Equifax or Harris, as an expert on privacy, or as the author of an analysis of opinion data (18.8% of cases). There was the same number of contributions ($n = 21$) from representatives of business as there was from representatives of consumer groups. However, witnesses from consumer organizations ($n = 10$) were more likely than business representatives ($n = 7$) to make reference to or cite data from Harris surveys in their testimony. However, five business representatives mentioned Westin specifically, but only one consumer representative mentioned his name in their testimony. I interpret this as an indication of a corporate attempt to capture the benefits of an association with an authoritative source that agreed with their policy preferences.

There were occasional references made to polls administered by news organizations, such as Time/CNN. There were a small number of references to polls administered or commissioned by the organization making testimony, such as the American Association for Retired Persons (AARP). Surveys of special populations, such as persons who had recently completed a polygraph examination, were also relatively rare (5.3%). Only two academic researchers presented the results of their own independent analyses of privacy-related public opinion.

Strategic representations of public opinion

Witnesses include references to specific assessments of public opinion because of the support those assessments lend to the arguments they hope to make in support of, or in opposition to, particular aspects of the privacy policies under discussion. Space limitations make it impossible to do more than provide a few examples of these representations. Three primary themes emerged in the testimony presented between 1970 and 1999: (a) the public is concerned, (b) there is more than one public, and (c) the majority of the public is reasonable. In addition to these themes, a small number of examples focused on specific policy options . . .

The public is concerned

Politicians respond to expressions of anxiety and fear among their constituents. That fear need not have an objective basis in fact, and those most concerned about a potential threat need not be those at the greatest risk (Bennett & Raab, 1998). The periodic emergence of threats to privacy on the policy agenda suggests that a substantial number of policy actors believe that representations of public anxiety have some strategic potential. As a result, they periodically seek novel ways of presenting these fundamental concerns (Hilgartner & Bosk, 1988).

Given the strategic nature of this testimony it is not surprising that the presentation of items from surveys was highly selective. Most witnesses limited their references to one or two questions from the polls they cited, and the items used most frequently were those that indicated the level of public concern or anxiety. Of the 64 witnesses whose testimony was reviewed for this study, nearly half (47%) made reference to the public's concern about privacy.

John Baker, Senior Vice President of Equifax, indicated that the general public was concerned about threats to privacy. He was unequivocal: '[T]he concerns about privacy are real. They are widespread' (*Amendments*, 1990, p. 52). Hubert Humphrey, III, the Attorney General of Minnesota, wrote to Esteban Torres, Chairman of the Subcommittee on Consumer Affairs, to offer his thoughts on proposed amendments to the Fair Credit Reporting Act. Humphrey cited the Equifax report (Equifax, 1990) in expressing his concern about the 'disturbing rise in the American public's concern that personal privacy is threatened' (*Fair Credit Reporting Act*, 1991b, p. 662).

Very little was made of the fact that, despite the apparent increase in the share of the public that is concerned about threats to privacy, there was no associated rise in reports of personal experience with such threats. The fact that the public knows so little about the ways in which personal information is used, and has little way of knowing that they have been victimized by its use, is rarely presented for consideration by policy makers (Sovern, 1999). In part, this may reflect the fact that questions that would emphasize this aspect of public concern have rarely been included in opinion surveys (Gandy, 1993).

There is more than one 'public'

In 1991, Westin introduced a three-group classification of privacy orientations (Equifax, 1991). He created an index in which respondents who had agreed with three or four privacy concerns were labeled 'high'; 'moderates' had agreed with two concerns; those who agreed with one or no privacy concerns were assigned to the 'low' concern group. Westin named these groups, respectively, 'the privacy fundamentalists,' 'the pragmatic majority,' and 'the unconcerned.' The pragmatic majority (57% of the American public in 1991) was then framed as the 'reasonable consumer' whose interests ought not be subordinated to the demands of the more radical fundamentalists (25% of the American public in 1991). Although Westin provided this and other more finely textured analyses of public opinion in his testimony, and in the reports published by the corporate sponsors of the surveys, few others who gave testimony referred explicitly to a tripartite, or any other, segmentation of the public. Depending upon the perspective they wished to convey, witnesses tended to talk about some sizeable majority as though it was a stable, coherent segment. Consumer advocates tended to talk about a concerned public. Business representatives talked about a reasonable public. These 'publics' were largely the product of their activation within the question frame, in that the ways in which the questions were posed helped to determine the character of the average response (Zaller, 1992).

The public is reasonable

Mary Culnan, a business school professor, relied upon her own research and several Harris surveys to make it clear that the public she envisioned would not object to businesses gathering and sharing their personal information as long as the information is actually 'relevant' or for 'compatible' purposes (*Financial Privacy*, 1999a, p. 148). Survey data included in her testimony reported the percentage of the public that felt that it was generally all right for corporations to use public record information if its use was appropriate. Culnan noted that 77% of respondents felt that it would be acceptable for automobile insurance companies to check accident and driving records of applicants, but that only 32% felt that it would be all right to use public record information for marketing purposes (*Financial Privacy*, 1999a). The general point of her testimony was that the reasonable consumer demands no more than what most people would recognize as fair information practices.

Specific policy options

Several Harris surveys provided data that witnesses interpreted as being in support of the right of consumers to 'opt-out' of relationships in which businesses would use personal information for marketing. Opting-out would require an affirmative act, such as checking a box on a form, which would supposedly limit secondary use of transaction-generated information. This was the version of 'consumer choice' that the industry seemed to prefer. 'Opt-in,' the policy supported by consumer activists, would require corporations to obtain explicit permission from individuals before personally identifiable information could be shared with third parties. Equifax surveys were used most often to demonstrate support for the corporate version of consumer choice.

In her testimony, Culnan (*Fair Credit*, 1991a) referred to the 1990 Equifax report in suggesting that the public 'did not object to the use of personal data for targeted marketing' if there were limits on the sharing of financial information, and if they had the opportunity to 'opt-out' of marketing lists entirely (p. 223). It is important to note, however, that none of the surveys cited in congressional testimony inquired specifically about whether the public preferred that 'opt-in' would be the default. Moreover, there was no mention of any surveys in which consumers were asked to express their preferences for one option over the other.

Despite the absence of *specific* survey items, Marc Rotenberg (*Financial Privacy*, 1999b), of the Electronic Privacy Information Center (EPIC), testified that there 'is plenty of data and plenty of polling information that shows that the American public, *if asked* [emphasis added], would much prefer an opt-in regime to an opt-out regime, and these questions have been asked by Time, CNN, by Lou Harris and other organizations' (p. 51).

The fact that none of the privacy surveys funded by Equifax explicitly asked consumers whether they preferred opt-in over opt-out as the policy default underscores the importance of being able to determine just which way policy-related questions are ultimately framed. The importance of question framing and interpretation was exemplified especially well in 1991. When the 1990 Equifax survey was first administered, respondents had been asked whether the use of consumer information by direct marketers was acceptable. Seventy-six percent of the public said that it was not. However, a follow-up survey was completed before the report was published. This reframed question made it possible for business representatives to report that when presented with a more 'fair and balanced' framing of the question, 67% of the public found direct marketing practices 'acceptable' (Equifax, 1990, pp. 70–73).

In an attempt to clarify the apparent confusion that resulted from the publication of these conflicting assessments of the public's views, Baker, Equifax's representative, noted that 'it is true . . . that there was a negative response in our survey last year to a question about marketing uses of information. When the marketing uses were not defined in the question and when the question ended with the statement, "and they do this without your permission," the statistic is correct of people saying they disapprove of the process. But two-thirds of the public approved the use of information to help companies advertise new services and market credit products when the process is explained to them' (*Amendments*, 1990, p. 106).

What Baker was suggesting, and what corporate strategy sought to establish as fact, was that the great majority of the public was reasonable, and that all they required was the 'right' information in order to choose. As a result, there would be no need for government to impose any additional requirements or constraints beyond the opportunity to 'opt-out' that the industry would reluctantly provide.

Summary and conclusions

Despite uncertainty about the power of public opinion, policy advocates continue to introduce strategic representations of public opinion into the policy process. This analysis suggests that private corporations are the primacy sponsors of this public opinion data. The use of reputable survey firms and respected academic advisors seems to have blunted the charge of self-serving bias in the framing of questions. At the same time, it seems clear that these surveys and their authors have played an instrumental role in 'steering' the policy debate toward a market-oriented standard of pragmatic self-regulation (Raab, 1999).

It seems likely, also, that, in the case of public policies that have the effect of defining consumer choice, public opinion surveys have been used to establish the legitimacy of a common industry practice after the fact. For example, the public was not invited to speak on the privacy policy options that they preferred until long after the policy actors involved in the management of the Video Privacy Protection Act of 1988 had succeeded in establishing 'opt-out' as the policy default in this class of transactions (Gandy, 1993).

Whether or not public opinion polls become a more *visible* resource for the management of personal information, as would be reflected in their citation in congressional floor debates, there is little doubt that the use of public opinion polls by policy entrepreneurs and activists will continue. The fact that policy scholars know so little about the ways in which interest groups help to shape government policy in general (Baumgartner & Leech, 1998) means that an even greater effort will have to be made to understand the ways in which these groups have been able to use a specific resource like public opinion data in the formation of privacy policy (Traugott, 2000). An important part of that effort should be directed toward understanding the process through which particular questions and policy perspectives come to be included in or excluded from surveys.

Note

1   This chapter is an extract from O.H. Gandy, Jr. (2003) Public opinion surveys and the formation of privacy policy, *Journal of Social Issues*, 59(2): 283–99.

References

Amendments to the Fair Credit Reporting Act: Hearing before the Subcommittee on Consumer Affairs and Coinage of the Committee on Banking, Finance and Urban Affairs, House of Representatives, 101st Cong., 2d Sess., 52 (1990; testimony of John Baker).

Bartlett, R. (1989) *Economics and Power: An Inquiry into Human Relations and Markets*. New York: Cambridge University Press.

Baumgartner, F. and Jones, B. (1993) *Agendas and Instability in American Politics*. Chicago: University of Chicago Press.

Baumgartner, F. and Leech, B. (1998) *Basic Interests: The Importance of Groups in Politics and Political Science*. Princeton, NJ: Princeton University Press.

Bennett, C. and Raab, C. (1998) The distribution of privacy risks: who needs protection? *The Information Society*, 14: 263–74.

Burstein, P. (1998) Bringing the public back in: Should sociologists consider the impact of public opinion on public policy? *Social Forces*, 77(1): 27–62.

Cohen, J. (2000) Examined lives: informational privacy and the subject as object, *Stanford Law Review*, 52(5): 1373–438.

Cook, T. (1998) *Governing with the News: The News Media as a Political Institution*. Chicago: University of Chicago Press.

Cook, F., Barabas, J. and Page, B. (2002) Invoking public opinion: policy elites and Social Security, *Public Opinion Quarterly*, 66(2): 235–64.

Davies, S. (1997) Re-engineering the right to privacy: how privacy has been transformed from a right to a commodity, in P. Agre and M. Rotenberg (eds) *Technology and Privacy: The New Landscape*. Cambridge, MA: MIT Press, pp. 143–65.

Davies, S. (1999) Spanners in the works: how the privacy movement is adapting to the challenge of Big Brother, in C. Bennett and R. Grant (eds) *Visions of Privacy: Policy Choices for the Digital Age*. Toronto, Ontario, Canada: University of Toronto Press, pp. 244–61.

Electronic Privacy Information Center (2002) *EPIC Bill Track. Tracking Privacy, Speech, and Cyber-liberties Bills in the 107th Congress*. Available at: http://www.epic.org/ privacy/ bill.track.html (accessed 28 February 2003).

Equifax, Inc. (1989) *1984 Annual Report*. Atlanta, GA: Equifax, Inc.

Equifax, Inc. (1990) *The Equifax Report on Consumers in the Information Age*. Atlanta: Equifax, Inc.

Equifax, Inc. (1991) *Harris-Equifax Consumer Privacy Survey 1991*. Atlanta: Equifax, Inc.

Etzioni, A. (1988) *The Moral Dimension*. New York: The Free Press.

Etzioni, A. (1999) *The Limits of Privacy*. New York: Basic Books.

Fair Credit Reporting Act: Hearing before the Subcommittee on Consumer Affairs and Coinage of the Committee on Banking, Finance, and Urban Affairs, House of Representatives, 102nd Cong., 1st Sess., 214 (1991a; testimony of Mary Culnan).

Fair Credit Reporting Act: Hearing before the Subcommittee on Consumer Affairs and Coinage of the Committee on Banking, Finance and Urban Affairs, House of Representatives, 102nd Cong., 1st Sess., 661 (1991b; letter from Hubert Humphrey).

Financial Privacy: Hearing before the Subcommittee on Financial Institutions and Consumer Credit of the Committee on Banking and Financial Services, House of Representatives, 106th Cong., 1st Sess., 16 (1999a; testimony of Mary Culnan).

Financial Privacy: Hearing before the Subcommittee on Financial Institutions and Consumer Credit of the Committee on Banking and Financial Services, House of Representatives, 106th Cong., 1st Sess., 51 (1999b; testimony of Marc Rotenberg).

Gandy, O. H., Jr. (1982) *Beyond Agenda Setting: Information Subsidies and Public Policy*. Norwood, NJ: Ablex.

Gandy, O. H., Jr. (1992) Public relations and public policy: the structuration of dominance in the information age, in E. Toth and R. Heath (eds) *Rhetorical and Critical Approaches to Public Relations*. Hillsdale, NJ: Erlbaum, pp. 131–63.

Gandy, O. H., Jr. (1993) *The Panoptic Sort: A Political Economy of Personal Information*. Boulder, CO: Westview.

Gaunt, P. and Ollenburger, J. (1995) Issues management revisited: a tool that deserves another look, *Public Relations Review*, 21(3): 199–210.

Ginsberg, B. (1986) *The Captive Public: How Mass Opinion Promotes State Power*. New York: Basic Books.

Harris Poll: Support is still strong for increased surveillance powers (2002, March 27). *The Wall Street Journal Online*. Available at: http://online.wsj.com/article/ 0,,SB1017770954712628960.djm,00.html (accessed 28 March 2002).

Herbst, S. (1993) *Numbered Voices: How Opinion Polling Has Shaped American Politics*. Chicago: University of Chicago Press.

Hilgartner, S. and Bosk, C. (1988) The rise and fall of social problems: a public arenas model, *American Journal of Sociology*, 94(1): 53–78.

Jacobs, L., Lawrence, E., Shapiro, R. and Smith, S. (1998) Congressional leadership of public opinion, *Political Science Quarterly*, 113(1): 21–42.

Kasperson, R. E. and Kasperson, J. (1996) The social amplification and attenuation of risk, *The Annals of the American Academy of Political and Social Science*, 545: 95–106.

King, R. (2001) *Statement of Rachel King on Anti-Terrorism Act of 2001 before the House Judiciary Committee*. Available at: http://www.aclu.org/NationalSecurity/National Security-.cfm?ID=9139&c=111 (accessed 28 February 2003).

King, E. and Schudson, M. (1995) The press and the illusion of public opinion: the strange case of Ronald Reagan's 'popularity', in T. Glasser and C. T. Salmon (eds) *Public Opinion and the Communication of Consent*. New York: Guilford, pp. 132–55.

Kollman, K. (1998) Outside lobbying, in *Public Opinion and Interest Group Strategies*. Princeton: Princeton University Press.

Ladd, E. and Benson, J. (1992) The growth of news polls in American politics, in T. Mann and G. Orren (eds) *Media Polls in American Politics*. Washington, DC: The Brookings Institution, pp. 19–31.

Leff, D., Protess, D. and Brooks, S. (1986) Crusading journalism: changing public attitudes and policy-making agendas, *Public Opinion Quarterly*, 50(3): 300–15.

Monroe, A. (1998) Public opinion and public policy, 1980–1993, *Public Opinion Quarterly*, 62: 6–28.

Nissenbaum H. (1998). Protecting privacy in an information age: the problem of privacy in public, *Law and Philosophy*, 17: 559–96.

Page, B. (1999) How public opinion affects reform, in S. Burke, E. Kingson and W. Reinhardt (eds) *Social Security and Medicare: Individual vs. Collective Risks and Responsibility*. Washington, DC: National Academy of Social Insurance, pp. 183–207.

Page, B. and Shapiro, R. (1992) *The Rational Public: Fifty Years of Trends in Americans' Policy Preferences*. Chicago: University of Chicago Press.

Preston, P. (2001) *Reshaping Communications*. London: Sage.

Raab, C. (1999) From balancing to steering: new directions for data protection, in C. Bennett and R. Grant (eds) *Visions of Privacy: Policy Choices for the Digital Age*. Toronto, Ontario, Canada: University of Toronto Press, pp. 68–93.

Regan, P. (1995) *Legislating Privacy: Technology, Social Values, and Public Policy*. Chapel Hill, NC: University of North Carolina Press.

Renfro, W. (1993) *Issues Management in Strategic Planning*. Westport, CT: Greenwood Publishing.

Sentry Insurance (1979) *The Dimensions of Privacy: A National Opinion Research Survey of Attitudes Toward Privacy.* Stevens Point, WI: Author.

Sharp, E. B. (1999) *The Sometimes Connection: Public Opinion and Social Policy.* Albany, NY: State University of New York Press.

Smith, H. J. (1994) *Managing Privacy: Information Technology and Corporate America.* Chapel Hill, NC: University of North Carolina Press.

Smith, R. (2000) *Ben Franklin's Web Site: Privacy and Curiosity from Plymouth Rock to the Internet.* Providence, RI: Privacy Journal.

Sovern, J. (1999) Opting in, opting out, or no options at all: the fight for control of personal information, *Washington Law Review*, 74(4): 1033–118.

Streitfeld, D. and Piller, C. (2002, 12 January). Big brother finds ally in once-wary high tech, *Latimes.com* Available at: http://www.latimes.com/news/nationworld/ nation/la-011902techshift.story

Traugott, M. (2000) *The Invocation of Public Opinion in Congress.* Paper presented at the meeting of the International Political Science Association, Quebec City, Canada, August.

USA PATRIOT Act of 2001, Pub. L. No. 107–56, 115 Stat. 272 (2001).

Visionics Corporation (2001) *Protecting Civilization from the Faces of Terror: A Primer on the Role Facial Recognition Technology Can Play in Enhancing Airport Security.* Jersey City, NJ: Author, 24 September.

Wessel, D. (2002, April 11). Evolving concepts of privacy in U.S. lead to push against telemarketers, *The Wall Street Journal Online* 11 April. Available at: http://online.wsj. com/article/0,,SB1018472873375533800.djm,00.html

Zaller, J. (1992) *The Nature and Origins of Mass Opinion.* New York: Cambridge University Press.

20

Spin control and freedom of information: lessons for the United Kingdom from Canada[1]

by Alasdair S. Roberts

A contradiction in reform?

The United Kingdom is entering an extraordinary period in administrative reform. It is a system of government in which, for many years, emphasis has been placed on the need for tight central control of media relations and other communications with the public. However, the Blair government has also committed itself to a new Freedom of Information Act (FOIA) which promises to create a broadly distributed power to gain access to government records. If journalists, legislators, and lobbyists exploit the potential of the new law, the capacity of government to maintain 'message discipline' and control of the policy agenda will be seriously undermined. In practice, how will these two contrary pressures – one for centralization of control over communications, the other for liberalization of access to documents – be reconciled?

The long-term trend toward centralization of control over communications functions within the United Kingdom's central government seems undeniable. As Bob Phillis has observed (Evidence to the House of Commons Public Administration Committee, 22 January 2004), authority for communications functions has been further concentrated within the Prime Minister's Office under the Blair government, with the task of news management 'tightly controlled' by the Prime Minister's press secretary 'and the machinery that he put in place'. The number of special advisors whose principal function is to handle contacts with the media has also grown substantially under New Labour (Committee on Standards in Public Life 2003, para 4.20). Communications specialists throughout government have been encouraged to take a more active role in policy-making, so that 'media handling [is] built into the decision-making process at the earliest stage' (Timmins 1997). Pressure on communications staff to 'raise their game' has led to widespread complaints about the politicization of career media officers (Committee on Standards in Public Life 2003, para 8.3; Government Communications Review Group 2004 . . .

The reasons for this continued drive toward centralization are complex. The Committee on Standards in Public Life suggested in 2003 that governments are responding to 'a dramatic change in media pressure', caused by a proliferation of media outlets, an erosion of media deference, and the advent of a twenty-four hour news cycle. Governments, it suggested, now live in a state of 'permanent campaign' (Committee on Standards in Public Life 2003, para 4.18). The encroachment of 'spin-culture' can be seen outside of government as well, as other institutions of British life sharpen their capacity to hone the messages which they project to the public (Manning 1998; Miller and Dinan 2000; Pitcher 2003). Even the Phillis Committee, while repudiating 'misleading spin' of government policies, argued, in its January 2004 report, for further concentration of communications responsibilities at the centre of government (Government Communications Review Group 2004).

The capacity to maintain message discipline depends as much on the ability to determine what is *not* said by government officials, as it does on the ability to coordinate what is said. In other words, it depends largely on the capacity to preserve secrecy. This point has been illustrated by the Hutton Inquiry, which exposed the Blair government's attempt to deal with the discordant messages about Iraqi military capabilities that were conveyed to journalists by a government official, David Kelly (Hutton 2004) . . .

Here is the paradox: the Blair government has also introduced legislation which could in fact seriously compromise government's ability to preserve secrecy. The United Kingdom's Freedom of Information Act (FOIA), which gives citizens a right of access to documents held by public authorities, was adopted in 2000 and will go into effect in 2005. The Blair government has promoted the law as a key element in a program of reform intended to revolutionize British politics. In 1997, Prime Minister Tony Blair said that the FOIA would break down the 'traditional culture of secrecy' within the UK government and produce a 'fundamental and vital change in the relationship between government and governed' (United Kingdom 1997, Preface). In 1999, Home Secretary Jack Straw lauded the FOIA as a landmark in constitutional history that would 'transform the default setting' of secrecy in government (Straw 1999).

These expressions of commitment to openness have been accompanied by an enthusiasm for a decentralized approach to the administration of the FOIA within central government departments. In some countries, responsibility for dealing with FOI requests is given to a central office located high in the departmental hierarchy. The implementation plan for the UK law is quite distinct, as a 2002 government report explained:

> For the majority of departments procedures for handling freedom of information requests are still to be determined . . . Some departments . . . will initially at least have some central co-ordination of requests for information in order to assess the level and type of demand. Other departments, notably the Ministry of Defence and the Home Office are planning for requests for information to be dealt with at a local level by the relevant policy official because of the wide range of departmental responsibilities.
>
> (Lord Chancellor's Department 2002, p. 19)

In short, some major departments plan a decentralized approach to FOIA administration, while others see centralized administration only as a transitional stage to accommodate uncertainties in the early stage of implementation.

The dangers inherent in this approach may not yet be fully appreciated by the Blair government. Evidence suggests that the new FOIA will be used extensively by journalists, legislators and advocacy groups who seek information for the purpose of scrutinizing or embarrassing the government, or shaping its policy agenda. The proportion of requests under the existing administrative code on access to government information coming from these sources increased fivefold between 1998 and 2002, and accounted for about 40 per cent of all requests in 2002 . . . The government presently anticipates that authority regarding the disclosure of this politically sensitive information will be devolved to the 'local levels' of its departments. This approach is radically at odds with the overall trend toward centralization of responsibility for governmental communications; is it tenable?

Canadian experience may show how the British government will deal with this tension. The structure of Canada's federal government is in many ways comparable to that of the United Kingdom. Authority is highly concentrated, often producing complaints about executive power that would be familiar to British observers. Canada also undertook an experiment with FOI legislation after the adoption of its Access to Information Act (ATIA), which marked its twentieth anniversary in 2003.

The lessons from Canada are sobering. The promise of increased openness has been undercut by the development of administrative routines designed to centralize control and minimize the disruptive potential of the FOI law. Special procedures for handling politically sensitive requests are commonplace in major departments. Information technology has been adapted to ensure that ministers and central agencies are informed about difficult requests within days of their arrival. Communications officers can be closely involved in the processing of these requests, developing 'media lines' and other 'communications products' to minimize the political fallout of disclosure.

These practices are largely hidden from public view. Nevertheless, they play an important role in shaping the substance of the right to information in Canada . . . [R]equirements for the approval of 'disclosure packages' by ministerial offices or central agency staff often produce unjustified delays in the release of documents. These procedures also enhance the capacity of government officials to anticipate and minimize the damage that may be done by disclosure of information.

. . . And so it seems likely that ministers and bureaucrats in the UK government may find similar ways of containing the disruptive potential of the new FOIA. This has two implications. First, it causes us to question the viability of current plans for a decentralized approach to FOIA administration. Second, it reminds non-governmental organizations of the importance of monitoring the development of internal practices which, although difficult to observe, may have profound effects on the right to information.

Amber lights and red files

Serious debate about the adoption of an FOI law in Canada began in October 1974, and eventually led to the adoption of a law – the Access to Information Act (ATIA) – in 1982. The law came into force in 1983. The rhetoric that accompanied the new law would be familiar to contemporary British observers. The ATIA, said the Trudeau government in 1977, would promote 'effective participation of citizens and organizations in the taking of public decisions', and provide 'an element of monitoring [of government] which will help to maintain the probity of administration, the consistency of handling of individual cases, and the quality of the analysis of policies and programs' (J. Roberts 2001) . . .

Support for a Canadian FOI law was . . . driven by concern about the undue concentration of executive power. In 1969, the political scientist Denis Smith lamented that Canadian government had been transformed into a 'thinly-disguised Presidential system', without the benefit of a strong legislature to balance presidential power (Smith 1977). A combination of circumstances – declining economic performance, constitutional instability, fiscal indiscipline and apparent abuses of power by the national police force – contributed to disillusionment with central government in Canada in the 1970s. The ATIA was one of several measures that were intended to constrain the executive and diffuse political influence more broadly. The sentiment which buoyed public support for the ATIA was articulated by Joe Clark, leader of the opposition Conservatives, in 1978:

> What we are talking about is power – political power. We are talking about the reality that real power is limited to those who have facts. In a democracy that power and that information should be shared broadly. In Canada today they are not, and to that degree we are no longer a democracy in any sensible sense of that word. There is excessive power concentrated in the hands of those who hide public information from the people and Parliament of Canada.
>
> (Osler 1999)

However, Canada's policy elites did not share Clark's keenness to diffuse executive power. In the 1980s and 1990s, policy-makers worried instead about challenges to national stability which seemed to be posed by secessionist pressures in Quebec, inter-regional conflict, economic liberalization, and growing indebtedness. Conservative and Liberal governments responded to these challenges by concentrating more authority at the heart of government, and developing a more sophisticated central capacity to poll public opinion and craft communications programs that advanced its agenda (Savoie 1999; Simpson 2001).

To ministers, the ATIA seemed at worst to pose a basic threat to order. In a 1993 court case involving an ATIA request for polling data on constitutional questions, the federal government argued that disclosure could undermine 'the very existence of the country' (*Canada (Information Commissioner) v. Canada (Prime Minister)* [1993] 1 F.C. 427. It seemed at best to serve only as a pointless irritant. 'In the vast majority of instances', said a senior Conservative minister after leaving government, 'embarrassment and titillation are the only objects of access-to-information requests' (Crosbie 1997). The disruptive effect of the ATIA was magnified as journalists, opposition politicians, and non-governmental organizations honed their ability to exploit the opportunities created by the Act . . . Throughout the 1990s, federal officials pursued three strategies designed to reduce the impact of the ATIA. The first was litigation aimed at confirming a restrictive interpretation of key provisions of the law. The second strategy consisted of repeated acts of omission: the consistent failure to include a series of new federal organizations under the ambit of the law (A. Roberts 2001). The third strategy, less easily observed, was the refinement of internal administrative routines designed to ensure special treatment for politically sensitive ATIA requests.

In 2003, Canadians were provided with a rare opportunity to learn more about these informal routines. A year earlier, the ATIA office within the federal Department of Citizenship and Immigration (known as Citizenship and Immigration Canada, or CIC) had undertaken a review of its procedures for handling politically sensitive requests. CIC receives more ATIA requests than any other department or agency in the Canadian government. Its review was prolonged, and involved close consultations with other major federal departments. The internal documents produced during this review became publicly available following an ATIA request by Ann Rees, a journalist who later revealed details about the handling of politically sensitive requests in reports for the *Toronto Star* newspaper (Rees 2003). The documents obtained by Rees provide a detailed view of the mechanisms used to manage politically sensitive requests within several federal departments . . .

The procedure for handling politically sensitive requests is known within CIC as the 'amber light process'. The name is telling: as it is to drivers, an amber light is a warning to officials to proceed with caution in their handling of an ATIA request. The aim of the process, according to a senior member of the CIC communications staff, is to 'achieve the objective of proactive issues management' on ATIA requests.

CIC's amber light process begins at the moment an ATIA request is received by the department. A 'risk assessment officer' reviews incoming requests to identify those which are potentially sensitive. In practice, there is a presumption of sensitivity for requests submitted by journalists or representatives of political parties, including the offices of Members of the Opposition. Standard procedure requires that notice about media or partisan requests should be sent to the Minister's Office and the department's communications office within one day. In addition, the ATIA office produces a weekly inventory of new and potentially sensitive requests for review by the Minister's Office and communications staff.

The Minister's Office may then choose to tag an ATIA request for special attention. For a request to be tagged – or 'amber lighted' in departmental jargon – 'there must be potential for the issue/incident to be used in a public setting to attack the Minister or the Department'. In 2002, about 20 per cent of requests identified as potentially sensitive by the ATIA office were also amber lighted by the Minister's Office.

The office that holds the records that relate to the request – known as the Office of Primary Interest (OPI) – is immediately advised that the request has been amber lighted. ATIA staff work with the OPI to 'identify and assess issues for sensitivity and media product development'. Communications staff will also work with the OPI to develop 'media lines' – a memorandum that outlines key messages that should be emphasized by departmental spokesmen in response to questions raised after the disclosure of information. 'House cards', which provide the Minister with responses to questions that may be raised in Parliament, are also prepared.

The complete 'disclosure package' – including documents which are to be released to the requester, along with the 'communications products' – is sent to the

Minister's Office for review. The role of the Minister's Office at this final stage is a sensitive matter for ATIA officers. The formal position is that the purpose of this review is to give the Minister's Office a warning or 'heads up' about the impending release, and not to allow an opportunity to question the ATIA officer's disclosure decisions. In practice, however, the Minister's Office may raise questions about disclosure decisions as well as the communications strategy. After approval by the Minister's Office, the disclosure package is returned to the ATIA office, and then sent to the requester. At the time of disclosure, the ATIA office also sends an email notice that contains the communications products for the request to senior managers within the department.

Comparable amber light procedures have been adopted within other major departments. According to internal documents, the Department of Foreign Affairs and International Trade (DFAIT) amber lighted between 50 and 70 per cent of its ATIA requests in 2002. In the Department of National Defence (DND), about 40 per cent of ATIA requests were seen by the Minister's Office. DND staff told CIC in March 2002 that amber lighting decisions were taken during a weekly meeting of officials from the Minister's Office, the Public Affairs office, and Communications office: 'If anyone has interest [in a request], then the file is flagged for viewing by the Minister's office'.

The Treasury Board Secretariat (TBS), the central agency responsible for policy on the administration of ATIA within federal departments and agencies, follows a similar routine. (In the TBS, sensitive requests are tagged simply as 'interesting'.) The same is true of the Department of Justice (DOJ), which provides advice to other departments on the interpretation of the ATIA. According to an internal manual, DOJ's ATIA office sends a weekly inventory of new requests to the Minister's Office, the Deputy Minister's Office, the Parliamentary Affairs Unit and the Communications Branch. In other internal documents, the Justice Department reported that 166 cases completed in 2002 were tagged as 'sensitive'. Of these requests, 81 were submitted by political parties and 33 by the media. This represents a substantial majority of all requests received from parties and the media.

At the very centre of government, politically sensitive ATIA requests are known as 'Red Files'. According to the procedures manual for the ATIA office of the Privy Council Office (PCO),

> Approximately once a week the [Office of the Prime Minister] is provided with a list of newly received requests. If they wish to see the release package of any of the requests they notify the [ATIA] Coordinator who passes on the information to the officer handling the request.

A check of PCO's ATIA caseload in October 2003 showed that 39 requests currently in process had been tagged as Red Files – probably about one-third of all requests in process within PCO at that time. Of these, 17 were identified as requests from the media, and another six as requests from Parliament. Most of these requests asked for material relating to high-profile policy debates; after this, the most common type of Red File request was for information about travel and hospitality expenses of ministers and PCO staff.

Within PCO, lower-level staff may also trigger the process of managing sensitive requests. For every ATIA request, staff within OPIs must complete a 'communications form' to identify the 'communications implications' of disclosure. If a request has communications implications, OPI staff are required to consult PCO communications staff to discuss the preparation of media lines and other communications products. The communications analyst is entitled to ask the ATIP officer for an opportunity to review the disclosure package before its release . . .

PCO's role in overseeing the ATIA system has sometimes been the subject of controversy. In 2002 a former director of research for the Liberal Party caucus complained that the PCO's 'Communications Co-ordination Group' (CCG) had become

> [an] egregious example of bureaucratic politicization . . . The CCG . . . is made up of the top Liberal functionaries from ministers' personal staff, along with several of the PMO senior staff, and the top communications bureaucrats from the supposedly non-partisan Privy Council Office . . . While the CCG's mandate is supposedly to 'co-ordinate' the government message, in practice much of the committee's time each week is taken up discussing ways to delay or thwart access-to-information requests.
>
> (Murphy 2002)

A senior PCO official later conceded to Rees that the office actively manages the government's response to sensitive requests received throughout government. 'It is our role', the official said, 'to make sure that . . . the department releasing the information is prepared to essentially handle any fallout' (Rees 2003).

Control enabled by technology

The administrative routines that have been developed to ensure special treatment for politically sensitive requests rely significantly on new information technologies. Within departments, ATIA databases have been adapted to streamline the process of tagging and tracking sensitive requests. A government-wide database has also been developed that allows central agencies to monitor incoming ATIA requests on an almost real-time basis.

Within federal departments, software initially acquired to aid in the management of ATIA caseloads has been adapted to facilitate the handling of politically sensitive requests. Today, most major federal departments use the same program – ATIPflow – to manage the flow of ATIA requests. ATIPflow was developed by a Ottawa-based contractor, PRIVASOFT, and widely adopted within the federal government in the 1990s. The use of case management software such as ATIPflow is not inherently problematic: on the contrary, it helps ATIA offices to track progress in processing requests, and collects statistics required for annual public reports on the operation of the law.

However, many department have altered their ATIPflow software to support the task of communications management. For example, several departments have broadened the range of categories that are used to describe requesters, typically by adding the categories 'Political Party' or 'Member of Parliament'. These categories are not required for the production of public reports on the operation of the ATIA. However, they serve an important purpose within departments, by making it easier to search the ATIPflow database to generate a list of potentially sensitive requests. Such categories are particularly important because ATIA offices are generally barred from disclosing the identity of a requester to other parts of the department. However, there are no prohibitions on the disclosure of the requester category.

ATIPflow software has also been adapted so that ATIA offices can identify whether a request has been tagged as a sensitive file (Roberts 2002). Again, this feature allows the ATIA office to exploit the search features of ATIPflow so that the process of compiling a inventory of sensitive requests is largely automated. Without ATIPflow – and these changes to the software – the process of managing the inventory of sensitive requests would be more complicated.

The task of monitoring sensitive requests is also simplified by a separate and government-wide database, known as the Coordination of Access to Information Request System (CAIRS). CAIRS is maintained by the Government Telecommunications and Informatics Services (GTIS), an agency within the Department of Public Works and Government Services. According to a TBS directive, all ATIA requests received by federal institutions must be entered into CAIRS within one day of receipt (Treasury Board Secretariat 2001) . . . ATIA offices in all federal departments and agencies are able to search the CAIRS database by several criteria, such as keywords in the substance of the request, or the category of requester.

The development of CAIRS was approved by Cabinet in 1988 and became operational in 1990. The system was substantially upgraded in 2001. The government says that CAIRS is designed 'to enable the government to monitor the progress of Access to Information (ATI) requests made, facilitate the coordination of responding to requests with common themes, and to facilitate communication and consultation with central agencies and institutions' (Government Telecommunications and Informatics Services 1999, p. 1). At the same time, CAIRS has been criticized as a tool for 'computer surveillance' of the entire federal ATIA system (Howard 1992).

The upgraded version of CAIRS is accessed by federal departments through a secure website. The access log for the CAIRS website was obtained through an ATIA request and analysed to determine which federal agencies rely most heavily on the database's oversight capabilities. An analysis of access log data from December 2002 to September 2003 is provided in [Table 20.1]. On the left side of [Table 20.1] is a breakdown of the frequency with which computers associated with various federal institutions executed searches on the CAIRS website. To execute a search, individuals must send information about search criteria to the CAIRS server from the main search page of the website. Searches were executed 10 204 times in the period under study. The access log maintains a record of the Internet Protocol (IP) address associated with the computer sending the data, and institutional affiliations for specific IP addresses can be identified. Table [20.1] suggests that at least 56 per cent of searches on CAIRS were executed by two central agencies – TBS and PCO . . .

It is also possible to analyse the access log to determine which institutions appear to conduct broad searches of the CAIRS database. Every execution of the CAIRS search feature results in a response in which the results of a search are returned to the

Table [20.1] Use of the search function on the CAIRS database

Searches executed (N = 10204)	%	Broad searches (n = 1675)	%
Treasury Board Canada/Finance Canada	41	Treasury Board Canada/Finance Canada	49
Privy Council Office	15	Privy Council Office	26
Indian and Northern Affairs	6	Public Works and Government Services	7
Public Works and Government Services	4	Indian and Northern Affairs	6
Foreign Affairs and International Trade	3	Foreign Affairs and International Trade	2
Justice	3	Canadian Heritage	1
Canada Customs and Revenue Agency	2	Environment	1
Environment	2	Industry	1

Note: Departments and agencies are listed by declining levels of activity. Several institutions that had lower levels of activity are not included.

Key: CAIRS = Coordination of Access to Information Request System.

user. The access log records how much data is conveyed to the user in each response. It is presumed that the amount of data conveyed in these responses is correlated with the number of requests that were responsive to the user's search criteria. This part of the analysis begins with transactions with the CAIRS server that involved the transmission of data from the server to the main search page. However, it only examines the top 20 per cent of these transactions, in terms of volume of data transmitted. The right side of Table [20.1] provides a summary of the institutions most frequently associated with these large searches. IP addresses associated with the two central agencies again appear to account for the preponderance of broad searches on the CAIRS database.

Generally, the results in Table [20.1] substantiate the view that the main purpose of CAIRS is to improve central agencies' oversight of the entire ATIA system. Certainly CAIRS was used for this purpose in the months following the terror attacks of September 11, 2001. In following weeks, the Security and Intelligence Secretariat of PCO told other departments that it should be consulted about requests for information 'pertaining to post-September 11, security measures, security policy and operations, security planning, and ongoing efforts to combat terrorism'. The Secretariat said in an internal memorandum that it would also 'regularly review the CAIR report' and ask to be consulted on files on its own initiative. The PCO later said that it undertook 184 'security-related access consultations' between 11 September 2001 and 31 March 2003. Security concerns may have been mixed with an interest in communications management. Perhaps three-quarters of the 'security-related' requests reviewed by PCO were submitted by journalists, Members of Parliament, or representatives of political parties.

Gauging the effect on statutory rights

The fact that major departments have developed special procedures for isolating politically sensitive requests may say something about the Canadian government's attitude toward the ATIA, but it does not necessarily follow that departments have compromised rights established under the law. To determine whether these procedures actually undermine access rights, further investigation is required. Analysis of data relating to the processing of ATIA requests within major departments suggests that these procedures do result in unjustifiable delays in the disclosure of information. It is more difficult to determine whether these procedures also result in indefensibly restrictive decisions about disclosure of information.

Delay in processing requests

Delay in processing ATIA requests can be very important, particularly for journalists, Members of Parliament or other party representatives. The news cycle has its own rhythm: an issue will not remain in the foreground indefinitely, and will soon be displaced by other topics. Delay can have the effect of substantially reducing the value of released information. At a certain point, the right to information can be substantially subverted by delay.

The stated policy of the government is that efforts at communications management should not delay responses to ATIA requests. The PCO says explicitly in its internal manual that its Red File procedure 'does not hold up the processing' of an ATIA request. Similarly, TBS says that efforts at interdepartmental consultation should 'under no circumstances . . . be used to delay or obstruct a request beyond the time limits set out in the Access to Information Act' (TBS 'Policy for the Coordination of Access to Information Requests', provided informally to the author in December 2003).

However, there is good reason to question whether these aspirations are achieved in practice. Responding to a 1999 investigation by Canada's Information Commissioner, DFAIT conceded that its 'cumbersome process for preparing communications advice on potentially sensitive issues' had been a significant source of delay in processing requests (Information Commissioner of Canada 1999, p. 19). In June 2000, the Information Commissioner (OIC) also warned DND that the ATIA 'creates no right for a minister or department to delay responses for political considerations including the need to serve the communications needs of the minister' (Information Commissioner of Canada 2000, pp. 63–8). Internal documents relating to CIC's review of its amber light procedure show that ATIA officers were similarly frustrated by bottlenecks and delays in the review process . . .

Damage control: an illustration

It is . . . difficult to quantify the extent to which the government's routines enhance its ability to minimize the political fallout from disclosure of information. But there is no doubt that the benefit to government departments is significant. A description of the government's management of one recent ATIA request illustrates how risks associated with transparency are managed – and also how the law may be bent to reduce those risks.

In November 2000, journalist Stewart Bell – a reporter for the *National Post* newspaper specializing in national security issues – filed an ATIA request with CIC.

Bell had been reporting on the connections between Tamil immigrant groups in Canada and Tamil terrorist groups in Sri Lanka, and the federal government's role in funding those immigrant groups. His request asked for records relating to the Tamil Eelam Society of Canada (TESC), which had connections to organizations already linked to terrorist groups by federal police and intelligence services. (This description of the handling of Bell's request is based on documents released by CIC and PCO in response to ATIA requests.)

Bell's request undoubtedly had 'communications implications' for the government. For the preceding five months, Finance Minister Paul Martin Jr had been criticized by Opposition Members of Parliament for attending a dinner organized by a group alleged to be a front for Tamil terrorists. Martin responded by denying the group's terrorist links and accusing Opposition MPs of bias against the Tamil community. Martin's defence was complicated when Reform Party MPs obtained emails written by Canadian diplomats expressing reservations about Martin's plan to attend the dinner.

Documents held by CIC (but not yet publicly released) threatened to intensify the controversy. Three years earlier, CIC's deputy minister had written a memorandum to CIC Minister Lucienne Robillard that asked for permission to stop funding for TESC because of internal concerns about its connection to terrorist groups. The Minister refused to terminate the relationship. 'We are to forget everything', a CIC official had explained to colleagues in an internal email, 'It is business as usual' (Bell 2002).

CIC 'amber lighted' Bell's ATIA request. A month later, the department also advised Bell that it intended to extend the statutory deadline for responding to his request by 190 days, to 25 June 2001. The case for an extension was strong: there were several thousand pages of relevant documents and these included many documents that could not be disclosed before consulting with other government departments.

Nevertheless, this delay dealt an advantage to CIC. In Spring 2001, it contracted with the auditing firm KPMG for a 'forensic audit' to determine whether TESC was spending CIC's money properly. The audit was commissioned, internal documents explained, 'because we thought that it was in the best interest of CIC and of the TESC to clear the air about various allegations that they were misusing public funds'. KPMG was instructed to complete its investigation by 29 June 2001 – that is, on roughly the same deadline as Bell's ATIA request. The investigation revealed no major improprieties.

In fact, CIC was unable to meet the 25 June deadline for responding to Bell's request. As interdepartmental consultations continued, CIC took other steps to avoid allegations of mismanagement. In January 2002, CIC officials met with TESC to resolve minor issues raised in KPMG's final report, which had been delivered the preceding month. A PCO memo suggests that CIC and other federal departments also developed a 'framework . . . [for a] package to stop this type of group funding terrorists'.

CIC was now in a better position to respond to the controversy that might arise following its disclosure of documents to Bell. In early February 2002, media lines were drafted that emphasized the positive findings of the KPMG audit and steps taken to ensure that TESC spent public funds properly. CIC officials were told that Bell would not be given a copy of the KPMG audit and the TESC action plan. His request had been interpreted to exclude documents created after November 2000.

However, CIC still did not respond to Bell's request – notwithstanding complaints from Bell about the delay. CIC's media lines explained that the issues raised by the KPMG audit 'relate to internal operations and aren't related to security concerns'. Nevertheless, the Security and Intelligence Secretariat of PCO told CIC that it wanted to review the Bell file under the special procedure for 'security-related' requests established following the attacks of 11 September 2001. The file was sent back to PCO for review in January 2002.

Because the file had been amber lighted, it also had to be reviewed by the Minister's Office within CIC. The ATIA office of CIC tried to expedite the response to Bell's request by sending the disclosure package to CIC's Minister's Office for review at the same time that the file was returned to PCO. But the Minister's Office deferred, asking to be advised about 'comments from PCO on this file, as well as exemptions recommended by PCO, if any'. Meanwhile, the Security and Intelligence Secretariat of PCO expressed its own concern about the proposed disclosures, and signalled its desire to review the matter with CIC's legal branch. The Secretariat finally agreed to the proposed disclosure on 14 March 2002.

CIC released its documents to Bell the next day – 483 days after the request had been filed, and 263 days past the statutory deadline. Bell's story was published in the *National Post* in May 2002 but received no attention in Parliament or follow-up in the media. In part this was because of delay, which sapped the story of much of its newsworthiness. Since the filing of the request, the Liberal government had won a large majority in a general election; controversy over the Liberal government's connections to the Tamil community had dissipated; and the CIC minister implicated in the 1997 documents had moved to another portfolio.

The newsworthiness of the story was also weakened by CIC's capacity to make a strong and immediate response. CIC had identified the spokesman responsible for handling Bell's story, and drafted his reply, over a month before it actually disclosed the information to Bell. Bell was required by professional norms to convey CIC's media line – that its 1997 concerns had been resolved by a later audit – in his story. This had the effect of squelching potential controversy. The fact that the audit had been commissioned four years after internal concerns had been voiced, and after the receipt of Bell's ATIA request, was unknown to Bell and unmentioned in the story.

Reconciling control and transparency

The handling of the Bell request was not unusual. It provides an illustration of the way in which Canadian government departments have designed internal routines to minimize the disruptive potential of the ATIA. These internal routines improve departments' capacity to control the timing of disclosure and rebut criticisms that may be made against the government after information is released. These routines provide strong protection for values that are important to players within government – such as control over the policy agenda and consistency in policy – at the cost of damage to values that are important to players outside of government, such as transparency and accountability.

These administrative routines are not easily observed, but play an important role in determining what the 'right to information' actually means in practice. I have argued elsewhere that these internal procedures may be described as constituting a 'hidden law' on access to information, which substantially restricts statutory rights for certain kinds of requesters (Roberts 2002). On the face of it, the law may appear to guarantee equal treatment for all requests – but in actual practice, journalists and partisans are treated differently. In general, their requests take longer to process. Statutory deadlines are more likely to be overrun. Relevant documents will be reviewed more closely. Special efforts will be made to enhance the government's capacity to rebut anticipated criticisms flowing from disclosure.

It is difficult to gauge whether such practices are commonplace in other governments, largely because they are not formalized in law or regulations; in addition, their existence may be actively denied by governments. Nevertheless there is some evidence that the Canadian federal government does not constitute an unusual case. In 2001, Ontario's Information Commissioner complained about informal procedures within provincial government departments that appeared to have an adverse effect on timely response and disclosure rates for politically sensitive requests. Even to the Commissioner, the exact requirements for handling sensitive requests remained unclear; nevertheless, they seemed to raise a 'systemic problem' of non-compliance throughout government (Information and Privacy Commissioner of Ontario 2001, pp. 4–6). Recent analysis has also shown that the British Columbia government has developed a central database that includes sophisticated mechanisms for tagging sensitive requests that could be related to administrative processes which cause undue delays (Roberts 2004).

Similar trends have been seen in Australia. 'As spin-doctors have moved closer towards centre stage in the operations of government', says Rick Snell, 'their impact on FoI has become potentially greater and more negative' (Snell 2002b, p. 194). Snell finds evidence of patterns of non-compliance in the handling of politically sensitive requests, followed by 'the use of a series of tactics to kill, swamp or divert attention away from the newsworthiness of any story or public use of released information' (Snell 2002a, b, p. 193).

Westminster systems, distinguished as they are by a concentration of executive authority, may be particularly likely to develop centralized procedures for handling sensitive requests. However, these procedures might be symptomatic of a more general problem. In many countries, public deference to government has declined precipitously. This has fueled a 'transparency revolution' that has affected all major social institutions, which is manifested in the rapid diffusion of FOI laws (Blanton 2002; Tapscott 2003). At the same time, however, policy elites have become anxious about the erosion of their capacity to govern in an era distinguished by the pace of social, economic and technological change. Concern about governmental competence in a time of 'rapid and profound change in the economic and institutional environment', was expressed in a 1996 meeting of OECD ministers, which concluded:

> Governments need to pursue more active communication policies, to keep control of their agendas and not just react passively to the pressure of events and emergency situations. Resisting excessive pressure from the media to influence the political and policy agenda was noted as both important and difficult.
>
> (OECD 1996)

This implies that the contradictions in reform in the United Kingdom – centralization of communication functions, and movement toward increased transparency – may be common to many other countries. The development of informal routines such as those used within the Canadian government may constitute a way of resolving the tension between the demand for transparency and elite anxiety about the decline of governability.

There are two broad implications for the development of freedom of information policy in the United Kingdom. The first relates to the likely viability of the proposed approach to the implementation of the FOIA. In November 2003 the Department of Constitutional Affairs reaffirmed its earlier view that a decentralized approach to FOIA, 'whereby requests are dealt with at the local level', would be common in many departments (Department of Constitutional Affairs 2003, pp. 24–5). This may prove untenable in practice. Perhaps a more realistic approach would be to develop formal and explicit procedures that accommodate the legitimate interests of ministers without compromising compliance with the requirements of the FOIA.

More generally, increased attention must be paid to internal procedures that may have a profound effect on the actual content of the right to information. The tendency in many jurisdictions has been for non-governmental organizations to pay disproportionate attention to statutory rules which, although easily observed and perhaps noxious in principle, will have only a marginal impact on the operation of law. For example, Canadian advocates of openness vigorously protested statutory amendments barring 'frivolous and vexatious' FOI requests which in practice affect only a small handful of requests (Roberts 1999). At the same time, informal procedures that eroded compliance in a much larger number of cases went unnoticed.

There may be an analogous difficulty with the recommendations contained in the January 2004 report of the Phillis Review of Government Communications. The report proposes several amendments to the FOIA which are expected to improve openness and restore trust in government (Government Communications Review Group 2004, p. 24). The merit of several of these amendments is undeniable. However, there is an element of misplaced emphasis in the report and the debate which it engendered. Great emphasis was given to the proposed elimination of the ministerial veto (Campaign for Freedom of Information 2004) – which, although egregious, is unlikely to be invoked regularly, if the experience of other jurisdictions is a guide. At the same time, the Phillis Review neglects the tension between the FOIA and its own call for a more centralized and better coordinated system of government communication – a tension that will be worked out in the less easily observed recesses of bureaucratic practice . . .

Note

1   This chapter is an extract from A. Roberts (2005) Spin control and freedom of information: lessons for the United Kingdom from Canada, *Public Administration*, 83(1):1–23.

References

Bell, S. (2002) Minister vetoed bid to stop Tamil funding, *National Post*, 29 May, p. A8.

Blanton, T. (2002) The world's right to know, *Foreign Policy*, July/August, 131: 50–8.

Campaign for Freedom of Information (2004) *'Abolish the Information Veto' Proposal Backed.* London: Campaign for Freedom of Information, 19 January.

Committee on Standards in Public Life (2003) *Ninth Report.* London: Committee on Standards in Public Life, April.

Crosbie, J. (1997) *No Holds Barred.* Toronto, ON: McClelland and Stewart.

Department of Constitutional Affairs (2003) *Annual Report on Bringing Fully into Force Those Provisions of the Freedom of Information Act 2000 which Are Not Yet Fully in Force.* London: Department of Constitutional Affairs, November.

Government Communications Review Group, (2004) *An Independent Review of Government Communications.* London: Government Communications Review Group.

Government Telecommunications and Informatics Services (1999) *Coordination of Access to Information Requests CAIR System: Replacement of Current System – Business Requirements.* Ottawa, ON: Government Telecommunications and Informatics Service, 24 September.

Howard, F. (1992) Information commissioner warns new access process will stem leaks, *Ottawa Citizen*, 3 July, p.A4.

Hutton, Lord (2004) *Report of the Inquiry to the Circumstances Surrounding the Death of Dr David Kelly.* London: The Hutton Inquiry, 28 January.

Information and Privacy Commissioner of Ontario (2001) *Annual Report 2000.* Toronto, ON: Office of the Information and Privacy Commissioner, 12 June.

Information Commissioner of Canada (1999) *Report Card on Compliance with Response Deadlines: Department of Foreign Affairs and International Trade.* Ottawa, ON: Office of the Information Commissioner, March.

Information Commissioner of Canada (2000) *Annual Report 1999–2000.* Ottawa: Office of the Information Commissioner.

Lord Chancellor's Department (2002) *Annual Report on Bringing Fully into Force Those Provisions of the Freedom of Information Act 2000 Which Are Not Yet Fully in Force.* London: Lord Chancellor's Department, 27 November.

Manning, P. (1998) *Spinning for Labour: Trade Unions and the New Media Environment.* Aldershot: Ashgate.

Miller, D. and Dinan, W. (2000) The rise of the PR industry in Britain, 1979–98, *European Journal of Communication*, 15(1): 53–5.

Murphy, J. (2002) Your candle's flickering, Jean, *Globe and Mail.* Toronto, ON, 17 May, p.A15.

OECD (1996) *Ministerial Symposium on the Future of Public Services.* Paris: OECD, March.

Osler, A. (1999) Journalism and the FOI laws: a faded promise, *Government Information in Canada, 17.* Available at: http://www.usask.ca/library/gic/17/osler.html

Pitcher, G. (2003) *The Death of Spin.* Chichester: Wiley.

Rees, A. (2003) Red file alert: public access at risk, *Toronto Star.* Toronto, ON, 1 November, p. A32.

Roberts, A. (1999) Retrenchment and freedom of information: recent experience under Federal, Ontario, and British Columbia Law, *Canadian Public Administration*, 42(4): 422–51.

Roberts, A. (2001) *Statement to the MPs' Committee on Access to Information*. Syracuse, NY: Campbell Public Affairs Institute. August 29.

Roberts, A. (2002) Administrative discretion and the Access to Information Act: an 'Internal law' on open government?, *Canadian Public Administration*, 45(2): 175–94.

Roberts, A. (2004) Treatment of sensitive requests under British Columbia's Freedom of Information Law, *Freedom of Information Review*.

Roberts, J. (2001) Green Paper on legislation on public access to government documents, in M. Drapeau and M.-A. Racicot (eds) *The Complete Annotated Guide to Federal Access to Information*. Toronto, ON: Carswell, pp. 5–43 (originally published 1977).

Savoie, D. (1999) *Governing from the Centre*. Toronto, ON: University of Toronto Press.

Simpson, J. (2001) *The Friendly Dictatorship*. Toronto, ON: McClelland and Stewart.

Smith, D. (1977) President and parliament: the transformation of parliamentary government in Canada, in T.A. Hockin (ed.) *Apex of Power: The Prime Minister and Political Leadership in Canada*. Toronto, ON: Prentice-Hall, pp. 308–25.

Snell, R. (2002a) Contentious issues management: the dry rot in FoI practice?, *Freedom of Information Review*, 102:62–5.

Snell, R. (2002b) FoI and the delivery of diminishing returns, or how spin-doctors and journalists have mistreated a volatile reform, *The Drawing Board: An Australian Review of Public Affairs*, 2(3): 187–207.

Straw, J. (1999) *House of Commons Debates*. London: House of Commons, 7 December.

Tapscott, D. (2003) *The Naked Corporation: How the Age of Transparency Will Revolutionize Business*. Toronto, ON: Viking Canada.

Timmins, N. (1997) Blair calls on Whitehall to raise its PR game, *Financial Times*. London, 2 October, 22.

PART 6
Mobility, privacy, ethics and resistance

We live in mobile societies. Although most people continue to think and talk about social life as though it can be easily explained using well-defined, clearly established parameters, domains or spheres – for example, the nation-state, family, culture, work, love, publicity, privacy and citizenship – the reality is that our lives are constructed around flows of information, capital, waste, technology, people, images, sounds, etc. (Castells 1996). Even the concepts 'society' and 'the social' have recently been interrogated as an 'enactment' that has as much to do with the assumptions driving social research as they do with the empirical world as it actually exists (Urry and Law 2004; see also Latour 2005). Think of the many layers of global flows that enter your daily life: music, television images, news stories, electronic mail, food, products, finance, literature, oil, pesticides, air pollution, environmental changes and, of course, travellers and tourists. Clearly, we interact with global flows on a daily basis even when we do not leave our homes.

The study of mobility has recently become all the rage in social and political theory, but there is nothing new to mobilities and flows. Zygmunt Bauman (2001), for example, explains this fact by conceptualizing the very structure of modernity (dating at least as far back as the sixteenth century) in terms of 'liquidity' or 'liquid modernity'. He argues that liquids, unlike solids, cannot easily hold their shape. Liquids spill, flow, run, splash and seep. Given the extraordinary mobility of liquids, we tend to assume that they are light and weightless, and that they are constantly on the move. We understand solids, by contrast, as durable and sturdy. Solids appear to be heavy and they project a sense of permanence (e.g., a huge boulder or a mountain). When liquids meet solids, it is the liquid that changes its shape, adapts and transforms before our eyes, while the solid holds steady, remains fixed and persists. If a glass of water spilled on a table, for instance, you would see the properties of the water change, but the table would remain the same. Or would it? Is it the properties of the liquid that have really changed? As Bauman points out, it is the nature of the liquid to change its shape. That's what liquids do. Beyond our vision or immediate perception, however, the liquid is actually soaking into the table and slowly changing its properties. Again, it is not the liquid that changes, for liquids are all about change. What is happening is that the liquid is 'melting' the solid, soaking into it, transforming it, and changing its constitution. While we 'see' the liquid change form, our vision is misleading.

Liquidity, for Bauman, is a fitting metaphor to capture the essence of modernity: melting of solids in the presence of liquids. Modernity, he contends, has always been a fluid or mobile process, and it has always been in constant, if imperceptible, motion, always susceptible to the forces of change. At certain times, societal arrangements might seem impossibly fixed or static (e.g., dictatorships), says Bauman, but the history of modernity is best conceptualized in terms of a process of 'melting of solids' of social structure. The first 'solid' to melt was traditional loyalty and customary rights that maintained social order. A new solid replaced the traditional, feudal order in the form of the panoptical society, with its bureaucratic systems of surveillance and social control. But this modern system, too, could not escape the processes of change, and we are at a point in modernity when we need to rethink the concepts of time, space, public, private, community and society, as they, too, are dissolving before (or beyond) our eyes. While there is nothing new to the forces of mobilities and flows that are dissolving the modern industrial structure, however, what is new is the rate or frequency with which we encounter global flows and the implications for ethics, security, liberty and democracy. In a world where co-presence is not required for action, where communication systems (e.g., video surveillance cameras and biometrically encoded identification cards) are used to regulate workers, citizens, migrants and travellers, and where time–space relations are dissolving (or melting), we face a new set of social, political, cultural and ethical challenges.

Section readings

The first reading passage, Chapter 21, directly addresses the theme of mobility. We have witnessed a shift over the past 100 years, Sheller and Urry argue, whereby the twentieth-century preoccupation with the preservation and protection of private life has been supplemented by a growing twenty-first-century preoccupation with the preservation and protection of public space. Trends towards the privatization of public space, in turn, pose implications for democratic citizenship. Sheller and Urry argue that while major approaches to the concepts public and private differ in the nuances of argumentation, each approach adheres to a static distinction between the public and the private. This is problematic for Sheller and Urry because such an understanding fails to take seriously the fluidities and mobilities that are contributing to the hybridization of those spaces commonly understood as 'public' and 'private'.

Against the grain of twentieth-century 'normative social thought', Sheller and Urry contend that the future of democratic citizenship depends on successfully negotiating and, necessarily, understanding, the new mobile world that is neither public nor private. One of the main problems with normative social theory is that it dichotomizes the public sphere and private space, conceptualizing the two domains as spatially fixed. This conceptualization is problematic because it presupposes an immobile public and a form of social life that is not 'in motion'. But public and private life has always been 'in motion', according to Sheller and Urry. To demonstrate the fluidity and mobility of social life, they examine the ambivalent democratic effects of automobility and information technologies – two aspects of everyday life in the West – and their concomitant implications for hybrid configurations of privacy in public (e.g., driving in a private automobile on a public city street), publicity in private (e.g., talking in a chat room from home), and more complex configurations of private–public–private–public space, such as providing private information (e.g., a password that happens to be your date of birth) to access a public service (e.g., the Internet) while driving a private automobile on a public street. We could add that the individual consumer driving in their 'private' car is constrained by 'public' speed limits, rules and directions, just as their 'private' Internet use is bound by 'public' rules (e.g., anti-pornography legislation). Things get more complicated, still, when we consider that 'public' money created the road to drive the 'private' automobile on, and that the 'private' technology used to access the 'public' (but partially 'private') Internet has left the user's 'private' information vulnerable to 'public' eavesdropping practices ushered in under new, 'public' laws after 9/11. The point Sheller and Urry make is that the materialization of the private and public have become too intermeshed, to the extent that the traditional notion of privacy makes little sense in a globalizing social context that uproots bodies from places and information from spaces.

What, then, are we to make of privacy legislation in a world of global informational mobilities? In the second reading passage, Chapter 22, Bennett and Raab examine 'the privacy paradigm'. The privacy paradigm, they contend, is comprised of a number of interrelated assumptions about the public and the private; about what constitutes threats to privacy; and about the rights and freedoms of citizens in a liberal democratic state. In its most common form, the privacy paradigm rests on the assumption that civil society is comprised of autonomous individuals who require access to a degree of privacy in order to fulfil their roles in the liberal democratic state. This paradigmatic understanding assumes that privacy pertains to individuals, and that forces exterior to the individual threaten the integrity of personal privacy. Under the auspices of information privacy and data protection, the privacy paradigm was set on a particular trajectory oriented towards granting individuals greater control over information collected by various organizations and agencies.

The liberal–modernist privacy paradigm, however, has not developed in the absence of criticism. While one group of critics has charged that liberal privacy protection opens opportunities for subversion and deceit, a second group has argued not only that the distinction between the public and private domain is false, but also that the test for democracy is not personal privacy. The test, rather, is the extent to which participatory parity is achieved (see Fraser 2003), conceptualized in Bennett and Raab's passage in terms of cooperation and community conscience. Given the excessive focus on data protection and individual liberty, however, there is only so far that privacy legislation can go to temper the expansion of surveillance societies and systems of control.

In the context of pervasive surveillance, therefore, we need to work towards social awareness and an ethics of surveillance. The third passage, Chapter 23, begins by pointing to the paradoxical character of surveillance as good and bad, helpful and harmful. In contrast to normative modern liberal theory, with its attendant emphasis on the public/private dichotomy, Sewell and Barker contend that information and communication technologies have ushered in an 'intense seismographic disruption' to the extent that a critical approach to the ethical dimensions of privacy needs to be formulated. The formulation of an ethics of surveillance, they contend, must foremost avoid the simplistic dualisms that continue to persist in policy debate.

To conceptualize an ethics of surveillance that avoids the 'antinomian' opposition of the public and private, Sewell and Barker begin by differentiating Panopticon from panopticism. They explain that the former corresponds to a particular form of social architecture (a prison, for example), but the latter is a cultural disposition or a general faith that the garnering of greater amounts of information will reveal the truth about the social world. Using surveillance in the workplace as a microcosm to address wider social forces, they explain this disposition in terms of a discursive ethic that is reproduced through the everyday work activities of labourers. By consenting to workplace surveillance, even if that consent is forced or difficult to refuse, workers contribute to the reproduction of power relations by entering into, and accepting, knowledge about surveillance practices (declaring, for example, that surveillance ensures quality customer service). Through the process of consenting to knowledge/power relationships, workers adopt mechanisms for self-surveillance in the form of 'rules of right' and 'rules of conduct'. For Sewell and Barker, a critical disposition to surveillance must entail scrutiny, analysis and evaluation.

The final reading passage, Chapter 24, addresses a significant but still limited theme in surveillance studies: resistance as a personal and a social ethic. David Lyon argues that post-9/11 systems of surveillance have shifted to the control side of the care–control spectrum characterizing contemporary surveillance practices, and that complacency is no longer an option for concerned citizens. Through the lens of 9/11 security responses, says Lyon, interlocking cultures of fear, control and suspicion have solidified. The resulting systems of surveillance, however, are not designed to simply target individual suspects. Rather, social sorting and categorical profiling are what characterizes globally integrated surveillance systems today. To rise to the challenges confronting citizens concerned with resisting surveillance, Lyon identifies three levels of analysis: social, political and technological. The message Lyon leaves us with, and the message that we choose to close the Reader with, is that something can be done about the pervasiveness of intrusive systems of surveillance. What is foremost necessary is awareness, understanding, compassion and responsible action.

Questions

Chapter 21 (Sheller and Urry)

1   People regularly talk about public space, private property, public debate and private information. Does such talk hide more than it reveals about the world today? Explain.
2   What are fluidities and mobilities? Generate a number of examples that touch your everyday life.
3   What are some of the ways that driving in a car represents the hybridization of public/private space?

Chapter 22 (Bennett and Raab)

1   What is the privacy paradigm?
2   In what ways does the privacy paradigm depend on, or reinforce, the distinction between the public and the private?
3   In what ways can information privacy legislation be understood to actually contribute to, rather than alleviate, systems of control?

Chapter 23 (Sewell and Barker)

1   What is a discursive ethics of surveillance?
2   Do you think that information and communication technologies pose new implications for an ethics of surveillance never before encountered?
3   How can you challenge power/knowledge surveillance relations in your workplace, school, or daily life?

Chapter 24 (Lyon)

1   What are some of the social challenges confronting those who seek to resist surveillance after the attacks on Washington and New York on 11 September 2001? Explain how this matters in your everyday life.
2   What are some of the political challenges confronting those who seek to resist surveillance after the attacks on Washington and New York on 11 September 2001? Explain how this matters in your everyday life.
3   What are some of the technological challenges confronting those who seek to resist surveillance after the attacks on Washington and New York on 11 September 2001? Explain how this matters in your everyday life.

Suggested reading

1   Whitaker, R. (1999) *The End of Privacy: How Total Surveillance is Becoming a Reality*. New York: New York Press.
Whitaker traces the development of surveillance technologies from World War II military intelligence to the information revolution. He conceptualizes surveillance in terms of power and social control, and suggests that we may be approaching a state of panopticism.
2   Bennett, C. and Regan, P. (2003) Surveillance and mobilities, *Surveillance and Society* (special issue), 1(4).
This special issue presents seven issues concerned with surveillance and mobilities. The papers assess what is meant by mobilities, the relationship between surveillance and mobility, and provides a typology of movement. The journal is available online, free of charge.
3   Urry, J. (2000) *Sociology Beyond Societies: Mobilities for the Twenty-First Century*. New York: Routledge.
A key contribution to the expanding field of mobilities, Urry's book argues that sociology must abandon its tradition foci if it is to meaningfully explain the world today. The book takes up themes of mobility such as travel, ideas, money and waste.
4   Castells, M. (1996) *The Rise of Network Society*. Malden, MA: Blackwell Publishers.
This book is the first of three books written on networked societies. The book offers an analysis of the socio-economic dynamics of the new age of information. Information is presented from the USA, Asia, Latin America and Europe.
5   Etzioni, A. (1996) *The Limits of Privacy*. New York: Basic Books.
This easy-to-read book presents five short case studies. Framed in the context of the privacy paradox, Etzioni raises important issues pertaining to HIV, ID cards, sex offenders and medical records.

References

Bauman, Z. (2001) *Liquid Modernity*. London: Polity.

Castells, M. (1996) *The Information Age: Economy, Society and Culture. vol. 1. The Rise of the Network Society*. Oxford: Blackwell.

Latour, B. (2005) *Reassembling the Social: An Introduction to Actor Network Theory*. Oxford: Oxford University Press.

Urry, J. and Law, J. (2004) Enacting the social, *Economy and Society*, 33(3): 390–415.

21

Mobile transformations of 'public' and 'private' life[1]
by Mimi Sheller and John Urry

One of the key dilemmas of the 20th century concerned the overwhelming power of the state and market to interfere in and to overpower 'private' life. By contrast, in the 21st century, the emerging social problem is seen as the erosion of the 'public' by processes otherwise understood to be 'private'. Thus participation in the public sphere of associational life and democratic communication has declined according to Wolfe (1989) and Putnam (2000), because commercialization and privatizing TV-watching have destroyed older feelings of solidarity and belonging to a community. The public spaces of cities, once the seedbeds of civility and social life, have been overrun by 'private cars' according to Habermas (1992), Sennett (1977) and Reclaim the Streets activists (Jordan, 1998). Private corporations have taken over once public institutions of schools, hospitals, prisons, transportation systems, postal services and the state itself, leading to a loss of democratic control, according to Nader (2000) and Klein (2000), while, according to Berlant (1997) and Bauman (2000), a politics of confessional intimacy and shaming has invaded the once public arena of political debate and arbitration of collective interests. On every front, it seems, the 'public' is being privatized, the private is becoming oversized, and this undermines democratic life . . .

Multiple publics and privates

. . . Social scientists and political theorists use the terms 'public' and 'private' in many, often contradictory, ways. Weintraub notes that 'different sets of people who employ these concepts mean very different things by them – and sometimes, without quite realizing it, mean several things at once' (1997: 1–2). He refers to four major approaches: the liberal-economistic model, the republican virtue (and classical) model, the 'sociability' or dramaturgic approach, and finally a range of feminist critiques/analyses. Emirbayer and Sheller (1999) have also pointed to the multiple contours of concepts of the public sphere oriented in different ways toward the economic, the political and the civil . . .

The first public/private distinction focuses on the boundary between the market and the state, of private *interests* versus public interests, or the private sector versus the public sector. Here the state is presumed to operate in the public interest, while economic actors pursue their own 'private' interests as calculating individuals or profit-maximizing corporations. Referring to this as the liberal-economistic model, Weintraub notes that 'this orientation defines public/private issues as having to do with striking a balance between individuals and contractually created organizations, on the one hand, and state action on the other' (1997: 8). Here the forms of inclusion and exclusion on either side of the boundary are state-determined; that is, they are grounded in law, contract, and the recognition of property and subjects before the law as either private or public. The private realm is predominantly economic in origins, motivation and orientation: it is about free markets (versus governmental hierarchies), Smith's 'invisible hand' (versus Hobbes's Leviathan) or capitalism (versus state socialism) . . .

In the second branch of social and political theory the public *sphere* is viewed as a space of rational debate and open communication mediating between the state and the private sphere of family life and economic relations. The private sphere is seen as part of civil society from which potential solidarity, equality and public participation can arise. Thus inclusion or exclusion from the public sphere occurs through the self-organization of social actors into associations that can act publicly or speak as the 'private citizens come together as a public'. Cohen and Arato refer to privacy as 'a domain of individual self-development and moral choice' (1992: 346), rather than simply as a realm of private economic interests. Such a view of the private also occurs within the civic republican tradition, which is largely concerned with the relation between the individual and the state, and subsumes private economic interests within a broader definition of a solidaristic civil society. Together these normative approaches can be thought of as defining a kind of 'political private'; the individual emerges as private citizen in relation to the state and ideally participates in a public sphere of communication, equality and deliberation . . .

. . . [A] third approach understands the private as more fundamentally rooted in private *life* and delineated by private *space*, in which the mechanisms of inclusion and exclusion revolve around social relations and physical and symbolic demarcations between different spaces (Sennett, 1977). This is the private sphere pertaining to the domestic, the familial, the personal, the bodily and the intimate inner world of the individual (Ariès and Duby, 1989; Elias, 1982). Privacy is viewed as much as a spatial arrangement as a social one, and is something marked off from the 'public spaces' of streets, parks and plazas (Weintraub, 1997: 17–25). This model of privacy also pertains to feminist approaches, which refer to everything outside the household as 'public', including economic institutions such as the workplace or corporations, *and* political institutions of the state *and* public spaces. A key concern here is with the exclusion of women from this array of public realms (Fraser, 1992; Pateman, 1989; Phillips, 1991).

Again there are several kinds of concern with the erosion of the public/private boundary. Some radical feminist theory rejects the notion of a separate private realm by highlighting the unavoidable intervention of the modern welfare state in the supposedly 'non-political' realms of the family, sexuality, child-rearing, control of one's body and so on (Pateman, 1998). Also relevant here is the shift from 'private patriarchy' to a new kind of 'public patriarchy' as women in many European societies have increasingly moved from the 'confines' of the 'private' household into the 'public' workplace and state institutions (Walby, 1990). Yet for others, the key problem in modern societies is the unravelling of traditional communities and associational practices. Putnam argues that this diminution of social activities and community ties has led to a decline of the 'social capital', which is necessary for a robust democratic society (2000).

Finally here, there is analysis of the media and forms of mass-mediated publicity in relation to questions of privacy. The Frankfurt School's critique of the mass media first identified how their increasing commodification undermined democratic communication and weakened citizenship. Foucauldians are concerned with the forms of surveillance and power which infiltrate the most 'private' realms of the family, the body and sexuality. This suggests that the very notion of a 'separate' private realm is an illusion in the first place, and the apparent boundary only exists so that state power can be exercised over bodies. At a more everyday level, there has been much publicity surrounding the media's invasion of the 'private' lives of public figures (see Richards et al., 1999). Media exposure transgresses the symbolic boundary that once kept such 'private' matters and people's personal lives hidden from public scrutiny . . .

Thus a more careful differentiation between distinctive understandings of the private and the public allows for a better reading of the multiple issues apparently raised by the erosion of the boundary between the two categories. There are many different kinds of 'erosion', pertaining to changes in legality and regulation, in civil institutions and associational ties, in uses of public space and the media. However, all such writers maintain an adhenence to what we have referred to as a static version of the divide between the public and the private. Is it still useful (or even possible) to maintain the boundary between a public and a private sphere? Can public interests and private interests be effectively separated? How can privacy and publicity be disentangled in the glare of media exposure? To address these questions, we argue, social theory will need to develop a more dynamic conceptualization of the fluidities and mobilities that have increasingly hybridized the public and private.

Moving within and between the public and private

We now turn to our own analysis of the links between these transformational processes, suggesting that the changing forms of physical and informational mobility that uproot bodies from place and information from space are key. The existing literature has been overly static and regional in its thinking, whatever distinction is drawn between the public and private domains. We show that cars, information, communications, screens, are all material worlds, hybrids of private and public life. Despite the heroic efforts of 20th-century normative theorists to rescue the divide, the various distinctions between public and private domains cannot survive. The critical theorists reviewed above each in different ways diagnosed the erosion of boundaries between public and private as the cause of democratic decline; maintaining or restoring the boundary, they imply, is crucial to the continuance of democratic citizenship in the contemporary world. We argue, in contrast, that the hybridization of public and private is even more extensive than previously thought, and is occurring in more complex and fluid ways than any regional model of separate spheres can capture.

Any hope for public citizenship and democracy, then, will depend on the capacity to navigate these new material, mobile worlds that are neither public nor private. In what follows we explore how mobilities are central to the reconstitution of publicity and privacy with far-reaching implications for the future of citizenship.

We begin our analysis first with civil society that is typically thought of as located within specific physical places (Cohen and Arato, 1992). Conceptually, it has been rooted in specific spatial zones of public sociality and at most involving connection through newspapers and the imagined communities of 'print publics' (Anderson, 1991). The power of civil society crucially depends on the 'space' between these public and private 'spheres'. Arendt, for example, located the origins of the public sphere in the Ancient Greek *polis*, based around the meeting of private citizens in the public space of the *agora* (1973). Tocqueville commented on the meetings, the voluntary associations and the democratic sociability of towns in America (1945). Habermas identified the origins of the bourgeois public sphere in the privatization of the conjugal family which fed into the literate public that formed within the coffee-houses, table societies and masonic lodges of late 18th-century European cities (1992; Cohen and Arato, 1992). In these idealized public places, an informed rational debate could take place at least among the elite men who could gain entry to these specific 'public' locales (Landes, 1988).

Thus the 'public sphere' of civil society has normally been conflated with that of 'public space' (Weintraub, 1997). But such spatial models of civil society do not attend to how people (and objects) *move*, or desire to move, between the supposedly private and the public domains. Indeed, it is often argued that the very freedom of mobility holds the potential to disrupt public space, to interfere with more stable associational life and to undermine proper politics. But focusing on movements within and across public space brings into view subaltern publics that have potentially disruptive politics (Ryan, 1997).

Historians have highlighted how both the public and private spheres have been circumscribed by various socio-spatial exclusions (Fraser, 1992; Kelley, 1996). Indeed while Ariès and Elias have carefully traced the material culture of private life as it emerged from the 16th to the 18th centuries, the contemporary analysts reviewed above have treated the private as spatially given rather than as something that is still evolving in relationship to the changing materialities of social life. What is held in common by these theorists of erosion is the way in which the capacity for inclusion/ exclusion is seen as spatially and materially fixed.

However, we suggest that public and private life have always been mobile, situational, flickering and fragmented. We focus on automobility and information technology as two key elements of modernity that have ambivalent effects on cultures of democracy. On the one hand, both sociotechnologies are seen as contributing to the decline of the public sphere, cars through their erosion of urban public spaces, and information technologies through the fostering of societies of surveillance and voyeurism, On the other hand, both technologies have also contributed to new processes of democratization. Cars have allowed for a 'sphere of personal freedom, leisure, and freedom of movement' (Habermas, 1992: 129), and have contributed to the peculiar 'auto-freedom' of modernity (Sheller and Urry, 2000). Likewise, information technology, especially the Internet, is envisioned as opening up new possibilities for global communication and democratization (Castells, 2001). The ambivalence of these opposing interpretations arises from how they put the public and the private against each other, while maintaining the boundary between them. What neither analysis recognizes is how both of these socio-technologies undo all divisions between public and private life through their machinic, mobile hybridities.

First then, automobility: this is a machinic complex of manufactured objects, individual consumption, environmental resource use and dominant culture that generates a specific character of domination over almost all contemporary societies (Sheller and Urry, 2000). It reconfigures the relation between place, space and the mobility of people and objects. The key feature leading to the flexible *and* coercive attraction of automobility is its formation as a 'quasi-private' mobility that subordinates other 'public' mobilities. We should not maintain a *regional* separation of the public versus the private, because its fluidities are simultaneously public *and* private. People move within and between the public and the private, at times being in effect in both simultaneously.

Automobility indeed constitutes a civil society of hybridized 'car-drivers', dwelling privately-within-their-cars, and excluding those without cars or without the 'licence' to drive from the car-dominated public realm. Such a civil society of automobility transforms public spaces into public roads, in which to a significant extent the hybrids of pedestrians, cyclists and even public transport users are marginalized. Only those moving (however slowly) in private vehicles can be *public* within a system in which public roads have been seized by the 'auto-mobile' private citizens cocooned within their 'iron-cages' (of modernity). A civil society of automobility, or the right to drive where and when one wants, involves the mobile transformation of once public space into road space, coercing, constraining and unfolding an awesome domination, such that nearly half of the land in LA, for example, is devoted to car-only environments.

As a rolling private-in-public space, automobility affords dwelling inside a mobile capsule that involves punctuated movement 'on the road'. Private zones of domesticity are reproduced on the road through social relations such as the 'back-seat driver' or the common dependence on a partner for navigation and map reading. A variety of services have become available without leaving the car, as the 'drive-in' becomes a feature of everyday life. Protected by seatbelts, airbags, 'crumple zones', 'roll bars' and 'bull bars', car-dwellers boost their own safety and leave others on the road to fend for themselves. In each car the driver is strapped into a comfortable armchair and surrounded by micro-electronic informational sources, controls and sources of pleasure, what Williams calls the 'mobile privatisation' of the car (Pinkney, 1991: 55).

And this is a private room, a moving private capsule, in which the sensing of the public world is impoverished. The speed at which the car must be driven constrains the driver to always keep moving. Dwelling at speed, drivers lose the ability to perceive local detail, to talk to strangers, to learn of local ways of life, to stop and sense the particularity of place. The sights, sounds, tastes, temperatures and smells of public spaces are reduced to the two-dimensional view through the car windscreen. The public world beyond the windscreen is an alien other, to be kept at bay through the diverse privatizing technologies incorporated within the contemporary car. Thus people remain inside their cars, while the 'coming together of private citizens in public space' is lost to a privatization of the mechanized self moving through the emptied non-places of public roads (Augé, 1995).

If automobility has afforded one set of mobile processes that change the materialization of the private and public, then new communication technologies offer further de-differentiation. In so far as citizenship rests on 'deliberation' or 'communicative action', all forms of communication have been reconfigured by new technologies and the new spatio-temporal patterns of social life through which they are made effective. People can now access 'public information' from 'private spaces' because of the availability of digital networks of electronic data and images. At the same time, however, private spaces and private information are now increasingly susceptible to public eavesdropping or tracking, whether by government agencies, marketing researchers or computer hackers. As public and private become so spatially intermeshed, privacy itself is transformed. Relationships involving new electronic media facilitate the obtaining of information about others, without those people knowing in general about the information flow or about the specific details (Lyon, 1994, 1997: 26–7). Examples include the use of databases to generate details of creditworthiness, surveillance cameras and satellites, computer hacking, the targeting of potential customers using information acquired from other sources, illegal tapping of phone calls, the use of GIS software to produce highly differentiated insurance rates, product choices and so on. These reconfigure humans as bits of information subject to computerized monitoring and control through various 'systems' of which they are typically unaware.

Thus individuals increasingly exist beyond their private bodies. Persons leave traces of their selves in informational space, and can be more readily mobile through space because of a greater potential for 'self-retrieval' at the other end of a network. If people bank electronically, for example, they are able to access their money in many parts of the world today; if they need to establish personal contact with family and friends, they can do so from most anywhere in the world. People are able to 'plug into' global networks of information through which they can 'do' things and 'talk' to people without being present in a particular place. 'Persons' occur as nodes in these networks of communication and mobility in so far as particular moving bodies become the repositories of 'narratives of the self': memories, plots, characters organized into a 'private life' (Giddens, 1991; White, 1992).

As a consequence, even the most intimate 'private' is no longer entirely 'personal' or 'inner-worldly'. Where the neural networks of the brain stop and the electronic networks of information begin is unclear. Parts of who one is may be stored on hard disks or digital circuits rather than in the 'old grey matter'. Much of what was once 'private' already exists outside of the physical body; the body can in some instances function as a hyperlink for gaining access to fragmented selves, or making connections with various nodes in the personal networks that no longer occur only within private spaces. The information revolution has implanted zones of publicity into the once-private interior spaces of the self and home.

Global mobilities

Moreover, the mobilities known as 'globalization' further de-differentiate the apparently 'public' and 'private' domains. Globalization can be seen in terms of global fluids constituted of waves of people, information, objects, money, images, risks and networks moving across regions in heterogeneous, uneven, unpredictable and often unplanned shapes (Mol and Law, 1994; Sheller, 2000; Urry, 2000). Such global fluids demonstrate no clear point of departure, just de-territorialized movement, at certain speeds and different levels of viscosity with no necessary end-state or purpose. They result from people acting upon the basis of local information but where these local actions are, through countless iterations, captured, moved, represented, marketed and generalized within multiple global waves often impacting upon distant places and peoples. Global fluids travel along various route-ways but, where they escape through the 'wall' into surrounding matter, they effect unpredictable consequences upon that matter. Fluids move according to certain novel shapes and temporalities as they may break free from the linear, clock-time of existing routeways – but they cannot go back, they cannot return since all times are irreversible. The messy complexity of relatively unfixed and mobile publics and privates can best be understood as emergent configurations of people, technologies and places within these global flows.

As a consequence of such global fluids, many apparently public institutions are no longer 'national'. We can distinguish at the global level between first, global civil publics which are concerned with orchestrating consumption and leisure flows, such as the Olympic movement, World Cups, CNN, MTV and so on (Roche, 2000). Second, there are global economic publics, such as the 'public' constituted by stockholders in the dominant 40,000 multinational corporations, the world financial institutions like the World Bank and IMF, or the bodies governing the flows of world trade such as the WTO, the World Intellectual Property Organization and so on. Third, global political publics operate both at the level of the organization of 'states' (EU, UN, UNESCO, IATA) and in the shape of international NGOs (e.g. Amnesty International, Global Exchange, Sisterhood is Global Institute) and social movements (the Zapatistas in Chiapas, Mexico, or the anti-WTO or anti-globalization campaigns) which envision a global mission. Each of these globals interacts with the others in a complex self-organizing and emergent set of fluidities that are simultaneously public-and-private (Urry, 2003).

Indeed, what we term the 'general public' is also transnational, knowing about and partly relating to these global institutions whose activities, procedures and rules help to constitute that public. Partly as a consequence 'publics' become much more fluidly 'cosmopolitan'. They are mobile, have a strong sense of mobile opportunities, have developed a notion that cultures travel and develop some orientation to the 'other' whose characteristics have been publicized and made visible (see Szerszynski et al., 2000). Related to this is the internationalizing of public spaces across the globe. Efforts to reclaim these public spaces have likewise moved beyond critiques of commodification to more playful interventions in the flows of car-traffic and brand-publicity, often using situated actions to 'jam' global flows (Klein, 2000; McKay, 1998).

And, most significantly, there has been the transformed staging of publicity. Citizenship has always necessitated processes of communication and the distribution of symbolic resources (Murdock, 1992: 20–1). Printing, especially of newspapers, was particularly significant in the 18th- and 19th-century development of the imagined community of the European nation, the public sphere and the growth of the nation-state (Anderson, 1991). In the 20th-century development of national citizenship, publicly owned radio broadcasting has been particularly significant. As Murdock notes: 'Where commercial broadcasting regarded listeners as consumers of products, the ethos of public service viewed them as citizens of a nation state' . . . (1992: 26–7) . . . The current mass media are comprised of extraordinary flows of visual images that reconstitute how human actions are conceived of and framed. Such continuous flows of images, and associated text, transform what was called the 'public sphere' into what we could conceptualize as a 'public screen', visible everywhere linked to global networks. This transformation further de-differentiates the previously separate spheres of the private and the public, local and global. Where once 'staging' was the operative metaphor for public events, now 'screening' is more appropriate to describe those contexts where privacy has been eroded and where supposedly private lives are ubiquitously screened . . .

Furthermore, the global media create global 'events' through simultaneous broadcasts. Indeed there are global events in which the world views itself; the event becomes global through its world-wide screening. Examples connected to global citizenship include the Live Aid concert, the release from prison of Nelson Mandela, the dramatic death and funeral of Princess Diana, the Rio Earth Summit, the Beijing Conference, and the *Brent Spar* episode. In the last example:

> . . . the communications deployed were second to none. The protestors had satellite telephones and a Mac computer that downloaded photographs and video footage to a media base in Frankfurt. Greenpeace employed its own photographer and cameraman to capture the images that ensured the story was splashed in papers and television screens across the world.
>
> (Pilkington et al., 1995: 4)

Greenpeace campaigners waved to the world from the *Brent Spar* oil rig and were recorded by the world's media who were invited by Greenpeace to use their facilities. Greenpeace spoke for the globe while appearing on the global *screen*.

And now such screens occur not only in the domestic space of the lounge, with the family gathered around its television, but also can be transmitted onto screens in airport lounges, bars, shops, waiting rooms, restaurants, shopping malls or the middle of Times Square in New York. McCarthy describes the huge extent of such 'ambient television', which 'produces the out-of-home TV audience as a mobile and elastic commodity' (2001: 24). Screens are leaving their moorings, so that global events can appear on the moving screens of an airplane, on a laptop computer on a train, on Internet connections within cars and so on. If the traditional threat to a democratic public revolved around issues of the 'staging' of events in a false or mindless 'mass acclamatory' public, the emergence of screening suggests a new set of tensions. Screening can also be thought of in the sense of filtering out the undesirable, of exercising surveillance and control. In other words, the power to shape, filter or 'screen' what appears on the global screen remains a significant issue of political contestation. The highly controlled screening of the Gulf War, the war in Afghanistan, and the war in Iraq, exemplifies the convergence of transport technologies for the moving of armies and weaponry, with the informational technologies by which bombs are guided to their targets and are televisually displayed hitting their targets for a globally watching TV audience on their screens, inside and outside the home . . .

Conclusion

. . . Contemporary social relations are shown to involve powerful, *mobile* networks, which are refolding what is public and what is private. The analysis of these networks is taking the social sciences way beyond the static, regional and fixed notions of public and private life characteristic of many 20th-century formulations, formulations in social and political theory that no longer suffice in the new century. The distinction between public and private domains should be dispensed with since nothing much of contemporary social life remains on one side or the other of the divide. Thus the problems of (and hopes for) democratic citizenship must be theorized in relation to these dynamic, multiple mobilities of people, objects, information and images, especially as these move in powerfully fused or hybridized forms . . .

Note

1 This chapter is an extract from M. Sheller and J. Urry (2003) Mobile transformations of 'public' and 'private' life, *Theory, Culture & Society*, 20(3): 107–25.

References

Anderson, B. (1991) *Imagined Communities: Reflections on the Origin and Spread of Nationalism*. London and New York: Verso.

Arendt, H. (1973/1958) *The Human Condition*. Chicago, IL: University of Chicago Press.

Ariès, P. and Duby, G. (1989) *A History of Private Life: Passions of the Renaissance*, vol. 3. Cambridge, MA, and London: Harvard University Press.

Augé, M. (1995) *Non-places*. London: Verso.

Bauman, Z. (2000) *Liquid Modernity*. Cambridge: Polity Press.

Berlant, L. (1997) *The Queen of America Goes to Washington City: Essays on Sex and Citizenship*. Durham, NC, and London: Duke University Press.

Castells, M. (2001) *The Internet Galaxy*. Oxford: Oxford University Press.

Cohen, J. and Arato, A. (1992) *Civil Society and Political Theory*. Cambridge, MA and London: MIT Press.

Elias, N. (1982) *The Civilizing Process*. New York: Pantheon.

Emirbayer, M. and Sheller, M. (1999) Publics in history, *Theory and Society*, 28: 145–97.

Fraser, N. (1992) Rethinking the public sphere: a contribution to the critique of actually existing democracy, in C. Calhoun (ed.) *Habermas and the Public Sphere*. Cambridge, MA, and London: MIT Press.

Giddens, A. (1991) *Modernity and Self-identity*. Cambridge: Polity.

Habermas, J. (1992) *The Structural Transformation of the Public Sphere: An Inquiry into a Category of Bourgeois Society*, trans. T. Burger. Cambridge, MA: MIT Press.

Jordan, J. (1998) The art of necessity: the subversive imagination of anti-road protest and Reclaim the Streets, in G. McKay (ed.) *DiY Culture: Party and Protest in Nineties Britain*. London and New York: Verso.

Klein, N. (2000) *No Logo*. London: Flamingo.

Landes, J. (1988) *Women and the Public Sphere in the Age of the French Revolution*. Ithaca, NY, and London: Cornell University Press.

Lyon, D. (1994) *The Electronic Eye: The Rise of the Surveillance Society*. Cambridge: Polity.

McCarthy, A. (2001) *Ambient Television*. Durham, NC, and London: Duke University Press.

McKay, G. (ed.) (1998) *DiY Culture: Party and Protest in Nineties Britain*. London and New York: Verso.

Mol, A. and Law, J. (1994) Regions, networks and fluids: anaemia and social topology, *Social Studies of Science*, 24: 641–71.

Murdock, G. (1992) Citizens, consumers, and public culture, in M. Shovmand and K. Shrøder (eds) *Media Cultures*. London: Routledge.

Nader, R. (2000) *The Ralph Nader Reader*. New York: Seren Stories Press.

Pateman, C. (1989) *The Sexual Contract*. Cambridge: Polity.

Pateman, C. (1998) The patriarchal welfare state, in J. Landes (ed.) *Feminism, the Public and the Private*. Oxford and New York. Oxford University Press.

Phillips, A. (1991) *Engendering Democracy*. Cambridge: Polity.

Pilkington, E., Clouston, E. and Traynor, I. (1995) How a wave of public opinion bowled over the Shell monolith, *The Guardian*, 22 June.

Pinkney, T. (1991) *Raymond Williams*. Bridgend: Seren Books.

Putnam, R. (2000) *Bowling Alone*. New York: Simon and Schuster.

Richards, J., Wilson, S. and Woodhead, L. (eds) (1999) *Diana: The Making of a Media Saint*. London: I.B. Tauris.

Roche, M. (2000) *Mega-events and Modernity*. London: Routledge.

Ryan, M. (1997) *Civic Wars: Democracy and Public Life in the American City During the Nineteenth Century*. Berkeley and Los Angeles: University of California Press.

Sennett, R. (1977) *The Fall of Public Man*. London and Boston, MA: Faber and Faber.

Sheller, M. (2000) The mechanisms of mobility and liquidity: re-thinking the movement in social movements. Available at: http://www.comp.lancs.ac.uk/sociology/soc076 ms.html

Sheller, M. and Urry, J. (2000) The city and the car, *International Journal of Urban and Regional Research*, 24: 737–57.

Szerszynski, B., Urry, J. and Myers, G. (2000) Mediating global citizenship, in J. Smith (ed.) *Global Environmental Change, the Public and the Media*. London: Earthscan.

Tocqueville, A. de (1945/1835) *Democracy in America*, 2 vols. New York: Vintage.

Urry, J. (2000) *Sociology Beyond Societies*. London: Routledge.

Urry, J. (2003) *Global Complexity*. Cambridge: Polity.

Walby, S. (1990) *Theorizing Patriarchy*. London: Basil Blackwell.

Weintraub, J. (1997) The theory and politics of the public/private distinction, in J. Weintraub and K. Kumar (eds) *Public and Private in Thought and Practice: Perspectives on a Grand Dichotomy*. Chicago, IL, and London: University of Chicago, Press.

White, H. (1992) *Identity and Control: A Structural Theory of Social Action*. Princeton, NJ: Princeton University Press.

Wolfe, A. (1989) *Whose Keeper? Social Science and Moral Obligation*. Berkeley: University of California Press.

22

The privacy paradigm[1]
by Colin Bennett and Charles Raab

Privacy and liberalism

We use the word 'paradigm' to denote a set of assumptions about a phenomenon or area of study which generally go unquestioned. These assumptions collectively set the agenda for research and for policy prescription. The paradigm produces an agreed understanding about the nature and scope of a particular problem. Paradigms are rarely explicitly interrogated, unless discoveries in knowledge and science force a community of scholars to confront their long-held and preconceived assumptions (Kuhn, 1970). Sometimes that interrogation can occur through the conduct of scientific inquiry; sometimes it can occur because of revolutionary changes in technology. The point is that paradigms are rarely questioned, because for the most part there is no necessity. We would argue that there is a set of unquestioned assumptions that surrounds the modern analysis of privacy protection in Western societies. We also hope to show that these assumptions are in need of careful scrutiny and revision in the light of recent technological developments and trends in the use of personal data in the state and the economy.

The privacy paradigm rests on a conception of society as comprising relatively autonomous *individuals*. It rests on an atomistic conception of society; the community is no more than the sum total of the individuals that make it up. Further, it rests on notions of differences between the privacy claims and interests of different individuals. The individual, with her liberty, autonomy, rationality and privacy, is assumed to know her interests, and should be allowed a private sphere untouched by others. In John Stuart Mill's terms, there should be certain 'self-regarding' activities of private concern, contrasted with 'other-regarding' activities susceptible to community interest and regulation (Mill, 1859).

The modern claim to privacy, then, is based on a notion of a boundary between the individual and other individuals, and between the individual and the state. It rests on notions of a distinction between the public and the private. It rests on the pervasive assumption of a civil society comprised of relatively autonomous individuals who need a modicum of privacy in order to be able to fulfil the various roles of the citizen in a liberal democratic state. Thus, as Warren and Brandeis comment in their seminal article on the right to privacy: 'Still, the protection of society must come mainly through a recognition of the rights of the individual. Each man is responsible for his own acts and omissions only' (Warren and Brandeis, 1890, pp. 219–20).

Shils is a twentieth-century proponent of this view that privacy reinforces the barriers between the individual and the state and within the contours of civil society (Shils, 1956, pp. 154–60). Privacy, for Shils, is essential for the strength of American pluralistic democracy because it bolsters the boundaries between competing and countervailing centers of power. Westin (1967) has provided perhaps the most eloquent statement of the importance of privacy for liberal democratic societies. In contrast to totalitarian regimes:

> [A] balance that ensures strong citadels of individual and group privacy and limits both disclosure and surveillance is a prerequisite for liberal democratic societies. The democratic society relies on publicity as a control over government, and on privacy as a shield for group and individual life . . . Liberal democratic theory assumes that a good life for the individual must have substantial areas of interest apart from political participation . . .
>
> (Westin, 1967, p. 24)

Westin goes on to address the specific functions that privacy plays. It promotes freedom of association. It shields scholarship and science from unnecessary interference by government. It permits the use of a secret ballot and protects the voting process by forbidding government surveillance of a citizen's past voting record. It restrains improper police conduct such as 'physical brutality, compulsory self-incrimination, and unreasonable searches and seizures' (Westin, 1967, p. 25). It serves also to shield those institutions, such as the press, that operate to keep government accountable.

Westin also argues that different historical and political traditions among Western nations were likely to create different results in the overall balance between privacy and government. In his view, England exhibits a 'deferential democratic balance', a combination in which there is 'greater personal reserve between Englishmen, high personal privacy in home and private associations, and a faith in government that bestows major areas of privacy for government operations'. West Germany exhibits an 'authoritarian democratic balance' in which 'respect for the privacy of person, home, office and press still gives way to the claims of official surveillance and disclosure.' The United States exhibits an 'egalitarian democratic balance, in which the privacy-supporting values of individualism, associational life, and civil liberty are under constant pressure from privacy-denying tendencies toward social egalitarianism, personal activism, and political fundamentalism' (Westin, 1967, pp. 26–7).

Whether or not these generalizations from the 1960s were, or still are, valid, it is no doubt interesting to hypothesize that the way the balance between privacy and community obligations and duties is struck within different democratic societies will vary according to different cultural traditions. The belief in privacy is arguably related to wider attitudes about participation in public affairs and about trust in the authority of governmental agencies . . .

We would therefore observe that privacy protection is normally justified in individualistic terms in the academic literature and in the popular mind. We each have a right or claim to be able to control information that relates to ourselves. Privacy has an aesthetic and humanistic affinity with individual autonomy and dignity. It can be justified in political terms in that it promotes the institutions of liberal democracy, and it has a number of utilitarian values by way of fostering the principle that only the 'right people should use the right information for the right purposes' (Sieghart, 1976). Whether justified in philosophical, political or utilitarian terms, privacy is almost always seen as a claim or right of individuals that is threatened by a set of social and technological forces. Privacy is something that 'we' once had; now it is something that public and private organizations employing the latest information and communications technologies are denying us.

This paradigmatic theme is represented in a large corpus of literature, written mainly by journalists, activists and academics, which has a polemical tone. Orwellian metaphors and imagery are naturally prolific, even though '1984' came and went without any palpable change in the attention paid to privacy questions. Among the early examples of the popular American literature are Packard's *The Naked Society* (1964) and Brenton's *The Privacy Invaders* (1964). Continually over the last thirty years or more, publishers in North America . . . Britain . . . and elsewhere have been attracted by this more polemical genre. The literature also encompasses a shifting anxiety over emerging technologies. This ranges from apprehension over the 'snooping devices' of the 1960s, to worries about the sophisticated trade in personal information revealed in Rothfeder's *Privacy for Sale* (1992), to the more contemporary concerns about the Internet discussed by Diffie and Landau (1998), and by Garfinkel (2000).

The importance of this literature arguably lies in its cumulative impact and message. A steady flow of horror stories about the intrusive nature of modern technology, about the abuse and misuse of personal data, and about the size and interconnectedness of contemporary information systems has probably had a steady impact on public and political consciousness (Smith, 1993). Moreover, many of these stories have then been picked up by the print and visual media, especially television. Big Brother imagery, together with accounts of how the powerless can be denied rights and services through the wrongful collection, use and disclosure of personal data certainly make good copy; they also make good films.[2]

Policy implications of the privacy paradigm

The pervasiveness of liberal assumptions within the literature has had a number of political and policy implications. Assuming that we each have privacy rights and interests, how can one frame a public policy to protect those rights? Philosophers, academic lawyers and other scholars have debated the meaning of 'privacy' from a variety of standpoints (e.g., Young, 1978; Schoeman, 1984). As a policy problem, however, the discourse settled around 'information privacy', a concept that arose in the 1960s and 1970s at about the same time that 'data protection', derived from the German *Datenschutz*, entered the vocabulary.

Concerns obviously differed among a number of advanced industrial states. However, a closely-knit group of experts in different countries coalesced, shared ideas, and generated a general consensus about the best way to solve the problem of protecting the privacy of personal information (Bennett, 1992, pp. 127–9). The overall policy goal in every country was to give individuals greater control of the information that is collected, stored, processed and disseminated about them by public, and in some cases, private organizations. Essentially, the common view was that this goal necessitates a distinction between the *subject* of the information and the *controller* of that information. This distinction is one of role rather than of person: although we are all 'data subjects', many of us are also 'data controllers', also known as 'data users'. By the 1980s, therefore, it is possible to discern the set of key assumptions upon which information privacy policy development rested.

The first assumption was that privacy is a highly subjective value. Concerns about the protection of personal information vary over time, across jurisdictions, by different ethnic subgroups, by gender, and so on. Consequently, public policy cannot second-guess the kinds of personal information about which a given population or group will be concerned at a given time. Public policy and law can only establish the rules, principles and procedures by which any individually identifiable personal information should be treated, and by which the worst effects of new technologies can be countered. Information privacy policy is based inevitably, therefore, on *procedural*, rather than *substantive*, tenets. It can put in place the mechanisms by which individuals can assert their own privacy interests and claims, *if they so wish*, and it can impose obligations on those who use personal data. But for the most part, the content of privacy rights and interests have to be defined by individuals themselves according to context.

It is generally difficult to define *a priori* those data that are inherently worthy of greater protection ('sensitive data'). It is often the shift of context – detaching personal data, through processing, from the circumstances of their original collection – rather than the properties of the data that lead to privacy risks when false conclusions are drawn about persons (Simitis, 1987, p. 718). In addition, the same information can take on very different sensitivity levels in different contexts. Our names in the telephone directory may be insensitive; our names on a list of bad credit risks or of sex offenders may be very sensitive. A name and address in a telephone directory may be insensitive for most people, but may be very sensitive for vulnerable persons who do not want to be monitored and tracked down. Whereas the name 'P. J. O'Reilly' is not particularly conspicuous in the telephone directory of an Irish town, it stands out in the telephone directory of a Chinese town. Little wonder that many people prefer to have unlisted telephone numbers. Examples of such people would be battered wives, doctors who perform abortions, celebrities, child protection staff, police officers, and so on.

For the most part, therefore, public policy cannot draw a definite line between those types of information that should remain private, and those that may be in the public domain. Law cannot easily delineate between those types of data that are particularly worthy of protection and those that are not. Despite this, however, data protection laws have distinguished between what are generally agreed to be 'sensitive' data – religious beliefs, political opinions, sexual preferences, health, and the like – and the rest. But this distinction, and the inventory of data deemed 'sensitive', have remained controversial.

A second conclusion stemmed from the observation that personal information cannot easily be regarded as a property right. Classic economic theorizing would contend that an imperfect marketplace can be rectified in one of two ways. First, one can give a value to personal information so that the costs and benefits of transactions are allocated more appropriately. But is very difficult to establish personal information as property in law, and then to define rights of action over its illegitimate processing. Consumers may have some bargaining power with a direct marketing firm that wants to trade lists of named individuals; citizens, however, have no bargaining power when faced with a warrant or any other potentially privacy-invasive technique backed up by the sanctions of the state. Let us recall that, at the outset of the privacy debate, it was the power of government agencies that were considered to pose the most significant challenges. It was therefore hard to resist the conclusion that the imbalance could only be set right by regulatory intervention. Consequently, information privacy was generally defined as a problem for public policy, rather than as an issue for private choice.

More recently, as critiques of the dominant approach have surfaced, the personal data processing practices of the private sector have arisen as equally significant concerns. Moreover, as Internet communications and e-commerce have risen to prominence, so a variety of market-based solutions have been proposed, all of which have been based on the premise that personal information can be given a property value, to be traded and exchanged within the personal information market (Laudon, 1996; Rule and Hunter, 1999; Lessig, 1999). Such arguments had, however, very little influence on the experts and legislators that grappled with the information privacy problem in the 1970s.

A third assumption concerned the relationship between information privacy and information security. These and related concepts (data protection, data security, confidentiality, etc.) have caused considerable confusion. Clarke notes that:

> The term 'privacy' is used by some people, particularly security specialists and computer scientists, and especially in the United States, to refer to the security of data against various risks, such as the risks of data being accessed or modified by unauthorised persons. In some cases, it is used even more restrictively, to refer only to the security of data during transmission. These aspects are only a small fraction of the considerations within the field of 'information privacy'. More appropriate terms to use for those concepts are 'data security' and 'data transmission security'.
>
> (Clarke, 1999, p. 3)

In other words, data security is a necessary but not a sufficient condition for information privacy. An organization might keep the personal information it collects highly secure, but if it should not be collecting that information in the first place, the individual's information privacy rights are clearly violated. Over time, it became clear that the European concept of 'data protection' was being used in much the same way as the term 'information privacy'. Some, however, see this term as overly technical and concentrating on the *data* rather than the *person* as the object of protection.

Finally, there has been a consensus that the focus of protection should be the individual, or the 'natural person' rather than some other entity. Therefore, organizations and corporations cannot have privacy rights. Some societies – in Scandinavia, for example – have attempted to embrace the rights of natural and legal persons in their data protection legislation, and Westin himself was certainly open to the possibility that groups and organizations could have privacy 'claims' (Westin, 1967, p. 7). Nevertheless, information privacy policy did develop, domestically and internationally, on the assumption that the interests of groups, corporations and other organizations in the information about them can and should be dealt with through other legal instruments.

These assumptions might not be accepted by every scholar and commentator. They were and are deeply contested. The basic point at this juncture in the analysis is that privacy protection policy was set on a particular trajectory as a result of some common assumptions about the nature of the information privacy problem. It is particularly noteworthy that the privacy paradigm is not only shared by intellectuals and popular commentators, but also by those who make and implement privacy protection policy in advanced industrial states. The policy responses that developed – data protection or information privacy statutes – were driven for the most part by a shared understanding among policy elites about the nature of the problem they were facing. Those shared assumptions, based on fundamental liberal principles, have had profound and widespread policy implications in every advanced industrial state.

The 'fair information principles' doctrine

From these realizations flows the doctrine of 'fair information principles' (FIPs), enjoining upon data controllers norms for the collection, retention, use and disclosure of personal information. The codification of these principles has varied over time and space. They appear either explicitly or implicitly within all national data protection laws, including those which, in the US, Australia, New Zealand and Canada, are called 'Privacy' Acts. They appear in more voluntary codes and standards (e.g., CSA, 1996). They also form the basis of international agreements . . . These include the 1981 *Guidelines* of the Organization for Economic Cooperation and Development (OECD, 1981), the 1981 *Convention* of the Council of Europe (CoE, 1981), and the more recent *Directive on Data Protection* of the European Union (EU, 1995). Over time, there has emerged a strong consensus on what it means for the responsible organization to pursue fair information practices responsibly.

While the codification of the principles may vary, they essentially boil down to the following tenets (Bennett and Grant, 1999, p. 6). An organization (public or private):

- must be *accountable* for all the personal information in its possession;
- should *identify the purposes* for which the information is processed at or before the time of collection;
- should only collect personal information with the *knowledge and consent* of the individual (except under specified circumstances);
- should *limit the collection* of personal information to that which is necessary for pursuing the identified purposes;

- should not use or disclose personal information for purposes other than those identified, except with the consent of the individual (the *finality* principle);
- should *retain* information only as long as necessary;
- should ensure that personal information is kept *accurate, complete and up-to-date*;
- should protect personal information with appropriate *security safeguards*;
- should be *open* about its policies and practices and maintain no secret information system;
- should allow data subjects *access* to their personal information, with an ability to amend it if it is inaccurate, incomplete or obsolete.

These principles are, of course, relative. However conceptualized, privacy is not an absolute right; it must be balanced against correlative rights and obligations to the community, and can be overridden by other important values and rights. Hixson (1987) conceptualizes 'balance' as the 'continuing struggle over the meaning of private and public, the jurisprudential debate over individual autonomy and collective welfare, between the person and the state, the individual and the community' (Hixson, 1987, pp. xv-xvi). An assumption of 'balance' underlies many of the official investigations into privacy policy. The US Privacy Protection Study Commission, for instance, began its analysis by declaring that 'the Commission has constantly sought to examine the balance between the legitimate, sometimes competing, interests of the individual, the record-keeping organization, and society in general' (US, PPSC, 1977, p. xv).

However, this concept is problematic both as a verb and a noun (Raab, 1999a). It does not discriminate between divergent conceptions of what it means, in practice, 'to balance'; nor does it provide criteria for judging when 'a balance' has been achieved. It is therefore not very informative to hear that 'a balance must be struck between privacy and the public interest', or that 'we have found the right balance' between the one and the other. Different people may go about finding a balance in different ways, and arrive at different substantive points of reconciliation between competing values, as we shall see shortly. Although the concept is related to the terminology of judicial decision, the achievement of a balance may ultimately be a matter of political negotiation, perhaps arriving at a consensus; or, alternatively, of authoritative assertion . . .

Critiques of the privacy paradigm

Not all commentators have accepted the logic outlined above. From the outset of the modern debate, there has been a lively but often marginalized critique of liberal political theory as a basis for privacy . . . First, some sceptics have noted that there is a definite negative dimension to the notion of privacy as the 'right to be let alone'. On the one hand, it draws attention to why one might want to be left alone, and invites the criticism that privacy rights are predominantly asserted by those who have the most to hide. Here is a quote from an early article by Arndt (1949): 'The cult of privacy seems specifically designed as a defence mechanism for the protection of anti-social behaviour.' He equates privacy with the almost pathological obsession with possessive individualism: 'The cult of privacy rests on an individualist conception of society, not merely in the innocent and beneficial sense of a society in which the welfare of individuals is conceived as the end of all social organisation, but in the more specific sense of "each for himself and the devil take the hindmost" ' (Arndt, 1949, p. 70).

A similar critique of the theory of information privacy was presented in a famous article by Posner (1978). Posner's central point is that the application of the principle of information privacy has an unfortunate corollary, namely that it allows people to conceal personal information in order to mislead and misrepresent their character. Others, including government institutions, 'have a legitimate interest in unmasking the misrepresentation' (Posner, 1978, p. 20). 'It is no answer,' he continues, 'that, in Brandeis's phrase, people have "the right to be let alone". Few people want to be let alone. They want to manipulate the world around them by selective disclosure of facts about themselves. Why should others be asked to take their self-serving claims at face value and prevented from obtaining the information necessary to verify or disprove these claims?' (Posner, 1978, p. 22).

A second line of attack has come from those who find the distinction between public and private problematic. They cannot be treated as separate entities but are complex concepts that operate on different dimensions according to whether one is analyzing access to information, the capacities in which agents enjoy that access, or in whose interest the access is sought.

By extension, feminists have criticized privacy for reifying a distinction between a private, domestic (female) world, and a public sphere that is chiefly the preserve of men (Pateman, 1983; Allen, 1985; Boling, 1996). Allen and Mack (1990) criticize Warren and Brandeis on these grounds: they 'were not critical of the ways in which homelife, assertions of masculine personality, and norms of female modesty contributed to women's lacking autonomous decision-making and meaningful forms of individual privacy.' They advocated 'too much of the wrong kinds of privacy – too much modesty, seclusion, reserve and compelled intimacy – and too little individual modes of personal privacy and autonomous private choice' (Allen and Mack, 1990, p. 477).

Thirdly, and from the perspective of democratic theory, some would also contend that the liberalism of Locke and Mill, upon which the theory of information privacy rests, represents just one version of democratic theory. Pateman (1970), for example, has contended that there are two general traditions of democratic theory. One is a liberal tradition rooted in 18th century natural rights theory; the other is derived from the view that the test of a democracy is not the protection of individual or minority rights, nor the degree of competition between centres of power. Rather, the test is the degree of participation, cooperation, community consciousness and so on – values that are not necessarily promoted by asserting the 'right to be let alone'.

This argument finds current reflection in the renewed interest in the communitarian theorizing of Etzioni (1999), which has resonated with contemporary political elites of the left and the right in both Europe and America. Etzioni explicitly attempts to point to a new 'communitarian concept of privacy' – 'one that systematically provides for a balance between rights and the common good' (Etzioni, 1999, p. 15).

His analysis of privacy builds on 'the sociological observation that although ideologies can be structured around a single organizing principle – like liberty, or a particular social virtue – societies must balance values that are not fully compatible' (Etzioni, 1999, p. 200). He contends that, insofar as the public sector is concerned, the balance is too often struck in favour of privacy, while private sector abuses often go unchallenged.

A communitarian position might even argue that some of the most creative civilizations in history – such as ancient Greece and Rome, and Renaissance Italy – flourished despite, or maybe because of, the lack of individual privacy. Public philosophies, including communitarianism, do not spring from an emphasis on the 'right to be let alone'. If information privacy, as it is conventionally construed, is a precondition of democracy, it is not of democracy *per se* but of a particular form, liberal democracy, the theoretical justifications for which were provided by Locke, Madison, and Mill, rather than by Jean-Jacques Rousseau. However, as we suggested earlier, there are alternative ways of looking at privacy, and these can serve other notions of democracy . . .

Thus the privacy debate has sometimes raised some insightful and controversial theorization about the concepts 'public' and 'private' and has echoed some of the claims and counterclaims within political theory generally. For the most part, however, political theorization about privacy has operated within the basic liberal paradigm. The privacy literature has assumed a distinction between the realms of the public business of the state, and the private spheres of individual life. It has also remained relatively unaffected by deeper questions about cultural relativity, or bias according to class, gender, race or other social categories . . .

Surveillance and the collective threat to individual privacy

. . . The liberal political theory that underpins the 'fair information practices' places an excessive faith in procedural and individual remedies to excessive intrusions. Thus privacy and data protection laws can only have a marginal impact on the development of surveillance societies; some would contend that they serve to legitimize new personal information systems and thus extend social control.

A formidable critique of the liberal theory of information privacy is given by Rule and his colleagues (1980). They claim that privacy and data protection laws are all well and good, but that they frame the problem in too narrow a fashion. The argument is that public policies that seek to 'balance' privacy rights with organizational demands for information may produce a fairer and more efficient use and management of personal data, but they cannot control the voracious and inherent appetite of all bureaucratic institutions for more and more information on individuals. They cannot halt surveillance, in other words. On the contrary, there are persuasive cases of the enactment of data protection law being used to legitimate the introduction of new surveillance systems. The essential problem for Rule, then, is the inherent tendency of bureaucratic organizations to want to collect and store more and more increasingly detailed personal information. This dynamic of complex organizations has its roots in the 18th century, and in the move towards rationalization and control of resources that accompanied industrialization (Beniger, 1986). Thus the 'solution' to increasing surveillance can only come from the cultivation of a looser, less discriminating and less efficient relationship between organizations and their clientele.

The idea that advanced industrial societies are creeping inexorably toward an unacceptable level of surveillance has influenced writers from a number of disciplinary and national backgrounds. Flaherty, a Canadian scholar of legal history and subsequently Information and Privacy Commissioner of British Columbia, gave the title of *Protecting Privacy in Surveillance Societies* to his comparative analysis of the operation of data protection laws (Flaherty, 1989). He begins: 'The central theme of this volume is that individuals in the Western world are increasingly subject to surveillance through the use of data bases in the public and private sectors, and that these developments have negative implications for the quality of life in our societies and for the protection of human rights' (Flaherty, 1989, p. 1). Flaherty demonstrates how countries that have established data protection agencies, including Germany and Sweden, have a better chance of stemming the tide than do countries like the US, whose privacy protection regimes rely solely on the individual assertion of privacy rights through the courts, and on weak oversight mechanisms. But his overall conclusion is sceptical. Echoing Rule's analysis, he suggests that '[a]t present, data protection agencies are in many ways functioning as legitimators of new technology. For the most part, their licensing and advisory functions have not prevented the introduction of threatening new technologies, such as machine-readable identity cards or innumerable forms of enhanced data banks; they act rather as shapers of marginal changes in the operating rules for such instruments of public surveillance' (Flaherty, 1989, p. 384).

As technological tools became smaller, less expensive, and more decentralized during the 1980s, other analysts have stressed rather different aspects of the problem. Marx's (1988) study of undercover police surveillance is a case in point. He demonstrates how incremental changes in technology, social values and the law have encouraged covert and deceptive police techniques with a variety of intended and unintended consequences. He shows how all covert surveillance has the tendency to blur the distinction between law enforcement and the lawless activities it is supposed to curtail. The range of new surveillance practices that Marx discusses allows him to suggest some more general characteristics of these new forms of social control.[3] 'The awesome power of the new surveillance,' Marx summarizes, 'lies partly in the paradoxical, never-before-possible combination of decentralized and centralized forms' (1988, pp. 217–19). This analysis led him, in more recent writing, to propose a completely revised 'ethics for the new surveillance' to replace what he regards as the outmoded and limiting 'fair information principles' doctrine (Marx, 1999).

Two other writers who have directed their attention as much to private as to public sector practices see other trends at work. Gandy (1993) draws upon a diversity of traditions to try to understand the implications for social control of new and sophisticated practices for the collection, classification, and manipulation of personal information in both sectors. He points out that a number of social theorists (Karl Marx, Ellul, Giddens, Weber, Foucault) contribute to an understanding of the system of disciplinary surveillance that continually seeks to identify, classify and evaluate individuals according to ever more refined and discriminating forms of personal data: '[t]he panoptic sort is a difference machine that sorts individuals into categories and classes on the basis of routine measurements. It is a discriminatory technique that allocates options and opportunities on the basis of those measures and the administrative models that they inform' (Gandy, 1993, p. 15). Gandy's analysis leads him to the conclusion that real consumer choice can only be implemented through 'opt-in' (positive consent) rather than 'opt-out' (negative consent) provisions.

Lyon (1994) employs more visual imagery to address much the same questions about surveillance. Drawing inspiration from much the same literature as does Gandy, he too contends that surveillance cannot be reduced to one social or political process. But whereas Gandy relies on contemporary empirical analysis of the surveillance practices of modern corporate and bureaucratic organizations, Lyon adopts a more historical approach. He links surveillance to theories of modernity, and speculates on the possibilities and implications of a more communitarian post-modern condition as a way to avoid the dystopic visions of both Orwell and Foucault. In this light, surveillance may have positive, as well as negative, ramifications (Lyon, 2001, pp. 53, 136–7).

The arguments of those who stress information privacy, and those who stress surveillance, have often been posited as diametrically opposed political stances. However, the distinction should not be exaggerated. The difference stems more from the starting-point: whether it is from the erosion of privacy and how the institutions of a liberal society might cope with the most dangerous and intrusive threats from new technologies; or whether it is from an interest in the changing impact and nature of social control and disciplinary practice. The processing of personal data by private and public institutions is, from this latter perspective, a way to shed light upon broader social and technological trends.

The privacy and surveillance literatures can often be regarded as two sides of the same coin. With few exceptions, most of the literature we have reviewed would share the following four assumptions:

- that privacy is an individual right;
- that privacy is something that we once had and is now eroding;
- that the source of the privacy problem is structural – the set of impersonal and remote forces that together contribute to the declining ability of individual agents to control the circulation of information that relates to them; and
- that the organizations that are responsible for privacy invasion can be observed, resisted and regulated because they are subject to a set of obligations that stem from principles as embodied in the laws of discrete and bounded liberal democratic states . . .

Conclusion: privacy and the liberal democratic state

The privacy paradigm, based on a conceptualization of distinct private and public realms, almost inevitably leads the debate to a discussion of how privacy conflicts with social or community values; this debate is prompted, for example, by the first assumption that we have identified. It leads often to the view that privacy and social values such as sociability, internal security, social welfare or government efficiency are necessarily antithetical. The problem here is not only the deeply contested and ambiguous quality of these concepts, but also that the promotion of privacy can itself be socially important.

Regan (1995) has gone far to develop the theory of privacy as a value for entities beyond the person. She writes:

> Most privacy scholars emphasize that the individual is better off if privacy exists; I argue that society is better off as well when privacy exists. I maintain that privacy serves not just individual interests but also common, public, and collective purposes. If privacy became less important to one individual in one particular context, or even to several individuals in several contexts, it would still be important as a value because it serves other crucial functions beyond those that it performs for a particular individual. Even if the individual interests in privacy became less compelling, social interests in privacy might remain.
>
> (Regan, 1995, p. 221)

Regan makes the important point that '[p]rivacy is becoming less an attribute of individuals and records and more an attribute of social relationships and information systems or communication systems' (Regan, 1995, p. 230). In this sense, it can be argued that excessive surveillance is bad not only for individuals, but also for society. Take a contemporary example: video-surveillance cameras (CCTV) in public places can be justified as a necessary remedy to deter and detect crime. On an individual level, they can be criticized as being overly intrusive, and may lead to mistaken identification with adverse consequences. On a societal level, we might properly question whether, as a society, we wish to go about our daily affairs with cameras recording our every movement, and enabling the compilation of comprehensive records of what we do, with whom, when, and where.

Moreover, such surveillance may have a chilling effect on associational activity, to the detriment of society. This argument is made in a similar critique by Schwartz (1999), who elaborates a theory of 'constitutive privacy' to replace 'the traditional liberal understanding of information privacy, which views privacy as a right to control the use of one's personal data' (Schwartz, 1999, p. 1613). In analyzing a variety of recent practices on the Internet, Schwartz is persuaded that the silent collection of personal information in cyberspace 'has a negative impact on individual self-determination; it makes it difficult to engage in the necessary thinking out loud and deliberation with others upon which choice-making depends' (Schwartz, 1999, p. 1701). As we saw, Westin's (1967) account of privacy also highlights certain political values, including freedom of association and the secret ballot. Among his 'four states of privacy' (Westin, 1967, pp. 31–2), intimacy and anonymity imply the ability of the individual to engage with with others, rather than signifying her withdrawal from society. These two 'states' therefore sustain participation in collective political life, including such modes of activity as associating politically with others or voting without the fear of surveillance . . .

The second of the four assumptions is that our privacy is eroding, vanishing, diminishing, and so on. We question such fatalism from a number of perspectives. We simply do not know whether we would have enjoyed higher 'levels' of privacy in the past. How does one calibrate a 'level' of privacy? Who are 'we'? These measurements are surely highly subjective and dependent on a range of diverse contextual circumstances . . . The mediaeval village or nineteenth-century industrial town was not a particularly privacy-friendly place. The argument about the erosion of privacy depends on the starting-point. Typically, the fatalistic contention means that organizations simply know more about our lives than they did in the past. If one were to reckon the sum total of information that external structures 'know' about us, that aggregation would be far greater than it would be for our predecessors who lived and worked in feudal and industrial societies. We therefore have less control over the amount and quality of the information that relates to us. Stated in this fashion, the problem becomes less one of stemming the collection of information, and more one of ensuring its appropriate use and disclosure. To the extent that this is so, the problem is inherently about social relations and their management.

Thirdly, therefore, the privacy value relates to more than the loss of human agency in the face of impersonal structural forces, whether bureaucracy, capitalism or technology. We would insist that the privacy problem has its roots in human agency as well as in structural conditions: '[p]rivacy problems arise when technologies work perfectly and when they fail. They arise when administrative, political, and economic elites have worthy motives, and when they do not. They arise through both human fallibility and infallibility' (Bennett and Grant, 1999, p. 4) . . .

Finally, and relating to our underlying theme about globalization, under our fourth assumption we wish to investigate the implications for privacy analysis and policy prescription when personal information knows neither organizational nor national attachments. The privacy paradigm, like liberalism, tends to be state-centric. We mean this in two different senses. First, the right to privacy is generally regarded as a benefit of state citizenship. These rights are conferred on us by virtue of our identities as Americans, Britons, Canadians, Germans, or whoever. The privacy and data protection laws that provide us with certain guarantees about our personal information reflect some essential principles of liberal democracy that are either enshrined in constitutions (such as the US Fourth Amendment) or are deeply embedded in the cultural and historical experiences of different societies.

Second, there is still an assumption that the primary threat to these rights emanates from within the state in which one is living, stemming from practices occurring within the boundaries of discrete states, whether in public agencies or in the private sector. This view was prevalent twenty years ago, when many of the European data protection laws were being promulgated, but contemporary discourse and policy prescriptions are still generally dictated by a paradigm which suggests that our personal information still tends to be held within organizations that are easily identifiable, stable, and that reside and operate within the boundaries of modern territorial states. However, many scholars, inspired by various themes prevalent in the literature on postmodernity, have questioned the empirical and theoretical reliance on the state for policy prescriptions in a range of policy sectors – the environment, consumer protection, taxation and so on. We raise similar questions with respect to privacy protection. Information and communication technologies, systems and practices involving personal data have changed dramatically over the past twenty years or so. When the problem is increasingly unbounded by state borders, how has this problem been redefined? What are the new policy instruments that have arisen? And what are the prospects for promoting this essential value within a globalized economy?

Notes

1   This chapter is an extract from C. Bennett and C. Raab (2003) The privacy paradigm, *The Governance of Privacy: Privacy Instruments in Global Perspective*. Burlington, VT: Ashgate, pp. 13–30.
2   For example, *The Handmaid's Tale; Gattaca; Enemy of the State*. We note, however, the reversal of effect for the 'Big Brother' label with regard to the overwhelmingly popular British television programme and other 'candid camera' productions which turn surveillance into mass entertainment.
3   He argues that there are ten attributes of the new surveillance:

- it transcends distance, darkness, and physical barriers;
- it transcends time; its records can be stored, retrieved, combined, analyzed, and communicated;
- it has low visibility, or is invisible;
- it is often involuntary;
- prevention is a major concern;
- it is capital- rather than labour-intensive;
- it involves decentralized self-policing;
- it triggers a shift from targeting a specific suspect to categorical suspicion of everyone;
- it is more intensive, probing beneath surfaces, discovering previously inaccessible information;
- it is more extensive, covering not only deeper, but larger, areas.

References

Allen, A. (1985) *Uneasy Access: Privacy for Women in a Free Society*. Totowa, NJ: Rowman and Littlefield.

Allen, A. and Mack, E. (1990) How privacy got its gender, *Northern Illinois University Law Review*, 10: 441–78.

Arndt, H. (1949) The cult of privacy, *Australian Quarterly*, 21: 69–71.

Bennett, C. (1992) *Regulating Privacy: Data Protection and Public Policy in Europe and the United States*. Ithaca: Cornell University Press.

Bennett, C. and Grant, R. (eds) (1999) *Visions of Privacy: Policy Choices for the Digital Age*. Toronto: University of Toronto Press.

Boling, P. (1996) *Privacy and the Politics of Intimate Life*. Ithaca: Cornell University Press.

Brenton, M. (1964) *The Privacy Invaders*. New York: Coward-McCann.

Canadian Standards Association (CSA) (1996) *Model Code for the Protection of Personal Information*, CAN/CSA-Q830-96. Rexdale: CSA, Available at: http://www.csa.ca/standards/privacy.

Chaum, D. (1992) Achieving electronic privacy, *Scientific American*, 267: 96–101.

Clarke, R. (1999) Introduction to dataveillance and information privacy, and definitions of terms. Available at: http://www.anu.edu.au/people/Roger.Clarke/DV/Intro.html

Council of Europe (CoE) (1981) *Convention for the Protection of Individuals with Regard to Automatic Processing of Personal Data (Convention 108)*. Strasbourg: Council of Europe.

Diffie, W. and Landau, S. (1998) *Privacy on the Line: The Politics of Wiretapping and Encryption*. Cambridge, MA: MIT Press.

Etzioni, A. (1999) *The Limits of Privacy*. New York: Basic Books.

European Union (EU) (1995) *Directive 95/46/EC of the European Parliament and of the Council on the Protection of Individuals with Regard to the Processing of Personal Data and on the Free Movement of Such Data*, Brussels, OJ No. L281 (The EU Data Protection Directive) (24 October 1995).

Flaherty, D. (1989) *Protecting Privacy in Surveillance Societies: The Federal Republic of Germany, Sweden, France, Canada, and the United States*. Chapel Hill: University of North Carolina Press.

Foucault, M. (1979) *Discipline and Punish: The Birth of the Prison*. New York: Vintage Books.

Gandy, O. (1993) *Panoptic Sort: A Political Economy of Personal Information*. Boulder, CO: Westview Press.

Garfinkel, S. (2000) *Database Nation: The Death of Privacy in the 21st Century*. Sebastopol, CA: O'Reilly.

Gavison, R. (1980) Privacy and the limits of the law, *Yale Law Journal*, 89: 421–71.

Gellman, R. (1993) Fragmented, incomplete and discontinuous: the failure of federal privacy regulatory proposals and institutions, *Software Law Journal*, 6: 199–231.

Gellman, R. (1996) Can privacy be regulated effectively on a national level? Thoughts on the possible need for international privacy rules, *Villanova Law Review*, 41: 129–72.

Gellman, R. (1997) Conflict and overlap in privacy regulation: national, international, and private, in B. Kahin and C. Nesson (eds) *Borders in Cyberspace*. Cambridge, MA: MIT Press, pp. 255–82.

General Agreement in Trade and Services (GATS) (1994) *General Agreement on Tariffs and Trade*. Geneva: The World Trade Organization. Available at: http://www.wto.org/english/tratp_e/serv_e/gatsintr_e.htm

Germany (1994) National Report 1993/1994, presented to the 16th International Conference of Privacy and Data Protection Commissioners, The Hague, 6–8 September.

Germany (1995) National Report 1994/1995, presented to the 17th International Conference of Privacy and Data Protection Commissioners, Copenhagen, 6–8 September.

Giddens, A. (1991) *Modernity and Self-Identity*. Standford, CA: Stanford University Press.

Gill, S. (1995) Globalisation, market civilisation, and disciplinary neoliberalism, *Millennium: Journal of International Studies*, 24: 399–423.

Goldberg, I. (2002) Privacy-enhancing technologies for the Internet, II: five years later, in R. Dingledine and P. Syverson (eds) *PET 2002 – Workshop on Privacy Enhancing Technologies*, San Francisco: PET.

Goldsmith, S. (1997) *Privacy: How to Live a Private Life Free from Big Brother's Interference*. Reading: Medina.

Greenleaf, G. (1995) The 1995 EU Data Protection Directive – an overview, *The International Privacy Bulletin*, 3: 1–21.

Harris – Equifax (1991) *Harris-Equifax Consumer Privacy Survey 1991*. Atlanta, GA: Equifax Inc.

Harris – Equifax (1992) *Harris-Equifax Consumer Privacy Survey 1992*. Atlanta, GA: Equifax Inc.

Harris – Equifax (1993) *Harris-Equifax Health Information Privacy Survey 1993*. Atlanta, GA: Equifax Inc.

Harris – Equifax (1994) *Equifax-Harris Consumer Privacy Survey 1994*. Atlanta, GA: Equifax Inc.

Harris – Equifax (1996) *Equifax-Harris Consumer Privacy Survey 1996*. Atlanta, GA: Equifax Inc.

Held, D., McGrew, A., Goldblatt, D. and Perraton, J. (1999) *Global Transformations: Politics, Economics and Culture*. Stanford, CA: Stanford University Press.

Henkel, M. (1991) The new UK evaluative state, *Public Administration*, 69(1): 121–36.

Henley Centre, The (1995) *Dataculture*. London: The Henley Centre.

Hewitt, P. (1977) *Privacy: The Information Gatherers*. London: National Council for Civil Liberties.

Hill, M. (1997) *The Policy Process in the Modern State*, 3rd edn. London: Prentice Hall.

Hine, C. and Eve, J. (1998) Privacy in the marketplace, *The Information Society*, 14: 253–62.

Hixson, R. (1987) *Privacy in a Public Society: Human Rights in Conflict*. New York: Oxford University Press.

Kuhn, T. (1970) *The Structure of Scientific Revolutions*, 2nd edn. Chicago: University of Chicago Press.

Laudon, K. (1996) Markets and privacy, *Communications of the Association for Computing Machinery*, 39: 92–104.

Lessig, L. (1999) *Code and Other Laws of Cyberspace*. New York: Basic Books.

Lyon, D. (1994) *The Electronic Eye: The Rise of Surveillance Society*. Minneapolis: University of Minnesota Press.

Lyon, D. (2001) *Surveillance Society: Monitoring Everyday Life*. Buckingham: Open University Press.

Marx, G. (1988) *Undercover: Police Surveillance in America*. Berkeley: University of California Press.

Marx, G. (1999) Ethics for the new surveillance, in C. Bennett and R. Grant (eds) *Visions of Privacy: Policy Choices for the Digital Age*. Toronto: University of Toronto Press, pp. 38–67.

Mill, J. S. (1859) *Three Essays*. Oxford: Oxford University Press.

Organisation for Economic Co-operation and Development (OECD) (1981) *Guidelines on the Protection of Privacy and Transborder Flows of Personal Data*. Paris: OECD. Available at: http://www.oecd.org/EN/relevant_links/0,,EN-relevant_links-43-nodirectorate-no-no-146-13,FF.html

Packard, V. (1964) *The Naked Society*. New York: David McKay.

Parker, R. (1974) A definition of privacy, *Rutgers Law Review*, 27: 275–96.

Pateman, C. (1970) *Participation and Democratic Theory*. Cambridge: Cambridge University Press.

Pateman, C. (1983) Feminist critiques of the public/private dichotomy, in S.I. Benn and G.F. Gaus (eds) *Public and Private in Social Life*. New York: St. Martin's Press, pp. 281–303.

Posner, R. (1978) An economic theory of privacy, *Regulation*, May/June, pp. 19–26.

Poster, M. (1990) *The Mode of Information*. New York: Polity Press.

Raab, C. (1999) From balancing to steering: new directions for data protection, in C. Bennett and R. Grant (eds) *Visions of Privacy: Policy Choices for the Digital Age*. Toronto: University of Toronto Press, pp. 68–93.

Regan, P. (1995) *Legislating Privacy: Technology, Social Values and Public Policy*. Chapel Hill: University of North Carolina Press.

Rothfeder, J. (1992) *Privacy for Sale*. New York: Simon and Shuster.

Royal Society, The (1992) *Risk: Analysis, Perception and Management*. London: The Royal Society.

Rule, J. and Hunter, L. (1999) Towards property rights in personal data, in C. Bennett and R. Grant (eds) *Visions of Privacy: Policy Choices for the Digital Age*. Toronto: University of Toronto Press, pp. 168–81.

Rule, J., McAdam, D., Stearns, L. and Uglow, D. (1980) *The Politics of Privacy: Planning for Personal Data Systems as Powerful Technologies*. New York: Elsevier.

Schoeman, F. (ed) (1984) *Philosophical Dimensions of Privacy: An Anthology*. New York: Cambridge University Press.

Schwartz, P. (1999) Privacy and democracy in cyberspace, *Vanderbilt Law Review*, 52: 1609–702.

Shils, E. (1956) *The Torment of Secrecy*. Glencoe, II: Free Press.

Sieghart, P. (1976) *Privacy and Computers*. London: Latimer.

Simitis, S. (1987) Reviewing privacy in an information society, *University of Pennsylvania Law Review*, 135: 707–46.

Smith, R. (1979) *Privacy: How to Protect What's Left of It*. Garden City, NJ: Anchor Press.

Smith, R. (1993) *War Stories: Accounts of Persons Victimized by Invasions of Privacy*. Providence, RI: Privacy Journal.

(US) United States (PPSC) Privacy Protection Study Commission (1977) *Protecting Privacy in an Information Society*. Washington, DC: Government Printing Office.

Warren, S. and Brandeis, L. (1890) The right to privacy, *Harvard Law Review*, 4: 193–220.

Westin, A. (1967) *Privacy and Freedom*. New York: Atheneum.

Westin, A. (1996) Testimony before the subcommittee on domestic and international monetary policy of the Committee on Banking and Financial Services, U.S. House of Representatives, Washington, DC, 11 June.

Young, J. (ed) (1978) *Privacy*. Wiley. New York:

23

Neither good, nor bad, but dangerous: surveillance as an ethical paradox[1]
by Graham Sewell and James R. Barker

Introduction

Today, surveillance is, literally and figuratively, everywhere we look as our burgeoning information and communication technologies [ICTs] continually confront us with new and more efficient forms of surveillance. Computer technologies can instantly digitise the faces of sports fans entering a stadium and compare their images to a data bank of known terrorists. Shoppers must submit to placing their purchasing behaviours under the surveillance of consumer profiling if they want discounts and preferential treatment. Internet technology rapidly makes personal financial, medical, and criminal information viewable for the savvy surfer. In the organization, supervisors, peers, and machines constantly monitor our activity.

Surveillance presents us with constant ethical paradoxes . . . Surveillance is useful but harmful; welcome but offensive; a necessary evil but an evil necessity. We support surveillance, so long as someone else is in its watchful eye. We find surveillance as something we have to do – even if it is only to protect ourselves or our organizations – but we do not particularly care for it. Hopefully it will hurt you more than it will hurt me . . .

The end of privacy?: A brief genealogy of the public and the private

. . . [W]e can make a number of observations concerning the traditional ethical debate on privacy within civil society.[2]

i)   Within the main streams of liberal thought (philosophy, political theory, and jurisprudence) the idea of an antinomian relationship between the 'public' and the 'private' has been relatively stable since the late eighteenth century. To be sure, it has had to respond to nineteenth century innovations including: demographic surveys, epidemiological surveillance, and positivistic sociology;[3] accounting practices;[4] and management science.[5] Later it also had to absorb the emergence of wireless telegraphy and broadcasting, but it has always displayed a notable degree of resilience in the face of such developments.

ii) Nevertheless, what actually constitutes legitimately private and public matters (i.e. what is to be protected from intrusion by the state or its agents and what is not) continues to be contested. Moreover, discussion of the 'private' and the 'public' is central to establishing the normative fabric of liberal democracies, including the ideas of citizenship, civic duty, the common good, and the role of the state.

iii) Despite the protestations of democratic inclusiveness, it is still in the gift of elites (intellectual, political, and judicial) to determine these normative priorities of liberal discourse. However, the spectacle of kings, princes, and courtiers fashioning social mores through ostentatious display has been superseded by a technocratic consciousness in which the legitimate boundary between the public and the private is established and presided over by *bien-pensant* citizens who are chosen (or, more likely, self-selected) on the basis of their privileged knowledge of ethical and practical considerations.

iv) To a large extent, the prevailing normative climate that surrounds the legitimate status of the public and private realms is coherent and stable enough so as to obviate the need for anything except minimal intervention by the state to preserve the status quo (for liberalism to operate it requires consent, thereby making minimal intervention the litmus test for the success or otherwise of the liberal political project).[6] Effectively, citizens recognize the legitimacy of the public/ private separation and police themselves accordingly.

But how has this ethical terrain – relatively stable throughout the modern period – fared in the face of the intense seismographic disruption caused by recent shocks inflicted by significant developments in the area of ICT? To be sure, many have predicted the effective 'End of Privacy' . . ., as ICT intrudes inexorably into our lives to such an extent that the liberal conception of the separation between the public and the private is rendered meaningless. Such a position runs the risk of sounding unduly fatalistic and technologically determinist – just because technology enables us to do these things then they will inevitably come about. It is also salutary to note that such predictions have a substantial pedigree and still remain (exaggerated press reports notwithstanding) unfulfilled to a large extent, suggesting that we should exercise caution before jumping to such extreme conclusion . . .

So, perhaps it is a mistake to be unduly pessimistic about the untrammelled intrusion of ICT into our lives as we are repeating, with some amendments, predictions made several decades ago. Technological rationalisation is not inevitable and liberal sentiments concerning the importance of privacy are deeply ingrained and, therefore, likely to be resilient even in the face of significant challenges. Indeed, we are struck by alacrity with which liberal states go about attempting to legislate against recent intrusions into privacy in much the same way that they always have done (although their success or otherwise is another matter). We are, however, even more struck by instances where by such intrusions are ingeniously subverted or simply ignored by those who are unwilling or unable to wait for the state to catch up, legislatively speaking.[7]

We should not, however, become complacent about our ability to arrest the shrinkage of the private domain. On the contrary, we should be constantly vigilant against the intrusions of ICT into our lives. Importantly, this vigilance should be alert to the qualitative differences between ICT and previous forms of surveillance as well as the continuities – it is not simply a case of 'more of the same'; ICT certainly increases the reach or immediacy of familiar forms of surveillance but it also enables new forms to operate that we have less experience of containing. One of the most significant of these is identified by Whitaker:[8] vast amounts of personal information are passing into corporate hands where it is far more complete, detailed (although not necessarily accurate), intrusive, and difficult to challenge than anything previously held by the state.

In these circumstances, we must also take into consideration the extent to which the dominant liberal conception of privacy is still useful under these changing conditions. Most notably, the ethical dimensions of liberal philosophical, political, and judicial attitudes toward privacy come into direct conflict with that distinct but nevertheless related intellectual tradition, economic liberalism. At a time when it is still fashionable to invoke the 'market' as a 'solution' to social problems then exploring changing attitudes towards privacy and surveillance in the workplace becomes all the more pressing . . .

Privacy, technology, and the workplace: navigating a complex ethical terrain

. . . Our main problem in developing a critical approach to the ethical status of privacy and surveillance in the workplace is that . . . the problem of privacy, as we saw above, is a mature ethical category within the liberal project that has been extended and revised in the face of changing intellectual, technological, and political developments. As a response to this complexity, we propose a simplified approach to privacy and surveillance; a form of applied ethics that rejects eschatology in favour of a much more modest, nominalist, and protean ethical disposition where the 'public' and the 'private' are not universal ontological categories but are constituted in localized contests over meaning . . .

Our reason for this is straightforward: we believe that the liberal conception of the tension between an individual's right to privacy and states' rights to intrude into that privacy places surveillance in the situation for which we are obliged to ascribe to it moral value. Therefore, it is seen as being either a virtuous thing that protects the Good Society from destabilisation or a pernicious intrusion into our basic and natural right to an existence without let and hindrance from others. Of course, in any practical sense the unworkable rigidity of such a dualism is soon revealed, especially when we realise that we often have highly ambivalent attitudes towards surveillance. Witness the introduction of sophisticated systems that appear to reduce street crime – for example, the use of closed circuit television cameras in city centres.[9]

Frequently such measures are accompanied by widespread public support tempered by a degree of skepticism and mistrust over the potential invasion of privacy.[10] We argue that such a framing of the problem is bound to err on the side of control whereby we commonly dismiss any misgivings with the popular aphorism, *if you've got nothing to hide, you've got nothing to fear*, thereby justifying almost any level of intrusion in the name of the Common Good. This perception that only ne'er-do-wells invoke privacy as a defense is also found in more scholarly ethical discussions. Take the following:

> Though we all acknowledge its value in the abstract, there are numerous grounds for puzzling over its significance, and for being suspicious of its value. The right to privacy is seen as creating the context in which both deceit and hypocrisy may flourish: It provides the cover under which most human wrong doing takes place, and then it protects the guilty from taking responsibility for their transgressions once committed. The right to privacy often stands in the way of vigorous public debate on issues of moral significance. Without the shade of privacy, many practices that are arguably legitimate though in fact illegal might be thoroughly debated rather than left unexposed and unexamined.[11]

For us, this position is much more troubling, if understandable. Schoeman, a US-based scholar, was writing in the wake of momentous cultural destabilisations brought about by events such as the exposure of the 'Military-Industrial Complex' as the chief architect of the Cold War, the activities of the Warren Commission, the anti-Vietnam War movement, and Watergate. In the face of these wounds inflicted on the liberal consensus, individual citizens, corporations, and even the institutions of government could no longer be trusted to operate on the basis of Good Faith alone. Instead, a climate of paranoia and mutual suspicion meant that ever more sophisticated systems of scrutiny were erected in all walks of life to such an extent that even something as apparently autonomous as cultural production (for example, films, televisions, and novels) did not simply reflect surveillance, they *were* a form of surveillance.[12]

In the light of such developments it is our view that the traditional liberal conceptualisation of the public and the private is less likely than ever to vouchsafe our ability to resist intrusions into our lives, especially our working lives. In response, we propose a way of thinking about the ethical implications of workplace surveillance that avoids appealing to 'natural' rights or unitary interests and does not assign moral status to surveillance in and of itself. Our way into this is to develop a critical stance towards an idea that has become a commonplace in recent studies of surveillance: Foucault's depiction of Jeremy Bentham's Panopticon.

Is there anything (useful) left to be said about the Panopticon?

. . . According to Jay,[13] Foucault was not the first 'rediscover' the Panopticon and identify its modern significance as the embodiment of a dystopian vision of total control. He bestows that honour on Himmelfarb.[14] There is also the suggestion that Jacques-Alain Miller[15] should at least get joint billing with Foucault in surveillance studies for recognising that the fetishizing of vision as a source of truth (literally, an enlightenment) was potentially coercive.[16] Take the following observation.

> The Panopticon is the temple of reason, a temple luminous and transparent in every sense: first because there are no shadows and nowhere to hide: it is open to constant surveillance by the invisible eye; but also, because totalitarian mastery

of the environment excludes everything irrational: no opacity can withstand logic.[17]

This is an instructive passage because it closely resembles Foucault's more extensive and historicized discussion of the Panopticon as a trope for social normalization through the rehabilitation of those deemed to be irrational, dissident, or recalcitrant. One possible analytical interpretation of the Panopticon as an idealised control mechanism is to observe the artefacts of contemporary surveillance and see how closely they measure up to this ideal. If we do so then it should come as no surprise to us that it never does; as we have pointed out elsewhere[18] the most useful way to think about the Panopticon in relation to surveillance is as a tropological device. In particular, we feel that we should treat the Panopticon as a synecdoche and metonym that, together, convey the idea of *panopticism.*

For us, one pragmatically useful outcome is that we do not need to dwell on the ability or otherwise of current forms of surveillance to achieve the totalising control so laboriously laid out in Bentham's treatises on the Panopticon (for an excellent discussion of this, see Boyne).[19] Indeed, what has been most notable for us is the failure of surveillance to deliver on its promises.[20] We take our lead here from Foucault who, on many occasions, noted not only that the total surveillance was impossible but also that even at heightened levels surveillance contained the seeds of its own downfall. This can be summed up by his aphorism, 'If one governed too much, one did not govern all – that one provoked results contrary to those desired.'[21]

In other words, that surveillance, by its very nature, 'manufactures' delinquents rather than simply reveals them to the world as subjects already fully formed and unchanging.[22] In this way *Discipline and Punish* is all about the ultimate failure of surveillance to render bodies docile, which suggests we must pose the question: Why does it remain such a popular and attractive proposition when we talk about the 'problems' of delinquency and disobedience?

Panopticism and the ethics of surveillance

Drawing a distinction between the Panopticon and panopticism is important in answering this perplexing question. If the former is an anachronism – an expression of Bentham's eighteenth century Utilitarianism (and later, his radicalism)[23] – then panopticism represents part of a much more resilient *disposition.* We suggest thinking of this disposition as a constellation of attitudes (attitudes, moreover, that are sometimes in conflict) that circle around a Nietzschean will-to-power ... This is expressed as a desire to increase power that will seize on any opportunity that the moment offers.[24] In specific relation to surveillance, the will-to-power is manifested as the occularcentric will-to-truth of post-Enlightenment thinking.[25] This rests on the assumption that the unimpeded gaze will reveal the essential truth about the subject. Foucault's Nietzschean inversions of this assumption – not that surveillance reveals truth but that surveillance *creates* truth – is central to his idea of Power/Knowledge[26] and, by extension, his critique of liberalism (and Communism too, for that matter).

But is panopticism still relevant when it has been observed that the occularcentrism of its founding trope – the Panopticon – has been superseded by forms of surveillance that are computerized and, therefore, no longer visual?[27] Deleuze[28] argues that whilst Foucault had largely anticipated this and incorporated it into his later thinking we would argue that panopticism, when thought of as part of a disposition (i.e. a particular articulation of a will-to-truth), can withstand this shift. Thus, although subjects need no longer be sequestered in time and space by an architectonic machine à la Bentham's Panopticon, in many institutional settings (especially the workplace) surveillance that extends beyond the reciprocal gaze to include other immediate physical senses (for example, electronic eavesdropping), the discursive (for example, email), and the symbolic (for example, internet usage) does not stand outside this disposition. On the contrary, to many it would appear to reinforce the belief that surveillance can reveal the essential subject by exposing an individual's innermost thoughts and desires.

As far as the problem of privacy is concerned, Foucault's observation that surveillance is bound up with the desire to reveal the transcendental, unified, and essential subject (i.e. to discover or 'know' one's true self and the truth about others through revelation) places overwhelming strain on the liberal notion of policing the boundary between the public and private. Because it is taken to be the case that only the irrational[29] or the illegal[30] hide behind the convenient excuse of privacy, ultimately there are no grounds upon which we can protect ourselves from intrusion. This is seen in more or less bizarre proposals that surface from time to time; indeed, Bentham himself suggested that each of the King's subjects be tattooed with a unique identifying mark.[31]

Today such sentiments are expressed in suggestions such as creating DNA profiles of all citizens or, in the workplace, subjecting all employees to drug tests. Refusal to comply with or even speak out against such proposals immediately places the individual under suspicion. Even the idea that privacy is an inalienable human right is of little help here for bitter experience shows us that, going all the way back to Warren and Brandeis,[32] 'on balance' liberalism tends to favour the 'common good' over individual rights. In order to counter this tendency, we feel it is timely to rethink the idea of privacy in such a way that we avoid the antinomian opposition of the public and the private that are inherent in liberal discussions of the problem . . .

Rescuing privacy as meaningful idea: toward a negotiated ethic of surveillance in the workplace

Taking on surveillance

. . . Under these conditions it becomes increasingly difficult to establish a space (literally and figuratively speaking) that is free from intrusion within the workplace. Of course, this has always been difficult; managers have tended to reserve the right to determine what is knowable and what must be known about subordinates – an expression of the will-to-truth, as it were (cf. Landes).[33] Indeed, for us this is the key point that delineates who is a manager and who is managed. In the past, resistance to this exercise of 'managerial prerogative,' whilst deemed to be undesirable in many quarters, was at least seen to be a rational expression of divergent interests.[34] However, under the influence of the rhetoric of unitary interests (i.e., 'Didn't you realise that we're all friends now?'), we find it increasingly difficult to mount an argument against surveillance. When organizations readily deem information gathering of 'hard' data on performance or 'softer' data on things like attitudes to be in everyone's interests, then nothing is considered worthy of remaining private. This is why to challenge the legitimacy of surveillance is seen to be a disobedient or irrational act. Nevertheless, and despite the invocation of unitary interests, responsibility for determining the kind of information that should be gathered is not democratized but remains in the hands of the technocratic managerial elite. In this way surveillance becomes aligned with subjugation in both a physical *and* a cognitive sense. Thus, a large component of such subjugation centres around issues of meaning; it is a necessarily discursive/ communicative phenomenon. That is, we, as organizational members, are implicated in the creation of the mechanisms of our subjugation by the course of our everyday interactions. By talking about surveillance in certain ways, by interacting under sur- veillance in certain ways, by participating in the surveillance of others in certain ways, we develop a *disposition* toward surveillance that invests it with certain power – a power that shapes and affects what we know about surveillance and how we 'ought' to use it on ourselves. This does not, however, imply a static and deterministic arrangement: by challenging the basis of this disposition we have the possibility of changing the power relationships that centre on surveillance. To be sure, there is no guarantee that these new relationships are any 'better' or more edifying that those they replace, but it does hold out the prospect of questioning the legitimacy of surveil- lance in a way that is less at risk from accusations of irrationality. An initial step toward developing this new disposition is to explore the discursive basis by which we invest surveillance with meaning.

Power/knowledge and rules of right: toward a micro-ethics of surveillance

Power/knowledge

Drawing on previous work,[35] we argue that meaning is created discursively through an intricate relationship of power/knowledge and rules of right.[36] Through the natural course of our discursive interactions, we humans will create meaning for ourselves by ascribing power relationships to important phenomena in our lives. For example, when we enter into a supervisory-subordinate relationship in an organization, we are ascribing a power relationship between ourselves as the subordinate and our boss as superior. That relationship will directly influence how we interact further – how we and our supervisor (or overseer) create further meaning for ourselves. We form power relationships with both material and symbolic objects. For example, in addition to the technological artefacts of production, corporate values and vision statements can become strong sources of power relationships.[37]

Surveillance provides a good example of how the material and the symbolic have a mutual importance. Take, for instance, the ubiquitous call-centre in which a person accepts a job as a telephone-based customer service representative. They enter into a power relationship with an organization whose desire is to scrutinize their work dir- ectly and in the minutest detail. That is, phone-based customer service representa- tives of, say, an insurance company, will have all or some of their telephone calls taped and evaluated by a supervisor for such things as length, 'accuracy,' or 'tone.' These representatives know that the organization demands the right to hold them under surveillance to ensure they meet their work requirements. In terms of power relationships, surveillance in the organization usually presents itself to us in such a form – supervisors retaining the power to observe workers and the workers consenting to such surveillance as a requirement of their job.

A key feature of this example is that both the subordinate service representative and the superior supervisor know about the power relationship consequent to surveillance; both parties know that the company uses surveillance. Moreover, both parties are aware of the ostensible reasons for this – for example, to improve the 'quality' of the service delivery or for use in training and rehabilitation. Thus, both parties know that the technical artefacts of surveillance gather data that is given meaning in relation to the implicit and explicit goals of the organization because the data are used to evaluate the subordinate's performance. Depending on the ethical stance of the firm, both parties will know whether or not the outcome of the surveillance actually gets used to improve the subordinate's work or rather gets used to punish the subordinate. Either way, the two parties will have some knowledge of how the power relationship they have created for surveillance in their organization works and affects them. Thus, our knowledge of power relationships gives those relationships meaning, or said another way, our knowledge of power relationships – what the relationships mean and how they work on us – makes the relationships meaningful for us.

Rules of right
To make our knowledge of power relationships manifest, we develop rules for how we exercise power relationships on ourselves.[38] These rules reflect what is taken to be 'right' as in true, correct, legitimate, and meaningful; ways of shaping our behaviour to conform with the power relationships we have developed. Returning to the example of our customer service representatives, under such 'rules of right,' the representatives will have to agree to having their phone calls held under surveillance – that is, they must recognise that one of the organization's 'rules of right' for surveillance is legitimate for to do otherwise would to be labelled irrational and make them vulnerable to normalization through 'therapies' such as retraining. As a consequence, they are acceding to having the results of surveillance used to evaluate their job performance – another rule of right.

Surveillance and the establishment of 'right conduct'
Together, power/knowledge and rules of right create powerful realities for us in the organization. We refer to this process as being 'generative'.[39] That is, we use power relationships, knowledge of those relationships, and rules of right to generate ways of 'right conduct' by shaping our behaviour in the organization so that we can make sense of what we (and what others) do. In this way we create practical meaning that helps us navigate the organizational day.

In relation to an ethics of surveillance, the power relationships we create concerning surveillance, the knowledge we form regarding those relationships, and the rules of right we create to shape our actions all reflect how we subjugate our private selves to public scrutiny in the organization. We (more or less) willingly submit ourselves to organizational surveillance because that is what we know how to do and because we are used to being observed. Recognizing this point opens up the ethical terrain in which surveillance operates.

Power/knowledge and rules of right create strong and aggressive formations of meaning that powerfully affect our organizational and personal lives. Indeed, this meaning impinges on most aspects of ethical substance; subjectification, practical asceticism, and moral telos. Viewed from a discursive stance, power/knowledge and rules of right are the processes through which we create a practical ethics of right conduct in an organization. We call this a micro-ethics because it focuses the ethical debate on developing local responses to specific issues rather than establishing a universal calculus of 'Good' and 'Bad' objects. Of course, living under the conditions of this limited ethical approach may not be an altogether pleasant experience – especially for, say, the customer service representatives who have surveillance used as a rod for their backs rather than to improve their work. We wish to avoid passing normative judgement on the moral status on this micro-ethics of right conduct for there is no reason to suggest that, under another set of rules of right, surveillance could not be used in other ways (say to protect employees from abusive customers, co-workers, or managers).

Thus, some arrangement of power/knowledge and rules of right in relation to surveillance are inevitable: they may be neither good nor bad, but they are necessary if we are to create useful meanings about what surveillance can do in our daily lives and whether surveillance is legitimate or not. Thus, our disposition toward surveillance will never be superseded by some morally utopian world where ICT is enrolled in the pursuit of the universal good of mankind. Conversely, to have no practical ethics of right conduct – to be completely amoral about ICT and surveillance, as it were – would be equally implausible. Indeed, it would likely lead to a descent into a Hobbsean war of all against all.

But is our usual method for creating meaning about surveillance dangerous and if so why? The power/knowledge and rules we create about surveillance can be used either for us or against us, to help us or to hurt us. What do we do about this ethical dilemma? We propose a simple (and, therefore, hopefully a practical) model of scrutiny that allows us to challenge taken-for-granted attitudes towards surveillance and its use in the workplace.

Developing a critical disposition toward surveillance

We have argued elsewhere[40] for the development of a critical disposition towards workplace surveillance that can be used to engage with its 'dangerous' side. From our perspective this critical disposition involves the exercise of constant vigilance along the following lines:

1. Scrutinizing the meaning of surveillance

The ability to scrutinize the meaning we attach to the use of surveillance in any particular setting involves a striving to determine how it becomes acceptable in our daily work interactions. Thus, as workers under surveillance, we should ask ourselves such questions as: Why is surveillance important? Why is surveillance necessary?

Who says we have to have surveillance of our work for the company to be successful? The key issue here is one of legitimacy, for if we determine how surveillance becomes a legitimate force in the organization, we will determine how it is valued. A focus on values will set in motion the intricate process of power/knowledge and rules of right. If we know how surveillance is valued, then we can discover how it becomes meaningful (Barker 1999).

2. Analysing power/knowledge and rules of right

The second element of a critical disposition toward surveillance requires rigorously analysing the process of how surveillance becomes meaningful for us. That is, we need to determine the power relationships we have created vis-à-vis surveillance and the rules of right we have in force that give surveillance meaning. The practical way to accomplish such a task is to work backwards. That is, we should first observe the rules we make about surveillance and then dismantle them to expose the ethical substrate upon which they are constructed. Image the following scenario: all customer service representatives must have their calls recorded. We must explore how and why this information is collected in order to determine the extent to which surveillance enmeshes us in power relations.

3. Evaluating surveillance

Any evaluation of how surveillance works in practice must involve more than a mere assessment of whether it measures up in terms of its technical abilities such as reach, accuracy, and coverage of its intended targets. It also requires us to go beyond its performative efficiencies to confront and challenge the basic reasoning behind its existence. For us this initially requires us to establish the 'essence' of surveillance[41] – that is, how do entities like the technical systems of surveillance become intelligible in some systematic and mutually comprehensible way? . . . For example, we might well ask: Who decides the purposes of surveillance and upon what ethical basis? Might the customer service representatives themselves, rather than their supervisors, be in a better position to decide on how to use surveillance to improve their work? The point here is 'Who determines how surveillance *ought* to be used?' This sense of *ought* (i.e., surveillance is contestable) rather than *is* (i.e., surveillance is uncontestable, just take it or leave it) becomes key for us for it lies at the crux of the public/ private convolution. In an ostensively free, market-driven society, ought not those who labour under surveillance have the power to determine how surveillance ought to be used on themselves? The answer certainly makes for an interesting organizational debate. It is our hope that such a willingly contested debate will enable us to negotiate new sets of power relationships, new approaches to what constitutes legitimate knowledge, and new rules of right for how we use surveillance – a new ethic for surveillance.

Concluding comments

. . . Although some (e.g., Flaherty)[42] have argued that the opportunities for privacy are actually greater in modern than in pre-industrial societies our own impressionistic evidence would suggest that we have never before been placed under such intense scrutiny from all quarters.[43] Clearly, ICT is deeply implicated in these changes and it is our assertion that the orthodox ethical approach to privacy has broken down and is no longer able to provide us with universal moral guidance as to how we conduct ourselves in terms of what is legitimately public and what is legitimately private (if it ever was). Indeed, under these circumstances the word 'privacy,' much like the word 'democracy,' becomes hopelessly degraded; a slogan to be used by anyone to justify their actions, however extreme or divergent. There remains, however, at least one interesting similarity that we can trace back to premodern societies: instead of aristocrats presiding over what is right in the way of conduct, we now have technocrats. In the modern period it is this technocratic consciousness, reflecting the will-to-power or will-to-truth, that dominates our disposition in relation to surveillance and privacy. In the workplace these technocrats are the managers and ICT experts who tell us what is good for us. Moreover, they increasingly tell us that it is everyone's interests to subjugate ourselves to surveillance. As we noted above, we must challenge this blind acceptance of the idea that 'if you have nothing to hide, you have nothing to fear'; that it is only madmen, criminals, and troublemakers who hide behind the excuse of privacy . . .[44]

Notes

1 This chapter is an extract from G. Sewell and J. R. Barker (2001) Neither good, nor bad, but dangerous: surveillance as an ethical paradox, *Information, Communication and Society*, 3: 183–96.

2 In this article we take civil society to be an inclusive term that stands for the domain over which liberal democracies consider themselves to exert legitimate jurisdiction.

3 Ian Hacking. Making up People. In Thomas C. Heller, Morton Sosna and David E. Wellbery, editors, *Reconstructing Individualism: Autonomy, Individuality and the Self in Western Thought*. Stanford, CA: Stanford University Press, 1986.

4 Keith W. Hoskins and Richard H. Macve. Accounting as Discipline: The Overlooked Supplement. In Ellen Messer-Davidow, David R. Shumway and David J. Sylvan, editors, *Knowledges: Historical and Critical Studies in Disciplinarity*. Charlottesville: University of Virginia Press, 1998; Mary Poovey. *The History of the Modern Fact: Problems of Knowledge in the Sciences of Wealth and Society*. Chicago: University of Chicago Press, 1993.

5 Harry Braverman. *Labor and Monopoly Capital: The Degradation of Work in the Twentieth Century*. New York: Monthly Review Press, 1974.

6 Oren M. Levin-Waldman. *Reconceiving Liberalism: Dilemmas of Contemporary Liberal Public Policy*. Pittsburgh: University of Pittsburgh Press, 1996.

7 Barker and Sewell (2000).

8 Whitaker (1999).

9 Jon Bannister, Nicholas R. Fyfe and Ade Kearns. Closed Circuit Television and the City. In Clive Norris, Jade Moran and Gary Armstrong, editors, *Surveillance, Closed Circuit Television, and Social Control*. Aldershot: Ashgate, 1998.

10 Barker and Sewell (2000).

11 Ferdinand Schoeman. Privacy: Philosophical Dimensions of the Literature.

In Ferdinand Shoeman, editor, *Philosophical Dimensions of Privacy*. Cambridge: Cambridge University Press, 1984, p. 1.

12 Stephen Paul Miller. *The Seventies Now: Culture as Surveillance*. Durham, NC: Duke University Press, 1999.

13 Jay (1994).

14 Gertrude Himmelfarb. The Haunted House of Jeremy Bentham. In Richard Herr and Harold T. Parker, editors, *Ideas in History*. Durham, NC: Duke University Press, 1965.

15 Jacques-Alain Miller. Jeremy Bentham's Panoptic Device. *October*, 41 (Summer): 3–29, 1987 [1973].

16 It is interesting to note that neither Foucault nor Miller acknowledge Himmelfarb, let alone each other.

17 J-A. Miller (1987: pp. 6–7).

18 Graham Sewell. Be Seeing You: A Rejoinder to Webster and Robins and to Jenkins. *Sociology*, 30: 785–797, 1996 and Barker and Sewell (2000).

19 Roy Boyne. Post-Panopticism. *Economy and Society*, 29: 285–307, 2000.

20 Barker and Sewell (2000).

21 Michel Foucault. Space, Knowledge, and Power. In Paul Rabinow, editor, *The Foucault Reader*. Harmondsworth: Penguin Books, 1984a, p. 242.

22 Michel Foucault. What is called 'Punishing'? In James D. Faubion, editor, *Essential Works of Michel Foucault, 1954–1984: Volume 3 (Power)*. New York: New Press, 2000.

23 Himmelfarb (1965).

24 Robert John Ackermann. *Nietzsche: A Frenzied Look*. Amherst, MA: University of Massachusetts Press, 1990.

25 Alan Sheridan. *Michel Foucault: The Will to Truth*. London: Tavistock Books and Jay, 1994 [1980].

26 Colin Gordon. Introduction. In James D. Faubion, editor, *Essential Works of Michel Foucault, 1954–1984: Volume 3 (Power)*. New York: New Press, 2000.

27 David Lyon. *The Electronic Eye: The Rise of Surveillance Society*. Cambridge: Polity Press, 1994.

28 Gilles Deleuze. *Foucault*. Minneapolis: University of Minnesota Press, 1988.

29 J-A. Miller (1987).

30 Schoeman (1984).

31 J-A. Miller (1987).

32 Samuel D. Warren and Louis D. Brandeis. The Right to Privacy [the Implicit Made Explicit]. In Ferdinand Shoeman, editor, *Philosophical Dimensions of Privacy*. Cambridge: Cambridge University Press, 1984 [1890].

33 Landes (1986).

34 Peter Fleming and Graham Sewell. *Looking for The Good Soldier, Švejk: Alternative Modalities of Resistance in the Contemporary Workplace*. Department of Management Working Paper 2000/18, University of Melbourne, Australia, 2000.

35 James R. Barker. *The Discipline of Teamwork*. Newbury Park CA: Sage, 1999 and James R. Barker and George Cheney. The Concept and the Practices of Discipline in Contemporary Organizational Life. *Communication Monographs* 61: 19–43, 1994.

36 This previous work includes an extensive ethnographic study of seven years duration.
37 Barker (1999).
38 Barker (1999).
39 Barker (1999).
40 Barker and Sewell (2000).
41 Martin Heidegger. *The Question Concerning Technology and Other Essays*. New York: Harper Row, 1977.
42 David Flaherty. *Privacy in Colonial New England*. Charlottesville, VA: University of Virginia Press, 1972.
43 This idea reflects the enduring legacy of the Chicago School of urban sociology, especially that the alienation associated with urban life leads to anomie.
44 J-A. Miller (1987) and Schoeman (1984).

References

Ackermann, R. (1990) *Nietzsche: A Frenzied Look*. Amherst, MA: University of Massachusetts Press.

Bannister, J. Fyfe, N. R. and Kearns, A. (1998) Closed circuit television and the city, in C. Norris, J. Moran and G. Armstrong (eds) *Surveillance, Closed Circuit Television, and Social Control*. Aldershot: Ashgate.

Barker, J. R. (1999) *The Discipline of Teamwork*. Newbury Park, CA: Sage.

Barker, J. and Sewell, G. (2000) *'Here's Looking at you': Surveillance as a Trope for Organizational Domination*. Department of Management Working Paper 2000/17, University of Melbourne, Australia.

Boyne, R. (2000) Post-Panopticism, *Economy and Society*, 29: 285–307.

Braverman, H. (1974) *Labor and Monopoly Capital: The Degradation of Work in the Twentieth Century*. New York: Monthly Review Press.

Deleuze, G. (1988) *Foucault*. Minneapolis: University of Minnesota Press.

Fleming, P. and Sewell, G. (2000) *Looking for The Good Soldier, Švejk: Alternative Modalities of Resistance in the Contemporary Workplace*. Department of Management Working Paper 2000/18, University of Melbourne, Australia.

Foucault, M. (1984a) Space, knowledge, and power, in P. Rabinow (ed.) *The Foucault Reader*. Harmondsworth: Penguin Books.

Foucault, M. (2000) What is called 'punishing'? in J. D. Faubion (ed.) *Essential Works of Michel Foucault, 1954–1984: Volume 3 (Power)*. New York: New Press.

Gordon, C. (2000) Introduction, in J. D. Faubion (ed.) *Essential Works of Michel Foucault, 1954–1984: Volume 3 (Power)*. New York: New Press.

Hacking, I. (1986) Making up people, in T. C. Heller, M. Sosna and D. E. Wellbery (eds) *Reconstructing Individualism: Autonomy, Individuality and the Self in Western Thought*. Stanford, CA: Stanford University Press.

Himmelfarb, G. (1965) The Haunted House of Jeremy Bentham, In R. Herr and H. T. Parker (eds) *Ideas in History*. Durham, NC: Duke University Press.

Hoskins, K. W. and Macve, R. H. (1993) Accounting as discipline: the overlooked supplement, in E. Messer-Davidow, D. R. Shumway and D. J. Sylvan (eds) *Knowledges: Historical and Critical Studies in Disciplinarity*. Charlottesville: University of Virginia Press.

Jay, M. (1994) *Downcast Eyes: The Denigration of Vision in Twentieth-Century French Thought*. Berkeley: University of California Press.

Landes, D. S. (1986) What do bosses really do? *Journal of Economic History*, XLVI: 585–623.

Levin-Waldman, O. M. (1996) *Reconceiving Liberalism: Dilemmas of Contemporary Liberal Public Policy*. Pittsburgh: University of Pittsburgh Press.

Lyon, D. (1994) *The Electronic Eye: The Rise of Surveillance Society*. Cambridge: Polity Press.

Miller, J.-A. (1987 [1973]) Jeremy Bentham's panoptic device, *October*, Summer, 41: 3–29.

Miller, S. P. (1999) *The Seventies Now: Culture as Surveillance*. Durham, NC: Duke University Press.

Packard, V. (1964) *The Naked Society*. Harmondsworth: Pelican.

Poovey, M. (1998) *The History of the Modern Fact: Problems of Knowledge in the Sciences of Wealth and Society*. Chicago: University of Chicago Press.

Sewell, G. (1996) Be seeing you: a rejoinder to Webster and Robins and to Jenkins, *Sociology*, 30: 785–97.

Sheridan, A. (1980) *Michel Foucault: The Will to Truth*. London: Tavistock Books.

Shoeman, F. (1984) Privacy: philosophical dimensions of the literature, in F. Shoeman (ed.) *Philosophical Dimensions of Privacy*. Cambridge: Cambridge University Press.

Warren, S. D. and Brandeis, L. D. (1984) The right to privacy [the implicit made explicit], in F. Shoeman (ed.) *Philosophical Dimensions of Privacy*. Cambridge: Cambridge University Press.

Whitaker, R. (1999) *The End of Privacy? How Total Surveillance is Becoming a Reality*. New York: New Press.

24

Resisting surveillance[1]
by David Lyon

The surveillance consequences of 9/11 provide an opportunity to rethink surveillance and also, I believe, to resist it. Thus far, already existing systems have been reinforced, increasing the tendency for cultures of control and of suspicion to be augmented. At least some of the intended outcomes of intensified surveillance are unlikely to be realized, whereas the unintended consequences are already appearing.

In the past few years, surveillance has become algorithmic, technological, pre-emptive, and classificatory, in every way broadening and tightening the net of social control and subtly stretching the categories of suspicion. It thus tends to undermine trust and, through its emphasis on individual behaviors, to undermine social solidarity as well. At the same time, it augments the power of those who institute such systems, without increasing their accountability. All these features have been amplified since 9/11.

Several years ago, when I first started researching and writing about surveillance, I endeavored to maintain an appropriate stance that was neither paranoid nor complacent. I argued (and still do) that surveillance of some kind is both socially necessary and desirable but that it is always ambiguous. The dangers and risks attending surveillance are as significant as its benefits. In contexts where I felt people were being alarmist and shrill I cautioned restraint and pleaded for more careful analysis. In contexts where complacency seemed to reign I tried to show that surveillance has real effects on people's life-chances and life-choices that can at times be very negative.

Since 9/11, however, the pendulum has swung so wildly from 'care' to 'control' that I feel compelled to turn more robustly to critique. While I still insist that attitudes to surveillance should be ambivalent, the evidence . . . obliges me to observe that oblique dissent will no longer do. Some instances of early twenty-first-century surveillance are downright unacceptable, as they directly impugn social justice and human personhood. They help to create a world where no one can trust a neighbor, and where decisions affecting people and polity are made behind closed doors or within 'smart' systems.

This is not merely a negative critique, however. Major challenges confront the world following 9/11. There is a need for positive suggestions about other ways forward. The challenges, I suggest, are analytical, political, and technological. That is, the challenges affect how the social world after 9/11 is understood; how it is ethically judged and what are taken to be priorities for action; and how people might participate in deciding what technologies are adopted. The world is even more complex, unstable, and risky after 9/11. But those are reasons for engagement with it, not withdrawal.

Drawing threads together

Surveillance as a central social process was already highly developed in most countries of the world before September 11, 2001. Modern societies are surveillance societies, even before they depend on digital technologies, but more fully so after computerization. Surveillance practices and processes were already being augmented by networked communication systems before 9/11, and change was accelerating. More and more surveillance cameras were being installed in urban areas, for example, not only in Britain and other European countries, but in North America and Asia as well. In many ways, however, the effect of 9/11 has been to accelerate the adoption of surveillance practices, such as Neighborhood Watch informers, and technologies, such as internet tracking. The attacks triggered intensified surveillance in many spheres.

Current evidence suggests that already existing trends in contemporary society are being reinforced since 9/11, especially the cultures of fear, control, suspicion, and secrecy. The first, fear, is easily amplified by the mass media, which was clearly seen just after 9/11 itself. The 'irrational' attacks, apparently 'from outside,' mean that 'no one is safe.' The endless replays of WTC footage themselves helped foster fear and eroded resistance to new surveillance regimes. The second, control, as David Garland has eloquently argued, is not a conspiracy of the powerful.[2] Rather, those in power have capitalized on certain social developments, especially the rise of the consumer-citizen and of privatized mobility, to institute forms of commodified control. These depend on calculating risks and on seeking information through surveillance.

The culture of suspicion follows from the first two. It is a consequence of dependence on a multitude of tokens of trust rather than on direct relations of trust, and of course it has been exacerbated by 9/11. The fear produced by the New York attacks, as Onora O'Neill argues, undermines trust in a peculiarly vicious way.[3] Finally, the culture of secrecy has always been a temptation of bureaucratic departments and governments, and it flies in the face of democratic practices. It too has mushroomed since 9/11.

. . . The laws passed in the wake of 9/11 often cover ground already covered by existing law, are unlikely to succeed in their stated aims of making terrorist attacks less likely, but are highly likely to have effects not explicitly intended by them. Similarly with new technological measures geared to minimizing risks of repeat attacks. Many are poorly suited to their purposes, while being lamentably conducive to other consequences. Of course, it is understandable that emergency powers, quickly-passed legislation, and hurriedly-installed technologies will have flaws, but the ironies of initiatives following 9/11 go beyond these. They hint at a lack of understanding of actual situations (how devious intelligent terrorist plotters are likely to be, or why net-worked attacks are not amenable to conventional centralized responses, for example). And they rely on time-honored solutions, technical fixes, and tighter controls, applied across the board.

Surveillance trends have solidified after September 11, especially those of social sorting. The much-publicized debates over 'racial profiling' places this in high relief, but the issues are broader than this. Negative discrimination toward those defined as 'Muslim/Arabs' is certainly occurring. This is one of the most insidious results of 9/11, not least because it connects suspicions with particular ethnic and religious groups regardless of on-the-ground realities. But social sorting is even more evident than before as a foreground feature of surveillance. All kinds of group may be included in the 'terrorist' category, and all kinds of activity, including casual chat, may be construed as suspicious. Such classification frequently takes place using human observers, but it becomes far more powerful when computer-assisted.

Other surveillance trends have also been accented since 9/11. One is the trend towards system integration. This is a goal that has long been shared by both technical system designers and by organization managers. The principle permits data – in this case personal data – to be shared across a range of departments or sections that today are typically networked. Searches and retrieval from remote sites are relatively straight-forward. System integration always militates against the principles of fair information handling. This is because such principles create friction in the system, slowing down disparate record linkages and refusing access to certain data. Yet integration performs many functions of centralization, such that power may in fact be more concentrated, even though it appears geographically to be dispersed. The so-called surveillance assemblage, which loosely links numerous data-sets and sources of information, may not itself be hierarchical, but this does not mean that power-pyramids are a thing of the past.

Last but not least, surveillance is being effectively globalized, a process that has been gathering speed since September 11. Personal data of all kinds are flowing more freely across borders, between airport authorities and police and intelligence agencies in the global north in particular. Already flowing data – especially via the internet – are subject to more and more checks and monitors. But if globalization originates in that very modern process of doing things at a distance, then it is clear that surveillance was set to be globalized from the start. The focused attention on personal details for management and control which comprises surveillance stretches increasingly over time and space, courtesy of new communication technologies. In terms of everyday practices, this touches directly on the 'delocalized border.' New measures move the information search away from the literal border as surveillance is globalized.

A further irony is this. The globalization processes that enabled the attacks of 9/11 to take place also enable efforts to apprehend potential terrorists. But in addition, they allow others to share information about negative aspects of surveillance and to warn others that not only the twin towers, but the towers of democratic involvement may also now be tumbling.

The lens of 9/11 responses also helps us see what sorts of direction are taken when states of emergency are declared and panic regimes take over. As we start to focus on this aspect of surveillance, some things seem scarcely credible. Certainly they appear contradictory. In the USA especially, the rush toward tight control appears to be reminiscent of highly authoritarian regimes of which the USA has been highly critical in the past. And the relentless hunt for enemies within is uncannily like that which occurred during the McCarthy era, only now 'terrorists' with particular ethnic backgrounds rather than 'communists' with particular national sympathies are the target. When surveillance turns ordinary citizens into suspects it is time for serious stocktaking.

Such social self-examination seems appropriate in the light of the apocalyptic aspects of 9/11 and the surveillance that is being established in its wake. Responses to 9/11 disclose already existing trends and simultaneously hint at a reckoning, a judgment. Normative approaches, already implicitly present in analysis and theory, need to be highlighted. It is one thing to be made aware of situations where freedoms are being constrained, human rights neglected, and people are suffering needlessly for things they have not done and for deeds they never contemplated; it is another to suggest what to look out for as warning signs as new measures are proposed, what sorts of alternative are appropriate, and why some kinds of response are preferable to others.

Meeting the challenges

Three major challenges confront those who would resist the surveillance consequences of September 11: grasping their social, political, and technological dimensions. By the first I refer especially to analysis done in the social sciences. Secondly, there are pressing ethical choices in a world where the politics of information are moving to center stage. And thirdly, understanding the technological dimensions of surveillance, especially after 9/11, is vital to any appraisal of what is going on in the world of identifying, locating, monitoring, tracking, and managing individuals and groups.

The social question

September 11, 2001 did not create the need for fresh concepts and new explanatory tools, but it does show how urgently they are needed now. Surveillance has to be understood today as social sorting, which has exclusionary consequences. Watching others has become systematic, embedded in a system that classifies according to certain pre-set criteria, and sorts into categories of risk or opportunity. These categories relate in turn to suspicion or to solicitation – and many others in between – depending on the purposes for which the surveillance is done. Such classification is very important to people's life-chances (as Max Weber would have put it) and choices. Surveillance is becoming a means of placing people in new, flexible, social classes.

How persons are 'made up' by surveillance systems, and with what consequences, is a vital question. If the 'data double'[4] that circulates through electronic systems does help to determine what sorts of treatment we receive from insurance companies, the police, welfare departments, employers, or marketing firms, then it is far from an innocent series of electronic signals. This is acutely true if ethnic, religious, or other contentious characteristics help comprise that data image. It also means that understanding how the coding systems work is also of utmost importance.

Struggles over classification are not new. What is new today is that classification processes are being automated, and used for a wide variety of tasks within increasingly dominant modes of risk management. Power over classificatory schemes, as Pierre Bourdieu argues, is central to the meaning of the social world. Law contributes to the codifying of classifications, as we saw with regard to definitions of terrorism. But technology buttresses this by removing further the human element, and by digitally facilitating the power of separation. Law and technology may seem remote to many, but their effects are felt locally, relationally, personally. As Bourdieu says: 'The fate of groups is bound up with the words that designate them.'[5] This could hardly be more true than for those today who are viewed first as 'Arabs,' 'Muslims,' or 'terrorists.' Surveillance practices enable fresh forms of exclusion that not only cut off certain targeted groups from social participation, but do so in subtle ways that are sometimes scarcely visible. Indeed, the automating of surveillance permits a distance to be maintained between those who are privileged and those who are poor, those who are 'safe' and those who are 'suspect.' This may be exclusion as domination, where the categories of outcast reflect deep and long-term tensions. But it may also be exclusion as abandonment in which the way is eased for some simply to 'walk by on the other side.'[6] So-called social defense technologies work the same way to keep out the proscribed persons as 'fast-track' 'preferred customer' technologies work to protect privilege.

This is a different kind of argument than is often made about surveillance. Especially in the USA, surveillance is often thought to be a threat to privacy. Editorial writers and activists complain about initiatives such as DARPA's Total Information Awareness as 'supersnoop' schemes that imperil personal freedoms.[7] But this is to misconstrue and underestimate the power of surveillance. To think of surveillance primarily as endangering personal spaces of freedom is highly individualistic. It also misses the point about surveillance contributing to social sorting mechanisms. To process personal data in order to classify groups is to affect profoundly their choices and their chances in life. This is why the *social* analysis of surveillance is so essential to a proper understanding. And it is even more vital after 9/11.

Although 9/11 has brought some questions to the fore, in the twenty-first century surveillance affects everyone all the time. Its intensity varies from country to country and from agency to agency but it is increasingly generalized. In the global north in particular, risk management regimes rely on surveillance for their ongoing data-processing. The addition of 'terrorist' categories to those already in operation dramatically deflects attention away from the routine and mundane operation of such systems. For most people, most of the time, insecurity and risk have precious little to do with anything as terrifying as terrorism. In homes and local communities it is items like the vagaries of the job market, the burden of debt, and the fracturing of relationships that constitute risk. Single mothers suspected of welfare fraud also have much to fear. For governments seeking to distract concern over poverty and inequality in their own countries and abroad, anti-terrorist surveillance provides an excellent decoy.

Another important caution: surveillance is not merely about new technologies. Ordinary people play a role within the surveillance process. The power of surveillance varies with circumstances, with the knowledge of the system held by its subjects, and with the responses that people make to the fact of being under surveillance. Sociologically, much power relates to economic factors; the rich tend to rule. Other aspects of power relate to status, to groups active in their pursuit of political goals, or to personal information held by those who have access to it. Power is always a social relationship, and it is always contested or contestable.

But power is also a resource. The more that power relates to data – retrievable information about groups and individuals that can be cross-checked to filter out particular persons – the more surveillance becomes, in principle, a political matter . . .

Compliance with surveillance is commonplace. Most of the time, and for many reasons, people go along with surveillance. It is a taken-for-granted fact of the modern world that we have to give our PIN at the bank machine, our driver's license to police, our health card number at the hospital. We assume that our employer, telephone company, and frequent flyer club will have a number for our records, and that when we vote in national or municipal elections our names will be listed. We assume that the benefits – security, efficiency, safety, rewards, convenience – are worth the price of having our personal data recorded, stored, retrieved, cross-checked, traded, and exchanged in surveillance systems. As ordinary subjects go along with surveillance, so the order constructed by the system is reinforced, and persons are 'normalized' (as Foucault would say) by the system. Since September 11, compliance has been even more marked, for many, with the additional 'fear factor.' At the same time, as we shall see, challenges have also appeared, the long-term consequences of which have yet to be seen . . .

Engaging a new politics

The political challenge connects with the social analytical challenge, and indeed flows out of it. It has many aspects, and here I touch on just three. The first is the basic political challenge presented by the surveillance aspects of responses to 9/11. The idea of free democratic participation in an open society is under assault. The second has to do with the 'dialectic of control' and raises the question of where leadership will come from in mitigating and reshaping surveillance practices. The third concerns the 'politics of the code.' This is a key aspect of politics in the twenty-first century, centering on the power of information and communication.

Whether seen in the lack of due process, the closed-door decisions of judges and politicians, the tendentious definitions of 'terrorist,' or the sheer authoritarianism of administrations engaged in the war on terrorism, democracy is in trouble after 9/11. Treating ordinary citizens as suspects, and simultaneously inciting them to spy on their neighbors, is an unlikely recipe for confidence in the political process. Placing security and military concerns at the top of the political agenda necessarily displaces freedom and democracy. They cannot coexist as equal priorities, at least under the current 'surveillance state' regimes that are emerging. The attempt to tighten border security to keep out all manner of aliens may effectively close the door on the real needs of both the world outside and the world within . . .

Since September 11, the kinds of agency, group, and movement that already challenged surveillance have redoubled their efforts. Recognizing that 9/11 provides new rationales for surveillance, along with a climate of fear and uncertainty, civil liberties groups and privacy commissions have been active in their critique and opposition to practices and technologies arising as a result of the attacks. Thus the Electronic Privacy Information Center (EPIC) and the American Civil Liberties Union (ACLU) have been prominent in voicing their unhappiness with new measures,[8] as have similar groups in other countries. Privacy International continues its invaluable work of documenting the growth of surveillance around the world, and of using Greenpeace-type publicity stunts to draw attention to the most blatant abuses. Liberty, in the UK, and Statewatch, in Europe more generally, play a cognate role. Also, government bodies that oversee data-protection and privacy have an important role. For instance, George Radwanski, the federal Privacy Commissioner of Canada, has been outspoken in his criticisms of the anti-terrorism law, as well as of matters like CCTV surveillance in Canadian cities – also growing since 9/11.

It is no accident that the activities of these groups have been strongly augmented since 9/11. In many countries surveillance has been intensified in the quest for security – but also in line with previous policy goals. So while Statewatch has appeared as a voice of dissent in Europe, other groups such as the Japanese Network Against Surveillance Technology (NAST) and the nascent Australian 'City-State' activities, have been formed to unite opposition to post-9/11 surveillance developments. It is particularly interesting to note the rising disquiet about surveillance in Japan. Although not directly related to post-9/11 developments, major protests and uncharacteristic civil disobedience followed the introduction of the national computerized registry of citizens in 2002. Yokohama City declared that it would only support a voluntary registry, while Kokubunji simply refused to cooperate. They held a 'disconnecting ceremony.'[9] Even in the USA, where for a while it appeared that emotional responses would drown dissent, several cities – including Berkeley, Cambridge, and Ann Arbor – have voted to defy the PATRIOT Act. It is significant how much may be achieved at a local level. Civil society and informal associations are an important alternative to the remoteness of rationalized risk societies.

The same kinds of technology that enable remote networked surveillance are also used to enable communication between those who dissent, above all using the internet. The groups mentioned above, which usually work both online and offline, are all attempting to use whatever means are at their disposal to open up public spaces. This is in sharp contrast with the efforts to close communication channels, and to envelop all significant decisions in a fog of secrecy. Such public spaces, to which democratic use of the internet is making important contributions, are crucial to any return to democratic practice after 9/11.

As the consequences of contemporary surveillance systems and of the specific fallout from 9/11 become clear, so it is likely that more attention will be focused on the code. As more systems are algorithmic, automating the social sorting processes, so awareness of the crucial role of software protocols is likely to rise. Ordinary people are, not unsurprisingly, interested in how facial recognition or racial profiling systems work. As Lawrence Lessig observes, cyberspace is already ruled by the law of the 'code,' it never was the realm of unrestricted freedom that some of its idealists imagined.[10] However arcane technical software codes may appear, they are never neutral, never innocent. They refer to the desires and purposes of those designing and implementing the systems, and will express their categories. And, as Lucy Suchman reminds us, categories have politics.[11]

Technological citizenship

The third major challenge confronting all who are concerned about surveillance, especially after 9/11, is technological. Remember, doing technology is not a foolish error. As I understand it, technology is part of the human calling to use wisely and fairly the earth's resources. Surveillance technologies themselves fall within this rubric as long as a just and appropriate balance is maintained between care and control.

The technology challenge has several aspects to it. At the most immediate level, those involved directly in technological efforts to combat terrorism – and any other perceived evil – have to confront the old conundrum of the likely effects of their work. It is a conundrum because until some system is installed and working at least some of its effects are unknown. But after it is installed, it may be too late to undo any potential damage. What is needed at this level is a keen awareness of the likely consequences, such that limiting measures can be built into the system. Groups such as Computer Professionals for Social Responsibility have been cognizant of these issues for some time. When social sorting is central to surveillance, the dangers of unfair treatment and prejudicial categorization should be highlighted so that potential damage can be minimized.

Beyond this, a time may yet come when the response to new surveillance proposals has, simply, to be negative – don't do it! For many reasons . . . the creation of new surveillance systems may be looked at skeptically. Missing the mark of networked terrorism, the possibilities of abuse, the likelihood of reinforcing social inequalities, the distraction from more appropriate responses – all these and more are good grounds for caution. But when powerful corporations are working with powerful government departments, and where there is public fear and political resort to fixes, those who speak for technological caution are likely to be voices crying in the wilderness. And yet in times like these it is precisely such voices that are needed.

At an even deeper level, it has to be acknowledged that the technological challenge is no longer merely one for technologists or for politicians to confront. It is not only that these matters are too important to be left to those people alone, but also that the challenge of technology is now one that involves everyone, in the intimate routines of everyday life. The development of technological citizenship[12] is called for, where the responsibilities and the privileges – and perhaps rights – associated with living in a world suffused with technology are a matter for ethical reflection and political practice. Such a process, if it is to succeed, will require some fundamental shifts in thinking . . .

The question of technology is also a challenge that, at least in the West, confronts some profound cultural claims about the power of technology. David Noble, for example, argues that a deep-seated religious project is expressed – notably in the USA – of transcendence through technology.[13] James Carey calls it the 'technological sublime,'[14] the dream of a world perfected through technology, especially information and communication technologies. To resist technological developments, then, may be, to some, tantamount to sacrilege or blasphemy. When the technicist approach is privileged, questioning it seems quirky if not perverse. It is the voices of prophets that cry in the wilderness, witnessing to the state of the world and to the light of another way. And prophets often get silenced.

Beyond suspicion and secrecy

. . . Surveillance after September 11 places before us some momentous challenges. Above all is the challenge of how to confront a closed-off world of social exclusion and how to resist the rise of classificatory, clandestine power. During the Renaissance the idea took root that peace and prosperity could be engineered through science and technology, and this idea was bolstered by the European Enlightenment. Since then, the attempted engineering of security has become a key priority, spawning the myths mentioned above,[15] and contributing to the very difficulties we now face. The problem is that the Renaissance and Enlightenment encouraged an inversion of priorities . . . an appropriate ethic begins by hearing the voice of the Other. And social care starts with acceptance – not suspicion – of the Other. Such an ethic does not exist in a cultural vaccum, however. It grows like green shoots in the soil of shared visions of desired worlds. But such visions seem in short supply today, when history is downplayed by mass media and securing the present preoccupies politicians. Attempts to engineer peace and security have become the default position in a world of amplified fears and truncated hopes. This 'fixing' mentality also tends to close off other options, as if they did not exist.

Jacques Ellul once noted, reflecting on the fate of ancient cities such as Babylon and Nineveh, that these cultures were closed, too, 'protected against attacks from the outside, in a security built up in walls and machines.'[16] Is there anything new under the sun? Yet against that, insists Ellul, is the vision of a city where doing justice and loving one's neighbor is put first. From that commitment to responsibility for the Other proceeds peace and prosperity, freedom and security, sought otherwise through false priorities. This is a city whose gates are never shut. It is a place of inclusion and trust. And its light finally banishes all that is now done in the dark.[17]

Notes

1 This chapter is an extract from D. Lyon (2003) Resisting surveillance, *Surveillance after September 11*. Cambridge: Polity Press, pp. 142–66.
2 David Garland, *The Culture of Control* (University of Chicago Press, 2001).
3 Onora O'Neill, *A Question of Trust* (Cambridge: Cambridge University Press, 2002), ch. 2.
4 Kevin Haggerty and Richard Ericson, 'The surveillant assemblage,' *British Journal of Sociology*, 54 (1), 2000.
5 Pierre Bourdieu, *Distinction: A Social Critique of the Judgment of Taste* (London and New York: Routledge, 1986), pp. 480–1. Thanks to Craig Calhoun for reminding me of this.
6 This distinction, plus one other, 'exclusion as assimilation,' comes from Miroslav

Volf, *Exclusion and Embrace: A Theological Exploration of Identity, Otherness, and Reconciliation* (Nashville: Abingdon, 1996), p. 75.

7   E.g. William Safire, 'You are a suspect,' *New York Times*, November 14, 2002 <www.nytimes.com/2002/11/14/opinion/14SAFI.html/> Good points are made but they do not go nearly far enough.

8   See the 2002 report, 'Bigger monster, weaker chains,' at <www.aclu.org/privacy/privacylist.cfm?c=39>

9   'Japan in uproar as "Big Brother" computer file kicks in,' <www.nytimes.com/2002/08/06/international/asia/ 06JAPA.html>

10   Lawrence Lessig, *Code and Other Laws of Cyberspace* (New York: Basic Books, 1999).

11   Lucy Suchman, 'Do categories have politics?' *Computer Supported Cooperative Work*, 2 (1), 1994: 177–90.

12   Ian Barns, 'Technological citizenship,' in Alan Petersen, Ian Barns, Janice Dudley, and Patricia Harris, *Post-Structuralism, Citizenship, and Social Policy* (London: Routledge, 1999).

13   David Noble, *The Religion of Technology: The Divinity of Man and the Spirit of Invention* (London: Penguin, 1997).

14   James W. Carey and James J. Quirk, 'The mythos of the electronic revolution,' *American Scholar*, 39 (1), 1970: 219–41, and 39 (2), 1970: 395–424.

15   Bob Goudzewaard, *Idols of our Time* (Downers Grove: Inter-Varsity Press, 1984), p. 66.

16   Jacques Ellul, *The Meaning of the City* (Grand Rapids: Eerdmans, 1970), p. 76.

17   Ibid., pp. 192–3.

Glossary of terms

algorithm: An algorithm is a problem-solving procedure. Regularly accomplished using a computer program, algorithms encrypt and decrypt information. Readers will be familiar with the use of algorithms in long division.

automation: Automated forms of surveillance do not require human beings at the point of contact. A wide range of automated functions exists today: bank machines, data mining techniques, facial recognition applications, and movement technologies.

Big Brother: A term popularized by George Orwell in his dystopian novel, *Nineteen Eighty-Four*, it is used to refer to intrusive forms of surveillance (see totalitarianism below). Usually, the term Big Brother is used in the context of government, but it is increasingly applied to employers, administrators and others who hold positions of authority and influence.

biometrics: Formally defined, biometrics is the scientific study of analysing biological data. A biometric is a measure of the body. Biometric measurements include fingerprints, iris scans, facial images and urine samples. Biometric verification is commonly used to verify or authenticate identities.

bureaucratization: Bureaucracy is an organizational structure characterized by regularized procedure, division of responsibility, rules, hierarchies and increasingly defined roles. Bureaucratic management of data is a form of surveillance, as most drivers who are forced to deal with the drivers' bureau are only too aware.

codes: Codes, or computer codes, are written sets of instructions for how a program will operate. They are rules, laws, or principles that arrange data or instructions. Codes, of course range from moral codes to computer codes. The latter is formally more popular in surveillance studies, although the former represents a very important part of monitoring suspicious behaviours.

computerization: Computerization simply refers to processes of control through computerization. However, the term also refers to the post-1960 era where computers were increasingly relied on to manage offices, consumerism, military, etc.

cookies: Cookies allow companies to trace consumers' web-based activity. They are implanted on a person's hard drive; they store data about what kinds of online activity occur. Students will probably recall using a website that 'remembered' past transactions.

data double: A data double is the virtual image of your embodied self. What this means is that we all have a digital presence through our consumer transactions and other personal information stored in a growing number of databases. Data doubles have become so important that it is tough to conduct business with companies in the absence of a data double (see also simulations).

data mining: Data mining is a component of the wider project of knowledge discovery in databases (KDD). It entails the 'discovery' of relationships in large databases. Using a range of virtual tools – neural networks, decision trees, rule induction and data visualization – data mining draws upon raw material from any number of online or offline activities or transactions using data algorithms to sift through large quantities of information. Originally applied in the research of artificial intelligence, the use of automated mining technologies allows for the efficient discovery of otherwise non-obvious, previously unknown information, facts and/or relationships.

digitalization: The process of transforming or transferring physical data into digital data. It is common today for books, records or audiotapes, paper files, and records of various sorts to be transferred into digital form.

disappearing bodies: A term used to denote social interaction (shopping, government, taxation, communication) that does not involve human co-presence. Over the last few hundred years, human beings have increasingly communicated and conducted interactions in the absence of one another. Writing was, of course, significant to the disappearance of bodies, but so, too, was the advent of paper and the dissemination of text. With advances in digital global communications, bodies are disappearing in many more social locations – and they are creating new social locations.

discourse: The ways language and other systems of communication are used to transmit cultural and historical meanings. They are the predominant linguistic and semiotic systems that people use to experience, make sense of and act in the world. A discourse can be anything from a gesture to sign posted on a wall. When a number of discourses come together to comprise a complex assemblage of cultural meanings (e.g., as laws, moral codes, origin stories), they constitute discursive formations.

distanciation: Distanciation is a term that was popularized by Anthony Giddens to denote the separation of space and time (a.k.a. time–space distanciation). Not dissimilar to disappearing bodies, Giddens based his analyses on Harold Innis's work (see Part I, this volume).

electronic monitoring: The use of electronic tracking devices to monitor human and non-human activity. The term electronic monitoring often conjures up images of electronic devices (e.g., ankle bracelets) used to monitor the movement of parolees. This is certainly one form of electronic monitoring. Other forms include breath tests for alcohol, blood pressure tests and measures of employee productivity levels.

entrepreneurial urbanism: In surveillance studies, entrepreneurial urbanism refers to the use of surveillance technologies (e.g., CCTV cameras) to monitor and regulate urban spaces. It involves a wide range of political, social, moral, technological and economic forces that intersect to produce various forms of social control.

fair information principles: Tracing to 1980, fair information principles were adopted by the Organization for Economic Cooperation and Development (OECD) and incorporated in its Guidelines for the Protection of Personal Data and Transborder Data Flows. They stipulate practices for access, choice, security and integrity in data management.

flows: Flows are the motion or characteristics of fluids. Social theorists have started to use the metaphor of liquids and flows to try to capture the nature of social life. Our lives are influenced by flows of money, people, ideas, images, products, etc. that constantly act on how we live (see also mobilities).

interpellation: A concept popularized in Western social thought by Louis Althusser. By interpellation, Althusser referred to the mechanisms through which ideology constitutes human beings as subjects. The constitution of subjects concerns the ways in which individuals come to define themselves and to make sense of their own subjectivity through social positions such as 'taxpayer', 'citizen' or 'middle class'. For Althusser, ideological state apparatuses such as media, education and the church interpellate, or 'hail', individuals in a way that situates them in certain subject positions. Those subject positions, in turn, fall in line with the desires and aspirations of the ruling class. Subsequent understandings of interpellation have removed the latter stipulation.

mobilities: Related to fluids, mobilities is the study of people and things on the move. Everything from people to boxes (e.g., couriers) are on the move in our global world, and scholars interested in mobilities are interested in how phenomena move, how they are regulated and understood, and the effects they have on social life.

new surveillance: A concept introduced by Gary Marx to refer to forms of surveillance that no longer involve the close monitoring of suspects. Marx excludes from the definition of new surveillance forms of monitoring that involve person-to-person watching. Instead, the new surveillance is about the use of technology; it tends to be involuntary, routine and remote; less visible, categorical, relatively cheap and automated; and it tends to involve multiple and intense measures that operate at a distance, often beyond the capacity of the human senses. It is important to note, too, that Marx emphasizes the supplemental nature of the new surveillance.

panopticism: A cultural disposition to know all and see all. Deriving from the metaphor of the Panopticon, panopticism is the cultural disposition to have members of society internalize the 'gaze' of the powerful and monitor their own behaviour. It is a rationality of control that aspires for total self-surveillance through the external threat from those in power.

Panopticon: An architectural design introduced by Jermey Bethham and popularized by Michel Foucault. The Panopticon, as applied to the prison, involves a centralized inspection tower surrounded by a semi-circular structure housing inmates in separate cells. There is an asymmetrical line of vision, whereby inspectors can see into cells but prisoners are not able to see into the tower to verify inspectors' presence. The ultimate purpose was to have prisoners internalize codes of conduct and discipline themselves.

primary definers: Primary definers is a term popularized by Stuart Hall and his colleagues in the late 1970s. Primary definers are individuals who enjoy social power and access to media of mass communications. Access to media enables the powerful to offer primary definitions of a situation or event. George W. Bush, for example, was a primary definer on the threat of international terrorism.

rhizome: Rhizomes are plants that grow in surface extensions through interconnected roots oriented in a vertical fashion. They grow across interconnected roots, throwing up shoots in different locations so that fracture or discontinuity in the root structure is inconsequential for the overall growth potential of the infrastructure. The concept of the rhizome was used as a metaphor to capture the contemporary character of surveillance by Haggerty and Ericson, and they contrasted the fluid structure of the rhizome to a centralized structure (or arborescent 'trunk').

risk: Over the past 15 years, the social theorization of risk has become institutionalized. At a basic level, risk is a probability or future-oriented event, occurrence, or happening. It is something that has not happened. Too often, we use the term risk as though it is a real, objective threat (e.g., the risk of smoking, obesity or terrorism). It is important to remember that risk is only a calculation or estimate, and that it can therefore be susceptible to many social and political forces and influences.

scales of social life: A term used by James Rule to differentiate population size and density. Surveillance systems change based on scales of social life.

simulations: A simulation is an artificial appearance or an abstraction from real events. It is the process of representing one set of phenomena through the use of a second set. Data doubling and surveillant assemblages involve simulations.

social control: Social control refers to a variety of mechanisms (e.g., norms, laws, rules) that are used to try to regulate individual and group behaviour. These mechanisms operate on the basis of reward and punishment. Social control mechanisms are often informal, and their targets range from physical violence to teenage sex.

society of strangers: A term used to characterize large-scale, heterogeneous, industrialized societies where citizens are strangers for the most part and who, consequently, interact through codes, PIN numbers, passwords and credit cards rather than on the sole basis of face-to-face, mutually trusting relationships.

superpanopticon: A general idea appearing in the work of Gandy and Poster to denote the use of databases and other large computer systems to monitor social life. For some observers, superpanopticon is a new development of bureaucratic surveillance.

surveillance: The garnering and processes of personal information to regulate, control, manage and enable human individual and collective behaviour. As the different sections of the book demonstrate, surveillance is a multifaceted, ambiguous process involving everything from person-to-person watching to surveillance systems operating on algorithms.

surveillance creep: Also known as 'function creep', it is the tendency for surveillance systems put in place for one reason to be used for other reasons. Students might appreciate the example of student loans monitoring: Canadian provincial governments use students' annual income tax information to cross-check income for student loan allocation.

surveillant assemblage: A term introduced by Haggerty and Ericson to denote the increasing convergence of once discrete systems of surveillance. The surveillant assemblage breaks the human body into a number of discrete signifying data flows.

synopticon: An opposite situation to panopticon (top–down, few to many surveillance) where the many watch the few. Modern television watching, for example, has been equated to synoptic surveillance, whereby millions of people focus on a few people. The term was popularized by Thomas Mathiesen in his (1997) article, 'The viewer society' (*Theoretical Criminology*, 1, (2): 215–34).

tokens of trust: A token of trust is a token or sign that is used to authenticate identities and verify a person's worth. For example, it is rare to enter a government building or a bank and not be asked for some form of identification or proof of ability to pay (e.g., a credit card). We live in a world where a person's word is increasingly dismissed in favour of some external token of trust.

totalitarianism: Totalitarianism means different things to different observers. In Part I of this volume, Giddens provocatively argues that totalitarianism is not a type of society but rather a type of rule. Generally, it refers to a centralized form of government that regulates, or seeks to regulate, all aspects of life.

Index

Publisher's acknowledgements

The authors and publisher wish to thank the following for permission to use copyright material:

Torpey, J 'Coming and Going' from *The Invention of the Passport* (Cambridge; Cambridge University Press) 2000. Reproduced with permission.

Foucault, M 'Panopticism' pp195-205 from *Discipline and Punish* translated by Alan Sheridan. Originally published as *Surveiller et punir: Naissance de la prison* by Éditions Gallimard 1975, Allen Lane 1975. Copyright © Alan Sheridan, 1977. Reproduced by permission Penguin Books Ltd. Reproduced in the USA and its dependencies, Canada and Phillipines by permission Georges Borchardt, Inc., for Éditions Gallimard.

Marx, G 'What's New About the New Surveillance?' *Surveillance and Society* Volume 1, Issue 1, 2002.

Bogard, W 'Surveillance, its Simulations and Hypercontrol in Virtual Systems' from *The Simulation of Surveillance* (Cambridge; Cambridge University Press) 1996. Reproduced with permission.

Haggerty, K and Ericson, R 'The Surveillant Assemblage' from *The British Journal of Sociology* Volume 51, Issue 4, 2000.

Hier, S 'Probing the Surveillant Assemblage' *Surveillance and Society* Volume 1, Issue 3, 2003.

Lyon, D Extract from 'Everyday Surveillance: Personal Data and Social Classification' in *Information, Communication and Society* Volume 51, Issue 1, 2002. Reprinted by permission of the publisher (Taylor & Francis Ltd, http://www.tandf.co.uk/journals).

Gandy, O 'Datamining and Surveillance in the Post-9/11 Environment' in Ball, K and Webster, F *The Intensification of Surveillance: Crime, Terrorism and Warfare in the Information Age* (London; Pluto Press) 2003.

Hansen, S 'From 'Common Observation' to Behavioural Risk Management' in

PUBLISHER'S ACKNOWLEDGEMENTS 393

International Sociology (© ISA) Volume 19, Issue 2, 2004. Reproduced by permission of Sage Publications Ltd.

Walby, K 'How Closed-Circuit Television Surveillance Organizes the Social' in the *Canadian Journal of Sociology* Issue 30, 2005.

Giliom, J 'Welfare Surveillance' in *Overseers of the Poor: Surveillance, Resistance and the Limits of Privacy* (Chicago; University of Chicago Press) 2001.

Graham, S and Wood, D 'Digitalizing Surveillance' in *Critical Social Policy* Volume 23, Issue 2, 2003. Reproduced by permission of Sage Publications Ltd.

Coleman, R 'Surveillance in the City' in *Crime, Media, Culture* Volume 1, Issue 2, 2005. Reproduced by permission of Sage Publications Ltd.

Haggerty, K and Moore, D 'Bring it on Home: Home Drug Testing and the Relocation of the War on Drugs' in *Social and Legal Studies* Volume 10, Issue 3 (London; Sage Publications) 2001.

Nellis, M 'News Media, Popular Culture and the Electronic Monitoring of Offenders in England and Wales' in the *Howard Journal of Criminal Justice* Volume 42, Issue 1, 2003. Reproduced by permission of Blackwell Publishing.

Gandy, O.H. Jr 'Public Opinion Surveys and the Formation of Privacy Policy' in the *Journal of Social Issues* Volume 59, Issue 2, 2003. Reproduced by permission of Blackwell Publishing.

Roberts, A 'Spin Control and Freedom of Information: Lessons for the United Kingdom from Canada' in *Public Administration* Volume 83, Issue 1, 2005. Reproduced by permission of Blackwell Publishing.

Sheller, M and Urry, J 'Mobile Transformations of 'Public' and 'Private' Life' in *Theory, Culture & Society* Volume 20, Issue 3, 2003. Reproduced by permission of Sage Publications Ltd.

Bennett, C and Raab, C 'The Privacy Paradigm' in *The Governance of Privacy* (London; Ashgate) 2003.

Sewell, G and Barker, J 'Neither Good, Nor Bad, But Dangerous' in *Information, Communication and Society* Volume 3, Issue 1, 2001. Reprinted by permission of the publisher (Taylor & Francis Ltd, http://www.tandf.co.uk/journals).

Lyon, D 'Resisting Surveillance' in *Surveillance after September 11* (Cambridge; Polity Press) 2003.

Every effort has been made to trace the copyright holders, but if any have been inadvertently overlooked the publisher will be pleased to make the necessary arrangement at the first opportunity.

Related books from Open University Press
Purchase from www.openup.co.uk or order through your local bookseller

SURVEILLANCE SOCIETY

MONITORING EVERYDAY LIFE

David Lyon

- In what ways does contemporary surveillance reinforce social divisions?
- How are police and consumer surveillance becoming more similar as they are automated?
- Why is surveillance both expanding globally and focusing more on the human body?

Surveillance Society takes a post-privacy approach to surveillance with a fresh look at the relations between technology and society. Personal data is collected from us all the time, whether we know it or not, through identity numbers, camera images, or increasingly by other means such as fingerprint and retinal scans. This book examines the constant computer-based scrutiny of ordinary daily life for citizens and consumers as they participate in contemporary societies. It argues that to understand what is happening we have to go beyond Orwellian alarms and cries for more privacy to see how such surveillance also reinforces divisions by sorting people into social categories. The issues spill over narrow policy and legal boundaries to generate responses at several levels including local consumer groups, internet activism, and international social movements. In this fascinating study sociologies of new technology and social theories of surveillance are illustrated with examples from North America, Europe, and Pacific Asia. David Lyon provides an invaluable text for undergraduate and postgraduate sociology courses, for example, in science, technology and society. It will also appeal much more widely to those with an interest in politics, social control, human geography, public administration, consumption, and workplace studies.

Contents

Introduction – Part one: Surveillance societies – Disappearing bodies – Invisible frameworks – Leaky Containers – Part two: The Spread of surveillance – Surveillant sorting in the city – Body parts and probes – Global data flows –Part three: Surveillance scenarios – New directions in theory – the politics of surveillance – The future of surveillance –Notes – Bibliography – Index.

208pp   0 335 20546 1 (Paperback)   0 335 20547 X (Hardback)

Printed in Great Britain
by Amazon.co.uk, Ltd.,
Marston Gate.